BT
10.45

PIŁSUDSKI'S
COUP D'ETAT

EAST CENTRAL EUROPEAN STUDIES
OF COLUMBIA UNIVERSITY

PIŁSUDSKI'S

COUP D'ETAT

by Joseph Rothschild

1966

COLUMBIA UNIVERSITY PRESS

NEW YORK AND LONDON

EAST CENTRAL EUROPEAN STUDIES
OF COLUMBIA UNIVERSITY

The East Central European Studies comprise scholarly books prepared at Columbia University and published under the auspices of the Institute on East Central Europe of Columbia University. The faculty of the Institute on East Central Europe, while not assuming responsibility for the material presented or the conclusions reached by the authors, believe that these studies contribute substantially to knowledge of the area and should serve to stimulate further inquiry and research.

The Communist Party of Bulgaria: Origins and Development, 1883–1936　　JOSEPH ROTHSCHILD

Yugoslavia in Crisis, 1934–1941　　J. B. HOPTNER

The First Partition of Poland　　HERBERT H. KAPLAN

Czechoslovak National Income and Product, 1947–1948 and 1955–1956　　THAD PAUL ALTON AND ASSOCIATES

Polish-Soviet Relations, 1932–1939　　BOHDAN B. BUDOROWYCZ

Hungarian National Income and Product in 1955
THAD PAUL ALTON AND ASSOCIATES

Politics of Socialist Agriculture in Poland: 1945–1960
ANDRZEJ KORBONSKI

Polish National Income and Product in 1954, 1955, and 1956
THAD PAUL ALTON AND ASSOCIATES

Comintern and Peasant in East Europe, 1919–1930
GEORGE D. JACKSON, JR.

Piłsudski's Coup d'Etat　　JOSEPH ROTHSCHILD

To Ruth

PREFACE

In May, 1926, the retired first marshal of Poland (since 1920), former chief of state (1918–22), and subsequent chief of the General Staff (1922–23), Józef Piłsudski, at the head of certain military units devoted to his person and with the enthusiastic approval of the political and social forces of the Polish Left, staged a successful coup d'état against the Polish parliamentary system dominated since the elections of November, 1922, by an agglomeration of Right and Center political parties. Though on the morrow of his victory Piłsudski moved swiftly and effectively to avert the devolution of his coup into a genuine social or even political revolution—to the disappointment of his recent allies on the Left—the coup nevertheless became one of the two crucial pivots of Polish political life between the two world wars. It signaled the failure of parliamentary democracy throughout East Central Europe (eventually, all the states of the area, with the exception of Czechoslovakia, succumbed to royal or military or political dictatorships), it aggravated within the Polish nation a rift which was not to be healed during the lifetime of the interwar republic, and its divisions run deep within Polish political memories to this day.

The present book is an inquiry into the causes, events, and consequences of this crisis of May, 1926. It is intended to be a contribution to the two academic disciplines of history and political science—as an analysis of a significant period in the political history of Poland and as a case study of the preparation, execution, and attempted consolidation of a coup d'état within a given set of historicopolitical and socioeconomic conditions. The book ends with the second great pivot of interwar Polish political life, the Brześć crisis of September, 1930, which in several ways closes the period of history inaugurated by the coup and serves as a verdict upon Piłsudski's attempted consolidation and legitimation of the power which the coup had put in his hands.

When originally contemplating the writing of this book in 1961, I was vastly impressed by the apparent analogy between interwar East Central Europe as a classic area of political fragility and economic poverty and the "new" nations which have emerged on other continents since World War II with comparable, albeit not identical, problems. This analogy had as its corollary the expectation of drawing explicit parallels between Piłsudski's experiment in "moral renovation" (*sanacja*) after the crisis of the Polish parliamentary system in 1926 and the various exercises in "guided democracy" and semi-dictatorship now being attempted in those other states, in regions where earlier efforts to import the Western parliamentary democratic model have, as in Poland, been confronted and defeated by the recalcitrance of local political and socioeconomic conditions. While my readers remain free, of course, to draw whatever comparative inferences they may wish from this study, I have become more cautious in regard to my original intellectual ambitions. The work has impressed on me an awareness that interwar Poland, despite her admitted and serious weaknesses, was not a "new" but a "restored" state, deeply conscious of her ancient political sovereignty and her traditional participation in the culture of Europe.

It is an honor and a pleasure to thank the friends and colleagues, scholars and administrators, who have facilitated and supported my work. At Columbia University, Professor Ludwik Krzyżanowski taught me to read and understand the Polish language, while Professors Peter Brock, Harvey L. Dyck, Alexander Erlich, Annette Baker Fox, Henry L. Roberts, Fritz Stern, and the late and lamented Matthew M. Fryde either discussed problems of research and interpretation with me or made helpful critical comments on earlier drafts of the manuscript. A former student of mine, Zvi Y. Gitelman, translated the pamphlet by Nagel, *Mai 1926,* from the Yiddish for me. Bolesław Rozwadowski of New York City reminisced to me about his uncle, General Tadeusz Rozwadowski, and lent me the biography of the latter by A. Jordan-Rozwadowski. Elsewhere, Kazimierz Bagiński of Phoenix, Arizona, lent me his copy of the extracts from the diaries of Maciej Rataj which record the latter's important role in the crisis of May, 1926, Jerzy Giedroyć of Paris sent me the typescript of the third volume of Wincenty Witos' *Moje wspomnienia* before its publication by the Institut Littéraire, and Stefan Arski of Warsaw likewise allowed me to read the typed draft of his book *My pierwsza brygada* prior to its publication. Drs. Zbigniew Landau of Warsaw and Antoni Czubiński and Krzysztof Skubiszewski of Poznań arranged to have books, microfilms, and photostats sent me from Poland since my visit there five years ago. Professors Tadeusz Daniszewski and Henryk Jabłoński of Warsaw replied to my inquiries concerning source materials, particularly for the Appendix.

I am also deeply indebted to the staffs of the various archives and libraries where this work was pursued, most particularly to the directors of the four archival collections housing the bulk of the unpublished and limited-circulation materials used in this study: the Józef Piłsudski Institute of America in New York City (Minister Wacław Jędrzejewicz and Colonel Adam Koc), the Bund Archives in New York City (Hillel Kempiński), the Piłsudski Historical Institute in London (Colonel Tadeusz Schaetzel), and the Archiwum Akt Nowych in Warsaw (Dr. Bronisława Skrzeszewska). Other collections where many valuable and often rare sources were found are those of the Library of Congress in Washington, D.C.; the Public Library, Polish Institute, and Yivo Institute in New York City; the Polish Research Center, British Museum, and School of Slavonic and East European Studies in London; and the university libraries of Columbia, Harvard, and Yale.

I have supplemented my utilization of written materials—both published and unpublished—with interviews of surviving participants in, and contemporary observers of, the events described and analyzed in this book. As their factual reminiscences were in almost all cases corroborated by the written materials, footnote citations have been made to the latter and the anonymity of most interviewees (which some of them requested) has been preserved. The three exceptions to this general policy involve cases where I am convinced that the information given me by two interviewees is correct but where I have failed to find identical written confirmation of it. All these interviewees and correspondents are herewith once again cordially thanked for sharing their time and their reminiscences with me.

Louise E. Luke, general editor for the East Central European Studies, and William F. Bernhardt, editor for Columbia University

Press, have done much to clarify, prune, and hence to improve my text. Mary Bickelhaupt and Janet Schmidt typed the manuscript with speed and accuracy.

Generous and appreciated financial support for this work has been given me by the American Council of Learned Societies, the Columbia University Council for Research in the Social Sciences, and the Columbia University Institute on East Central Europe.

Columbia University   JOSEPH ROTHSCHILD
May, 1966

CONTENTS

CONTENTS

MAPS

PART ONE

THE BACKGROUND

ABBREVIATIONS

AGLŻ   Akta Generała Lucjana Żeligowskiego (Papers of General Lucjan Żeligowski). 40-plus folios.

AKL   Akta Komisji Likwidacyjnej (Documents of the Commission to Investigate the Military Events of the Coup). 25 folios.

BBWR   Bezpartyjny Blok Współpracy z Rządem (The Nonpartisan Bloc for Cooperation with the Government)

KPP   Komunistyczna Partia Polski (Communist Party of Poland)

NPR   Narodowa Partia Robotnicza (National Labor Party)

POW   Polska Organizacja Wojskowa (Polish Military Organization)

PPS   Polska Partia Socjalistyczna (Polish Socialist Party)

PZ   Józef Piłsudski, *Pisma Zbiorowe* (Collected Writings). 10 vols. Warsaw, 1937–38.

CHAPTER I

THE IDEOLOGICAL, POLITICAL, AND ECONOMIC BACKGROUND

The Polish Commonwealth, before its partition and destruction in the second half of the eighteenth century at the hands of Austria, Prussia, and Russia, had been a multinational state governed by a Polish and Polonized Lithuanian–White Russian–Ukrainian nobility. The constitutional principles of this state had been federalistic and decentralistic. During the nineteenth and twentieth centuries memories of it fed the various insurrectionary movements against the partitioning powers, while the chief bearers of this insurrectionary tradition came to be the "state-orientated" strata of Polish society: the intelligentsia (drawn from gentry and bourgeoisie), the workers and socialists, and a part of the radical peasantry. The culmination of the tradition (disregarding for the moment the upheavals of 1944 and 1956 that fall outside the range of this narrative) was Józef Piłsudski's Legionary movement of World War I, which insisted on active Polish belligerence against tsarist Russia to effect the resurrection of Poland as an independent state. Its revolutionary posture, its struggle against tsarist Russia, its insistence on independent statehood, and its rejection of ethnic chauvinism and clericalism rendered this insurrectionary tradition a movement of the Left despite its historicism and its partly aristocratic pedigree.

The revolutionary decades of the mid-nineteenth century had ushered into East Central Europe a new type of national patriotism. In the case of Poland its protagonists were less committed than the adherents of the first, insurrectionary tradition to the memories of and aspirations for independent statehood, and more inclined to view the state as but an instrument—even a dispensable one—for the development, as a primary value, of the "organic" nation. The progress of the nation was to be furthered not by romantic, history-inspired, and ultimately abortive insurrections but by slow, "positive" economic and cultural endeavor. Rejecting the multinational federalistic traditions as well as the antibourgeois political and institutional biases of the prepartition Polish Commonwealth,[1] this school of nationalism, whose main social bearers were the middle class and the more prosperous peasantry, became a Polish analogue of the strictly ethnic nationalisms of the peasant-and-bourgeois nations of East Central and Eastern Europe that lacked an aristocracy. Its leading political expression eventually came to be the National Democratic camp, which, though organized in the last two decades of the nineteenth century as a reaction against the apoliticism of the original, purely economic and cultural positivism of the mid-century, had by the eve of World War I, under the twin shocks of the social revolutionary ferment of 1905 in the Russian-ruled areas of Poland and of the tough Germanization pressure in the Prussian areas, reconciled itself to continued Polish political incorporation in the tsarist and Habsburg empires. In the restored Polish Republic after 1918, the protagonists of this tendency vehemently insisted that ethnic Poles be masters in their own house and, as a corollary, were strongly reluctant to concede any participation in political life to Poland's minorities (German, Jewish, Ukrainian, White Russian), who accounted for more than 30 percent of her population.[2] This school was by then chauvinist even when socially

---

[1] These two stances were interrelated. The absence of ethnic nationalism together with an aristocratic contempt for capitalist activities in the ideology of the ruling establishment of the prepartition Commonwealth had allowed Germans and Jews to play preponderant roles in the urban middle class.

[2] According to the census of 1921, in which nationality was determined by ethnic definition, out of a total population of 27,177,000 there were 18,814,000 Poles (69.2 percent). In 1931 mother tongue became the operational definition of nationality. The census of that year gave 21,933,000 (68.9 percent) who spoke Polish as their mother tongue among a total population of 31,916,000. In 1921 there were 2,110,000 Jews (7.8 percent), while in 1931 the number of Yiddish speakers was 2,489,000 (7.8 percent) and of Hebrew speakers 244,000 (0.8 percent). The German population declined during the decade from 1,059,000 (3.9 percent) to 741,000 (2.3 percent). Of the eastern minorities, the Ruthenians in 1921 numbered 3,898,000 (14.3 percent), the White Russians 1,060,000 (3.9 percent), and 49,000 (0.2 percent) people—mainly in Polesie— gave their nationality simply as "local" (*tutejsi*). By 1931 the linguistic criterion indicated 3,222,000 (10.1 percent) speaking Ukrainian, 1,220,000 (3.8 percent) Ruthenian, 990,000 (3.1 percent) White Russian, and 707,000 (2.2 percent "local" dialects. The minorities accounting for less than 1 percent of the population were the Lithuanians, Russians, and Czechs. These official statistics, it should be noted, have been challenged as distorted and unreliable by spokesmen for the ethnic minorities.

progressive, and its intense nationalism had led it into political alliance with clericalism, for the Roman Catholic faith was regarded as one of the major repositories of the essence of Polish nationhood.

In foreign policy, the adherents of the first tradition, state-oriented and insurrectionary, looked primarily to expansion and consolidation toward the east, where the prepartition Commonwealth had held vast Lithuanian, White Russian, and Ukrainian lands in a quasi-federal relationship with Poland proper. To put it baldly, they were primarily anti-Russian (and later anti-Soviet), whereas the second, positivist-nationalist camp was more fearful of German expansionism as the age-old and presumably permanent threat to the Polish nation. In contrast to Piłsudski's military activities against Russia in World War I, the National Democrats endorsed the war effort of the tsarist empire, in which they saw both a Slavic shield against the German aggressor and a vast market for those Polish industries which their "positivist-organic" orientation was fostering.

Well before the conclusion of the war and the emergence of an independent Polish state, different geopolitical and ethno-political theories as to the proper extent and role of that state in East Central Europe had come to the fore. The National Democrats would in principle have been content with a Poland limited toward the east to more or less ethnically Polish areas, whereas Piłsudski feared that such a state would be too small and weak to avoid becoming a German or (more likely) a Russian satellite. He therefore revived the "Jagiellonian idea" of a multinational Polish–Lithuanian–White Russian–Ukrainian federation (under Polish leadership) and launched a war against Soviet Russia in 1920 to realize it. Alas, Piłsudski's correct awareness of the relative weakness of a Poland generally confined to Polish-populated areas was not matched by an appreciation of the impossibility of permanently imposing such a Jagiellonian rollback upon twentieth-century Russia and the Ukraine. His campaign of 1920 fell between two stools. Thanks to Russia's momentary postwar and postrevolutionary weakness, it did result in the incorporation into Poland of extensive White Russian- and Ukrainian-populated areas. Yet the centralistic constitution which the National Democrats and their allies gave the country in 1921, as well as their generally chauvinistic stance, offended these large minorities, rendering them unassimilable to any Jagiellonian policy ambitions. Russia, in turn, was alienated without being permanently weakened by these territorial losses to Poland.

There was also in the restored Poland after 1918 a group of conservative landowning nobility with ideological headquarters in Wilno and Kraków. Although identifying themselves during the partition period with the tsarist and Habsburg empires, they still embodied the state-oriented traditions of the prepartition Commonwealth. During the first years of the restored Republic they were excluded from public political power by the electoral principle of the rural masses that "peasants elect peasants"; they were also self-excluded by their reluctance to adapt themselves to the political processes and rules of the game as played in a parliamentary republic. Uncomfortably associated, *faute de mieux,* with a Right-Center political coalition before Piłsudski's 1926 coup,[3] these conservative aristocrats were, however, in a deeper sense alienated from the Piast Peasant Party by its professed, but hardly militant, espousal of land reform and from the National Democratic-led Right by that camp's raucous chauvinism and bourgeois-urban political outlook. They were actively wooed during and after the crisis of 1926 by Piłsudski, who regarded them (exaggeratedly) as a class (they were in fact only a stratum or coterie) with a state-building tradition desperately needed by a

[3] The elections of November 5, 1922, for the Sejm, the lower but more powerful of the two houses of the National Assembly, gave 163 seats out of a total of 444 to a bloc of Right-wing and allied parties and 70 to the Centrist but nationalistic Piast Peasant Party. This party, which until these elections had generally declined collaboration with the Right, then reversed itself after a final alliance with the Left during the two presidential elections of Gabriel Narutowicz and Stanisław Wojciechowski by the National Assembly in December, 1922. Led by Wincenty Witos, the Piast Peasant Party became a perennial ally of the Right from the middle of 1923. This coalition thereafter effectively dominated the Sejm, but it failed to give Poland stable governments. A more radical peasant party, named Wyzwolenie (Liberation), had 49 seats; the Socialists (Polska Partia Socjalistyczna—PPS), 41; and other Center and Left parties, 32, of which 18 went to the nonsocialist National Labor Party (NPR). The non-Polish ethnic minorities elected 89 Sejm deputies, of whom 65 formed themselves in to a National Minorities bloc that was potentially in a pivotal position should the Right-Center combination ever founder. In the Senate elected on November 12, 1922, the Right was proportionately even more strongly represented, in part because of higher age qualifications for the vote. It held 48 of the 111 seats, with 17 going to Piast, 8 to Wyzwolenie, 7 to the PPS, 3 to the NPR, 27 to the National Minorities, and 1 miscellaneous.

Poland on the verge of disintegration thanks to incessant party and factional strife. Nor was Piłsudski deterred from this endeavor by the consideration that a rapprochement with these conservatives could be effected only at the price of repudiating the expectations of his earlier and traditional comrades of the Left. His impatience with domestic political strife had, by 1926, come to be extended to parties per se. An adequate appreciation of the institutional as well as the political power of Polish parties during the years before the coup and an understanding of Piłsudski's exasperation with them require a brief review of the origins and provisos of the constitution of restored Poland.

The Polish constitution of March 17, 1921, had been drafted by a commission of nine members designated early in 1919 by a unicameral Constituent Sejm elected on January 26, 1919, and initially dominated by the parties of the Right.[4] The chairman of the drafting commission was Professor Edward Dubanowicz of Lwów University, a constitutional lawyer closely associated with the Rightist National Democrats, who later was even to flirt with monarchism. The Right feared that Piłsudski—whom it detested as a prewar Socialist, as the organizer of the Legionary struggle against Russia and thus as *de facto* wartime ally of Germany (which the Right regarded as Poland's major and hereditary foe), as the protagonist of federalist notions for organizing East Central Europe and therefore as the presumed champion of Poland's ethnic minorities, and as the incarnation of the Polish insurrectionary-statist tradition with its contempt for the Right's own positivist-organic outlook—would become president since he was so obviously the spectacular hero of Poland's resurrection as an independent state. The Right therefore decided to tailor the constitution to suit its own apprehensions and gave Poland a basic charter providing for an emasculated presidency and an omnipotent

---

[4] At the time of the January, 1919, elections, the Polish frontiers, especially in the east, were still indefinite. The elections took place only within the areas controlled by Polish authorities on January 26, 1919, and later in Pomerania, Poznania, and Wilno. In effect, therefore, the eastern minorities were excluded from representation in this Constituent Sejm, which kept itself in power during the first four crucial years of the organization of the new state. For details, see *Dziesięciolecie Polski odrodzonej, 1919–1928*, pp. 184–85.

legislature. The state institutions of the Republic were thus shaped *ad personam*—a fatal political procedure.[5] (Particularly crippling for any presidential ambitions which Piłsudski might have entertained was Article 46, which, while making the president titular head of the armed forces, prohibited his exercising command in wartime.) Ironically, just as the Right in 1919–21 violated its own general belief in a strong executive and, for fear of Piłsudski, proceeded to cripple the presidency as an institution, so in May, 1926, the Left, out of resentment against the policies of the Sejm's dominant Right-Center coalition, was to help this same Piłsudski stage a military coup d'état against the parliamentary institutions which the Left in principle championed.

Piłsudski's response to the constitutional engineering of the Right was to refuse to permit his name to be placed in nomination at the time of the first presidential election of December 9, 1922. He had been chief of state since the resignation of the wartime Regency on November 14, 1918, and had been unamimously confirmed in that title and post by the Constituent Sejm on February 20, 1919. Politically, the source of his authority during these early years had been a general, pervasive sense of national acclamation in recognition of his wartime exploits as leader of the armed struggle for a revived Polish state.[6] Upon his declining election to the largely ceremonial office of the presidency under the new constitution, the National Assembly (Sejm and Senate) on December 9, 1922, elected his friend Gabriel Narutowicz on the fifth ballot by a vote of 289 to 227. The winning coalition was composed of the Left, the Center, and the National Minorities. A week later, on December 16, 1922, while opening an exhibition in Warsaw, the new president was assassinated by a Rightist fanatic, Eligiusz Niewiadomski, because he had been elected with the aid of non-Polish votes. This murder deepened the chasm between the Right and Piłsudski, for Niewiadomski's trial brought out the fact that Piłsudski would have been the preferred victim. Niewiadomski was executed in the Warsaw Citadel on January 31, 1923, and his grave became a place of pilgrimage for the Right.[7]

[5] See the accounts by the Rightist constitutional ideologist Dubanowicz, p. 37, and by the National Democratic parliamentary leader Głąbiński, pp. 455–58.
[6] See Romeyko, "Pierwsze dni niepodległości i zamach stanu," pp. 81–100.
[7] Fiderkiewicz, *Dobre czasy,* p. 82.

Piłsudski never forgave the National Democrats and other Right parties for what he regarded as their moral responsibility for the murder of Poland's first president.[8]

On December 20, 1922, the same Left–Center–National Minorities coalition, by a vote of 298 to 221, elected to the presidency another political colleague of Piłsudski, a prewar Socialist and the founder of Poland's cooperative system, Stanisław Wojciechowski. The victorious coalition broke up soon thereafter as Wincenty Witos took his Piast Peasant Party into partnership with the Right in the spring of 1923.

The office to which Wojciechowski had been elected under the constitution of March 17, 1921, was weak in the manner of the French presidency under the Third Republic. Elected by the National Assembly for a seven-year term, the president had neither legislative initiative nor a veto, and he could dissolve the Sejm, the lower but stronger house, only with the assent of three fifths of the total number of 111 Senators in the presence of at least half the 444 Sejm deputies, the Senate thereby dissolving itself simultaneously. In fact, these provisions for dissolution by the president were a dead letter, and their ineffectiveness became an important factor contributing to the crisis of 1926. Equally inoperative was the power of the Sejm to dissolve itself by a two-thirds vote.

In effect, executive power rested with the cabinet, which was dependent on a Sejm majority. The large number of parties—there were at least ten sizable Polish parties during the early 1920s, not counting the half-dozen or more associations of ethnic minority parties [9]—and

[8] "This crime did more than any other stroke of fate to make the Marshal [Piłsudski] an embittered man. . . . The gravest consequence of the assassination . . . was probably its effect upon Piłsudski's mind. . . . He had no reserves of patience, and the notion that the Right were murderers fermented in his brain." Reddaway, p. 171. The deputies of the Right had, as a body, boycotted Narutowicz's inauguration on December 11. See Thugutt, p. 101.

The assassin Niewiadomski (1869–1923) was a painter and professor of art history. For eyewitness descriptions of the murder, see Iłłakowiczówna, pp. 73–78, and Skotnicki, pp. 209–13. The stenographic record of the trial and Niewiadomski's apologia, written in prison, have been published under the titles *Proces Eligjusza Niewiadomskiego* and Niewiadomski, *Kartki z więzienia*.

[9] Daszyński, *Sejm, rząd, król, dyktator*, p. 28. The most detailed calculation available indicates that, on the eve of the 1926 coup, there was a grand total of 59 political parties in Poland, of which 31 were represented in the Sejm and/or the Senate; in these two bodies their members organized themselves into about 20 parliamentary clubs. Of the total of 59 parties, 26 were Polish, and 33 expressed ethnic minority politics. See Czubiński, *Centrolew*, p. 32, citing Alicja Bełcikowska in *Biuletyn Polityczny*, April, 1926.

their tendency toward splits, schisms, excessive maneuvering for office, and frequent change of partnerships rendered the Sejm majorities highly unstable. Ministerial upheavals were consequently frequent. The cabinet which Piłsudski ousted by his coup of May, 1926, was Poland's fourteenth since November, 1918—not counting *replâtrages* of portfolios within any one cabinet.

This instability tended to weaken the ministers in relation to both party leaders and individual deputies. The minister, frequently so transient as to be unable to familiarize himself adequately with the work of his department, was often bullied by his party's leaders into transforming both its policy and its personnel into a party rampart. Individual deputies, acting as messengers for powerful interests and constituents, shamelessly applied pressure on both ministers and civil servants. The government, in turn, would try to secure a deputy's support through judicious use of state credits, import and export licenses, land leases, forest concessions, state deliveries, and the administration of the alcohol and tobacco monopolies.[10] Ironically, the deputies who on the one hand habitually exceeded their authority by constant interference with administration would simultaneously shirk their basic legislative and budgetary responsibilities through excessive recourse to delegated legislation and to ex post facto legalization of economic and fiscal departures by the cabinet.[11] A raucous and intensely partisan press aggravated the general political debasement and maximized the timidity of the ministers.

While corruption and venality were probably not as extensive as the public thought them to be,[12] the very belief in their pervasiveness and ubiquity proved fatal to the prevailing political order. By 1926 the Sejm, though elected by universal suffrage, was out of touch with

[10] Krzyżanowski, pp. 51–52.

[11] This tendency reached its apogee under the longest-lived cabinet of the pre-1926 period, that of Władysław Grabski, which was in office for nearly two years, from December 19, 1923, to November 14, 1925.

[12] The public's lack of confidence in the governmental apparatus sank to such a low level that unofficial lynch courts sprang up to mete out private justice. Thus on April 17, 1926, as the former minister of posts (1919) and of finance (1923), Hubert Linde, was being tried on charges of malfeasance in the administration of the funds of the Postal Savings Bank, he was shot down in the streets by vigilantes who lacked confidence in the ability or willingness of the public courts to administer true justice. See Porczak, *Rewolucja majowa,* pp. 38–39. For the report of the subsequent trial of the assassin, see *Ilustrowany Kurjer Codzienny,* June 19, 1926.

a public craving stronger and more disciplined and responsible government.[13] The beneficiary of this decline in the prestige of the Sejm elected in 1922 in particular, and of parliamentary politics in general, was Piłsudski, who in May-July, 1923, had followed up his earlier refusal of the presidency by resigning from his military functions and withdrawing into ostentatious—but intensely political— retirement at his country house in Sulejówek, near Warsaw.

In addition to the faulty distribution of institutional powers under the constitution of March 17, 1921, a cause of the sorry tendency toward political deterioration was the heritage of the eighteenth-century partitions, which not only had rent asunder the Polish nation and distributed it for over a century among three foreign powers with different political institutions and economic patterns [14] but also had severed the Poles of the Prussian and Russian parts from positive participation in political life. Deprived of the opportunity to gain experience and responsibility in public service, they came to regard "the state" as foreign and hostile, while to bribe its officials, cheat it on taxes (especially direct taxes), and flout its regulations could be regarded as acceptable or even patriotic. This heritage plagued the restored Polish state in its initial years when only the economically poor but politically experienced former Austrian area of Galicia was in a position to furnish it with trained administrators. By the middle 1920s, however, this situation was rapidly improving as the Polish universities graduated state administrators and economic managers of ability and dedication. Popular contempt for public authority as something alien and to be cheated also declined, as did its curious corollary, the initial postwar expectation that the new Polish state had come primarily to give favors rather than to require sacrifices. In this area,

[13] See Karpatowicz, p. 102.

[14] "On the day of their political unification, the three parts of Poland did not constitute a single economic unit. They had different systems of civil, commercial, and fiscal legislation. They belonged to differing customs units, to differing money and credit systems. . . . Before 1914 imports into the Polish area came, to the extent of 83.3%, from Russia, Germany, and Austria; from other countries came only 8.5% *while trade between the three occupied areas themselves amounted to only 8.2% of the total imports.* Exports from the Polish areas to Russia, Germany, and Austria amounted to 85% of total exports, those to other countries to 7%, *while the trade between the occupied areas amounted to only 8% of the total exports of these areas.*" Zweig, p. 13 (italics mine). Communications between the three parts were as minimal as trade, despite the fact that the Vistula basin is a natural economic unit.

too, the initial spendthrift period of "overdraft" had given way by the mid-1920s to a spirit of duty, work, and self-discipline. Unfortunately for Poland, parliamentary political life lagged behind this new and healthier spirit animating the society and economy, thus increasing public exasperation with a Sejm which appeared to cling to the earlier habits of self-indulgence and irresponsibility already being rapidly abandoned by the public.[15]

The assassination of President Gabriel Narutowicz on December 16, 1922, elicited the formation, later that same day, of a nonparty cabinet headed by General Władysław Sikorski. Piłsudski, who had advised the acting president, Marshal (Speaker) of the Sejm Maciej Rataj, to name Sikorski prime minister, replaced the latter as chief of the General Staff, an office which Piłsudski viewed as potentially more critical than either the presidency or the premiership. In an apparently deteriorating political situation, Piłsudski, who was also designate commander in chief in the event of war, thus seemed to have successfully established his own control over the army and to have "kicked upstairs" an eventual military and political rival. In May, 1923, however, Piłsudski's strong institutional position was undermined as the Right-Center coalition ousted General Sikorski's nonparty government and formed a coalition cabinet headed by Piast leader Wincenty Witos,[16] in which Piłsudski's inveterate National

---

[15] On this point I disagree with the Socialist leader, Daszyński, who argued that Polish society was worse, that is, more selfish, irresponsible, and frivolous, than the politicians. See Daszyński, *Sejm, rząd, król, dyktator, passim.* See also W. Grabski, pp. 296–307.

[16] On May 17, 1923, Witos laid the groundwork for his coalition with the Right by the Pact of Lanckorona, in which he promised not to go beyond a modest degree of land reform in return for the Right's support of his ambition to be prime minister. On May 26 Sikorski was overthrown by this partnership (supplemented by the votes of the National Minorities) on the pretext that a parliamentary-party regime would be more democratic than Sikorski's nonparty government. On May 28 Witos was installed as prime minister, in effect the hostage of the Right, which dominated his cabinet. His alliance with the Right and his betrayal of the expectations of the peasantry for radical land reform led to the secession from his Piast Party of Left-wing groups led by Jan Dąbski and Jan Bryl. In January, 1926, some of these defectors founded the separate Peasant Party (Stronnictwo Chłopskie). For the terms of the Pact of Lanckorona, see Głąbiński, pp. 527–28. For the negotiations which led to it, see Dymek, pp. 143–60. For Dąbski's and Bryl's reaction and response, see Więzikowa, pp. 280–310.
Sikorski, it seems, did not forgive the politicians of this Right-Center coali-

Democratic enemies played the dominant role and which promptly assigned organizational control of the armed forces to his professional and political foes.

Regarding the new regime as composed of men bearing the moral responsibility for the assassination of President Narutowicz, and aware that it was determined to purge the state apparatus of its opponents, Piłsudski decided to dissociate himself totally from Witos' Right-Center cabinet by resigning his various military appointments. He thereupon retired to the country house (Milusin) at Sulejówek, ten and a half miles east of Warsaw, that his army comrades had presented to him. Piłsudski emphasized that the reasons for his resignation from the key post of chief of the General Staff were political and had nothing to do with the work of that body.[17] To underline his differences with the government, he ostentatiously refused to use his pension for himself, assigning it to the Stefan Batory University in Wilno, the city of his childhood. Henceforth he supported himself and his family through lecture fees and royalties from his writings. These lectures, interviews, and writings were intensely polemical and political, their language often violent.[18]

The new government lost little time in taking its revenge and promptly on June 27, 1923, introduced draft legislation to dismantle the military organizational structure which Piłsudski had erected during the preceding years.[19] When a day later, on June 28, the Sejm grudgingly adopted a resolution (by 162 to 88 votes, the rest of the 444 deputies not voting) to the effect that the departing "Marshal Józef Piłsudski, as chief of state and commander in chief, has deserved well of the nation," the minister of the interior, Władysław Kiernik, of the Piast Peasant Party, succumbed to the threats of the Right to oust him if he reproduced this resolution in public notices—as pro-

---

tion for toppling him. Though his quarrel with Piłsudski was as stubborn as theirs, he was to behave enigmatically when the same coalition found itself under Piłsudski's attack in the coup of May, 1926. The Right had already been hostile to Sikorski when he stepped into the assassination crisis on December 16, 1922, and was still suspicious when he later succeeded Sosnkowski as war minister on February 17, 1924. See the memoirs of General Berbecki, p. 182, and of the politician Głąbiński, p. 524.

[17] See his farewell speech to the officers of the General Staff in Piłsudski, *PZ*, VI, 19.

[18] His first publication after retirement was a lengthy biographical pamphlet in memory of the murdered President Narutowicz, reprinted in *ibid.*, pp. 36–59.

[19] For details, see below, pp. 29–32.

vided by law—and failed to do so.[20] The Right also sought to connect Piłsudski with two former Legionnaires and army officers, Walery Bagiński and Antoni Wieczorkiewicz, who were arrested in July, 1923, on charges of espionage and sabotage for Soviet Russia.[21] He was accused of dastardly private and public crimes in whisper campaigns and was spied upon at Sulejówek,[22] and the atmosphere around him became increasingly bitter.[23] In a speech at a farewell banquet tendered in his honor by about two hundred friends and supporters on July 3, 1923, in the Sala Malinowa of the Hotel Bristol in War-

[20] This incident is recounted in an unpublished portion of the typescript memoirs of President Ignacy Mościcki preserved in the archives of the Piłsudski Historical Institute in London.

[21] The Right also hoped—with some plausibility—to link Piłsudski with certain insurrectionary incidents of November, 1923, in Kraków. As for Bagiński and Wieczorkiewicz, they were condemned to death, pardoned by the President, scheduled for deportation to Soviet Russia in exchange for two Poles, and murdered by a Polish police official on March 29, 1925, as they were being taken to the border crossing-point. The murderer, one Muraszko, was let off with two years' detention. For details, see *Sprawa Józefa Muraszki*, p. 106; Rek, "Sprawa Bagińskiego i Wieczorkiewicza," pp. 4–5; Z. Landau and J. Tomaszewski, "O polityce zagranicznej polski w latach 1924–1925," pp. 736–37.

It has been suggested that Bagiński and Wieczorkiewicz were in fact Polish counteragents within the Communist movement, killed in error, or, alternatively, that they were from the beginning of the affair the innocent victims of a police provocation and of a rigged trial. See, for example, Pragier, "Spisek" and "Wierzyć," pp. 2 and 3.

[22] On March 18, 1924, there opened in Warsaw the court-martial of one Lieutenant Stanisław Błoński of the Second (Intelligence) Department of the General Staff on the charge of having made false depositions. Błoński had stated that in October, 1923, he had been requested by his superior, Major Eugeniusz Pieczonka, who in turn was allegedly acting on the instructions of General Stanisław Haller, chief of the General Staff, to spy on Piłsudski at Sulejówek, for which purpose money and assistants would be put at his disposal. On March 21, 1924, Piłsudski testified at the Błoński trial that he had indeed been spied upon over many years. (His testimony is reprinted in Piłsudski, *PZ*, VI, 212–17.) On November 19, 1924, the trial was suspended as a result of the prosecution's withdrawal of its charges against Błoński. For Błoński's later role in the coup of May, 1926, see below, p. 116, n. 43. He was an ex-Legionnaire, while both Pieczonka and Haller were veterans of the old Austrian army, inclined to be hostile to Piłsudski.

[23] Among the offenses alleged against Piłsudski were the theft of Poland's royal regalia and treasonable relations with the Bolsheviks during the campaign of 1920. The latter allegation was a distortion of the nature of Piłsudski's contacts with Lenin during the autumn of 1919, when each regarded the Denikin army as a threat to his own position since that army was both anti-Soviet and dedicated to regaining imperial Russia's frontiers, which had included the lion's share of Poland.

saw, he expressed his deep disappointment with trends in Poland, which he alleged was sinking into a political and moral swamp, and explained that he was retiring because he regarded the Right-Center politicians then in power as responsible for both the attempted character assassination of his own person and the all too successful physical assault on the life of President Narutowicz.[24]

The Right-Center cabinet, in which Witos, though prime minister, was in effect the willing hostage of the Right, fell on December 14, 1923, in consequence of its failure to assuage the peasants' hunger for radical land reform or to stem a disastrous inflation. When Witos took office in May, 1923, the U.S. dollar had brought 53,375 Polish marks. By November the dollar fetched 6,050,000 Polish marks.[25] Witos' inability to halt the steeply spiraling cost of living led to serious labor unrest which in Kraków took on insurrectionary proportions early in November.[26] Witos was brought down by a combination of the Socialist (Polska Partia Socjalistyczna—PPS) and radical Peasant (Wyzwolenie and the secessionist groups from Piast led by Jan Dąbski and Jan Bryl) parties. Witos' cabinet was replaced on December 19, 1923, by a supraparty cabinet headed by the financial expert Władysław Grabski, who had once before been prime minister for a month in the summer of 1920 (June 23–July 20) and who had also served during two extended periods as finance minister (December 13, 1919–November 26, 1920; January 13–July 1, 1923). Grabski now took on the finance portfolio as well as the premiership.[27]

Grabski's cabinet was a mixture of politicians and experts, and it governed largely through delegated legislation—an indication of the Sejm's declining authority and prestige and a first step toward its eventual impotence. On January 11, 1924, a reluctant legislature granted Grabski extraordinary economic decree powers (which it had

[24] The speech is reprinted in Piłsudski, *PZ*, VI, 24–35. The banquet was attended by representatives of the arts and sciences and politics, including the first postwar premier, the Socialist Jędrzej Moraczewski, who also addressed the gathering, as did some other guests.

[25] Zweig, p. 36.

[26] Violence also erupted in Borysław and Tarnów. Troops were called out to quell the disturbances.

[27] In the interval between Witos' fall and Grabski's installation, the Wyzwolenie leader, Stanisław Thugutt, had made an abortive attempt to form a parliamentary cabinet. See Thugutt, pp. 111–13.

not given Witos), and thereafter it habitually, if petulantly, tolerated Grabski's energetic measures. President Wojciechowski, in turn, gave Grabski all his institutionally limited support.

For twenty-three months Grabski governed with vigor. On April 14, 1924, he replaced the hopelessly inflated mark with a new unit, the złoty, equivalent at par to the Swiss gold franc and with an official U.S. dollar parity of 5.18. The old mark was exchanged for the new złoty at a ratio of 1,800,000 to one. Simultaneously, the issuance of the złoty was conferred on a new Bank Polski (Bank of Poland), founded on April 15 with a capital of 100,000,000 złoty, in place of the crippled Polska Krajowa Kasa Pożyczkowa (Polish National Loan Bank). Taxes were henceforth collected with resolution after being revalorized to the new currency.[28]

Supported by public opinion, Grabski refused to place the country under the fiscal control of the League of Nations since such supervision was considered an infringement on sovereignty.[29] As a result, however, foreign money markets became rather inhospitable for the floating of Polish loans, and their terms of interest became harsh. Although the złoty remained stable for some time in relation to foreign currencies, internal prices began to rise steeply after December, 1924, thus leading to sharply adverse trade balances. Contributing to this shift in trade was a decline in the world price of three major Polish export items—coal, lumber, and sugar.[30] The budget could not be balanced nor price and wage control maintained. Indeed, wages in many industries were geared to the rising cost of living. The return on a capital levy was also disappointing, as was the 1924 harvest, which reduced agricultural export possibilities. Finally, on June 15, 1925, Germany halted its imports of Polish coal and launched a tariff war, causing great hardship and sharply rising unemployment in

[28] Smith, pp. 147–50; Krzyżanowski, pp. 58–60.
[29] Tomaszewski, pp. 77–122; Z. Landau, "Władysław Grabski a pożyczki zagraniczne," pp. 1187–88, 1197.
[30] W. Grabski, p. 81. Trade balances, as given in Kutrzeba, pp. 284–85, were:

	Imports (in złoty)	*Exports (in złoty)*
First half of 1924	712,944,000	656,491,000
First half of 1925	1,047,469,000	630,085,000

Poland, which until then had found in Germany a market for about half of her products.[31]

Grabski's program was overly ambitious, attempting to superimpose an expansion of the state's economic activities and the construction of state factories on the task of financial stabilization. Already on May 29, 1925, Vice-Premier Stanisław Thugutt had resigned from the cabinet in order to be free of responsibility for the worsening economic situation and because of political and administrative differences with Premier Grabski.[32] In July the złoty plunged so seriously from its gold moorings that Foreign Minister Count Aleksander Skrzyński and the vice-president of the Bank Polski, Dr. Feliks Młynarski, were sent to New York in vain attempts to raise further substantial Ameri-

[31] Under the terms of the Upper Silesia Convention of 1922, Germany was committed to importing, duty-free, 500,000 tons of Polish coal per month until June 15, 1925. After that date she halted the import of Polish coal and soon thereafter of a whole series of Polish agricultural, metallurgical, and timber products, thereby starting a tariff war in which the Poles quickly retaliated. Affected were about 27 percent of Poland's total exports and 16 percent of her imports but only 3.5 percent and 3 percent of Germany's exports and imports. The German aims were clearly political, being tied both to a specific demand for concessions to the German minority in Poland and to the general policy of crippling her. A laboriously negotiated treaty to halt the tariff war was signed on March 17, 1930, but the Reichstag failed to ratify it. The negotiations, which had begun as early as January, 1925, had been broken off six times, mainly for political reasons. The struggle was finally halted with the general German-Polish détente of the mid-1930s, when a *Zollfriedensprotokoll* was signed on March 7, 1934. For details, see Kruszewski, pp. 294–315; Sokulski, pp. 54–65; and Ratyńska, pp. 77–103.

Some data on German-Polish foreign trade during the interval between the Upper Silesia Convention and the customs war of 1925–34 are also given in Czubiński, "Przewrót majowy," p. 89. Citing Franciszek Fiedler, *Tło gospodarcze przewrotu majowego* (Kraków, 1927), p. 48, he presents the following estimates of German-Polish trade as a percentage of all Polish foreign trade:

Year	Polish imports from Germany (in percent)	Polish exports to Germany (in percent)
1922	37.0	49.5
1923	43.6	50.6
1924	34.6	43.2
1925 (first half)	34.0	50.0

Polish-Soviet trade, in turn, was virtually nonexistent throughout the interwar period, and Polish cities which before World War I had produced for the Russian market—Łódź, Zawiercie, and Żyrardów, for example—were hard hit.

[32] See W. Grabski, p. 147, and Thugutt, pp. 6, 124.

can loans.[33] (Dillon, Read & Company had floated a loan in the spring of 1925 for the disappointing net sum of $23.5 million at 8 percent.)[34] Approaches to London proved equally unavailing.

By August, 1925, the gold reserves of the Bank Polski were dangerously depleted in consequence of the widening gap in the balance of payments, and a new depreciation of the złoty set in. Finally, on November 12, 1925, the president of the Bank Polski, Stanisław Karpiński, refused to sell any further gold or foreign securities to support the parity of the złoty.[35] Grabski resigned the next day, declining to remain in office even on a caretaker basis pending the formation of a new cabinet and urging the formation of a government of national unity to confront the country's desperate situation. Left no choice, President Wojciechowski had to accept the resignation on November 14, 1925. Significantly, the Grabski cabinet had been overthrown by public unrest and by the Bank Polski, not by the Sejm, which as late as October 23 and November 11 had given Grabski narrow but adequate votes of confidence,[36] nor by the President, whose particular *homme de confiance* Grabski remained.[37] The cabinet's fall was thus interpreted as a failure not only of democracy but even of semidemocracy, for democracy was assumed to have already failed with the granting of discretionary decree powers to Grabski on January 11, 1924.

Another drastic inflationary spiral began immediately. Unemployment increased steeply. Public disillusion was profound, for the great sacrifices made since 1923 appeared to have been in vain.

Piłsudski was clearly the beneficiary of the general atmosphere of

[33] Skrzyński's trip was also an aspect of Poland's pre-Locarno diplomatic maneuvers. See his letter of June 27, 1925, to Prime Minister Grabski as quoted in Balcerak, p. 276.

[34] Z. Landau, "Pożyczka dillonowska," pp. 79–85.

[35] Z. Landau, "Władysław Grabski a pożyczki zagraniczne," p. 1204.

[36] About 180–90 to 150–60. The opposition consisted of the extreme Left, the National Minorities, and Witos' Piast Peasant Party. The Socialists tolerated Grabski to the end for fear of worse. See Chrząszczewski, *Od sejmowładztwa do dyktatury,* p. 143; H. Jabłoński, pp. 442–43; and W. Grabski, pp. 232, 237.

[37] For his earlier, relatively successful financial reforms, Grabski had been rewarded by a grateful and impressed President Wojciechowski with Poland's highest order, that of the White Eagle. The two men were related through the marriage of their children.

crisis and frustration.[38] But his day had not yet come.[39] The parties decided on one more try at a broad parliamentary coalition, and on November 20, 1925, a cabinet headed by the foreign minister of the outgoing Grabski cabinet, Count Aleksander Skrzyński, took office.

Inauspicious was the manner in which the Skrzyński cabinet was formed. The parliamentary leaders of the five member parties—National Democratic, Christian Democratic, Piast Peasant, National Labor, and Socialist (the Wyzwolenie Peasant Party was the one major Polish group to decline participation or support)—distributed the portfolios and then invited Skrzyński (who had been foreign minister under Sikorski from December 16, 1922, to May 26, 1923, and again under Grabski since July 27, 1924) as a nonparty man to head this cabinet. The Prime Minister (who also retained the foreign affairs portfolio) was thus virtually an outsider in his own government. He owed his position to the fact that the party leaders did not trust each other sufficiently to agree on an outstanding political figure as prime minister[40] and to the expectation that his high reputation in the West (he had accommodated Poland's foreign policy to the Locarno system) would facilitate Poland's quest for loans and credits there.[41] Known as the government of "national concord," this five-party coalition was a particularly inept one, composed as it was of parties with diametrically contradictory fiscal and economic theories in a situation of immediate and intense fiscal-economic crisis. The National Democrats had insisted on holding the ministries of Finance

[38] The Socialist leader, Ignacy Daszyński, had spent the summer of 1925 writing a laudatory biographical brochure of Piłsudski, to whom he obviously expected Poland to turn in her travail and in whose democratic inclinations he still had confidence. See Daszyński, *Wielki człowiek w Polsce.*

[39] The pro-Piłsudski historian Pobóg-Malinowski, *Najnowsza historia*, II, 469, asserts that on the morrow of Grabski's fall Piłsudski was persuaded by Maciej Rataj, the marshal of the Sejm, tentatively to agree to join a nonparty cabinet of outstanding individuals but that nothing came of this plan because the Sejm politicians were not yet ready for it and President Wojciechowski applied no pressure on them to accept it.

[40] See Morawski, "Przewrót majowy," p. 1, and Krzyżanowski p. 72. For the same reason, the critical Ministry of the Interior was assigned to the civil servant Władysław Raczkiewicz.

[41] *Frankfurter Zeitung*, April 22, 1926. Skrzyński's main, indeed virtually exclusive, interest was foreign policy. Even during his premiership he spent extended periods abroad in his simultaneous capacity as foreign minister.

(Jerzy Zdziechowski) and Education (Stanisław Grabski, brother of ex-premier Władisław) as their price for entering the cabinet, while the Socialists were determined to force pump-priming and welfare spending upon the government through their control over the ministries of Public Works (Jędrzej Moraczewski) and Labor and Welfare (Bronisław Ziemięcki). Though the assignment of the War Ministry to General Lucjan Żeligowski had briefly purchased what amounted to Piłsudski's initial benevolent neutrality, the cabinet was wracked by too many internal contradictions to be able for long to avoid a schism or to take a strong position on any controversial issue.

On February 7, 1926, Minister of Public Works Moraczewski resigned on the issue of the cabinet's inability to resolve the chronic dispute over the proper organization of the supreme command of the armed forces to Piłsudski's satisfaction and reportedly also as an expression of dissent from Zdziechowski's conservative economic program. Significantly, Moraczewski's replacement, Norbert Barlicki, who took office on February 13, was selected not by Skrzyński but by the Socialist Party leaders.

In March and April, 1926, the złoty broke.[42] Bank deposits were withdrawn in panic and twenty banks failed. Industrial unemployment inched toward the disaster figure of 350,000–400,000—a third of the labor force—which did not even include youths entering the labor market for the first time or the several million "superfluous" village poor.[43] Demonstrations of unemployed and riots—with attendant loss

---

[42] The official dollar-złoty rate rose between April 6 and 21 from $1 = 7.9 zł. to $1 = 9.9 zł., a 25 percent rise in two weeks. On the free market the dollar brought 12 złoty on April 20. *Frankfurter Zeitung,* April 21, 1926.

[43] While historians and economists are unanimously of the view that Poland's economic situation was calamitous at this time, there is disagreement among pro- and anti-Piłsudskists whether all the economic indicators—including that of unemployment—were persistently deteriorating up to the time of Piłsudski's coup in mid-May, 1926, or whether some easement had already preceded it. The pro-Piłsudskists (e.g., Pobóg-Malinowski, *Najnowsza historia,* II, 465–72, 502–4) seek to demonstrate a worsening situation right up to the time of the coup, followed by a sharp improvement immediately afterward—and caused by it, thanks to Piłsudski's personal ability to elicit confidence and to the wisdom of his policies. Anti-Piłsudski critics (e.g., Z. Landau, *Plan Stabilizacyjny, 1927–1930,* pp. 31–39) argue that the corner toward recovery had already been turned in the early spring of 1926—weeks before the coup—without any contribution by Piłsudski. This problem will be discussed below, pp. 279–81. Here it suffices to say that even though the presentation of statistical evidence by the anti-Piłsudskists is the more impressive one, and it appears to be true that an

of life and subsequent arrests—took place in the streets of Kalisz, Łódź, Lublin, Lwów, Stryj, Warsaw, and Włocławek.[44] Calls for dictatorship became ever more general and open. Even those who opposed dictatorship demanded early constitutional revision so as to strengthen the president and give him effective power to dissolve the Sejm.[45]

The Rightist (National Democratic) finance minister, Jerzy Zdziechowski, insisted on a thoroughly deflationary policy toward the crisis: namely, severing the automatic correlation of wages to prices (the abolition of the cost-of-living bonus); dismissing 18,000–25,000 railroad workers; sharply reducing (by about 35 percent) compensation payments to the sick, the disabled, and the aged; raising taxes by 10 percent—except for the tax on real property—and instituting a head tax of five złoty per person; and raising the price of gas, electricity, oil, salt, tobacco, matches, and alcohol so as to "commercialize" these state enterprises and monopolies.[46]

The Socialists also wished to balance the budget but not at the shameless expense of workers, employees, and civil servants. They were caught in a double embarrassment. Initially they suggested saving expenditure by reducing police and army outlays but dropped the latter proposal at the request of their former comrade Piłsudski,[47] whom many among them still considered one of their own. Initially, also, they had agreed to a three months' reduction in the cost-of-living

"objective" improvement of certain economic indicators had set in already during March–April, 1926, this was not sufficient to lessen the "subjective" political atmosphere of panic and crisis that persisted up to the moment of Piłsudski's coup and supplied grist for his mill.

In a vain attempt to relieve the appalling burden of unemployment by opening up the Russian market to Polish industry, a group of Sejm deputies from ultra-Left and National Minority parties traveled to Moscow early in 1926 for trade talks that turned out to be abortive. See Fiderkiewicz, "Wyprawa posłów polskich," p. 4.

[44] *Frankfurter Zeitung,* February 10, April 3, 9, 10, 15, and 27, 1926.

[45] This was the common theme of three books published in the spring of 1926 by men of such differing political positions as the Socialist Daszyński, the National Christian Dubanowicz (who, ironically, was the main author of that constitution for whose revision he was now calling and who in 1919–21 had insisted on a weak presidency out of fear of Piłsudski), and Piast leader Witos. See Daszyński, *Sejm, rząd, król, dyktator;* Dubanowicz, *Rewizja konstytucji;* Witos, *Czasy i ludzie.* The various political parties were also demanding more or less radical changes of the constitutional and electoral laws.

[46] See *Frankfurter Zeitung,* April 12, 19, and 27, 1926; Zweig, p. 41; and Próchnik, *Pierwsze piętnastolecie,* p. 217.

[47] *Frankfurter Zeitung,* April 19, 1926.

bonus of state employees but, embarrassed by the Communist pressure on their left and the outraged response of those affected, refused toward the end of March to extend this concession.[48] Then they also demanded an immediate investment of 300,000,000 złoty in construction and industry so as to break the unemployment curve, a capital levy to raise 85,000,000 złoty, and an increase in the real property tax.[49] Upon Zdziechowski's refusal to consider such a policy, Sejm Marshal Rataj summoned a conference of political leaders on April 18, 1926, that proved to be abortive.[50] The discussion was more formal than genuine since each side had for days been warning that it would not retreat. Failing to force the substitution of their own fiscal-economic program for Zdziechowski's, the Socialists on April 20 withdrew their ministers Norbert Barlicki (Public Works) and Bronisław Ziemięcki (Labor and Welfare) from the cabinet.

The next day Skrzyński offered President Wojciechowski the resignation of his entire cabinet but was persuaded to delay this step until the Zdziechowski budget estimates for May and June had been accepted by Sejm and Senate in order to avoid a governmental vacuum at the critical time of the workers' May Day demonstrations.[51] The Right and Center leaders, who had been negotiating with each other during Easter at the Zakopane resort in the Tatra Mountains for a renewal of their Lanckorona Pact of 1923, urged Skrzyński to replace the departing Socialists with members of their own parties and to carry on the government on such a reconstructed basis. At that time, however, Skrzyński was convinced that Poland could not be governed against both Piłsudski and the Socialists.[52] He therefore provisionally

---

[48] *Le Temps,* March 28, 1926; Krzyżanowski, pp. 72–75. Civil servants and employees of the national government with their families numbered 2,132,000 in 1925 (or 8 percent of the population). If local government employees had been added, the total would perhaps have been 10 percent. See X.X.X., p. 9.

[49] Porczak, *Rewolucja majowa,* p. 40; Pobóg-Malinowski, *Najnowsza historia,* II, 472.

[50] Those attending were Rataj, Prime Minister Skrzyński, Ignacy Daszyński and Zygmunt Marek for the Socialists, Jerzy Zdziechowski and Stanisław Głąbiński for the National Democrats, Wincenty Witos for Piast, Karol Popiel for the National Laborites, and Józef Chaciński for the Christian Democrats.

[51] See Kutrzeba, p. 290, and Krzyżanowski, p. 75. The Left criticized, as allegedly partisan and unconstitutional, Wojciechowski's refusal to accept Skrzyński's resignation. See "Le coup d'état de Varsovie," p. 4.

[52] Morawski, "Przewrót majowy," p. 1; *Frankfurter Zeitung,* April 9 and 22, 1926; *Le Temps,* April 23, 1926. Skrzyński announced that he would not attempt to head a cabinet based on only one political grouping.

reassigned the two portfolios on a nonparty basis (Public Works to Mieczysław Rybczyński; Labor and Welfare to Jan Jankowski), and, with May Day as well as the national holiday of May 3 peacefully behind him and the May–June budget estimates passed, he resigned on May 5, 1926, thereby opening Poland's last and most severe cabinet crisis prior to the coup. The Right and Center leaders, intoxicated by their Easter negotiations at Zakopane, chose to disregard the skepticism of Skrzyński concerning the feasibility of governing Poland against both Piłsudski and the Socialists and to ignore a warning from General Sikorski that it would be fatal to attempt another Right-Center cabinet until the army command question had been settled.[53] Their formation of a Witos-led cabinet on May 10 provoked Piłsudski's and the Left's violent riposte of May 12.

In the area of foreign as well as domestic policy, Poland's vulnerabilities were starkly emphasized in the year immediately preceding the coup of May, 1926. Warsaw's failure to raise substantial Western loans during the economic crisis of 1925 testified to Germany's success in sapping international confidence in Poland at a time when the two antagonists were locked in their tariff war. The multilateral Locarno Treaties of October 16, 1925, which acknowledged Germany's insistence on differentiating the legal-political validity of her western and eastern frontiers, were also a substantive defeat for Poland. Not only did Locarno legitimate by implication, as it were, Germany's anti-Polish territorial revisionism, but it also exposed the unreliability of Poland's French ally, then striving for an independent understanding of her own with Germany, and it emphasized Britain's indifference to Poland's security interests vis-à-vis Germany. Moreover, Germany's rapprochement with France and Britain at Locarno did not prevent her continued cooperation with Russia to Poland's detriment. Indeed, half a year after Locarno, these two historic enemies of Poland reaffirmed their Rapallo rapprochement of April 16, 1922, with the Berlin Treaty of April 24, 1926. Though overtly only a nonaggression and neutrality agreement, this pact nevertheless appeared in fact to confirm Poland's isolation. It thus contributed to the

[53] Pietrzak, ed., "Jak doszło" i "Przewrót," p. 138. Sikorski was, indeed, in Zakopane at the time of these Right-Center political negotiations but he denied having participated in them when questioned by the war minister. AGLŻ, 26/114–15.

general sense of political malaise in Poland, to the increasing suspicion of prevailing policies, personalities, and institutions as bankrupt, and hence to the widespread readiness—born of hope and
despair—to look to Piłsudski as a savior.

Though foreign policy developments were thus one of the background aspects of Piłsudski's coup of May, 1926, this event nevertheless—and contrary to many expectations both domestic and foreign—
marked less of a break in the continuity of Poland's diplomatic policy
and position than in her internal politics. The power factors of the
international system proved less amenable to Piłsudski's control and
more refractory to his intended alterations than did Poland's domestic
political structure.

CHAPTER II

THE MILITARY BACKGROUND

Though lacking formal military training, Józef Piłsudski, as the war-time commander of the First Legion Brigade [1] and thus as the leader of the armed anti-Russian struggle for the restoration of an independent Polish state, regarded himself as the father of the Polish army and the nation's first soldier. With the rank of First Marshal of Poland (conferred on his name day, March 19, in 1920), he felt himself entitled to insist on the implementation of his military views, whether he was on active service or in ostensible retirement. These views brought him into sharp conflict with other political leaders and senior officers.

The officer cadre of the army of resurrected Poland was drawn from several sources. There were the veterans of Piłsudski's wartime Legionary movement and of its underground arm, the POW (Polska Organizacja Wojskowa—Polish Military Organization). Like Piłsudski, they were generally without formal military training before World War I but thought that they merited the special recognition of the nation by virtue of their heroic exploits on behalf of Polish independence during that war. Piłsudski's most loyal supporters were former Legionnaires, though not all Legion veterans were devoted to him; those from the Second Brigade generally attached themselves to his rivals, Generals Józef Haller and Władysław Sikorski. During the war the Second Legion Brigade had acquired an Austro-Polish political orientation in contrast to the commitment to an independent Poland of the Piłsudski-led First Brigade. The Third Brigade, raised in the former Russian share of Poland upon the expulsion of the Russian

[1] The name "Legion" evoked memories of those earlier Polish Legionnaires who had fought alongside the revolutionary and Napoleonic French armies after 1797 for the restoration of Poland and the renovation of Europe.

army by the Central Powers in 1915, assimilated the political outlook of Piłsudski's First Brigade.[2]

The onetime Legion and POW officers were in constant friction with those who had entered the Polish army from the former imperial Austrian army, by whom they were regarded as incompetent amateurs. The Legion and POW veterans reciprocated by looking down on the ex-Austrians as only lukewarm Poles, more devoted to the House of Habsburg than to the cause of Poland's resurrection.[3] The senior ex-Austrians, particularly the former General Staff officers among them, were a rather cohesive group and were suspected not only of helping each other to promotion but of blackballing outsiders.[4] Their leaders were Generals Stanisław Haller, Tadeusz Rozwadowski, Count Stanisław Szeptycki, and Włodzimierz Zagórski. All were hostile to Piłsudski, forcefully resisting his coup in May, 1926, and, despite their alleged professional apoliticism, many among them harbored Rightist political attachments. Piłsudski's animosity toward these former Austrian General Staff officers was, in turn, so strong that he warned President Wojciechowski against them and publicly criticized their traditions and styles of work.[5]

Sometimes confused with, but not strictly belonging to, this ex-Austrian coterie was the group of officers identified with General Władysław Sikorski. As chief of the Military Department of the Galician Naczelny Komitet Narodowy (Supreme National Committee) during World War I, Sikorski had identified himself with the Austro-Polish solution to the Polish problem and thereby had come into lifelong friction with Piłsudski, who, though also fighting tsarist Russia, remained politically aloof from the war aims of the Central Powers.[6] In the army of restored Poland, Sikorski nurtured the Honor i Ojczyzna (Honor and Native Country) circle of officers, which was apparently organized on Masonic models, though flexible in its admissions policy.

---

[2] See Lipiński, "Wywiad u marszałka Piłsudskiego w Sulejówku z dn. 10. II. 1924 r.," p. 74. The Third Legion Brigade was led by the future generals Bolesław Roja and Mieczysław Norwid-Neugebauer.

[3] *Ibid.,* pp. 66–68.

[4] Loessner, p. 162.

[5] Piłsudski, *PZ,* VIII, 258, 283.

[6] See J. Rzepecki, "Rozejście się Sikorskiego z Piłsudskim w świetle korespondencji Izy Moszczeńskiej z sierpnia 1915 r.," pp. 728–39.

Founded in 1921, this secret organization was dissolved in 1925.[7] Popularly termed the "H_2O" group, it had been feared by the Rightist parties as a criminal-Masonic conspiracy. Genuine Masonic cells also existed in the army, though their extent was difficult to trace.[8]

Officers from the former tsarist Russian army were generally politically passive, except for a strong pro-Piłsudski sentiment among many of their seniors, perhaps partly because of the Marshal's great political interest in the *kresy,* or eastern borderlands of Poland, whence many of them had originated. Among their leading representatives were General Lucjan Żeligowski, who seized Wilno for Poland on October 9, 1920, and was war minister in the spring of 1926 in the last cabinet before Piłsudski's coup; General Wacław Iwaszkiewicz, the defender of Lwów and commander of the Polish southern front in the Polish-Soviet campaign of 1920; and General Daniel Konarzewski, who became Piłsudski's vice-minister of war after May, 1926, and helped him reorganize and popularize the army. In contrast, General Józef Dowbór-Muśnicki, who had commanded the First Polish Corps (organized in July, 1917) within the Russian army, sharply opposed Piłsudski's coup in 1926. He had, however, retired in 1920, declining a command in the Polish-Soviet war that year.

Only a few Polish officers had previously served in the German-Prussian army. Their senior representative was General Kazimierz Raszewski, the last commander of the German Wandsbecker Husaren regiment, who in the Polish army subsequently commanded for a time the Poznań Military District. He was a monarchist and an opponent of Piłsudski. There were also some officers who entered the Polish army from the local Polish forces organized in Poznania province in 1918 during the German collapse.

Finally, mention must be made of the contingent that entered the army from the Polish corps organized in 1918 in France under the command of General Józef Haller. After serving in the Austrian army from 1895 to 1910, Haller had resigned his commission to devote himself to the Polish independence movement. He had commanded

[7] Lisiewicz, pp. 47–53; Marian Kukiel, letter to the editor, *Zeszyty Historyczne,* IV (1963), 175–76; Pragier, "H₂O i bomba Trojanowskiego," p. 2.
[8] See Katelbach, "Loże," pp. 199–208, and Hass, "Zamach majowy 1926 r.," p. 4.

the Second Legion Brigade in World War I but crossed over to the Russian lines during the night of February 15–16, 1918, in protest against what he regarded as the Central Powers' betrayal of the Polish cause to the Ukrainians at the Brest-Litovsk negotiations. Brought to France later in the year, he commanded there the Polish corps that became the first organizational model for the Polish army. Like his cousin General Stanisław Haller of the Austrian General Staff group, Józef Haller was a vigorous foe of Piłsudski.

To forge professional unity among these conglomerate military traditions and to give formal military education to the Legion and POW veterans who lacked it, French instructors were imported after the war. They suspected Piłsudski and his ex-Legion and POW cohorts of Germanophilism and favored the Józef Haller corps veterans above all others. Symbolically, the round *maciejówka* military cap of Piłsudski's Legions and prewar Riflemen (sing.: Strzelec; pl.: Strzelcy) was replaced by the Haller corps' square *rogatywka* (the traditional headgear of the gentry and the Cracovian peasantry) in the Polish army uniform. Piłsudski alone refused to adopt the latter.

Piłsudski wished to limit the influence of the French mission on the Polish army, and after the May, 1926, coup it was eventually terminated, in part because its work was nearing completion but chiefly because of friction with Piłsudski and the Piłsudskists.

The army was always the apple of Piłsudski's eye. In the first two postwar cabinets, that of Jędrzej Moraczewski (November 18, 1918–January 16, 1919) and initially in that of Ignacy Paderewski (January 16–December 9, 1919), Piłsudski, as *Naczelnik Państwa,* or chief of state, had not permitted the appointment of a war minister but only of provisional directors to that ministry (until February 27, 1919), since he wished to establish personal ascendancy over the army. In the spring and summer of 1920, Piłsudski, as *Naczelny Wódz,* or commander in chief, personally led the Polish armies in the war against Soviet Russia. Subsequently, the war minister from August 9, 1920, until the formation of the first Right-Center cabinet under Wincenty Witos on May 23, 1923, was Piłsudski's devoted friend and chief of staff during the Legion campaigns of World War I, his companion during the latter months of the Magdeburg imprisonment of

1917–18, General Kazimierz Sosnkowski.[9] Piłsudski's control over the army was reinforced more directly when in December, 1922, he took on the post of chief of the General Staff in place of General Władysław Sikorski. On Piłsudski's advice, Sikorski had been named premier by the acting president, Sejm Marshal (Speaker) Maciej Rataj, on December 16, 1922, to head a nonparty cabinet in the crisis created by the assassination that day of President Narutowicz.

During these years of his great organizational control, Piłsudski attempted to give the army a command system conforming to his notions of the proper degree of military independence from political restraints and to his expectations of the probable type of future war that the army might be obliged to wage.

On January 7, 1921, Piłsudski, in his capacity as commander in chief, issued a decree [10] creating two high-level military institutions:

(1) The Full War Council (Pełna Rada Wojenna), an advisory body to be composed of the president of the Republic as its presiding officer, the war minister and his vice-minister, the general designated in advance to be commander in chief in wartime, the chief of the General Staff and his two deputies, those generals designated as field commanders of corps in wartime and serving as army inspectors in peacetime, and a maximum of three other generals nominated annually by the war minister. The sphere of competence of the full council was to discuss and give advice on questions of military training, armaments, mobilization, communications, technology, fortifications, and other issues on which the president or war minister might wish to consult it.

(2) The Inner War Council (Ścisła Rada Wojenna), a smaller

[9] In the spring of 1917, after the February Revolution in Russia and America's entry into the war on the Allied side, Piłsudski had differentiated more categorically than heretofore the war aims of his Polish Legionary movement from that of the Central Powers. Upon his advising the Legionnaires to refuse to swear an oath of lasting solidarity with the German and Austro-Hungarian armies, the Germans arrested him and Sosnkowski on July 22, 1917, and interned them until the end of the war. The First and Third Legion Brigades largely heeded Piłsudski's recommendation and were dissolved. The Austro-Polish Second Brigade, in contrast, remained faithful to the Central Powers until its disillusionment over the concessions made to Ukrainian territorial aspirations at the Brest-Litovsk conference the following February.

[10] The decree is reprinted in Piłsudski, *PZ,* Vol. VIII, Appendix I, pp. iii–v.

but more powerful body to be composed of the general designated as commander in chief in wartime, who was to serve as its presiding officer, the chief of the General Staff, his second deputy, who was to head the secretariat of this Inner War Council but to have no vote in it, and the generals designated as field commanders of corps in war-time (peacetime army inspectors). The rather weakened war minister could attend meetings "according to need and his convictions" but had no control over either the designate commander in chief for wartime or the army inspectors. The functions of this Inner War Council were to prepare, in cooperation with the General Staff, operational war plans which would be binding on the war minister and to pass on the qualifications of all unit commanders from regi-mental colonels upward. Needless to add, the chairman of this Inner War Council and designate commander in chief in the event of war was Piłsudski himself.

By thus rendering the war minister, who was responsible to the parliament (Sejm), powerless in respect to the war-operational machinery, Piłsudski hoped to immunize the fighting army from politi-cal interference. This arrangement simultaneously limited effective civilian-parliamentary control over the armed forces. Piłsudski antici-pated that the constitution which was about to be adopted would locate the center of political power in the Sejm and thus in the political parties; and his decree of January 7, 1921, was an attempt to remove the army in advance from this parliamentary political control.

The next two years, however, brought a steady erosion of Piłsudski's institutional power in Poland. The adoption in March, 1921, of the new constitution, with its proparliamentary and antiexecutive bias, was followed by the calamitously divisive presidential elections of December, 1922, after which he ceased to be chief of state. Finally, the formation of Witos' Right-Center cabinet in May, 1923, forced Piłsudski into relinquishing as well his military posts—chief of the General Staff (May 30), chairman of the Inner War Council, and designate commander in chief in the event of war (July 2)—and retiring from public office. He regarded the new regime as one com-posed, in effect, of the murderers of Narutowicz, and it, in turn, had no use for him. The chieftaincy of the General Staff and that of the

War Ministry were transferred to two of Piłsudski's professional and political rivals from the former Austrian army, General Stanisław Haller and General Count Stanisław Szeptycki respectively. The latter promptly drafted a new plan of military organization. It was approved by the cabinet on June 18 and presented to the Sejm on June 27, 1923, to replace Piłsudski's decree of January 7, 1921, which the Right-Center political coalition had viewed as a sinister attempt on Piłsudski's part to render the army his personal *imperium in imperio* within the Polish state and which it regarded as having become obsolete with his retirement.[11]

Free from the constraints of military discipline, Piłsudski used his retirement at Sulejówek for a vigorous campaign with word and pen against Szeptycki's new army command project, which bore certain strong similarities to the one France had abandoned as obsolete in 1911.[12] It removed the president of the Republic from the Full War Council, which was transformed into an advisory body to the war minister, to be composed of the minister as chairman, the chief of the General Staff, the chief of Army Administration, and the inspector general of armies and the other inspectors. The prime minister also had access to its meetings. The inspector general of armies was apparently presumed to be—but not explicitly designated as—the commander in chief in the event of war. Both he and the chief of the General Staff were each immediately and exclusively responsible to the war minister. The Inner War Council, which Piłsudski had regarded as the key to the proper insulation of the armed forces from political interference in the basic professional function of preparing for war, was eliminated.

In theory this system appeared to have the political virtue of ensuring ultimate civilian-democratic control over the armed forces,

---

[11] See Dąbrowski, *Zagadnienie obrony narodowej w wojnie nowoczesnej, passim.* Szeptycki's organizational plan is reprinted in Piłsudski, *PZ,* Vol. VIII, Appendix I, pp. vi–viii. Szeptycki had been Austrian governor-general of Lublin in 1917–18 (resigning in protest against the concessions made to the Ukrainians by the Central Powers in the negotiations at Brest-Litovsk) and commander of the Polish northern front during the Polish-Soviet campaign of 1920. He was a brother of the Uniate Metropolitan of Lwów, Roman (Andrei) Sheptyts'kyi (1865–1944), who was a world-famous patron of the cultural and national aspirations of the Ukrainian minority of Poland.

[12] Podoski, p. 187, and J. Revol, *Histoire de l'Armée Française* (Paris, 1929), p. 211.

all of which were made directly responsible to the war minister, who, in turn, was answerable to the Sejm. In fact, however, the kaleidoscopic instability of Polish cabinets and the habit of irresponsible interference by Sejm deputies with administration meant that the Szeptycki plan carried the threat of transforming the armed forces into a political football—a risk heightened by the relatively impotent projected position of the inspector general of armies in relation to both the war minister and the chief of the General Staff and one excessively dangerous for such a vulnerable state as the new Poland, precariously placed between hostile Germany and Russia. This fault was so manifest that the Szeptycki plan was stillborn. Its author's tenure as war minister ended on November 5, 1923. In any event, Witos' Right-Center cabinet fell a few weeks later, on December 14, 1923, largely as a result of its inability to cope with the country's monumental economic difficulties.[13]

Stanisław Thugutt, leader of the Leftist Wyzwolenie, next tried to form a cabinet. He offered the War Ministry to the retired but still immensely influential Piłsudski, who insisted as a precondition on the scrapping of the Szeptycki project and reversion to his own army-command organization decree of January 7, 1921. Thugutt agreed but failed to form a government.[14] The financial expert Władysław Grabski then succeeded and on December 19, 1923, installed his supraparty cabinet of experts, which was to last for two years, until November 14, 1925—longer than any other between 1918 and 1926. Grabski, who originally wished to effect Piłsudski's return to the army, reappointed as his first war minister Piłsudski's veteran collaborator, General Kazimierz Sosnkowski, who had already held this portfolio for nearly three uninterrupted years until the Szeptycki interval.

Sosnkowski, hoping to solve this issue by compromise, introduced a proposal to appoint Piłsudski inspector general of armies (and designate commander in chief in war) and simultaneously to declare this post to be of cabinet rank and thus equal to that of the war minister. This plan was denounced as unconstitutional by the civilian politicians and rejected as unsound by Piłsudski.[15] For these reasons,

---

[13] See above, pp. 12–15.
[14] Thugutt, p. 113, and Piłsudski, *PZ*, VI, 145–46.
[15] Pietrzak, ed., "Jak doszło" i "Przewrót," p. 130, and Pobóg-Malinowski, *Najnowsza historia*, II, 457–58.

and because of budgetary differences with Grabski, who was finance minister as well as prime minister,[16] Sosnkowski resigned and was succeeded at the War Ministry on February 17, 1924, by Piłsudski's most serious rival, General Władysław Sikorski. An attempt, made in January with the support of President Wojciechowski,[17] to persuade Piłsudski to return to active service as the designate commander in chief in wartime, had aborted because Piłsudski's conditions were still too sweeping to be acceptable to the Rightist parties on whose toleration the Grabski government depended. [18]

Sikorski quickly withdrew the Szeptycki project on February 25 and presented his own, which was endorsed by the cabinet on March 10 and sent to the Sejm on March 14, 1924, for legislative consideration.[19] It provided for a Council for the Defense of the State, a kind of inner war cabinet with a civilian majority, presided over by the president of the Republic and including as well the prime minister, the ministers of foreign affairs, of war, of finance, of the interior, of commerce and industry, of railroads, the chief of the General Staff, and the inspector general of armies. This council was to examine and coordinate general defense problems and measures. For direct operational planning, the Sikorski project provided a Council of War under the chairmanship of the war minister and consisting further of the inspector general of armies, the chief of the General Staff, the chief of Army Administration, the various inspectors, and two other generals nominated by the war minister. The inspector general of armies and the chief of the General Staff were to be each directly responsible to the war minister and to cooperate with each other in preparing operational plans, in which work the inspector general had the right to issue "directives" (but not "orders") to the chief of the General Staff.

[16] It appears that Sosnkowski vainly appealed to President Wojciechowski for support against Grabski on this issue of military appropriations. See Aleksandra Piłsudska, *Wspomnienia,* p. 289, and W. Grabski, pp. 33–34.

[17] Until shortly before the coup of May, 1926, President Wojciechowski had persistently sought to facilitate Piłsudski's return to the army. See Benedykt, p. 1, and AGLŻ, 32a/29, 31, 61, 246.

[18] See Piłsudski's press interview with the Warsaw *Kurjer Poranny* of January 10, 1924, and his letter to the editor of *Polska Zbrojna,* August 27, 1924, which are reprinted, respectively, in his *PZ,* VI, 145–47, and VIII, 45–46.

[19] Sikorski's project is reprinted in Piłsudski, *PZ,* Vol. VIII, Appendix I, pp. ix–xiii.

Through an intermediary—a procedure deeply resented by Piłsud-ski—Sikorski had asked for Piłsudski's comments about this project, and on February 29, 1924, Piłsudski replied with a withering letter alleging that the plan was an inept aping of the French one of 1920 and that it paid no attention to the profoundly different conditions prevailing in Poland. He charged that the project failed to allocate clearly the respective functions and powers of the war minister, the chief of the General Staff, and the inspector general of armies—the last being far too weak—and that it opened the army to political interference and intrigue.[20]

Though Sikorski proceeded to present his project to the cabinet and the Sejm despite these criticisms, during the course of the year he nevertheless did work out some alterations, which were accepted by the cabinet on December 5, 1924. This revised version specifically designated the inspector general of armies as the commander in chief in wartime, gave him somewhat greater but still not categorically clear authority over the chief of the General Staff, but without the power to select the latter, and again left both these officers directly responsi-ble to the war minister, who in turn was accountable to the Sejm.[21] These latter provisos provoked Piłsudski's rejection of the project at a conference on December 11, 1924, attended by Premier Grabski, Piłsudski, Sikorski, Marshal of the Sejm Maciej Rataj, Vice-Premier (without portfolio) Stanisław Thugutt, and Sejm deputy Stefan Dą-browski, who was *rapporteur* for the bill on the military affairs com-mittee of the Sejm and an important Rightist, that is, anti-Piłsudski, politician. Piłsudski refused to consider accepting the position of inspector general of armies as long as its powers and independence were in his view inadequate, and he regarded the entire plan as animated by a profound suspicion of this office and a desire to curb its incumbent, which he was invited to become.[22]

[20] This letter was made public by Piłsudski the following year on August 15, 1925, and is reprinted *ibid.*, VI, 209–11.

[21] Sikorski is said to have discussed his proposed revisions with French political and military circles during his visit to Paris of October–November, 1924. See Malicki, p. 229. His amended project is reprinted in Piłsudski, *PZ*, Vol. VIII, Appendix I, pp. xiii–xvii.

[22] For a recollection of this meeting, see Thugutt, pp. 125–26. Immediately afterward Piłsudski made public his reasons for rejecting the amended Sikorski project and for refusing to serve as inspector general of armies under its terms

Henceforth, relations between Sikorski and Piłsudski, already tense since their World War I differences over Sikorski's Austro-Polish leanings, were to become increasingly bitter. Sikorski and his supporters complained that Piłsudski seemed not to comprehend that the army must be the army of the state and the government, not of the retired commander in chief, and that he confused the necessary apoliticism of the army with mere loyalty to his own person as its creator.[23] Piłsudski and his partisans, in turn, charged that Sikorski's entire mode of conduct and allegedly sincere desire to facilitate Piłsudski's resumption of the functions of the designate commander in chief in wartime (inspector general of armies) were sheer hypocrisy, designed to mollify public demand for Piłsudski's return in a worsening political and economic climate—a demand expressed, for example, in a resolution adopted at the Legion reunion in Lublin on August 10, 1924 [24]—while Sikorski was in fact frustrating this return with an organizational plan that he knew in advance would be unacceptable to Piłsudski.[25] In response to officially inspired rumors that Piłsudski had approved the revised Sikorski project, Piłsudski issued a vehement denial on August 15, 1925, and made public his letter of February 29, 1924, criticizing the original Sikorski formulations to prove that he had been opposed to them from their very inception.[26]

Meanwhile, during the first half of 1925 the military affairs com-

---

in an interview published in the *Kurjer Poranny,* December 12, 1924, and reprinted in his *PZ,* VIII, 122–27.

[23] Sikorski, p. 15, and Pietrzak, ed., "Jak doszło" i "Przewrót," p. 132. This latter item consists of two unsigned memoranda written either by Sikorski or by a political confidant of his and preserved in the Warsaw Archiwum Akt Nowych, S. Kauzik Collection. For a defense of Sikorski's project on the grounds that it ensured civilian control over the armed forces through the war minister's supremacy over them and his simultaneous accountability to the Sejm, see Kukiel, "Jeszcze o przełomie majowym," p. 16.

[24] See Piłsudski, *PZ,* VIII, 43. It was in response to this resolution that the government publicly announced its desire to appoint Piłsudski inspector general of armies. *Ibid.,* p. 45.

[25] For charges of bad faith and opportunistic careerism leveled against Sikorski, see Piłsudski's letter in the *Kurjer Poranny,* August 15, 1925, reprinted in his *PZ,* VIII, 209–10; Daszyński, *W pierwszą rocznicę,* p. 21; Porczak, *Rewolucja majowa,* p. 32; and Pobóg-Malinowski, *Najnowsza historia,* II, 458. For Sikorski's rejection of these allegations and protestations of sincerity toward Piłsudski, see the sources in note 23 above.

[26] Piłsudski, *PZ,* VIII, 209–10; VI, 209–11.

mittee of the Sejm was still considering and further amending the revised Sikorski project. Here the parties of the nationalistic Right, motivated by political and personal antipathy to Piłsudski and determined to render his return to the army either impossible or at least merely ceremonial, further worsened (in Piłsudski's view)[27] the Sikorski project by making the transient prime minister rather than the more permanent president the chairman of the proposed Council for the Defense of the State—which, in the light of its designated membership, would be little more than a cabinet committee of predictably short-lived ministers—and by strongly confirming the subordination of the inspector general of armies to the frequently changing and politically vulnerable war minister. They also introduced various amendments to weaken the inspector general of armies altogether, behaving once again as they had during the constitutional discussions of 1919–21 over the powers of the president.[28]

The Right's vindictiveness toward Piłsudski and seeming indifference to sound organizational principles were embarrassing to Sikorski, who was anxious to differentiate his quarrel with Piłsudski from the Right's and who insisted that his aim was to wed the best of the Legions' tradition and enthusiasm with the professional expertise of the officers from the former partitioning armies.[29]

The PPS was also in a dilemma. On the one hand, as one of its leading Sejm deputies, Dr. Herman Lieberman, explained to the Sejm military affairs committee, the Socialists regarded Piłsudski's return to the army as indispensable, for they considered him Poland's most reputable military figure. On the other hand, they opposed his notion that the inspector general of armies should be independent of the war minister and not accountable to the Sejm. The Socialists deplored the use of the army for partisan political purposes as strongly as

[27] Piłsudski's embittered reaction to the Sejm committee's version of the Sikorski bill was given in an interview published in the *Kurjer Poranny,* July 27, 1925, and reprinted in his *PZ,* VIII, 191–94.

[28] The chief tactician of the Right on this issue was the Christian National *rapporteur* for the bill, deputy Stefan Dąbrowski, who published an elaborate defense of his (and the Right's) position in his book *Zagadnienie obrony narodowej w wojnie nowoczesnej: Organizacja rządu i naczelnego dowództwa.* The Sejm committee's project is reprinted in Piłsudski, *PZ,* Vol. VIII, Appendix I, pp. xviii–xxiv.

[29] Sikorski, p. 15, and Pietrzak, ed., "Jak doszło" i "Przewrót," pp. 130–31, 143.

attempts by military figures to remove themselves from civilian control.[30] The Polish Socialists had shared in the prewar tradition of armed struggle for independence and now took a positive attitude toward the military establishment. They insisted, however, on civilian supremacy and vainly sought to persuade their onetime party comrade, Piłsudski, to moderate his adamant stand.[31] Piłsudski replied that his insistence on the autonomy and preponderance of the inspector general of armies as designate commander in chief in wartime was soundly grounded in the geopolitical situation of Poland as well as in the valid principle of immunizing the army from partisan political influences. Situated between two powerful neighbors, Poland, he argued, was a potential object of aggression, and in the opening phases of a war her army would be obligated to conduct a defensive campaign. Since the military initiative would be with the offensively deployed foreign foe, the Polish commander in chief must be free to improvise and take immediate decisions. This, however, necessitated thorough preliminary control on his part over his forces and required that even in peacetime the future commander in chief must have undiluted authority over the General Staff and its chief, who drafted war plans, as well as over the inspectors who would command the various field corps in battle.[32] Finally, Piłsudski's insistence on the autonomy of the army command was also rooted in his conviction that a major cause of the decline and disappearance of the old Polish Commonwealth had been the neglect of the military establishment by the society, the kings, and the Sejms of the century preceding the partitions [33]—and that it was at all costs essential to ensure against a repetition of this sad history.

The entire issue, meanwhile, still hung suspended. Piłsudski's

[30] Porczak, *Rewolucja majowa*, p. 32, and Daszyński, *W pierwszą rocznicę*, pp. 18–22.

[31] Pietrzak, ed., "Jak doszło" i "Przewrót," p. 131.

[32] See Piłsudski's press interview in the *Kurjer Poranny* of January 20, 1926, reprinted in his *PZ*, VIII, 259–64. Piłsudski also developed this argument at length at a secret meeting of about thirty of his supporters held in the second half of 1925 in the Warsaw home of his devoted supporter Kazimierz Świtalski. This meeting is described in the recollections of one of its participants, Sławoj-Składkowski, "Wspomnienia z okresu majowego," p. 109. Other such "secret" meetings—of which the authorities were in fact well informed— took place in the home of General Jakub Krzemieński.

[33] See his lecture of January 24, 1926, on this theme as reprinted in his *PZ*, VIII, 264–76.

prestige in the country was such that the Sejm dared not enact an army organization project of which he disapproved, while the Rightist parties were strong enough in the legislature to prevent the adoption of one conforming to his demands. The financial and economic crisis was simultaneously becoming acute, and on November 13, 1925, Grabski submitted his cabinet's resignation, which a reluctant President Wojciechowski accepted the next day.

Piłsudski immediately seized the opportunity to demonstrate his strength. At two o'clock on the afternoon of November 14, 1925, he appeared at the Belweder palace, the presidential residence, and handed Wojciechowski a memorandum, which he obliged the President to sign, cautioning him against permitting any further assaults on the "moral interests" of the army. Without mentioning names, the memorandum asserted that such infringments had already occured twice—a clear allusion to the appointments of Szeptycki and Sikorski as war minister.[34] Warning that the army could no longer permit its honor to be sullied by being made the object of political bargaining among Sejm politicians and ambitious generals, Piłsudski declared that he considered himself justified in undertaking this intervention with Wojciechowski by virtue of his positions as former chief of state, as creator of the Polish army, as its victorious commander (in 1920), and as the bearer of its highest rank (First Marshal of Poland). Wojciechowski, in reply, confessed himself powerless to intervene to halt the general political rot.[35] The President thus doubly exposed his weakness: in accepting, and even signing a receipt for, an ultimatum from Piłsudski[36] and in bewailing his inability to halt the admitted deterioration of the political and social situation of the nation.

The next day, November 15, there occurred an extraordinary demonstration at Piłsudski's country home in Sulejówek. Allegedly to commemorate the seventh anniversary of Piłsudski's return to

[34] Piłsudski confirmed that he had these two officers in mind. See his interview in the *Kurjer Poranny* of January 14, 1926, reprinted in his *PZ*, VIII, 257.

[35] Piłsudski's memorandum is reprinted in his *PZ*, VIII, 247–48, and in Malicki, pp. 255–56. A detailed account of the meeting is given in Benedykt, p. 1, and other references to it may be found in Krzyżanowski, p. 70.

[36] Sikorski bitterly resented this act and complained that it undermined the army's confidence in the President. See Sikorski, p. 4.

Warsaw from German imprisonment at Magdeburg (the precise anniversary was on November 10), a large number of pro-Piłsudski officers from the Warsaw garrison—estimates vary from 400 to 2,000, including 20 generals—assembled at Sulejówek to pay tribute to Poland's First Marshal.[37] Their spokesman, the Legion veteran General Gustaw Orlicz-Dreszer, gave a short speech recalling the glorious days of November, 1918, when Piłsudski was Poland's uncrowned dictator,[38] begging Piłsudski not to absent himself from public life in the difficult days through which Poland was currently passing, and assuring him that not only the loyal hearts but also the victorious swords of the assembled officers were at his disposal. To this transparent invitation to stage a coup d'état, Piłsudski replied equivocally. Confessing his deep disappointment with Poland's political history since his return from Magdeburg, when he had virtually incarnated Poland by national acclamation, he expressed his conviction that justice must eventually be done and that those who delayed it were weakening the state. He concluded by asking for continued comradeship in the days ahead among all those present.[39]

At about the same time, the officers of other garrisons—among them the strongly pro-Piłsudski garrison at Wilno—also sent Piłsudski declarations of their loyalty.[40]

Sikorski, furious at what he regarded as a political demonstration

[37] The lowest figure, 400, is given in P. Bartel, *Le Maréchal Pilsudski*, p. 233, and R. Landau, p. 215. Verax, p. 513, says 415 officers participated, while Loessner, p. 186, and Reddaway, p. 210, speak of 1,000 assembled well-wishers—which is also the figure cited in Piłsudski, *PZ*, VIII, 248. The high estimate of 2,000 is made in Wrzos, p. 67.

[38] On his return to Warsaw from Magdeburg on November 10, 1918, Piłsudski inherited the legislative and executive powers of the previous regimes in Congress Poland and Western Galicia. He was recognized as the *Naczelnik* (Chief)—the title once borne by the great Kościuszko in 1794—and his authority was indeed virtually dictatorial. He quickly arranged that elections to a Constituent Sejm take place on January 26, 1919. On February 20, 1919, he surrendered his supreme powers to this Constituent Sejm, which confirmed him as chief of state but declared itself to be the legal bearer of state sovereignty.

[39] Orlicz-Dreszer's and Piłsudski's speeches on this occasion are reprinted in Piłsudski, *PZ*, VIII, 248–51. An interesting claim that Orlicz-Dreszer's seemingly indiscreet speech had actually been drafted by Piłsudski is made by the former's brother, Zygmunt Dreszer, p. 4.

[40] In Wilno, General Stefan Dąb-Biernacki and Colonels Jan Kruszewski and Stanisław Skwarczyński—three ex-Legionnaires—renamed the "Szeptycki barracks" the "Piłsudski barracks." For this and other details, see Czubiński, "Przewrót majowy," p. 121, and Porczak, *Rewolucja majowa*, p. 34.

and breach of discipline, used his authority as caretaker war minister pending the formation of a new cabinet to relieve Orlicz-Dreszer from his command of the Second Cavalry Division in Warsaw and transfer him to the Third Cavalry Division in Poznań—a city and garrison thoroughly National Democratic (Rightist) in outlook, where a partisan of Piłsudski would be utterly isolated. Orlicz-Dreszer, rather than accept this banishment, went on leave.[41] Sikorski, apparently fearing an imminent coup, took other extensive administrative precautions.[42]

Nevertheless, the double show of Piłsudskist strength on November 14 and 15 had a catalytic effect on the political situation. On November 20, 1925, the parties formed a broad-spectrum coalition cabinet under Prime Minister (and Foreign Minister) Count Aleksander Skrzyński stretching from Right to Left, from the National Democrats to the Socialists, and including also the Christian Democrats, the Piast Peasants, and the National Laborites. A week later, on November 27, 1925, the War Ministry was assigned to a nominee of Piłsudski, General Lucjan Żeligowski of the former tsarist Russian army. Sikorski was exiled eastward to command the Lwów Military District after Prime Minister Skrzyński had been personally warned by three members of the inner Piłsudskist entourage (members of the so-called colonels' group which was to become politically prominent in the 1930s) that Sikorski's retention as war minister would elicit serious consequences.[43] The Socialists had endorsed these Piłsudskist objections to Sikorski, about whom the Right also had its reservations; finally, President Wojciechowski was himself also opposed to him.[44]

[41] Kmicic-Skrzyński, p. 3 (an unpublished typescript in the archives of the Piłsudski Historical Institute in London).

[42] On November 14, 1925, Sikorski had ordered the disarming of a number of paramilitary and youth organizations in the capital, among them the Riflemen, Sokol gymnasts, Scouts, and Association of Rural Youth. He also provisionally nominated Colonel Władysław Anders to command the Warsaw garrison. See Czubiński, "Przewrót majowy," p. 121; Pietrzak, ed., "Jak doszło" i "Przewrót," p. 132; and Malicki, pp. 257–58.

[43] The three Piłsudskist troubleshooters were the ex-Legionnaires Bogusław Miedziński, Kazimierz Świtalski, and Bolesław Wieniawa-Długoszowski. The last was at this time still on active military service as a cavalry colonel. All three figured prominently in the May coup and its aftermath.

[44] Rataj, pp. 316–17, 341–42; AGLŻ, 32/17; and Głąbiński, p. 546. For Sikorski's awareness and resentment of Wojciechowski's hostility, see his "Kartki z dziennika," p. 4.

One of Żeligowski's first ministerial acts was to recall Orlicz-Dreszer to Warsaw, thereby provoking the withdrawal in protest of General Stanisław Haller (of the former Austrian army) as chief of the General Staff on December 15, 1925.[45] Haller, it will be recalled, had succeeded Piłsudski as chief of the General Staff upon the latter's angry resignation on May 30, 1923. He was a dedicated foe of Piłsudski, and his current fears were soon justified as Orlicz-Dreszer quickly plunged into active conspiratorial preparation for the May, 1926, coup.

Since Prime Minister Skrzyński, serving also as foreign minister, was preoccupied during the initial weeks of his premiership with implementing the recently concluded Locarno Treaties, the pro-Piłsudski elements in his cabinet waited till the beginning of the new year before launching their offensive on the army command question. Then, on January 7, 1926, the Socialist minister of public works, Jędrzej Moraczewski, who had been Poland's first prime minister from November 18, 1918, to January 16, 1919, and who was a close political associate of Piłsudski, raised the question of Piłsudski's return to active service at a cabinet meeting.[46] Skrzyński, whose main interest was foreign affairs and who sought domestic tranquillity so as to be able to devote himself to this interest, was convinced that Piłsudski's return was essential to secure such tranquillity. His hands were tied, however, by the need to balance between the Left and the Right members of his coalition, and since the Right remained adamantly opposed to facilitating Piłsudski's return to the army, the cabinet could do no better than to request the Sejm to expedite its consideration of the army command bill (that is, Sikorski's revised and amended project) and to resolve the question one way or another.[47] Simultaneously, Skrzyński undertook negotiations with Pił-

[45] Haller's lengthy and sharp letter of resignation is in AGLŻ, 26/7–9. Though formally continuing to bear the title of chief of the General Staff, Haller took an extended leave. His functions were assigned to General Edmund Kessler as acting chief, after both Piłsudski and Żeligowski failed to persuade Sosnkowski to accept the post. *Ibid.*, 26/28–29, 32/14–15.

[46] Daszyński, *W pierwszą rocznicę*, p. 22, asserts that Moraczewski suggested appointing Piłsudski once again to be chief of the General Staff. Other sources do not specify this particular office, nor does the official cabinet communiqué on this episode, cited in the next footnote.

[47] See the cabinet communiqué of January 11, 1926, reprinted in Piłsudski, *PZ*, VIII, 251.

sudski, who continued to insist as a preliminary condition on the withdrawal of the Sikorski project in all its versions [48]—a step which the Right vetoed. After waiting in vain for a resolution of this problem for exactly a month from the day he had first raised the issue, Moraczewski resigned from the cabinet on February 7, 1926, officially for reasons of health but in fact in protest against Skrzyński's failure to meet Piłsudski's terms.[49] Two days later, on February 9, 1926, Piłsudski announced that he, too, was breaking off his negotiations with Skrzyński.[50] The next day, February 10, a troubled War Minister Żeligowski insisted on the withdrawal of the Sikorski project and the introduction of one acceptable to Piłsudski, but the profoundly divided cabinet again procrastinated and could only agree to consult the executive committees of the parties composing it.[51]

Meanwhile, Piłsudski was sustaining his pressure with press interviews, letters to editors, public speeches, and audiences with President Wojciechowski.[52] On March 21, 1926, he gave a public lecture on the theme of "The Commander in Chief in Theory and Practice" to an audience of several thousand in Warsaw, who transformed the occasion into a mass public demonstration for him. The disastrously deepening economic crisis and the ominous international situation, for which the public tended to blame the parliamentary system in general and the Rightist parties in particular, were steadily increasing the appeal of Piłsudski as the nation's potential savior. His opponents were forced on the defensive. In strictly military terms, too, there was increasing concern on the part of responsible persons to end the

[48] Piłsudski's letter on this point in the *Kurjer Poranny* of January 13, 1926, is reprinted in his *PZ*, VIII, 252–53. See also *ibid.*, p. 277, and AGLŻ, 32a/3.

[49] The *Frankfurter Zeitung*, February 10, 1926, speculated that another reason for Moraczewski's resignation was his dismay over the conservative fiscal and tax policies of the National Democratic finance minister, Jerzy Zdziechowski. That the resignation was a strictly personal action, not authorized by the PPS, is insisted upon by Pragier, "Ostatni rząd przedmajowy," p. 2. Moraczewski was replaced as minister of public works on February 13 by another Socialist, Norbert Barlicki.

[50] Piłsudski's interview of February 9 is reprinted in his *PZ*, VIII, 277–80.

[51] *Ibid.*, p. 280; AGLŻ, 32a/30–31.

[52] Piłsudski's various utterances on the army command question from the fall of the Grabski cabinet on November 14, 1925, to his last interview with President Wojciechowski before the coup cover pp. 247–332 of Vol. VIII of his *PZ*.

long interregnum at the level of the supreme command, for without a designated commander in chief in the event of war, the army inspectors worked in a void, the chief of the General Staff became immersed in the *ad hoc* problems of the war minister, and the Inner War Council was reduced to redundancy.[53]

Finally, on May 4, 1926, came the breakthrough: the cabinet agreed to withdraw the modified Sikorski army command project and to permit Żeligowski to introduce a new one which, though it did not have Piłsudski's formal endorsement, was nevertheless basically in conformity with his views, since it gave the inspector general of armies, who was again designated as wartime commander in chief, control over the General Staff and its chief, and also restored the chairmanship of the Council for the Defense of the State to the president.[54] By now, however, it was too late. The cabinet, already weakened by Moraczewski's resignation on February 7 and the subsequent withdrawal of the Socialists Ziemięcki and Barlicki over fiscal and economic issues on April 20, fell on May 5, the day after Żeligowski's project had been sent to the Sejm, thereby inaugurating Poland's last governmental crisis before the coup.

It is difficult, even in retrospect, to make a judgment whether the various protagonists in these constant discussions on the organization of the army command structure had consistently negotiated in good faith. Piłsudski, eventually, professed to believe that he was being toyed with and that, despite disclaimers to the contrary, the prevailing political establishment was determined to frustrate his return to the army. This suspicion was quite correct so far as it attached to the Rightist camp of politicians and the generals allied with them. It was almost certainly false in regard to such figures as President Wojcie-chowski, Prime Ministers Grabski and Skrzyński, War Ministers Sosnkowski and Żeligowski, perhaps even Sikorski. As Piłsudski's manner, in turn, became ever more irascible and his public statements increasingly peremptory, the other figures tended to gain the impression that he had ceased to be interested in working toward a negotiated solution and was confident of being able to ride the crest

[53] AGLŻ, 32/4; 32a/262, 264.
[54] Żeligowski's project is reprinted in Piłsudski, *PZ*, Vol. VIII, Appendix I, pp. xxv–xxix.

of politico-economic crisis and public frustration to total victory.[55] Finally, even many responsible persons otherwise well disposed toward Piłsudski were disturbed by his insistence that the designate commander in chief for war be invested even in peacetime with a degree of autonomy and authority which appeared to them to be excessive and incompatible with the political and constitutional principles of parliamentary democracy.

[55] See the memoirs of the deputy chief of President Wojciechowski's Civilian Chancellery, Chrząszczewski, "Kartki z mego pamiętnika," No. 21, pp. 2 and 7. Even the pro-Piłsudski Żeligowski developed the impression that by April, 1926, Piłsudski was no longer interested in Żeligowski's efforts to facilitate the Marshal's return to the army by a statutory settlement and preferred a thoroughgoing crisis. See AGLŻ, 32/55–56, 32a/132.

PART TWO

THE COUP D'ETAT

CHAPTER III

MAY 5–12: A WEEK OF
MOUNTING TENSION

The resignation of Prime Minister Aleksander Skrzyński and the fall of his cabinet on May 5 were not at first viewed with particular alarm nor regarded as initiating an extraordinary crisis. The early formation of still another in Poland's chronic series of coalition cabinets was awaited,[1] and the Right-Center alliance, freshly recemented at the Zakopane negotiations during Easter, was expected to lead to a new government without any particular difficulties.[2] Indeed, the main attention of the politicians was for a brief period still focused on the new (May 4) army command project of outgoing War Minister Żeligowski and its political implications. In the Senate, the National Democratic presiding officer (marshal) of that body, Wojciech Trąmpczyński, recognizing that General Żeligowski's plan was to facilitate Piłsudski's resumption of active command, delivered on May 5 a bitter attack against Piłsudski, denying him any qualifications for higher command (as allegedly displayed by his decisions during the Polish-Soviet campaign of 1920 and his tenure as chief of the General Staff in 1922–23) and denouncing his prospective return to the army as a catastrophe for Poland over which the Germans could well rejoice.[3] On the same day there was an angry falling-out between

[1] See *Kurjer Warszawski,* May 5 and 6, 1926.
[2] This coalition could muster a minimum of 212 Sejm deputies. With Christian Nationalist and Catholic People's support, it could count on 238 votes. See "Le coup d'état de Varsovie," p. 15.
[3] Porczak, *Rewolucja majowa,* p. 44, and Malicki, pp. 276–77. Trąmpczyński was from Poznań, in the former Prussian part of Poland, and hence particularly anti-German. His speech provoked a sensation in the army and elicited sharp protests by a number of pro-Piłsudski officers led by General Edward Rydz-Śmigły, whose letter of protest to President Wojciechowski is published in Nagel, pp. 16–18.

Żeligowski and the Senate's military affairs committee apropos of that body's discussion of a hostile interpellation, referring to Piłsudski's activities, which had been addressed some weeks earlier to the War Minister by about forty overwhelmingly Rightist senators.[4] It thus seemed at first that this issue would overshadow the simultaneous cabinet dissolution, especially as the Piast Peasant Party's Wincenty Witos was proceeding with apparent confidence to assemble a successor cabinet.

The Piast leader first sought to ascertain whether he could purchase the neutrality of the Socialists by omitting the extreme Right—the antirepublican Christian Nationalists—from his prospective Right-Center cabinet.[5] Upon being disabused of this hope, he shrewdly withdrew into the background as President Wojciechowski (who disliked and disapproved of Witos) invited the Christian Democrat Józef Chaciński and the Piast Jan Dębski [6] to try their chances at assembling parliamentary majorities.[7] Dębski, perhaps reluctant to be suspected of betraying his party chief, Witos, apparently made no vigorous efforts. Chaciński, in turn, hoped to form a Right-Center coalition of the National Democratic, Piast Peasant, Christian Democratic, and National Labor parties which would hopefully enjoy the toleration of the extreme Rightist Christian Nationalists and of the parliamentary Left. He gave up, however, on being warned of the latter's vigorous opposition unless he accepted the rather implausible condition of basing himself on the Left's own political and economic program. Against this ultimatum, a qualified promise of support by the Christian Nationalists was politically worthless.[8] Meanwhile, the

[4] AGLŻ, 32/59–60, 33/258–69; *Kurjer Warszawski*, May 6, 1926. The text of the senatorial interpellation and of Żeligowski's preliminary written reply to it is in *Polska Zbrojna*, April 22 and 23, 1926.

[5] He sounded the Socialist leaders Norbert Barlicki and Mieczysław Niedziałkowski. See *Kurjer Warszawski*, May 5, 1926.

[6] Jan Dębski is not to be confused with the Jan Dąbski who had seceded from Piast in 1923 and cofounded the more radical Stronnictwo Chłopskie in 1926. Furthermore, the Christian Democratic Party is not to be confused with the Christian Nationalists. It was moderately conservative in contrast to the latter's Right extremism.

[7] *Kurjer Warszawski*, May 6, 1926. Witos was quite content to desist temporarily because the distribution of prospective portfolios was provoking quarrels in his camp. For Wojciechowski's dislike of Witos, see Głąbiński, p. 535.

[8] He had conferred with Zygmunt Marek (PPS), Józef Putek (Wyzwolenie), and Edward Dubanowicz (Christian Nationalist). Rataj, p. 362, and *Kurjer Warszawski*, May 7, 1926.

four Polish parties of the parliamentary Left (Socialist, Wyzwolenie, Klub Praca, Stronnictwo Chłopskie) decided to maximize their bargaining and veto power by forming a consultative bloc for the duration of the cabinet crisis.

It was once again Witos' turn. He began auspiciously by getting the prestigious Skrzyński to agree to continue serving as foreign minister. When the Left bloc announced its total hostility to Witos' prospective cabinet, however, Skrzyński retracted his pledge, claiming that it had been postulated on the assumption that Witos' cabinet would be broad enough to win the toleration of the Left.[9] Witos withdrew. An attempt by Sejm Marshal Maciej Rataj to find a way out came to nought because his own Piast Peasant Party remained committed to its leader Witos.[10]

As the newly organized Left bloc had so far been the primary *tombeur* of the preceding efforts, President Wojciechowski next requested the Socialist Zygmunt Marek to try his hand at cabinet building. To discover whether a Left-Center coalition was feasible, Marek sounded Witos, Chaciński, and Piłsudski. The cool response of the first two having convinced him that his own premiership was impracticable,[11] Marek thereupon offered the Left bloc's support for a government headed by Piłsudski, who declined, alleging poor health.[12] Since he was physically up to the rigors of a coup d'état a few days later, more plausible reasons for Piłsudski's refusal are that he had no confidence in the Left's ability to sustain a majority and/or that he did not want to be exclusively associated with it.[13]

Right-Center and Left-Center parliamentary combinations having proved abortive, President Wojciechowski now resorted to what had

[9] *Kurjer Warszawski,* May 8 and 9, 1926; Witos, *Moje wspomnienia,* III, 84–85; Rataj, p. 363. Skrzyński declared himself convinced that no regime opposed by both Piłsudski and the Socialists could last. His foreign policy ("the spirit of Locarno") had been most consistently supported by the Left. Just after the fall of his cabinet, Skrzyński had attacked the Christian Nationalists for coveting republican portfolios while endorsing monarchism. *Berliner Tageblatt,* May 5, 1926.

[10] Rataj, pp. 363–64; Kutrzeba, p. 290.

[11] *Kurjer Warszawski,* May 9, 1926; Rataj, p. 364.

[12] This was revealed in the testimony given at the Brześć trial on October 27, 1931, by the Socialist defendant Barlicki and witness Niedziałkowski. See *Sprawa brzeska,* pp. 56, 194. Also Singer, pp. 96–97, and Chrząszczewski, "Kartki z mego pamiętnika," No. 22, p. 2.

[13] Benedykt, p. 1. A report that Piłsudski declined to be premier but indicated a readiness to head the War Ministry in a Left-Center cabinet led by Marek is in *Kurjer Warszawski,* May 9, 1926.

probably all along been his first preference: he requested Władysław Grabski to attempt a repetition of his supraparty government of 1923–25. Determined finally to cut through some of Poland's chronic and fundamental political problems, Wojciechowski and Grabski agreed during a night conference of May 8–9 that the latter would go to the Sejm with a strong dual demand for a constitutional amendment giving the President the power to dissolve the legislature and for a regulation of the army command issue so as to strengthen the President's legal authority in military affairs.[14] Expecting the politicians to be unenthusiastic, Grabski hoped to strengthen his image among the public as a man above parties by retaining Skrzyński and Raczkiewicz in their respective portfolios of foreign affairs and the interior, by making the legal expert Professor Wacław Makowski his minister of justice, and by persuading Piłsudski to accept the position of war minister or at least to nominate his own candidate for this portfolio.[15]

Grabski's strategy was apparently also to deactivate Piłsudski politically through reactivating him militarily. By being given control of the army, Piłsudski might hopefully be withdrawn from the political maelstrom in which he was increasingly becoming the focus of expectations for the country's dissatisfied and disillusioned.[16] Grabski's hopes were dashed at an afternoon conference on May 9 of himself, Wojciechowski, and Piłsudski during which the last-named declined to head the War Ministry under Grabski or to recommend an alternative candidate.[17]

Though unsuccessful, these maneuvers on the part of Wojciechowski and Grabski for an extraparliamentary solution of the crisis, with their implication of Piłsudski's return to power in the army, had the

[14] Dołęga-Modrzewski, p. 3. Dołęga-Modrzewski is a pseudonym of Stanisław Kauzik, an economist who was Grabski's close political confidant and a witness to this night conference. During World War II Kauzik was a high political functionary in the Polish underground.

[15] J. Zdziechowski, "Wspomnienia o Stanisławie Wojciechowskim." Jerzy Zdziechowski was offered the Finance Ministry, which he declined. Though a National Democrat, he was no "mere" politician and qualified as something of a financial expert.

[16] See Radek and Stefanovich, p. 33.

[17] See Piłsudski's rather enigmatic press release published in *Kurjer Poranny* on May 10, 1926, and reprinted in his *PZ*, VIII, 332. It appears that Piłsudski bore Grabski a grudge for having retained Sikorski as war minister during Grabski's previous premiership.

effect of a red flag on the Right-Center politicians and galvanized them into hurriedly patching together a cabinet under Witos' premiership that could count on a Sejm majority of approximately twenty.

The National Democratic leader, Stanisław Głąbiński, informed the President of this development just in time to interrupt still another effort to avoid a "Witos solution." After his negative meeting with Grabski, Piłsudski had, in the course of a further conversation with Wojciechowski, agreed to become war minister in a reconstituted Skrzyński cabinet provided that he could nominate three additional ministers. These would be Jędrzej Moraczewski and Bronisław Ziemięcki, to return to their former portfolios of public works and labor and welfare, and Kazimierz Bartel to be minister of railroads.[18] Piłsudski further agreed to Skrzyński's continuing to combine the foreign affairs post with the premiership. He reported this news to a caucus of Left and Center political leaders late on May 9, fully expecting the crisis to be resolved according to these terms.[19] Piłsudski's hopes evaporated, however, because the President, despite profound misgivings, felt duty-bound to give priority to a parliamentary majority, such as the Witos-led Right-Center coalition of which Głąbiński informed him during the night, over a Skrzyński-Piłsudski combination with dubious prospects of obtaining a vote of confidence. Furthermore, Skrzyński's own feelings toward this alternative option were reported to have been unenthusiastic.[20]

The Right-Center cabinet which Witos now proceeded to assemble was composed of National Democrats, Christian Democrats, and

[18] Bartel was leader of the Klub Praca, a parliamentary fraction which had seceded from Wyzwolenie in April, 1925. It was left-of-center with strong technocratic leanings and, at this time, the political group to which Piłsudski felt closest.

[19] See the two articles by Wacław Grzybowski, then secretary of the Klub Praca, at whose home this caucus met: "Spotkania i rozmowy z Józefem Piłsudskim," p. 93, and "Premier Kazimierz Bartel," p. 104. This development is also discussed by two other close partisans of Piłsudski: Schaetzel, "Przełom majowy," p. 6, and Sławoj-Składkowski, "Wspomnienia z okresu majowego," p. 115. A still later recollection of the episode is that in Walewski, p. 116.

[20] Arski, p. 410. At this time, though in connection with a different set of negotiations, Skrzyński told Witos that he felt obliged to withdraw from politics for a while. Witos, *Moje wspomnienia*, III, 85. Witos was aware of the President's animosity and was reportedly prepared to threaten a presidential crisis as well as a cabinet crisis unless Wojciechowski designated him premier. *Frankfurter Zeitung*, May 10, 1926.

National Laborites, as well as his own Piast Peasant Party. Though Christian Nationalists of the extreme Right were omitted and though as many as nine portfolios were retained by the incumbents who had last held them under Skrzyński,[21] the over-all complexion of this government was far more Rightist than the preceding one owing to the omission of the PPS. It was indeed reminiscent of Witos' earlier cabinet of 1923, which had reneged on radical land reform, presided over a hyperinflation, and provoked the workers of Kraków into insurrection in November 1923. A direct provocation to Piłsudski, furthermore, was the assignment of the War Ministry to the ex-Austrian General Juliusz Malczewski, who would inevitably withdraw Żeligowski's army command project of May 4 and revert to a solution unacceptable to Piłsudski. Indeed, on being invited to accept the ministerial position, Malczewski had indicated to his political interviewers that he regarded Piłsudski's influence in the army as nil and the Marshal himself as a has-been.[22] Piłsudski had good reason to fear a purge of his supporters from the army under Malczewski's administration.[23]

The only significant noncontroversial appointment in Witos' cabinet was that of the career diplomat Kajetan Morawski to head the Foreign Ministry. This had the approval of the outgoing Skrzyński, of Piłsudski, and of the PPS, all of whom were eager—as was Witos—to keep foreign policy immune from the sharpening internal crisis.[24] On the other hand, the fact that the portfolios of public works and labor and welfare were left on an "acting" basis with the same non-political ministers to whom they had been provisionally assigned in the last weeks of the Skrzyński cabinet failed to mollify the Left.

Witos inaugurated his return to power by throwing the gauntlet to his foes in a press interview just prior to his formal installation. Announcing his intention to govern with a "strong hand," Witos explicitly challenged Piłsudski to cease his behind-the-scenes political

[21] For the names and the portfolios, see Markert, ed., p. 677.

[22] Głąbiński, p. 549. The interlocutors were the National Democrat Głąbiński and the Piast Władysław Kiernik, who was Skrzyński's and Witos' minister of agriculture. Malczewski's previous post was commander of the Warsaw Military District.

[23] See Smogorzewski, *Le Jeu complexe des partis en Pologne,* p. 30; Nagel, p. 11; Grzędziński, "Fragmenty pamiętnika," p. 388.

[24] Morawski, "Przewrót majowy," p. 1, and Benedykt, p. 1.

manipulations, to halt his Delphic utterances on military questions, and to make his bid for power and influence in the open political arena.[25] Witos' reference to a strong hand was understood to imply a purge of prefects (*starosta*) throughout the country, to be followed by new, "managed" elections in the venerable "Austrian" manner of his native Galicia. He intended then to proceed to force through constitutional amendments to strengthen the presidency (which, ironically, Piłsudski also desired) and the Senate, in addition to revising the electoral laws so as to liquidate small political parties (thus rendering cabinets more durable) and reduce the representation of the ethnic minorities. Finally, he proposed to transfer the adjudication of election disputes from the courts to the purged bureaucracy.[26] As for his explicit, even taunting, challenge to Piłsudski, Witos apparently was confident that it would not be accepted. At the congress of his Piast Peasant Party held at Tarnów in April, 1925, Witos had openly expressed his opinion that there was no place in contemporary Polish public life for Piłsudski, who, like Clemenceau, had played out his role and should recede from the political stage.[27] Similarly, the powerful National Democratic politician Stanisław Grabski (brother of the ex-premier) had in February, 1926, privately referred to Piłsudski as a "political corpse." [28]

Witos' major miscalculation was his failure to recognize, or to take into account, the fact that his parliamentary majority was not a true reflection of his real strength in the country, which the Sejm no longer mirrored accurately. The mounting unemployment crisis,

[25] Witos presented this challenge in the form of special interviews granted to the *Nowy Kurjer Polski* and the *Ilustrowany Kurjer Codzienny.* The former paper published the interview on May 9 (the issue is preserved in the AGLŻ, appended to folio No. 33); the latter refrained, allegedly because it considered Witos' remarks too inflammatory. For a detailed recollection of this episode by the then parliamentary correspondent of the *Ilustrowany Kurjer Codzienny,* see Walewski, pp. 117–19.

[26] Witos spelled out this program in his pamphlet *Czasy i ludzie,* published in February, 1926. See also Kukiel, "Jeszcze o przełomie majowym," p. 16, and Daszyński, *W pierwszą rocznicę,* p. 11. As regards the Senate, Witos proposed either to widen its power or, should this prove unfeasible, to abolish it altogether.

[27] Witos quoted in Starzewski, p. 240, and in an unpublished portion of the memoirs of President Ignacy Mościcki preserved in the archives of the Piłsudski Historical Institute in London. See also Sieroszewski *et al.,* eds., p. 76, and Anusz, p. 17.

[28] AGLŻ, 32a/32.

the renewed fluctuation of the currency, the memories of his unfortunate regime in 1923, all had an exasperating effect on the masses. To these was now added the further irritant of revelations deeply compromising to some of Witos' closest political associates, which emerged during a current trial in Warsaw of some leaders of a fascist conspiratorial organization, the Pogotowie Patriotów Polskich (Action Squad of Polish Patriots).[29]

The four embittered parties of the Left bloc greeted the Witos cabinet with a manifesto on May 11, denouncing it as a government of reaction, exploitation, incompetence, and national weakness, against which they would wage persistent opposition.[30] Piłsudski, for his part, granted an interview on May 10 to his favorite newspaper, Warsaw's *Kurjer Poranny* (Morning Courier), in the course of which he warned that by no means did he regard the cabinet crisis as closed with the formation of a government of men as notoriously indifferent to the "moral interests" of the state and the army as Witos and his cohort allegedly were. He went on to denounce Witos, W. Grabski, Szeptycki, and Sikorski in vitriolic terms as the inaugurators of a regime of corruption and malfeasance which had demoralized the public service and the army under their respective ministerial stewardships between 1923 and 1925 and which would now be resumed. Of Malczewski, Piłsudski had an abysmally low opinion and feared that this War Minister had been selected to serve as Witos' tool for misusing the army for partisan purposes. Piłsudski doubted, he confessed, that

[29] The trial lasted from May 4 to May 21, 1926, and was reported at length in the pages of *Kurjer Warszawski, Ilustrowany Kurjer Codzienny,* and *Nowy Kurjer Polski.* The Pogotowie Patriotów Polskich (PPP) had been organized at the close of 1922 and aimed to seize power by armed force. It first came to the notice of the police in February, 1923, and was broken up by arrests in January, 1924. Numbering 1,200 civilian, military, and clerical members, it hoped to introduce into Poland a regime modeled on Mussolini's. Prominent figures compromised during the trial were General Stanisław Szeptycki, the Piast politician Władysław Kiernik, and National Democratic leader Stanisław Głąbiński. All three had served in Witos' 1923 cabinet, during the tenure of which the PPP had enjoyed an alarming degree of official toleration. Kiernik, who had been minister of the interior at that time, was now scheduled to be Witos' minister of agriculture, while Głąbiński, vice-premier and minister of education in 1923, was the kingmaker behind Witos' current cabinet of May, 1926.

The sentences meted out to the six fascist defendants on May 21, 1926, were preposterously light and were quashed on appeal in February, 1928.

[30] The manifesto is reprinted in Bełcikowska, *Walki majowe,* p. 8; she erroneously dates it as May 12.

Polish soldiers would be prepared to lay down their lives in battle for such a government as that under Witos. He concluded the interview with a warning that he would not cease to struggle against the regime of unbridled parties which ignored the higher interests of the state while concentrating only on private enrichment.[31]

Witos decided to use this press interview as the first occasion to demonstrate his intention to govern with a strong hand. Though not yet formally sworn into office, he instructed the Ministry of the Interior to confiscate the May 11 issue of the *Kurjer Poranny* in which Piłsudski's remarks appeared. This gesture was quite futile, since thousands of copies had already been distributed, and the provincial papers in Kraków, Łódź, and Wilno, as well as the Yiddish and foreign press, had reprinted the interview.[32]

In its effect on public opinion, the unsuccessful attempt to suppress Piłsudski's interview backfired against Witos. So also did a rumor, launched apparently by individuals close to the new Prime Minister, that Piłsudski might be arrested and indicted for the allegedly calumnious content of his remarks.[33] Indeed, Witos' enemies went over to the counterattack. One of the leaders of the Left bloc confidently threatened that "they [the new government] confiscate our journals, but we shall confiscate their men. If they want a fight, they will get one."[34] Demonstrations in favor of Piłsudski and against Witos erupted—not altogether spontaneously—during the late afternoon and evening hours of May 11 in the streets and cafés of Warsaw.[35] In order to

[31] *Kurjer Poranny,* May 11, 1926, reprinted in Piłsudski, *PZ,* VIII, 333–36.
[32] *Frankfurter Zeitung,* May 12, 1926; "Le coup d'état de Varsovie," p. 17.
[33] The origin of this rumor was attributed to the new Christian Democratic minister of the interior, Stefan Smólski, and it was given wide currency in a special edition of *Rzeczpospolita* (Republic), his party's press organ.
[34] Senator Jan Woźnicki, of Wyzwolenie, in *Przegląd Wieczorny,* May 11, 1926, quoted in Smogorzewski, *La Pologne restaurée,* p. 302. The *Przegląd Wieczorny* was the evening edition of the *Kurjer Poranny.*
[35] For details, see *Dokumenty chwili,* I, 4. The orchestras of the cafés were required to play the marching song of Piłsudski's Legions, "My pierwsza brygada" (We are the first brigade), by roving bands of officers, soldiers, and civilians shouting such slogans as "We shall not let Poland be robbed," "We will not permit the army to be bartered away," "Down with the Right-Witos gang," "Long live Commander in Chief Piłsudski." Some minor scuffles occurred, but the mood of the capital's population was generally sympathetic to Piłsudski and to these demonstrators. The organizer of the supposedly spontaneous demonstrations was Piłsudski's former adjutant, Lieutenant Colonel Bolesław Wieniawa-Długoszowski. This is conceded in Sławoj-Składkowski, "Wspomnienia z okresu majowego," p. 116.

maximize the righteous indignation of the Warsaw public against Witos, a fabricated report was planted that Piłsudski's house at Sulejówek had been fired on during the night of May 11-12 by paramilitary hoodlums acting at the behest of Witos' Right-Center coalition.[36] This fictitious news provided the pretext for a number of nearby regiments to rush from their garrisons toward Sulejówek to protect their former Commander in Chief and, in the afternoon of May 12, to march with him on Warsaw for his test of strength with the government. This seeming spontaneity of Piłsudski's coup d'état, however, is belied by the extensive conspiratorial preparation which preceded it.

The rising tension seemed to leave immune only President Wojciechowski, who, exhausted by the week-long negotiations and assuming that the formation of the Witos cabinet had concluded the crisis, had decided on May 11 to leave Warsaw early the next morning for a rest at the presidential summer residence of Spała, sixty miles to the southwest. Malczewski, on the other hand, disquieted by suspicious troop dispositions made by his pro-Piłsudski predecessor at the War Ministry, Żeligowski, had resolved on that day to order up to Warsaw certain regiments whose officers were presumed to be anti-Piłsudski. It was also suspected that he intended to arrest a number of Piłsudski's protégés in the army.[37] Convinced that a violent showdown

[36] The attack was alleged in a special late edition of *Przegląd Wieczorny,* May 11, and denied in *Kurjer Warszawski,* May 12. Years later the *Kurjer Poranny* conceded that it was a ruse. For a report that Wieniawa-Długoszowski had "arranged" for a few shots to be fired in the air near Piłsudski's house in order to furnish an alibi for the coup d'état which now erupted, see Górnicki, "Ostatni rokosz z Warszawie," p. 9. That the incident was Bogusław Miedziński's invention is suggested in Arski, p. 415. Mme Piłsudska, in neither her *Memoirs* nor her *Wspomnienia,* makes any mention of an attack on their home. Had one occurred, she would undoubtedly have alluded to it in justification of her husband's subsequent actions. Piłsudski himself is reported to have referred to an attack on his children in Sulejówek when he confronted President Wojciechowski on the Poniatowski bridge on the afternoon of May 12. See Karbowski, p. 334, and Rzepecki, *Wspomnienia,* p. 18. The episode is termed "more or less imaginary" in Morawski, "Przewrót majowy," p. 2.

[37] Wieniawa-Długoszowski was indeed arrested at his residence early on May 12, presumably for organizing the previous day's street and café disturbances. Lieutenant Colonel Józef Beck (the foreign minister of the 1930s) achieved his release by warning Malczewski that a large part of the officer corps would regard this action as an intolerable affront. See Wierzbiński, p. 91. Though Malczewski had already suspected a Piłsudski-Żeligowski plot on May 11, his summons for reinforcements to come to Warsaw did not go out before May 12. See AKL, 5/4, and Jachieć, p. 337.

was imminent, Acting Minister of Foreign Affairs Morawski put through an emergency call to General Kazimierz Sosnkowski, who, as Piłsudski's deputy and closest colleague in the Legions during World War I, as the perennial war minister during the early years of the restored Polish Republic, and currently as commander of the Poznań Military District, enjoyed wide prestige and general influence in the army. Morawski requested Sosnkowski to come to Warsaw in order to avert a catastrophe. Sosnkowski came but during the evening of May 11 telephoned to Morawski the sad news that his mission was too late, that events were irresistibly moving toward a clash, and that he was returning to his post in Poznań.[38]

The devastating information that Sosnkowski had learned at about the same time as the War Minister was that under the screen of Żeligowski's parting orders—too late revoked by Malczewski—the 7th Regiment of Uhlans (lancers), commanded by one of Piłsudski's former adjutants, Colonel Kazimierz Stamirowski, had in the afternoon of May 11 left its barracks at Mińsk Mazowiecki (twenty-four miles east of Warsaw) and, armed with live ammunition, had gone to the training camp at Rembertów in the environs of Warsaw, very close to Piłsudski's suburban home at Sulejówek.[39] The next morning, after the alleged night attack on Piłsudski's house, units of the regiment were moved up to screen Sulejówek. The regiment refused to obey Malczewski's order to return to its Mińsk Mazowiecki base. Indeed, Stamirowski had illegally summoned to Rembertów from its base at Siedlce (fifty-five miles east of Warsaw) the 22d Infantry Regiment, commanded by his fellow Legionnaire and devotee of Piłsudski, Colonel Henryk Krok-Paszkowski. The latter commandeered a train that brought two battalions of his regiment to Rembertów in the early afternoon of May 12, just in time to link up with Piłsudski's march on Warsaw.[40]

---

[38] Morawski, "Przewrót majowy," p. 1.

[39] For details, see Karbowski, p. 329. The arrival of the 7th Uhlans at Rembertów was unexpected by General Rudolf Prych, commander of the training camp, who went to the War Ministry in Warsaw the next day to ascertain the true situation. Malczewski placed certain units of the Warsaw city garrison on strictest alert later in the evening of May 11.

Rembertów and Sulejówek are, respectively, six and ten and a half miles east of Warsaw.

[40] AKL, 15/11–12. Stamirowski's messenger to Krok-Paszkowski was the future minister of industry and commerce (1934–35), Henryk Floyar-Rajchman. In later years Stamirowski left the army for a political role in the Pił-

Piłsudski had left his Sulejówek home in midmorning on May 12, had collected his protective screen of troops at Rembertów, and had then set out for Warsaw. His advance guard occupied Praga, on the eastern bank of the Vistula river, directly across from Warsaw, in the early afternoon and temporarily disarmed the local police forces.[41] Piłsudski himself, accompanied by his troubleshooter Lieutenant Colonel Bogusław Wieniawa-Długoszowski, arrived several hours later and drove toward the Poniatowski bridge leading into Warsaw, fully expecting the capital to put itself at his disposal without resistance.

News of this march on Warsaw began to grip the city shortly after noon. The money market, as usual, reacted sharply, and the dollar-exchange value of the złoty plummeted. Still before noon, Malczewski had summoned to Warsaw more regiments that he expected to be loyal to the government, had prohibited all troop movements except at his own explicit orders, had named General Tadeusz Rozwadowski—also one of Piłsudski's rivals from the former Austrian army—to command the defense of Warsaw, and had recalled to the capital General Stanisław Haller—another ex-Austrian foe of Piłsudski's—to assist in its defense. (Haller, it will be recalled, had gone on extended leave from his post as chief of the General Staff in the previous December in protest against Żeligowski's blatantly pro-Piłsudski personnel arrangements.) [42]

The cabinet had been in emergency session since the morning. For several hours, however, Witos had neglected to inform Wojciechowski at Spała of the situation or to request his return to Warsaw. His lame explanation that in the press of events he had forgotten about the President is suspect.[43] Knowing of Wojciechowski's dislike of Witos

---

sudski camp, becoming president of the Polish Western Association and director of a state bank. The Germans killed him at Oświęcim (Auschwitz) in October, 1943.

[41] The units accompanying Piłsudski on this march were the 7th Uhlan Regiment, the two battalions of the 22d Infantry Regiment, and certain miscellaneous training and maneuver units stationed at Rembertów. Their number totaled about 2,000. Other units joined Piłsudski later in the day. For details, see Czubiński, "Przewrót majowy," p. 128; *Dokumenty chwili*, I, 8; Strumph-Wojtkiewicz *et al.*, p. 12; *Kurjer Warszawski*, May 13, 1926.

[42] Haller flew up from Kraków in the early evening. See his *Wypadki warszawskie*, p. 7.

[43] Morawski, "Przewrót majowy," p. 1. In his own recollections, written in exile in the 1930s, Witos believed that he had informed the President promptly of the situation. His memory appears to be in error. See Witos, *Moje wspomnienia*, III, 92.

and the new cabinet, the Prime Minister may well have feared that the President would side with Piłsudski, his old colleague of the pre-World War I Socialist underground movement, and utilize the current crisis to oust the government. If such were Witos' apprehensions about Wojciechowski, he little knew his man. Ironically, Piłsudski made the same miscalculation about his former comrade, his preferred candidate in both presidential elections of December, 1922.

Wojciechowski having belatedly been sent for at the suggestion of Morawski, acting minister of foreign affairs, the government issued a communiqué in midafternoon confirming that certain army units at Rembertów had mutinied in response to false rumors (presumably a reference to the alleged firing on Piłsudski's house during the previous night). The population was requested to remain calm and to support the legal (Witos) government in its defense of the capital and the constitution. Simultaneously, a manifesto to the army was issued over the signatures of Wojciechowski, Witos, and Malczewski, ordering it to preserve honor and discipline by obedience to the legitimate authorities, as required by the military oath. Those who had violated this obligation were sternly recalled to an awareness of it. Finally and simultaneously, a state of emergency, with suspension of civic rights, was decreed in the city and province of Warsaw as well as in the adjacent Siedlce and Łuków counties of Lublin province and in Piłsudski's native Wilno province, where he was known to have many fervent civilian and military partisans.[44] These official proclamations having been issued, President Wojciechowski—without the cabinet—betook himself through the tension-filled streets of Warsaw to the Poniatowski bridge for a final confrontation with Piłsudski.

The situation at the bridge was dramatic. The eastern (Praga) end was held for Piłsudski by Stamirowski's 7th Uhlans and Wieniawa-

[44] The texts of these three decrees are in *Dziennik Ustaw Rzeczypospolitej Polskiej,* 1926, No. 46, Item 281, and *Dokumenty chwili,* I, 5–6. The last one meant, under Article 124 of the constitution of March 17, 1921, the suspension of personal liberty (Art. 97), of inviolability of home and hearth (Art. 100), of freedom of the press (Art. 105), of secrecy of correspondence (Art. 106), of the rights of assembly, combination, and association (Art. 108).

The publication of the three public announcements sharply increased the bustle in the capital. Many, however, still predicted that the affair would end with yet another conventional reshuffling of the cabinet. Only the subsequent appearance of armed military units rushing to block the Vistula bridges against Piłsudski brought them to a full realization of the exceptional seriousness of this crisis. Not since 1915 and 1920 had Warsaw seen such urgent military activity. See *Dokumenty chwili,* I, 6–7.

Długoszowski's 1st Light Cavalry Regiment.[45] Their entrance into the capital, however, was blocked by machine gunners of the Infantry Officer School (postgraduates of the Cadet Corps), who, obeying the orders of the legally constituted government, had been hastily sent during the afternoon to hold the Warsaw end of the span. At about 5 P.M. Wojciechowski's car arrived and drove onto the bridge. Alighting, the President handed Stamirowski a note demanding to speak with Piłsudski, who presently approached, acompanied by General Gustaw Orlicz-Dreszer and Colonels Wieniawa-Długoszowski and Stamirowski. The two principals drew aside toward the balustrade for a conversation *à deux*. There are several accounts of what then took place, but they coincide heavily and vary from each other only on inessential points.[46] Piłsudski, apparently believing that Wojciechowski sympathized with and would facilitate his show of force, requested access to Warsaw, where a cabinet allegedly injurious to the honor of the army had entrenched itself. Wojciechowski insisted that the Republic, which he incarnated as its President, could not and would not surrender to rebellion. He demanded the withdrawal of Piłsudski's troops. Somewhat taken aback but still hopeful, Piłsudski replied that nothing was easier and that this presidential request would be complied with as soon as the Witos government (which he knew the

[45] The 1st Light Cavalry Regiment was part of the Warsaw garrison. This regiment had not marched with Piłsudski from Rembertów but had crossed over to his side as the other units entered Praga from the east. Wieniawa-Długoszowski, though not its current commander (the post was then held by a Lieutenant Colonel Jan Głogowski), was long associated with and enjoyed enormous influence in the regiment. Further information on Wieniawa-Długoszowski will be found in the Biographical Register at the end of this volume.

[46] For Piłsudski's version, see his *PZ,* IX, 15. Wojciechowski wrote but never published his side of the story, which is related in a handwritten memoir currently in the possession of his son-in-law, Władysław Jan Grabski. See the latter's article "Ostatnie rozmowy Piłsudskiego z Wojciechowskim," pp. 3, 11, and especially Arski, pp. 408–9, 418, where a photographic reproduction and a transcription of Wojciechowski's account are given. A number of the infantry officer candidates and cadets stationed on the bridge by the government were in a position to overhear snatches of the Piłsudski-Wojciechowski conversation and subsequently published their recollections. Among these are: (1) Piątkowski, *Wspomnienia z "wypadków majowych" 1926 roku*—a pamphlet to which are appended the reminiscences of several other eyewitnesses of this event; (2) Rzepecki, *Wspomnienia,* p. 23; (3) Józef Kuropieska, whose recollections appear in Karbowski, p. 334. For secondary—but also fairly unanimous—accounts, see Strumph-Wojtkiewicz *et al.,* p. 15; P. Bartel, *Le Maréchal Piłsudski,* p. 237; P. Bartel, "Josef Pilsudski," p. 304; R. Landau, pp. 232–34; Mettler, p. 219; *Dokumenty chwili,* I, 9; *Kurjer Warszawski,* May 13, 1926.

President to dislike) was dismissed. Wojciechowski remonstrated that the Witos government was the legal one and that Piłsudski must state his grievances and desires to it in a legal manner. To this Piłsudski replied bitterly that for himself the legal road was closed under such a government but that he intended no harm to Wojciechowski. At this point Wojciechowski icily said that the issue did not concern persons but Poland. He thereupon broke off the interview, extricated himself from Piłsudski's grasp on his coat lapel, ordered the infantry officer candidates to bar entry into Warsaw to Piłsudski and his units, and drove back to the cabinet meeting.

Arriving there (in the Namiestnikowski palace), Wojciechowski emphatically informed the assembled ministers that he would not tolerate Piłsudski's rebellion and would insist on resisting it by force even though he knew that certain members of the cabinet preferred to compromise.[47] This allusion was quite valid, particularly in regard to Witos, who was a tough *political* infighter but had no stomach for civil war in the name of the majesty of the Republic and of the Law. Possibly under the private urging of Sejm Marshal Rataj, Witos was seeking to incline the cabinet toward resignation when Wojciechowski's intervention stiffened its position and preempted the government's choice of response to the coup.[48] But for the President's unexpected toughness, Piłsudski's hope of achieving his purpose through an armed demonstration without the necessity of actually using force would have been realized. It is therefore ironical that both Piłsudski and Witos miscalculated in their mutual expectation that Wojciechowski's dislike of Witos and old comradeship with Piłsudski would incline him to side with the latter in the current crisis.[49]

[47] For details of this dramatic scene, see Morawski, "Przewrót majowy," p. 1.
[48] Schaetzel, "Ustalenie faktów," p. 6. Witos' former secretary blurs this episode out of deference to his patron, while Witos' own allusions to it are extremely cagy. See Dzendzel, p. 5, and Witos, *Moje wspomnienia*, III, 92–95.
[49] That Piłsudski had expected Wojciechowski to mediate the crisis by inclining the Witos cabinet toward capitulation is indicated by Piłsudski's subsequent interview of May 25, 1926, in the *Kurjer Poranny*, reprinted in his *PZ*, IX, 14–20.
It is interesting to contrast the behavior of Wojciechowski in 1926 with that of French President René Coty in an analogous situation, that of the Gaullist coup in 1958. A suggestive comparison of Piłsudski and De Gaulle has been undertaken in Roos, "Józef Piłsudski i Charles de Gaulle," pp. 11–20. Roos finds that De Gaulle, who served on the French military mission in Poland during the 1920s, was consciously influenced in his ideas and style by Piłsudski.

Wojciechowski's uncompromising stand can be partly explained as the reaction of a man who felt himself betrayed. Just a few days earlier, when Piłsudski had appeared at the presidential Belweder palace to be offered and to decline the War Ministry during the abortive experiment to form a supraparty cabinet under W. Grabski, Wojciechowski had been solemnly and personally assured by Piłsudski that the Marshal would never resort to force against the legitimate authorities and that this had been made categorically clear to those of his partisans in the army who were urging him to stage a coup d'état.[50] Implicitly accepting these assurances, Wojciechowski had calmly left Warsaw for Spała early on May 12, having dismissed the warnings of the cleric, Aleksander Cardinal Kakowski, and the fears of the National Democrat Głąbiński and of Witos that a Piłsudski coup was brewing.[51] Against this background of events, Wojciechowski's strong sense of constitutional proprieties and legal rectitude was now reinforced by a feeling of personal outrage to Piłsudski's resort to force.[52]

Meanwhile, on the Poniatowski bridge, it was the reputedly nerveless soldier Piłsudski, rather than the supposedly timid civilian Wojciechowski, who was shaken by their conversation and its prospective consequences. At first he sought to bluff his way out of the dilemma by asking the infantry officer candidates, in his best would-be Napoleonic manner, whether they, as his "children," would really shoot at the First Marshal of Poland, and was informed that they would execute their orders. He also sought to incite the defection to his side of the officer in charge, Major Marian Porwit, by appealing to Porwit's sense of comradeship with Piłsudski as a fellow ex-Legionnaire and comember of the order of *Virtuti Militari,* composed of men who had distinguished themselves in the Polish cause during World War I or

[50] W. J. Grabski, p. 11.

[51] *Ibid.,* p. 11; Głąbiński, pp. 545–46; Witos, *Moje wspomnienia,* III, 83. Wojciechowski allegedly told the Cardinal to concern himself with ecclesiastical, not political, matters.

[52] The public apparently would not believe that the hitherto reserved Wojciechowski could be the lion of the government during these days of crisis. False rumor had it that he was eager to compromise but was prevented from acting by being held a virtual prisoner by Witos and the anti-Piłsudski generals. See Bełcikowska, *Walki majowe,* p. 22, and *Kurjer Poranny,* May 13, 1926 (special issue).

in the Polish-Soviet campaign of 1920.[53] At last persuaded that these
efforts to achieve a crossing over the Poniatowski bridge through
primitive exercises in psychological warfare were in vain, Piłsudski
ordered Colonel Krok-Paszkowski to take his battalions of the 22d
Infantry Regiment northward to the Kierbedź bridge and try to force
his way into Warsaw over that span.[54] But he seems not to have had
much confidence in the success of this maneuver since he supposed
the Kierbedź bridge to be also blocked by units mobilized by Malczewski. Having given his instructions to Krok-Pazkowski, Piłsudski
left the Poniatowski bridge in a deep depression, fearful that the failure of his armed demonstration to achieve its purpose had cost him
his power, authority, and prestige. Returning to Praga, he sat in a
barracks there—shocked, gloomy, and randomly musing about the
fate of the First Polish Corps in the tsarist Russian army in 1917.[55]

The day was saved for Piłsudski in the military dimension by two
developments, neither of which was initiated by him. The unit holding the Kierbedź bridge, the 36th Infantry Regiment of Lieutenant

[53] For details of these incidents, see Piątkowski, p. 5; Rzepecki, *Wspomnienia,* pp. 23–24; P. Bartel, *Le Maréchal Pilsudski,* p. 237; *Ilustrowany Kurjer
Codzienny,* May 27, 1926. In September, 1939, Porwit held an important command in the defense of Warsaw.

[54] Picheta, p. 3. In 1926 Picheta was a captain and battalion commander in
the 22d Infantry Regiment. See also his remarks appended to Piątkowski, p. 24.

[55] Benedykt, p. 1. Another eyewitness reporter of Piłsudski's depressed
mental state at this time was W. Grzybowski. See his "Spotkania i rozmowy z
Józefem Piłsudskim," p. 93.

Wieniawa-Długoszowski stayed behind on the bridge to observe developments, was arrested by the government troops, and was held in a military
prison in Warsaw until the Piłsudski forces overran that part of the city (Dzika
street) and freed him later that same evening. As for the military situation on
the Poniatowski bridge, the government forces (infantry officer candidates), by
agreement with their foes (1st Light Cavalry, the 7th Uhlans having been withdrawn elsewhere), occupied the main span sometime between 5:30 and 6:00
P.M. but made no attempt to advance into Praga. At 7:00 P.M. the main body
of the Cadet Corps (from which the Infantry Officer School was drawn), commanded by Colonel Gustaw Paszkiewicz and also loyal to the government,
crossed through Praga from the east, coming from Rembertów (whence they
had been recalled from summer training by Malczewski). The Piłsudski units,
not wanting to be caught in a cross fire between Porwit's and Paszkiewicz's
troops, permitted the latter to pass unhindered through the Praga bridgehead
and over the bridge into Warsaw. For details, see Mercik, pp. 103–4; Wrzos,
p. 68; Piątkowski, pp. 3, 26. The Infantry Officer School and the Cadet Corps
were to provide the backbone of the government forces during the next days
of fighting. Colonel Paszkiewicz was commandant and Major Porwit was director of studies for both units.

Colonel Kazimierz Sawicki, now refused to accept any more orders from Malczewski, placed itself at the disposal of Piłsudski, and, accordingly, opened the bridge to Krok-Paszkowski's and other Piłsudskist units. The energetic Orlicz-Dreszer promptly took over *de facto* command of these forces from the numbed hands of Piłsudski and decisively exploited this new opportunity. The troops poured across the Kierbedź bridge.[56] As they debouched into Warsaw they clashed with defending units of the 30th Infantry Regiment (Colonel Izydor Modelski commanding). Shots were exchanged. Dead and wounded fell. A political crisis had turned into a violent coup d'état.

[56] Jellenta, "Relacja" (an unpublished memoir by an officer of the 36th Infantry Regiment, in the archives of the Józef Piłsudski Institute of America, New York City), p. 1; Krok-Paszkowski's report in AKL, 15/12. See also the interview of Orlicz-Dreszer in Wrzos, p. 68. His chief of staff in these operations was the future foreign minister, Lieutenant Colonel Józef Beck. Sawicki and several other officers of the 36th Infantry Regiment were Legion veterans, predisposed emotionally toward Piłsudski. Sawicki was destined, as a general, to participate in the Polish Home Army's Warsaw uprising in 1944. He survived both that battle and his subsequent German captivity to become, after the war, one of the directors of the Piłsudski Historical Institute in London.

CHAPTER IV

PIŁSUDSKI'S EXPECTATIONS AND PLANS

That his political demonstration should have degenerated into a military battle was a source of dismay and anguish to Piłsudski. That he, the restorer of the Polish state, the creator of its army, the protagonist of a strong presidency, should lead a revolt against the state authorities, sunder the unity of the army, and stand across the barricades from the president were facts which were to haunt and trouble the remaining nine years of his life.[1] The root of his miscalculation was the assumption that his prestige was so high that armed resistance to his demands was inconceivable.

A considerable body of evidence attests to the fact that Piłsudski expected no fighting. The military forces alerted to support his demonstration were quite small. They included no artillery, consisting, instead, quite heavily of cavalry, which would be difficult to utilize effectively in the event of street fighting. Indeed, when Orlicz-Dreszer remonstrated with Piłsudski about this point just before the confrontation with Wojciechowski on the Poniatowski bridge, Piłsudski assured him that there would be no fighting. On leaving Sulejówek that morning, Piłsudski had told his wife to expect him home for lunch at 2:30 o'clock. He anticipated marching unopposed into Warsaw and dictating his demands from the General Staff headquarters on Saxon Square (Plac Saski).[2]

For the upset of these calculations, Piłsudski subsequently (and

---

[1] Aleksandra Piłsudska, *Wspomnienia,* p. 291. The point is also made in an unpublished manuscript memoir by General Stanisław Skwarczyński, preserved in the archives of the Piłsudski Historical Institute in London.

[2] Orlicz-Dreszer, interviewed in Wrzos, p. 68, and Aleksandra Piłsudska, *Wspomnienia,* p. 290. Piłsudski's optimism was apparently contagious, for Orlicz-Dreszer gave assurances to other officers that there would be no fighting, as indicated in the unpublished memoir by Skwarczyński.

correctly) held Wojciechowski responsible.[3] Witos, after all, was prepared to capitulate. But instead of playing the assigned role of dismissing the cabinet, the President had stiffened its opposition. How could Wojciechowski's personality have been so badly misread by Piłsudski, who had known him so long? In later years, Piłsudski's partisans would argue that if only the two could have met privately in a room of the Belweder palace, instead of publicly on the Poniatowski bridge under circumstances which were bound to heighten Wojciechowski's sense of his presidential prerogatives, then all would have ended well and as expected.[4]

At first Piłsudski could not come to terms with the failure of his calculations. Hence his initial despondency after the interview on the bridge. Hence, also, his resort immediately thereafter to a multitude of improvised mediation missions. He simply had no plan of action in the event of resistance and fighting.

To the cheers of the citizenry, a depressed Piłsudski followed his troops into Warsaw shortly before 9 P.M. on May 12. After a stopover at the old Royal Castle just beyond the Kierbedź bridge, he transferred his headquarters to the Warsaw Garrison Headquarters (Komenda Miasta) on Saxon Square. There he told representatives of the press that he was physically and morally exhausted, that though opposed in principle to force and violence, he had decided on the present test of strength and had a moral right to do so because he had fought all his life for honor, virtue, and courage instead of for private material gain. He concluded with an implied but clear bid for the support of the working class and of his former comrades of the Socialist movement by denouncing, in his peroration, the prevailing excessive injustice toward, and exploitation of, those who gave their labor to others.[5] He then immediately launched or encouraged a number of overlapping attempts to mediate the crisis and avoid further fighting. Had he, at this moment, been prepared to accept the responsibility for

---

[3] Piłsudski, *PZ,* IX, 15. See also the semiofficial biography *Józef Piłsudski, 1867–1935,* pp. 124, 126; the account by a leading Piłsudskist publicist, Stpiczyński, pp. 97–98; as well as Verax, p. 515. Wojciechowski's toughness was also a stunning surprise to Piłsudski's archrival Sikorski. See Sikorski's "Kartki z dziennika." For the same reaction within the cabinet, see the recollections of Witos' secretary Dzendzel, p. 5.

[4] See Benedykt, p. 1.

[5] Piłsudski, *PZ,* IX, 9.

further casualties and some possibly sharp combat, Piłsudski could in all probability have overrun all of Warsaw and overthrown the reeling government during the evening of May 12.[6]

The parties of the Left bloc had already made one mediation effort on their own. Upon Wojciechowski's return from the Poniatowski bridge, a delegation of their leaders had requested an interview with the President for the purpose of resolving the crisis through political compromise.[7] Wojciechowski had declined to receive them and, through an adjutant, directed them to the cabinet as the proper body for political negotiations. The Left-bloc politicians refused, however, to approach Witos and informed Wojciechowski that in their eyes he bore full responsibility for further developments.[8]

They stuck to this decision when, a few hours later, Jan Dębski of Witos' own Piast Peasant Party suggested to the Socialists that they confer with Witos, who, anxious to avoid civil war, could (Dębski believed) be persuaded to compromise.[9] Although evidence is lacking, one may conjecture that the politically flexible Witos, who shared none of Wojciechowski's righteous determination to defend legality even at the price of civil war, may himself have inspired Dębski's approach to the Socialists. In any event, this group once again declined to confer with Witos and referred Dębski to a joint Left-bloc resolution issued during the afternoon flatly demanding the cabinet's resignation if serious disturbances were to be avoided.[10]

The Socialists' decision not to involve themselves in bilateral negotiations with Witos when they momentarily expected his imminent col-

[6] See Srokowski, p. 91.

[7] The men involved were Zygmunt Marek and Mieczysław Niedziałkowski of PPS, Juliusz Poniatowski of Wyzwolenie, and Kazimierz Bartel of Klub Praca. *Documenty chwili*, I, 9. Wojciechowski's personal adjutant asserts that before the Poniatowski bridge episode, that is, immediately after Wojciechowski's return from Spała, PPS leader Norbert Barlicki had made two vain pleas by telephone to speak to the President. Comte, "Granaty nad Belwederem," No. 23, p. 11.

[8] Bełcikowska, *Walki majowe*, p. 13. For the Socialists' versions and interpretations of this episode, see Daszyński, *W pierwszą rocznicę*, pp. 24–26; Porczak, *Rewolucja majowa*, p. 49; Próchnik, *Pierwsze piętnastolecie*, p. 234. The Socialists argued that, by his refusal to receive the Left-bloc delegation, Wojciechowski had violated the requirement of presidential political neutrality and had become a partisan of the Right-Center coalition.

[9] *Dokumenty chwili*, I, 9. Dębski's overture was made shortly after 8 P.M. on May 12.

[10] This resolution was issued in reply to the three governmental proclamations of the afternoon. See above, p. 59. Its text is reprinted in *Dokumenty chwili*, I, 9.

lapse may also have been strengthened by a meeting of some of their leaders with Piłsudski which is alleged to have occurred in Praga at about 8 P.M.[11] In any event, it is noteworthy that Piłsudski's subsequent comments to the press were obviously phrased to appeal to the workers and the Socialists.[12] It is also manifest, however, that he was eager not to become exclusively dependent on the Socialists as mediators or supporters.

Thus Piłsudski had been busy with other mediation moves since soon after entering Warsaw. In one of these, Sejm Marshal Rataj was the go-between. Piłsudski subsequently claimed that he had set in motion the Rataj mission.[13] Others assert that he took advantage of Rataj's own initiative, undertaken as part of an afternoon agreement between Rataj and the Left bloc that the former would intercede with Piłsudski while the latter sought access to Wojciechowski.[14] As was the case with Dębski's overture to the Socialists, one cannot rule out the possibility that Rataj's approach to Piłsudski was undertaken with the approval of the compromise-inclined Witos.[15] In any event, sometime during the evening of May 12 Sejm deputy Marian Zyndram-Kościałkowski of the Klub Praca, which was then the party closest to Piłsudski, arranged a meeting between Rataj and Piłsudski in the latter's Warsaw headquarters.[16] Here Piłsudski, insisting that he possessed a preponderance of force that was growing by the hour, nevertheless volunteered to postpone its application till the next day if Rataj could manage during the night to mediate Piłsudski's quarrel with the government and achieve the withdrawal of the Witos cabinet through negotiation. In that case, the demonstration of power could

[11] Górnicki, "Ostatni rokosz w Warszawie," No. 21, p. 9. Górnicki surmises that Niedziałkowski, who had earlier vainly sought to see Wojciechowski, was among those Socialists who conferred with Piłsudski.

[12] Piłsudski, PZ, IX, 9.

[13] Ibid., p. 15. This claim is supported in Pobóg-Malinowski, Najnowsza historia, II, 481, and in Wiek Nowy, May 13, 1926.

[14] Ilustrowany Kurjer Codzienny, May 15, 1926; Dokumenty chwili, I, 13.

[15] See Wierzbiński, p. 129; P. Bartel, Le Maréchal Pilsudski, p. 239.

[16] Piłsudski, PZ, IX, 15, gives the time of this meeting as 9 P.M.; Dokumenty chwili, I, 13, as midnight. The latter source asserts that Rataj approached Zyndram-Kościałkowski, whereas the Wiek Nowy, May 13, 1926, and Ilustrowany Kurjer Codzienny, May 14, 1926, claim that Zyndram-Kościałkowski, on Piłsudski's behalf, invited Rataj to call on Piłsudski. The last-mentioned source lists Tadeusz Hołówko, Piłsudski's expert for Ukrainian questions, as accompanying Zyndram-Kościałkowski.

still be halted before devolving into a coup d'état. Rataj thereupon betook himself to the presidential Belweder palace, to which the Witos cabinet had meanwhile fled after the entry of the Piłsudski units into Warsaw. There he was firmly rebuffed by Wojciechowski, who refused to negotiate with rebels and expressed his conviction that the "festering abscess" of Piłsudski's extralegal power must at last be lanced.[17] Wojciechowski's determination was undoubtedly strengthened by the knowledge that reinforcements for the government were already arriving and more were on the way. Rataj reported the failure of his mission first to Piłsudski, at the latter's headquarters, and then to various deputies and the press at the Sejm building.[18]

A number of other mediation missions were proceeding either simultaneously with or subsequent to Rataj's. Thus General Żeligowski, the recent war minister, essayed an abortive feeler toward the Belweder palace on Piłsudski's behalf during the evening of May 12.[19] Piłsudski also urged such of his political supporters or agents as ex-premier Jędrzej Moraczewski (PPS), Bogusław Miedziński, Juliusz Poniatowski, and Jan Woźnicki (Wyzwolenie) to intercede.[20]

As all of these individuals of the Left and Center to whom Piłsudski had turned during the evening of May 12 had gotten no satisfaction from the government or the President, Piłsudski turned the next day to some conservative political figures and large landowners in the belief that they would have more influence with the Right-Center cabinet. Although the government's army units vigorously attacked his own throughout that day of May 13, Piłsudski remained on the military defensive in Warsaw in the hope that these fresh mediators would manage to find an escape from his dilemma and enable him

[17] *Ilustrowany Kurjer Codzienny*, May 15, 1926, and S. Haller, pp. 21–23. Haller was in the Belweder palace during Rataj's visit. Piłsudskist propagandists, unwilling to believe that Wojciechowski could repulse their hero, later falsely suggested that Witos and the ex-Austrian generals in the Belweder palace had prevented Rataj from seeing Wojciechowski, thereby aborting the mediation mission. See Bełcikowska, *Walki majowe*, p. 22, and R. Landau, p. 237. Also, though less categorically, Mettler, p. 219. They even report claims that Wojciechowski attempted to launch compromise appeals on his own but was blocked by Witos.

[18] *Wiek Nowy*, May 13, 1926. The deputies were Bartel (Praca), Dębski and Niedbalski (Piast), Marek and Niedziałkowski (PPS).

[19] Karbowski, p. 341; Pobóg-Malinowski, *Najnowsza historia*, II, 481.

[20] *Ilustrowany Kurjer Codzienny*, May 15, 1926; Pobóg-Malinowski, *Najnowsza historia*, II, 481.

to win his political demands without having to unleash a full-scale civil war.

He began this round by summoning Stanisław Mackiewicz ("Cat"), the editor of the ultraconservative Wilno paper *Słowo* (Word), to the Warsaw Garrison Headquarters. To Piłsudski's proposal that Mackiewicz organize a mediation committee, the latter responded with a disclaimer of his own political influence and a counteroffer to persuade Prince Zdzisław Lubomirski (one of the Regents of World War I) and Aleksander Meysztowicz—two prominent conservatives—to undertake this mission.[21] At about the same time Cardinal Kakowski's suffragan, Bishop Stanisław Gall of Warsaw, offered his good services as an intermediary to Piłsudski.[22] Believing that a combined effort by ecclesiastical dignitaries and prestigious conservatives might enjoy a good chance of success, Piłsudski requested Mackiewicz to proceed as offered.

Mackiewicz contacted Władysław Glinka, founder and president of the Land Credit Society (Towarzystwo Kredytowe Ziemskie)—a private bank for large landowners—who quickly gathered together at his home a group of wealthy, prominent, conservative, aristocratic magnates including, in addition to Lubomirski and Meysztowicz, such worthies as Count Adam Tarnowski, Count Leon Łubieński, Margrave Wielopolski, and Count Antoni Jundziłł. Mackiewicz related Piłsudski's request. He and Meysztowicz argued in favor of accepting the invitation to mediate because it would bring the large landowners into close contact with Piłsudski, whose support might some day be crucial to them and who would probably prove a more reliable ally in the long run than Witos. Glinka and Jundziłł declined to have anything to do with the ex-Socialist Piłsudski. Lubomirski, in turn, was in favor of mediation to halt an incipient civil war but insisted that in doing so the mediators must not let themselves become the instrument through which Piłsudski would realize his political goals.[23]

[21] Mackiewicz, p. 174.

[22] The Cardinal himself was in Rome during the days of the coup. That the intervention of the ecclesiastical dignitaries had been sought by Klub Praca leader (and post-coup premier) Kazimierz Bartel is suggested in W. Zyndram-Kościałkowski, p. 2.

[23] This account is based on a memorandum of the meeting written by Glinka and found after World War II among the papers of Jan Stecki which have been deposited in the library of the Catholic University of Lublin. Stecki was a

Lubomirski, Meysztowicz, and Mackiewicz then left to meet with Piłsudski at the railroad station in Praga. By now it was the late afternoon of May 13 and Piłsudski's troops, occupying the northern section of Warsaw but held to defensive tactics, had been absorbing punishing counterattacks from the government forces throughout the day. Their posture could not be maintained much longer. Unless he achieved a quick political solution, Piłsudski would either (*a*) have to capitulate, (*b*) launch a full-scale attack with all its possible consequences, or (*c*) owe his victory exclusively to the Socialists, who were just in the process of launching a general strike on his behalf.[24] As he dreaded all of these possibilities, it is not surprising that Lubomirski found him gloomy and dejected.[25] Piłsudski began by assuring his visitors that he had not intended to attack or to involve the constitution, the President, or the Sejm. He then requested them to assemble a delegation of six or seven persons of various political complexions—including at least one Socialist—to which he would present his political conditions for a cease-fire. He would withhold his military offensive till shortly before midnight in order to give them time to launch this effort. (It was then between 5 and 6 P.M.)

Lubomirski and Meysztowicz went to the aristocratic Hunt Club (Klub Myśliwski) and began phoning various people. Some, including Bishop Gall and Count Łubieński, now refused to participate. Others couldn't leave their homes owing to the street fighting or had been trapped by it away from their homes. In any event, the telephone service was cut off at 10 P.M. Thus this attempt, too, collapsed.[26] Its significance lies not only in the fact that it serves as further proof that Piłsudski was surprised and appalled to have met with armed resistance to his would-be nonviolent show of force but also in the evidence it presents that he already desired the old conservative forces of Po-

---

Christian Nationalist leader of the landed interests who had been minister of the interior under the Regency in 1918 but after 1928 was affiliated with the Piłsudskist BBWR (on which see chapter XIV). Glinka's memoir was published as an article: "W rocznicę przewrotu majowego."

[24] See below, pp. 125–27.

[25] Lubomirski's impression as told to Morawski on May 16. Morawski, "Przewrót majowy," p. 2.

[26] Glinka, p. 6. In his press interview of May 25, 1926, Piłsudski spoke candidly about Rataj's mediation efforts but very guardedly—without mentioning names—about that of the three conservatives. See Piłsudski, *PZ*, IX, 15–16.

land to rescue him from his hitherto exclusive political identification with the Left. If successful, this strategy would have the additional virtue of splitting these conservatives from the detested National Democratic camp. Piłsudski was to return to this effort immediately after the coup.

Piłsudski had given his support to yet one more attempt at mediation during the evening of May 13. Where politicians had failed, soldiers were now to try their luck. At about the same time as Lubomirski and Meysztowicz were telephoning their political acquaintances, three former ministers or acting ministers of war, the senior generals Lucjan Żeligowski, Stefan Majewski, and Aleksander Osiński, appeared at the Belweder palace to plead for a cease-fire in the name of the all-too-frail unity of the young Polish army. General Stanisław Haller, chief of the General Staff for the government forces, apparently still fearful lest Wojciechowski weaken, advised War Minister Malczewski not to permit the three generals to see the President. His anxiety was groundless. Wojciechowski ordered them to be presented and vigorously rebuked them for putting rebels and officers loyal to their oath on an equal plane. He refused to entertain any notions of cease-fire or mediation.[27]

Thus expired the string of mediation attempts so eagerly elicited or supported by the chagrined Piłsudski.[28] He had no choice now but to

[27] S. Haller, pp. 47–48. Żeligowski and Osiński were from the old tsarist Russian army, Majewski from the former Austrian one. For the dates of their ministerial incumbencies, see Markert, ed., pp. 676–77. Osiński and Majewski confided to S. Haller at the Belweder palace that Żeligowski had suggested the intervention to them. Haller asserts that they appeared to feel uncomfortable in their roles of would-be mediators between a legal government and rebels. Upon being rebuffed by Wojciechowski, the three generals were detained for some time inside the perimeter of the government's defenders. Within the hour, Żeligowski wrote out a request for retirement from the army, which is appended to AGLŻ, 32/79. After the conclusion of the coup, however, he was named by Piłsudski to head the commission of inquiry to ascertain how all military units had conducted themselves during its course (cited as AKL). His definitive retirement was thus postponed to August 31, 1927.

That Piłsudski supported, even though he may not have initiated, the intervention of the three generals is suggested by the fact that, before their arrival, his headquarters had telephoned a request to the Belweder palace that they be received there. Srokowski, p. 96. However, see also AGLŻ, 32/70, 72. Further information on Żeligowski will be found in the Biographical Register at the end of this volume.

[28] There is an obscure and undocumented allegation of yet another such effort by the conservative professor Marian Zdziechowski of the University of

employ his military might, which had grown considerably as fresh reinforcements arrived from various provincial garrisons throughout May 13. Early the next morning he launched a full-scale attack on the government forces in central and southern Warsaw.

It would be a profound error to assume that, merely because he had not expected actual fighting to erupt, Piłsudski had neglected to make careful preparations for his planned show of force. The reverse is indeed the case. He appears to have acted on the plausible assumption that, the more thorough his preparations, the less would be the risk of outright violence. His planning proceeded on both the political and the military levels.

In the political dimension, it is probable that even without any efforts by him or on his behalf Piłsudski would have been the beneficiary of the deteriorating economic and political situation of the preceding years. There was a dual aspect to this trend: (*a*) the exasperated public tended increasingly to look to him for salvation, and (*b*) vested power interests came to view him as a "lesser evil," preferable to social revolution. For Piłsudski to capitalize on this trend, however, it was essential that no alternative candidate for savior of Poland emerge. Hence Piłsudski's ceaseless efforts to discredit his only potential extrapolitical rival in authority and prestige, General Władysław Sikorski.

Sikorski, who was politically ambitious and had a high opinion of himself, was for a time seriously regarded as a potential strong man by some circles convinced that the rotting parliamentary regime required overhaul or replacement.[29] In fact, President Wojciechowski became so disquieted by reports to this effect that in November, 1925, he summoned Sikorski (who was then about to be replaced as war minister by Żeligowski) to the Belweder palace and warned him against staging a coup. Sikorski vigorously denied any such inten-

Wilno, in Pobóg-Malinowski, *Najnowsza historia,* II, 481. No evidence has been found to support this and Pobóg-Malinowski admits that it is only a surmise on his part.

[29] Pobóg-Malinowski, *Najnowsza historia,* II, 460; Morawski, *Tamten brzeg,* p. 164. Among the early supporters of Sikorski was the PPS leader Herman Lieberman, who had strongly recommended him for the premiership at the time of the Narutowicz assassination in December, 1922.

tion.[30] In the long run, moreover, it became obvious that Sikorski's name did not arouse sufficient mass appeal in the country nor make quite enough of an impact on the army to compete successfully against Piłsudski's image. Hence a number of his erstwhile supporters transferred their allegiance to Piłsudski and so informed Piłsudski's intimate assistants, Orlicz-Dreszer and Wieniawa-Długoszowski.[31]

Piłsudski himself had not been idle during the years of his ostensible retirement to Sulejówek after May, 1923. He conducted his preparations for a political comeback on three planes: public, confidential, and conspiratorial. In the public forum, his constant stream of lectures, interviews, and pamphlets was intended to maintain a vivid impression of himself as the unique Polish champion of public integrity and of the common man's aspirations. Three press organs stood at Piłsudski's disposal and supported him in this campaign of soliciting public support: the daily *Kurjer Poranny* (Morning Courier), the weekly *Głos Prawdy* (Voice of Truth), and the monthly *Droga* (The Way). In the confidential arena, he cultivated pivotal political figures and established especially close relations with the technocratically oriented Klub Praca (Work) group.[32] The conspiratorial work came last and was heavily delegated to Bogusław Miedziński[33] for civilian and to General Gustaw Orlicz-Dreszer for military preparations.[34] Piłsudski apparently found the idea of entangling the army in

[30] Sikorski's recollection of this incident was told to Colonel A. K. Kędzior, who appended it to Piątkowski, p. 31. Skrzyński is alleged to have warned Wojciechowski against Sikorski. For other allusions to Wojciechowski's suspicions of Sikorski, see the latter's "Kartki z dziennika," p. 4, and Witos, *Moje wspomnienia*, III, 83, 85. Plausible, albeit hearsay, evidence that Sikorski was indeed indulging in political and military intrigues is contained in some letters addressed by active officers to War Minister Żeligowski, preserved in his AGLŻ, 32a/26–27; 33/46.

[31] Ostrowski, p. 6, and Morawski, *Tamten brzeg*, p. 164.

[32] In 1925–26 the Klub Praca consisted of six Sejm deputies and four senators. Its membership changed after Piłsudski's coup.

[33] Miedziński had first demonstrated his skill and indispensability for this kind of work when he had kept alive Piłsudski's political organization in World War I by organizing the clandestine Konwent after the arrest of Piłsudski and Sosnkowski by the German authorities on July 22, 1917. The Konwent remained in existence in restored Poland until its dissolution by Piłsudski in 1927. In 1926 Miedziński was formally a Sejm deputy for Wyzwolenie.

[34] Z. Dreszer (brother of the general), pp. 4–5, and Romeyko, "Maj 1926. Zwierzenia generała Kutrzeby," pp. 6–7.

politics distasteful and hesitated for a long time before authorizing Orlicz-Dreszer to proceed on this course.[35]

In mid-September, 1925, a few weeks before the fall of the Grabski cabinet but well after the resumption of Poland's fiscal-economic crisis, Piłsudski had summoned the leader of the Klub Praca, Professor Kazimierz Bartel, and urged him to prepare himself to undertake the premiership in a Piłsudskist government to be formed after the now seemingly inevitable collapse of the current system based on party representation in the Sejm. Bartel accepted this mandate and began a thorough study of the country's economic and political problems: interviewing experts, organizing conferences, appointing study groups, etc.[36] Several more conversations took place in the following months (the last one preceding the coup occurred on May 9), in the course of which Piłsudski discussed virtually all political issues except foreign affairs with Bartel and, in turn, was briefed on the progress of the latter's programmatic preparations. Piłsudski's own political recommendations at this time were in the direction of moderation and gradualism on sociopolitical issues, such as, for example, land reform. Though technically still a private personage, Piłsudski already acted, in the course of his meetings with Bartel, like the future master of Poland. On one occasion he wondered aloud whether Poland might not, after all, require in the twentieth century that interval of enlightened absolutism which she had avoided—perhaps to her detriment— in the eighteenth.[37] Simultaneously, however, he remained careful to preserve intact his connections with the parliamentary Left and Center

[35] In the autumn of 1923, shortly after his retirement to Sulejówek, Piłsudski was informed that some of his supporters intended to organize a clandestine political organization on his behalf. He replied at that time that they were free to act as they believed proper in their capacities as politicians but that they must under no circumstances involve the army in their plans or infringe on its apoliticism. See Baranowski, pp. 179–80, and the review of his book by Paweł Hulka-Laskowski in *Wiadomości Literackie*, XV, No. 789 (December 4, 1938), 5. Baranowski was the bearer of the plan to Piłsudski.

[36] W. Grzybowski, "Premier Kazimierz Bartel," pp. 99–101. In addition to his political activities, Bartel was professor of mathematics at the Lwów Polytechnic. He had been an effective minister of railroads during the Polish-Soviet campaign of 1920.

[37] W. Grzybowski, "Spotkania i rozmowy z Józefem Piłsudskim," p. 92. Grzybowski, as secretary of the Klub Praca, was often present at these meetings. Marian Zyndram-Kościałkowski, one of the Klub Praca's Sejm deputies, was also closely involved in this work.

parties and to establish some new ones with significant conservative-aristocratic (but not National Democratic) political figures.

The military-conspiratorial aspects of preparing Piłsudski's intended demonstration of power were facilitated by the fact that the Polish officer corps was not a unitary body but had been only recently patched together, after more than a century of partition, from several different—and rivalrous—traditions. Piłsudski could, in general, count on the personal loyalty of those who had emerged from the Legionary and POW background of World War I (except the Second Brigade veterans), while some of the older officers from the former tsarist Russian army were also either his active supporters or benevolent neutrals.

It was neither possible nor necessary nor even desirable to initiate all of Piłsudski's military admirers into the planning for his show of force. All that was needed was to involve those who would be in a position to add real strength to the undertaking and—conversely—to remove from pivotal posts those who were known or suspected foes. To ensure the appropriate personnel assignments, it was necessary that Piłsudski reacquire control over the War Ministry, which had been lost during the incumbencies of Szeptycki and Sikorski (1923–25), both of whom had aroused Piłsudski's ire. This preliminary goal was achieved on November 27, 1925, with the assignment of that ministry to Żeligowski.

Though he was subsequently to deny it, circumstantial appearances suggest that Żeligowski worked hand in glove with the pro-Piłsudski forces. At the very least, he allowed himself to be used by them, turning a blind eye as his staff facilitated the conspiracy. First came some major transfers of central headquarters officers, followed by a "weeding through" of key unit commanders and their staffs. Sikorski's banishment of Orlicz-Dreszer from Warsaw was revoked, thereby provoking the departure of the ex-Austrian Stanisław Haller from his post of chief of the General Staff. Thus two birds were killed with one stone. Orlicz-Dreszer, brought back to the capital as inspector of cavalry for the Warsaw Military District and chief of the Cavalry Department of the War Ministry, soon took charge of the detailed preparatory work for Piłsudski's intended armed demonstration. The hitherto chief and deputy chief of Army Administration, the ex-Austrian Majewski and Żymierski (the latter, though a Legionnaire, had been politically at odds with Piłsudski since 1917), were replaced, respectively, by the pro-Piłsudski ex-Russian Konarzewski and the ex-Legionnaire Norwid-Neugebauer.[38] Similar developments occurred in the Second (Intelligence) Department of the General Staff, where the ex-Legionnaire Ścieżyński was designated chief in place of the ex-Russian and "Hallerite" Bajer, and in its Third (Training and Operations) Department, where the former Legion and POW officers Burhardt-Bukacki and Beck were given the principal appointments.

Where the commanders of operational units were regarded as hostile or doubtful, attempts were made to seed their staffs with loyal Piłsudskists who might, in a critical moment, be able to outmaneuver their commanders. The headquarters of the military districts of Warsaw, Lublin, Grodno, Łódź, and Brześć were infiltrated to a particularly advanced degree.[39] Soundings were taken by Piłsudski's close associates to determine the sympathies and expected reactions of officers whose political views were unknown.

Many extant memoirs testify to these activities. Thus, in the spring of 1926, the then Lieutenant Colonel Ludwik Kmicic-Skrzyński, at the time chief of staff of the Second Cavalry Division in Warsaw, was told by Orlicz-Dreszer to prepare his unit for possible participation in an eventual military operation that Piłsudski might find necessary in order to "rescue" the Polish state from its current "chaos."[40] Similarly, in the second half of April, 1926, Captain Henryk Picheta, a battalion commander of the 22d Infantry Regiment stationed in Siedlce, was asked by Krok-Paszkowski, his regimental colonel,

[38] Konarzewski had been the senior general participating in the demonstrative homage of the officers to Piłsudski at Sulejówek on November 15, 1925, at which Orlicz-Dreszer had clearly hinted at a coup d'état. For further information on these several officers, see pp. 91–115, and the Biographical Register.

[39] Pietrzak, ed., "Jak doszło" i "Przewrót," p. 133. See also S. Haller, p. 10.
Żeligowski claimed—casuistically though perhaps strictly speaking correctly— that he was not party to any conspiratorial preparations for an armed demonstration on Piłsudski's behalf and that it was purely fortuitous that his own personnel assignments and transfers of the first half of 1926 subsequently facilitated the coup of May 12–15. AGLŻ, 32/68; 32a/115, 133, 144, 148, 155, 203.

[40] Kmicic-Skrzyński, p. 3.

whether he could be counted on to support a coup d'état by Piłsud-ski.[41] Krok-Paszkowski, in turn, had been initiated into the conspiracy by General Mieczysław Trojanowski, another ex-Legionnaire and currently commander of the Ninth Infantry Division.[42] Colonel Wieniawa-Długoszowski, meanwhile, was "scouting" the Infantry Officer School and the Cadet Corps in Warsaw [43]—to no avail; they proved to be the mainstay of the government during the May fighting. Colonel Walery Sławek, Piłsudski's closest personal friend since their association in the pre-World War I Socialist underground, now on the reserve list but still well connected in the army, probed among provincial garrisons, allegedly promising higher pensions to the impoverished married officers should Piłsudski return to power.[44] Regardless of the truth of such charges, it may be presumed that some opportunists now made the proverbial jump onto what they supposed would prove to be the winning bandwagon. Certain paramilitary and patriotic organizations, such as the revived Riflemen and the Polish Organization of Liberty (Polska Organizacja Wolności), were infiltrated and mobilized on behalf of Piłsudski. As the conspiratorial network became more elaborate during April, 1926, certain officers of proven devotion to Piłsudski were released from their provincial garrison assignments to assist Orlicz-Dreszer in Warsaw.[45]

Piłsudski himself ostensibly remained aloof from the conspiratorial work, simply indicating by his public activities that he was "at the disposal" of the nation. In fact, however, by April he was deeply immersed in the clandestine activities on his behalf. On one occasion he attended a secret meeting of Orlicz-Dreszer's preparatory task force. He appears to have been startled by the assumption of some

[41] Picheta, p. 3. The same question was put to other junior officers in the regiment.

[42] Krok-Paszkowski, "Relacja" (unpublished memoir in the archives of the Piłsudski Historical Institute in London).

[43] Rzepecki, *Wspomnienia*, p. 14.

[44] Pietrzak, ed., "Jak doszło" i "Przewrót," p. 134. It is also asserted here that the Wilno conservatives were promised a restoration of Lithuania's "Jagiellonian autonomy" in respect to "Crown Poland" in order to persuade them to support Piłsudski. These accusations came from circles close to Sikorski (if not from Sikorski himself) and hostile to Piłsudski.

[45] S. Skwarczyński, "Relacja" (unpublished memoir in the archives of the Piłsudski Historical Institute in London). He and six other officers were transferred from the First Legion Division in Wilno, the commander of which was General Dąb-Biernacki, another Piłsudskist.

of its members that a battle would have to be fought to overthrow an undesirable government, thus rendering necessary the mobilization of maximum force by the Piłsudskists. He deprecated these seemingly alarmist views as a case of rolling out cannons to shoot at flies.[46] On another occasion, he forgot himself and discussed his most secret plans with Orlicz-Dreszer in the presence of an officer who was not a party to the conspiracy, Colonel Tadeusz Kutrzeba of the General Staff.[47]

On April 18, as the internal crisis within the Skrzyński cabinet was coming to a head, War Minister Żeligowski ordered certain units (including Stamirowski's 7th Uhlan Regiment) to assemble on May 10 at the Rembertów training ground (between Sulejówek and Warsaw) for special maneuvers. The inspirer of this order was Wieniawa-Długoszowski, who had been strategically placed by the conspirators as first officer on the inspectorate staff of the War Ministry.[48] The acting chief of the General Staff, General Edmund Kessler (who was not a party to the conspiracy), immediately protested to Żeligowski

---

[46] *Ibid.*

[47] The background to this curious incident is as follows: Kutrzeba, who was a military historian as well as a staff officer, had in 1924 published (under the pseudonym "Miles") a book entitled *Commanders in Chief* to which Piłsudski had written a long preface (reprinted in his *PZ,* VI, 169–96). Piłsudski thought well of Kutrzeba's work and in this preface had referred to him as "my friend" (p. 185). In the spring of 1926 Kutrzeba was at work on a treatise dealing with the Polish-Soviet campaign of 1920 and requested an interview with Piłsudski to check certain points. He was invited to Sulejówek in March or April and, on his arrival, found Orlicz-Dreszer also waiting in Piłsudski's anteroom to confer with the Marshal. Piłsudski entered and, unmindful of Kutrzeba's presence, gave Orlicz-Dreszer his "final directives" as to which officers and units were to be used for his coming show of force. Orlicz-Dreszer then begged Kutrzeba to keep silent about what he had overheard and the latter promised to do so, even though he was an ex-Austrian officer. During the May battle in Warsaw, Kutrzeba fought on the government side against Piłsudski and helped to arrange the concluding cease-fire terms. He was reappointed to his General Staff functions immediately afterward and in 1928 was promoted to command the Superior War Academy (Wyższa Szkoła Wojenna). In September, 1939, Kutrzeba commanded the Poznanian army group against the Germans. He had revealed his secret knowledge of Piłsudski's 1926 plans to Colonel Romeyko while going to the funeral of Orlicz-Dreszer (killed in an airplane crash at Gdynia) in July, 1936. See Romeyko, "Maj 1926. Zwierzenia generała Kutrzeby," pp. 6–7.

[48] S. Skwarczyński, "Relacja." Witos, at the time leader of Piast but not in the cabinet, claims to have come into possession of hard proof of these putschist preparations on April 19 but to have been unable to persuade Skrzyński of their authenticity. Witos, *Moje wspomnienia,* III, 75–80.

in a letter of April 20 that the units designated for these maneuvers were fractional, selected seemingly at random from several divisions, and did not collectively compose a suitable operational body for maneuvers.[49] In fact, there was of course nothing random about the choice of units. The principle of selection had merely been political rather than military. The machinery for a coup was now ready and required but a suitable moment to be set into motion.

That moment came with the political crisis inaugurated upon the resignation of Skrzyński on May 5. By May 8 it was clear that the crisis would prove to be a severe and perhaps a shattering one. On that day Żeligowski, in one of his last acts as caretaker war minister, issued an order about which he failed to inform his successor Malczewski of the incoming Witos cabinet. It named Piłsudski to command the maneuvers scheduled to begin two days later at Rembertów.[50] By the time Malczewski had oriented himself in the War Ministry and canceled the maneuvers, it was too late. Only the Cadet Corps, of the units assembled at Rembertów, obeyed his orders and returned to Warsaw on May 12 to defend the government against Piłsudski. Malczewski was further hampered by the fact that the staff of the Warsaw Military District was riddled with partisans of Piłsudski who sabotaged his orders. Hence Sawicki's unreliable 36th Infantry Regiment was sent to hold the Kierbedź bridge against Piłsudski and promptly defected, thereby presenting him a bridgehead in Warsaw.[51]

The elaborate conspiratorial preparations preceding Piłsudski's march on Warsaw on May 12 demonstrate that his move on that day was far from being a spontaneous response provoked by the alleged night attack (May 11) on his Sulejówek home. Indeed, already during the afternoon of May 11, that is, before that pretext became available, Wieniawa-Długoszowski was confidentially informing other initiates into the plot that Piłsudski would march on Warsaw the next day with the 7th Uhlan Regiment.[52] Yet, though the preparations had been made, the final occasion for the coup seems to have come un-

[49] Górnicki, "Ostatni rokosz w Warszawie," p. 8.

[50] Jordan-Rozwadowski, p. 114.

[51] After Malczewski's assumption of office, Orlicz-Dreszer was summoned to present himself at the Warsaw Garrison Headquarters. Fearing arrest, he refused. See Kmicic-Skrzyński, p. 3.

[52] Interview of October 4, 1963, with Colonel Adam Koc; S. Skwarczyński, "Relacja."

expectedly. As late as the morning of May 10, Piłsudski had sent Wieniawa-Długoszowski to the French embassy to arrange a visit by Piłsudski to ambassador Jules Laroche for the afternoon of May 12.[53] Mme Piłsudska, in turn, was scheduled to preside as patroness over a huge charity-benefit reception in the Warsaw town hall on the evening of May 12.[54] These may, of course, have been ruses to mislead the government. Orlicz-Dreszer's brother, indeed, traced Piłsudski's definitive resolution to set in motion his prepared "armed demonstration" to the predawn hours of May 10. In any event, even some of the Marshal's close intimates were taken by surprise when finally, and abruptly, they were alerted to stand by for imminent action.[55]

Thus everyone involved in the coup was each in his own way surprised by it. Piłsudski was surprised that he would have to fight. Wojciechowski was surprised that Piłsudski had resorted to illegal action. Witos and Piłsudski were both surprised by Wojciechowski's toughness. Piłsudski's associates were surprised when the time came to put their plans into effect. (Eventually the Left parties which supported him were to be surprised by the uses to which he would soon put his newly seized power.) There is much irony in this pervasive sensation of ultimate surprise, for Warsaw had been periodically flooded with rumors of a coup—to be staged by Piłsudskists or by the Right—since the beginning of the year. It had been prophesied for early January, then for Piłsudski's name day of March 19, then for May Day (May 1), and finally for the national holiday of May 3. On the last occasion the capital was so jittery that the Cadet Corps and the Infantry Officer School were issued live ammunition to put down an expected seizure of power by Piłsudski.[56] The Right, in turn, had brought some paramilitary toughs from the so-called Union of Hallerites (Związek Hallerczyków) up to Warsaw from the National Democratic strongholds of Poznania and Pomerania early in May.[57] The universal nervousness had, in fact, prolonged the formal life of the Skrzyński cabinet until after these critical anniversaries were over lest

[53] Laroche, p. 30.

[54] Rzepecki, *Wspomnienia*, p. 17; Skwarczyński, "Relacja."

[55] Z. Dreszer, p. 4, and interview with Colonel Adam Koc of October 4, 1963.

[56] Piątkowski, p. 1.

[57] J. Haller, p. 261. The Hallerites were veterans of the Polish corps that had served in France in 1918 under General Józef Haller.

Poland be without a government during them. That Piłsudski finally chose the formation of the Witos cabinet as the occasion for launching his stroke, rather than a mechanically predetermined date, shows that he had political aims and claims to advance and was not motivated by a mere hunger for personal power. His tragedy rested in the circumstance that, in acting to realize his goals, he had to take the responsibility for fracturing the fragile unity of the new Polish state and army and involving them in fratricidal strife.

CHAPTER V

THE BATTLE: THE COUNTERATTACK
OF THE GOVERNMENT FORCES

The initial impetus of Piłsudski's units as they poured across the Kierbedź bridge and fanned out over northern Warsaw during the early evening hours of May 12 was soon slowed by the double check of Piłsudski's alarmed quest for mediation and of determined rearguard resistance by units loyal to the government, particularly the Cadet Corps and the Infantry Officer School.[1] However, that first sweep of the Piłsudski forces had been sufficiently wide (from the Royal Castle southward to the War Ministry building on Nowowiejska street)[2] to bring into their perimeter many of the key governmental buildings, the important railroad stations, and the main telephone exchange—possession of which was to be of critical importance during the next three days. The crowds in the streets were demonstratively friendly to the Piłsudski forces, and the fact that Orlicz-Dreszer was in immediate command helped to solidify the support of the workers and of the Left, among whom this general enjoyed considerable popularity.[3]

Later that evening the Piłsudskist headquarters were organized. Orlicz-Dreszer's assumption of direct military command was formalized and Beck's role as his chief of staff for the current operation was confirmed. Other officers were assigned to take charge of intelligence, transport, organization, and other services. Piłsudski designated as chief of the General Staff (an assignment without much substance

[1] For details, see Mercik, pp. 106–8; Piątkowski, pp. 8–10; and Bełcikowska, *Walki majowe,* pp. 14–17. Also AKL, 11/36, annexes 1 and 2.

[2] To facilitate the perusal of this chapter, the reader is referred to the accompanying map No. 1.

[3] *Dokumenty chwili,* I, 12, and Hass, "Zamach majowy 1926 r.," p. 4.

until after the domestic fighting was over), General Stanisław Burhardt-Bukacki, who had come over to his side from the government
forces' headquarters earlier in the evening.[4] On May 13, since his
mediation efforts were failing to bear fruit, Piłsudski made a number
of provisional governmental assignments, of which the most important were those of Klub Praca leader Kazimierz Bartel as commissar (that is, *de facto* acting minister) for railroads, and of Roman
Knoll (previously envoy to Soviet Russia and to Turkey but currently
in Warsaw) as commissar for foreign affairs. Legion veteran and
army physician General Felicjan Sławoj-Składkowski was named
commissar for Warsaw (an appointment with a jurisdiction analogous
to that of the *wojewoda* [governor] of a province), while Generals
Jan Romer and Stanisław Małachowski were designated commissars
for the strategic rail-hubs of Lublin and Łódź respectively. Through
these cities reinforcements to either side in Warsaw could be sent or
blocked.[5] These appointments were Piłsudski's first tentative moves
toward establishing an alternative government.[6]

[4] Burhardt-Bukacki (1890–1942) had led a nonsocialist paramilitary organization in pre-World War I Galicia which he had merged with Piłsudski's
socialist Riflemen at war's outbreak in 1914 to form the nucleus of the
Legions. During the day of May 12 he had been at Malczewski's headquarters
in his capacity as second deputy chief of the General Staff for Training and
Operations (by appointment of Żeligowski). During the September, 1939, campaign he was to be sent on a vain mission to France to plead for a Western
offensive against the Germans so as to relieve the overwhelming pressure on
Poland.

[5] As Piłsudski had expected an immediate political victory in the capital on
the strength of an armed demonstration to be made with nearby units, little
preliminary attention had been given to organizing "follow-up" operations in
the provinces. When these were required by virtue of the government's resistance, they were made in haste and often in ignorance. Thus General Romer,
commander of the Lublin Military District, was named commissar there by
Piłsudski, but, though sympathizing with the Marshal's political and administrative goals, he remained at least formally loyal and obedient to the Wojciechowski-Witos government—as explained by him in J. Romer, pp. 317–18.
(Sikorski, on the other hand, with some justice, accused Romer of having in
fact hedged during the coup. See Sikorski, p. 14.) In Łódź, in turn, Piłsudski's
choice as commissar, General Małachowski, was only a divisional commander.
To arrest his authority, he had to "depose" the military district commander
(General Władysław Jung) and intern the provincial governor (*wojewoda*
Ludwik Darowski). See AKL, 10/10, 11/12. Both Romer and Jung were
veterans of the former Austrian army, while Małachowski came from the tsarist
Russian one.

[6] A full list of Piłsudski's various governmental and military assignments at
this time may be compiled by consulting *Kurjer Warszawski*, May 14 and 15,
1926; Bełcikowska, *Walki majowe*, p. 22; W. Grzybowski, "Premier Kazimierz
Bartel," p. 104; and Arski, p. 422.

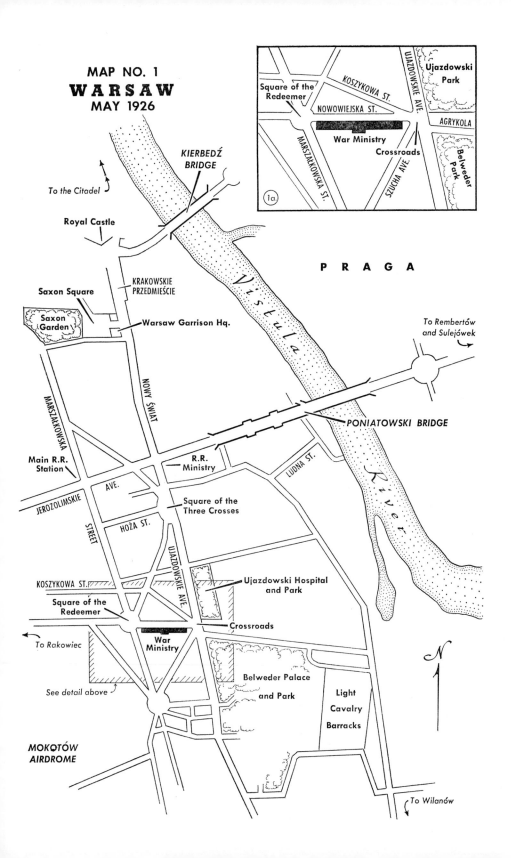

MAP NO. 1
WARSAW
MAY 1926

To the Citadel

KIERBEDŹ BRIDGE

Royal Castle

KRAKOWSKIE PRZEDMIEŚCIE

Saxon Square

Saxon Garden

Warsaw Garrison Hq.

NOWY ŚWIAT

MARSZAŁKOWSKA

Main R.R. Station

R.R. Ministry

AVE.

JEROZOLIMSKIE

STREET

HOŻA ST.

Square of the Three Crosses

UJAZDOWSKI AVE.

LUDNA ST.

Vistula

PRAGA

To Rembertów and Sulejówek

PONIATOWSKI BRIDGE

River

KOSZYKOWA ST.

Square of the Redeemer

To Rakowiec

War Ministry

See detail above

Ujazdowski Hospital and Park

Crossroads

Belweder Palace and Park

Light Cavalry Barracks

MOKOTÓW AIRDROME

N

To Wilanów

UJAZDOWSKIE AVE.

Ujazdowski Park

KOSZYKOWA ST.

Square of the Redeemer

NOWOWIEJSKA ST.

AGRYKOLA

MARSZAŁKOWSKA ST.

War Ministry

Crossroads

SZUCHA AVE.

Belweder Park

1a.

The Wojciechowski-Witos government, in its turn, had responded to Piłsudski's attack with energy and resolution once the Prime Minister's original inclination to yield had been overruled and overtaken by events. Both the cabinet and the loyal generals had withdrawn from their endangered locations in north-central Warsaw after Piłsudski's units swept over the Kierbedź bridge, and had repaired southward to the presidential Belweder palace.[7] Here a redoubt was established, originally consisting chiefly of the Infantry Officer School and the Cadet Corps (which were withdrawn from the Poniatowski bridge after the Piłsudskists had outflanked it) but reinforced during the night of May 12 and on May 13 by several additional regiments.

This initial retreat and entrenchment by the legal forces brought them a number of military and political benefits. First of all, the geographical separation between the two rival headquarters now clarified the affiliation of the many high military officers in the capital at that time. In a coup d'état situation, the conspirators have the initial advantage of knowing who are the initiates into their intrigue, while the legal side is handicapped in being obliged to determine under pressure, in haste, and with risk who will prove loyal. The means of ascertaining this information was provided by the withdrawal of the government and its military protectors to the Belweder palace and the resultant establishment of a clearly loyal redoubt and headquarters in southern Warsaw. From there orders were issued which obliged senior commanders to show their hand. This benefit,

---

[7] The cabinet had been in session in the Namiestnikowski palace on Krakowskie Przedmieście, while the loyal generals had been meeting at the General Staff headquarters on Saxon Square. It was during the withdrawal to the Belweder palace that Burhardt-Bukacki had defected to Piłsudski. For accounts of this withdrawal operation by participants, see Morawski, *Tamten brzeg,* p. 148, and S. Haller, pp. 12–17. It was screened by cordons of the Infantry Officer School and the Cadet Corps. For recollections of men from these units, see Mercik, pp. 106 ff.; Piątkowski, pp. 8–10; Rzepecki, *Wspomnienia,* pp. 27–30.

Sławoj-Składkowski—whom Piłsudski was to name commissar for Warsaw a few hours later—claimed to have seen, from a window of the War Ministry building, President Wojciechowski among the retinue of retreating ministers and generals and therefore to have ordered his troops to hold their fire. Acting Foreign Minister Morawski, on the other hand, wrote that Wojciechowski had left for the Belweder palace considerably earlier than the cabinet. Cf. Sławoj-Składkowski, "Wspomnienia z okresu majowego," p. 145, and Morawski, *Tamten brzeg,* pp. 147–48. The latter version is indirectly confirmed in the recollections of Wojciechowski's personal adjutant, Comte, "Granaty nad Belwederem," No. 23, p. 11.

on balance, outweighed the disadvantage that the very speed of the withdrawal had left stranded behind Piłsudski's lines some officers who wanted to join the legal side.[8]

Politically, the retreat to the Belweder palace was a shrewd move for the government to make, for it enabled the controversial Witos cabinet to cover itself with the mantle of the nonpolitical presidency. By thus identifying their own political constellation with the highest authority of the state—indeed, with "The State" as such—Witos and his Right-Center colleagues were enabled to draw on the services of those civil and military officers who in fact sympathized with Piłsudski but who felt duty-bound and oath-bound to defend the president and the principle of constitutional legality which his office symbolized to them.[9] Conversely, the cabinet's removal to the Belweder palace forced Piłsudski into the unwelcome and even painful situation of appearing to attack the presidential institution as he pursued his effort to overthrow the Witos regime. Thus his constant endeavor, nurtured since the restoration of Polish independence, always to be seen to act so as to increase the authority of the state and particularly of its executive authorities was seriously compromised.[10]

Nevertheless, the important political advantage which accrued to the government by virtue of its withdrawal to the Belweder palace had to be paid for with a military sacrifice which was to prove increasingly serious during the next three days of fighting. To establish their defensive perimeter around the palace—which had no intrinsic military significance apart from its political symbolism—the government's generals were obliged by the thinness of their available man-

[8] Since the afternoon the war minister, General Juliusz Malczewski, had taken personal charge of interrogating officers found on the streets of Warsaw so as to ascertain their affiliation. Popławski, p. 3.

[9] An example was Colonel Gustaw Paszkiewicz, commander of the Cadet Corps and of the Infantry Officer School. who confessed to Acting Foreign Minister Morawski that those were his sentiments. Morawski, *Tamten brzeg,* p. 157. It is possible that Colonel Tadeusz Kutrzeba may also have felt this way. One of Piłsudski's original Legion comrades, Colonel Stanisław Skotnicki-Grzmot, likewise held his Poznań-based 15th Uhlan Regiment loyal to its constitutional oath despite his friendship for Piłsudski. Subsequently promoted to general nevertheless, he fell in the September, 1939, campaign.

[10] Indicative of just how aggravating this reversal of his self-assigned role was to Piłsudski are the press communiqué issued by his headquarters on May 13, 1926, reprinted in *Dokumenty chwili,* I, 17, and his press interview of May 25, 1926, by the *Kurjer Poranny,* reproduced in Piłsudski, *PZ,* IX, 15.

power to relinquish the city's main railroad stations, upon which they would be dependent for the arrival of reinforcements, as well as the chief telegraph and telephone facilities, which were important for communication with the provinces. The Belweder concentration thus became a beleaguered and isolated camp, dependent for contact with the rest of Poland on the embryonic air force and its radio facilities, neither of which was an adequate substitute for railroads and telegraph facilities.[11] From the strictly military point of view, it would have been preferable to concentrate the defense around these crucial transport and communication points or—better yet—to have abandoned Warsaw, with its largely pro-Piłsudski population, and withdrawn to the National Democratic, that is, anti-Piłsudski, regions of western Poland, whence a counterattack might have been launched with the strong and loyal regiments stationed in the provinces of Pomerania and Poznania. For understandable reasons, however, it was feared that a flight by the President from his capital and residence might well prove politically fatal.[12] As an insurance measure, two cabinet members—the Christian Democratic minister of justice, Stefan Piechocki, and the Piast Peasant minister of industry and commerce, Stanisław Osiecki—were flown out to Poznań at noon on May 13 with plenipotentiary reserve powers.[13]

In any event, the crippling implications of the isolation of the Belweder units were not to become fully apparent for another day or two, until the loss of the Warsaw railroad stations was compounded by the effects of a nationwide refusal of the Socialist-affiliated railroad workers' union to transport reinforcements for the Wojciechowski-Witos government to Warsaw. In the meantime, the situation did not

[11] For the role of communication facilities during the coup, see Hauke-Nowak, "Nieznany raport o telefonach, telegrafie i radiu w czasie przewrotu majowego 1926 roku w Warszawie."

The Mokotów military airdrome lay within the Belweder perimeter. Its garrison, under the influence of General Włodzimierz Zagórski, remained loyal to the legal government. Zagórski had been relieved as commander of the air force by Żeligowski in April, 1926, but was reappointed by Malczewski on May 12. A professional officer in the imperial Austrian army, he had been "seconded" in 1914 for service with the Legions, where his relations with Piłsudski were rancorous.

[12] Morawski, *Tamten brzeg*, pp. 149–50; S. Haller, p. 20.

[13] *Ilustrowany Kurjer Codzienny*, May 17, 1926. S. Haller (p. 43) reports that Witos had proposed to fly to Poznań himself but that Wojciechowski had successfully interceded against this plan. Witos (*Moje wspomnienia*, III, 102) says he independently reversed his original intention.

seem at all hopeless to the Belweder defenders. The Cadet Corps and the Infantry Officer School skillfully and successfully defended the perimeter during the night of May 12.[14] By the next morning the 10th Infantry Regiment from Łowicz and the 57th and 58th Infantry Regiments from Poznań, which had meanwhile arrived at a small freight depot (the so-called sixth station) on the western outskirts of Warsaw and had marched by a roundabout route from there to the Belweder area, would be ready to go into action.[15] The Belweder defenders also had some additional, secondary forces at their disposal. Among these were an air regiment and an antiaircraft unit at the Mokotów airdrome, a fraction of the 21st Infantry Regiment, an ordnance battalion, the presidential guard, and a cannon. Also present in the Belweder perimeter was a fairly large number of unattached officers, as well as members of National Democratic youth associations. The former were organized into an auxiliary Officer Legion by General Rudolf Prych, who was cut off from his command at the Rembertów training camp, and were deployed to help defend the Mokotów airdrome and the rear of the Belweder palace.[16] The Rightist youths, in turn, were put at the disposal of the generals by the National Democratic minister of education, Stanisław Grabski, and were used as couriers and for reconnaissance.[17] Finally, there existed a potentially strong pocket of supposedly loyal troops behind Piłsudski's lines. This was Colonel Izydor Modelski's 30th Infantry Regiment, which had shut itself up in the Citadel in northern Warsaw

[14] Exhaustively detailed descriptions of this phase may be found in many sources: S. Haller, p. 18; Jordan-Rozwadowski, p. 116; Piątkowski, pp. 8–11; Mercik, pp. 107–8; Rzepecki, *Wspomnienia,* pp. 27–31; Sławoj-Składkowski, "Wspomnienia z okresu majowego," p. 145; Karbowski, p. 339; Strumph-Wojtkiewicz *et al.,* p. 28.

[15] Piłsudski's staff had intended to trap and capture these reinforcements for the legal government upon their expected arrival at one of the major railroad stations. This hope was foiled by Colonel Tadeusz Kurcyusz, the Belwederians' transport chief, who intercepted them at the "sixth station." The 10th Infantry Regiment had arrived at 2 A.M. and the other pair in the morning. AKL, 14/3a, and S. Haller, pp. 26, 31, 33.

[16] Srokowski, p. 95, and S. Haller, p. 34. Some units of the Cadet Corps were also assigned to Prych's command. For the reason for his presence in Warsaw, see above, p. 57, n. 39.

[17] Jordan-Rozwadowski, p. 117; S. Haller, p. 30. In his memoirs (*Moje wspomnienia,* III, 113), Witos bitterly complains of the paucity of such Rightist civilian help in May, 1926, and contrasts it with the Right's ability to dominate the streets of Warsaw at the time of President Narutowicz's election and assassination in December, 1922.

after its brief clash with Piłsudski's troops upon their emergence from the Kierbedź bridge. Its existence opened up the possibility of catching Piłsudski's units in a pincer movement by simultaneous attacks on them from the Belweder area (south) and the Citadel fortress (north). As Piłsudski himself was meanwhile refraining from pressing his attack while the mediation efforts were grinding fruitlessly on, the aggressively minded Belweder defenders decided to go over to the offensive early on May 13.

The organization of the legal government's command structure at the Belweder palace was relatively complicated, thanks partly to the veritable surfeit of senior officers available. The formal commander in chief under President Wojciechowski was the war minister, General Juliusz Malczewski. He was, however, excessively nervous and given to hysteria; thus he did not exercise effective command.[18] Leadership devolved upon another ex-Austrian, General Tadeusz Rozwadowski, hitherto the army's inspector of cavalry, who was given the *ad hoc* designation of "Commander of the Defense of Warsaw and Director of Military Actions." [19] His chief of staff in this command was Colonel Władysław Anders, upon whom much of the actual responsibility for the later phases of the operations of the government forces was soon to fall, inasmuch as Rozwadowski became ill on the third day (May 14) of the fighting.[20] General Stanisław Haller returned to his post as chief of the General Staff, from which he had gone on leave the previous December 15, but this position had as little substance during the days of the coup as did Burhardt-Bukacki's assumption of the identical appointment in Piłsudski's camp.[21] Also present in the Belweder palace was General Edmund Kessler, who

[18] See Witos, *Moje wspomnienia*, III, 96 ff.; Kukiel, "Jeszcze o przełomie majowym," p. 16; Piątkowski, pp. 8–10, 18. For an extended sketch of Malczewski, confirming these personality traits, see Romeyko, "Przed i po maju 1926 r.," VII, No. 4, 289–94.

[19] A former Habsburg lieutenant general, Rozwadowski had won the Austrian army's highest distinction for valor, the Order of Maria Theresa, in World War I. In restored Poland, he had defended Lwów against the Ukrainians in 1918–19 and had served as chief of the General Staff during the Polish-Soviet campaign of 1920. He died on October 18, 1928.

[20] On Anders' subsequent career, consult the Biographical Register.

[21] Pro-Piłsudski historians subsequently refused to acknowledge Haller's resumption of the post on May 12 in their chronological tables of chiefs of the General Staff. See *Dziesięciolecie Polski odrodzonej, 1918–1928*, p. 303. In World War II, Stanisław Haller was taken captive by Soviet forces in September, 1939, and was subsequently killed in the Katyn forest massacre. See Zbyszewski, "Generał Haller," p. 106.

had been acting chief during Haller's furlough, as well as Colonel Tadeusz Kutrzeba, who had earlier inadvertently come to know but not to betray Piłsudski's plans for an "armed demonstration." General Włodzimierz Zagórski, as has been mentioned, commanded the government's air units at the Mokotów field, while Colonels Michał Bajer, Tadeusz Kurcyusz,[22] and Franciszek Kleeberg [23] were in charge of intelligence, transport, and quartermaster problems respectively. Active in operational and tactical roles were Generals Marian Kukiel,[24] chief of the army's historical bureau, Michał Żymierski,[25] who busied himself attempting to guide additional reinforcements to the Belweder perimeter, and Anatol Kędzierski, the commander of the 57th and 58th Infantry Regiments freshly arrived from Poznań. Colonel Gustaw Paszkiewicz commanded the Cadet Corps and the Infantry Officer School.[26] To the extent that it is meaningful to speak of sectors in as confined an operational area as

[22] Kurcyusz's account of his actions during the coup is in AKL, 2/35. Consult the Biographical Register for his later career.

[23] For further information on Kleeberg, consult the Biographical Register.

[24] In July, 1917, Kukiel and Żymierski (see next footnote) had been among the few exceptions to the general refusal of the Piłsudskist First and Third Legion Brigades to take an oath of loyalty to the German and Austro-Hungarian armies. In 1925 Kukiel had angered Piłsudski with an article on the Battle of Warsaw of 1920, which Piłsudski felt minimized and distorted his own role in that Polish victory. (See Piłsudski, *PZ*, VIII, 218–44.) After the events of May, 1926, Kukiel was placed at the (inactive) disposal of the war minister until 1930, when he retired from the army to accept a lectureship in history at Kraków. Further information on Kukiel will be found in the Biographical Register.

[25] Żymierski's real name was Łyżwiński, but he had changed it before World War I to dissociate himself from a brother who had committed a bank robbery in Kraków. During the war he had served as a Legion officer and hobnobbed with Austro-Polish aristocrats. Though a man of proven bravery, he already enjoyed a certain notoriety as a *blagueur* and *hochstapler*. In the postwar Polish army he identified himself with the group of Piłsudski's foes from the old Austrian army. In 1925, as deputy chief of Army Administration under War Minister Sikorski, he was involved in unsavory financial dealings, accepting defective gas masks for the army and receiving money from the firm which supplied them. Although investigated and preliminarily exculpated once before May, 1926, Żymierski was tried again after Piłsudski's coup. In September, 1927, he was sentenced to degradation of rank, expulsion from the army, and five years' imprisonment. See Lubodziecki, "Sprawa Michała Żymierskiego." Further information on Żymierski will be found in the Biographical Register.

[26] Paszkiewicz, who had a laudable record in the Polish-Soviet campaign of 1920, fought energetically on behalf of the Wojciechowski-Witos government in May, 1926, even though his sympathies were apparently with Piłsudski (see note 9 above). Afterward he publicly declared himself a partisan of Piłsudski's post-coup system. For further information on him, see the Biographical Register.

the Belweder perimeter, one might say that Kukiel commanded the right wing, Kędzierski the center, and Paszkiewicz the left flank, while Żymierski was supposed to bring up the expected reserves.

The over-all political complexion of the Belweder officers, particularly of the senior generals among them, was "Austrian," conservative, anti-Piłsudski.[27] Haller, Malczewski, Rozwadowski, Zagórski, Żymierski, and former War Minister (1923) Stanisław Szeptycki (who was seeking to send the government reinforcements from the southwest) were known to look down upon the veterans of Piłsudski's wartime Legions and underground POW with contempt. These generals, in turn, were themselves despised and feared by the Piłsudski camp and by the Polish political Left as arrogant promotion-manipulators with reactionary reflexes.[28] Concerning three of them—Rozwadowski, Zagórski, and Żymierski—there floated rumored charges of corruption and malfeasance.[29] Thus, at the very moment

[27] Of the Belweder officers listed here, Generals Haller, Malczewski, Prych, Rozwadowski, and Zagórski had been career officers in the imperial Austrian army, as had Colonels Kleeberg and Kutrzeba. Generals Kukiel and Żymierski, though Legion veterans, had been politically at odds with Piłsudski at least since the crisis of July, 1917, over the oath of loyalty to the Central Powers. Generals Kędzierski and Kessler, as well as Colonels Anders, Bajer, Kurcyusz, and Paszkiewicz, were from the tsarist Russian army. Lieutenant Colonel Stanisław Rostworowski—Kędzierski's chief of staff and in World War II the commander of the underground Home Army in the Kraków area until his capture and execution by the Germans in the summer of 1944—was a veteran of the anti-Piłsudski Second Legion Brigade.

[28] See, for example, Daszyński, *W pierwszą rocznicę,* p. 27.

[29] These accusations were published in an anonymous pamphlet entitled *Zbrodniarze* (Criminals), the second in a series of brochures issued by the "Library of Moral Regeneration" (Biblioteka Odrodzenia Moralnego) which, in turn, was sponsored by the pro-Piłsudski journal *Głos Prawdy* (a weekly before May, 1926, later a daily). It is possible that the anonymous author of *Zbrodniarze* was the editor of *Głos Prawdy,* Wojciech Stpiczyński, a wounded Legion veteran and Piłsudski's leading journalistic shield-bearer. (For details on Stpiczyński's career of political journalism, see Singer, pp. 64–66, and Grzędziński, *Maj 1926,* pp. 62–66). *Zbrodniarze* was serialized during 1927 in the Polish-American weekly *Robotnik Polski* (The Polish Worker), published in Detroit, Michigan. It is in that version that I read it.

Briefly, Rozwadowski was already under investigation before the coup for suspected financial abuses of sundry kinds. The post-coup Piłsudski regime, in fact, held him a prisoner for a whole year (until May 18, 1927) and prepared to indict him, but he died on October 18, 1928, before a trial could be held. See Jordan-Rozwadowski, pp. 119–22, and AGLŻ, 26/71–79, 32/54–55. Also Badeni, "O Generale Rozwadowskim," and Czarkowski-Golejewski, "Walki majowe i audiencja w Belwederze."

Zagórski was accused of accepting kickbacks from, and owning stock in, a

when Piłsudski was appealing to the workers, the peasant poor, and the ethnic minorities with his ringing denunciation of exploitation and injustice,[30] the public political impact made by the names of the senior generals gathered during the night of May 12 at the Belweder palace was unfortunate. Nevertheless, the aroused and by now even bellicose President Wojciechowski was closer to them during the next days of fighting than to the civilian cabinet ministers whom he suspected (in some cases correctly) of being disposed to compromise.[31]

In addition to their subjective inclinations, another factor inducing the Belweder generals to launch an offensive on the morning of May 13 was the consideration that there were few food supplies or ammunition reserves within the narrow confines of their perimeter as originally stabilized during the preceding night. Simply to survive, it was necessary to advance into parts of Warsaw where food shops and barracks would provide an opportunity to replenish these two items. Accordingly, the 10th Infantry Regiment, which had arrived from Łowicz during the night, was ordered to capture the barracks of the (Piłsudskist) 1st Light Cavalry Regiment on the eastern flank of the Belweder concentration,[32] while units of the Cadet Corps and the Infantry Officer School were to open a path to the north by taking the massive complex of the War Ministry, which stretched east-westward the entire distance between the so-called Crossroads (Na Rozdrożu) and the Square of the Redeemer (Plac Zbawiciela) along the southern side of Nowowiejska street.[33]

Lacking artillery support and harassed by civilian snipers of the Piłsudskist Rifleman organization, both attacks soon stalled. Then Kukiel took personal charge of the assault on the light cavalry

Franco-Polish firm with which he had placed the Polish army's orders for airplanes. AGLŻ, 26/102–3; AKL, 16/1. The Żymierski affair is discussed in note 25 above.

[30] See above, p. 66; also *Frankfurter Zeitung*, May 15, 1926.

[31] Morawski, "Przewrót majowy," p. 2.

[32] Jachieć, pp. 338–39.

[33] The War Ministry building was held for Piłsudski by a hastily assembled contingent under the command of General Felicjan Sławoj-Składkowski, shortly to be named commissar for Warsaw and a future minister of the interior and prime minister. He has described this episode in detail in his "Wspomnienia z okresu majowego," pp. 145–48. The tactical commander of the attacking cadets and officer candidates has also published his recollections. See Piątkowski, pp. 11–15. The official report of the Cadet Corps on its role in the fighting is in AKL, 8/3.

barracks, into which was now thrown the 58th Infantry Regiment, freshly arrived from Poznań. Its sister unit, the 57th Infantry Regiment, was simultaneously sent to reinforce the storming of the War Ministry. This became the scene of the heaviest combat as the ministry building was fought for room by room. By the early afternoon, both operations had met with success.[34] In the light cavalry barracks the Belwederians captured roughly 400 military prisoners and about 80 civilian Riflemen. What was more important, they also found much-needed supplies of food and ammunition, as well as two additional cannon, thus achieving one of the main purposes of their offensive. Upon taking the War Ministry, they found that only the recruits were left to surrender, the officers having departed in time for the Piłsudskist command post at the Warsaw Garrison Headquarters on Saxon Square to the north.[35]

With the light cavalry barracks and the War Ministry bastion in their possession, the troops of the legal government now fanned out northward in a semicircular arc. By late afternoon they had cleared the Piłsudskists out of the area of the Square of the Three Crosses (Plac Trzech Krzyży) and had reached the east-west axis of Jerozolimskie (Jerusalem) avenue. Still their patrols pushed onward, some getting as far north as the Saxon Garden (Ogród Saski) just to the west of Piłsudski's headquarters.[36] For a brief period, even the main telegraph office, the main railroad station, and the Railroad Ministry building, from which the Piłsudskists were organizing the interdiction of the transport of further reinforcements to the Belwederians, passed behind the latter's lines; the main telephone station

---

[34] Kukiel's and Kędzierski's subsequent reports on these actions are in AKL, 2/24 and 14/3a. Folio 14/6, subfolders 1–9, of that archive preserves the voluminous documentary records of the Belwederian units involved from May 12 until their return to barracks on May 18.

[35] S. Haller, p. 35, scoffingly imputes cowardice or at least impropriety to the Piłsudskist officers in relating this circumstance. Sławoj-Składkowski, "Wspomnienia z okresu majowego," p. 147, explains that he and the other defending officers in the War Ministry building had been explicitly recalled to Piłsudski's headquarters by Orlicz-Dreszer and that they were obeying these orders, not running away from a fight. This is confirmed by the bearer of Orlicz-Dreszer's orders, who adds that he had been instructed to threaten Sławoj-Składkowski and the other officers with arrest unless they obeyed—which he knew they would be reluctant to do for fear of being suspected of pusillanimity. See Kmicic-Skrzyński, p. 6.

[36] For details, see Dokumenty chwili, I, 16, and Grzędziński, "Fragmenty pamiętnika," p. 485.

was left in a no-man's-land between the lines. Unaccountably, the generals of the legal government seemed oblivious of the decisive importance of these points and ignored their prizes, thus enabling Bartel (Piłsudski's commissar for railroads) and his staff to continue their unobtrusive but effective work inside the Railroad Ministry building.[37]

If the Belwederians' attack had been reinforced or even sustained at this point, it might have smashed the Piłsudskists. That, at least, was the view of their chief of the General Staff, Stanisław Haller, whose optimism was immensely buoyed by a report that Piłsudski and his immediate entourage had withdrawn across the river to Praga for fear of being overrun or surrounded at the Saxon Square headquarters.[38] At any rate, this was the last moment when the government forces still had a chance of success in Warsaw. By the next day, the strangulation effect of the railroad strike against their reinforcements coming from western Poland, together with the massive augmentation of Piłsudski's strength by units from eastern garrisons, rendered their situation in the capital hopeless and confronted them with the fateful dilemma of capitulation or total civil war between Poland's but recently (1918–20) reunited provinces.

Rozwadowski's analysis was, however, the very reverse of what the situation required, although understandable in the light of the information available to him as of the early evening of May 13. Pessimistic about his immediate tactical situation and optimistic regarding his long-run prospects, he feared that his flanks were too exposed and his forces too meager to permit further advances that night.[39] Simultaneously, he was confident that additional reinforcements—already close—would manage to get through to him. He

[37] Hauke-Nowak, p. 13; Grzędziński, "Fragmenty pamiętnika," pp. 462, 485; W. Grzybowski, "Premier Kazimierz Bartel," p. 104. The main railroad station was then located at the northwest corner of Marszałkowska street and Jerozolimskie avenue, where the Palace of Culture was erected after World War II. The Railroad Ministry stood near the intersection of Nowy Świat and Jerozolimskie avenue, where the Polish United Workers Party (that is, the Communist Party) now has its headquarters.

For the crucial importance of the railroad strike against the Wojciechowski-Witos forces, see below, chapter VII.

[38] S. Haller, p. 38, and Witos, *Moje wspomnienia,* III, 101. Piłsudski did cross to Praga on May 13 to confer with the would-be conservative mediators but there is no evidence that he was fleeing Warsaw.

[39] S. Haller, p. 38; Kędzierski in AKL, 14/3a.

decided, therefore, to postpone the resumption of his offensive until their expected arrival the next day.

Meanwhile, Rozwadowski had been disappointed in his hopes of catching the Piłsudskists in a pincer movement, the second prong of which should have been Colonel Izydor Modelski's 30th Infantry Regiment to the north of their concentration. After having been the first unit to engage the Piłsudskists in combat upon their emergence from the Kierbedź bridge the previous evening, this regiment had withdrawn into its barracks in the Citadel, which was thereupon blockaded by Colonel Kazimierz Sawicki's 36th Infantry Regiment, this unit having earlier gone over to Piłsudski. Inside the Citadel was also quartered the 21st Infantry Regiment of Colonel Romuald Żurakowski, which initially was neutral, although one or two of its platoons had been impressed into the Belwederians' service by General Stanisław Haller.[40] Modelski, who had been brought to Warsaw from a provincial command toward the end of Sikorski's tenure as war minister, had over-all responsibility for the Citadel's precincts.

During the night of May 12, as part of his plan to attack the Piłsudskists the next morning, Rozwadowski had sent orders to Modelski to make a southward sally out of the Citadel in concert with the northward attack of the Belweder forces. Rozwadowski explained, in this instruction, that it was urgent to liquidate the Piłsudskists before their expected reinforcements arrived and that therefore the assault on their headquarters must be prosecuted with great vigor. It was essential to capture or kill Piłsudski and the other rebel leaders.[41] A copy of this order, which was being taken to the Citadel by officers dressed in civilian clothes attempting to slip through Piłsudskists' lines, was intercepted and brought to Orlicz-Dreszer. The Belwederians' readiness to contemplate killing Piłsudski, which contrasted sharply with the latter's considerable concern to avoid fighting in general and to spare Wojciechowski in particular, aroused much bitterness in Piłsudski's headquarters, where there reigned an utter inability to comprehend the fact that, in Rozwadowski's eyes, Pił-

[40] S. Haller, pp. 16–17.
[41] The original of Rozwadowski's order to Modelski is in AKL, 5/9. Its text has been repeatedly published, e.g., in Bełcikowska, *Walki majowe,* p. 26, in Strumph-Wojtkiewicz *et al.,* p. 48, and in Bojan-Błażewicz, pp. 17–18.

sudski was not a national hero intervening to save the state from chaos but a mere rebel.[42]

Regardless of whether or not Modelski received another copy of Rozwadowski's orders (Haller suggests that he did), his subsequent behavior was extraordinarily passive. At about noon on May 13, his fellow regimental commander in the Citadel, Żurakowski, had allowed himself to be persuaded by two of his staff officers to opt for Piłsudski. Modelski, not feeling sure of his own officers, had then proposed to Żurakowski an agreement whereby the two regiments would remain in their respective barracks, leaving the gate to the Citadel (which was Modelski's responsibility) unsecured, and had informed his Belweder superiors accordingly. In midafternoon, Burhardt-Bukacki, Piłsudski's newly designated chief of the General Staff, entered the Citadel and, with some bravura, simply announced that in Piłsudski's name he was relieving Modelski of command. Modelski unresistingly allowed himself and two of his majors to be arrested and his regiment to be taken over by the Piłsudskists.[43] Thus did Rozwadowski lose his northern pincer and the chance of catching Piłsudski in a cross fire, while the latter, by the same token, was enabled to secure his rear as a preliminary to his own offensive of the next day.[44]

Rozwadowski's military loss was paralleled by a political blunder. In the course of the earlier advance by the legal government's forces, Piłsudski's artillery had shelled the Belweder palace courtyard and Zagórski's planes had thrown some bombs on Piłsudski-occupied points in Warsaw. Each side claimed that its own action was only a

[42] For an example of this Piłsudskist sense of shocked incomprehension, see Malicki, pp. 284–85. The account of the interception of Rozwadowski's order is in AKL, 2/3b. The interceptor was the then Lieutenant W. Karbowski.

[43] This account of developments in the Citadel is based on AKL, 2/36 and 5/19; S. Haller, pp. 35–38; and Karbowski, pp. 347–55. Żurakowski was a veteran of the tsarist Russian army. Modelski was initially an Austro-Polish Legionnaire (like his patron Sikorski) and then a (Józef) Hallerite.

[44] *Dokumenty chwili*, I, 16, and Srokowski, p. 94. There is a certain parallelism between Modelski's passivity in the Citadel and the enigmatic position adopted by his patron Sikorski in the Lwów Military District to the southeast. (See below, pp. 105–8.) Piłsudski, through the beneficiary of Modelski's inertness, was appalled by it. (See Pobóg-Malinowski, *Najnowsza historia*, II, 477.) Accordingly, Modelski was retired from the army in 1927. Further information on him will be found in the Biographical Register.

retaliation for the other side's initial escalation of weaponry.[45] Neither action inflicted much physical damage, but in terms of public relations the Belwederians were the losers, for the stigma of a readiness to bomb the civilian population of their own capital now attached to them. The Piłsudskists elaborated on this theme to attribute a particular bloodthirstiness to Zagórski, who was alleged to have personally led the raids, and to charge that but for the noble disobedience of his young pilots, who were said to have deliberately dropped most of their bombs in open fields, he would have decimated the capital.[46] Actually, Zagórski was obeying Rozwadowski's orders, and his purpose had presumably been not to terrorize the population—although in fact bombs did kill some civilians and panic others—but rather the triple one of interdicting the arrival of Piłsudski's reinforcements, interrupting the concentration of his forces for their attack, and destroying from the air Piłsudski's headquarters on Saxon Square.[47] These goals were not achieved and the political loss incurred in their attempt was considerable.

It was thus clear, by close of day on May 13, that each side had lost its opportunity to score an immediate victory.[48] The unnerved Piłsudski had failed to exploit his advantages of manpower superiority and of surprise the previous evening and, instead of seizing the Belweder palace, had desperately cast about for mediators. Rozwadowski, rather than risk a final assault on Saxon Square with his available forces during the evening of May 13, had chosen instead to con-

[45] See S. Haller, pp. 32–33, and *Frankfurter Zeitung,* May 14, 1926. The Piłsudskists, who had neglected to bring along any artillery for their original "armed demonstration," had captured six pieces in Warsaw at the beginning of the fighting. Piłsudski, *PZ,* IX, 12.

[46] Bełcikowska, *Walki majowe,* p. 21. On the question of Zagórski's alleged personal role in the bombings, see the controversy between Schaetzel, "Przełom majowy" (who endorses this allegation), and Kukiel, "Jeszcze o majowej wojnie domowej i generale Zagórskim" (who disputes it). The testimony in AKL, 18/85, also deals with this matter.

[47] Jordan-Rozwadowski, p. 117, and Romeyko, "Przed i po maju 1926 r.," VII, No. 3, 287. There was a report that two of Zagórski's planes were shot down by Piłsudskist fire; see the *Ilustrowany Kurjer Codzienny,* May 18, 1926, and *Dokumenty chwili,* I, 15. Grzędziński, *Maj 1926,* p. 92, says four of Zagórski's pilots died in these actions.

[48] Lively journalistic descriptions of that day's fighting are the contemporary observations by Wilhelm Stein in the *Vossische Zeitung,* May 20, 1926, and by Kisch, "Warszawa w dzień po przewrocie."

solidate his gains of the day and await reinforcements. Perhaps the loss of the Citadel tipped his balance toward that option. In any event, it was clear that the conflict was henceforth to be a race for reinforcements, and this meant that the disposition of various provincial garrison commanders had become crucial. Reinforcements, however, must be more readily available than merely being potentially on call in the provinces. As long as both rival headquarters elected to remain in Warsaw, the effectiveness of reinforcements depended on their transport to the capital, and this fact superimposed a political dimension on the conflict's military one; for transportation required the cooperation of the railroad workers, whose main trade union, in turn, was closely affiliated with the PPS.

CHAPTER VI

THE BATTLE: THE RACE FOR
REINFORCEMENTS

Since Piłsudski had foreseen no fighting but instead had expected an immediate political victory as a result of his "armed demonstration," he had paid little attention to the matter of mobilizing reinforcements. Even after the disastrous meeting with President Wojciechowski on the Poniatowski bridge, it was not Piłsudski or Orlicz-Dreszer but rather the alert Colonel Stanisław Skwarczyński (who had been transferred in April, 1926, from his post in Wilno to Orlicz-Dreszer's conspiratorial staff in Warsaw) who took the initiative to summon three regiments from Kutno, Łomża, and Pułtusk—all within a radius of seventy-five miles of Warsaw.[1] It was not, however, until the Belwederians' energetic counterattack of May 13, that the Piłsudskists became seriously concerned with the problem of reinforcements. Malczewski, by contrast, had been summoning provincial contingents to the government's defense since May 12.

As the contradictory orders and summonses flowed into provincial garrison headquarters, a kind of emergency plebiscite occurred among the commanders of corps, divisions, and regiments. With but few exceptions, junior officers and other ranks accepted the decisions of their commanders as to which orders to obey and which to ignore. Three choices were open: to support Piłsudski, to obey the government, or to find plausible grounds for remaining neutral or inactive. Except for the veterans of the old Austro-Polish Second Brigade, the ex-Legionnaires—who in sociological terms were essentially uni-

[1] S. Skwarczyński, "Relacja." Further information on Skwarczyński will be found in the Biographical Register. To facilitate the perusal of this chapter, the reader is referred to map No. 2.

N

Baltic Sea

LATVIA

LITHUANIA

DANZIG
(GDAŃSK)

Gdynia

EAST
PRUSSIA

• Wilno

• Grodno

WHITE
RUSSIAN
SSR

Niemen R.

GERMANY

Grudziądz

• Brodnica

Bydgoszcz

• Toruń

Inowrocław

Włocławek

Poznań

Września

Kutno

Leszno

Kalisz

• Łowicz

Krotoszyn

Łódź

• Spała

Piotrków

Częstochowa

Tarnowskie Góry

Katowice

Cieszyn

Kraków

Nowy
Targ

Zakopane

Łomża

Ostrołęka

• Białystok

Nieśwież

Pułtusk

• Ostrów Mazowiecka

WARSAW

• Siedlce

• Brześć

Mińsk Mazowiecki

Dęblin

Lublin

Chełm

Bug R.

Pripet R.

S. S. R.

U.

Vistula R.

Vistula R.

San R.

• Tarnów

Nowy Sącz

Lwów

• Przemyśl

• Brzeżany

Stryj

• Stanisławów

UKRAINIAN
SSR

CZECHOSLOVAKIA

RUMANIA

HUNGARY

0   100   200 Miles

MAP NO. 2
POLAND
MAY 1926

*Some of the Polish Garrisons Involved
in the Race for Reinforcements*

formed members of the Polish intelligentsia, sharing its characteristic messianic outlook—overwhelmingly supported Piłsudski. The professional officers from the traditionally rather reactionary and clubby former imperial Austrian army declared for the government. While a number of the older ex-tsarist officers were Piłsudskists, no clear pattern of response is discernible among this most professionalized contingent of the Polish officer corps. Many of the commanders who sought to avoid committing themselves—and some of them existed within all the preindependence career groupings—appear to have taken their cue from former War Minister Sikorski, currently commanding the Lwów Military District in southeastern Poland.[2] The geographical pattern which emerged, supplementing the one based on career biographies, is that Piłsudski drew most of his reinforcements from eastern garrisons and the Belwederians theirs from the western regions, formerly parts of Prussia, where the National Democratic camp was politically dominant.

One of the few exceptions to this geographical generalization was the garrison of Kutno, sixty-five miles due west of Warsaw—but still within the formerly Russian, not Prussian, part of Poland. There the 37th Infantry Regiment under the Legion veteran Lieutenant Colonel Władysław Bortnowski had already been alerted on May 12 by Skwarczyński to aid the Piłsudskists. Bortnowski deployed one of his battalions in Kutno with orders to impede and delay the Poznanian and Pomeranian reinforcements for the legal government, and with two others forced his way to Warsaw on May 13, despite repeated bombing attacks on his troop train by Zagórski's airplanes. The next day Bortnowski's units were to have their revenge on Zagórski as they participated in the Piłsudskists' capture of the Mokotów airdrome.[3]

Other Piłsudskist barricades were set up around Łódź, southwest of the capital, by General Stanisław Małachowski, whom Piłsudski had named commissar there.[4] These, however, proved to be less crucial than had been anticipated. For reasons to be discussed presently, the would-be reinforcements coming to the relief of the Bel-

[2] Sikorski, pp. 14–15, and Berbecki, pp. 191–93.

[3] AKL, 4/44; S. Haller, pp. 40, 44; and Rzepecki, *Wspomnienia,* p. 52. Further information on Bortnowski will be found in the Biographical Register.

[4] AKL, 10/10. The next month, Piłsudski promoted Małachowski to the command of the Łódź Military District.

wederians from southwestern Poland were halted short of Łódź on their way to the capital and the ones from the west and northwest chose instead to force their way through the Kutno obstructions. Małachowski also sent parts of one regiment (the 31st of infantry) to Warsaw to aid Piłsudski.

As has been noted, the bulk of Piłsudski's reinforcements arrived from the east, particularly his native northeast. From Pułtusk came the 13th Infantry Regiment and from Ostrołęka the 5th Cavalry Regiment, which, like Stamirowski's 7th Uhlans, was part of Orlicz-Dreszer's old Second Cavalry Division.[5] In answer to the Belwederians' successes of May 13, the greater parts of two infantry regiments (the 1st and 6th) and one of field artillery (the 1st) were promptly dispatched to Piłsudski by train from Wilno by the former high Legion officer (1914–17) and underground POW commander (1917–18) General Edward Rydz-Śmigły, at the time an army inspector with headquarters in Wilno. Despite being attacked by Zagórski's planes, these units arrived in Warsaw during the early hours of May 14.[6] Rydz-Śmigły would have sent even more but for the potential dangers of leaving the Polish-Lithuanian and Polish-Soviet frontiers exposed.[7] Knowing of Rydz-Śmigły's dedication to Piłsudski, the Belwederian generals had already sent orders on May 12 to General Józef Rybak, commander of the Brześć Military District, to intercept any Piłsudskist reinforcements attempting to pass through his area of responsibility. On May 13 Rybak was further instructed to attack from the rear any which might penetrate through to Warsaw. He did neither, subsequently asserting that these orders had never reached him.[8] In any event, Rybak would have been at a disadvantage had he attempted to execute such instructions, for the Piłsudskist network was extensive within his command. It included, among others, Colonel Henryk Krok-Paszkowski, whose 22d Infantry Regiment based at Siedlce had already joined Piłsudski on his march from Sulejówek to Warsaw, Major Henryk Floyar-Rajchman, who had summoned Krok-Paszkowski to this demonstration, and General Mieczysław Trojanowski, who

[5] Piłsudski, *PZ*, IX, 16.
[6] AKL, 10/4–6.
[7] Czubiński, "Przewrót majowy," p. 129. On Rydz-Śmigły's later career, see the Biographical Register.
[8] S. Haller, p. 29, and Rzepecki, *Wspomnienia*, p. 51.

had initiated him into the conspiracy. As far as is known, Rybak made no attempt to recall Krok-Paszkowski's regiment to its base.[9] Rybak himself had been closely acquainted with Piłsudski since serving as the Austrian General Staff's liaison to Piłsudski's paramilitary movement before World War I.

Also passive in regard to Rydz-Śmigły's energetic activity on behalf of Piłsudski was General Leon Berbecki, a veteran of both the tsarist Russian officer corps (till 1906) and the Legions, and in May, 1926, commander of the Grodno Military District within which Wilno was located. In his memoirs Berbecki asserts that he was obliged to adopt a neutral position toward the conflict in Warsaw by the need to devote all his attention to the vulnerable Polish–East Prussian frontier.[10] He professed to have feared a German attempt to take advantage of Poland's domestic difficulties by launching a sudden invasion, and therefore to have coordinated a neutral policy toward the fighting in the capital with Sikorski, who commanded along the equally sensitive Polish–Soviet Ukrainian border (Lwów Military District). Sikorski's own reflections here flatly contradict Berbecki's statement, asserting, instead, that Berbecki was clearly and unconditionally on Piłsudski's side.[11] It must be conceded that both Berbecki's conduct in 1926 and his justification of it three decades later were rather lame. A plausible conjecture is that, given the hostile official attitude toward the Piłsudski regime which prevailed in Poland when Berbecki published his memoirs (1959), he was then too embarrassed to admit that he had helped it to power in 1926. This suspicion is strengthened by the ostentatiously indignant tone with which Berbecki insists on his subsequent disillusionment over Piłsudski's failure to institute radical social

[9] AKL, 4/55 and 4/66–67. Rybak's own exceedingly uninformative official report is in folio 15/10. After the coup, Rybak was promoted to army inspector by Piłsudski. In August, 1926, Trojanowski succeeded Rybak in the command of the Brześć Military District. Trojanowski died as a prisoner of the Germans in the Mauthausen Concentration Camp in April, 1945.

[10] Berbecki, pp. 191–93. Although a Legionnaire in World War I, Berbecki, together with Kukiel and Żymierski, had been among the few exceptions to the general refusal of the Piłsudskist First and Third Legion Brigades to take an oath of loyalty to the German and Austro-Hungarian armies in July, 1917. Pobóg-Malinowski, Najnowsza historia (1st ed.), I, 332.

[11] Sikorski, p. 14.

reforms, sweeping land distribution to poor peasants, and other such measures.[12]

Sikorski, an officer of extensive professional self-confidence and of considerable political ambition, played an enigmatic role during the coup. He and Piłsudski had been politically cool to each other ever since their differences over Austro-Polonism during World War I and professionally stiff in their relations since the Polish-Soviet campaign of 1920, in which each regarded himself as having turned the key to the final Polish victory.[13] Their subsequent angry controversy over the organization of the army high command at the time of Sikorski's tenure as war minister (1924–25) had left both men deeply embittered. Yet, though he was by 1926 an obvious enemy of Piłsudski, Sikorski also had no love for Witos' Right-Center political coalition which three years earlier, in May, 1923, had overthrown his own cabinet and ousted him from the premiership (1922–23). As he now contemplated Witos' discomfiture and received his urgent appeals for help,[14] Sikorski found it difficult to resist the temptation to indulge in a certain amount of *Schadenfreude,* especially since he had warned against the formation of another Right-Center cabinet pending the settlement of the army command controversy.[15]

Already on May 12, Sikorski had been summoned from Lwów to Warsaw by Witos and Malczewski and instructed to bring loyal reinforcements with him. This order was repeated the next day at the insistence of Witos, whose memoirs assert his intention to give Sikorski supreme command of the government's troops.[16] Apparently, Witos was belatedly seeking to effect a closing of ranks of all Piłsudski's enemies. Rozwadowski, however, had in the meantime (between the government's two summonses) independently radioed Sikorski that

[12] Berbecki, p. 193. Shortly after the coup, Berbecki was transferred to command the Toruń Military District. In time, he was promoted to army inspector. He spent World War II in German captivity.

[13] See Piłsudski, *Rok 1920* (Warsaw, 1924), and Sikorski, *Nad Wisłą i Wkrą* (Lwów, 1928).

[14] Witos, *Moje wspomnienia,* III, 94.

[15] See above, p. 23, n. 53. Unless otherwise indicated, the information presented here and on the following pages comes from Sikorski's diary, "Kartki z dziennika."

[16] AKL, 14/2; S. Haller, p. 27; and Witos, *Moje wspomnienia,* III, 98. This is confirmed in the memoirs of Witos' secretary Dzendzel, No. 416, p. 6.

his presence in Warsaw was not essential. Whether Rozwadowski's motive was jealousy of the man by whom he was himself scheduled to be replaced, or confidence that Piłsudski could be defeated with the forces already at hand in Warsaw and arriving from the west, or nervousness about a possible Soviet incursion into southeastern Poland, or a combination of these considerations, remains a mystery.[17] At any rate, Sikorski, during the evening of May 13, sent a message by air-courier asking to be excused from either coming himself or sending reinforcements from Lwów. In explanation, he cited (*a*) alleged Soviet troop movements along the border; (*b*) alleged insurrectionary ferment among the Ukrainian population of southeastern Poland; (*c*) the reluctance of the Socialist railroad personnel to transport reinforcements for the government's cause; (*d*) the reluctance of many of his subordinate officers to fight for the incumbent government; (*e*) the presence of a superfluity of generals in the Belweder.[18]

Of these five excuses, the first two were indeed dangerous possibilities without, however, being factual occurrences at the time;[19] the third was not to be a crippling obstacle until the next day; the fourth appears, indeed, to have been valid as regards the officers of three of Sikorski's regiments (the 19th, 26th, and 40th of infantry); while the fifth is suggestive of rivalry on his part with the Belwederian generals and hints at a fear that he might not be given a sufficiently elevated command if he were to come to Warsaw.

Deeply disturbed by Sikorski's communication, the Belwederians now sent him a third message, agreeing to dispense with his personal appearance but unconditionally ordering him to dispatch one infantry regiment and three artillery batteries to Warsaw. Sikorski radioed his

[17] AKL, 12/28. There are hints of professional rivalry between the two generals in Sikorski's diary and in Witos, *Moje wspomnienia*, III, 98. This latter source (III, 105–8) also contains repeated references to Rozwadowski's general optimism, of which mention was made above. Finally, Polish nervousness concerning Soviet intentions was, ironically, reciprocated by Soviet suspicions that the coup was but a screen for Polish aggressive designs upon the Soviet Union. See Poznański, p. 3, and *Ilustrowany Kurjer Codzienny*, May 15 and 18, 1926.

[18] S. Haller, pp. 44–45; AKL, 5/15 and 4/11.

[19] Sikorski's diary also refers to the menace of Ukrainian subversion, but the only specific examples of political activity in his area which it cites were all simply local expressions of the anti-Witos stance taken by the Polish parties forming the Left bloc. It records no case of Ukrainian obstreperousness, let alone of insurgency, to buttress his excuses.

compliance early on May 14 but simultaneously warned that the infantry regiment which he was sending in execution of the order was "spiritually devoted" to Piłsudski.[20] If so, one wonders why Sikorski elected to send this unit, instead of a more reliable one. Also intriguing is the fact that he combed these contingents out of the most remote southeastern pocket of his command, the garrisons of Stanisławów and Brzeżany, whence transportation to Warsaw was most awkward and long.

In any event, the time for reinforcements was overdue. Since many of the military garrisons and railroad stations along the shortest route between the Lwów Military District and Warsaw were under Piłsudski's control by May 14, Sikorski's reinforcements to the government had to be dispatched in a roundabout direction—first due westward, then northward. By the time the advance units reached Kraków in the southwest, the fighting had ended and they proceeded no farther.[21] Others never got beyond Przemyśl, where a part of the infantry placed itself at the disposal of that military district's chief of staff, Lieutenant Colonel Mieczysław Wyżeł-Ścieżyński, an ex-Legionnaire and an active Piłsudskist who had already detached approximately one battalion of his own troops to Piłsudski's aid.[22]

Sikorski's equivocal conduct during the coup; the resentful or contemptuous references to Piłsudski, Wojciechowski, Witos, Malczewski, the Belweder generals, and the Right-Center coalition with which his diary abounds; the boasts which it contains that other officers throughout Poland placed themselves at his disposal and looked to him for guidance during the crisis; his dispatch (by plane) of a liaison officer to Berbecki in Grodno to consult on coordinating their responses; and his teletyped conversation with the Poznanian command in the same vein[23]—all suggest that what Sikorski really hoped for was that the two camps in Warsaw would battle each other to a stalemate, leaving

[20] Bełcikowska, *Walki majowe,* p. 31.
[21] Tadeusz Skwarczyński, p. 1. (This Skwarczyński was an officer in the detachment which reached Kraków. He is not to be confused with Stanisław Skwarczyński, who was one of the Piłsudskist activists and whose unpublished memoir in the Piłsudski Historical Institute in London has been frequently cited.)
[22] Popławski, p. 3; Rzepecki, *Wspomnienia,* p. 53; S. Haller, p. 45.
[23] Berbecki, pp. 191–93; AKL, 13/407.

him to impose a settlement and therewith to acquire decisive political power.[24]

The roll call of senior officers who chose neutrality or ambiguity during the coup is not exhausted with Rybak, Berbecki, and Sikorski, though the last-named may well have been the only one to entertain political as well as professional ambitions. The commander of the Lublin Military District lying between Sikorski's district and Warsaw, General Jan Romer, formally remained loyal to the government despite having been named commissar by Piłsudski.[25] Yet, when his instructions to his subordinates not to obey a Piłsudskist summons to Warsaw on May 13 were disobeyed, Romer took no corrective or preventive action. Indeed, his memoirs concede that he was rather glad that he lacked the means to enforce his restraining order. Though having emerged from the old Austrian army, Romer had been personally devoted to Piłsudski ever since the Polish-Soviet campaign of 1920, in which Piłsudski had defended him against accusations of having prematurely and unnecessarily abandoned the town of Osowiec to the Bolsheviks during their July advance.[26]

While, in general, Romer's intervention had the result merely of delaying by a few hours the departure for Warsaw of Piłsudskist reinforcements from his district, in one case it led to tragedy. The Legion veteran Colonel Mieczysław Prus-Więckowski, commander of the 7th Infantry Regiment stationed at Chełm, could find no other way than suicide out of the dilemma of being caught between Piłsudski's appeal and Romer's prohibition. Nevertheless, his regiment,

[24] After the coup, Sikorski retained command of the Lwów Military District until March 19, 1928. Piłsudski's confidant, Colonel Adam Koc, was meanwhile assigned to him as chief of staff, with the supplementary function—many suspected—of observing Sikorski's possible political activities. (See Grobicki, p. 101.) From 1928 until 1939, Sikorski had no military functions and was at the disposition (unused) of the war minister. During these years he became a focus of opposition to both the domestic and the foreign policies of the Piłsudski regime, deploring in particular its apparent readiness to minimize the alliance with France which he regarded as the keystone to Poland's security. He visited France virtually every year and gradually built up a "brain trust" of like-minded persons which included, among others, General Kukiel and Colonel Modelski. (See Ligocki, p. 15, and Bednarczyk, p. 7.) Further information on Sikorski will be found in the Biographical Register.

[25] AKL, 4/28–29, 4/54.

[26] J. Romer, pp. 319, 344–45. In contrast to his warm feelings for Piłsudski, Romer hated Rozwadowski. (*Ibid.*, pp. 266–67, 270.) Shortly after the coup, Piłsudski promoted Romer to be an army inspector.

as well as the 8th and 9th of infantry (the last commanded by another ex-Legionnaire, Colonel Zdzisław Maćkowski), arrived in Warsaw in time to aid Piłsudski in the final battles of May 14.[27] These three regiments composed the Third Infantry Division commanded by General Kazimierz Fabrycy, a staff officer in the First Legion Brigade during World War I, a devoted Piłsudskist, and now the effective leader of activity on Piłsudski's behalf in the Lublin Military District.[28]

Another case of straddling similar to Romer's, with a *de facto* bias toward Piłsudski, occurred in the southwestern part of the country and affected units stationed in the Kraków and Łódź Military Districts. Here the critical rail junction for communication with the rest of Poland was the city of Częstochowa, where General Stanisław Wróblewski of the old Austrian army had his headquarters as a division commander. At the outbreak of the coup, Wróblewski, on Malczewski's orders, had sent some troops toward Warsaw to aid the Belwederians. Subsequently, however, as other reinforcements for the government, coming from Silesian and Cracovian garrisons farther to the south, sought to pass through Częstochowa on their way to Warsaw, Wróblewski delayed them on various technical pretexts. By the time General Stanisław Szeptycki, currently an army inspector with headquarters in Kraków, had intervened to clear Wróblewski's bottleneck, it was May 14—too late for the detained reinforcements to affect the outcome of the battle in Warsaw.[29] Stanisław Wróblewski's

[27] AKL, 3/24, 4/24, 4/32, and 10/2–3. The 8th was garrisoned in Lublin, the 9th in Zamość.

[28] Fabrycy's account of his activities during the coup is in AKL, 10/2. Further information on him will be found in the Biographical Register.

[29] AKL, 2/18, 3/56, 4/63–64, 5/74, and 10/8; S. Haller, p. 43; and Rzepecki, *Wspomnienia*, p. 52. The units involved were the 2d and 4th Podhalian (Tatra mountaineer) Regiments from Nowy Sącz and Cieszyn (Teschen), the 6th Artillery Regiment from Kraków, and the 3d Uhlan Regiment from Tarnowskie Góry. They were under the over-all command of General Andrzej Galica, one of the more interesting figures in the Polish army. A Legion veteran, engineer, dramatist, and poet, an enthusiast for Tatra mountaineer mores and style of life, Galica formally obeyed the orders of the Belwederians but appeared to have been quite content to be halted at Częstochowa (AKL, 10/8, 13/464, 13/470). In September, 1926, Piłsudski transferred Galica from his line command along the southwestern frontiers to the administrative post of commander of the Przemyśl Military District. As this was formally a promotion, it could be interpreted as a gesture of reconciliation by a Piłsudski eager to demonstrate his desire to bind up the wounds of the coup. On the other hand, the Przemyśl assignment was less alluring to Galica than his previous operational command

apparent shift of position may have been the consequence of a telephone call from his brother, General Jan Wróblewski, the deputy
commander of the Warsaw Military District and one of the few former
Austrian officers to side unequivocally with Piłsudski. When asked to
account for his actions by Szeptycki, however, Stanisław Wróblewski
denied that political or ulterior motives were responsible for the delays imposed upon the government's reinforcements at Częstochowa
and insisted that the incident was the result of a genuine technical
misunderstanding. After the coup, he was to claim the reverse—that
he had acted in deliberate support of Piłsudski.[30] In any event, within
a month both Wróblewski brothers were promoted by Piłsudski to the
command of military districts—Stanisław in Kraków, Jan in Warsaw.
Prime Minister Witos, in his turn, reproached Szeptycki for insuffi-
cient zeal and speed in clearing the Częstochowa bottleneck.[31] Whatever resentments Witos may have harbored toward Szeptycki since the
latter's service as war minister in the Witos cabinet of 1923, there is
no doubt that Szeptycki, like most of his ex-Austrian army colleagues,
was an irreconcilable enemy of Piłsudski, completely committed to
preventing the Marshal's return to power, and that the other Belweder
generals trusted him, for they gave him charge of all attempts to
arrange transports to Warsaw from southern and western Poland.[32]

As has been mentioned, the bulk of the Belwederians' aid came
from western Poland. There, in the former Prussian parts of the state,
National Democratic sentiment had long been prevalent and Piłsudski
was always unpopular. Two military districts, those of Poznań and
Toruń, were located in the area.

The commander of the Poznań Military District, since his retirement as war minister in February, 1924, had been General Kazimierz
Sosnkowski. Piłsudski's devoted friend even before World War I, his
chief of staff with the Legions during that war, his companion in Ger-

---

and hence could also be viewed as a punishment for not having explicitly
declared for Piłsudski in the May crisis. In any event, there was no permanent
political breach between Piłsudski and Galica. Further information on Galica
will be found in the Biographical Register.

[30] Rzepecki, *Wspomnienia*, p. 48; S. Haller, p. 44; AKL, 10/8 and 4/34.
[31] Witos, *Moje wspomnienia*, III, 101.
[32] S. Haller, p. 42.

man internment at Magdeburg in its later stages, Sosnkowski was still one of Piłsudski's closest collaborator's at the time of the latter's withdrawal from all state posts in the summer of 1923. After Piłsudski's "retirement" to Sulejówek, however, and especially with Sosnkowski's assumption of the Poznań command, the two men drifted apart. Sosnkowski's departure from the War Ministry in February, 1924, it will be recalled, had been preceded and partly caused by Piłsudski's rejection of his army organization plan. During the next two years in Poznań, Sosnkowski was apparently "socialized" to some extent into the National Democratic atmosphere prevailing there. Piłsudski, in turn, after failing in November, 1925, to persuade Sosnkowski to become chief of the General Staff simultaneously with Żeligowski's assumption of the War Ministry, thereafter excluded Sosnkowski from his planning in 1926 for the "armed demonstration" to assert and seize political power.

On May 11, 1926, Sosnkowski had come from Poznań to Warsaw, either as a result of Acting Foreign Minister Morawski's emergency appeal, or because he was in any event scheduled to confer with Morawski preparatory to proceeding to Geneva to serve as Poland's chief delegate to the disarmament conference scheduled to open May 18.[33] On arrival in Warsaw, he quickly learned of the imminent crisis. It is established that Sosnkowski did not meet Piłsudski, but what did take place is not clear. According to later pro-Piłsudski historiography, Piłsudski, fearing that Witos intended to annex the prestige of Sosnkowski's name to the dubious Right-Center political combination, sent a double message to Sosnkowski, urging him not to accept any appointment by Witos and to return immediately to his command in Poznań. Only the second, laconic part of this communication was allegedly delivered to Sosnkowski and was heeded by him. So dismayed is he purported to have been, however, over Piłsudski's seeming reluctance to trust him sufficiently to make him a party to the conspiracy that, upon arriving back in Poznań, he attempted suicide.[34] This version—needless to emphasize—minimizes the previous political estrangement between the two men and attributes Sosnkowski's

[33] See above, p. 57, and AKL, 16/22.
[34] Pobóg-Malinowski, *Najnowsza historia*, II, 483–84.

action exclusively to an erroneous impression, deduced from an accidental failure of communication, that Piłsudski had repudiated him as a dependable comrade.

That Sosnkowski was wounded by a pistol shot in his office in Poznań after his return from Warsaw is beyond dispute. Although there were reports at the time that the shooting was the deed of a young officer of Rightist sympathies, eager to eliminate the man whom he erroneously assumed still to be Piłsudski's closest confidant,[35] it appears more probable—both by virtue of the norms characterizing relations between junior and senior army officers and by virtue of Sosnkowski's personality—that the wound was indeed self-inflicted. Nevertheless, many circumstances of the episode remain matters of controversy. Did Sosnkowski seriously attempt suicide or merely intend to inflict a wound sufficient to render himself *hors de combat* and thus be absolved from having to commit himself in the civil strife? [36] This problem is further compounded by a certain degree of ambiguity as to the seriousness and even the precise location of the wound.[37] Sosnkowski had the reputation of being a Hamlet-like figure—brave, intelligent, but indecisive. However, this personality trait does not

[35] *Polska Zbrojna,* May 19, 1926; *Deutsche Zeitung,* May 20, 1926; J. Haller, p. 264.

[36] This is believed by several knowledgeable survivors of the inner Piłsudskist circle whom I have interviewed and who prefer to remain anonymous. This motive is also suggested in Wierzbiński, pp. 132–33, and Rzepecki, "Jeszcze o maju 1926," p. 348. Sosnkowski, under oath, laconically avowed on May 23 at the official army investigation that he had shot himself but did not discuss his motives or intention. AKL, 16/24.

[37] That the wound was serious—the bullet entering the body on the right side of the chest and emerging under the left shoulder blade—is stated in the official testimony of the attending surgeon, Professor Dr. Antoni Jurasz, given on May 25, 1926, and recorded in AKL, 16/24. Pobóg-Malinowski (*Najnowsza historia,* II, 483–84) also insists that the shot came within a hairbreadth of proving fatal, and J. Haller (p. 264), who was in Poznań at the time, speaks of a heavy chest wound. As early as May 15, however, that is, two days after the event, the *Kurjer Warszawski* reported that there was no reason to fear for Sosnkowski's life. Arski, p. 414, locates the wound in the upper arm, while one of my interviewees puts it in the abdomen. The latter suggested as a hypothesis that Sosnkowski may have aimed for the heart but that someone else intervened just in time to deflect the bullet. This version gives a new twist to the reports of a young officer being involved, but it and Arski's account vary excessively from the surgeon's testimony as to the location of the wound.

European military men, when seriously attempting suicide, conventionally shoot themselves in the head. All sources agree that the shot was not aimed at that part of Sosnkowski's anatomy.

solve the problem, since suicide and artifice might each tempt such a person in a dilemma. In any event, if the suicide attempt was indeed genuine, its motivation is more likely to have been a paralysis of decision-making than grief over a presumed withdrawal of confidence by Piłsudski, from whom Sosnkowski had already become somewhat alienated.

Obscure as is the problem of motive, the sequence of events in Poznań is fairly clear. Whether as a result of Piłsudski's injunction, or on instructions from the government, or because he independently felt his proper place in the impeding crisis to be at his command post,[38] Sosnkowski returned from Warsaw to Poznań, where he found his deputy, General Edmund Hauser of the old Austrian army, processing Malczewski's summons for help. Hauser requested Sosnkowski's signature on the prepared marching orders dispatching the reinforcements to the government in Warsaw. There are two versions as to Sosnkowski's response. According to Hauser, he is supposed to have remarked cryptically that in such times everyone must let his actions be dictated by his conscience—and thereupon to have entered his private office, from which a shot was heard shortly. The second, Piłsudskist, account has Sosnkowski categorically refuse to sign the orders, whereupon Hauser demands the surrender of his sword preparatory to placing him under arrest, at which point Sosnkowski withdraws into the inner office. Then follows the shot.[39]

These dramatic developments did not prevent or even materially delay the sending of Poznanian reinforcements to the beleaguered Belwederians in Warsaw. The 57th and 58th Infantry Regiments had already slipped through Łódź during the night of May 12, before the Piłsudskist efforts to barricade the railroads became effective. More reinforcements were dispatched the next day. Hauser skillfully deployed his Kalisz garrison so as to check the insurgent Małachowski in Łódź and sent the bulk of his subsequent relief forces to smash

[38] See Romeyko, "Przed i po maju 1926 r.," VII, No. 4, 279–83, and Morawski, *Tamten brzeg*, p. 146.

[39] AKL, 14/4 versus *Kurjer Poranny*, May 20, 1926. Whatever may have been the degree of estrangement between Piłsudski and Sosnkowski before these events, the political breach hardened after them. Piłsudski continued to give Sosnkowski high military assignments—promoting him to army inspector—but rigorously excluded him from political influences and responsibilities. Further information on Sosnkowski will be found in the Biographical Register.

through the other Piłsudskist barrier at Kutno, where he occupied the railroad station with sappers and paramilitary volunteers from Poznań. Repairing the railroad tracks which the Piłsudskists had sabotaged to delay them, the Poznanian troops laboriously pushed on toward Warsaw.[40] By the morning of May 14 they had made it as far as Łowicz, approximately forty-five miles west-southwest of Warsaw, where they were met by General Żymierski of the Belwederians, who had come out by car to take command of them. Owing to the paralyzing strike of the railroad workers and the tightening Piłsudskist noose around Warsaw, Żymierski decided to detrain these reinforcements at the suburb of Ożarów, still nine miles short of Warsaw, and to march from there. In the course of the afternoon, however, he became enmeshed in a series of peripheral skirmishes at the approaches to the capital and failed to break through to the government's defenders. Meanwhile, at Ożarów, more reinforcements were piling up from both Poznanian and Pomeranian garrisons.

Pomerania, like Poznania, was also politically anti-Piłsudski. Here again, the National Democratic camp and its allied workers' offshoot, the NPR, virtually monopolized local electoral and administrative power. The Piłsudskists hoped to swing the Toruń Military District, which largely overlapped with this province, into their camp. General Leonard Skierski, a veteran of the tsarist Russian army, a backer of Piłsudski, and an army inspector, attempted the same maneuver that Rydz-Śmigły so successfully employed in the northeast, that is, to usurp *de facto* control of the area's garrisons. In Toruń, however, the military district commander, the ex-Austrian General Władysław Hubischta, turned the tables, arresting Skierski and dispatching massive reinforcements to the aid of the government in Warsaw.[41] These units, like the later Poznanian ones, also detrained and became immobilized at Ożarów during the evening and night of May 14. By the next morning eight Poznanian and Pomeranian regiments, totaling approximately 6,000 effectives, had piled up there—quite apart from

[40] AKL, 14/3e, 14/4, and S. Haller, p. 43. Hauser also sent some airplanes to the aid of the Belwederians.

[41] Hubischta's official report is in AKL, 15/1. Skierski was released on May 17, after the coup. In World War II he was imprisoned by the Soviets and perished in the Katyn forest massacre. Hubischta was retired from the army in April, 1927, and died in January, 1933.

the three with which Żymierski was maneuvering at the outskirts of the capital. For various reasons to be analyzed presently, they never participated in the Warsaw battle.

Also detoured and blocked from joining in the combat was the 71st Infantry Regiment, upon which the Belwederians had counted even though it was garrisoned at Ostrów Mazowiecka, fifty-five miles northeast of Warsaw, in an area rather solidly controlled by the Piłsudskists. Its commander, Colonel Mieczysław Boruta-Spiechowicz, an officer in the Second (that is, anti-Piłsudski) Legion Brigade during World War I, had telegraphed the War Ministry for instructions on the morning of May 12, at a time when Malczewski was still resident there, and had been told to prepare his regiment for action. During the night of May 12 he had telephoned the Ministry—unaware that it had meanwhile been seized (temporarily) by the Piłsudskists—to announce that his unit was mobilized and awaiting orders. Norwid-Neugebauer, the Piłsudskist deputy chief of Army Administration, without informing Boruta-Spiechowicz of the true situation at the Ministry, deceptively assured him that there were more than enough troops on hand in Warsaw and instructed him to return his men to their barracks. This ruse successfully delayed the regiment's departure for Warsaw until May 13, when Rozwadowski managed to send it his own instructions. These were to enter Warsaw from the north, link up with Modelski's garrison in the Citadel, and strike the Piłsudskists from the rear.[42]

Not only Modelski's surrender of the Citadel prevented the execution of these orders. Once again, as was the case with the later Poznanian and Pomeranian regiments, the strangulation of transportation by the railroad workers proved too much of a hindrance for the government forces to overcome. Boruta-Spiechowicz's troop train was shunted onto a dead-end track at Ząbki, still four and a half miles short of Praga on the eastern, that is, wrong, side of the Vistula river. Attempting to march on foot to Warsaw, his men became entangled in wasteful skirmishes with Sawicki's 36th Infantry Regiment and other Piłsudskist units, in the course of which two of Boruta-Spiecho-

[42] Sławoj-Składkowski, "Wspomnienia z okresu majowego," p. 146, and S. Haller, pp. 28, 35. For Norwid-Neugebauer's appointment by Żeligowski, see above, p. 77. Further information on Norwid-Neugebauer will be found in the Biographical Register.

wicz's companies defected to the Piłsudskists.[43] His regiment thus disintegrated without making a contribution to the defense of the government.

The race for reinforcements resulted in an organizational and logistical success for Piłsudski. Simultaneously, however, it dealt him a staggering psychological and moral defeat. He had confidently assumed—and was eager to demonstrate—that in a showdown the army would obey him, its former commander in chief, rather than its current, transient, if constitutional, authorities.[44] This proved not to be the case. The army was not, as Piłsudski had fondly believed, "his." Officers and men were prepared to resist him by force, either because —as was the case with most of the senior ex-Austrian generals—they despised his style, his background, and his politics, or—what was probably true of most of those heeding the orders of the government— because legal authority proved to be more impelling in a crisis than charismatic appeal. By the third day of the coup, May 14, Piłsudski enjoyed a military advantage over Wojciechowski and Witos in Warsaw. He owed it, however, not to any rallying of a cohesive army behind its first chief but to the conspiratorial preparations which preceded his show of force and to the political support of the Left, crystallizing after the launching of the coup in the decisive transport strike of the Socialist railroad workers.

[43] AKL, 8/11; Grzędziński, "Fragmenty pamiętnika," pp. 444, 462; Rzepecki, *Wspomnienia,* p. 50. The defectors were led by that Lieutenant Błoński whose protest that he had been instructed to spy on Piłsudski had aroused a political scandal in 1924. Further information on Boruta-Spiechowicz will be found in the Biographical Register.

[44] See Pobóg-Malinowski, *Najnowsza historia,* II, 478.

CHAPTER VII
THE STRIKE: POLITICAL POWER
DECISIVE

Before World War I, Józef Piłsudski had been a leader of the Polish Socialist Party in the tsarist Russian empire, where it was an illegal, underground, revolutionary movement. The Party subscribed to the dual goals of a socialist order and independent Polish statehood. Whereas these two principles were regarded as interdependent by the movement's ideologues, Piłsudski came in time to focus his interest exclusively upon the second one. Socialism ceased to interest him and he eventually sought to manipulate the PPS simply as an instrument for conducting a militant and violent struggle for Poland's liberation from tsarist Russia. By 1906 the Party was seriously split over this strategy. Many leaders and members were repelled by Piłsudski's exclusive concentration on national goals and insurrectionary methods, while a smaller but aggressive section endorsed his priorities without, however, accepting his growing indifference to socialism per se and as an ultimate goal. After 1908, therefore, he shifted the primary institutional base of his political activities from the PPS—even from his own wing of the PPS—to various paramilitary organizations, culminating in the Riflemen, which the Austrian authorities permitted him to develop in Galicia as a potential Polish auxiliary force for use in an eventual war against tsarist Russia. The Riflemen, in turn, numbering over 7,000 by June, 1914,[1] became the nucleus of the Legions, whose exploits during World War I in the cause of Poland's resurrection elevated Piłsudski, their creator, to the position of national hero and chief of state in the restored Poland of 1918.

However, Piłsudski's parting with the Socialists was not abrupt or,

[1] Pobóg-Malinowski, *Najnowsza historia* (2d ed.), I, 629.

for a long time, even clear. In November, 1912, he had still been sent as a delegate by his own more insurrectionary and nationalistic section of the PPS to the Austrian Social Democratic Party's congress in Vienna, and as late as March, 1914, on the eve of World War I, a Party council of that wing, meeting in Lwów, had again confirmed him as a member of its directorate.[2] It appears that in his own mind his departure from the Party occurred in the course of the war and was confirmed by the achievement of independence.[3] When a PPS delegation called on him in November, 1918, on the morrow of his triumphant elevation to national leadership, and addressed him in the traditional Socialist style as "comrade," Piłsudski demurred. The metaphor in which he expressed his objection is picturesque: "Gentlemen, I am no longer your comrade. In the beginning we followed the same direction and took the same red-painted streetcar. As for me, I got off at 'Independence' station. You are continuing the trip till you reach the 'Socialism' stop. My best wishes accompany you, but . . . call me mister." [4]

Despite this repudiation, the Socialists still continued for a long time to think of Piłsudski as one of their own. The Party had helped to sustain the prewar Riflemen financially, and many of its members had both belonged to that organization and subsequently fought in the Legions. Their sense of loyalty to Piłsudski was dual and often blurred: they regarded him as both military chieftain and political leader. Many Socialists, furthermore, remained confident that, subjectively, Piłsudski continued to see his mission as championing the exploited and the poor against the powerful and the privileged—a general reputation, albeit vague, which was to stand him in good stead in the 1926 crisis. Thus, many leaders of the PPS initially persuaded themselves that only the formal dignity of his role as chief of state had required Piłsudski's postwar rebuff and that, as a matter of political fact, he expected and depended upon the Party's support. During the first two years of independence, the years when the nation's energies were devoted primarily to carving out the frontiers of the new state in many battles against several neighbors, the PPS had

2 *Ibid.*, p. 601.
3 Aleksandra Piłsudska, *Wspomnienia*, p. 228.
4 Quoted in Smogorzewski, *La Pologne restaurée*, p. 324.

willingly given him its support, applauding even Piłsudski's invasion of the Soviet Ukraine in April, 1920, and accepting the seizure of Wilno which he instigated in October of that year.[5] The Polish Socialists had never disavowed their strong nationalism, and they endorsed Piłsudski's federalistic ideas for the organization of the western areas—the old Jagiellonian lands—of the former tsarist Russian empire.[6] Indeed, many of those who in 1906 had denounced Piłsudski's exclusive concentration on the armed struggle for national independence had, since the restoration of that independence in 1918, returned to the fold of his former wing, the so-called Revolutionary Fraction, of the Party, now enlarged, legalized, and reconstituted in postwar Poland as the unified PPS. The rest of his former opponents within the Socialist movement had gone over to communism.[7]

As Poland turned in the early 1920s from the problems of military struggle and frontier vindication to the domestic ones of political organization and economic renovation, the "Piłsudski question" remained critical to the internal life of the PPS. With Piłsudski's shadow as a potential savior of the nation from political and economic disintegration looming ever larger across the Polish landscape, and with his general reputation as a man of the Left surviving into this period, many in the PPS tended to look to him for a Socialist-Bonapartist solution to the country's troubles. This sentiment was so widespread and deep that at the 19th congress of the PPS, held in Kraków at the turn of the year 1923-24, the veteran leader Feliks Perl, chairman of the Party's Central Executive Committee and editor of its daily *Robotnik* (Worker), felt obliged to caution his comrades against the expectation that a Piłsudskist dictatorship could be the lever for transforming Poland into a socialist society. Piłsudski, he warned, was no longer a Socialist and the PPS, if it persisted in its illusions about him, ran the risk of itself becoming his instrument rather than vice versa. The effect of this admonition was heightened by the fact

[5] Pobóg-Malinowski, *Najnowsza historia,* II, 256. For an illustration of a Polish Communist leader's frustrated reaction to this enduring PPS regard for Piłsudski, see Łańcucki, I, 189–90.

[6] Lewandowski, pp. 81–87. For Piłsudski's territorial and political program for these borderlands, see Dziewanowski, "Piłsudski's Federal Policy."

[7] Dziewanowski, *The Communist Party of Poland,* p. 77.

that Perl had himself belonged to Piłsudski's branch of the PPS before World War I.[8]

It was not easy, however, for Perl to convince his party. The only apparent alternative to championing a Bonapartist bid for power by Piłsudski—with the attractiveness of its seemingly "revolutionary" and "militant" implications—was the "responsible" but unpopular policy of supporting, or at least tolerating, the cabinets of Grabski (December 19, 1923–November 14, 1925) and Skrzyński (November 20, 1925–May 5, 1926), both of whose economic policies demanded painful sacrifices by the working class and the intelligentsia. A third, theoretical alternative—that of independent revolutionary action—appalled the PPS leadership. Polish society was deemed to be too underdeveloped and immature for a socialist revolution, and a premature attempt to launch one could only result in one or more disasters: Communist rioting, reactionary putsch, civil war, German-Soviet intervention. Thus, at the time of the assassination of President Narutowicz on December 16, 1922, and again when the workers of Kraków, Borysław, and Tarnów arose in insurrectionary ferment from November 5 to 8, 1923, the PPS had acted to smother the violence and restore order. Nevertheless, this policy of restraint and responsibility became ever more difficult for the Socialists and imposed increasingly severe internal strain on their party. By May, 1926, they could no longer sustain it and hence suspended their hitherto consistent and principled support for parliamentary-constitutional approaches to the nation's problems.

The mounting pressure within the PPS to cease support for the Grabski and Skrzyński experiments had come from two directions. To begin with, there existed a Leftist minority less apprehensive than the Party leadership about the possible risks of adopting a politically and socially radical stance and articulating the interests of the increasingly afflicted and angry proletariat. These Leftists became progressively more outraged over the glaring discrepancy between the pauperization inflicted on the workers and poor peasants on the one hand, and the loose tax morality permitted to the bourgeois and

[8] Two speeches by Perl on January 1, 1924, quoted in Próchnik, *Pierwsze piętnastolecie*, p. 192, and in Roos, *Geschichte der polnischen Nation*, p. 113. Perl had belonged to Piłsudski's PPS–Revolutionary Fraction from 1906 to 1912, had headed a splinter group from it during the next year, and had reunited with it at the outbreak of war in 1914. He died on April 14, 1927.

landed classes on the other.[9] They demanded that the PPS champion and lead the social ferment which this situation was provoking. After much agitational and factional activity within the PPS, a group from this wing eventually seceded in June, 1926, a month after Piłsudski's coup, to organize itself as the distinct Left-PPS (PPS-Lewica). A year later it claimed 5,000 members and 10,000 by mid-1928—the latter figure being probably a somewhat inflated one. As the parent PPS itself moved to the left in later years under the multiple impacts of disillusionment with the post-coup governments, persuasion by those Leftists who had remained within it, and secession by the explicitly Piłsudskist wing of the Party, the Left-PPS ceased to attract members out of the PPS and itself became subverted from within by the Communists. By mid-1929 the Communists had transformed it into one of their legal "fronts," ousted the original founders, and elected their own candidate, Władysław Gomułka, to the General Secretariat of the Left-PPS at its first congress, held in Warsaw on July 20–21, 1929. The Left-PPS was declared subversive and was dissolved by the government on February 3, 1931, the day after the conclusion of its second two-day congress, which had been held in Łódź and at which all 350 participants had been arrested.[10]

However, a far more serious internal problem than this "Leftist" one had been posed to the PPS in the years before the May, 1926, crisis by the activities of its fervently Piłsudskist wing. A bid for power by the Marshal was, after all, a far more imminent and plausible culmination to the political and economic crisis of that period than a proletarian revolutionary upheaval. Hence the Party's need to have a strategy for that eventuality was more imperative. The Piłsudskists within the PPS were not a formally organized faction but rather a group of comrades from among those Party members who had fought under Piłsudski in the Polish national cause during World War I. Though by no means all of the Socialist veterans of those

[9] See Krzyżanowski, pp. 42–45.

[10] Hass, "PPS Lewica, 1926–1931," *Mówią Wieki*, II, No. 3 (March, 1959), 1–7, and the much longer study by the same author under the same title in *Najnowsze Dzieje Polski: Materiały i Studia z okresu 1914–1939*, IV (1961), 59–99. The Left-PPS periodicals were *Głos Pracy* (Voice of Labor), a weekly for trade unionists published in Kraków from February 22, 1926, until April 3, 1927 (45 issues), and *Robociarz* (The Laborer), a political weekly also published in Kraków beginning on July 4, 1926. The group had cells in more than a dozen cities and towns.

campaigns were numbered among these Piłsudskist praetorians, the experience and the memory of having served with him made such a deep and lasting psychological impact upon many that it became difficult in the postwar years to discriminate whether they were PPS members devoted to the Marshal or Piłsudskist agents within the Party. They were particularly strong in its Warsaw District Committee, which, at the time of the insurrectionary episode of November, 1923, in Kraków and other towns, had sought to commit the PPS to a "revolutionary" tactic of exacerbating the crisis so as to bring Piłsudski to power.[11] Their leaders were the ex-Legionnaires Jędrzej Moraczewski (prime minister [1918–19] and minister of public works [1925–26]), Rajmund Jaworowski, and Marian Malinowski ("Wojtek").

The PPS "center" leadership, under the intellectual guidance of Feliks Perl, managed to stave off a Piłsudskist offensive. Indeed, the 19th PPS congress, meeting shortly after the critical events of November, 1923, not only heard Perl's warning that the Party risked becoming a Piłsudskist tool but heeded it by adopting a resolution requiring members to apply for and receive the permission of the Presidium of the Party's Central Executive Committee before attending reunions of the wartime Legions and underground POW. Membership in the Riflemen, Legions, and POW had also to be registered with the central party apparatus, which was controlled by Perl and his allies. Thus did the Party seek to ensure its autonomy in regard to Piłsudski and avert the danger of being tripped into a possibly fatal adventure on his behalf. The congress also resolved to support the Grabski government.[12]

In the subsequent years 1924-26, however, this strategy of supporting the Grabski and later the Skrzyński constellations for fear of worse was increasingly undermined by the deepening general crisis which both the Leftist and the Piłsudskist oppositional wings exploited to embarrass the central PPS leadership. Through seemingly revolutionary appeals for extraparliamentary solutions to the nation's problems, the issues were blurred, Piłsudski was presented as a more

11 Hass, "Kształtowanie się lewicowego nurtu w Polskiej Partii Socjalistycznej na tle sytuacji wewnątrzpartyjnej (listopad 1923–maj 1926)," p. 78.

12 *Ibid.*, pp. 80, 82. The 19th congress sat December 30, 1923–January 1, 1924.

"radical" alternative, and the central leadership was thrown on the defensive. An apparent defection from that central "line" occurred in September, 1925, when the veteran Galician Socialist leader, Ignacy Daszyński, who had hitherto loyally accepted Perl's policy, published a dithyrambically laudatory biographical pamphlet on Piłsudski.[13] This seemed to be premonitory of the leadership's impending retreat, defeat, or disintegration on the Piłsudski problem.

At the 20th PPS congress, the last before Piłsudski's coup, held in Warsaw at the turn of the year 1925–26, Perl won a Pyrrhic victory. The Party was persuaded to support Skrzyński but on condition that he be presented with an ultimatum to enact its key economic and political demands for coping with the crisis. It was also generally assumed that Moraczewski, who was one of the two Socialist ministers whom the Party contributed to Skrzyński's cabinet and who would present its demands, would in fact act on Piłsudski's behalf and at his behest within the government. Since War Minister Żeligowski was also in effect a Piłsudskist Trojan horse in the cabinet, Skrzyński initially enjoyed the benevolent toleration of Piłsudski and of the Piłsudskists in the PPS. Perhaps an additional, if marginal, reason for the support of the latter was that they may have been uneasy over the other, militantly Leftist pressure upon Perl within the Party and apprehensive about the incalculable but possibly disintegrative consequences of prematurely destroying Skrzyński before Piłsudski was prepared to assume power.[14]

By February 7, 1926, however, Moraczewski's efforts to facilitate Piłsudski's resumption of *de facto* control over the army and thus of power in the state had proved unavailing and he resigned.[15] Thereafter the Piłsudskists within the PPS no longer accepted responsibility

[13] Daszyński, *Wielki człowiek w Polsce.*

[14] The 20th congress sat December 31, 1925 to January 3, 1926. Some Leftist defections to the Independent Peasant Party (Niezależna Partia Chłopska)— a Communist "front"—took place toward the end of January. Local cooperation by Left-PPS groups (then still within the parent party) with the Communist Party occurred in Kraków in February and in Lublin in March, 1926. These Polish developments coincided with and appear to have been expressions of a general international Communist drive during 1925 and 1926 for "unity of action" between Communist parties and trade unions on the one hand and Socialist parties on the other. See J. Rothschild, *The Communist Party of Bulgaria* (New York, 1959), pp. 265–67.

[15] See above, pp. 41–42.

for sustaining Skrzyński, and Perl's central group was left to bear the burden alone. Moraczewski's successor as minister of public works, Norbert Barlicki, was indeed of this central, non-Piłsudskist faction; but his selection availed nothing, for National Democratic Finance Minister Jerzy Zdziechowski's deflationary economic program proved intolerable even to this compromise-seeking central sector of the PPS. Desperately casting about for a device to honor the Party's ideological-programmatic commitments and yet to maintain the Skrzyński coalition against a background of violent demonstrations by the unemployed and an ominous air of expectancy on the part of the Piłsudskists, the PPS leaders offered to accept another National Democrat in place of Zdziechowski. When this proposal was declined, they withdrew from the cabinet on April 20. Their parliamentary spokesman, Zygmunt Marek, confided at the time to his National Democratic counterpart, Stanisław Głąbiński, that the non-Piłsudskists in the PPS had assented to this step only with trepidation and reluctance.[16] Simultaneously with its withdrawal from the cabinet, the PPS leadership explained itself in a "Manifesto to the Working People"—among whom the Marshal was popular and the coalition strategy not appreciated. Here assurances were given that the Party definitely wished to see Piłsudski restored to control of the army.[17]

At this time the PPS leaders may still have hoped—as Grabski did —to pull the sting of Piłsudski as a political threat by satisfying his military demands. Even in the political dimension, however, their hesitancy toward him was as nothing compared to their revulsion over the prospect of another Right-Center attempt at government, reminiscent of Witos' disastrous regime of May-December, 1923. Hence, during the critical week of May 5–12, 1926, the PPS had offered its collaboration to Piłsudski in an abortive effort to avert that other, infinitely more feared, alternative.[18] When Witos nevertheless formed such a cabinet on May 10, the PPS—like Piłsudski—responded with bitter opposition.

To have offered cooperation to Piłsudski in order to prevent a de-

---

[16] Głąbiński, p. 545.

[17] PPS "Manifesto to the Working People," quoted in Hass, "Kształtowanie się lewicowego nurtu w Polskiej Partii Socjalistycznej na tle sytuacji wewnątrz-partyjnej (listopad 1923–maj 1926)," p. 101.

[18] For the relations of Grabski and the PPS with Piłsudski during the tense week of May 5–12, see above, pp. 49–51.

plored political experiment was one thing. To collaborate in an armed coup d'état against a legal—if hated—government was a rather different proposition and one which the PPS leaders hesitated to accept. On May 11 they had joined their comrade parties of the Left bloc to denounce the Witos cabinet as one of reaction, exploitation, incompetence, and national weakness. The next day, as news and rumors of Piłsudski's march on Warsaw flooded the capital, they issued a similar manifesto through the agency of their own Central Executive Committee, explicitly denouncing the "fascists, monarchists, and profiteers" allegedly composing the Witos government and rendering it one intolerable to the worker and peasant masses.[19] Significantly, neither statement mentioned Piłsudski.

Whereas the PPS central leadership thus initially sought to avoid identifying the Party's own response to the new government with that of Piłsudski, the latter's supporters and agents within the Party had other intentions. Through the instrumentality of the Warsaw District Committee of the PPS, which they dominated and of which Jaworowski was the municipal "boss," the Piłsudskists within the Party managed to preempt its response to the coup by unofficially organizing a railroad strike against the government's reinforcements and then blackmailing the Party's Central Executive Committee into an official endorsement of this action. The railroad workers, it will be recalled, had particular reason to be enraged at the deflationary economic policy of Zdziechowski, whom Witos had retained as finance minister.

This sequence of events was dramatic as the Central Executive Committee, under Perl's chairmanship, deliberated the Party's proper response to the coup during a round-the-clock session in Warsaw on May 13. Although hostility to the Witos regime was unanimous, the Perl leadership group still argued against immediate endorsement of Piłsudski's coup pending clarification of the Marshal's political intentions.[20] Persuaded that the Socialist affiliation of the key railroad workers' union put into the hands of the PPS the decisive weapon for

---

[19] Reprinted in *Dokumenty chwili*, II, 11, and in Czubiński, "Przewrót majowy," p. 130. For the joint Left-bloc statement of May 11, see above, p. 54.

[20] See the testimony subsequently given on this point by the PPS leader and former minister (1926) Norbert Barlicki while testifying on October 27, 1931, as a defendant at the notorious Brześć political trial. *Sprawa brzeska*, pp. 55–56. Barlicki had supported Perl in 1926 on the "Piłsudski problem" in the PPS.

determining the outcome of the politico-military confrontation then taking place in Warsaw, they opposed striking in Piłsudski's support except as a *quid pro quo* for specific commitments and assurances to be given by him. Jaworowski, on behalf of Piłsudski and through the instrumentality of the PPS Warsaw District Committee, had, however, since the previous evening, been arguing, lobbying, propagandizing, and preparing for an immediate and unconditional strike against the Witos government. More importantly, his agitational activities were being endorsed organizationally by the president of the main railroad workers' union, Adam Kuryłowicz, who had been cooperating closely with Piłsudski's military staff at least since the night of May 12.[21] Then, on May 13, the senior among the PPS Piłsudskists, former premier and minister Moraczewski, stunned the Central Executive Committee in the midst of its strategy deliberations by announcing that the railroad workers would strike against Witos and for Piłsudski no matter what the PPS leadership resolved and that their union had, in fact, already issued strike orders. Although this second assertion was still technically premature at the moment, Moraczewski's implied warning of an incipient split between the workers and the Party leadership which might leave the latter isolated was effective in triggering it into an immediate endorsement of a strike without awaiting political pledges from Piłsudski. The strike could thereupon be promptly activated into high gear thanks to Jaworowski's and Kuryłowicz's preparatory work.[22]

At eight o'clock on the evening of May 13, the official strike manifesto was finally broadcast.[23] Ironically, it came at the end of a day of startling military successes by the Belwederians in the course of which they could have seized the headquarters from which the strike was to be organized had they but realized its crucial importance. The

[21] Grzędziński, *Maj 1926,* p. 28. Grzędziński, a Legion veteran and former adjutant to Piłsudski, a lieutenant colonel in May, 1926, was one of two officers on Piłsudski's staff during the coup who were assigned to work on transportation arrangements. The other one was a former Rifleman and POW veteran, Lieutenant Colonel Janusz Gąsiorowski. Further information on both officers and on the trade unionist Kuryłowicz will be found in the Biographical Register.

[22] Arski, p. 425, citing the oral recollections of that meeting given him in 1938 by Norbert Barlicki, and Wierzbiński, pp. 97, 122–25.

[23] Text in Strumph-Wojtkiewicz *et al.,* pp. 51–52, and in *Dokumenty chwili,* I, 20.

manifesto called for a general as well as a transport strike, to begin the next day (May 14) and to continue indefinitely until explicitly halted. Exceptions would be permitted for workers in water and electricity facilities, bakeries, and hospitals. The purposes of the strike were declared to be to support Piłsudski and his heroic troops, to overthrow the Witos cabinet and to oust President Wojciechowski (whom Piłsudski, unlike the PPS, refrained from criticizing in public statements at this time), and to replace them by a worker-peasant government (a goal which Piłsudski was also not endorsing).

The strike order—echoed by the other parties of the Left bloc [24] — was successfully executed. Indeed, the railroad strike was already unofficially and selectively under way by the time the order was issued. At critical rail junctions throughout Poland—Lublin, Łódź, Częstochowa—as well as at the approaches to Warsaw—Ożarów, Ząbki—the government's troop trains were sidetracked, uncoupled, and blocked, and traffic ground to a halt. Simultaneously the trade unionist Adam Kuryłowicz and the PPS functionary Bronisław Ziemięcki, in cooperation with Piłsudski's commissar for railroads, Kazimierz Bartel, and his military staff officers, were arranging that the railroadmen haul specifically identified Piłsudskist reinforcements to Warsaw.[25] The fact that the Witos cabinet gave its military officers authority to conscript railroad workers and subject them to martial law [26] availed it nothing. After May 13 the Belwederians ceased to receive reinforcements and were isolated from the rest of the country.

The external triumph of the strike, however, cannot disguise the fact that the internal PPS rift over the "Piłsudski problem" was simply plastered over but not healed. On May 13, the day of the strike manifesto, Jaworowski's explicitly Piłsudskist Warsaw District Committee

[24] Extensive quotations from the manifestos of all the Left-bloc parties are reprinted in the embittered memoirs of Witos, *Moje wspomnienia,* III, 117–20. See also Bełcikowska, *Walki majowe,* p. 25.

[25] See Ziemięcki's testimony of November 18, 1931, as a witness at the Brześć trial in *Sprawa brzeska,* p. 207; also Arski, pp. 422–23. Ziemięcki had been minister of labor under Moraczewski (1918–19) and under Skrzyński (1925–26), and his relations with the workers were good. He was fated to be shot by the Germans in February, 1943. Some details concerning the effects of the railroad strike at various junctions and stations in May, 1926, are in *Ilustrowany Kurjer Codzienny,* May 17, 1926, and Porczak, *Rewolucja majowa,* p. 52.

[26] S. Haller, p. 41.

issued a supplementary appeal "To the Working People of Warsaw" which, paraphrased, argued as follows: Witos, the hangman of the people of Kraków (an allusion to the insurrectionary incidents of November, 1923), has again dared to reach for power with his cohort of reactionaries, robbers, and exploiters. Opposed to him stands Piłsudski, the creator of independent Poland, who in 1918 had worked with Moraczewski's first postindependence government to give Poland republican institutions, including universal, secret, direct, equal, and proportional suffrage, as well as to guarantee the workers an eight-hour day. Now, when this Piłsudski protests against the provocation to the democratic and working people which the formation of the Witos cabinet represents, Witos responds by opening fratricidal strife. Witos is prepared to drown Poland's democratic structure, her political and social freedoms, in a sea of blood rather than relinquish power. He must be overthrown and Wojciechowski's betrayal of democratic Poland in appointing him must be punished. The instrument of this democratic and republican vengeance is Piłsudski's army, in whose support we have proclaimed a general strike.[27]

This statement, in its historical allusions, sought to recall and to perpetuate Piłsudski's traditional reputation as a man of the Left, as a champion of political republicanism and social democracy, without committing him to a specific course of subsequent action. It also reflected Piłsudski's current insistence that his march on Warsaw had been intended merely as a "demonstration" against Witos, who must himself now bear the responsibility for the subsequent eruption of actual fighting. In its pointed coupling of Piłsudski with Moraczewski, furthermore, the Warsaw District Committee's appeal attempted to convey an image of Piłsudski and the PPS as mutual auxiliaries.

A different note was struck in an editorial appearing on May 14 in the central organ of the PPS, Perl's *Robotnik*.[28] Although equally vehement and even insulting in its denunciation of the "blackest reactionary alliance of fascists, monarchists, and profiteers" which was said to constitute the Witos government, this statement made no mention of Piłsudski and instead called upon workers and citizens in general to support the PPS in its struggle for a democratic Poland and socialism.

[27] Text in *Dokumenty chwili*, I, 20, and in Bojan-Błażewicz, pp. 20–21.
[28] Text in Witos, *Moje wspomnienia*, III, 117.

However deep may have been the reticence of some PPS leaders toward Piłsudski, there is no doubt that the strike which their party authorized—and which was enthusiastically implemented by the workers—proved decisive.[29] Although Piłsudski and his publicists refused to acknowledge it,[30] the undeniable—and ironic—fact is that he owed his victory in May, 1926, to the PPS-affiliated railroad workers. The irony here is triple. First of all, the PPS had not initially been unanimous in the fateful decision to throw its full support—gratis—behind Piłsudski's coup. In the second place, it was not destined to share the fruits of his victory or to succeed in imparting to his subsequent system a Socialist direction.[31] Thirdly, Piłsudski's own attitude toward the PPS and its political potential was at least as cautious and reserved as that of the Perl group toward him once his expectations of a quick victory on May 12 were disappointed and the government's resistance confronted him with the threat of a genuine civil war. Though workers, Socialists, and generally "Leftist" civilians flocked en masse to his banner as the fighting developed,[32] Piłsudski became as concerned after May 12 to exclude uncontrolled and potentially volatile mass participation in the combat as he had earlier been eager to avoid fighting altogether. He did not wish to be identified with or indebted to any one—that is, Leftist—political constellation. Still less did he wish to see the elevation—or degeneration—of his military coup into a civil war or a social revolution. Hence his reluctance to acknowledge the political circumstances to which he

[29] This is the conclusion of such diverse analysts of the coup as Witos' acting foreign minister, Morawski (*Tamten brzeg*, p. 151), the Socialists Zaremba (p. 100) and Porczak (*Rewolucja majowa*, p. 52), the anonymous author of "Le coup d'état de Varsovie," p. 20, the German historian Roos (*Geschichte der polnischen Nation*, p. 114), and the Canadian student of Polish affairs Rose (*The Rise of Polish Democracy*, p. 172). For a related but more general (and also correct) argument to the effect that Piłsudski's victory was less a military one than a reflection of the fact that he represented public opinion more validly than did Witos' discredited Sejm majority, see the tract by the Cracovian professional economist Krzyżanowski, p. 41.

[30] See Piłsudski, *PZ*, IX, 12–27, and Bełcikowska, *Walki majowe*, p. 28.

[31] The PPS organ *Robotnik* was to be the first newspaper subjected after the coup to the harassing confiscations of Piłsudski's commissar for Warsaw, Sławoj-Składkowski. The conservative Kraków lawyer and historian Klemens Bąkowski presciently noted in his diary on May 13 that the workers were deceiving themselves in their enthusiasm for Piłsudski. See Bąkowski, p. 18.

[32] See Mieszkowski, pp. 4–5, and Katelbach, *Spowiedź pokolenia*, p. 137, for eyewitness impressions.

owed his military preponderance in Warsaw as May 15 dawned. Hence, also, his deliberate sabotage of the endeavors of workers and sympathetic civilians to participate in the fighting. He instructed his staff that such volunteers be given obsolete rifles and unsuitable ammunition, that they be organized into a "workers' battalion" closely supervised by his proven officers, and, finally, that they be kept away from the actual theater of operations. As he candidly conceded to his intimates, "The army will cease firing at my command, but I don't know if the civilians will." [33] Immediately after the coup, Piłsudski issued strict orders that all these civilian volunteer participants be disarmed.[34] Communist offers of aid, brought to Piłsudski's Saxon Square headquarters by Sejm deputy Jerzy Czeszejko-Sochacki, were peremptorily rebuffed, and attempts by the Communist Party to organize supportive rallies were broken up by Piłsudski's gendarmes.[35] In a sense, Piłsudski acted in May, 1926, as the PPS had done in December, 1922, and again in November, 1923—to contain the level of violence and avert a revolutionary eruption emerging out of a political crisis.

Were Piłsudski's fears of a radicalization of his military intervention into a social upheaval rational? In one sense—his own subjective

---

[33] Mackiewicz, p. 174, and Pobóg-Malinowski, *Najnowsza historia,* II, 482. Piłsudski's reluctance to permit a role in his coup to civilians applied primarily to their unorganized, spontaneous activity and to voluntary participation by groups (such as the Socialists) beyond his direct aegis and outside his unquestioned control. It did not apply, on the other hand, to such notoriously—if unofficially—Piłsudskist organizations as the Polska Organizacja Wolności (Polish Organization of Liberty), a civilian group dedicated to perpetuating the political and comradely traditions of the wartime underground Piłsudskist POW, or to the postwar Riflemen, revived in 1919 as a patriotic and paramilitary organization ostensibly devoted to educating and training the public to an awareness of and a capacity to fulfill its responsibilities toward national defense. Ideologically in rapport with Wyzwolenie, this postwar group served virtually as an auxiliary army to Piłsudski during the coup. Its activities at that time are cited in AKL, 2/31; *Dokumenty chwili,* I, 13 and 34; Bełcikowska, *Walki majowe,* p. 14; S. Haller, p. 36; and Piątkowski, p. 15. For a rather vague claim that Piłsudski eventually also acceded to the importunate requests of certain Jewish youth groups to be permitted to serve him in an auxiliary capacity, see Nagel, p. 48.

[34] *Ilustrowany Kurjer Codzienny,* May 18, 1926.

[35] "Jak się zachowali komuniści w dniach majowych?" *Robotnik Polski* (Detroit), January 22, 1928, p. 2; *Kurjer Warszawski,* May 15, 1926; Sławoj-Składkowski, "Wspomnienia z okresu majowego," p. 152. For an extended discussion of the Communist role in the coup and of the coup's reverse impact on the power conglomeration within the Communist Party, see the Appendix.

one—the answer must be positive. Given the extremely cautious and even conservative uses to which Piłsudski was to put his power after the coup, and given his determination—not publically expressed until the fighting was over—that there were to be no revolutionary consequences to his coup,[36] even the relatively modest political expectations of the PPS and its partners in the Left bloc must have appeared as corrosively revolutionary threats. The objective situation is more difficult to evaluate in retrospect. Both the Communists and their sworn foe within the PPS, the tough Piłsudskist Jaworowski, professed to believe—the former hopefully, the latter fearfully—that "power was lying in the streets" and that the political situation was indeed revolutionary.[37] In Warsaw the workers were demanding arms. From the provinces came scattered reports of peasants invading state forests and attempting spontaneous partitions of estates. Clashes between demonstrating masses and the police occurred in a number of towns.[38] The over-all impression which the surviving historical evidence suggests is, however, one of hopeful expectation reposed in Piłsudski rather than of serious revolutionary momentum. The Communists were too weak and myopic, the peasant forces too fragmented, the Socialists too skeptical, to push a determinedly unreceptive Piłsudski in a radical direction or to overwhelm him with an independently unleashed revolutionary juggernaut. Both his political allies of the Left and his foes of the Right-Center government were to permit him to close out the coup with a limited military action on May 14.

[36] See Piłsudski's interview in the *Kurjer Poranny,* May 25, 1926, reprinted in his *PZ,* IX, 18.

[37] For the Communist evaluation of a revolutionary situation, see Kowalski, *Zarys historii polskiego ruchu robotniczego w latach 1918–1939,* I, 288. For Jaworowski's reported remarks to the same effect, see Wierzbiński, p. 122.

[38] *Ilustrowany Kurjer Codzienny,* May 15, 17, and 26, June 4, 12, and 13, 1926.

CHAPTER VIII

MAY 14-15: THE END OF THE
MILITARY PHASE

By the night of May 13, the time, the opportunity, and, indeed, the necessity for Piłsudski to resume the military initiative was at hand. The surrender of the Citadel to his chief of the General Staff during the afternoon had insured him against tactical encirclement within Warsaw. The decision of the Socialists and their affiliated trade unions to launch a railroad and general strike against the government promised him an impending strategic advantage around the capital for the immediate future. The morale of his troops, who had absorbed the punishing counterattacks of the Belwederians throughout the previous day, required a riposte on his part. He must strike while the iron was hot.

Though extending his self-imposed restraint on resuming the military offensive as long as the aristocratic-conservative Lubomirski-Meysztowicz-Mackiewicz mediation mission still seemed to provide a glimmer of hope for a political solution during the evening of May 13 (and until his own reinforcements from Wilno arrived during the night), Piłsudski had nevertheless prepared the psychological grounds for resuming his assault with a declaration issued by his headquarters to the press sometime after the fall of the Citadel.[1] It began by arguing once again that he had intended no fighting or bloodshed but only an armed demonstration against the evil Witos cabinet. It insisted that

[1] The text of the statement is reprinted in *Dokumenty chwili*, I, 17; Nagel, pp. 44–46; and Bełcikowska, *Walki majowe*, pp. 32–33. The first two date its issuance as of the evening of May 13 and the last as of dawn on May 14. In view of Bełcikowska's occasional inaccuracies on matters of timing, I have chosen to accept the dating of the other sources. An additional reason for so doing is that the Witos government appears tangentially to have replied to this statement in one of its own, issued late on May 13. See below, p. 144, n. 22.

the fighting had been provoked by Witos' stubbornness and that the first shots were fired on Rozwadowski's order. Nevertheless, to demonstrate his pacific good faith, Piłsudski had leashed his troops since the night of May 12 even though they could easily have overpowered the government forces at that time and seized the Belweder palace. In thus restraining them, he had desired to provide emphatic proof that in no sense was his action directed against the President residing in the Belweder. In fact—the statement continued—Piłsudski had definite information to the effect that Wojciechowski, too, had been making simply superhuman efforts to halt further bloodshed and had repeatedly sought to contact Piłsudski for this purpose. These would-be overtures by Wojciechowski, as well as the mediation attempts of Rataj, had, alas, been frustrated by that unregenerate foe of peace—Witos.

On this note of righteous indignation the statement closed. Its misrepresentation of Wojciechowski's position may have reflected wishful thinking as well as intended exoneration of Piłsudski. Its spurious depiction of Witos as diabolically and gratuitously bellicose was designed to present Piłsudski's impending resumption of offensive activity as simple and just retribution.

While massive reinforcements were arriving for him during the night of May 13, Piłsudski's headquarters issued a further communiqué in the predawn hours. Beginning with yet another repetition of the (correct) assertion that Piłsudski had not wanted to provoke bloodshed, it went on to boast of his currently prevailing superiority of armed might in Warsaw and to allege that, the other side having resorted to atrocities such as letting the wounded bleed to death, shooting civilians and maltreating military prisoners, and using (Rightist) civilian snipers to shoot at his troops from the rear, Piłsudski now felt himself morally obliged to undertake what he also had the power to accomplish—the liquidation of the entire affair with the greatest dispatch through an all-out offensive.[2]

---

[2] The text is reprinted in Bełcikowska, *Walki majowe,* p. 29, and in Bojan-Błażewicz, pp. 21–22.

Piłsudski was to repeat the allegation of atrocities in his post-coup interview in the *Kurjer Poranny* of May 25, 1926, reprinted in Piłsudski, *PZ,* IX, 18. The facts appear to have been as follows: since even the Belwederian generals Haller and Kukiel implicitly concede that the hysterically inclined Malczewski reviled, abused, and struck some prisoners, this charge can be accepted as con-

Another motive which, though unmentioned by him, should have contributed to Piłsudski's resolution to bring his coup to a speedy close was the consideration that, in the long run, time was on the side of his enemies. With every passing hour during which the Belwederians remained in the field and in control of the presidential palace, the advantage of their legality per se would grow in its impact upon the straddlers, the hesitators, and the politically inactive but law-respecting officers and citizens throughout the country. While ready to acknowledge a successful *de facto* seizure of power, such people were likely to drift toward the legal government's side in the eventuality of long-drawn-out civil strife. Time was also running out on Piłsudski in the military operational sense. By the morning of May 14 he had reached the peak of his strength in Warsaw, while most of the Poznanian and Pomeranian reinforcements destined for his enemies were still mobilizing in their garrisons or massing at the approaches to Warsaw. Sooner or later, some of them were bound to break through his encirclement of the Belwederians and, by forced marches from the suburbs where their trains had been halted, circumvent the railroad strike. Eventually, too, in the absence of a quick settlement in Warsaw, the outraged Rightist bastions of western Poland would be encouraged to persist in organizing a counterinsurrectionary or quasi-secessionist Vendée in their provinces. That would confront Piłsudski with the worst of his nightmares—the escalation of his intended "armed demonstration" into full-scale civil war, resulting in the tearing apart of the young Polish state and, by eliciting German and/or Soviet intervention, inviting its possible extinction. It was in-

---

firmed. (See S. Haller, p. 37, and Kukiel, "Jeszcze o majowej wojnie domowej i generale Zagórskim," p. 6.) Another allegation, that the immunity of the Ujazdowski Hospital was violated, is more difficult to clarify. That such a violation did occur is an established fact, but which side first fired upon or from the hospital grounds was heatedly disputed. (See Bełcikowska, *Walki majowe*, pp. 25 and 35; S. Haller, pp. 37 and 53; Rzepecki, *Wspomnienia*, p. 32; and *Ilustrowany Kurjer Codzienny*, May 18 and June 16, 1926.) Further, the Belwederians do not appear to have denied Piłsudskist charges that Rozwadowski callously and brutally rejected a telephoned plea that the wounded lying in no-man's-land between the opposing lines be given first aid under the curtain of a few minutes' cease-fire. Several wounded then bled to death for lack of medical attention. (See Bełcikowska, *Walki majowe*, pp. 25 and 35.) Finally, the Piłsudskist charge that the Belwederian command had ordered the summary execution of armed civilian captives is answered with the claim that these were turned over to the police. (See Bełcikowska, *Walki majowe*, p. 25, and S. Haller, p. 36.)

deed imperative that Piłsudski utilize his immediate advantage in Warsaw to liquidate the affair in short order.

Having allowed his embattled as well as his newly arrived—but also fatigued—regiments a few hours' rest, Piłsudski at last opened his final assault upon the Belwederians on the morning of May 14, with himself in charge of the operation. By now he had the equivalent of fifteen regiments at his disposal in Warsaw, without even bothering to make use of those units which had come over to him from the government side on the previous day.[3] The front now ran from the Vistula river westward along Ludna street to the Square of the Three Crosses, then along Hoża street to Marszałkowska street, on to the railroad station then located at the crossing of Marzałkowska street and Jerozolimskie avenue, and from there into the suburbs. The Mokotów airdrome to the southwest of this line was still held by the Belwederians. As a result of paralysis on the railroads, it had become their sole physical link with the rest of Poland, and their commanding generals were determined to hold it. They had recently been enabled to reinforce its defense thanks to the fact that the Engineering Officer School had managed during the night of May 13 to break out of a Piłsudskist encirclement of its quarters and make its way to the Belweder perimeter. Part of the Cadet Corps was also deployed to protect the airdrome.[4]

The government's defending generals were concerned primarily over this left, suburban flank at the airdrome and remained confident of their ability to withstand the Piłsudskists in the heart of the city.[5]

---

[3] Piłsudski apparently never utilized Modelski's 30th Infantry Regiment or the two companies of Boruta-Spiechowicz's 71st Infantry Regiment which had defected to him on May 13. During the night of May 13, some units of the 55th Infantry Regiment, which was one of those coming from Poznania to the relief of the Belweder perimeter (it was garrisoned in Leszno), also resolved not to let themselves be used against Piłsudski. As a result, this regiment, too, remained aloof from the battle. Its commander, Colonel Józef Kustroń, a prewar Rifleman and wartime Legionnaire, was to perish as a general in the September, 1939, campaign.

[4] Details concerning these military dispositions of May 14 are in AKL, 14/3, subfolders 1–9, and, in published accounts, in Bełcikowska, *Walki majowe*, p. 32; Jordan-Rozwadowski, p. 117; Rzepecki, *Wspomnienia*, pp. 34 and 48; Mercik, p. 109.

[5] See, for example, S. Haller, p. 51.

Yet the grim fact was that their resources were simply too modest and their line too thin for a sustained defense of their perimeter. The accretion of the Engineering Officer School was no compensation for the failure of their major expected reinforcements to break through to them. But for this minor accession, they were still confined to the units—by now fatigued and overextended—with which they had fought so aggressively on May 13: the Cadet Corps and the Infantry Officer School, the 10th Infantry Regiment from Łowicz, the 57th and 58th from Poznań, various secondary and fractional units such as the presidential guard, an ordnance battalion, and part of the Citadel-based 21st Infantry Regiment. Finally, the air and antiaircraft regiments at Mokotów would be well-nigh useless in ground fighting. All in all, this was simply not enough. Sometime after noon the Mokotów airdrome fell, following shortly upon the loss of the Superior War Academy building, which had protected the approach to it on Koszykowa street. The government's defenders in the eastern and central sectors of the front, between the Vistula river and Marszałkowska street, who had been relatively successfully resisting several Piłsudskist assaults during the morning, were now obliged to pull back. In midafternoon the War Ministry building on Nowowiejska street was stormed by the Piłsudskists and the fighting thus approached the immediate vicinity of the Belweder palace.[6]

It was clear that the fate of the shrinking Belweder perimeter depended on a speedy link-up with it by the additional reinforcements from western Poland, whose advance guards were then being conducted toward Warsaw by General Żymierski from the suburban stations where the railroad strike had obliged them to detrain. Żymierski, upon making contact with three Poznanian regiments that morning, had left one, the 14th of field artillery, at the western suburb of Ożarów with orders to follow on and pushed ahead toward the capital with two others, the 56th and 68th of infantry. However, his decisions and commands were indecisive and unrealistic. While time was of the essence, he frittered away the morning at the suburban locality of

---

[6] When the Mokotów airdrome fell, General Zagórski, defending it to the last, was almost captured by paramilitary Piłsudskist Riflemen. See Piątkowski, p. 15.

The War Ministry building had changed hands three times in the course of the coup.

Mory, several miles short of the Mokotów airdrome, waiting for the remaining artillery regiment at Ożarów to catch up with him. When he finally did resume his advance, instead of deploying his regiments compactly, he dispersed them thinly over a wide arc, issued frequent, confusing, and apparently contradictory orders to their subunits, and allowed them to become entrapped in secondary skirmishes. By the time his patrols reached the Rakowiec area, due west of Mokotów, it was midafternoon, the airdrome had just fallen, the Belweder perimeter had been truncated, and a link-up with it was no longer possible.[7]

In the Belweder palace, tension and irritability were mounting in proportion to the worsening of the military situation. President Wojciechowski, who had repeatedly manifested a determination to retain for himself direct supervision of military operations and immediate access to his generals—much to the annoyance of the constitutionally responsible Prime Minister Witos—had that morning "exiled" the civilian ministers to the upper floor of the Belweder and instructed the military on the ground floor to communicate with none but himself and—for form's sake—Witos.[8] Now, upon the fall of the Mokotów airdrome and the War Ministry building, with the failure of Żymierski to break through the Piłsudskist encirclement manifest and an attack on the Belweder itself imminent, Wojciechowski turned to his military staff for counsel. Haller, with the assent of Malczewski, Rozwadowski, and Anders, advised a withdrawal southward—the direction where the Piłsudskist net was still loosest—to Wilanów, the royal residence built by King John III Sobieski (reigned 1674–96) approximately five miles south of Warsaw. From there, contact with, or further retreat to, western Poland could be attempted. Major Porwit, however, believed that the hostile encirclement of the Belweder area was already too tight to permit withdrawal, and the unstable Malczewski now vacillated toward this view. Wojciechowski

[7] This account of Żymierski's movements on May 14 is based primarily on AKL, 14/3f, and on that of his fellow Belwederian general, S. Haller, pp. 58–63. Haller concedes (p. 63) that, though having originally great confidence in Żymierski, he began by early afternoon to suspect Żymierski's competence and good faith. Prime Minister Witos complained in his memoirs that the generals in the Belweder remained mindlessly optimistic about the prospects of Żymierski's arrival until long after such hopes had ceased to be warranted. See Witos, *Moje wspomnienia*, III, 106–8.

[8] Witos, *Woje wspomnienia*, III, 99, 105, and S. Haller, p. 53.

thereupon ordered that preparations be made to defend the Belweder to the last man.[9]

The Belweder being a nineteenth-century palace rather than an old castle, it had no prepared fortifications and provided only limited opportunities for improvising any. Furthermore, the cabinet demurred against what it regarded as Wojciechowski's exaggeratedly romantic and politically naïve responses. He seemed to be behaving less like a President confronting a grave state crisis than an old Socialist underground fighter (which he had once been) trapped in his hideout by the tsarist *okhrana.* He even went so far as to propose to the ministers that the army units be ordered to fight their way out of the Piłsudskist ring while the cabinet defend itself to the last man in the Belweder with a supply of revolvers which he had available.[10] It never came to any such drastic resort because the ministers' objections received support from Colonel Anders, who managed to persuade the President that withdrawal toward Wilanów was still practicable provided it be initiated immediately.

The evacuation of the Belweder took place between 3 and 4 o'clock in the afternoon. (The Piłsudskists were to enter the virtually deserted palace at approximately 5 P.M.) Wojciechowski was by then so annoyed with his senior generals, especially the hysterical Malczewski who attempted to surround the operation with all manner of histrionic mummery, that he placed the relatively junior Colonel Anders in charge.[11] Though wounded by a rifle bullet in the leg the previous evening, Anders, as Rozwadowski's chief of staff, had already been bearing the burden of *de facto* direction of the government forces throughout the day.[12] His energy and directness impressed a Wojciechowski weary of the mutual contradictions, professional jealousies, personal quirks, and mindless optimism of his senior generals.

While the withdrawal was not a panicky flight and although the retreating column managed to frighten off one hostile patrol which

[9] Particulars are in Comte, "Granaty nad Belwederem," No. 24, p. 11; S. Haller, pp. 63–65, who observes that Malczewski was by then thoroughly unnerved; and *Ilustrowany Kurjer Codzienny,* May 18, 1926. For Major Porwit's identity, see above, pp. 62–63.

[10] Morawski, "Przewrót majowy," p. 2.

[11] For details, see S. Haller, p. 67, and Comte, "Granaty nad Belwederem," No. 24, p. 11.

[12] Srokowski, p. 95.

stumbled upon it, the militarily destructive consequences of "order, counterorder, disorder" were incipiently in evidence. Most of the 10th Infantry Regiment was left behind and some units of the Infantry Officer School were cut off or got lost.[13] The ministerial automobiles, which would be indispensable in the event of a subsequent attempt at a dash into western Poland, were left behind, either because the Piłsudskists had sabotaged the tires or because the chauffeurs had deserted or because of panic or owing to patches of sandy road and potholes.[14] Nevertheless, by making an eastern detour around the suburban villages of Czerniaków and Służew—already occupied by Piłsudski's reinforcements from Wilno—the bulk of the government's forces, together with the President and the cabinet, managed to make their way by early evening to Wilanów. While some harassment by Piłsudski's paramilitary Riflemen during this retreat was a nuisance, a far more painful experience was to hear the sound of cannon fire from the west, where Żymierski's attack was being pounded to a halt in Rakowiec.[15] With the Piłsudskists holding Służew and Czerniaków between Rakowiec and Wilanów, this meant that the withdrawal had failed to bring the government into effective contact with its would-be reinforcements.

During the withdrawal, the cabinet—and particularly Prime Minister Witos—suffered a jarring psychological blow as three ministers surreptitiously forsook the retreating column and returned to Warsaw. Two of them, Józef Radwan (Land Reform) and Mieczysław Rybczyński (Public Works), were nonparty officials and could be forgiven by Witos for wanting to withdraw from the political crisis (even though Acting Foreign Minister Morawski disdained to resort to the same available pretext for opting out of continued involvement). The desertion of Railroad Minister Adam Chądzyński of the NPR, however, enraged Witos, who was already predisposed to suspect Chądzyński of bad faith because of the minister's earlier helpless and phlegmatic response to the illegal Piłsudskist troop movements of May 12. At that time Chądzyński had advised against dis-

---

[13] Jachieć, pp. 342–43, and Piątkowski, pp. 16–18.

[14] Dzendzel, p. 6; Witos, *Moje wspomnienia,* III, 110; Rzepecki, *Wspomnienia,* p. 36.

[15] Piątkowski, pp. 18–19, and Rzepecki, *Wspomnienia,* p. 36. The Belweder-Wilanów withdrawal is also described in Brudkowski, pp. 12–13.

connecting railroad switches and taking other technical measures to halt or delay the insurgent troops as futile. Now he left his Wilanów-bound colleagues and returned to Warsaw, where he was promptly captured by the Piłsudskists but was released the next day (May 15) upon the personal intervention of Piłsudski's commissar for rail-roads—and new prime minister—Kazimierz Bartel.[16]

At Wilanów an outward calm reigned and the sound of gunfire was at last hushed as the government and its military advisers discussed their next steps. The course of action which they eventually decided upon is known from the record of events, but the trend of their preceding discussion is rendered difficult to reconstruct by the fact that two of the key participants have left rather rancorous memoirs designed to demonstrate that the virtuous author-protagonist was forced by the weakness or cowardice of others into accepting a regrettable decision to surrender. Thus Haller argues that the heroic Belweder army was betrayed by a gang of spineless politicians determined on a shameful peace at the cost of honor, while Witos insists that his cabinet was deserted by a timorous Wojciechowski and misled by incompetent military advice. Morawski, alone of those participants who have published their recollections,[17] implies no particular righteous fortitude for himself but claims that the cabinet was stampeded into panic by a final message from Sikorski in Lwów, which allegedly arrived in the midst of the Wilanów deliberations, citing purported Ukrainian subversive ferment and Soviet troop movements as the reasons for Sikorski's failure to render aid to the government and implying that a continuation of the strife could have disastrous consequences in the borderlands and along the frontiers of eastern Poland.

Each of these accounts is valuable but must be examined carefully. Haller is correct on matters of sheer fact but obtuse in his unwilling-

[16] Witos, *Moje wspomnienia,* III, 96–97, 110, 112; *Kurjer Warszawski,* May 16, 1926. Chądzyński was one of Witos' holdovers from the preceding Skrzyński cabinet. As leader of the NPR, Chądzyński had a certain amount of influence upon Catholic workers in general. As minister of railroads since November 20, 1925, he had some standing with railroad employees in particular. Bartel's considerate treatment of him was probably an expression of the new regime's strong desire to liquidate the strike and the other sociopolitical manifestations of the crisis as quickly as possible.

[17] S. Haller, pp. 71–81; Witos, *Moje wspomnienia,* III, 110–16; Morawski, *Tamten brzeg,* pp. 154–55.

ness to consider seriously the politicians' appraisal of the possibly catastrophic political consequences of broadening the scope of military operations. Witos is justified in his complaint that the generals' blind optimism throughout the preceding two days had given the cabinet a false impression of the imminence of reinforcements and thus of victory. His attempt to portray Wojciechowski as having maneuvered a reluctant cabinet into premature resignation does not, on the other hand, ring true, and the chronological recital with which Witos seeks to buttress his account of what took place in Wilanów is factually erroneous and internally contradictory. Morawski rightly suggests that the overwhelming majority of the cabinet was skeptical of the utility of continuing the fight and worried lest it escalate into civil war and elicit foreign intervention. But, though he correctly summarizes the substance of Sikorski's report, he errs insidiously as regards its arrival time, for this Sikorski message, itemizing the alleged political and military dangers in the Lwów area, had been received in Warsaw the previous evening by air courier.[18] Sikorski's last report had been sent by radio on the morning of May 14 and it was now impossible for him to communicate with the utterly isolated Wilanów refugees. Thus, Morawski's depiction of Sikorski, whose failure to render effective assistance had indeed been a devastating blow, as the exclusive catalyst in the cabinet's loss of nerve is too pat and contrived. It was, after all, the government's responsibility to evaluate Sikorski's reports rather than to be panicked by them. To affix responsibility on him for this consequence is an inverted argument. Nevertheless, Morawski's rather laconic account is certainly correct in its larger claim that the Wilanów deliberations proceeded under a heavy weight of concern for the internal and external security— indeed, over the very survival—of the Polish state.

It is not, of course, surprising that the discussions held and the decisions taken at Wilanów during the evening of May 14 should have provoked frayed tempers into mutual animosities. After all, both the government and its generals had been toughly confident virtually throughout the entire course of the crisis, and when the

---

[18] See above, p. 106. Haller reports that this message of May 13 from Sikorski had been given to the cabinet at the time of its receipt. Wojciechowski's prohibition to the generals against communicating with the ministers (see above, p. 137) was not issued until May 14. S. Haller, pp. 45, 53.

realization of imminent defeat finally broke through their euphoria during the late afternoon of May 14 it hit with a shattering impact. To understand their bewildered sense of unexpected collapse, it is necessary to appreciate the sanguine assurance which had preceded it, and to convey an adequate impression of that earlier euphoria, it is necessary at this point to have recourse to the awkward but un-avoidable device of a brief flashback.

Wojciechowski's pugnacity, the generals' buoyancy, and the arrival of the first (and last) reinforcements at the Belweder early on May 13 had exerted a stiffening effect on the ministers, including Witos, whose original reluctance to fight and proneness to compromise were suspended by the prevailing and contagious optimism. On May 13 the cabinet had determined to prosecute the struggle *à outrance,* first from Warsaw and, should its position in the capital ultimately become untenable, then from loyal Poznań. To prepare for this turn of events, and as insurance against all negative eventualities, two ministers, Stefan Piechocki (Justice) and Stanisław Osiecki (Industry and Com-merce), were dispatched by plane to Poznań with plenipotentiary powers, including reserve authority to launch a general mobilization.[19]

Simultaneously with its resolution to fight on with utmost vigor, the Witos cabinet had decided upon a general proclamation to the public during the morning of May 13. Signed by every member of the cabinet, this statement began with the confident claim that those who had originally been stunned by the temporary initial success of the insurgents were now coming to recognize that legality and constitu-tionality must triumph over sedition and treason. The government of the Republic, headed by the President—the proclamation continued—was at its post and its strength was growing hourly as more military contingents manifested their loyalty to the Republic and fulfilled their soldierly honor. The insurgents, in order to excuse their shameful treachery, had not scrupled to invent the defamatory charge of a supposed attack by the government on the life of Piłsudski (a refer-ence to the fabricated night attack of May 11 on his Sulejówek home). But this would avail them little in the long run, for already many of those who had initially permitted themselves to be thus

[19] Witos, *Moje wspomnienia,* III, 102.

enticed into participation in this criminal revolt had become conscience-striken and had returned to fealty to the President of the Republic as the supreme chief of the armed forces of the state. The Belweder palace being currently the seat not only of the head of state but also of the government, it had become the symbol of the rule of law as well as of patriotic fidelity, and the nation's outstanding generals—here followed twelve names—had rallied to its defense against the rebellion. The proclamation concluded with an appeal to all citizens to rally to the President and to cooperate with the government in stifling a rebellion which, in provoking fratricidal strife, was declared to have endangered the existence and the future of the state.[20]

Breathing confidence, conveying an expectation of victory, exploiting to the maximum the argument of the government's legality, closely identifying the controversial cabinet with the suprapartisan President and the supposedly nonpolitical armed forces—indeed, with the State as such—this proclamation set the initial tone for a series of increasingly triumphant and tough statements broadcast to the army, the country, and the world by the Belwederian ministers and generals in the course of that day (May 13) of their military successes. In one of these, "Mister" (not "Marshal") Piłsudski's shameful revolt against the constitutional authorities was declared a tragic warning to future generations, an act exposing him as a hundredfold more dangerous to the Polish state than any external foe.[21] In another governmental statement of the evening of May 13, Piłsudski was denounced as a self-nominated dictator, acting from motives of purely personal power-hunger without any general political or social purposes whatsoever, who, in order to hide the utter political poverty of his completely groundless rebellion, had sought to provide himself with

---

[20] The text is reprinted in *Dokumenty chwili,* II, 7–8, and in Bojan-Błażewicz, pp. 16–17.

Piłsudski sought to exploit in his own interest the dubious associations of some of the generals listed in the proclamation as supporting the government. His headquarters issued a communiqué drawing attention to the fact that among them were men against whom heavy accusations of corrupt and criminal activity had been levied—a reference, presumably, to Rozwadowski, Zagórski, and Żymierski. The Piłsudskist communiqué is summarized in Bełcikowska, *Walki majowe,* p. 18.

[21] The text is reprinted in Karbowski, p. 341. Karbowski is under the erroneous impression that this statement was issued during the night of May 12, which cannot be because it also refers to some of the military developments of the afternoon of May 13.

some seeming legitimacy by spreading lying allegations of a supposed attempt on his own life and false claims of presidential sympathy with his perfidy, and whose appointment of "commissars" exposed his essentially Bolshevik style.[22] War Minister Malczewski also issued an appeal to the intermediate-rank and noncommissioned officers of the Piłsudski camp, intimating an amnesty for those who immediately abandoned Piłsudski and reverted to loyal obedience to the President of the Republic.[23] From Poznań, finally, the two ministers who had been sent there earlier in the day circulated an extremely belligerent notification to Polish diplomatic missions abroad, insisting that Piłsudski must henceforth be regarded and treated as an outlaw. This statement had actually been drafted for them by the Rightist Sejm deputy Stefan Dąbrowski who, over the past several years, had been using his powerful position on the Sejm's military affairs committee to block any army command organizational project that would have facilitated Piłsudski's return to active service. Now on May 13, 1926, armed with plenipotentiary powers from the cabinet, intoxicated by the vitriolically anti-Piłsudski atmosphere of Poznań, and confident that the impending defeat of Piłsudski's insurrection provided the opportunity once and for all to eliminate him from Polish public life, Piechocki and Osiecki dispatched Dąbrowski's blustering and abusive diatribe over the unauthorized signatures of Prime Minister Witos and Acting Foreign Minister Morawski, much to the latter's subsequent embarrassment.[24]

Pride goeth before a fall, and within a day of their robust claims and hard harangues the government and its generals found themselves defeated and isolated. Upon their arrival at Wilanów toward evening

[22] The text is in Witos, *Moje wspomnienia*, III, 102–3. The closing "commissar" allusion refers to Piłsudski's designating Bartel, Knoll, Sławoj-Składkowski, Romer, and Małachowski by that title. The allusion was a red herring, since the Polish title "Komisarz" is neutral and has no Bolshevik connotations. The reference to Wojciechowski pertains to the Piłsudskist insinuations that Wojciechowski wished to negotiate but was prevented from doing so by his belligerent Belweder entourage.

[23] The original is in AKL, 5/13. The text is reprinted in Witos, *Moje wspomnienia*, III, 103.

[24] Morawski, *Tamten brzeg*, pp. 160–63. Arski (p. 421) appears to have confused this document with the one cited in note 21 above.

on May 14, a preliminary, unofficial, but crucial cabinet meeting was called to examine what options for further action remained open.[25] President Wojciechowski attended and Generals Rozwadowski and Haller were invited to join Malczewski as spokesmen for the loyal army. The generals, still manifesting their resilient—indeed, their elastic—optimism, ardently urged immediate efforts to slip through the Piłsudskist encirclement in order to continue the struggle from a friendlier base than the Warsaw area. War Minister Malczewski proposed marching further southward in the direction of Dęblin, while Chief of the General Staff Haller recommended a westward breakout toward Poznań.[26] By this time, however, both Wojciechowski and Witos were satiated with the unreliable prognoses of the military men. The President irritably recalled their contradictory advice of that afternoon concerning the proposed evacuation of the Belweder area and objected to the proposed incognito flight by the Head of State through rebel lines inside his own country as mortifying. The Prime Minister, for his part, could neither forgive nor forget the generals' earlier unwarranted predictions of speedy victory and unfulfilled promises of an imminent arrival by Żymierski with reinforcements. Now, in Wilanów, Witos insisted that whether or not to continue the fight was a political, not a military, decision, to be taken by the government, not the generals.

In the political discussion which then ensued, Witos declared himself categorically against further fighting lest Poland be rent asunder in a civil war which might provoke insurrection by her refractory minorities and invite partition by her hostile neighbors. He was supported by the preponderant majority of his civilian ministers with the exception of the National Democrat Jerzy Zdziechowski (Finance), who argued that capitulation to Piłsudski was impermissible. Whether Zdziechowski seconded Haller's suggestion of withdrawal to Poznań

---

[25] The following résumé of the deliberations at Wilanów is collated from the sources cited in note 17 above.

[26] The officers—if not the noncoms—of the Dęblin garrison (15th Infantry Regiment), though located across the Vistula river on the edge of the generally pro-Piłsudski Lublin Military District, were loyal to the Wojciechowski-Witos government. Poznań was completely reliable but perhaps riskier to march toward at the time in view of the tighter Piłsudskist encirclement in that direction.

to continue the struggle or avoided committing himself to any definite course of action at all is in dispute.[27] Witos' Piast Peasant colleague Władysław Kiernik (Agriculture) apparently endorsed Zdziechowski's unwillingness to surrender but in a feeble and indecisive manner. National Democratic Minister of Education Stanisław Grabski, who had for many years championed a policy of Polonizing the minorities and restricting their national cultural development, now was particularly disturbed over the threat of uprisings by the Ukrainians, as reported earlier by Sikorski. He therefore endorsed Witos' view that the fighting must be halted to avert any such eventuality.[28] General Malczewski's final contribution to the discussion in his capacity as war minister was to fall to the floor in a loud weeping spell.

Toward 7:00 P.M., at the conclusion of one and one-half hours of discussion, the cabinet resolved to appeal for a cease-fire in order to preserve the essential unity of the nation and the army and thus to avert the ominous threats to the integrity of the state and its frontiers.[29] Wojciechowski, for his part, decided to resign the presidency, citing his current inability to execute effectively the functions of the office and his wish to avoid the humiliation of having to resume contacts with Piłsudski. An irreconcilable discrepancy over the causal interrelationship of these two decisions persists in the sources. General Haller presents the President's decision to resign as the consequence of the cabinet's cease-fire resolution—though he concedes that Wojciechowski regarded the latter as the only feasible course of action under the circumstances. Prime Minister Witos, on the other hand, accuses

[27] Morawski, *Tamten brzeg,* p. 154, versus S. Haller, p. 76.

[28] There was a report in the *Ilustrowany Kurjer Codzienny,* May 17, 1926, that Grabski had urged transfer of the government to Poznań to enable it to continue the struggle. This is directly contrary to the account of the eyewitness S. Haller (p. 76) and may be a case of confusing Grabski with Zdziechowski. Haller's recollections are supported by the (then) Piłsudskist publicist Mackiewicz, p. 174. Further information on the Grabski brothers will be found in the Biographical Register.

[29] This is the reason given in the official minutes of the meeting, published in Bełcikowska, *Walki majowe,* p. 41. There is no reason to doubt it, for it is also cited in S. Haller, p. 76, and Morawski, *Tamten brzeg,* pp. 154–55—both of whom were participants. Further confirmation is provided by Eugeniusz Romer (brother of the Lublin Military District commander, General Jan Romer), who interviewed members of the Wojciechowski-Witos government immediately after the coup and published his findings and reflections in *Rady i przestrogi, 1918–1938,* p. 45.

Wojciechowski of having bludgeoned into capitulation a cabinet ready to continue the struggle by summoning—as a preliminary to the cabinet's formal deliberations—Sejm Marshal Rataj from Warsaw to be on hand for any forthcoming resignations and to set armistice machinery into motion, and then, during the course of the discussion, by insisting on going through with his own previously expressed intention to resign and urging the cabinet to do likewise. While it is conceivable that Wojciechowski was by then ready to end his hitherto consistent belligerency and to acknowledge defeat, it is difficult to accept Witos' rather feebly advanced claim—flatly contradicted by all other sources—that a cabinet majority was ready and willing to continue resistance. Witos' rather confusing recital of the chronology of that evening's events casts further doubt on the accuracy of his memory.[30]

The cabinet's resolution to sue for a cease-fire and Wojciechowski's to resign his office having been taken in one sequence or another, the President insisted on personally informing General Kędzierski and Colonels Anders and Paszkiewicz—three of the Belwederians' immediate combat commanders. They deplored the decisions. Kędzierski intimated that Poznań might not accept them, while the two colonels argued that military honor forbade loyal officers to surrender to rebels. Wojciechowski, though appreciating these considerations, nevertheless maintained that Polish *raison d'état* required the immediate cessation of civil strife. He extracted their promise—which Anders initially hesitated to give—to abide by the coming cease-fire and not to renew hostilities except on the explicit orders of Sejm Marshal Rataj, upon whom presidential powers would shortly devolve as soon as Wojciechowski's resignation was officially tendered.[31]

[30] S. Haller, p. 77, versus Witos, *Moje wspomnienia*, III, 114–16. To cite but one example: Witos tells of President Wojciechowski's releasing the loyal army contingents from further obligations under their oath on page 111, that is, several pages *before* he narrates his version of the Wilanów cabinet deliberations. Thereby the unalert reader may be induced into thinking that Wojciechowski had forced the government into capitulation by first depriving it of its military arm.

[31] AKL, 14/3a, and S. Haller, pp. 77–78. General Kukiel was apparently overlooked in this presidential gesture of courtesy and gratitude to the Belwederians' combat commanders. Anders' initial recalcitrance in accepting the cease-fire is confirmed in Morawski, *Tamten brzeg*, p. 155, and Witos, *Moje wspomnienia*, III, 115.

The emissaries dispatched to contact Rataj in the Sejm building in Warsaw were the official presidential chaplain, Father Marian Tokarzewski, and the chief of the President's military chancellery, Major Kazimierz Mazanek. They bore a letter signed by Wojciechowski and Witos, dated 7:15 P.M., requesting Rataj's immediate presence in Wilanów to receive a declaration from Wojciechowski, to be made in the presence of the cabinet, the purpose of which would be to halt further bloodshed. An immediate cease-fire was also requested.[32] Upon receipt of this note at 10:00 P.M., Rataj reported its contents to Piłsudski, who promised to issue the appropriate instructions for a cease-fire to his units immediately.[33] Then, toward midnight, Rataj appeared in Wilanów, accompanied by Piłsudski's troubleshooter (and Orlicz-Dreszer's assistant), Lieutenant Colonel Józef Beck. Witos lamely insists that these developments in no way prejudiced his cabinet's continued existence or compromised its freedom of action since he had so far merely countersigned a presidential letter in which a desire for a purely military cease-fire was indicated.[34] This pretended naïveté, however, is quite unconvincing, for the decisive political point-of-no-return had been passed and the inevitable denouement of the cabinet's own resignation now followed at an anticlimactic second, formal cabinet session from which the military was excluded. Three documents were then handed to Rataj: (1) Wojciechowski's letter of resignation, which simply alluded to a situation rendering impossible the fulfillment of his oath of office and cited Article 40 of the constitution, according to which a resigning president's powers devolve upon the marshal of the Sejm pending the election of a successor; (2) a one-sentence letter of resignation signed by Witos on behalf of his entire cabinet; (3) the minutes of the recent cabinet discussions.[35]

In his new capacity as acting president, Rataj accepted the cabinet's resignation without requesting the ministers to remain at their

[32] For the text of this note, see Witos, *Moje wspomnienia*, III, 114.
[33] Bełcikowska, *Walki majowe*, p. 40.
[34] Witos, *Moje wspomnienia*, III, 114.
[35] The official minutes as published in Bełcikowska, *Walki majowe*, p. 41, telescope the decisions taken at the two cabinet sessions into one protocol. All resolutions are there represented as having been adopted unanimously, and no clue is given as to the tenor of the preceding discussion. The protocol has recently been reprinted in Czubiński, "Przewrót majowy," p. 133, and in Zakrzewska, pp. 35–36.

posts on a caretaker basis (as was the custom after "ordinary" cabinet crises). He then summoned Generals Malczewski, Rozwadowski, and Haller, thanked them for having defended the legal government, and ordered a cessation of all further military action.[36] Rataj, who had originally sharply opposed Witos' formation of the Right-Center cabinet as dangerously provocative given the prevailing political situation, now avoided all recrimination and even gave an impression of sympathizing with what was, after all, a legal government overthrown by force. Apparently convinced from the beginning that Piłsudski would eventually triumph, he had deliberately remained outwardly neutral in order to be available as an intermediary at the fighting's end.[37] Upon his return to Warsaw in the early hours of May 15, Rataj first conferred with representatives of various political parties and presently issued a press communiqué announcing the Wilanów resignations, his own assumption of presidential functions, and his expectation of immediate consultations with Piłsudski.[38] This last reference unveiled the real power constellation in Warsaw: Rataj's authority was legal and formal; Piłsudski's power was military and political. Indeed, Piłsudski's headquarters went so far as to issue an announcement at dawn on May 15, just before Rataj's press communiqué, making the technically false but politically revealing claim that Wojciechowski had signed his presidential powers over to Piłsudski, recognizing him as uniquely suitable and qualified to rule Poland. The dissolved Witos government would be replaced by a new one, composed of honorable and worthy people, on whose composition Piłsudski was working with Rataj. Meanwhile—the statement concluded—Piłsudski had ordered all army units to observe a cease-fire pending their return to garri-

[36] S. Haller, p. 83.

[37] For Rataj's earlier mediation mission during the evening of May 12, see above, p. 68. His opposition to Witos' acceptance of the premiership is expressed in his own diary, pp. 361–63, and in the memoirs of Witos' secretary Dzendzel, p. 5. For his apparent sympathy with the plight of the Belwederians in their final extremity, see Morawski, *Tamten brzeg,* p. 155. Years later, after Poland's defeat in September, 1939, Rataj claimed that, though in 1926 he had made himself available to mediate Piłsudski's assumption of power, he had already suspected him of having no clear idea of how to use it. At the time of this reminiscence, Rataj was bitterly holding Piłsudski responsible for Poland's recent disaster. See S. Korboński, *W Imieniu Rzeczypospolitej* (Paris, 1954), p. 13.

[38] *Dokumenty chwili,* I, 27. Rataj's communiqué was issued at 6:15 A.M., May 15.

son.[39] Since such an announcement would scarcely have been issued by his headquarters unless it conformed to Piłsudski's general view of the situation, it indicates that, though prepared to accept such legal niceties as acknowledging Rataj's formal role of acting president, he was determined to retain in his own hands effective control over political developments and military dispositions.

At Wilanów, meanwhile, the Witos cabinet was placed in temporary protective custody, to guard its members from hostile civilians and paramilitary mobs coming from the direction of Warsaw. President Wojciechowski, however, was permitted to leave for Spała (where his family was) during the morning of May 15. Before departing, Wojciechowski issued a farewell message of gratitude to all officers and men who, during the recent days, had remained loyal to the Republic. He also expressed particularly warm personal thanks to Major Porwit, who had first stood by him to bar Piłsudski's way at the Poniatowski bridge three long days earlier.[40]

Still before Wojciechowski's departure, there arrived in Wilanów at approximately 8:00 A.M. a Major Witold Morawski (a cousin of the acting foreign minister). He had driven through the Piłsudskist lines from Ożarów, the suburban station nine miles west of Warsaw, to report to President Wojciechowski—of whose resignation he had not heard—that powerful reinforcements assembled there from western Poland were ready to go into action at the behest of the legal government. Close on Morawski's heels, and giving emphasis to his report, came a cavalry squadron from one of these Ożarów units (the 15th Uhlan Regiment from Poznań).[41] The situation at Ożarów was as follows: Throughout the previous day and night (May 14), the railroad strike had forced the detraining there of further massive reinforcements coming to the rescue of the Wojciechowski-Witos government from the military districts of Poznań and Toruń. The Poznanian regiments were commanded by General Stanisław Taczak, the Pomer-

---

[39] The statement was signed by Piłsudski's chief of the General Staff, Burhardt-Bukacki, and published in *Dokumenty chwili,* I, 26. It was issued at 5:40 A.M. The original draft is in AKL, 5/60.

[40] Rzepecki, *Wspomnienia,* p. 38. The Witos cabinet members were released from internment at Wilanów during the afternoon of May 16.

[41] AKL, 14/3a, and S. Haller, p. 84. Further information on Morawski will be found in the Biographical Register.

anian (Toruń) ones by General Kazimierz Ładoś, who, as senior officer, took over control of the whole Ożarów group as well as Żymierski's units, whom the Piłsudskists had beaten back that afternoon at Rakowiec. In addition to the three regiments with Żymierski, Ładoś disposed of four infantry, two cavalry, and one field artillery regiment, one horse artillery battery, and some armored cars at Ożarów—a grand total of over eight thousand men.[42] It is therefore not surprising that the still belligerent senior Belwederian generals, now in Wilanów with the approximately two thousand troops remaining since the retreat from Warsaw, should have viewed the information brought them by Major Morawski early on May 15 as creating an entirely new situation. Their itch to renew the fight was only whetted when, almost immediately after the arrival of the cavalry squadron which followed Morawski, several Piłsudskist artillery shells were fired on Wilanów—either in error or as a warning—and Piłsudskist cavalry was observed sealing closed the southern gap in the ring of encirclement around Wilanów.[43]

Wojciechowski being now a private individual without public authority and the Witos cabinet having resigned, General Rozwadowski, as the senior among all the anti-Piłsudski generals, took charge. He sent Morawski back toward Ożarów with instructions to Ładoś to march southeastward toward the Wilanów contingents. Simultaneously he ordered the units at Wilanów to prepare to break out of the Piłsudskist ring in a northwesterly direction for a link-up with the Ożarów group. Such marches, even if intended only as preparatory maneuvers into stronger positions, were obviously bound to provoke renewed hostilities with the Piłsudskist forces lying between Ożarów and Wilanów. Rozwadowski was ready, perhaps even eager, to run this risk. It was averted by the purposive and accidental actions of

---

[42] The units with Żymierski were the 56th and 68th Infantry Regiments from Krotoszyn and Września and the 14th Field Artillery from Poznań. Also now at Ożarów were the 61st Regiment from Bydgoszcz, the 64th from Grudziądz, the 67th from Brodnica, and the 69th from Gniezno—all infantry—the 15th and 17th Uhlan (cavalry) Regiments from Poznań and Leszno, the 17th Field Artillery Regiment from Gniezno, and a battery of the 7th Horse Artillery and some armored cars from Poznań. Exhaustive details are in the official reports of Ładoś and Taczak and their unit commanders in AKL, 15/4–9 and 14/3b–3j, 4, 5.

[43] Kędzierski in AKL, 14/3a; Rzepecki, *Wspomnienia*, pp. 37–38. One uhlan was killed and several were wounded by the artillery.

others. First of all, General Kędzierski and the junior officers of the Cadet Corps (to the evident satisfaction of their commander, Colonel Paszkiewicz) refused to obey Rozwadowski on the ground that his orders were rendered illegal by Acting President Rataj's earlier command to cease all further military action.[44] Then Witos, although no longer having any official authority, also pleaded against flouting Rataj and the constitution—in the name of which, after all, the Belwederians had fought their three-day battle.[45] Rozwadowski thereupon desisted and sent a message to Rataj informing him of the availability of the Ożarów group, hoping that it would at least strengthen Rataj's hand in his political negotiations with Piłsudski even if it had come too late to turn the balance toward a military defeat of Piłsudski. Major Morawski, finally, was captured by the Piłsudskists on his way back to Ożarów, thus preventing Rozwadowski's orders from reaching Ładoś. Meanwhile, Piłsudski had sent an emissary to Ładoś that morning to inform him of Wojciechowski's resignation and the conclusion of a cease-fire. Ładoś had agreed to maintain a temporary truce while he sent one of his officers to Warsaw to be shown the appropriate documents by Rataj and confirm their validity. Shortly after noon this was accomplished, and Ładoś thereupon promptly put his units at Rataj's disposal and obeyed the Acting President's order against further military activities. Simultaneously, General Szeptycki, coordinator of the transportation of reinforcements to the legal government from southern and western Poland, halted all his activities and units.[46] The military combat phase of the coup d'état was finished.[47]

[44] Kędzierski in AKL, 14/3a; Mercik, pp. 110–11; and Piątkowski, p. 20. Mercik, then a captain, was the instigator of this "legal mutiny" of the younger officers. Rozwadowski's controversial orders to Ładoś and Kędzierski are in AKL, 5/14 and 14/3a.

[45] Morawski, *Tamten brzeg,* p. 157.

[46] S. Haller, pp. 87–89. Thanks to the railroad strike and the earlier delays at Częstochowa, none of the units forwarded by Szeptycki had gotten closer to Warsaw than Piotrków—still eighty miles southwest of the capital.

[47] Casualty estimates for the three days of fighting varied widely and wildly. The official Warsaw municipal statistics, compiled from reports by the army, hospitals, and cemeteries, numbered 371 killed and 918 wounded (among whom were, respectively, 176 and 313 civilians). *Kronika Warszawy,* II, No. 5 (May, 1926), 89. Extensive damage had been inflicted on the façades of buildings in the combat zone and paving blocks and trolley rails had been torn up for barricades.

A number of politico-military problems remain to be considered. It seems appropriate at this point to draw attention to the fact that Ładoś' preparations to bring his Ożarów group into the battle had been extraordinarily deliberate and slow, given the imperative need for speed if the government was still to be rescued. While every minute counted, the evening and night of May 14 had passed without any attempt to strike from Ożarów toward Warsaw or Wilanów. Indeed, Ładoś was not planning to throw his troops into action before midafternoon on May 15.[48] It may be that objective difficulties accounted for this slow pace. It may also be that Ładoś saw the political handwriting on the wall, plausibly concluded that the railroad and general strike ensured Piłsudski's imminent victory, and decided that vigorous military intervention by the Ożarów contingent would only needlessly prolong the bloodshed without altering the outcome. Although he was one of the higher ex-Austrian officers in the Polish army and therefore presumably without any particular sympathies toward Piłsudski, Ładoś may have been blessed with greater political subtlety than Rozwadowski, Malczewski, *et al.* and have deliberately acted so as to abbreviate rather than extend the civil strife.[49]

Given the decisive role of the railroad strike, one may well ask if the Belwederians could have at any time avoided or trumped its impact. Two alternative options suggest themselves. Had the government evacuated exposed and hostile Warsaw—so obviously the target of Piłsudski's conspiratorial preparations and so vulnerable to a blockade—at the moment of the outbreak of the coup on May 12 and withdrawn to the friendly hinterland of Poznań, it not only would

[48] Czubiński, "Wielkopolska i Pomorze wobec zamachu stanu w maju 1926 r.," p. 177.
[49] This conjecture was endorsed by the late Dr. Otton Pehr, a former PPS leader in Pomerania and Ładoś' neighbor in the town of Grudziądz. Interviewed in New York on July 16, 1963, Dr. Pehr said that General Ładoś had confided to him afterward that he (Ładoś) had been reluctant to rekindle the obviously dying flames of battle during the last hours of the coup. Nevertheless, Ładoś was retired a year after the coup, in May, 1927, at the early age of fifty. The other senior officer commanding the "western" regiments at Ożarów on May 15, Taczak, was one of the few Polish generals to have emerged from the imperial German army, in which he had been a major. In December, 1918–January, 1919, he had been the first commander in the uprising of the Poznanian Poles against the Germans. After the 1926 coup he was appointed commander of the Lublin Military District in November, 1928, but was on the retired list by 1930.

have escaped the isolating effect of the railroad strike but it could also have gone on to conduct extended resistance, accumulate massive resources for a counterattack, and perhaps capitalize on the growing advantage of its legality. Against this prognosis, however, must be weighed the negative and possibly fatal consequences of abandoning the capital to such a politically prestigious rebel as Piłsudski. Alternatively, if the Belwederian forces could have sustained the momentum of their advance on May 13 in Warsaw and either captured or killed Piłsudski while his initial stroke was still temporarily blunted and while they still held major sections of the capital, the railroad strike might have been rendered irrelevant. As events turned out, it ensured Piłsudski's military victory. The question henceforth was to be what he would do with the political power this victory now gave him.

PART THREE

THE ATTEMPTED
CONSOLIDATION AND
LEGITIMATION
OF POWER

CHAPTER IX

MODERATION AT THE CENTER, PACIFICATION IN THE PERIPHERIES

Since both sides in the coup were ultimately concerned for the survival, safety, and integrity of Poland, each had acted so as to contain the level of violence, avert a drift toward civil war, and avoid foreign intervention. Piłsudski and Witos, though now utterly repugnant to each other, were equally appalled at the specter of the Warsaw clashes getting out of control and provoking the disintegration of the restored Polish state. From the beginning Witos had sought to avoid an armed clash. By May 14 and 15 in Wilanów, even the originally belligerent Wojciechowski and the more astute among the military had come to agree with him that those righteously fanatical officers who were prepared to run the risks of extending or renewing the violence must be overruled. Piłsudski, for his part, after his desperate efforts at mediation had to be abandoned and he temporarily lost personal control of the fast-moving developments which enveloped the coup, still remained shrewdly careful to limit the destructiveness and the duration of military activities as well as the politico-social violence which he was prepared to permit his supporters. Hence his ultimate determination to close the coup in a series of short, sharp engagements on May 14, lest—through delay—it extend itself. Hence, also, his sabotage of attempts at *armed* Socialist (or other Leftist) participation in the fighting. The same concern to avoid unnecessary physical destruction and hence political embitterment accounts for Piłsudski's deliberate limitation on the use of artillery (of which he had an adequate supply by May 14) by his forces. Indeed, throughout the three days of fighting his officers were constrained to hold all casualties—their own, the foe's, the Warsaw population's—to a minimum.[1] That even at the height of battle and on the threshold of victory he anticipated utilizing Rataj as an intermediary to "legalize" the coup rather than concluding it with an establishment of his own overt dictatorship is indicated by Piłsudski's stern reprimand to Orlicz-Dreszer, his right hand, when some of the latter's troops violated the "extraterritorial" immunity of the Sejm building's (that is, Rataj's) precincts during the morning of May 14.[2]

It would, however, be a profound error to misinterpret Piłsudski's desire initially to avoid and then to limit armed hostilities as indicating any reticence to assert decisive political power in Poland. The difficulty was that his vision of the nation's problems and destiny required that this power of his be both legal and ultimate. If Piłsudski was now prepared to accept and even to welcome Rataj's intercession to end the fighting, he was nevertheless determined to assert his own control over subsequent developments. If he acknowledged such constitutional proprieties as Rataj's role of acting president and, subsequently, the legislative sovereignty of the Sejm, it was because he expected them to screen and to facilitate rather than to frustrate or to limit his own power and also to serve him as legal blocks against a real revolution. The failure of contemporary politicians to appreciate this ambivalence of Piłsudski's apparent respect for public institutions as formal, legal entities, combined with his simultaneous intolerance of their politico-institutional restraints on his own power, was to result in four years of mutual exasperation until an embittered and exhausted Piłsudski eventually moved toward a more overt form of authoritarianism in 1930.

The first now to be painfully taught (or retaught) this lesson of Piłsudski's political style was Rataj, who, as a leading personality in the Piast Peasant Party and as marshal of the Sejm, had hitherto been one of the pivotal political figures of Poland with every prospect and

[1] The Piłsudskists had initially lobbed some shells at the Belweder palace and courtyard but had then desisted on Piłsudski's personal orders. They had also directed some horse artillery fire at the Superior War Academy building, which had to be taken before they could capture the Mokotów airdrome on May 14. Karbowski, p. 358, and Czarkowski-Golejewski, p. 1. For Piłsudski's concern to hold all casualties to a minimum, see Strumph-Wojtkiewicz *et al.*, p. 72.

[2] See Benedykt, p. 1. The troops had not entered the Sejm building itself but only the grounds of its enclosure. Piłsudski nevertheless had them withdrawn, rebuked Orlicz-Dreszer, and tendered an apology to Rataj.

expectation of ever-increasing power and influence.[3] Accordingly, when the coup transferred the dignity of the acting presidency onto his shoulders during the night of May 14, Rataj initially appeared to have thought of himself as a pillar rather than a funnel of power in Poland.

On his predawn return to Warsaw from Wilanów on May 15 with the Wojciechowski and Witos resignations in his pocket, Rataj had conferred with representatives of various political parties. Unable to contact the National Democratic leader, Stanisław Głąbiński, he had nevertheless consulted a Piast Peasant leader (and vice-marshal of the Sejm), Jan Dębski; the vice-chairman of the PPS parliamentary club, Mieczysław Niedziałkowski; and the leader of the Klub Praca (and Piłsudski's recently designated commissar for railroads), Kazimierz Bartel. Dębski, it will be recalled, had been one of several politicians invited by Wojciechowski to try to form a cabinet during the post-Skrzyński interlude of May 5–10 and had then, upon the outbreak of the coup on May 12, attempted an abortive mediation mission via the PPS. Niedziałkowski had been one of the Left-bloc leaders who had made a vain effort during that same evening of May 12 to get through to President Wojciechowski in order to urge him to avert an explosion by dismissing Witos. Bartel, finally, had been studying the country's problems and preparing himself for the premiership ever since Piłsudski urged this course on him in September, 1925.[4] Now, during the early hours of May 15, Rataj informed Bartel that he intended to authorize Dębski to form a broadly based "government of national reconciliation"—an intention which Rataj tried to transform into a *fait accompli* by "leaking" it to the press.[5] Perhaps Rataj hoped that Dębski's wartime service in the Legions and the POW would now render him acceptable to Piłsudski despite his current prominent position in Witos' party. Bartel, instead of remonstrating, simply reported this development to Piłsudski at 8:00 A.M.[6]

[3] See Singer, pp. 43–46.

[4] Further information on Dębski, Niedziałkowski, and Bartel will be found in the Biographical Register. On Bartel, see also note 10 below.

[5] *Ilustrowany Kurjer Codzienny,* May 17, 1926.

[6] W. Grzybowski, "Premier Kazimierz Bartel," p. 104. Dębski might also have been presumed to be *persona grata* to Piłsudski for having introduced in 1923 the parliamentary resolution that Piłsudski had served the nation well. See above, p. 13.

Half an hour later Piłsudski, who was in any event scheduled to confer with Rataj, appeared at the Sejm building. Preoccupied with worry that the Poznanian and Pomeranian army units to the west of Warsaw might still attack him after all, and impatient at being expected at this juncture to concern himself with politico-administrative questions, Piłsudski simply demanded that Bartel be named prime minister. Rataj acceded. An experienced and sophisticated political tactician, Rataj was stunned and somewhat frightened at the incongruity of Piłsudski's implicit expectation of having decisive power and his simultaneous irritation with administrative and personnel issues—matters which, Rataj knew, were the mortar and brick of political power.[7] Rataj, nevertheless, not only bowed to Piłsudski's wish to have Bartel named premier but also yielded to Niedziałkowski's demand, expressed as a condition of PPS toleration (the railroad and general strike was still in force and was not revoked till later in the day), that, in place of Rataj's desired broad government of reconciliation, the entire Right, as well as the NPR, be excluded from Bartel's victory cabinet.[8] To the enraged consternation of the political Right and the Belwederian generals,[9] Rataj made no attempt to use Ładoś' powerful Ożarów army group as a bargaining lever. From this day onward his power waned irretrievably. Rataj ceased personally to be a crucial figure, his Piast Peasant Party lost its pivotal political position, and the Sejm over which he presided declined in institutional power in relation to the cabinets and to Piłsudski.

Ironically, it was now Bartel who, despite his extensive preparations for the post, refused to accept the premiership unless Piłsudski joined him in an overt, explicit official capacity. Perhaps he, too, was con-

[7] See W. Grzybowski, "Spotkania i rozmowy z Józefem Piłsudskim," p. 94. Piłsudski himself, sedulous to foster an impression of utter legality and propriety, was subsequently to insist—wrongly—that Rataj had acted on his own, unpressured free will in appointing Bartel. See his interview in the *Kurjer Poranny* of May 25, 1926, reprinted in Piłsudski, *PZ*, IX, 17.

[8] *Ilustrowany Kurjer Codzienny*, May 17, 1926.

[9] For example, S. Haller, p. 89. In subsequent weeks, the Right reproached Rataj so fiercely for having allegedly betrayed it that on June 18 he resigned as marshal of the Sejm in protest. He was reelected a few days later, after three ballots, by 176 Left and Center votes over 128 for the National Democratic leader, Głąbiński. For details, see *Frankfurter Zeitung*, June 19, 1926; Rataj, pp.373–75; and Malicki, pp. 317–19. Further information on Rataj will be found in the Biographical Register.

cerned over Piłsudski's romantically cavalier indifference to the pro-saic structural aspects of government and was fearful that Piłsudski would leave him in the lurch and withdraw into a veiled, irresponsible, ostensibly "purely military" but actually all-powerful strong-man role. Piłsudski relented, agreeing to become Bartel's war minister.[10] The public and the politicians expected that this was but preliminary to Piłsudski's eventual election as president and hence to official, in-stitutional responsibility for guiding Poland's destiny.

Bartel thereupon accepted the premiership on the understanding—shared by Piłsudski and Rataj—that his cabinet would serve until the National Assembly's pending election of a new president. While the Socialists demanded the exclusion of the Right, the National Democrats resolved, in any event, to have nothing to do with the new cabinet and thus to oblige those who had launched the coup d'état to accept sole responsibility for settling it.[11] Bartel decided to avoid the twin dangers of appearing to depend on the Left and of needlessly exacerbating the Right by forming a nonpartisan cabinet of experts and technicians, which would have been his and Piłsudski's preference even without these disparate pressures of the parties. Having given much thought to the problem over the past eight months, Bartel had a cabinet list ready to present to Rataj by 7:00 P.M. that evening when he, Piłsudski, and Piłsudski's intimate con-fidant, Bogusław Miedziński, called on the Acting President, who had meanwhile spent the day informing representatives of various political parties of current developments.[12]

[10] W. Grzybowski, "Spotkania i rozmowy z Józefem Piłsudskim," p. 94. Piłsudski indirectly and cryptically confirmed this version of what happened in his interview in the *Kurjer Poranny* of May 25, 1926, reprinted in his *PZ,* IX, 17.

Bartel, an autodidact, had raised himself from locksmith to university pro-fessor (of descriptive geometry at the Lwów Polytechnic). He had impressed Piłsudski as minister of railroads during the Polish-Soviet campaign of 1920. Elected to the Sejm in 1922 on the label of the Wyzwolenie Peasant Party, he had split away from Wyzwolenie in April, 1925, to found the ten-member Klub Praca, which soon came to enjoy Piłsudski's patronage. Between May, 1926, and March, 1930, Bartel was to be prime minister five times. He gave his name to a style of government, the *bartlowanie,* characterized by elastic stubbornness and the avoidance of a definitive deadlock in dealing with the Sejm. Further information on him will be found in the Biographical Register.

[11] This resolution is reprinted in *Dokumenty chwili,* I, 31.

[12] *Ibid.,* I, 28 and 31.

Bartel supplemented his authority as prime minister by retaining for himself the Railroad Ministry, which was his own specialty and currently particularly important in view of recent developments. In addition to Piłsudski as war minister, the cabinet consisted of General Kazimierz Młodzianowski as minister of the interior, the civil servant Gabriel Czechowicz as finance minister, the Warsaw University law professor Wacław Makowski as minister of justice, the mining engineer, economist, and civil servant Hipolit Gliwic as minister of industry and commerce, the Warsaw Polytechnic professor Witold Broniewski as minister of public works, and the civil servant Stanisław Jurkiewicz as minister of labor and welfare. In addition, the following were named acting ministers: The diplomat August Zaleski—foreign affairs; Professor Józef Mikułowski-Pomorski—education; Dr. Józef Raczyński (a civil servant)—agriculture and land reform.

A number of considerations are suggested by the nomination of these men. They combined considerable political experience with nonaffiliation to the parliamentary parties. Młodzianowski (the interior), an earlier commandant of the Cadet Corps and lately *wojewoda* of Polesie province, may have been selected to mollify the former, which had been the backbone of the Belwederians in the recent combat, and to control the possibly restive Ukrainian and White Russian minorities, with whom he had presumably become familiar during his recent service in the east. As a veteran of the First Legion Brigade, he also enjoyed Piłsudski's confidence. Czechowicz (finance), hitherto an undersecretary in his ministry, had opposed Zdziechowski's pre-coup deflationary financial policies and was expected (erroneously, as it turned out) to pursue a more adventurous, "Leftist" fiscal course.[13] It may therefore have been an intentional desire to achieve a cabinet balance on economic matters that motivated the appointment of Gliwic (industry and commerce), formerly commercial counselor and chargé d'affaires at the Polish legation in Washington, D.C., a man with good Anglo-American business contacts as well as close connections to Polish mining and metallurgical industrial circles and—perhaps therefore—with ready access to

---

[13] Daszyński, *W pierwszą rocznicę,* p. 33. See also Z. Landau, "Wpływ zamachu majowego na gospodarkę polską," p. 508. For the subsequently notorious "Czechowicz affair" of 1928–29, see below, pp. 333–39.

Piłsudski.[14] Similarly, Raczyński (agriculture and land reform), though also a civil servant and now holding his portfolio only on an "acting" basis, was reputedly on good terms with the large landowners, which was quite in conformity with Piłsudski's own current desire to attract to his side this supposedly "state-building" stratum of the nation.[15]

Zaleski's appointment to the Foreign Ministry elicited considerable surprise, for the general press speculation had been that Skrzyński would resume his tenure of that portfolio. But while Skrzyński's former skillful conduct of Polish foreign policy had elicited the esteem of European diplomats and the respect of the Polish Left, he had aroused Piłsudski's wrath by affiliating Poland to the Locarno Treaties system (October, 1925), which Piłsudski regarded as a spineless accommodation to France's betrayal of her Polish ally.[16] That Bartel did not share Piłsudski's tendency to take his frustration over Locarno out on Skrzyński is indicated by reports that Skrzyński had, in fact, initially been offered his old portfolio in Bartel's new cabinet but had declined.[17] Regardless of whether it was a veto by Piłsudski or a refusal by Skrzyński (or both) that accounted for the latter's failure to be in the cabinet, there is no doubt that Zaleski was more *persona*

[14] Between 1923 and 1926 Gliwic had been received several times by the ostensibly retired Piłsudski in Sulejówek—an unusual distinction. These visits occurred during Gliwic's home visits from Washington and after his permanent return to Poland in 1925 to become director of the Commercial Section of the Ministry of Commerce and Industry. For details, see *Ilustrowany Kurjer Codzienny*, June 4, 1926; Dawson, p. 590; Górnicki, "Ostatni rokosz w Warszawie," No. 20, p. 8.

[15] Czubiński, "Przewrót majowy," p. 144.

[16] Piłsudski, *PZ*, VIII, 293, and Beck, p. 268. In retrospect, Piłsudski's reaction to Locarno, though understandable, appears too irascible. While Locarno—with its failure to provide the same international guarantees for the Polish-German as for the Belgian-German and Franco-German frontiers—was indeed an unhappy development for Poland, Piłsudski failed to appreciate that her diplomatic isolation would have been even more acute had Skrzyński simply boycotted the conference. The over-all relevance of Piłsudski's coup to Polish foreign policy is discussed below, chapter XVI.

For Polish press speculation on the morrow of the coup that the foreign affairs portfolio would again revert to Skrzyński, see, for example, *Ilustrowany Kurjer Codzienny*, May 17, 1926, and *Dokumenty chwili*, I, 29.

[17] Smogorzewski, *La Pologne restaurée*, p. 310; Lapter, p. 64; and Morawski, *Tamten brzeg*, p. 157. Interviewed by the *Ilustrowany Kurjer Codzienny*, May 18, 1926, Bartel alluded vaguely to the allegedly poor state of Skrzyński's nerves as making it impossible for him to accept a portfolio. Skrzyński was to die in an auto accident on September 25, 1931.

grata to Piłsudski, for he, too, had been critical of Locarno.[18] He possessed the additional virtue of being personally well acquainted with Great Britain since his residence there as a propagandist for the Polish cause during World War I—and Britain's attitude would manifestly be a crucial factor for Poland's international security in view of the increasingly uncertain state of the Franco-Polish alliance. Nevertheless, Zaleski was initially given his portfolio only on an "acting" basis (until June 25, when it was regularized), suggesting that Bartel may still have hoped to keep the door open for his eventual replacement by Skrzyński, who was, after all, also a protagonist of firmer Anglo-Polish relations, or that Piłsudski was awaiting a suitable opportunity to confer this portfolio on someone else altogether, someone who could bring in extensive political support or be particularly suitable in initiating a *détente* with Germany.[19]

As for the new war minister, Piłsudski's induction into that office marked the first time that he had taken an oath of loyalty to the constitution of March 17, 1921, which had not yet existed when he had become head of the restored Polish state at the conclusion of World War I. To a legal fetishist of his type, a man of greater respect for the forms and sources of law than for its spirit and substance, this proved to be an important psychological and therefore ultimately political limitation on his future momentum toward eliminating the parliamentary structure authorized by that constitution.

In sum, the Bartel cabinet was a nonpolitical but centrist one, characterized by a bias toward the intelligentsia and the technocratic elite. Besides Piłsudski, who was *sui generis,* it consisted of four professors of more or less technical subjects (Bartel, Makowski, Broniewski, and Mikułowski-Pomorski), an army officer with civil-administrative experience (Młodzianowski), and five veteran bureaucrats (Czechowicz, Gliwic, Jurkiewicz, Zaleski, and Raczyński). Four among them (Bartel, Makowski, Raczyński, and Mikułowski-Pomor-

18 Singer, p. 98; Krasuski, p. 42.

19 The name of Prince Janusz Radziwiłł was apparently under consideration in this connection. See Laroche, p. 47. Ironically, Zaleski happened to be in Warsaw during the May crisis because he was in the process of being transferred as envoy from Rome to Tokyo. This was something of a demotion, and it may have been provoked either by the National Democrats (as claimed in Singer, p. 98) or by Skrzyński (as suggested in Morawski, *Tamten brzeg,* p. 160). Both explanations are plausible. Though Skrzyński and Zaleski did not care much for each other, they were both in the bad graces of the Right.

ski) had held cabinet rank on previous occasions when technical expertise had been needed—not counting Piłsudski's earlier service as chief of state and commander in chief. Though this was certainly not the cabinet of reconciliation among the parties which Rataj had desired, even less did it fulfill the Socialists' hopes for a victory cabinet of the Left. With the exception of Piłsudski and Czechowicz, there was no one in it to alarm the propertied classes, and even in the case of these two, the fears of social and economic radicalism which they originally inspired were quickly to be proved unjustified.[20]

The Socialists and the two peasant parties of the Left bloc had vainly sought to apply pressure on Bartel through a series of similarly phrased resolutions adopted at various party conferences in the course of the afternoon of May 15. They demanded the immediate dissolution of the Right and Center-dominated Sejm (elected in 1922 and indeed no longer representative of public opinion), the elevation of Piłsudski to the presidency, the formation of a worker-peasant cabinet, fundamental improvements in policies toward the ethnic minorities, and the punishment of a number of ministers in previous cabinets who were alleged to have embezzled public funds.[21] The PPS resolution, adopted at a joint session of the Party's Central Executive Committee and its parliamentary delegation, also pointedly thanked the working class for having ensured Piłsudski's recent victory and requested that it remain alert to further appeals of the Party, for the struggle against reaction was not yet definitively won. The resolutions of the Wyzwolenie Peasant Party and of the Stronnictwo Chłopskie both contained additional demands for land reform— the latter specifying that there be no compensation to previous owners. Wyzwolenie explicitly threatened to withold support from any government other than one of a "distinctly Leftist and socially radical character." Of the four parties which had formed the Left

---

[20] For the dates of the previous cabinet service of some of the members, see Markert, ed., pp. 673–76. The subsequent careers of a number of these men are interesting and are sketched in the Biographical Register.

[21] The texts are reprinted in *Dokumenty chwili*, I, 30–31. The PPS accused the following former ministers of corrupt practices: Wincenty Witos, Jerzy Zdziechowski, Władysław Kiernik, Stanisław Osiecki, Wojciech Korfanty, Władysław Kucharski, and Jan Moszczyński. For the dates of their tenures of office, see Markert, ed., pp. 674–77. Most of them issued public denials of any wrongdoing which were published in the *Kurjer Warszawski* during the second half of May. Some of them were subsequently investigated and purged.

bloc on the morrow of Skrzyński's fall and at the beginning of the entire crisis, only Bartel's Klub Praca—understandably—now issued no such resolution lest it embarrass him even by implication.

The three Left parties were, however, in a difficult position. On the one hand, they were being accused of rendering the solution of the crisis unnecessarily difficult through their allegedly excessive and truculent demands.[22] On the other hand, they found it impossible in the rush of events to educate the public—especially their own supporters—to an understanding of their possible differences with and striving for autonomy from the victorious Piłsudski and his premier-designate. The past and recent efforts of the Perl leadership group to disentangle the PPS from the Piłsudski camp had failed. The same was true of Wyzwolenie, while the Stronnictwo Chłopskie was still too young and untested (having been founded only in January) to exert much leverage. Furthermore, the Left's seemingly most powerful weapon of the moment—the strike—was, in fact, a doubly dubious one. First of all, amidst the masses' current postvictory euphoria, so eminently focused on the person of the Marshal, the PPS leaders might well hesitate to force an immediate test of the railroadmen's and other workers' primary allegiance between the Party leadership and Piłsudski. The powerful and resourceful Piłsudskist faction within the bosom of the Party was likely to break discipline on such an issue. Secondly, even in the event the workers heeded the non-Piłsudskist PPS leadership in a showdown, a decision on its part to sustain a transport and general strike for an extended period in the pursuit of "worker-peasant" political goals obviously implied a readiness to face and to force some critical—even revolutionary—consequences. While the PPS leaders might have followed Piłsudski in a revolutionary direction, they were not prepared for such responsibility on their own. Nor were they eager to risk a test over control of the strikers. Having served to defeat Witos and intimidate Rataj, the strike was revoked on May 15 before it could become a challenge to Piłsudski.[23]

---

[22] This charge was leveled in the important *Ilustrowany Kurjer Codzienny,* May 17, 1926.

[23] *Ibid.* The return to work was apparently immediate everywhere except in radical Kraków, where it was briefly delayed. *Ibid.,* May 18, 1926. Bartel ordered a doubling of work shifts on the railroads.

Thereafter the Left bloc could comfort itself with the reflection that Bartel's cabinet, though something of a disappointment and obviously not one to indulge in radical economic or political experiments, was after all simply a stopgap pending the National Assembly's early election of a new president.[24] The Left, and the country in general, also expected that the two chambers of the Assembly would in any event be dissolved shortly and that the subsequent elections would produce a resounding victory for the Left.[25] On May 16 the Supreme Council of the PPS issued what amounted to its first election manifesto, appealing for working-class support, reaffirming its traditional political, economic, social, and ethnic programs, inviting the comradeship of its Left-bloc partners but repudiating that of the Communists and their suspected "fronts," and demanding the punishment of those Belwederian officers alleged to have behaved barbarically during the recent battle.[26] In the interval until the election of a new president, Bartel sought to mollify the Left and to encourage it to persist in its politically restrained and strictly legal course by accepting a PPS suggestion for extensive emergency public works credits.[27]

By this time, Piłsudski and Bartel had a far more serious pacification problem on their hands than the toothless growling of the Left. The country's former Prussian areas were defiant and gave alarming signs of transforming themselves into a counterinsurrectionary Vendée to resist the new government. Even secessionist threats were being heard from the western provinces.

As has been shown, the military districts of Poznań and Toruń,

[24] On at least two occasions—a press announcement of May 15 and a government manifesto of May 16—Bartel himself confirmed this view of his cabinet's role. The texts are reprinted in Bełcikowska, *Walki majowe*, pp. 44–47.

[25] Bartel suggested a dissolution and new elections in a press conference on May 24. His remarks are published in Maciejowski, pp. 17–19.

[26] The text is reprinted in *Dokumenty chwili*, I, 40. It insinuated that two parties were Communist "fronts": the Independent Socialist Labor Party (NSPP) and the Independent Peasant Party (NPCh). For brief discussions of the first, see Drobner, *passim,* and A. L., "Socjalizm polski na drodze ku konsolidacji." For the second, see Jarecka, "Stosunek N.P.Ch. do przewrotu majowego i Piłsudskiego w świetle materiałów policyjnych," and, by the same author, *Niezależna Partia Chłopska, passim.* Also, Garlicki, "N.P.Ch." I am persuaded that the PPS exaggerated in intimating that the first of these parties, the NSPP, was a mere Communist "front." See below, p. 313, n. 5.

[27] *Ilustrowany Kurjer Codzienny,* May 22, 1926.

largely overlapping with the provinces of Poznania and Polish Pomerania (Pomorze), had supplied most of the Wojciechowski-Witos government's armed force during the coup. Not only Ładoś' entire group at Ożarów, not only Żymierski's three regiments at Rakowiec, but about half of the Belwederian force proper had come from these two western areas of Poland. Nor was this simply an organizational accident, for in their readiness to send troops to Warsaw against Piłsudski, the corps headquarters in Poznań and Toruń thoroughly reflected the political sentiments prevailing in their provinces.

Most of the interbellum Polish province of Pomerania and a slice of Poznania had been annexed by Prussia in the first partition of Poland in 1772. The rest of Pomerania, together with the bulk of Poznania, had followed with the second partition in 1793. Their historical experience during the period of well over a century until the reincorporation of the two provinces into the restored post-World War I Poland had served to differentiate the political, psychological, and economic styles of the Pomeranians and Poznanians from those of their brother-Poles who had meanwhile lived in the Austrian and Russian empires. Their nationalism was more explicitly anti-German, their political ideologies more "bourgeois," their economic institutions often healthier, than the anti-Russian, socialist or peasant-ist or aristocratic patterns prevailing in the generally poorer areas which had emerged after 1918 from under Habsburg and Romanov administration. Though without heavy industry, Poznania and Pomerania were relatively rich thanks to an efficient agriculture and its associated processing industries. They were the classic loci in Poland of an energetic peasantry and an enterprising *economic* bourgeoisie, whereas to the south and east the peasantry was on the whole more primitive and the middle class was preponderantly made up of the intelligentsia and professional strata—usually with a semi-aristocratic "szlachta" self-image. (The *economic* bourgeoisie in these other areas—particularly in Galicia and the eastern *kresy*—was heavily Jewish.) Even the landscape reflected these differences, being in Poznania and Pomerania one of frequent small towns rather than the endless vista of fields, forests, and villages interspersed with an occasional city which prevailed in much of the rest of Poland.

In the restored state, these western Poles manifested a Catalan-like stance of strong regional identity combined with a contemptuous and resentful pride toward their compatriots. Though passionately anti-German, they regarded themselves as the sole bearers in restored Poland of such positive, "Prussian" cultural virtues as efficiency, punctuality, perseverance, and industriousness. Convinced that they alone worked hard, the westerners came to feel themselves exploited by what appeared to them as the economically parasitical but politically dexterous Galician, Congress Kingdom, and eastern *kresy* Poles. Their sense of grievance was fed by the economic dislocations consequent upon their separation from Germany, by the subsequent chronic financial turmoil, and, finally, by the sacrifices required after the eruption of the Polish-German tariff war in June, 1925.[28] Politically led by their farmer-landowners, their bourgeoisie, and their Roman Catholic clergy, overwhelmingly in the camp of National Democracy and its allies (even the workers here generally supported the NPR rather than the PPS), the Poznanians and Pomeranians came to see in Piłsudski the personification of all the vices and policies which they despised and feared in Poland. In their eyes he appeared as the *déclassé* son of a Polish-Lithuanian gentry family with insurrectionary traditions, a man of cavalier contempt for money and sublime inability to earn it through "rational" economic enterprise or skill, a Socialist terrorist before the war, a *de facto* ally of the Germans during the war, and—finally—an irresponsible adventurer pursuing preposterous Jagiellonian dreams on the Ukrainian steppes and in the White Russian marshes after its conclusion. Their response to his coup was one of rage, and it was strengthened by the assimilation to their views of most of the civil and military bureaucracy stationed in the two provinces.[29]

Upon news of the coup reaching Poznań, military reinforcements were promptly dispatched to the Belwederians, the students of the local university staged an anti-Piłsudski rally, and a protest parade

[28] See above, p. 17, n. 31.

[29] For some examples of the western Poles' sense of superior probity, etc., see Wapiński, pp. 15–20. Even Piłsudski's former friend and collaborator Sosnkowski had not remained immune to the spirit of Poznań. The same could perhaps also be said of Skotnicki-Grzmot. The core of the civil bureaucracy in the two provinces was locally recruited.

of 10,000 marchers followed.[30] The student rally was addressed by the Rightist Sejm deputy Stefan Dąbrowski, who had worked so effectively in the past to frustrate Piłsudski's return to the army, while the parade was "reviewed" by the anti-Piłsudski, retired Generals Józef Dowbór-Muśnicki and Kazimierz Raszewski. They were promptly joined in the mobilization of a Poznanian "volunteer army" to march against Piłsudski (in addition to the regular contingents being sent) by General Józef Haller, currently the Polish army's inspector of artillery and a veritable incarnation of anti-Piłsudskism.[31] Already during the evening of May 12, the Poznań offices of certain neutral or pro-Piłsudski national newspapers, such as the *Ilustrowany Kurjer Codzienny* (Illustrated Daily Courier) and the *Przegląd Poranny* (Morning Review), had been sacked.

The belligerency of the local population and of the three generals received legal succor with the arrival on May 13 of ministers Piechocki and Osiecki bearing plenipotentiary powers from Warsaw. A state of emergency was imposed on Poznania and Pomerania the next day, the dissemination of news unfavorable to the Wojciechowski-Witos government was banned, the railroad strike was prohibited and rendered ineffective within the two provinces, and the vitriolic message declaring Piłsudski an outlaw was dispatched abroad.[32] Gathering momentum, the locally powerful *Kurjer Poznański* (Poznanian Courier) published a fiery editorial on May 15, denouncing Piłsudski as one who "for us, has ceased to be a Pole" and vowing to resist him come what might.

The climax of this western explosion did not come, however, until after the Wojciechowski-Witos government's capitulation, which the Poznanians and Pomeranians initially flatly refused to accept. When the *wojewoda* of Pomerania, Stanisław Wachowiak, though sympathetic to the local anti-Piłsudski sentiments, finally agreed during the night of May 15–16 to acknowledge the Rataj-Bartel-Piłsudski government after inspecting Wojciechowski's and Witos' letters of resignation, which had been flown to Toruń for his personal verifi-

[30] *Ilustrowany Kurjer Codzienny,* May 15, 1926.
[31] Further information on Józef Haller, a cousin of the Belwederians' chief of the General Staff, Stanisław Haller, will be found in the Biographical Register.
[32] See above, p. 144. Poznań city, where Piechocki was a lawyer, was his Sejm constituency.

cation, he was promptly denounced by the local community leaders and subjected to an attempted quarantine by his fellow public officials. There was even a tentative plot to arrest him.[33] For his part, Dowbór-Muśnicki, sought to incite Hubischta, commander of the Toruń Military District, to resist Wachowiak's acceptance of the *fait accompli* by sending him a false report to the effect that Rataj had managed to telephone to Poznań the news that he (Rataj) was a virtual prisoner in Warsaw, deprived of his freedom of action and movement.[34] The *wojewoda* of Poznania, Count Adolf Bniński, though in possession of as much accurate information as Wachowiak, threw in his lot with the local extremists and lent himself to this and other deceptions designed to inflame resistance to the new government in Warsaw. Thus, with Bniński's acquiescent encouragement, twenty-three deputies and ten senators from that province met in Poznań city on May 16 and adopted a defiant resolution refusing to acknowledge the validity of Rataj's actions (among which was the appointment of the Bartel cabinet) on the ground that he was deemed to be acting under compulsion. The resolution further insisted that no future president elected by a National Assembly meeting in Warsaw could be accepted as legitimate, since the capital was declared to be intimidated by insurrectionary bayonets. After insisting that no laws or decrees or directives currently issuing from Warsaw had to be obeyed, the resolution somewhat incongruously concluded with an appeal for the restoration of law and order.[35]

A day later, on May 17, a similar meeting of fifteen Silesian deputies and senators gathered in their province's capital of Katowice. Most of Silesia, like Pomerania and Poznania, had been part of Germany (Prussia) before 1918, but in many respects Silesia differed from those two provinces historically, economically, and politically. Silesia had not been taken from Poland during the eighteenth-century partitions but had been lost much earlier, in the fourteenth century, to the Bohemian crown. In 1526 it passed into the possession of the

[33] Wapiński, p. 34. Wachowiak had been a National Laborite Sejm deputy for a Poznanian constituency (he was a native of Poznań province) from 1922 to 1924 before becoming *wojewoda* of Pomerania in the latter year.

[34] Czubiński, "Wielkopolska i Pomorze wobec zamachu stanu w maju 1926 r.," p. 179.

[35] The text is reprinted in *Dokumenty chwili*, II, 19–20.

Habsburgs, who later lost most of Silesia to Prussia in a series of wars and treaties between 1740 and 1763. Developing into one of Europe's major areas of heavy industry, Silesia had been subjected to a cultural and linguistic re-Polonization since the last third of the nineteenth century. On the strength of this modern national resurgence, rather than of her medieval historical claims, Poland, after World War I, had reacquired parts of Prussian Silesia and a slice of that fragment which had earlier remained Austrian (Teschen or Cieszyn or Těšín Silesia). She had successfully fortified her Silesian demands with three armed anti-German uprisings in the province between August, 1919, and May, 1921.

Silesia, as the nation's heavy industrial arsenal, enjoyed a favored position in restored Poland, including the unique legal privileges of a provincial diet and a certain degree of administrative and legislative autonomy (Law of July 15, 1920). Politically, the leading Polish party—owing to the combination of an industrial economy with a devotedly Catholic population—was by far that of the Christian Democrats: clerical, nationalistic, anti-Piłsudski, but not as far to the Right as the National Democrats who dominated Poznania and Pomerania. The NPR and the PPS also had some local strength, a fact that further conduced to relative moderation. The province's most powerful political personality was Christian Democratic leader Wojciech Korfanty, a former deputy to the Prussian Diet (1904–18) and the German Reichstag (1903–12), where he had been the *enfant terrible* of Polish nationalism.[36]

[36] On Korfanty, see Morawski, *Wspólna droga*, pp. 104–15. One of the organizers of the Silesian uprisings of 1919–21, Korfanty had been vice-premier toward the close of Witos' 1923 government. An outspoken enemy of Piłsudski, he was removed by the Bartel cabinet from the presidency of the Silesian Bank on May 26, 1926, on charges of corruption, which had actually been preferred against him in 1925 when Władysław Grabski was premier. Korfanty had, in fact, reneged on a promise given by him in December, 1925, to resign the bank presidency. A Sejm Marshal's Court (a court of honor, not of law) investigated in the autumn of 1927 and found Korfanty's actions as head of the bank to have been incompatible with his role as Sejm deputy, as well as deficient in expected standards of propriety. However, no indictment was preferred since no law had been violated. (Pragier, "Sąd nad Korfantym.") In March, 1928, Korfanty was reelected to the Sejm but declined to take his seat in order to avoid another "conflict of interest" inquiry. He was one of the political foes of Piłsudski incarcerated in the notorious Brześć episode of 1930 (see below, pp. 353–58). Korfanty lived in exile in Czechoslovakia from 1935 until March, 1939, and died in Warsaw on August 17, 1939.

Now, the demands made by the Silesian deputies and senators at their meeting of May 17, 1926, in Katowice, presided over by Korfanty, were less provocative than the resolution adopted the previous day in Poznań. With the largest German minority of any Polish province to caution them,[37] with the memory of three sharp Freikorps-style battles against the Germans (1919–21) to sober them, with some already acquired autonomy to placate them, and with a strong industrial proletariat—largely Catholic but not politically reactionary—to inhibit them, Korfanty and his fellow anti-Piłsudski Silesian leaders confined their counterchallenge to a set of demands that the National Assembly meet in a city other than Piłsudski-dominated Warsaw to elect the next president, that the interned Belwederians be released, and that paramilitary organizations be disarmed and their demonstrations prohibited. (The Piłsudskist Riflemen were meant here.) Simultaneously, they appealed to the Silesians to preserve calm and discipline.[38]

In Pomerania, the bellicose Toruń paper *Słowo Pomorskie* (Pomeranian Word) was publishing, as late as May 18, utterly false accounts of developments in Warsaw. Under such misleading headlines as "Good news from Warsaw," "General Rozwadowski at the head of the army," "Army ready for battle," it sought to give the impression that the combined Wilanów-Ożarów contingents under Rozwadowski and Ładoś were about to attack and destroy Piłsudski's forces and that *wojewoda* Wachowiak's submission to the new regime had therefore been premature and unnecessary. The paper's editors, belonging to a fringe group of extremists which reportedly was being encouraged by Dowbór-Muśnicki from Poznań, were prepared to go as far as separatism and secession.[39] They demanded the convocation of a "Sejm for the West" under which the western provinces would

[37] In that part of former Prussian Silesia which finally was assigned to Poland, 44.2 percent of the voters had opted for Germany in a plebiscite on March 20, 1921. In Poland's slice of Cieszyn Silesia, 20 percent of the population was German.

[38] The text of this resolution is published in *Dokumenty chwili*, II, 20.

[39] See Czubiński, "Wielkopolska i Pomorze wobec zamachu stanu w maju 1926 r.," pp. 180, 187. One of the fringe group's leaders, a Count Mielżyński, was in telephonic communication with Dowbór-Muśnicki. It must be borne in mind that these separatists were Poles, not the local Germans. For the latter, who interpreted the May crisis as evidence for their contention that Poland was but an ephemeral *Saisonstaat*, see *ibid.*, pp. 199–201.

draw in upon themselves to become a center of pure "Piast Polonism" uncorrupted by eastern accretions (a reference to the medieval native dynasty and its geographical heartland—not to Witos' modern peasant party). Wachowiak, though sharply denounced by them for his "unreliability," refused to indulge the separatists, and his firm attitude influenced General Hubischta to subordinate himself to the new central authorities in Warsaw on May 18. These two chief civil and military officers in the province acted not out of any liking for Piłsudski but for fear of trouble from the local German minority (18.7 percent in Pomerania according to the Polish census of 1921) and—even more strongly—from a concern over the revisionist designs of the German Reich upon the so-called Polish Corridor, which was a part of Polish Pomerania. In other words, their motives were a particular application of the general considerations which had inclined the Witos government to yield during the night of May 14. In addition, of course, the habit of obedience to the administrative center tended to reemerge as the situation in the capital became clarified.

In Poznania, where the local German minority accounted for 16.7 percent of the population (1921 Polish census) and toward which German annexationist hunger was only slightly less voracious than in the case of the "Corridor," antisecessionist sobriety also eventually prevailed, but it was applied to the situation in a more extortionate manner than in Pomerania. The strategist of Poznania's manipulative maneuver of accommodation to Warsaw was Marshal of the Senate Wojciech Trąmpczyński, a local National Democratic favorite son who had represented the Poznań Poles in the Prussian Diet (1910–18) and in the German Reichstag (1912–18) before and during World War I, who had then been marshal of restored Poland's first Sejm (1919–22) and subsequently of her Senate (since 1922). On May 16, disquieted by the Vendée-like rumblings from Poznań, Bartel had requested Trąmpczyński—who was in Warsaw during the coup—to go to Poznań and calm it in the national interest, taking along documentary evidence of Wojciechowski's resignation.[40]

Trąmpczyński arrived in Poznań to find an explosive situation. On May 17 a force of 1,400 paramilitary volunteers from the army that Haller, Dowbór-Muśnicki, and Raszewski were organizing to fight Piłsudski was reported to have reached Kutno from Poznań and there

---

[40] *Dokumenty chwili,* I, 37, 39.

was barely persuaded to desist from marching on Warsaw.[41] On May 19 the *Kurjer Poznański* followed up its incendiary editorial of four days earlier with this warning: "The crisis is far from terminated. One might even say that it has only begun. He who sows the wind reaps the tempest. Thus will it be with the Piłsudskist rebels. The western provinces of Poland have the mission of saving the state." Trąmpczyński's strategy under these circumstances was the dual one of assuaging this volatile situation and simultaneously using it as a lever to ensure the National Democratic camp a continuing pivotal, if not preponderant, role in national politics. Thus, while genuinely seeking to avert another explosion in the west, he hoped to blackmail Warsaw with the threat of the western "wild men," whom only concessions to his camp could pacify. On May 20, accordingly, he issued an appeal to the Poznanian public, denouncing intentions to resume hostilities, forbidding allegiance to certain self-proclaimed secessionist or vigilante authorities, and insisting on obedience to *wojewoda* Bniński—not to Prime Minister Bartel or to Acting President Rataj in Warsaw—as the bearer of state authority pending the election of a new president by the National Assembly.[42] With considerable bluster, most of the Poznanian Right fell into line behind Trąmpczyński. Bniński banned all Socialist and trade union meetings in the province and ordered the censorship of all newspapers and periodicals entering it in order to immunize the local euphoria against outside facts and thus to strengthen his own and Trąmpczyński's leverage.[43] On May 20 the deputies and senators who four days earlier had repudiated Rataj and defied Warsaw, now joined by some local worthies in an *ad hoc* Organization for the Defense of the State (Organizacja Obrony Państwa), issued another truculent but shrewder statement proclaiming Poznania to be the base where lawful political tendencies in Poland would first crystallize before liberating the rest of the coun-

[41] AKL, 10/10; *Kurjer Warszawski*, May 18, 1926. The *Frankfurter Zeitung* of May 18, seemingly hopeful of a disintegrative civil war in Poland, inflated this report into a force of 6,000 Hallerite volunteers reaching Żyrardów. This was echoed in the anti-Piłsudski French *Journal des débats politiques et littéraires*, XXXIII, No. 1682 (May 21, 1926), 814. Kutno and Żyrardów are, respectively, 65 and 27 miles west of Warsaw.
[42] The text is published in *Kurjer Warszawski*, May 20, 1926.
[43] *Ilustrowany Kurjer Codzienny*, May 22, 1926. The censorship was lifted on May 25. *Ibid.*, May 27, 1926.

try from social revolutionaries. "Capitulation to rebellion and anarchy" was refused and Trąmpczyński's appeal of earlier that day to rally to Bniński was endorsed. Simultaneously, a telegram was sent to Rataj demanding the transfer out of Warsaw of all military units other than its regular garrison, the disarming of the Piłsudskist paramilitary Rifleman organization, and the removal from the cabinet of the direct authors (unnamed) of the recent coup d'état.[44] Thus was staked out a hopefully strong Rightist position preparatory to the impending presidential election.

It was not, however, an easy maneuver, for the Trąmpczyński-Bniński "line" was repudiated by both more intransigent and more moderate groups. Whereas the Pomeranian extremists toyed with separatism, those in Poznania were torn between that style of subversion and the stronger urge to reopen hostilities with a march on Warsaw. The first course was suggested in a characteristically mindless fashion by the Poznań Reserve Officer Association, which proposed that Bniński proclaim himself an independent chief executive of an autonomous Poznania, refusing allegiance to the new government until the *bona fides* of whoever would be elected president could be scrutinized.[45] The Association apparently did not concern itself with the problems of how such an ostrichlike policy could affect the results of that presidential election or of what was to be done in case the victor was found to be beyond the Poznanian margin of acceptability. Its proposal serves as evidence of how blinding Poznania's self-imposed censorship was proving to be. The second extremist alternative, that of renewing the armed quest for the military victory which had so recently seemed within their grasp, was propagated most determinedly by Generals Józef Haller and Dowbór-Muśnicki and was en-

---

[44] Texts and résumés of these various pronouncements were published in *Ilustrowany Kurjer Codzienny*, May 22, 1926. As might have been expected, the ubiquitous deputy Stefan Dąbrowski was a leader of this Organization for the Defense of the State. In Pomerania, its equivalent was named the Committee of National Defense (Komitet Obrony Narodowej). Initially some members of the Piast Peasant Party belonged to it but shortly withdrew.

[45] *Frankfurter Zeitung*, May 22, 1926. In a variation on this theme, a Professor Grabowski of Poznań University proposed that the western provinces proclaim their autonomy under the presidency of General Raszewski. See Léontin, "Les Evénements de Pologne," p. 298.

thusiastically endorsed by most of the local university students.[46]

Thus, western Poland's response to Piłsudski's victory and Bartel's government ran the gamut from Wachowiak's and Hubischta's simple acknowledgment, to Korfanty's pouting one, through the Trąmpczyński maneuver of partial boycott so as to reserve National Democratic claims at the center, to the Haller and Dowbór-Muśnicki itch for a second military round, and ended with the marginal separatists in whose camp Generals Dowbór-Muśnicki and Raszewski may also have had a foot. These variant postures were illustrated when Poznań welcomed home its returning regiments from Warsaw on May 20 with a ceremonial parade that took on the atmosphere of a religious ceremony of dedication to a crusade. Trąmpczyński, Bniński, Osiecki, Haller, Dowbór-Muśnicki, Raszewski, and other politicians and political generals vied for ovations and sought more or less subtly to utilize the great emotion of the moment for their respective policies and positions.[47] But it was all in vain: they had overplayed their hands. The agents who punctured their several bubbles were the moderate wing of the NPR, which *wojewoda* Wachowiak encouraged, the ever-pragmatic Witos, and the unexpectedly restrained Piłsudski.

On that day of bluster and drama, May 20, the Poznanian NPR deputy Antoni Ciszak, a locksmith, had gone from Poznań to Warsaw, where he denounced western Polish intransigence, declared that the workers of Poznania would have nothing to do with separatism, called for putting a seal upon the recent crisis by electing Piłsudski to the presidency, and demanded the early dissolution of the current, no longer representative Sejm and Senate.[48] Though suspended by the Party a week later, on May 27, Ciszak was joined in his opposition to the intransigent line of its national leadership by another disaffected

[46] Czubiński, "Wielkopolska i Pomorze wobec zamachu stanu w maju 1926 r.," p. 183; *Ilustrowany Kurjer Codzienny,* May 22, 1926; and *Berliner Tageblatt,* May 25, 1926.

[47] There is an exhaustive description of this pageant in Maciejowski, p. 3. The local bishop participated, as did the French and Czechoslovak consuls, who perhaps desired subtly to demonstrate their countries' preference for Piłsudski's foes since the Marshal was known to be skeptically disposed toward France and unfriendly to Czechoslovakia. The German vice-consul was also present, presumably viewing with satisfaction the internal split among the parts of Poland.

[48] *Ilustrowany Kurjer Codzienny,* May 22, 1926.

member, deputy Ludwik Waszkiewicz. Supported unobtrusively by Pomeranian *wojewoda* Wachowiak, who had been a deputy for the Party from 1922 to 1924, they extricated the western NPR from the immediate cabal of defiance against the new government in Warsaw.[49] Furthermore, convinced that the Party's close association with the National Democrats was stunting its development and distorting its political stance, they broke away during July-August, 1926, to organize a separate Left-NPR (NPR-Lewica), which—like the parent Party—had its greatest strength in the west. It eventually entered the Piłsudski camp, becoming the Marshal's main—if still modest— source of support in the country's western regions. Witos, meanwhile, had been in Poznań toward the end of May, quietly exerting his influence on behalf of moderation and acceptance of the Warsaw developments.[50] Piłsudski, though publicly professing to be unworried by all the western thunder and declaring his confidence that time would heal the breach between Warsaw and Poznań,[51] took the precaution of sending the prestigious and conservative Count Adam Tarnowski to the west to incline the landed interests there toward moderation.[52] Even more efficacious in calming the restless and initially outraged Right was Piłsudski's subsequent over-all policy of permitting no social revolutionary consequences to his coup.

All these developments served to lance the counterinsurgent abscess in the west, which slowly accommodated itself to the *faits accomplis* which had occurred in Warsaw. Much sound and fury remained to be expended, however, and the Poznanians took out some of their frustration in a nasty campaign of provocation and repression against the relatively weak local PPS minority. On May 31, the day scheduled

---

[49] *Berliner Tageblatt,* May 25, 1926, and *Ilustrowany Kurjer Codzienny,* May 29, 1926. Waszkiewicz, in contrast to Ciszak and Wachowiak, was not strictly a "westerner," having been elected to the Sejm from the industrial center of Łódź, his native city.

[50] *Kurjer Warszawski,* May 28, 1926; *Ilustrowany Kurjer Codzienny,* May 30, 1926.

[51] Piłsudski interviews in *Le Matin* (Paris) of May 24 and 26 and in *Kurjer Poranny* (Warsaw) of May 25, 1926, reprinted in Piłsulski, *PZ,* IX, 13, 16, 21. In the Polish interview he referred to the Poznanian effervescence as a *wojna kokosza* (hen war)—a reference to a Fronde-like revolt of the gentry in 1537.

[52] *Ilustrowany Kurjer Codzienny,* May 27, 1926. Tarnowski had enjoyed a distinguished diplomatic career in the Austro-Hungarian service, having been chargé d'affaires in London (1910) and ambassador to Bulgaria (1911–16) and to the United States (1917).

for the presidential election—in which *wojewoda* Bniński stood as the candidate of the Right—Poznań cut itself off from all telephonic and telegraphic communication with Warsaw. As late as June 8 and 10, two extremist deputies called for Pomeranian autonomy and insulted Piłsudski in speeches made near Toruń and in Grudziądz—but by then merely irritated their audiences.[53] The public authorities were also becoming impatient. On June 3, *wojewoda* Wachowiak—acting at the urging of General Skierski and with the authorization of Interior Minister General Młodzianowski—had reimposed the recently lifted state of emergency on Pomerania in order to cope with the secessionist fulminations of the *Słowo Pomorskie* and the province's other wild separationists.[54] In mid-June, General Hauser, acting commander of the Poznań Military District during Sosnkowski's recuperation from his gunshot wound, went to Warsaw to complain to War Minister Piłsudski—whom he had opposed to the best of his ability during the coup—about the continuing subversive activities of the retired generals Dowbór-Muśnicki and Raszewski.[55]

In the long run, the May crisis, by puncturing so many illusions, served to integrate the former Prussian provinces more organically with the rest of Poland and to weaken their political provincialism. Over the next two years, the Piłsudski-Bartel regimes conducted a slow but steady bureaucratic purge to end the Rightist stranglehold upon the local administration. In August, 1926, the Piłsudskist Michał Grażyński was appointed *wojewoda* in what had hitherto been Korfanty's personal bailiwick of Silesia.[56] In October, Interior Minister General Młodzianowski was transferred to be *wojewoda* in the critical province of Pomerania. As for Poznania, the purge there

[53] *Ilustrowany Kurjer Codzienny,* May 30 and June 14, 1926.

[54] Czubiński, "Wielkopolska i Pomorze wobec zamachu stanu w maju 1926 r.," pp. 188, 203. Wachowiak was replaced as *wojewoda* by Młodzianowski in October, becoming chief director of the important national exhibition in Poznań to celebrate the impending tenth anniversary of Poland's recovered independence. Further information on him will be found in the Biographical Register.

[55] *Ilustrowany Kurjer Codzienny,* June 19, 1926. Other details of the western "Vendée" are in AKL, 3/3 and 5/74–77.

[56] Grażyński, as a POW officer, had been a military leader in the Silesian anti-German uprisings of 1919–21. As *wojewoda* from 1926 to 1939, he was known for his rigorous determination thoroughly to Polonize the province's political, economic, and cultural character, repressing its German survivals. Further information on him will be found in the Biographical Register.

was slower and initially more cautious, but by the time of the parliamentary elections of March, 1928, the Right's monopolistic grip on political power in this province had also been loosened. In June of that year, the axe finally fell on *wojewoda* Bniński.[57] With his removal, the unofficial but politically palpable quasi autonomy of National Democratic Poznania may be said to have come to a close.

[57] A native of the province, Bniński was *wojewoda* of Poznania from 1923 to 1928. Further information on him will be found in the Biographical Register.

CHAPTER X

THE ARMY AFTER THE COUP

Piłsudski's most immediate concern on the morrow of the coup was for the army. To rescue it from the allegedly degenerating influences of politicians and political generals had, after all, been one of the main—if not the main—declared reasons for launching his intended armed demonstration against the Witos government. Piłsudski had been profoundly shaken when, in responding to the crisis, the army had split into fratricidal strife instead of—as he had expected—rallying to himself as its former commander in chief. Formally, the cleft within the army which then ensued was repaired by the evening of May 15 when Rataj, unwilling to utilize for political leverage the fact that Ładoś' Ożarów group stood at his immediate disposal, transferred to Piłsudski as war minister full authority over all armed forces and complete responsibility for liquidating the military aftermath of recent events.[1] Not so easily healed was the army's moral and psychological schism. The unity of an army is, after all, something organic. Once ruptured, it cannot be mechanically pasted together again. The unity of an army, furthermore, derives its moral cohesion from internal and external obedience to constituted authority. Piłsudski was well aware that, except for a few senior—mainly former Austrian—generals who had derived personal and political satisfaction from fighting him, the bulk of his foes in the recent combat had taken up arms in conformity to their oath, in fulfillment of their duty as they saw it, in defense of the state's legal authority against a rebel, with no particular enthusiasm for the persons of Witos and Wojciechowski or for the institutions of the Sejm and the Right-Center cabinet. Piłsudski had now to bind up the wounds, to establish his legitimacy, and to reconcile these late opponents to his victory. But since he was ultimately a political, not a professional, soldier, he was determined somehow to combine this task of reunification with the simultaneous transforma-

---

[1] Rataj's decree is reprinted in *Dokumenty chwili,* I, 33.

tion of the army into his own instrument—the reflection and the weapon of his own policies.

Despite the multiplicity of its preindependence origins and experiences, the Polish officer cadre on the eve of Piłsudski's coup had been characterized by high professional morale and a developing sense of corporate unity—except at its very summit, where the political tensions among Piłsudski, Sikorski, Szeptycki, *et al.* were keen. While memories and comradeships from earlier service careers survived and were cultivated, the common effort of the Polish-Soviet campaign of 1920 had been the starting point of a process—subsequently reinforced by the passage of time and by internal institutional pressures— of fusing the disparate parts of the officer corps into a whole. By 1926 its internal psychology was "federalistic": dedication to the central notion of the Polish national army was combined with "sectional" sentiments still attaching to its original component parts— Legions and POW, Austrian, German, and Russian armies, Haller corps, etc.[2] Given a sufficiently long period of domestic peace, it seems likely that the balance among these loyalties would increasingly have shifted toward the central and away from the parochial objects and that friction among the latter would probably have abated. But domestic peace was not given the army. The cantankerous quarrel between Piłsudski and his rivals had provided a discordant tone ever since 1923, and the bitter days of civil strife in May, 1926, threatened to unravel whatever real internal unity had so far been achieved.

Piłsudski's task was not facilitated by the closing contribution to the crisis of embittered President Wojciechowski, who, after informing his military entourage at Wilanów during the night of May 14 of the cease-fire and his decision to resign, had remarked that every officer would have to consult his conscience whether he could continue to serve in the kind of army which would emerge from the affair.[3] This implied suggestion that resignation was the imperative of honor echoed so resonantly during the following days that eventually the Rightist press, as well as General Sikorski and the recent acting foreign minister, Morawski, intervened to counsel against such protest resignations from either the military or the foreign service as sterile

[2] See Kopański, p. 302.
[3] S. Haller, p. 79.

and as simply playing into the hands of the Left in its desire for a radical political purge of the state apparatus.[4] Another initial obstacle to Piłsudski's mission of reunification was the gusto with which some of his own ardent but myopic paladins proceeded to celebrate their victory by punishing the recent "enemy." This became apparent in the provocatively tough and humiliating "surrender" conditions which they wished to impose on the Wilanów contingents and which were only averted because of the intercession of Kutrzeba (who had inadvertently been privy to Piłsudski's plans but had fought for the Belwederians) with his friend Orlicz-Dreszer.[5]

Piłsudski's own approach to the dual problem of renewing the army's solidarity and simultaneously consolidating his own hold upon it was characteristically dialectical. Those officers who, in his conviction, had fought against him purely in obedience to orders or from a sense of their sworn duty he desired to reintegrate into the army and even—where appropriate—to promote as a gesture of acknowledgment to the army's collective professional ethos. Simultaneously, he was determined to eliminate his politico-personal antagonists among the senior generals, but—not wishing to give the appearance of a purge—he would utilize for this purpose the conveniently available charges of corruption and dereliction which had been leveled against a number of them. In the process he intended to cashier those officers whom he regarded as guilty of poltroonery or purely opportunistic fence-straddling during the May crisis. The ultimate legal-organizational keystone to this intended reform and renewal of the armed forces would be a definitive settlement of the chronic and vexing supreme command problem in accordance with Piłsudski's own theories and on his own terms.

The elimination of his overt, quasi-political enemies from the army was achieved relatively easily. A few, such as the two Hallers and

---

[4] "Les absents ont toujours tort" warned the influential Rightist *Rzeczpospolita* in an editorial of May 21, 1926, advising against resignations. For Sikorski's and Morawski's similar positions, see Pietrzak, ed., "Jak doszło" i "Przewrót," p. 145, and Morawski, "Przewrót majowy," p. 2.

[5] Piątkowski, p. 21. Particularly determined to inflict punishment on those who had opposed Piłsudski was General Stefan Dąb-Biernacki, a Legion veteran, who had come to Warsaw in command of the regiments which Rydz-Śmigły had sent from Wilno to aid Piłsudski and who had already aroused attention with his ostentatious Piłsudskist zeal in November, 1925. Further information on him will be found in the Biographical Register.

Szeptycki, obliged Piłsudski by requesting retirement.[6] Malczewski was detained under rigorous conditions in Wilno for having abused and maltreated the Piłsudskist cavalrymen whom the Belwederians had captured on May 13. As his behavior had obviously been the expression of nervous excitability rather than cold malice, he was released, a broken man, toward the end of October, 1926, and retired in January, 1927.[7] Rozwadowski and Zagórski were also held captive in the same Wilno prison on charges of having engaged in fiscal abuses in their earlier respective capacities of inspector of cavalry and chief of the Air Department of the Polish army. The former was released on parole on May 18, 1927, and died on October 18, 1928, without ever having been given a formal trial. The latter was held prisoner until early August, 1927, and then vanished under mysterious circumstances which aroused suspicions of political murder.[8] During 1927 Żymierski was drummed out of the army for corruption, and Modelski was prematurely retired because of his passive surrender of the Citadel on May 13.[9] The highest political card of all, Sikorski, was more difficult for Piłsudski to take without publicly exposing his

[6] J. Haller, p. 266; *Kurjer Warszawski*, May 21, 1926; *Ilustrowany Kurjer Codzienny*, May 22, June 13 and 19, 1926. For the subsequent fates of the two Hallers, see above, p. 90, n. 21, and the Biographical Register. Szeptychi died in 1950.

[7] Daszyński, *W pierwszą rocznicę* p. 28.

[8] This notorious Zagórski affair is again the subject of recent inquests, among them: L. Hass, "Tajemnicze zniknięcie," *Mówią Wieki*, II, No. 12 (December, 1959), 14–17, and "Jeszcze raz o generale Zagórskim," *Tygodnik Powszechny*, XIV, No. 8 (February 21, 1960), 7; Kukiel, "Jeszcze o majowej wojnie domowej i generale Zagórskim," *Wiadomości*, XIV, No. 693 (July 12, 1959), 6; S. Pomorski, "Jak zginął gen. Zagórski," *Nadodrze*, No. 7 (1959), p. 3; J. Rawicz, *Generał Zagórski zaginął* (Warsaw, 1963).

The jailer of the three generals in Wilno was the same Dąb-Biernacki who had already been itching to punish the defeated Belwederians in the immediate aftermath of the coup. Berbecki has since alleged that Dąb-Biernacki was sadistically severe in his treatment of these prisoners, that he initially kept them cold and hungry and deprived them of books and correspondence, etc. See Berbecki, p. 195. In June, 1926, however, Berbecki, as commander of the military district in which the prisoners were being detained, had denied these very same allegations when made by Józef Haller. AKL, 16/9.

[9] Also sentenced was General Bolesław Jaźwiński, charged with tolerating abuses in the administration of the Military Geographical Institute, which he had directed. Ironically, Jaźwiński had apparently been attempting to make his way over the Poniatowski bridge to join Piłsudski in Praga on that fateful afternoon of May 12, when he was halted and reprimanded by Wojciechowski and thereupon remained in Warsaw with the Belwederian camp. He became paralyzed and died soon afterward. AKL, 2/27.

hand as a purger of the army. Uninvolved in the May fighting, Sikorski was also free of accusations of corruption. Objectively considered, furthermore, Piłsudski was profoundly indebted to Sikorski, who, had he promptly thrown his Lwowian regiments, his military influence, and his public prestige into the scales against Piłsudski during the May crisis, could have seriously delayed and perhaps even altered its outcome. Accordingly, Sikorski was left in command of the Lwów Military District until March, 1928, when the immediate furor over the coup had died down, meanwhile being obliged to accept as his chief of staff (and suspected surveillant) the Legion and POW veteran Colonel Adam Koc, a close confidant of Piłsudski. Kukiel, similarly uncontaminated by allegations of financial impropriety though also known as one of Piłsudski's bêtes noires in the army, was at first simply put at the (unutilized) disposal of the war minister and eventually retired in 1930.[10]

Piłsudski handled the reconciliation aspect of his resumed control over the army with overt panache and finesse. On May 22 he issued an eloquent and moving Order of the Day, the style of which showed him at his romantic and political and human best. Insisting that it was her soldiers who had earlier restored independence to Poland and who had now been required to rescue her yet again from the morass of political strife, he appealed to the army to rededicate itself to brotherhood so that it might be an example of patriotic selflessness to the nation. Warning that no foreign foe should misinterpret the recent fratricidal strife as indicating that Poland would lie helpless and divided in the face of external aggression, and eloquently evoking the memories of common travail and triumph in the Polish cause in 1920, Piłsudski pledged the army to a renewed comradely solidarity. Still appalled over the late bloodshed, for which he seemed to feel some emotional and moral sense of responsibility despite his polemical and political insistence that others were exclusively to blame, he concluded this Order of the Day with the obviously anguished plea, "May God who is merciful forgive us our sins and withhold his avenging arm;

[10] For Sikorski's and Kukiel's subsequent careers, see above, p. 108, n. 24, p. 91, n. 24, and the relevant entries in the Biographical Register. Sikorski had poured fresh oil onto his feud with Piłsudski by sending a cabled warning on May 16, 1926, that no vengeance must be inflicted on those who had served the legal government during the coup and that all the interned must be released immediately lest the sparks of civil war flame up anew. AKL, 13/408.

and as for us, let us set about our work to strengthen and rejuvenate our land." [11] As a gesture toward that reconciliation for which he was appealing, Piłsudski forbade any medals or citations to be awarded for even the most impressive military performances during the May fighting. He made it a point to praise the cadets and infantry officer candidates for the skill and courage which they had manifested in fighting against him. His new minister of the interior and their former commandant, Młodzianowski, also came to pay the regime's compliments to these recent champions of the Belwederians and future cadres of the entire officer corps.[12] Paszkiewicz and Porwit, though transferred from the command of these units, were in due time promoted—as were such other Belwederian lions as Anders, Kleeberg, Kutrzeba, and several regimental commanders.[13] Yet, even in this, one of his finest moments, Piłsudski managed to spoil the effect by unconcernedly and even with some bravado remarking to a French journalist on the day after his affecting plea for solidarity that he now expected quite a few duels to be fought among officers in repercussion to the recent events.[14] The swashbuckling urge of the bellicose *szlachcic* seemed always to strain within him to break out of the confines of the statesman of vision.

Piłsudski's legal instrument for remolding the Polish army and the officer corps in his own image was a new and definitive regulation of the hitherto obstinately troublesome supreme command problem. On June 8, as a preliminary measure and as one aspect of a cabinet reshuffle, Bartel had accepted a demand by Piłsudski that the Marshal's own organizational decree of January 7, 1921, be revalidated,

[11] The text is reprinted in Piłsudski, *PZ, IX,* 10–11. There was a report in the *Berliner Tageblatt* on May 25, 1926, that, despite Piłsudski's express instruction as war minister that the Order be read to all units, it was not read to those stationed in still embittered Poznania.

[12] Mercik, p. 111, and Piątkowski, p. 22.

[13] For later details on some of these officers, see the relevant entries in the Biographical Register. There subsequently developed a widespread but unsubstantiated rumor that Piłsudski requested Kutrzeba, who soon became commandant of the Superior War Academy, to give him private lessons in military tactics. See Barbier, p. 299. (Barbier was First Secretary at the French embassy in Warsaw during much of the 1920s.)

[14] Interview in *Le Matin,* May 24, 1926, reprinted in Piłsudski, *PZ, IX,* 12–13.

that a prospective commander in chief for wartime be designated, that the war minister be obliged to accommodate himself to that future commander in chief in all matters pertaining to the defense of the state, and that the war minister's other responsibilities toward the president, the prime minister, and the Sejm be strictly defined.[15] Four days later, on June 12, Piłsudski was appointed president of the Inner War Council provided by the terms of his 1921 decree, thereby becoming, in effect, both war minister and the designate commander in chief for wartime. Finally, to clear the ground, the Bartel government withdrew all other supreme command projects pending before the Sejm. By now these amounted to the Szeptycki draft law of June, 1923, the two Sikorski versions of March and December, 1924, the Dąbrowski-inspired Sejm committee revisions of 1925 upon the second Sikorski draft, and the last-minute Żeligowski project of May, 1926—not to mention Sosnkowski's unformalized project of early 1924.

Piłsudski's 1921 decree having, however, been issued in something of a constitutional vacuum, before the definition of the functions and powers of the president and the Sejm by the terms of the constitution of March 17, 1921, had been accomplished, an updating and formal synchronization of his plan with that constitution was now appropriate. On August 6, 1926—the twelfth anniversary of the entry of the Legions into action in World War I—a presidential decree effected this revision. (The necessary powers had been conferred on the president by a constitutional amendment four days earlier.) [16] Drafted by Piłsudski, this settlement finally established the position of inspector general of the armed forces, to whom the General Staff, its chief, and the various army inspectors were to be subordinate and who was designated to function as commander in chief in wartime. These explicit provisos filled some gaps in the 1921 decree, the text (if not the intention) of which had left the chief of the General Staff hovering

---

[15] Piłsudski's letter to Bartel is reprinted in his *PZ*, IX, 37–39. He wrote it in reply to a formal request by Bartel that he remain as war minister in the new cabinet. Piłsudski made his agreement conditional upon Bartel's acceptance of these demands.

[16] See below, pp. 226–28. The text of the presidential regulation of August 6, 1926, is in *Dziennik Ustaw Rzeczypospolitej Polskiej*, 1926, No. 79, Items 444–45. The text of the 1921 decree is reprinted in Piłsudski, *PZ*, Vol. VIII, Appendix I, pp. iii–v.

between *de facto* responsibility to the future wartime commander in chief and *de jure* subordination to the war minister. The last-named was now assigned purely to peacetime administration and was excluded from the work of war preparation and planning, which became the preserve of the inspector general of the armed forces. Presidential decrees and ordinances pertaining to the army, including organizational and personnel matters, would, moreover, henceforth be countersigned exclusively by this war minister—who thereby accepted political responsibility—and no longer by the prime minister. Piłsudski thus wished to make "strictly" military matters the exclusive preserve of the president and the senior officers (to whose ranks the war minister would belong despite his operational inferiority to the inspector general of the armed forces). Whereas a prime minister could be expected, thanks to the political pressures upon him, to press for the limitation of military budgets, Piłsudski hoped that the more autonomous president, whom he was thus seeking to propel into more active involvement with these matters, would be inclined to support the army's budget requests. In the final analysis, of course, the cabinet and the Sejm would still legislate the size of the budget and of the annual call-up, but, while prepared formally to respect this principle of civilian control, Piłsudski hoped to attenuate it in practice by— among other devices—enlisting presidential, "nonpartisan" prestige behind the requests of the military.[17]

On August 27, 1926, a presidential decree issued at the recommendation of the cabinet, which in turn was acting on the counsel of War Minister Piłsudski, appointed Marshal Piłsudski to the post of inspector general of the armed forces. Since the entire reorganization structure had been designed to Piłsudski's plans and to suit his ideas and personality, the insertion of this keystone into its arch elicited little surprise. And since Piłsudski was destined to occupy the two posts of war minister and inspector general uninterruptedly until the day of his death on May 12, 1935 (twice also holding the premiership for a total period of two years), any friction which the somewhat anomalous relationship of these offices to each other might otherwise have provoked was averted. He was henceforth to be the politico-

[17] See I. Mościcki, "Wspomnienia," *Niepodległość,* p. 198, and Podoski, p. 195.

administrative head of the army as well as the nation's first soldier and strategist.[18]

On October 25, 1926, a supplementary presidential decree created the Committee for the Defense of the State (Komitet Obrony Państwa), of which the president of the Republic was to be chairman, with the inspector general of the armed forces as its *rapporteur*. The committee was prohibited from taking any resolutions without consulting the inspector general, who prepared its agenda and communicated its decisions to the appropriate ministries with powers to enforce execution through standing military bureaus attached to the ministries. Other statutory members of the committee were to be the premier and the ministers of war, foreign affairs, finance, and the interior. In practice, the chief and deputy chief of the General Staff and the chief of Army Administration generally attended meetings but were voteless. This decree also had the dual purpose of maximizing the inspector general's authority over planning, control, supervision, and command as well as of increasing the president's fund of military information and hence of influence in respect to the more partisan and directly political cabinet ministers.[19]

Organizationally and structurally, the army changed but little at levels below that of the supreme command after the coup. Owing to Poland's precarious international position and to the generous patriotism of the nation, it also remained, as heretofore, one of Europe's largest armies, oscillating for the next decade between 260,000 and 290,000 standing peacetime effectives (not counting reserves)—to which should be added a Frontier Surveillance Corps of 26–28,000, a State Police Force of approximately 30,000, a gendarmery, and a navy which by 1937, on the eve of the European crisis, numbered four destroyers, three submarines (two more under construction), five torpedo boats, and a river flotilla. The air arm was an integral part

[18] The official appointment of Piłsudski as inspector general is reprinted in Malicki, p. 322. His terms as prime minister were from October 2, 1926, to June 27, 1928, and from August 25 to December 4, 1930.

[19] Podoski, p. 191. See also H. Mościcki *et al.*, eds., Part IV, chapters I and V. The text of the decree of October 25, 1926, is in *Dziennik Ustaw Rzeczypospolitej Polskiej*, 1926, No. 108, Item 633. The constitution of April 23, 1935, which entered into effect a few days before Piłsudski's death but had been drafted to formalize his system of rule, was to confirm explicitly this autonomy of the inspector general from the cabinet and his exclusive—if formal—responsibility to the president alone (Article 63).

of the army.[20] Thanks to the system of conscription and the country's generous manpower reserve, Poland could mobilize approximately 1,250,000 trained men in case of war.

The implementation of Piłsudski's subjectively sincere wish to knit this enthusiastic and dedicated military establishment into a seamless, whole garment was to confront frustrating counterforces. For one thing, among his most enthusiastic champions were men—less far-sighted and more primitively vindictive than he—who insisted on punishing some of the Belwederian officers. Tragically, their rancor could most easily expend itself on those who bore least responsibility—the middle- and junior-ranking officers among their late foes. In an army of approximately 18,000 commissioned officers, War Minister and Inspector General Piłsudski could obviously not scrutinize the promotion dossiers of any but the relatively senior ranks. It was administratively impossible for him to enforce equity for the others against the bias of his own praetorians, upon whom he did— in the final analysis—rely. The younger officers who had been on the "wrong" side in the May crisis and who were subsequently passed over or encountered delays in promotion soon coined a new adjective to describe their plight—*zmajowany,* or "May-ed." [21]

But his cohort's urge for vengeance was not the only obstacle to Piłsudski's intended reintegration of the officers corps. Devoted though he was to the idea of regeneration through reunion, he could not free himself from his implicit conviction that the army's and Poland's best human and moral material—the essential building blocks for their reconstruction—consisted of his old Legion comrades and those who had supported him in his recent armed retribution against Witos' allegedly unworthy coterie of malefactors. By the time Poland celebrated the tenth anniversary of her independence in November, 1928, Piłsudski's closest coworkers in the inspector generalcy of the armed forces—the men who were intended to be the key operational corps commanders in wartime and whose selection was therefore Piłsudski's most critical professional decision—were Sosnkowski, Osiński, Rydz-Śmigły, Norwid-Neugebauer, Burhardt-Bukacki, Dąb-Biernacki, Or-

[20] Retinger, pp. 203–20, and Carency, p. 221. According to League of Nations figures, Poland had the world's fourth largest army in the early 1930s, on the eve of Hitler's rearmament of Germany. At that time, only the armies of France, Italy, and the Soviet Union exceeded Poland's in size.

[21] See Grobicki, p. 100; Piątkowski, p. 23; and Kopański, pp. 149–50.

licz-Dreszer, Skierski, Rybak, and Romer. All but the first two of them had either actively or passively supported the May coup d'état, and six of the ten were old Legionnaires. In the following years many high-ranking officers who had supported the Belwederians in 1926 but could not at that time be conveniently purged, since they had acted in obedience to orders and not from any demonstrably political motives, were nevertheless retired, even though they were no older than many retained on the active list. Among them, for example, were most of the prominent Poznanian and Pomeranian officers: Hauser, Hubischta, Kędzierski, Ładoś, Rostworowski, and Taczak.

Piłsudskists, meanwhile, were not only promoted to the commanding positions within the army but were also frequently "loaned" from it to the civilian administrative apparatus—a process which incurred the double danger of militarizing the state while weakening the army by diverting its officers from their proper professional concerns.[22] Only in his last years did Piłsudski become sufficiently impressed by this threat to military performance to establish the principle that an officer accepting an extended nonmilitary assignment ought not thereafter to be restored to an active army command. This rule, however, did not halt the recruitment of Piłsudskist officers into key positions in the state apparatus, though it attenuated the deprofessionalization of the remaining officer corps. Within the army, ex-Legionnaires were favored for admission to the elite Superior War Academy, and the obligatory entrance examination was at times waived for them.[23] Many who were promoted after 1926 were less capable than those who were retired to make way for them, as even one of the highest military beneficiaries of the new regime and one of its friendliest wellwishers acknowledged.[24] The army's opportunists, as expected, now tried to assimilate to the revived Piłsudskist-Legionnaire style; after the September, 1939, catastrophe, they were to be just as avid to disown it.

By the outbreak of war in 1939, the Polish officer corps was far more "Piłsudskist" than it had been at the close of its last previous campaign, that against Soviet Russia in 1920. When the Verification

---

[22] See Kirchmayer, pp. 241–43; Stünzner, p. 680; Eichler, p. 26; Romeyko, "Przed i po maju 1926 r.," IX, No. 3, 193–202.

[23] Grudziński, p. 6.

[24] J. Romer, p. 326, and AGLŻ, 32a/137, 142, 143, 147. Also see Kopański, pp. 149–50.

Commission to integrate and synchronize the new army's multi-ori-gined officer corps completed its work shortly after that earlier war, only about 10 percent of those holding commissions had emerged from Piłsudski's Legions. By 1939 this category accounted for 70 per-cent of all commanders of infantry divisions (active and reserve) and 54 percent of the commanders of cavalry and motorized armored brigades. In sum, 65 percent of the commanders of large units were ex-Legionnaires, as were the inspector general, the chief of the Gen-eral Staff and his deputies, the minister and vice-ministers of war.[25] It is true, of course, that to a limited extent age favored the Legion veterans, for even the senior among them tended to be younger than the senior ex-Austrian, ex-Prussian, and ex-Russian officers and hence to survive these during the two decades of Polish independence. Never-theless, masses of younger officers from the armies of the partitioning powers also had entered the Polish army upon its re-creation and accounted for the bulk of that 90 percent which was not of ex-Legion-naire status in 1920. Their opportunities for promotion were mani-festly not equal to those of Piłsudski's own favored reservoir for higher commanders, and they were often discharged at a suspiciously early age by *ad hoc* medical boards.[26]

Apart from these statistical considerations—though related to them —stands the problem of determining whether the internal emotional and psychological wounds inflicted on the army by the May, 1926, split eventually healed. The solution of this problem has been ren-dered particularly difficult by the later superimposition onto it of the even more painful controversy concerning responsibility for Poland's September, 1939, disaster—a disaster in which the Polish soldier was not outfought so much as the military doctrine of his supreme com-mand was exposed as outdated. As might have been expected, the political debate over the 1939 catastrophe reveals certain analogies to that of the historians who seek to grapple with the causes of Poland's disappearance as an independent state in the eighteenth century. The Piłsudskists argue that the Polish army was professionally competent,

[25] Grudziński, p. 6; Kopański, pp. 302–3.
[26] See Grudziński, p. 6, and Romeyko, "Przed i po maju 1926 r.," VIII, No. 1, 259, for references to officers being prematurely retired on unconvincing medical grounds. A recent claim is that, in the immediate aftermath of the coup, 30 generals and 235 colonels and lieutenant colonels were retired—not one of whom was an ex-Legionnaire of the First or Third Brigades. Stawecki, p. 330.

internally united, and at one with the nation on the eve of World War II, that the wounds of 1926 had healed, that responsibility for the catastrophe rests exclusively with Poland's voracious neighbors and passive allies, and that the subsequent inquests into the so-called question of internal responsibility are transparently political attempts by Sikorski-ites (and later by Communists) to disparage the achievements of the Piłsudski era. Their opponents, while conceding that even a vastly improved Polish army could not—given the disparity in over-all national power—have been expected actually to defeat the Germans and Soviets, nevertheless insist that the breach of 1926 was never closed, that the officer corps subsequently became excessively politicized and hence militarily impaired, and that both Piłsudski and his successor as supreme commander, Rydz-Śmigły, were professionally incompetent and were in any event too immersed in political activities to devote that full attention to the army which Poland's precarious situation required of her designated commander in chief. A truly apolitical and competently led army, they insist, could have given a better account of itself. Finally comes the charge that a proper inquiry into and reconstruction of the army had been prevented while they still might have done some good—in the 1930s—by the regime's recourse to the blackmail of patriotism, to the elevation of the army's popularity into a cult, and to the equation of criticism of its high command with disloyalty and lack of patriotism.[27] This quarrel itself contains its own irony, quite apart from the tragedy of its subject. The Piłsudskists, having earlier claimed total credit for Poland's resurrection between 1914 and 1920 and hence the exclusive right to govern and administer the country during the interwar period, were saddled after 1939—equally extravagantly—with sole blame for the September calamity.

[27] See, for example, Benedykt, "O przełomie majowym," Pobóg-Malinowski, *Najnowsza historia*, Vol. III, chapters XXII and XXIII, and Sławoj-Składkowski, *Nie ostatnie słowo oskarżonego, passim,* presenting the Piłsudskist argument, versus the anti-Piłsudskists Kownacki, *Gdyby dziadek żył, passim,* Kozłowski, *Wojsko polskie, 1936–1939, passim,* but especially the Introduction, Kirchmayer, *Kampania wrześniowa,* Part III, and Kukiel, "Jeszcze o przełomie majowym." Exceedingly vitriolic in presenting this last argument is the brochure of Niemczyk, *Rachunek sumienia.*
For a recent example of the parallel debate concerning the responsibility for Poland's partition in the eighteenth century, see the discussion among professors Oswald P. Backus III, Oscar Halecki, and Joseph Jakstas in the *Slavic Review,* XXII, No. 3 (September, 1963), 411–55.

CHAPTER XI

ELECTING A PRESIDENT

Piłsudski's post-coup policy in the political realm paralleled his military procedures. Here the analogues to reconciliation and renewed fraternity were moderation and adhesion to legality, while corresponding to the Piłsudskist reconstruction of the army an attempt was launched to superimpose on Poland's discordant multiparty system a new, inclusive, disciplined camp of Piłsudskists sworn to no particular policy other than the regenerative purging (*sanacja*) of the state.

Piłsudski's decision to forego an explicit dictatorship and instead to prompt Acting President Rataj to summon the Bartel cabinet had been his first gesture toward legality, just as the composition of that cabinet had turned into an unmistakable demonstration of moderation. This trend was then sustained by the prompt release of Witos' interned ministers, followed by a decision the new cabinet took at its first session during the evening of May 16 to rescind the state of emergency that Witos and Wojciechowski had imposed on Warsaw and other areas on May 12. Simultaneously the Bartel government issued a manifesto to the nation, emphasizing the constitutional legality of its convocation (even if done without a formal parliamentary vote of confidence), promising to submit its resignation upon the early election of a new president, but appealing to the public to recognize that a mere restoration of law and order would not be enough unless it was accompanied by a genuine moral regeneration of Polish public life. The government promised to address itself energetically and immediately, through appropriate decrees and suitable actions, to the task of extirpating administrative decay, partisan rapaciousness, and personal cupidity from its own realm of the state apparatus, and simultaneously demanded service, cooperation, and obedience from the public.[1] Thus, together with its demonstration of legality and moderation, the new Piłsudski regime launched its campaign of purification, its *sanacja,* which was always to be more of a general political stance, even a frame of mind, than a specific policy program. *Sanacja,* in fact, came to imply an amalgam of buttressing the Piłsudskist executive in relation to the multiparty Sejm, superordinating the Piłsudskist state over the allegedly politically immature society, purging from that Piłsudskist state apparatus its incompetent and/or inconvenient personnel,[2] and cultivating a mystique of Piłsudski as the nation's heroic father, wise guide, and benevolent protector.

The press was requested and was expected to use its influence with the public so as to facilitate the implementation of the government's immediate and long-range intentions. Already on the evening of May 15, Acting President Rataj had appealed to the press to help pacify the country and return it to law and order. Then Interior Minister Młodzianowski, while echoing Rataj's sentiments, expanded on them to explain the government's intentions. Likening the recent coup to the bursting of an ulcer, he solicited the aid of the press in ensuring that the noxious matter extruded from that ulcer be not permitted to enter and poison the nation's blood stream. Denying any intentions to resort to dictatorial methods, Młodzianowski nevertheless insisted that the government had the right and the obligation to cleanse the state administration of improprieties but promised not to conduct such a purge in a narrowly partisan manner. He expected the press to help create an atmosphere conducive to the calm election of a new president and the rejuvenation and reunification of the nation under the leadership of the government.[3] Once again, as had been the case in the military arena, where some of Piłsudski's more truculent supporters had desired to proceed to an immediate and rigorous crackdown, so here too some of his more parochial followers were eager to

[1] The text of this government manifesto of May 16 is in *Dokumenty chwili,* I, 39–40. Its concluding passage was probably drafted with the combustible situation in western Poland in mind.

[2] A "nonpartisan" purge of state functionaries regarded as ethically or professionally unsuitable was decided upon at the first session of the Bartel cabinet on May 16. See the cabinet minutes as published by Zakrzewska, "Za kulisami przewrotu majowego." See also Rataj, pp. 390, 396.

[3] Rataj's and Młodzianowski's comments to the press are reproduced respectively in *Dokumenty chwili,* I, 32, and II, 25–26.

impose preliminary censorship on the press as a standard feature.[4] Even the more liberal Premier Bartel warned that he had no margin of tolerance for newspapers which infringed on the requirements of public order, and—as if to emphasize the government's equal detachment from all prevailing parties regardless of whether they had supported or opposed the recent coup—he threatened to confiscate the Socialist *Robotnik* as readily as any Rightist paper should it violate those requirements. Aware, however, of the power of the press to strengthen or to subvert a government's public image, Bartel opposed inflicting gratuitous humiliations on it or putting arbitrary difficulties in the way of its reporters.[5]

The country's various political parties, economic interests, and corporate bodies were impressed but yet disconcerted by the new regime's apparent moderation, determined aloofness from all partisan constellations, and oracular though cryptic pledges of purification and renovation. They sought to force it to show its hand and simultaneously to incline it toward their own policy preferences. The press began to hedge and to hector. The Rightist and Center-affiliated newspapers, deploring what they referred to as the futile and misguided "Aventine secession" of the west Polish irreconcilables, advised a wait-and-see attitude toward Bartel—whose integrity and idealism they acknowledged—and warned the Left not to push Bartel and Poland further toward a real revolutionary abyss.[6] The deeply conservative Association of Landed Proprietors (Związek Ziemian) met on May 18 and, apparently gratified by the government's moderation so far but also nervous lest it succumb to Leftist and Left-Peasantist pressures for radical land reform, resolved that all outstanding social questions called for cold, calm, dispassionate deliberation in an atmosphere of law and order. The land problem in particular—the resolution concluded—must be approached with due regard for the legitimate

[4] *Ibid.*, I, 35–36. It appears that the itch to impose such censorship was particularly strong in the office of the new commissar for Warsaw, General Sławoj-Składkowski.

[5] *Ilustrowany Kurjer Codzienny*, May 18, 1926; *Dokumenty chwili*, I, 37. The admonition alluding to *Robotnik* was prophetic; this paper was the first subsequently to suffer confiscation of an issue at the hands of Sławoj-Składkowski.

[6] *Dokumenty chwili*, II, 13–25; *Kurjer Warszawski* and *Ilustrowany Kurjer Codzienny*, May–June, 1926, *passim*.

claims of justice, patriotism, and religious faith. In other words, the government was reminded that in vast areas of eastern Poland a breakup of the large estates would benefit the White Russian and Ukrainian peasantry—often Orthodox in religion—at the expense of the Polish Catholic proprietors. Ten days later, on May 28, a group of industrialists and bankers published a statement which was already far less anxious about the government's intentions toward their sector of the economy and explicitly declared their confidence in the Bartel-Piłsudski regime.[7]

The Left bloc, as expected, did its best to counter such conservative pressures, inducements, and flattery upon the new regime. Its press directed a steady stream of specific policy demands and recommendations at the government. Its four constituent parties—including Bartel's own Klub Praca—issued a declaration on May 20 emphasizing that the recent coup d'état must become the starting point for the full implementation in Poland of a true democracy, based on right and justice. Piłsudski's victory having, in their view, demonstrated the possibility of achieving that goal, the Left-bloc parties further endorsed the new government's intention of launching a "purification drive," urged Piłsudski's prompt elevation to the national presidency, and demanded the immediate dissolution of the discredited Right-and-Center-dominated Sejm and Senate, to be followed by early elections.[8]

Piłsudski himself was understandably intent to retain the free hand he had acquired by emerging from the coup in triumph and without acknowledged debts to any political party, not even to the Socialists for the railroad strike. It was also to his interest, having once decided against an explicit dictatorship, to sustain the aura of expectant awe in which the public now held him, by being Delphic, yet high-minded

---

[7] The resolution of the landed proprietors (signed by Count Maurycy Zamoyski, Jan Stecki, et al.) is in Dokumenty chwili, II, 19, and that of the industrialists and bankers (also with signatures) is in the Ilustrowany Kurjer Codzienny, May 30, 1926.

[8] The text of the Left-bloc declaration of May 20 is in Dokumenty chwili, II, 20–21. In addition to Bartel's Klub Praca, the parties signing it were the PPS, Wyzwolenie, and Stronnictwo Chłopskie. The Ukrainians endorsed this Left-bloc demand for new elections. Having extensively boycotted the elections of November, 1922, they now desired to undo that blunder and elevate their parliamentary representation to its due demographic level.

and "strong," in his public utterances. Such a stance was rendered all the more desirable—even necessary—by Piłsudski's lack of explicit views in most areas of public policy other than military and foreign affairs. Piłsudski was able successfully to project this desired image of independence, power, and integrity, while simultaneously suggesting hidden reserves of ideas and wisdom, in a series of intelligently presented and cleverly utilized foreign and domestic press interviews conducted during the last week of May.[9] Stressing that any hesitation which might be discerned in his actions since the successful conclusion of the coup was exclusively over the means, not the determination, to rescue Poland from her perilous straits through strong government, Piłsudski went on to pride himself at having managed to "legalize" his coup without resort to political dictatorship and at having effected a revolution of power without any socially or institutionally revolutionary consequences. Acknowledging that these developments had disappointed some of his (Leftist) supporters, who had hoped for a period of purge-dictatorship, Piłsudski explained that any dictatorship, no matter how benevolent or reformist, would only have retarded the necessary and desirable political maturation of the Polish people. Claiming to have friends in both political camps, Piłsudski protested that he wanted to have nothing to do with such notions and labels as "Left" and "Right." Indeed, he insisted, these very terms had no rational meaning in Poland: socially, she could not afford to imitate either Soviet Russian or fascist Italian experiments; politically, her so-called Right had presented the perverse spectacle (in relation to the general historical stance of the European Right) of envenomed hostility to strong executive authority, first in tailoring the constitution so as to emasculate the presidency, then in assassinating the first elected holder of that office (Narutowicz). As for himself, Piłsudski was at pains to argue that his respect for the dignity of the presidency was such that he had gone out of his way and even discommoded his military operations in a vain effort—spoiled by others—to avoid involving its incumbent (Wojciechowski) in the recent crisis. As regards the immediate future of the office, he did not wish to be the only

[9] These interviews are reprinted in Piłsudski, *PZ,* IX, 11–30. The original order of their publication had been: *Le Matin* (Paris), May 24; *Kurjer Poranny* (Warsaw), May 25; *Le Matin,* May 26; *Kurjer Poranny,* May 27 and 29, 1926.

presidential candidate. He hoped that others would emerge before the pending election (which Rataj on May 22 had announced for May 31) and that all the candidates would collectively demand the constitutional strengthening of the presidency and collectively repudiate any *pacta conventa* which might be solicited from them by political parties or pressure groups. After the election, Sejm and Senate should disperse in order to give the government a chance to govern without the ubiquitous petty interference by the legislators, which was the bane of the country's political life. This, indeed, was the main long-term reform which Poland required: the valid principle of the political responsibility of the government to the legislature having become corrupted into a morass of collusion between government and parties, of influence peddling, wirepulling, and personnel packing by deputies and senators among ministers and administrators, it was imperative that the entire executive branch—president, cabinet, administration— be emancipated from this chronic oppression and empowered, at last, truly to govern.

Though there was much that was incisive, sensible, and shrewd in these comments by Piłsudski, they contained little that was reminiscent of the spirit of that denunciation of social injustice with which he had bid for Leftist support on the evening of May 12, when the fate of his "armed demonstration" still hung in the balance. Apart from his rejection of Soviet and fascist models as inappropriate for Poland (with which the PPS would have agreed), Piłsudski's only social comment in these post-coup press interviews was a twice-repeated and—in context—gratuitous denunciation of *nouveaux riches* elements as having allegedly achieved a stranglehold on the country's state and political institutions through systematic, and hitherto unpunished, corruption. These remarks could plausibly be interpreted as a veiled appeal to the old, conservative, established aristocracy to reactivate itself politically and help Piłsudski to recover the state from the clutches of a traditionless, *arriviste,* National Democratic bourgeoisie. In this sense, the passages can be read as a continuation of the approach Piłsudski had made to the conservative aristocracy on May 13 in soliciting its mediation to end the Warsaw fighting. It is also worth noting that, whereas the Left bloc was demanding the dissolution of Sejm and Senate so that a more genuinely representative legislature might be elected, Piłsudski suggested only their adjournment in order to free the executive branch from their harassing presence.

It would be an error cynically to dismiss, as mere rationalization, Piłsudski's explanation that his refraining from making himself dictator had been motivated by a desire to encourage the public's political maturation. Though the political and military strength which the Belwederians had mobilized during the coup did indeed indicate that a Piłsudskist dictatorship would have met with serious difficulties, perhaps even provoking renewed fighting,[10] and though an attempt to establish such a dictatorship would therefore have thrown Piłsudski into unwelcome sociopolitical dependence on the Left and hence was unacceptable to him, yet there is also no doubt of Piłsudski's utter sincerity in viewing himself as the teacher of the nation, paternally guiding it toward the moral and political responsibilities of democracy. It was precisely out of the friction between this romantic, *noblesse oblige,* tutorial self-image and Piłsudski's equally sincere and strong belief that Poland's safety required the retention and maximization of decisive power in his own hands that so much political frustration and personal tragedy was to be generated over the next decade.

Against the background of the approaching presidential election, Piłsudski's handling of his press interviews had admirably served his purpose. While the Left was skeptical of the pride he took in having avoided all the sociopolitical consequences which might have been provoked by the recent military and political upheaval, it was nevertheless mollified by his agreement with it—even though for different reasons—that the current legislature had proved a negative quantity in the political scales. The Left was also gratified that, without explicitly announcing it, Piłsudski seemed to take his own presidential candidacy for granted. The view that he was basically and ultimately a man of the Left was still prevalent within this group and accounts for much of the Leftist determination to elevate him to the presidency, thereby—hopefully—reactivating the potential dynamism of the recent crisis. Yet the very "moderation" and "responsibility" manifested in

[10] Not only were bellicose elements strong in Poznania and Pomerania, but Sikorski in the southeast also claimed to have been ready and determined to reopen armed hostilities had Piłsudski made himself dictator. See Sikorski, pp. 14–15.

Piłsudski's press interviews also served to convince many non-Leftist, "moderate" and "responsible" elements, not hitherto or otherwise friendly to him, that Piłsudski could and should be entrusted with a strengthened chief executive office, if only to reunite *de facto* and *de jure* power in the state and enable him to keep his "wilder" supporters in line.[11]

Piłsudski's own final intervention before the election took the form of a remarkable speech delivered on May 29 to an impressive assemblage of influential Sejm deputies and senators whom Bartel had gathered so that they might hear Piłsudski expound unofficially but authoritatively on his view of the political problems involved in the forthcoming presidential election. Not wishing to evoke echoes of the ill-fated first presidential election of 1922, when the issue of the National Minorities' contribution to Narutowicz's victory had proved so bitterly divisive, Bartel had invited no representatives of their parties to this meeting. The unmollified National Democrats nevertheless boycotted it, though some Christian Nationalists did attend together with representatives of all the other important Polish parties.[12]

Piłsudski opened a sharp speech by brusquely refusing to discuss his recent coup d'état, declaring that, as his own conscience was not troubled over it, he saw no reason to account for it to anyone else. He then immediately proceeded to locate the main cause of Poland's weakness and misery in the morass of unpunished corruption which swamped her state institutions. Ruefully recalling that his stature had been such that he could easily have made himself dictator at the moment of Poland's resurrection in 1918, he explained that he had instead summoned the Constituent Sejm because he had then believed

[11] See Porczak, *Rewolucja majowa,* p. 55, for Leftist hopes, versus the "responsible" expectations of E. Romer, pp. 41–50. A brother of General Jan Romer, a renowned geographer, and one of Poland's most distinguished intellectuals, Professor Eugeniusz Romer published his arguments for electing Piłsudski president in the *Kurjer Lwowski* of May 27, 1926. On that same day, Poland's biggest and most influential newspaper, the *Ilustrowany Kurjer Codzienny,* also came out for Piłsudski's presidential candidacy, expressing its confidence that he would permit no revolutionary deepening of the recent crisis.

[12] Estimates of the total number attending vary from thirty (*Ilustrowany Kurjer Codzienny,* May 31, 1926) to over one hundred (Pobóg-Malinowski, *Najnowsza historia,* II, 488). Both of these sources give some of the names of those attending. Another extensive list, of 23 names, is in Wierzbicki, p. 218. For the National Democratic decision to boycott the affair, see Głąbiński, p. 552.

in the nation's moral regeneration. Alas, instead of such a regeneration, the state had been taken over by knaves and scoundrels. Democracy itself had become discredited through partisan strife and excess. All this evil had been directed against the state as such and against its chief executive in particular. He himself had been hounded with slander; Narutowicz had been murdered and the instigators of this murder had gone unpunished; Wojciechowski had been intimidated into despairing impotence by the ruthlessness and selfishness of Polish political life. Now he, Piłsudski, once again had the opportunity to make himself dictator on the morrow of the recent crisis and once again—but for the last time—was desisting. He would make one final trial to determine if Poland could be ruled without recourse to the whip and give the politicians—the deputies and senators—one more chance freely to elect a suprapartisan, truly national president. After that, they must disperse in order to give that president and the government a chance to govern. With his own candidacy they could do as they wished. Elected or not, he would continue to wage war against villainy and corruption in the state. If they bungled this, their last chance to set the nation's political house in order, he would no longer protect them from the anger of the street when the next revolutionary wave burst over them. He had no desire to rule through the whip, which he had learned to hate under the preindependence partitioning powers, and he hoped that the politicians would not cause him ultimately to regret not having resorted to it. In the final analysis, however, there was always the army, which had given life to the Polish state and had remained its one moral and creative island while the rest of the nation's political life and public institutions had sunk into a bog of contempt and derision.[13]

The speech, delivered in a deliberatively provocative and belligerent manner, was a strange performance, suggesting that Piłsudski was not clear as to what precisely he wanted and was frustrated over his current role. In principle eager to legitimize his position, he was simultaneously conscious of his unique power and role, and thus resented owing such a legitimation to the compromised and therefore

[13] The speech was published in the *Kurjer Poranny* of May 30, 1926, and is reprinted in Piłsudski, *PZ*, IX, 30–33.

possibly compromising Sejm and Senate. Hence his threatening references to the street (that is, revolution) and the army (that is, praetorianism). It seems likely that Piłsudski had genuinely, if somewhat naïvely, hoped—as his earlier press interviews had repeatedly suggested—that several distinguished and prestigious presidential candidates would present themselves and that these, acting as a kind of *ad hoc* national council of sages under his own leadership, could collectively enforce on and extract from the Sejm and Senate certain constitutional amendments to strengthen the powers of the presidency.

The Right was offended by the substance of the speech. The Left was embarrassed. Itself highly critical of the current Sejm and Senate as allegedly unrepresentative, the Left was disconcerted by the insulting tone of Piłsudski's references to politicians, parties, and parliamentary life as such. In Poznań, the still choleric Right-wingers of the Organization for the Defense of the State announced through the *Kurjer Poznański* of May 31 that their province would never recognize an election of Piłsudski to the presidency after such implicit threats and explicit insults as were contained in his speech of May 29. The time and particularly the place of the election were also proving controversial. The government had originally hoped to schedule it earlier than May 31 but had been obliged to await the relative tranquilization of the western areas. The Right in general, and the Poznanian-Pomeranian Right in particular, was also demanding that the election be transferred from the capital to a city less intimidated by Piłsudskist bayonets than Warsaw was stated to be.[14] As the constitution did not specify the locale of a presidential election, there was some sentiment—with which Acting President Rataj was initially reported to agree—for appeasing the Right by holding the election in the medieval capital of Kraków.[15] In the end, however, after consultations among Rataj, Bartel, and Piłsudski, Warsaw was selected in

[14] Various Rightist demands to this effect are reprinted in Stroński, pp. 521–23; Strumph-Wojtkiewicz *et al.*, p. 123; *Dokumenty chwili,* II, 19–20; *Kurjer Warszawski,* May 21 and 23, 1926; *Ilustrowany Kurjer Codzienny,* May 31, 1926. See also Gauvain, "La Crise polonaise," No. 1682, p. 814.

[15] The *Ilustrowany Kurjer Codzienny,* which was itself published in Kraków, endorsed this city as a compromise solution (an alternative to Warsaw and Poznań) in an editorial of May 22, 1926.

order to demonstrate to the nation and the world that calm and tranquillity and freedom reigned once again throughout Poland, particularly in her recently embattled capital.[16]

Speculation about presidential candidacies was widespread and intense. Piłsudski was, of course, the nominee of his own entourage and of the Left bloc. Among his recent enemies in the Warsaw battle, the ever-pragmatic Witos, always ready to acknowledge and respect force, was in favor of giving Piłsudski a clear run and thus letting him demonstrate what he intended to do with the power which he had wrested to himself by the coup.[17] The more ideological and less detached Right, however, insisted that it had an obligation to oppose and seek to defeat Piłsudski. Some Rightists, to make their moral point, proposed voting for the resigned Wojciechowski, who was, however, unavailable. Rataj refused to stand as a Right-Center compromise candidate, announcing that he was not yet ready to abandon active politics for the largely ceremonial functions of the presidency. One may speculate whether that was indeed his real or main motive for not running against Piłsudski. There seems, on the other hand, no reason to doubt that Trąmpczyński was both sincere and correct when he removed himself from consideration with the blunt remark that his candidacy would be regarded by both Piłsudski and the Left as a provocation. Roman Dmowski, the ideological mentor of the National Democratic camp, also declined to let his name be entered, and a rumor that the choice would fall on the internationally renowned pianist Ignacy Paderewski quickly fell flat with the realization that the public's memories of his earlier premiership (January 16–December 9, 1919) were not the happiest and that he had lived abroad most of the time since then. The possibility of again nominating the National Democrat Count Maurycy Zamoyski, a former ambassador to France (1919–24) and foreign minister (January 19–July 27, 1924), who had been the Right's defeated candidate against the subsequently assassinated Narutowicz in December, 1922, was also briefly explored and promptly abandoned, since there was no hope of persuading any

[16] See Rataj's explanatory comments of May 22, 1926, to the press, cited in Maciejowski, p. 5. The report that he had originally favored Kraków is in *The Times* (London), May 19, 1926.
[17] See Witos' testimony of October 28, 1931, as a defendant at the Brześć trial in *Sprawa brzeska*, p. 80, or *Proces brzeski*, p. 67.

section of the peasantry to accept the candidacy of this largest latifundist in all Poland. Somewhat shrewder was a suggestion to nominate the conservative and distinguished Kraków historian Michał
Bobrzyński, who, however, removed himself from consideration with
the comment that he could not, in good faith, take an oath to the current constitution. General Józef Haller and the National Democratic
parliamentary leader, Stanisław Głąbiński, were also briefly considered
as possible candidates for the Right. In addition, the names of the
former premier and foreign minister, Skrzyński, and of General
Sosnkowski were speculated about as eventual nonpartisan, suprapolitical, national compromise candidates.[18]

Finally, on May 31—election day—the Right selected as its candidate the National Democratic *wojewoda* of recalcitrant Poznania,
Count Adolf Bniński. This dubious choice apparently strengthened
Piłsudski's chances since several Christian Democrats promptly declared that they would vote for him in preference to Bniński, and in
the final balloting many Party members appear to have followed their
example. Piast formally gave its members a free vote, but behind the
scenes Witos was successfully urging his party colleagues to support
Piłsudski.[19] The NPR split, its Ciszak-Waszkiewicz offshoot having
already declared for Piłsudski on May 28 and the parent leadership
now conceding a free vote.[20] The Left-bloc parties having resolved
collectively and individually to vote for Piłsudski, it remained but for
the Communists, their minor allies, and the National Minorities to
adopt positions.

This last problem, the stand of the National Minorities, was potentially inflammable. The fact that their "non-Polish" votes had given
Narutowicz his margin of victory over Zamoyski on December 9, 1922,
had led to recrimination and assassination. Zealous, in principle, to
demonstrate that he could reconcile the National Minorities to the Polish state, and personally free of chauvinistic xenophobia, Piłsudski was

[18] This discussion of the search for presidential candidates is abbreviated
from many editorials and articles appearing between May 20 and 30 in the
Ilustrowany Kurjer Codzienny, Kurjer Warszawski, Berliner Tageblatt, and
Frankfurter Zeitung.

[19] For the preelection maneuverings of the Christian Democrats and of
Witos, see, respectively, Maciejowski, p. 34, and Pobóg-Malinowski, *Najnowsza
historia,* II, 489.

[20] *Ilustrowany Kurjer Codzienny,* May 30, 1926, and Maciejowski, p. 34.

immediately concerned, however, to avoid the kiss of death of receiving the presidency from their hands. Hence the government's otherwise gratuitously arbitrary timing in dissolving the last surviving unit of the Ukrainian gymnastic—and onetime paramilitary—society Sich toward the end of May.[21] Hence, also, Bartel's exclusion of the National Minorities from the audience of Piłsudski's preelection speech of May 29. More than mere sops to the Right, these gestures appear as calculated efforts to jostle the National Minorities—at least the eastern, Slavic ones—into abstention instead of support for Piłsudski in the presidential voting. This, at any rate, is in part what resulted. While the German and Jewish parliamentary delegations eventually endorsed Piłsudski,[22] the Ukrainians and White Russians cast blank or invalid ballots.[23] It must be borne in mind, however, that, even without these immediate preelection affronts to them, the eastern, Slavic minorities were by mid-1926 already substantially disenchanted with Polish political institutions as such, including, to some extent, the Piłsudskist camp.[24]

The voting took place amidst stringent precautions against a repetition of the tragic events which had been elicited by Narutowicz's election. By order of Commissar General Sławoj-Składkowski, public meetings and the sale of alcohol had been banned in Warsaw as of the afternoon of May 29 and food prices were frozen. Police patrols were heavy.[25] One of the statutory Sejm seats being vacant at the moment, the total number of eligible electors was 554 (443 deputies and 111

---

[21] *Ilustrowany Kurjer Codzienny,* May 27, 1926. The name Sich refers historically to a fortified Cossack settlement. The modern gymnastic society of that name, founded in 1900 among the Ukrainians of the Habsburg empire, was originally analogous to the Czech Sokol. The Polish authorities had suppressed the general association in 1924 but at least one unit had survived into 1926.

[22] Halpern, p. 25, and *Schulthess' Europäischer Geschichtskalender,* 1926, p. 367.

[23] This was urged by the influential Ukrainian newspaper *Dilo* (Action—published in Lwów), as reported in *Ilustrowany Kurjer Codzienny,* May 31, 1926. See also Maciejowski, p. 34.

[24] See the skeptical remarks about Piłsudski by the White Russian leader Bronislav Tarashkevich, quoted in *Kurjer Warsawski,* May 27, 1926. He recalled that the eastern minorities had supported Wojciechowski in the second presidential election of December, 1922, only to have him side with the Right against them on ethnic minority issues. Piłsudski might well prove to be no better from their point of view.

[25] *Ilustrowany Kurjer Codzienny* and *Berliner Tageblatt,* May 30, 1926. The Piłsudskist weekly *Głos Prawdy* reported rumors of another Rightist assassina-

senators). The result of the balloting, as announced by Rataj toward noon on May 31 was 292 votes for Piłsudski, 193 votes for Bniński, and 61 blank or invalid ballots. Eight electors had been absent.

Though the vote was secret, it is possible to reconstruct the political content of the figures. As a result of defections, splits, and amalgamations, the partisan composition of the National Assembly had altered somewhat since the parliamentary elections of November, 1922. By May, 1926, the Right bloc, strictly speaking, consisted of 130 National Democrats, 28 Christian Nationalists, and 9 formally independent but closely associated deputies and senators. Totaling 167 members in the two chambers, it accounted for most of Bniński's 193 votes, the remaining 26 having been provided by some Christian Democrats and National Laborites. These two parties, of which the former had run on the Right-bloc electoral list in 1922 but had subsequently organized itself as a separate—though generally allied—parliamentary club, now totaled, respectively, 48 and 21 deputies and senators.

Piast, prompted by Witos, threw the bulk of its 66 votes to Piłsudski. Nevertheless, the three members of the Party who had held portfolios in the cabinet overthrown by the coup—Witos, Kiernik, and Osiecki—absented themselves from the balloting as a moral gesture. Piłsudski also received the 121 votes of the Left bloc, consisting of 48 Socialists, 33 deputies and senators of Wyzwolenie, 30 of the Stronnictwo Chłopskie, and the Klub Praca's 10. A handful of miscellaneous independent and radical Leftist electors also appear to have voted for Piłsudski, as did a substantial number of Christian Democrats and National Laborites. The rest of Piłsudski's 292 votes came from the 22 Germans and 47 Jews of the 111 electors representing National Minority parties. The 28 Ukrainians, 13 White Russians, and 1 Russian account for most of the 61 blank and invalid ballots. Among these ballots were six made out to the local Communist leader, Stanisław Łańcucki, and one to the Polish-born organizer of the Soviet Cheka, Felix Dzerzhinsky. (At this time there were six Communists in the Sejm. The "extra" ballot bearing a Communist name was probably cast by one of the seven deputies of the closely allied Independ-

tion plot which allegedly justified the presence in Warsaw of large numbers of pro-Piłsudskist Riflemen, whose disarming and dispersal were being demanded by the Right.

ent Peasant Party, the rest of whom either cast blank ballots or voted for Piłsudski.) The unaccounted remainder of the blank ballots is likely to have been cast by stray Christian Democrats, National Laborites, or members of Piast.[26]

Piłsudski's election to the presidency by the constitutionally required absolute majority of the National Assembly elicited enthusiastic demonstrations among the Warsaw crowds and troops. The Socialists scheduled a huge parade. In an ostentatiously theatrical ceremony, the election was even verbally "reported" by a military honor guard to the Tomb of the Unknown Soldier and to the nearby equestrian statue of the national hero and Napoleonic marshal, Prince Józef Poniatowski. To universal consternation, however, Piłsudski declined to serve. In a letter significantly written on War Ministry stationery, he explained that his strategy in permitting himself to be nominated and elected had been simply to legalize retroactively his recent coup d'état. This achieved, he now refused to serve in a position which was constitutionally too feeble to encompass his energies. Nor could he forgive or forget the murder of Narutowicz or certain brutal assaults on his own children, for which members of the National Assembly bore moral responsibility. Hence, his conscience did not permit him to accept office from its hands even though he appreciated the fact that at least this time it had not been so hypocritical as to elect him unanimously— an improvement over the proceedings of February 20, 1919.[27]

From virtually every point of view—moral, historical, political, psychological—this performance of Piłsudski's was deplorable. In preening himself on having allowed the balloting to take its course in order thereby to legalize his coup, he seemed to have forgotten that the darkest events of Poland's earlier history—including her very partitions—had thus been "legalized" by cowed and degraded Sejms. He

[26] The numerical estimate of party strengths in Sejm and Senate as of May, 1926, is based on *Ilustrowany Kurjer Codzienny*, May 31, 1926. For the figures as of the morrow of the elections in November, 1922, see above, p. 6, n. 3.

[27] The letter is reprinted in Piłsudski, *PZ*, IX, 33–34. The cryptic and unexplained allusion to attacks on his children appears to refer to alleged "buzzings" by Zagórski's airplanes of Piłsudski's Sulejówek home—where his wife and young daughters were then domiciled—during the coup. Piłsudski had already expressed his indignation about this in his press interview in the *Kurjer Poranny* of May 25, reprinted in his *PZ*, IX, 18–19. Mme Piłsudska's *Memoirs* and *Wspomnienia* make no mention of it.

was also apparently unaware of the incompatibility of insisting, on the one hand, that the election had legalized his coup while simultaneously declaring his moral revulsion against the body which had elected him. The humiliation he thereby inflicted on the National Assembly and the debasement to which his stratagem had subjected the presidency, moreover, were hardly compatible with his frequent, virtually obsessive claims to have been motivated in his recent "armed demonstration" by a compelling need to elevate the prestige of state institutions in the eyes of the Polish public. The obscure allusion to alleged—probably fictional, and in any event trivial—threats against the lives of his small daughters was an effrontery at a time when several hundred Polish families were still mourning their dead, killed in the course of his coup d'état. The institutional powers of the presidency were indeed weak, but—as subsequent developments showed—the National Assembly was amenable to strengthening them. Piłsudski's action, per contra, had the opposite effect. As the manifestly most powerful political personality in the country at this moment, he ensured the continuing political impotence of the presidency through his manner of declining the office, thus guaranteeing that its eventual incumbent would be a relative cipher, a creature of and a screen for Piłsudski, a man obviously not the republic's first citizen in any politically convincing sense during Piłsudski's own lifetime. The coup and the vote of May 31 had given Piłsudski a unique opportunity to combine charismatic and institutional power, to restructure and correct the governmental-constitutional system of Poland—and he had thrown it away, revealing once again his characteristically ambivalent approach to power. Eager to wield the substance of power, he suspected its public forms as potential restrictions on his personal freedom of action. At the same time, he also feared lest its official incarnation by himself—as president, for example—be taken as an implied inhibition on the nation's freedom to mature out of his tutelage, a maturation for which his "better part" always hoped.[28]

It was subsequently argued that to have accepted his election to the

[28] For a suggestive discussion of the dialectic of power and freedom in Piłsudski's psychology and thought, see the forewords by his intimate collaborator and subsequent (1929) premier, Kazimierz Świtalski, to the fifth and ninth volumes of Piłsudski, *PZ*. Also interesting, if erratic, is the discussion of Piłsudski's personality in Malaparte, chapters III and VI.

presidency after having for so long criticized the constitutional emascu-
lation of the office would have appeared as unprincipled on Piłsudski's
part.[29] Yet, first to permit and then to refuse the election made an
even more perverse impression. Another suggestion—that Piłsudski
was unwilling to accept the diversion from direct control over military
matters which his elevation to the presidency would have required [30]—
while plausible, also fails to justify the supposed "legalization" maneuver of first permitting his nomination and election to proceed
before declining to accept. Furthermore, the National Assembly might
conceivably have been prepared to address itself to this difficulty in
its subsequent constitutional revisions. In any event, Piłsudski's attention to the army over the next decade was to be far from exclusive of
other political concerns. It seems evident, in retrospect, that Piłsudski
was chagrined that the election had not been and could not be that
cathartic exercise in national reconciliation and political renovation
for which he had in some sense hoped and which he and Bartel had
sought to elicit by their actions and policies over the past fortnight.
The vote thus also brought home to him the fact that his strenuous
efforts before, during, and since the coup to remain aloof from the
Left, to present himself as a suprapolitical guardian of national interests and state institutions, as the olympian nemesis of all transgressors
and malfactors regardless of party affiliation, had been in vain. To the
National Democrats and particularly to their western militants he
remained a partisan, unacceptable figure. Hence his bittersweet reference to the nonunanimity of the presidential vote. Hence his decision
not to serve, for his conception of the presidency required that its
incumbent be imposing and capable of strong action, yet universally
respected and able to foster general concord. Conscious, on the one
hand, of the extraordinary power which the recent crisis had focused
in his own person, Piłsudski was also aware—and the vote of May 31
sharply reminded him—that he was too controversial to fit his image
of the presidency. He could make and win a coup, but not harmonize
the nation to a collective effort of rededication. Piłsudski had sensed
this before the presidential vote, and it had accounted for the irascible
manner in which he had simultaneously berated the legislators and

[29] Poralla, p. 93.
[30] *Frankfurter Zeitung,* June 1, 1926.

invited their "legitimation" of the coup. His awareness of it also explained a vain attempt on his part to persuade the prestigious former Regent, Prince Zdzisław Lubomirski—to whom he had already turned for one of the coup's abortive mediation efforts—to become a presidential candidate, one uniquely capable, Piłsudski believed, of harnessing all political camps, including even the National Minorities, to cooperative endeavor and of inducing the conservative, supposedly state-oriented aristocracy to resume an active role in Polish public life. But Lubomirski refused even indirectly to sanction Piłsudski's coup d'état by accepting Wojciechowski's office.[31]

His appeal to Lubomirski having fallen on deaf ears, and being unwilling to serve himself, Piłsudski was nevertheless obliged to indicate some alternative choice to his stunned supporters, especially as Rataj, on learning of Piłsudski's declination, had immediately scheduled a second election for the next day, June 1. Among those whom Piłsudski considered recommending were his prewar PPS comrade, wartime political collaborator, and postwar *homme de confiance* as premier in 1922, Artur Śliwiński, who by 1926 was out of politics.[32] Another was the distinguished professor of comparative European literature at the university of Wilno, Marian Zdziechowski, who declined.[33] Bartel, in any event, was impressing on Piłsudski the importance of nominating someone more acceptable to the near-mutinous Left than the conservative Zdziechowski, and more symbolic of the modern technological problems which confronted Poland than

[31] For Piłsudski's appeal to Lubomirski, see Morawski, *Tamten brzeg*, p. 159.
[32] Artur Śliwiński had joined Piłsudski's wing of the PPS in 1907; during the war he had presided over the National Central Committee of independence-oriented Polish parties (1915–16) and had been a member of the Provisional Council of State (1917–18) authorized by the Central Powers occupying Poland at that time. He had then served as vice-mayor of Warsaw until 1922, when he was Piłsudski's candidate for premier in a celebrated tug-of-war with the Constituent Sejm's Rightist-dominated majority. Ironically, his mother was killed by a stray bullet during the coup. For a discussion of his potential presidential candidacy in 1926, see Skotnicki, p. 274.
[33] M. Zdziechowski, p. 2. Zdziechowski speculates—probably correctly—that his being considered for the presidency represented a general gesture by Piłsudski toward political conservatism and a particular one toward the Stefan Batory University in Wilno, of which Marian Zdziechowski was then rector and which Piłsudski had already patronized during his Sulejówek "retirement." Marian Zdziechowski is not to be confused with the National Democratic financial expert and former minister (1925–26) Jerzy Zdziechowski. For an extensive biographical sketch, see Kościałkowski, "Marian Zdziechowski."

the historian and theater director Śliwiński. He recommended his professorial colleague at the Lwów Polytechnic, the famous electrochemist Ignacy Mościcki, who as a young man had worked with Piłsudski in the illegal prewar PPS and had subsequently made his international reputation as a scientist at Fribourg in Switzerland and at Lwów and had also proved outstandingly successful as the director of the extensive Silesian nitrate works at Chorzów after they passed into Polish possession in 1922.

Piłsudski endorsed Mościcki's name with alacrity,[34] but part of the Left proved recalcitrant. Humiliated by Piłsudski's contemptuous repudiation of his election after all their work and propaganda on his behalf, offended by his deliberate flirtation with conservatives, outraged by his blithe assumption that they must follow, sheeplike, wherever he led, the PPS, Wyzwolenie, and Stronnictwo Chłopskie determined to assert their independence of him. As Rataj refused another plea to stand as a compromise candidate and instead threw his influence behind Mościcki,[35] the PPS resolved to nominate its current parliamentary chairman, Dr. Zygmunt Marek. Since Bartel had originally sponsored Mościcki and was in any event Piłsudski's man, the PPS had no illusions that his Klub Praca could be induced to support Marek. It had, however, good reason to be disappointed when its partners in the Left bloc, Wyzwolenie and Stronnictwo Chłopskie, after some hesitation, eventually also yielded to the considerable pressure being applied on them to back Mościcki. Rataj was simultaneously aiding Witos in shepherding the Piast Peasant Party into Mościcki's pasture, whither most of the NPR followed after some hesitation. The Right once again nominated Bniński, whom this time the Christian Democrats, reverting to their traditional alliance, also endorsed. The Germans and Jews, after toying with the notion of a *pro forma* minorities' candidate, eventually decided to vote for Mościcki, while the Slavic eastern minorities (Ukrainians and White Russians) again remained officially aloof. The Communists and their allies decided to cast their ballots for Dr. Alfred Fiderkiewicz, a deputy of the "fellow-traveling" Independent Peasant Party, whose

[34] See his remarks of June 1 in praise of Mościcki in Piłsudski, *PZ*, IX, 35–36. For a slightly different version of this sequence, see Popiel, pp. 46–51.
[35] Rataj, p. 410. See also *Kurjer Warszawski,* June 1, 1926.

candidacy, not having been endorsed by the legally required minimum of fifty signatures, was technically invalid.[36]

Of the 545 deputies and senators who appeared on June 1 for this second presidential election within two days, 215 voted for Mościcki, 211 for Bniński, 56 for Marek, while 63 cast blank or invalid ballots. Piłsudski thus had failed to transfer his own majority intact to Mościcki. The PPS and a few other Leftists had preferred to make the futile but necessary gesture of voting for Marek, while most of the Christian Democrats had redefected to Bniński. The structure of the blank and invalid ballots had remained basically stable, though those cast on the previous day by undecided Christian Democrats may this time have been replaced by members of the Stronnictwo Chłopskie unwilling to chose between Mościcki and Marek.

Mościcki's total not being an absolute majority of the National Assembly, a second ballot was taken immediately after the first. The Socialists, having once demonstrated their independence, now yielded to Bartel's entreaties, withdrew Marek's candidacy, and declared for Mościcki as an act of "republican discipline" against the Right. As a result of this decision and of a handful of desertions (probably again Christian Democratic) from Bniński, the total votes for Mościcki now reached 281, while Bniński retained 200. One ballot obstinately again bore Marek's name, and 63 others were also once again invalid or blank. Mościcki's total was barely adequate to meet the constitutional requirement of an absolute majority of the 555-member National Assembly and, like Narutowicz's in 1922, would not have been reached without a substantial increment of German and Jewish minority support.

This time, however, the Left seemed more discomfited by the election than the Right. Though Piłsudski as a person remained anathema to the National Democratic camp, it had taken his measure as a poli-

---

[36] This résumé of the results of the various party caucuses is based on Maciejowski, pp. 44–47; *Kurjer Warszawski*, June 1, 1926; and Fiderkiewicz, *Dobre czasy*, p. 316. Before settling on Marek as its candidate, the PPS had also briefly considered two other, somewhat more prominent, leaders, Ignacy Daszyński and Norbert Barlicki.

Fiderkiewicz received the votes of the seven colleagues of his own party, of the six overt Communists, and of the five deputies of the White Russian Hramada (Throng), a nationalistic and revolutionary peasant party. They were numbered among the invalid ballots.

tician and correctly deduced that he was no social radical or political revolutionary. The conservative strata went further and became available for active cooperation with him. Both of these political orientations took Mościcki's election in their stride, as did the Center, which had contributed many votes to it. The Left, however, already disturbed by the results, or rather lack of expected results, of the coup and offended by Piłsudski's conduct in the matter of the election, was now to be further disquieted by his symbolically significant gesture of insisting that Mościcki's inauguration take place in the Royal Castle rather than in the Sejm building. The PPS was so deeply affronted by this implied attack on parliamentary sovereignty that most of its members boycotted the inauguration on June 4.[37] But worse was to come. With the election of his candidate safely behind him, Piłsudski now refused the Left that dissolution of the legislature and scheduling of new elections which Bartel's clear indications to this effect and Piłsudski's own obscurer allusions had been giving the Left reason to expect, thereby helping to keep it in line. Convinced that three years of socioeconomic crisis had channeled the political mood of the country in its own direction, and confident that the recent coup had even accelerated this trend, the Left was most eager to harvest its expected victory in early elections. The results of many local elections over the next few months were to confirm and spur its confidence in this regard.[38]

By the same token, however, Piłsudski preferred to retain the current Sejm with its chastened, defeated, cowed, confused, and now split Right-Center majority. This Sejm could be expected to prove far more docile than a new, representative one, dominated by a triumphant and confident Left. Since its maximum five-year life span did not expire

---

[37] *Kurjer Warszawski*, June 4, 1926. Colonel Krok-Paszkowski commanded the honor guard at the inauguration. The six Communist deputies did attend it—to create a scene by shouting for the release of political prisoners, work for the unemployed, land for the landless, a worker-peasant government for Poland, social revolution for the world, etc.

That the PPS was correct in interpreting the change in the locale of the inauguration as an effort by Piłsudski to elevate the prestige and autonomy of the executive in relation to the legislative branch of government is confirmed in I. Mościcki, "Wspomnienia," *Niepodległość*, p. 196. For the same reason, Piłsudski caused the official presidential residence to be transferred from the Belweder palace to the Royal Castle. Piłsudski himself then moved into the former.

[38] Próchnik, *Pierwsze piętnastolecie,* p. 263.

until November, 1927, Piłsudski saw no reason for dissolving it prematurely. For the next few weeks his regime took refuge behind the difficult dissolution clauses of the constitution, even though he had the effective power and the national prestige to compel their implementation. But even after the adoption on August 2 of a constitutional amendment giving the president clear and simple power to dissolve the chambers on a proposal by the cabinet, Piłsudski declined to permit its exercise by Mościcki.[39] Before risking elections, Piłsudski needed more time to woo the conservatives and to build up his own, extensive political camp. To permit the continued functioning of the current legislature was, furthermore, a harmless and propagandistically useful demonstration of his commitment to moderation and legality. In the aftermath of the coup, Piłsudski's policy was circumscribed by the following premise: any tendencies on his part toward social radicalism or explicit dictatorship would have stiffened the resistance of the Right and alienated the supposedly state-oriented conservatives. Piłsudski, in turn, would then have been forced to rely on the Left for the consolidation of his power. Such an alliance, however, was politically repugnant to him, quite apart from the fact that his personal inclinations were neither socially radical nor overtly dictatorial. Hence his watchwords became moderation, legality, and regeneration. Since he was convinced that this necessary regeneration of Poland—indeed, her very security—required his own control or at least supervision of her state apparatus, he was destined to be forced, in time, into an exasperating policy of manipulating, coercing, undermining, and eventually emasculating those public institutions to whose official retention he had committed himself under the rubric of moderation and legality. Thus his style came to require splintered parties, a submissive Sejm, and an obedient president. Yet he remained pathetically aware of the self-defeating nature of this campaign of emasculating the nation's autonomous governmental institutions while seeking to educate it to political maturity. His awareness of this contradiction accounts for the tortured quality, the combined brutality and hesitancy, of Piłsudski's reluctant yet inevitable vendetta against parties, legislature, and constitution over the next years.

Only the new President—who inaugurated his assumption of office

[39] See below, p. 226, for this amendment and above, p. 9, for the original constitutional provisions for dissolution.

with an appeal to the nation in which he took up the new *sanacja* themes of unity, work, and moral regeneration—gave Piłsudski no difficulties. Though Mościcki was to reveal himself as an unexpectedly resourceful and stubborn politician after Piłsudski's death in 1935, he was to be his pliant instrument prior to that time. Mościcki appeared to find this role neither chafing nor humiliating but entirely appropriate. As he explained on one occasion to the chief of his civilian chancellery, as a scientist he believed in expertise: for illness, he would consult a physician; for building a house, he would contract an architect; for governing Poland, he would rely on Piłsudski.[40] As he was otherwise a detached, self-confident, and intelligent man, this reverential deference on Mościcki's part toward Piłsudski—which was typical of the attitude prevailing within the Piłsudskist retinue—is indicative of the enormous and impressive charismatic power of the Marshal's personality.[41]

[40] See the reminiscence of Hełczyński, p. 230.

[41] Ignacy Mościcki was born on December 1, 1867, at Mierzanów, near Płock, in what was then Russian-occupied Poland. His father had been a participant in the Polish insurrection of 1863 against tsarist Russia. Educated in Warsaw and Riga, the young Mościcki became involved in the Socialist revolutionary underground and was obliged to flee to London in 1892 as a result of having been involved in an attempt to assassinate the Russian governor-general in Warsaw. In 1897 he was named an assistant in physics at the Swiss university in Fribourg and four years later was advanced to be the director of its experimental electrochemistry laboratory. Though he attended one International Socialist Congress, his political interests became peripheral to his scientific work, in which he developed new synthetic nitrate and acid production techniques. At one point he proposed a major hydroelectric and nitrate development project for Galicia, a proposal that received the technical endorsement of a predecessor as president of Poland, Narutowicz, then a professor of hydraulic engineering at Zurich. Owing to lack of financial support, this program never came to fruition. By 1912 Mościcki's professional renown was such that a new chair for electrochemistry was created for him at the Lwów Polytechnic in what was then Austrian Poland. There he also established an Experimental Chemical Institute and published many scientific papers. In addition to these functions, in July, 1922, he was appointed to direct the newly acquired, hitherto German, state-owned nitrate works at Chorzów (formerly Königshütte) in Silesia. As president of the Republic after the 1926 coup, Mościcki lent dignity and grace to ceremonial state functions. After Piłsudski's death in 1935, he became politically more active. In September, 1939, he fled with the government to Rumania, from where he was allowed to retire in December—after American diplomatic intervention—to Switzerland. He died there, at Versoix, on October 2, 1946. His immediate predecessor as president, Wojciechowski—on whom Mościcki paid a courtesy call soon after the 1926 election at the insistence of the guilt-laden Piłsudski—also survived the war, as well as the death of his son at the hands of the Germans at Oświęcim (Auschwitz). He died on April 9, 1953, at the age of eighty-four, in a suburb of Warsaw.

CHAPTER XII

AMENDING THE CONSTITUTION

The inherent tendencies of the Piłsudskist system of *sanacja* were not, of course, immediately apparent—or at best only partially and dimly so—to either the protagonists or the observers of the Polish drama in 1926. In the initial postpresidential election period, Piłsudski was to withdraw somewhat from the political limelight to devote himself to his pressing military concerns, leaving the center of the public stage to Prime Minister Bartel, who undertook an enterprising, yet delicate, campaign to consolidate and extend the regime's consensual base.

Bartel's first action after Mościcki's inauguration was to honor the commitment he had made on assuming office, of submitting the resignation of his cabinet to the new president. Mościcki, after consulting Piłsudski,[1] requested Bartel to form another government, and the Prime Minister thereupon endeavored to widen the composition of his cabinet, and hence its hoped-for support, in several political and social directions. Toward the Left, the Ministry of Agriculture was offered to the Wyzwolenie Peasant Party leader, Juliusz Poniatowski, while the Piłsudskist PPS veteran Jędrzej Moraczewski was invited to become vice-minister of railroads. Both declined for the time being. On the reverse tack, there was a plan—also premature and probably fathered by Piłsudski rather than Bartel—to bring the influential conservatives Aleksander Meysztowicz and Prince Janusz Radziwiłł into the government.[2]

Though such dramatic extensions of the cabinet's ideological spectrum were not yet quite feasible, Bartel was able to make a start by enlisting the Christian Democratic deputy and engineer Paweł

---

[1] Mościcki, "Wspomnienia," *Niepodległość,* p. 197.
[2] Meysztowicz was being considered for the justice portfolio and Radziwiłł for that of foreign affairs.

Romocki to take over the direction of the Railroad Ministry on June 14. Romocki's dual political and technical attributes are a significant clue to Bartel's governmental approach and theories. Though prompt to make political overtures which might hopefully elicit an increment of prestige and strength for his government, either by swaying or disrupting a party previously disposed to be negative, Bartel was even more concerned with the technical qualifications of his personnel and believed, somewhat innocently, that he could outflank the political parties and indirectly strengthen his government far beyond any support which they might lend to it by earning for it a general, public reputation for technocratic, managerial expertise. Herein he saw both the challenge and the opportunity with which the coup had confronted the Polish political system. Hence Romocki the engineer was invited to become a full minister while the politically far more significant ex-premier (1918–19) and ex-minister of public works (1925–26), Moraczewski, had been offered only the vice-ministerial post.[3] Hence also the tendency of the other new ministers whom Bartel brought into his reconstructed cabinet to sharpen yet further its already prominent leanings toward the technocratic elite and the intelligentsia.

The engineer Eugeniusz Kwiatkowski, whom Mościcki had made the technical director of the Chorzów nitrate works in 1923, was now brought into the government as minister of industry and commerce and promptly proceeded to make a scintillating public reputation as the developer of the Baltic port of Gdynia and of its railroad connections with the Silesian industrial basin.[4] The ministries of Land Reform

[3] Romocki had once served as director of the War Ministry's Industrial Commission. He now found Bartel's technocratic views on the proper allocation of power within the government to be congenial and resigned his "partisan" (Christian Democratic) Sejm mandate shortly after entering the cabinet, in which he remained until June 27, 1928. On September 27, 1926, his ministry's responsibility was expanded from railroads to all transportation.

[4] Piłsudski, though acknowledging Kwiatkowski's managerial abilities, always denied him any competence as a statesman, politician, or economic theorist. Nevertheless, Bartel and Mościcki were able to hold Piłsudski's skepticism at bay and retain Kwiatkowski in the cabinet until August, 1930, when Piłsudski insisted on dropping him and returning him to industrial management at Chorzów and Mościce. Despite repeated pleas by Mościcki to rescind this "exile," Piłsudski remained adamant and Kwiatkowski could not be brought back into the government until after Piłsudski's death, when he was elevated to be finance minister and vice-premier in charge of all economic matters. Further information on Kwiatkowski will be found in the Biographical Register.

and Agriculture were again separated. The former was assigned on June 20 to Witold Staniewicz, hitherto a professor of agronomy and agricultural economics at Wilno University and the Lwów Polytechnic,[5] while the agriculture portfolio was transferred the next day from Józef to Aleksander Raczyński, an economist, lawyer, and university lecturer (at Lwów). On July 7 Professor Antoni Sujkowski, an anthropogeographer and statistician, became minister of education. Meanwhile, the official leadership of the Finance Ministry had also changed hands as the still controversial Gabriel Czechowicz returned to the relative obscurity but great power of its undersecretaryship, surrendering for the time being its cabinet portfolio to a onetime senior official from that same ministry, Czesław Klarner. A former vice-minister of finance (1924–25) and minister of industry and commerce (1925) in the suprapartisan cabinet of Władysław Grabski, Klarner was a man whose close connections with Polish big business and industrial circles made his replacement of Czechowicz appear as something of a concession to these groups as long as his predecessor was still suspect in their eyes. Initially eager to secure the transfer of the finance portfolio to Gliwic, who now left the cabinet, these powerful economic interests were to be quickly reassured not only by Klarner's categorically conservative fiscal policies but also by the soon verifiable "respectability" of his deputy Czechowicz.[6] The rest of Bartel's reconstructed cabinet consisted of the presumed technical expert holdovers from his first one: himself (Premier), Piłsudski (War), Zaleski (Foreign Affairs), Młodzianowski (Interior), Makowski (Justice), Jurkiewicz (Labor and Welfare), and Broniewski (Public Works).

Bartel's apolitical, managerial approach to government—his readiness to permit the parties to cooperate with his technocratic cabinet but not to contest its competence or agenda—was now to reveal itself in full measure. While the sense of strain in Bartel's mind between government and politics bore some analogy to Piłsudski's own tensions

---

[5] Staniewicz had been adjutant to General Żeligowski in "Middle Lithuania" during 1920–22. He then embarked on his academic career, which he was to resume after leaving the cabinet in 1930. Returning first as professor to Wilno, he became rector there in 1933. He broke with the Piłsudski camp in 1930 in protest over its brutal incarceration of political opposition leaders in the Brześć fortress-prison.

[6] Z. Landau, *Plan Stabilizacyjny, 1927–1930, passim.*

about the power of government to rule in relation to the freedom of society to mature, and to his ambivalence on the theme of substantive power versus the legal responsibilities of public office, Bartel's position was both more intellectualized and more programmatic. Bartel now took the initiative in establishing several advisory committees for various socioeconomic policy areas, on each of which sat "theoretician-experts" (often academics) and "political" spokesmen for the affected interest groups. The committee on industrial problems, for example, was chaired by deputy Andrzej Wierzbicki, a leader of big business and chairman of the Polish equivalent of a chamber of industry and commerce. Heading the committee on agriculture was senator Jan Stecki, president of the Association of Landed Proprietors, while that for labor and welfare issues was presided over by the PPS specialist and former minister (1918–19, 1925–26) for that field, Bronisław Ziemięcki. Thanks in part to the work and advice of the latter committee, a series of progressive regulations and policies in the areas of factory hygiene, accident insurance, and sickness compensation was formulated by the government over the next two years.[7] Often consulting these and similar committees parallel with or even before discussing the relevant problems in the cabinet, Bartel hoped thus to control and energize the governmental bureaucracy by bringing "outside" expert and representative views and interests to bear on it, without, however, funneling these views through the political parties. Conversely, the interested social groups and forces would learn of the government's policy views without recourse to the machinery of the parties. Since, however, Wierzbicki, Stecki, Ziemięcki, *et al.* had party affiliations (National Democratic, Christian Nationalist, Socialist, etc.) and since the advisory committees were indeed active and influential, Bartel could argue and sincerely believe that his regime was by no means an aloof bureaucratic one and that the nation's social and political interests were adequately represented in it—in consultative roles. This concept of cooperation among the "objective" technocratic experts in the government, the "independent" theoretical experts from the universities, and the "subjective" but informed and politically articulate interest groups was Bartel's idea of good government. He also acknowledged the ultimate veto power of

[7] Kowalski, *Zarys historii polskiego ruchu robotniczego,* I, 298, and Z. Landau and J. Tomaszewski, *Zarys historii gospodarczej Polski, 1918–1939,* p. 116.

the political forces in the form of the parliamentary censure vote. Let, however, the "subjective" political forces claim direct policy-making and executive power, and Bartel would become indignantly un-comprehending.[8]

Bartel, it will be recalled, had recommended the dissolution of Sejm and Senate in the immediate aftermath of the coup, while still under the strong, and negative, impression of habitual Right-Center viola-tions of his notions of proper governmental procedures. He reversed himself, however, upon ascertaining that the Left desired such a dis-solution, to be followed by new elections, precisely in order to replace the Right-Center majority with its own and to assume direct govern-mental and policy-making power.[9] Bartel's refusal to indulge the Left in this strategy and his retraction of his earlier stand on dis-solution were no mere blind subservience to Piłsudski. Bartel's ration-ale, in fact, was both more doctrinaire and more naïve than Piłsud-ski's, who understood and rejected the Left on its own political terms. Bartel, on the other hand, reacted to the Left-bloc demands for new elections as if it were perverse in principle to aspire to partisan ag-grandizement at a time when so much social, economic, legislative, and administrative work was pending. As an expression of his belief that governmental responsibility and party politics were incompatible, that a minister could be "objective" only if free of partisan affiliation, Bartel formally resigned from his own Klub Praca on June 14.[10]

First priority among the pending governmental business, whose urgency allegedly relegated new elections to the category of irrelevant frivolity, was assigned by Bartel to amending the constitution in the direction of strengthened executive power. The Klub Praca, which on May 20, that is, before the presidential elections, had joined with

[8] Bartel sketched out these views in three short discussions: *Niedomagania parlamentaryzmu; Kilka uwag o praktyce parlamentarnej w Polsce;* and in his introductory remarks to the volume *Współpraca rządu z sferami gospodarczemi państwa,* pp. 1–2. See also W. Grzybowski, "Premier Kazimierz Bartel," pp. 106–9, and Wierzbicki, pp. 224–25.

[9] Bartel's original recommendation of an early dissolution and new elections was noted above, p. 167, n. 25. His subsequent reversal on this point is re-corded in an entry in Rataj's diary on June 12, following a conversation between them. Rataj, p. 370. See also Daszyński, *W pierwszą rocznicę,* pp. 34–37.

[10] *Ilustrowany Kurjer Codzienny,* June 16, 1926. He was succeeded as party leader by Marian Zyndram-Kościałkowski.

its three partners in a collective Left-bloc call for immediate dissolution and new elections, now agreed with Bartel at its party conference of June 9–10 to postpone that demand until after the legislative adoption of certain indispensable structural and constitutional
changes in the state apparatus.[11] The other three Left-bloc parties,
however, made no attempt to hide their deep chagrin and profound
sense of betrayal over the government's new antidissolution position—
in fact, over its entire post-coup policy and mode of conduct. There
were scenes of stormy protest in the chambers. The PPS, Wyzwolenie,
and Stronnictwo Chłopskie introduced a joint proposal for the self-
dissolution of the legislature. Caucuses of these parties adopted
militant resolutions demanding dissolution, a leftward socioeconomic
course, and the purge of compromised ministers and functionaries of
earlier Right-Center governments. They warned against frittering
away the potential for change introduced by the coup.[12] PPS leader
Herman Lieberman explicitly denounced Piłsudski's proud claim to
having made "a revolution without revolutionary consequences" and,
on behalf of the Party, insisted that the logical political consequences
of the coup be implemented, beginning with the dissolution of the
Right-Center dominated legislature. Rather hollowly he warned, or
rather pleaded, that unless Piłsudski met the PPS halfway it could not
continue to consider itself obliged to support him.[13] In a more philo-
sophical vein, socialist intellectuals expressed disillusionment with the
entire "suprapolitical" trend of "moral" regeneration through "expert"
government which had emerged as the governmental ideology. Denouncing the official refusal to acknowledge the political content of
socioeconomic and constitutional-structural issues, or even to recognize the existence of social classes and political parties, these intellectuals (often affiliated with smaller Marxist groups) went on to
console the PPS with the reflection that in the long run the Party
would be healthier for having been disabused of the illusion that "the
great man"—Piłsudski—would do its work and implement Socialist

---

[11] *Ibid.*, June 12, 1926. For its earlier call of May 20 for dissolution and
elections, see above, p. 197.

[12] *Ibid.*, June 12, 13, 1926; Porczak, *Rewolucja majowa*, p. 55.

[13] Malicki, p. 316, and *Ilustrowany Kurjer Codzienny*, June 16, 1926. See
above, p. 198, for Piłsudski's boast to having made "a revolution without
revolutionary consequences."

goals in Poland without Socialists having to work or fight for them.[14] The Party's subsequent policy was to demonstrate that the PPS still had a long way to go before being finally and definitively cured of its illusions about Piłsudski, illusions which Piłsudski did little to foster or encourage and with which the Party gratuitously deceived itself. For the time being, the PPS, together with the rest of the Left, was mortified by its failure to make a dent in Piłsudski's politics and—as Lieberman's pathetic admonition indicates—still hopeful that he would yet relent.

Though prepared to bargain on the details of his government's legislative program, Piłsudski remained adamantly committed to his general policies and original priorities. His press organs warned that continued refusal by the Left to address itself to the task of constitutional revision and its persistent demands for the sociopolitical "deepening" of the coup could well provoke another crisis which would this time culminate in a military dictatorship pure and simple.[15] Bartel, more moderately, insisted that there was enough serious work facing the legislature to make new elections unthinkable before six months hence at the earliest.[16]

The government's project for constitutional amendments was drafted largely by Prime Minister Bartel and Minister of Justice Makowski. As approved by the cabinet on June 16, it incorporated the following points: granting the president power to dissolve the legislature upon the recommendation of the cabinet, with all ministers countersigning the statement of dissolution; conferring a suspensive veto over legislation upon the president; giving the government standing authority to issue decrees having the force of law in the interval between legislative sessions or between a dissolution and new elections (this latter interval to be extended to a maximum of 120 days); imposing an upper limit of four months on the consideration by the chambers of the government's budget proposals.[17] Through the

[14] For example, Werder, pp. 105–8. His article appeared in *Walka* (Struggle), a periodical devoted to socialist theory and political analysis published under the auspices of the Jewish Socialist Bund. In 1928 it was transferred from Kraków to Warsaw, where it henceforth appeared under the name *Nasza Walka* (Our Struggle).

[15] *Kurjer Poranny,* cited in *Ilustrowany Kurjer Codzienny,* June 16, 1926.

[16] Bartel cited in *Ilustrowany Kurjer Codzienny,* June 13, 1926.

[17] Folkerts, appendix.

medium of Sejm Marshal Rataj, to whom these draft amendments were officially conveyed on June 17, the government elicited the reactions of the parties. Simultaneously, its press launched a series of threatening and intimidating attacks on the legislature which were of such virulence as to provoke Rataj to protest.[18]

The Right and the Center wanted to couple these governmental proposals to strengthen the executive with drastic additional alterations of the constitution, as well as of the electoral laws, in the direction of weakening both minor and National Minority parties. Proportional representation should be eliminated or at least its effects neutralized, the voting age raised, and the eastern electoral districts gerrymandered. These moves were declared necessary to ensure not only that cabinets would henceforth be more stable but also that they would be based on ethnically Polish parliamentary majorities. Without such supplementary changes in the electoral system, the proposed amendment allowing for more frequent dissolutions and hence elections would allegedly prove futile, for the same kaleidoscopic electorate would return the same fragmented and hence unmanageable legislatures as heretofore. The Right also would have liked an amendment to strengthen the Senate. As for the government's proposals to confer greater powers on the executive, Right and Center now agreed to their utility.[19] Though nominally to be exercised by the president, these powers were, after all, to be substantively under the control of the cabinet. In any event, Piłsudski was not the president, and the Right had by now learned that its constitutional surgery of 1919–21 had in some ways cut off its own nose to spite his face.

The three remaining Left-bloc parties had by this time so thoroughly convinced themselves of the compelling necessity to replace the current Sejm and Senate that they endorsed the proposed conferral of dissolution powers upon the president. Their Jacobin distaste for the latently Caesaristic implications of this measure was held in check by the projected limitation that the president could so act only on the cabinet's recommendation. A more immediate lure was their hopeful expectation that, once the constitution was amended, the government would finally initiate new elections. Otherwise the

[18] Rataj's protest letter is recorded in his *Pamiętniki,* pp. 371–72.

[19] Groth, pp. 169 ff. Also Folkerts, pp. 37–41, and Dąbrowski, "Zamach majowy i kryzys państwa," p. 2.

proposed amendment would appear to be meaningless. Confident that his interests as well as his sentiments would direct Piłsudski to an effort to humble his traditional parliamentary foes, the Left underestimated his tactical adroitness and failed to anticipate that the requested dissolution power might be more useful to him as a reserve club with which to threaten the Right and the Center than as a keen sword to wield for the benefit of the Left. As both Piłsudski and Bartel were shrewd enough never explicitly to foreclose their option on this point, that is, their choice of dissolving or honoring the legislature's quinquennial mandate, it served as a carrot before the Left and a whip over the Right, inducing each to harness itself to the government's legislative program.

Apart from the enticing dissolution prospect, which it rationalized as inherently democratic, the Left was alarmed by the rest of the government's amendment proposals. It denounced them not only as a miserable substitute for a genuine—and badly needed—social and economic program, but as a reactionary assault on parliamentary democracy through executive arrogation. Stronger or at least more stable cabinets might indeed be desirable, but not at the price of structurally emasculating the legislature. If parliamentary irresponsibility was now to be exorcised through bureaucratic omnipotence, then the cure would prove worse than the disease and the vaunted regeneration of the nation become its own caricature.[20]

The Sejm convened on June 22 to begin its official consideration of the government's amendment proposals and promptly referred them for study to its constitutional commission. On July 16 this body reported out an amalgam of the government's project and the Right-Center program. In the ensuing debate, the National Minorities supported the Left in staving off this latter part, which the government also deprecated as untimely.[21] In view of Piłsudski's well-established hostility to multiparty strife and confusion, it appears inconceivable that he was a proponent in principle of proportional representation. Yet it is also clear that he had every political reason to permit its survival at the present time, when abolition would have been such a blatant victory for his traditional foes while he had as yet no massive

[20] Daszyński on behalf of the Left, cited in Próchnik, *Ignacy Daszyński,* pp. 76–77.
[21] Groth, pp. 178–203.

political party of his own. Piłsudski had not repudiated the Left simply to fall captive to the Right and the Center but to secure his own autonomy and hegemony. Indeed, lest the process of revision turn into a partisan victory of the Right and lest the Left, already alienated, be driven to utter despair, Piłsudski's ministers now made one absolute and two relative concessions on points about which the Left felt particularly strongly. The proposed suspensive presidential veto on legislation was buried; the time available for legislative scrutiny of the budget was extended from four to five months; and the maximum interval between a dissolution and new elections reverted from 120 to the previous limit of 90 days (Article 26).

On July 22, 1926, the essentially intact if somewhat expanded government project for constitutional amendment passed the Sejm by a vote of 246 to 95. Though more than a hundred deputies abstained or absented themselves, the result satisfied the constitutional requirement of a two-thirds majority of votes cast within a quorum of at least half the total membership (Article 125). The project was accordingly promulgated as the law of the land on August 2, after an effort by the Senate to extend its own powers had been rebuffed.[22] Voting against the amendments were the Socialists, the Slavic minorities, and the Communists with their Independent Peasant Party ally. Since Bartel's Klub Praca supported the amendments, while the Wyzwolenie and Stronnictwo Chłopskie deputies split between approvers and abstainers, the vote tolled the effective end, for the time being, of the Left bloc as a cohesive political force.

As extensive chicanery was to characterize the official governmental interpretation of the constitution in subsequent years, it is appropriate to examine the amendments of August 2, 1926, in some detail. To the later rage of the Left, the Sejm, in investing the government with the power of dissolution, had divested itself of its former right of self-dissolution. In issuing an order of dissolution, the president was required to act on the recommendation of the cabinet and to specify the reason for the action. This particular reason, once utilized, could not serve to justify any further dissolutions within the five-year electoral span. Additional dissolutions, in other words,

[22] *Dziennik Ustaw Rzeczypospolitej Polskiej,* 1926, No. 78, Item 442.

would necessitate alternative reasons—a purely formal limitation on the dissolution power. The final, official version of this amendment omitted the requirement, contained in the original government draft, that all ministers must countersign the dissolution decree. It thus facilitated the eventual procedure of dissolution by eliminating this explicit requirement of unanimity. Another "gift" by the Sejm to the government, which the latter had not originally solicited, was an amendment to the effect that a parliamentary motion of censure against the cabinet or any one minister could not be voted on at the same session at which it was submitted. The purpose here was to prevent "snap" governmental crises. A further measure designed to raise the dignity and propriety of legislative conduct was an amendment specifying that a deputy who violated the conflict-of-interest prohibition on buying or leasing state property or concessions (Article 22) should lose his mandate as well as the said acquisitions.

As for the budget: the government's draft was to be submitted to the Sejm at least five months before the next fiscal year. If the Sejm had not acted on it within three and a half months, it was to go automatically to the Senate. Failure by the latter to act within one month was to be regarded as tantamount to approval. Modifications introduced by the Senate must be approved or rejected by the Sejm within a subsequent period of two weeks. Failure to act was to be regarded as tantamount to acceptance of the Senate's modifications. The final budget thus went into effect within a maximum period of five months (3½ plus 1 plus ½) from the date of its presentation to the Sejm. This final budget was either the government's draft as modified by Sejm and/or Senate or its original draft if both chambers failed to act. If the Sejm explicitly and totally rejected the government's budget draft, a dissolution and elections were presumed to follow. In the ensuing interval until the new legislature convened, both the budgetary and the military call-up provisions of the current year remained in effect.

The new presidential decree powers were relatively complicated: in the interval between a dissolution and the convening of a new legislature, the president could, "in case of urgent state necessity," promulgate ordinances having the force of law. The following spheres, however, were immune to attempted change by such presidential action: the constitution itself; the system of local self-government; the budget; the statutory strength of the army; the public debt; international treaties which affected the state's frontiers, its financial burden, or the legal rules binding on its citizens; the Sejm's responsibility for declaring war and concluding peace; the constitutional responsibility of ministers; the electoral laws. In addition to conferring on the president this decree power in the interval between Sejm sessions, the amendment also authorized enabling acts under which the Sejm and the Senate might grant to the president general or specific decree powers for designated time spans. Only the authority to change the constitution itself could not thus be delegated to the president. Both the former "interval" decrees and the latter enabling act decrees required the countersignature of all ministers and would lose their validity unless presented to the Sejm within fourteen days after its next session following their promulgation. Whether the Sejm could void them by a simple resolution to that effect or only by the more complicated procedure of passing—with the concurrence of the Senate—a statute of repeal in the form of an ordinary law was eventually to become the basis of an intensely argued quarrel, with the regime insisting that mere negative Sejm resolutions were *interna collegii* and without legal effect on the validity of such presidential decrees.

On August 2, the day that the amendments went into effect, the first Enabling Act was passed, giving the president sweeping authority to "harmonize existing laws with the constitution and enforce those of its provisions which call for . . . special laws; reorganize and simplify the state administration and put in order the legal system of the country, the administration of justice, and the social services; ensure budgetary equilibrium, stabilize the currency and the economic reconstruction of the state, particularly as regards agriculture and forestry. . . ." Limited only by the reservations itemized above for the "interval" decrees and a few specific additional conditions, this delegation of power was granted until the convening of a new Sejm and was so extensive as to virtually amount to plenipotentiary legislative and administrative authority. This time the National Democrats and that branch of the NPR still allied with them had joined the PPS and the Slavic minorities in vainly voting against this sweeping investment of power.[23]

Armed with the new decree prerogatives (of which it was to make massive use), as well as the threat of dissolution to hold over the legislature's Right-Center majority, the Piłsudski-Bartel regime apparently expected that these weapons would more than compensate for its failure to secure a suspensive presidential veto on legislation.[24] It could not foresee that it would shortly be confronted by a hostile Sejm majority drawn from all political directions and that in lieu of a veto it would be obliged to resort to the awkward device of repeated presidential prorogations of Sejm sessions to prevent that "negative" majority from passing "hostile" legislation.

Indeed, the Piłsudski-Bartel regime had maneuvered itself into an awkward corner by its very moderation in the handling of the immediate post-coup political, social, and constitutional problems. Instead of eliciting gratitude and cooperation by its self-restraint in not resorting to dictatorship, in refraining from arbitrarily promulgating a new constitution, and in confining itself to legally eliciting from the Sejm a necessary minimum of relatively modest changes,[25] the regime was presently to learn to its chagrin that it had aroused part of the Right to obstreperous militancy and provoked most of the Left into mulish resentment. The vote on the Enabling Act of August 2, in which parts of the Right, Left, and National Minority camps aggregated their votes against the government, was a premonition of difficulties to come, and they came almost immediately.

The Right was eager to demonstrate that it still had teeth. The Center, which had earlier given critical support to Piłsudski in the presidential elections, now wished to reassert its pivotal role. Accordingly, the two groups decided to make an issue of the replacement of two *wojewodas*, those of Silesia and Volhynia, by the regime's own nominees, as well as of its allegedly "soft" policy toward the ethnic

---

[23] The text of the Enabling Act is in *Dziennik Ustaw Rzeczypospolitej Polskiej*, 1926, No. 78, Item 443. The pattern of the vote adopting it is discussed in Smogorzewski, *La Pologne restaurée*, p. 321.

[24] See Delmas, p. 57.

[25] See Minister of Justice Makowski's contribution to *Dziesięciolecie Polski odrodzonej, 1918–1928*, p. 178, and Bernus, "Pilsudski et la politique polonaise," p. 789.

minorities. Censure motions were therefore pressed against Interior Minister Młodzianowski, who had direct charge of *wojewoda* assignments and who had designated a special commission to review ethnic minority policy, and against Education Minister Sujkowski, who had given encouragement to the idea of a Ukrainian university. On September 24 the motions were carried by majorities of 144 to 83 (Młodzianowski) and 176 to 81 (Sujkowski).[26] The Jews, despite their high regard for Piłsudski and Bartel and their obverse antipathy to the Right and the Center, had nevertheless regretfully joined in the vote against Sujkowski, who appeared to favor a *numerus clausus* on their access to higher education and whom, as minister, they held responsible for failing to prevent certain anti-Semitic manifestations in institutions of higher education, especially in Lwów.[27] Bartel thereupon resigned on behalf of his entire cabinet, but, after telephoning Piłsudski (then vacationing at Druskieniki in the northeast), who insisted on unyielding firmness, Bartel re-formed the identical cabinet on September 27. This was to be an early but typical example of Piłsudskist legal casuistry: the constitution specified that a censured minister must resign, and this had duly occurred. The constitution did not, however, explicitly prohibit such a minister's reappearance in the immediately subsequent cabinet, and this is what Piłsudski now engineered. Not only was Bartel himself reportedly unhappy over this violation by trickery of the general spirit if not the precise letter of Poland's constitution,[28] but the political parties were deeply offended. However, as Piłsudski now blackmailed the Right and the Center with the threat of immediate dissolution should they again censure Bartel's cabinet, they were obliged to seek another device to flex their muscles without running the risk of early elections. Their response was to move a reduction in the government's supplementary budget estimates for the final quarter of the year from 484 to 450 million złoty. The Left, outraged by Piłsudski's preceding affront to the very principle of parliamentary democracy, but not yet ready for a break with him, was divided in its response, with the PPS particulary exasperated by the regime but paralyzed by its own hesitation.

[26] Ortel, p. 123. Slightly different statistics are given in Malicki, p. 323, and Rataj, p. 402.

[27] Halpern, pp. 25–26; *Frankfurter Zeitung*, September 27, 1926.

[28] See Rataj, p. 403.

The Right and Piast were also joined by many National Minority votes (other than those of the Jews, who abstained) to carry the reduction by a Sejm vote of 206 to 94 on September 30.[29] The embarrassed Bartel insisted on resigning. Two days later Piłsudski accepted a presidential mandate to form and head a new cabinet.

Thus, four and a half months after his coup d'état, Piłsudski was finally obliged to accept public, official, legal responsibility for leading the government. While his ordinary preference was for wielding control less directly, his sense of personal honor now required him to step into the central post of prime minister to lead the fight for his system against the politically "unnatural" but collectively dangerous agglomeration which was forming to harass it. His response was dual: arranging an unprecedented presidential prorogation of the tormenting legislature on the very day of his assumption of office (October 2), he then promptly utilized the ensuing respite to launch his long-range plan of fracturing, neutralizing, and bullying the hostile phalanx. A prompt manifestation of this strategy was to be his selection of ministers.

To clear the ground, Młodzianowski and Sujkowski were replaced. The former, a soldier-administrator to whom the problems of dealing with the Sejm parties had proved baffling and exasperating, now took over as *wojewoda* of Pomerania from Wachowiak and transferred the interior portfolio to General Sławoj-Składkowski, who had been commissar for Warsaw since the coup. Sujkowski's Education Ministry was taken over on an "acting" basis by Bartel, who also functioned as Piłsudski's deputy premier, frequently presiding over and generally coordinating the cabinet.[30] Piłsudski initially invited Klarner to remain as finance minister, but this conservative and correct economist–

---

[29] An informative article on this episode is in the *Frankfurter Zeitung*, October 1, 1926, where the vote, however, is given as 212 to 94, which deviates slightly from the official count. See also Ortel, p. 124, and Pobóg-Malinowski, *Najnowsza historia*, II, 495. The Senate had already approved this reduction on September 28 by a vote of 40 to 37.

[30] Sławoj-Składkowski, *Strzępy meldunków*, p. 85, and W. Grzybowski, "Premier Kazimierz Bartel," p. 111. On January 9, 1927, Bartel transferred the education portfolio to Gustaw Dobrucki, by profession a physician, politically a Rifleman and Legion veteran who as a Senator since 1922 had moved from Piast to Wyzwolenie and in 1925 to the Klub Praca.

Młodzianowski died in 1928 and Sujkowski in German-occupied Warsaw in December, 1941.

public servant made his acceptance conditional on Piłsudski's undertaking to keep expenditures, particularly military expenditures, within authorized budgetary limits.[31] Unwilling to give such a pledge, Piłsudski recalled the less punctilious Czechowicz to this portfolio. But the real political *pièce de résistance* which Piłsudski now produced was the appointment of two members of Left parties and two from the conservative-aristocratic stratum to his cabinet. PPS leader Jędrzej Moraczewski resumed his former portfolio of public works. Wyzwolenie Peasant Party deputy Bogusław Miedziński assumed the position of minister of postal and telegraphic services when that portfolio was reactivated by presidential decree on January 19, 1927.[32] The conservatives Aleksander Meysztowicz and Karol Niezabytowski became ministers of justice and agriculture respectively.[33] The rest of

[31] *Frankfurter Zeitung,* October 3, 1926, and Z. Landau, *Plan Stabilizacyjny, 1927–1930,* p. 82.

[32] Miedziński, like Moraczewski, had belonged to Piłsudski's "Revolutionary Fraction" of the PPS before World War I and had been active in the paramilitary Rifleman organization. During the war he had been in the Legions and the POW and had performed crucial political services for Piłsudski after the latter's arrest in 1917. Subsequently for a time head of the Intelligence Department of the General Staff (the so-called *dwójka,* or *deuxième bureau*), he had been elected a Sejm deputy on the Piast label in November, 1922, but had transferred to Wyzwolenie in protest against Piast's lukewarm response to the Narutowicz murder and against Witos' alliance with the Right. He was to be reelected to the Sejm as a declared Piłsudskist in 1928, becoming editor in chief the next year of the *sanacja's* semiofficial journal, *Gazeta Polska,* at which time he relinquished the Ministry of Posts. A leading polemicist for the regime, its parliamentary budget *rapporteur* at the turn of the decade, vice-marshal of the Sejm from 1935 to 1938, marshal of the Senate during 1938–39, Miedziński played a political role that was consistently more crucial than his official titles tended to indicate.

[33] Meysztowicz, it will be recalled, had participated in one of the abortive attempts to mediate during the coup. A Pole from the Wilno region, he had been a member of the tsarist Russian Council of State from 1909 to 1917 and the political leader of "Middle Lithuania" during 1921–22, before its official incorporation into Poland. He was now to serve as minister of justice until December 22, 1928. In 1933 he was appointed a secret papal chamberlain by Pope Pius XI and died in the Vatican in 1943. The Polish Left used to enjoy taunting him with the fact that in September, 1904, he had participated in a ceremony of homage to the memory of Empress Catherine the Great, a principal culprit in the eighteenth-century partitions of Poland. The occasion had been the unveiling of a statue of the empress in Wilno.

Niezabytowski had been a deputy to the tsarist Russian Duma from his native Minsk area from 1911 to 1913. In 1919 he had served as the chief Polish Red Cross official in the White Russian frontier area. He was to serve as minister of agriculture until December, 1929, when Bartel, forming his last pre-"colonels" civilian cabinet, dropped him as a concession to the Left and

the cabinet remained as before, that is, Piłsudski as war minister, Zaleski at the foreign office, Staniewicz as minister of land reform, Jurkiewicz of labor, Romocki of transport, and Kwiatkowski of industry.

Though Moraczewski and Miedziński were long known as partisans of Piłsudski within their respective parties and as belonging to the Marshal's closest entourage, and though both PPS and Wyzwolenie promptly made it clear that these two new ministers were acting on their own responsibility and not as party representatives,[34] Piłsudski's recruitment of them into his cabinet was nevertheless a demonstration of his intention to bend or break the established political pattern to his will. By harnessing together such a seemingly disparate team as these two "Leftists" with the other pair of conservatives and, in turn, with the "lapsed" Christian Democrat Romocki and the rest of the technocratic contingent originally selected by Bartel, Piłsudski gave notice that he would seek to superimpose on Poland's traditional, ungovernable, multiparty chaos a new, positive, "state-constructive" solution drawn from the "healthy" elements of all social and political orientations.

While Piłsudski's construction of this cabinet signaled his eventual political goals, the system of administration which he now developed was characteristic of his personal political style. The public, official ministers were chosen for their technical expertise or for the political support which they could bring him from certain classes or against certain parties. As such they enjoyed Piłsudski's confidence. But his own, personal control over the entire state apparatus and political system was to be exercised by a contingent of close confidants who were now "seeded" at second-ranking but crucial points into the various government departments and public agencies to supervise them for Piłsudski. Veterans of the First Legion Brigade and of the POW (typically alumni of their intelligence departments), these

---

Center opposition. His policy as minister since the onset of the world agricultural depression in 1928 had been to maintain high grain prices at all costs. This had angered not only the urban consumer of bread (in political terms, the PPS) but also the small peasant who bought corn to fatten his livestock for the market (that is the various Center and Left peasant parties).

[34] Próchnik, *Pierwsze piętnastolecie*, p. 256, and Tymieniecka, "Rozłam w PPS w 1928 roku," p. 813. See also the bulletin of the PPS Central Executive Committee of November 19, 1926, reprinted as Appendix No. 1 in Stęborowski, pp. 411–15.

men—Beck, Car, the brothers Jędrzejewicz, Koc, Matuszewski, Miedziński, Pieracki, Prystor, Sławek, Starzyński, Świtalski, and others—were the nucleus of the "colonels' group" which was to impress its image on Poland so powerfully in the 1930s, when Piłsudski abandoned the *bartlowanie* (Bartel style) for more authoritarian methods of rule. For the time being, they functioned out of the limelight (only Miedziński being given a portfolio early in 1927) as Piłsudski's personal task force, but they soon conveyed a characteristic *ambiance* of self-conscious toughness mixed with personel selflessness to the political and administrative style of the Polish state.

CHAPTER XIII

MANEUVERING FOR POLITICAL CONSOLIDATION: INITIATIVES AND RESPONSES

Piłsudski's tenure as premier began with a rather nasty set of incidents for which he bore no direct personal responsibility but which indicated that a number of his "harder" young disciples were quite capable of emulating some of the least edifying methods of the Right. The former National Democratic finance minister (1925–26), Jerzy Zdziechowski, who had criticized the Piłsudski-Bartel regime with particular eloquence during the recent discussion on the supplementary budget estimates, was "punished" for his presumption by being dragged out of bed and severely clubbed by several "unknown" culprits in army officers' uniforms who broke into his home on the night of September 30. Similarly assaulted were the admittedly scurrilous National Democratic satirist Adolf Nowaczyński and the Rightist journalist-novelist Tadeusz Dołęga-Mostowicz.[1] Though the Polish press was still free to castigate such methods of dealing with critics of the regime—and did so most severely—and though these methods were by no means as yet typical of the regime's techniques of rule, they were already premonitory of the more authoritarian procedures of the 1930s, of the Brześć affair and the Bereza Kartuska concentration camp. The irony of these developments lay in the fact that, having seized political power from the Right, the Piłsudskists also found themselves adopting something of the style of the Right, originally unveiled with the assassination of Narutowicz. Characteristically, the assailants of Zdziechowski, Nowaczyński, and Dołęga-Mostowicz were never found and the official investigations of these episodes were soon suspended. Moreover, it was an ominous though perhaps unre-

[1] *Frankfurter Zeitung* and *The Times* (London), October 2, 1926. See also Mackiewicz, pp. 209–14, and Pobóg-Malinowski, *Najnowsza historia,* II, 501,

lated coincidence that shortly thereafter a decree was promulgated through which the regime sought to curb the admittedly often abused freedom of the press.

Piłsudski himself was meanwhile playing for far higher stakes than mere petulant revenge. His attention was ever more strongly focused on the strategy of winning the conservative landed and industrial strata over to his side, a strategy toward which he had begun to move even before the coup, and to which one of his mediation efforts during its course and some of his pronouncements and actions since then had already given expression. Such a strategy, if successfully realized, would have the following virtues in Piłsudski's eyes: It would convincingly demonstrate his own political camp to be suprapartisan, seemingly "all-national," rather than simply personal or merely Leftist. It would deprive the National Democrats—whom Piłsudski always regarded as a cancer—of the respectability and money with which the conservatives had hitherto endowed them. It would rally behind his own endeavor to elevate the State above the Society a social stratum with historic state-service traditions, a stratum which the political system of the new Polish state had until now condemned either to political withdrawal or, *faute de mieux,* to a not particularly congenial association with the National Democrats. Sufficiently sober politically not to share all of the conservatives' substantive socioeconomic views, Piłsudski was nevertheless imbued psychologically with a romantic vision of the state-supportive, albeit conservative, aristocracy as the indispensable ingredient for consolidating his and the state's power. His determination to concretize the vision and apply the strategy had motivated the inclusion of Meysztowicz and Niezabytowski in his cabinet and was now to account for the spectacular gesture of his cordial exchange of felicities with the collective Polish aristocracy on the Radziwiłł estate.

On October 25, 1926, Piłsudski came to the ancestral castle of the Polish-Lithuanian Radziwiłł family at Nieśwież in northeastern Poland, in order posthumously to confer the golden *Virtuti Militari* medal on the tomb of Major Stanisław Radziwiłł, once an adjutant to Piłsudski, who had fallen in the Polish-Soviet campaign of 1920. Piłsudski was enough of a romantic for this explanation of his visit to Nieśwież to be genuine but too much of a politician for it to be the exclusive reason. He wanted a rapprochement with the conservative aristocracy, and it, in turn, was substantially ready to meet him half-way. Indeed, among its shrewder political heads, Prince Janusz Radzi-wiłł had seen the handwriting on the wall as early as the autumn of 1925 and had then advised his conservative confreres to mend their fences with Piłsudski.[2] Now the magnates presented themselves in serried ranks to witness the Nieśwież ceremony and attend a subse-quent banquet tendered by the Radziwiłłs in Piłsudski's honor.[3] At last here was a head of government in Poland who took them seri-ously, who claimed he needed them, and who did not appear to regard their favor as an embarrassment. Even Prince Eustachy Sa-pieha, who in January, 1919, had masterminded (together with Jerzy Zdziechowski and others) an abortive coup d'état against the Pił-sudski-Moraczewski government in Warsaw, now toasted the Marshal in the most fulsome terms as the nation's savior from the creeping anarchy of the Sejm-party system. Though Piłsudski's own public remarks on this occasion were an appropriately subdued eulogy of the fallen major combined with warm praise for the family which had contributed him and so many of his ancestors to the service of Po-land,[4] the affair was generally and correctly regarded as an immensely significant political stroke on his part—another challenge to his in-creasingly fretful supporters of the Left, but even more provocatively a gauntlet thrown to his perennial enemies of the National Demo-cratic Right.[5]

What gains did the Nieśwież strategy bring Piłsudski and what price did he have to pay for them? The immediate political results

[2] Koitz, p. 236.

[3] Among the noble families represented were the Czapski, Czartoryski, Czetwertyński, Giecewicz, Lubormirski, Obiezierski, Plater, Potocki, Mycielski, Radziwiłł, Sapieha, Tyszkiewicz, and Żółkiewski clans. Meysztowicz and Nieza-bytowski came as members of Piłsudski's retinue. Stanisław Mackiewicz, the editor of the ultraconservative Wilno *Słowo,* was the only journalist present at the affair. The *Frankfurter Zeitung* of October 27, 1926, gives the rather high estimate of 400 persons attending.

[4] Piłsudski, *PZ,* IX, 47–48.

[5] Mackiewicz interprets Nieśwież—incorrectly, I believe—as primarily in-tended by Piłsudski to signal his public rupture with the Left (Mackiewicz, p. 186). French, German, and even Soviet foreign observers had the greater shrewdness to perceive it as an attempt to destroy the Right by peeling the conservatives away from the National Democrats. See Gauvain, "Le Prétendu mouvement monarchiste en Pologne," pp. 748–49; Hurwicz, p. 10; Vonsovski and Rudomimo, pp. 88–89.

were gratifying. Agrarian magnates and strong industrialists both threw in their lot with his regime. Though distinct in their functional economic roles and by no means inevitably unanimous in their policy priorities, these two sets of economic vested interests nevertheless overlapped in Poland in a hybrid feudal-capitalistic system of inter-locking family and corporate directorates. As a result of extensive for-eign investments and control, capitalism in Poland, as a system of industrial production, had outstripped the development of a capitalist class assured and self-confident in the exercise of power. Hence the older landed aristocracy was enabled to step into this breach and wield a disproportionately heavy degree of political and social influ-ence. The snob value of an aristocratic name on the board of directors of an industrial or commercial enterprise was highly esteemed in the world of *arriviste* bourgeois entrepreneurs. Prince Janusz Radziwiłł, for example, in addition to his family's vast landed properties, en-joyed a multiplicity of capitalistic connections. While Piłsudski's Nieśwież visit, because of its setting, could be regarded primarily as an appeal to the more specifically landed agrarian element of the Polish "establishment," it was supplemented by a parallel conference of Bartel's with the leading textile industrialists of Łódź.[6] The busi-ness world's pacesetters, it will be recalled, had already declared their confidence in Piłsudski before these Nieśwież-Łódź gestures, at a time when the agrarians were still cautious. Now the latter joined them and the commitment to the regime of the industrialists' "roof" organiza-tion, the Lewiatan, became an outright one.[7]

There were, however, some differentiations within the conservative camp. The ever-reckless Prince Eustachy Sapieha, leader of the more exclusively agrarian and politically rather primitive aristocracy of the northeastern border regions, stood for unconditional cooperation with Piłsudski's regime. The politically more serious Prince Janusz Radzi-wiłł, whose influence was considerable among the economically and

[6] W. J. Rose, *The Rise of Polish Democracy*, p. 175. "Nieśwież" will, how-ever, be used below as shorthand for both arms of this policy of wooing the large agrarian and big business interests.

[7] Lewiatan (Leviathan) was the informal appellation given to the Central Association of Polish Industry, Mining, Commerce, and Finance (Centralny Związek Polskiego Przemysłu, Górnictwa, Handlu i Finansów). For its post-coup rapprochement with Piłsudski, see Brus, p. 56. Andrzej Wierzbicki was its current chairman and Prince Janusz Radziwiłł a vice-chairman.

politically more modern part of the aristocracy that had both industrial and landed interests and lived in Warsaw and Kraków, wished
(like the PPS leadership during the coup) to be assured of a *quid pro
quo* in return for endorsing Piłsudski's *sanacja*.[8] In Poznania and
Pomerania—as might have been expected—the conservatives' acknowledgment of Piłsudski was most reluctant and went no further
than a readiness on the part of some to move to a political mid-point
between Piłsudski's camp and their recent Rightist allies. But at least
this did involve a readiness to work with the regime in Bartel's
technical-administrative sense, a readiness which became perceptible
by December, 1926.[9] Finally, an occasional great magnate—for example, Count Maurycy Zamoyski—and some elements of the medium-
range landed proprietors remained unreconciled to Piłsudski and close
to the National Democrats.[10] Among the parliamentary parties, the
Christian Nationalists were internally most affected by the conservative
dilemma over the proper response to Piłsudski's wooing. Senator Jan
Stecki brought a part of this party, together with the Association of
Landed Proprietors, to Piłsudski's support, while deputy (and professor) Stanisław Stroński remained faithful to the alliance with the
National Democrats. In consequence, Stroński found himself deprived
in 1928 of the editorship of his newspaper *Warszawianka* (Varsovi-
enne), which was subsidized by the aristocracy.[11]

Piłsudski's Nieśwież overture proved, in sum, to be eminently successful, and the reasons for this success were historical, cultural, and
political. A large part—indeed, the preponderant part—of the conservative aristocracy had never found the alliance with the raucous,
xenophobic, bourgeois, nonhistorical National Democratic camp to
be congenial. It had no confidence in the ability or right of the
National Democrats to rule. Furthermore, a part of the conservative
stratum was deeply ingrained with a strong legally (though not politically) liberal strain, particularly the prestigious Cracovian aristocracy
of the former Habsburg lands, who believed, as a matter of principle,
in the rule of law and who were offended by a number of proto-

[8] Okulicz, p. 3, and Czubiński, *Centrolew,* p. 35.
[9] W. Grzybowski, "Premier Kazimierz Bartel," p. 112.
[10] See Smogorzewski, *La Pologne restaurée*, pp. 328–30.
[11] Singer, p. 57.

totalitarian, "mass"-societal National Democratic political reflexes and modes. Piłsudski, who was genealogically descended from the Polish-Lithuanian gentry of the Wilno region, had enjoyed respectful political contacts with the Cracovian aristocracy during World War I. As a result, these two sectors of the conservative camp were particularly predisposed to exempt themselves from the National Democratic vendetta against him and to accept a rapprochement on mutually acceptable terms with him. Finally, during 1925, the entire landed aristocracy had been specifically disturbed by the manifest readiness of the National Democrats, who in turn were under renewed pressure by their other ally, the Piast Peasant Party, to accept a more ambitious and energetic—though in fact still very modest—land reform program than the estate-owners thought proper. Thus, by the time of Piłsudski's Nieśwież overture, the bulk of the aristocracy was quite ready to cut itself loose from and turn the tables on these uncomfortable and only dubiously reliable National Democratic allies.[12]

The price which Piłsudski had to pay for the support of the conservatives in terms of socioeconomic policy orientations was less than anticipated, thanks in large part to the fortuitous circumstance that the extended British coal miners' strike of 1926 gave an unexpected boost to Polish coal exports, a boost so massive as to pull the entire industrial sector of the economy into a period of expansion and prosperity. As for agriculture, the fact that the 1926 harvest was considerably below expectations rendered the landowners somewhat docile toward the government, to which they looked for protection and succor. There then followed a brief but politically soothing period of high agricultural prices until the onset of depression at the end of the decade. Many of the great landed families, furthermore, because of their diverse interests and connections, shared in the benefits of the simultaneous industrial and business recovery. For the time being, therefore, Piłsudski's administration made no legislative innovations in agriculture. While it did not meet the expansive hopes of the two peasant parties in the Left bloc at the time of the coup—hopes for a radical assault on the big estates—neither did it retreat from the admittedly moderate land reform law of December 28, 1925, which

[12] Already during the days of the May coup, the leading conservative press organ, the Kraków *Czas* (Time), had been benevolently neutral toward Piłsudski. See Bąkowski, p. 19.

provided for comfortable acreage maxima, full compensation, and initially free disposal by the owners of excess land. Until the onset of the world agricultural crisis in 1929, the Ministry of Land Reform scrupulously implemented—indeed, substantially exceeded—the stated goal of the 1925 law that 200,000 hectares (494,200 acres) be repartitioned annually. Piłsudski's government also promoted the consolidation of scattered strips into compact farms, particularly in the central and eastern districts. Moreover, it supplemented the 1925 law with good credit facilities for the peasant beneficiaries.[13]

Thus, for a number of reasons, Piłsudski was not obliged to pursue quite as conservative a course as Nieśwież appeared initially to imply and as he had earlier in 1926 indicated might be required by the then disastrous economic situation. At that time, between January and March, 1926, he had hinted to some conservative spokesmen who had come to Sulejówek to sound him out that he regarded not only the land reform law but also the eight-hour industrial workday and the prevailing system of social security as excessively indulgent given the then perilous condition of the economy. Whether this was a seriously considered statement in favor of retrenchement or, more likely, simply a political effort to reassure the conservatives of his own "soundness,"[14] Piłsudski found himself, after the coup and after Nieśwież,

---

[13] The general maximum under the 1925 law was to be 180 hectares (445 acres). In suburban and industrial areas, it was to come down to 60 hectares (148 acres), while in the eastern districts, where the landlord represented the Polish element amidst a sea of Ukrainian and White Russian peasants, the maximum was permitted to rise to 300 hectares (741 acres). For details concerning the law and its implementation, see Pronin, pp. 133–41; Kagan, pp. 264–65; Markert, ed., pp. 73–77; Zweig, pp. 129–36; and Ajnenkiel, "Z dziejów reformy rolnej w Polsce, 1918–1939," pp. 6–8.

[14] Glinka, p. 6. Also Baranowski, p. 199. That the latter hypothesis is the more probable one is indirectly confirmed by the fact that, at about the same time, the Piłsudskist "colonel"-economist Stefan Starzyński published a pamphlet seeking to give the impression that Piłsudski was an economic "Leftist." This was an expansion of an argument he had earlier presented in the Piłsudskist monthly *Droga* (The Way). Starzyński's brochure bears the prefatory date April, 1926, and is entitled *Program rządu pracy w Polsce* (Program of a Government of Work in Poland). The fact of the matter is that, apart from a belief in the sanctity of balanced budgets, Piłsudski was indifferent to economic issues per se. He did not understand them, and even his commitment to balanced budgets was rather that of the economic philistine than of the serious conservative. He therefore had no qualms about using economic programs for politically manipulative purposes and could open his camp to protagonists of a wide spectrum of economic views. Starzyński, for example, though a member

the beneficiary of an economic situation which freed him from having to implement a drastic and divisive program. Only after the onset of the world depression—first agricultural, then industrial—at the turn of the decade did a negative economic situation again confront him with new dilemmas.

Meanwhile, Nieśwież extracted its indirect price in the response of the two groups most threatened and offended by it: the National Democrats and the Left.

At a stirring political rally in Poznań on December 4, 1926, Roman Dmowski, the redoubtable oracle of National Democratic ideology, founded a new organizational expression of that ideology which he named the Camp of Great Poland (Obóz Wielkiej Polski). With this action Dmowski translated the really dynamic political base of National Democracy from a conventional political *party* (though this remained active) into a new-style public political *movement*. For the time being, he was prepared to surrender the *state* apparatus to Piłsudski and to concentrate instead on impregnating Polish *society* with his ideology. Advancing the characteristically vicious yet enticing explanation that the May coup and its consequences had been a violent fraud perpetrated on the honest Polish nation for the benefit of a parasitical Masonic-Jewish conspiracy, Dmowski concluded that the only proper response to the coup was the formation of a hierarchically disciplined, solidarity-instilling, suprapartisan "movement"-organization which would effectively mobilize the healthy elements of the Polish nation against the sinister conglomeration of corrosive Jews, subversive Masons, denationalized Piłsudskists, and effete aristocrats which was allegedly holding Poland in thrall through control of a mechanically impressive but spiritually barren state apparatus.[15]

In its appointive, hierarchical organizational structure, its elitist-militaristic nomenclature (for example, Dmowski was the grand camp

of the inner Piłsudskist brain trust, was at this time genuinely Leftist in his economic thinking. Shortly *after* the coup, he even toyed with the idea of joining the PPS. See Z. Landau, *Plan Stabilizacyjny, 1927–1930*, p. 13.

[15] Dmowski, p. 473, and his speech at the founding of the Camp of Great Poland, reported in *The Times* (London), December 6, 1926. The Polish conservative papers *Czas* (Kraków) and *Słowo* (Wilno) commented in disbelief that Dmowski talked as if the Polish state had fallen into the hands of the enemies of the Polish people. This was precisely his conviction.

commander [Wielki Oboźny] surrounded by his Grand Council [Wielka Rada]; below them came the provincial camp commanders, etc.), its refusal to elaborate a concrete political program, its anti-rationalistic rhetoric of "organic" modes of thought and action, its pietistic ultranationalism, the Camp of Great Poland was rolling with the newly fashionable European tide of Right-radical totalitarian movements. This trend, which in Poland had been held in abeyance as long as the National Democrats were in tandem with their conservative and peasant allies, now flowered into malevolent splendor when concessions no longer had to be made to these fair-weather friends.[16]

The Camp of Great Poland was thus an initially oblique but ultimately decisive reply to Piłsudski's attempted isolation of the National Democrats at Nieśwież. Let Piłsudski have his conservative allies, let the freshly disappointed Left and the ever-opportunistic Center play their futile and frustrating game of parliamentary hide-and-seek with the regime. Dmowski and his Camp of Great Poland would outflank them all. And indeed, by the time Piłsudski's government finally dissolved Dmowski's Camp on March 28, 1933, after having suppressed it in its Poznanian and Pomeranian strongholds in November, 1932, the nationalistic youth, particularly the academic youth, had been largely captured by Dmowski's Polish brand of Right radicalism.[17] So

[16] There are many scattered accounts of the Camp of Great Poland, among them: Ajnenkiel, "Materiały do dziejów politycznych Polski w latach 1924–1927," p. 445; Garlicki, "Obóz Wielkiej Polski," p. 32; Roth, p. 23; Smogorzewski, *La Pologne restaurée*, pp. 332–35. It is interesting to note that General Stanisław Haller, the Belwederians' chief of the General Staff during the May coup, was a member of the Camp's twenty-man Grand Council. Former Finance Minister Jerzy Zdziechowski also was associated with it.

[17] Dmowski's own writings provide the best and most devastating view of the quality of his thought. Virulently anti-Semitic, passionately anti-Socialist, pathologically suspicious of presumed Masonic conspiracies, profoundly fearful of the German threat to the Polish nation's survival, Dmowski had been a cofounder of the National Democratic Party in 1897. A "new-style" Polish nationalist, he was led by his fear of the Teutonic menace into persistent yet ineffectual efforts before and during World War I to reach a compromise with the tsarist government under which Polish political and economic aspirations could be satisfied within the rubric of the Russian empire. Thus, at the time of the Russo-Japanese War (1904–5), he opposed a project of Piłsudski's to solicit Japanese support for an anti-tsarist Polish insurrection. As leader of the Polish club in the second and third Russian Dumas (1907–12) and as a consultant on Polish policy to the tsarist government during the first phase (1914–15) of World War I, Dmowski continued his vain pursuit of a Russian-

powerful and pervasive was the impact of this ideology that the Piłsudskist regime found itself reduced in the 1930s to competing by
imitation, to attempting—somewhat shamefacedly—to reabsorb the
youth by assimilating and sponsoring a quasi-totalitarian style of its
own. The effort was halting, halfhearted, pathetic—and too late. The
conquest of institutional power in 1926 had since dwindled to ideological stagnation, and the strategy of isolation with which Piłsudski
had hoped politically to cripple the National Democrats had psychologically been turned against his own regime. Piłsudski's personal
charisma still sufficed to obscure this trend during his own lifetime,
but after 1935 his epigoni found themselves desperately casting about
for some sort of moral and ideological legitimation of their rule.[18] Not
only was the nationalistic youth lost to Right radicalism, but analogous if less invidious radicalizing tendencies in the Peasant and Socialist camps had alienated their youth from the regime and its system of
rule.

Piłsudski's coup, his reconciliation with the conservatives at Nieśwież, and Dmowski's riposte with the Camp of Great Poland—these

---

Polish compromise in the context of general Slavonic solidarity. By the winter
of 1915–16, however, Russian political recalcitrance and military weakness
made necessary the transfer of Dmowski's locus of action to the West, where
he founded the Polish National Committee at Paris in August, 1917. His active
propagation of the Polish cause among the British, French, and American governments led to his recognition as head of the Polish delegation to the Versailles Peace Conference. Once the Polish state had been born, Dmowski
vigorously opposed Piłsudski's federative plans toward its eastern neighbors and
minorities. His political power in the new Poland, however, was never comparable to Piłsudski's nor, indeed, to his own extensive moral and psychological
influence. An inactive deputy to the Constituent Sejm of 1919–22, Dmowski
subsequently only briefly held a public office as foreign minister under Witos
from October 27 to December 14, 1923. The May coup had found him on a
trip to western Europe. If one wished to personalize interwar Polish history as
a contest between *sanacja* and *endecja,* between Piłsudski and Dmowski, one
might conclude that the former's political victory in the struggle for control of
the state apparatus was counterbalanced, if not outweighed, by the latter's ideological saturation of bourgeois society. (*Endecja* is the verbal coinage made
from the Polish pronunciation of the initial letters of *N*ational *D*emocrat—
*N*arodowa-*D*emokracja.)

[18] It would be interesting—but beyond the scope of this study—to investigate
whether this need to cultivate the regime's domestic popularity was a causal
factor for some of its flamboyant and provocative foreign policy initiatives
during the post-Piłsudski years; for example, in the truculent ultimatums of
1938 to Lithuania and Czechoslovakia.

three interrelated developments confronted the hierarchy of the Polish Roman Catholic Church with a policy problem. Though Dmowski personally returned to the Church's fold only in the last year of his life (he died on January 2, 1939), his hopes for the Camp of Great Poland included an expectation of mutual support between the Camp and the Church in the campaign to restore the nation to spiritual and political health by purging the degenerative secular, Socialist, Judaeo-Masonic, foreign poisons which had supposedly been malevolently injected into it. Since nationalism and Catholicism were historically and culturally fused in Poland, Dmowski insisted that the Camp and the Church owed each other mutual political support in the struggle to return the country to its original, organic, pristine heritage.[19]

Before these developments of 1926, the domestic Polish political situation had been relatively unproblematical for the Church. The Right-Center phalanx which emerged after the 1922 elections subsumed within itself virtually all the reliably Catholic classes and forces of the nation—from conservative aristocracy through nationalistic bourgeoisie to Christian workers and believing peasants—and was therefore naturally an object of the Church's benevolent solicitude. Furthermore, since this Right-Center constellation was either the actively ruling coalition (Witos, 1923 and 1926), or an indispensable "tolerator" of suprapartisan cabinets (Grabski, 1923–25), or a participant in all-party emergency cabinets (Skrzyński, 1925–26), support for it meant that the Church was not obliged to brace itself in the unpleasant posture of opposition to the government. Now, as the year 1926 drew to a close, this happy situation was no more. Catholic aristocrats, Catholic nationalists, Catholic workers, Catholic peasants were split. Some supported the new government, others opposed it, still others wavered. Furthermore, the central core of the new regime—Piłsudski, Mościcki, Bartel, and their entourage of colonels and technocrats—were religiously indifferent and made little pretence of being practicing Catholics.

Piłsudski's coup d'état had aroused the impassioned indignation of many ecclesiastical dignitaries, and it is plausible that, left to its own

[19] In the years after his founding of the Camp of Great Poland, Dmowski wrote a series of brochures and books on this and related themes under such titles as *Kościół* (The Church), *Naród i Państwo* (Nation and State), *Przewrót* (Overthrow). See also the apposite quotation from one of his speeches in Czubiński, *Centrolew,* p. 38.

discretion, the Polish Catholic hierarchy might have adopted a negative posture toward his regime. Thus, for example, at the burial mass for those who had fallen in the Warsaw street fighting, Father Józef Panaś, who in World War I had served as chaplain to the (anti-Piłsudski) Second Legion Brigade and was currently chief chaplain of the Przemyśl Military District, tore his medals from his breast and threw them at the feet of Piłsudski's representative, General Orlicz-Dreszer.[20] In the following months, several priests and bishops barred members of the Piłsudskist Rifleman association from their services or refused to celebrate special masses on Piłsudski's name day (March 19).[21] The Polish Church seethed with resentment and suspicion.

Vatican *raison d'état,* however, required that Church-state relations in Poland not be permitted to degenerate to a level of mutual irritation and alienation. Good relations were essential to ensure the full implementation of the generous concordat which Poland had concluded with the Holy See on February 10, 1925. Good relations were also personally desired by Pope Pius XI, who, as Msgr. Achille Ratti, had served as apostolic visitor (1918–19) and papal nuncio (1919–21) to Poland and had during these years—which included the Polish-Soviet campaign of 1920—developed a relationship of mutual cordiality with the then chief of state and commander in chief, Józef Piłsudski. Simultaneously, he appears to have been left distinctly unimpressed by the National Democratic-led Right-wing camp. After his elevation to the papacy, he expressly ordered Bishop Prince Adam Sapieha (Kraków) and Archbishop Józef Teodorowicz (Lwów) to resign Polish senatorial seats to which they had been elected on the Rightist label in November, 1922. They eventually complied in March, 1923.[22] The Pope's readiness, in 1926, to adopt a more favorable view than many Polish Catholic ecclesiastics of Piłsudski's new—even though usurpatory—regime may also have been conditioned by the prevailing European expectation that Piłsudski's foreign policy would be fundamentally anti-Soviet.

The Pope took a series of discreet yet unmistakable steps to signal

[20] AKL, 3/116, 5/77.

[21] For details, see Daszyński, *W pierwszą rocznicę,* p. 54, and Pobóg-Malinowski, *Najnowsza historia,* II, 499–500.

[22] Jurkiewicz, *Watykan a Polska,* p. 43. Teodorowicz had earlier been a Christian Nationalist deputy to the Constituent Sejm of 1919–22.

his positive attitude toward Piłsudski. By chance, the archbishop of Warsaw, Aleksander Cardinal Kakowski, had been in Rome at the time of the coup. Upon his return he received Premier Bartel in a widely advertised audience on May 27 to convey the Pope's benediction for Marshal Piłsudski and the Bartel government. Two days later, Kakowski paid a well-publicized return call on Bartel, after having in the interval issued a plea for harmony, condemned any renewal of hostilities (an implied rebuke to the Poznanian-Pomeranian extremists), and appealed for the election of a president who would harmonize relations between Church and state by respecting the rights of both.[23] He then received Mościcki upon the latter's election to the presidency. By another fortuitous circumstance, the primal Polish see of Gniezno-Poznań happened to be vacant at the time of Piłsudski's coup, the previous incumbent, Edmund Cardinal Dalbor, having died on February 13, 1926. Bypassing a number of more senior but politically overcommitted churchmen, Pope Pius XI nominated the bishop of Katowice, August Hlond, to the primal see on June 24, 1926, and elevated him to the cardinalate a year later, on June 20, 1927. Unidentified with any domestic Polish political direction, having spent much of his adult life in Vienna as an administrator of the Salesian Order, Hlond was an eminently suitable representative of Church interests *stricto sensu* in relation to the Polish state, and his subsequent relations with the Piłsudski regime were generally characterized by cooperation and mutual respect.

The government, as was to be expected, was gratified by the papal overtures and sought to reciprocate their policy implications. As a gesture of good will, President Mościcki attended the opening meeting of a four-day Catholic Congress which took place in Warsaw on August 27–30, 1926, and was welcomed by Cardinal Kakowski with a greeting friendly in tone and businesslike in substance: Polish Catholics were ready to support the government and in return expected it to respect the religious sentiments and convictions of the overwhelmingly Catholic majority of the nation.[24] Three months later, to allay rumors which were being given currency in the Rightist press to

[23] *Ilustrowany Kurjer Codzienny,* May 29 and 30, 1926; *Dokumenty chwili,* II, 32.
[24] Kakowski's address is reprinted in Jurkiewicz, *Watykan a Polska,* p. 46.

the effect that the Bishops' Conference of November 30–December 1, 1926, had adopted resolutions critical of the government, Primate Archbishop Hlond handed Justice Minister Meysztowicz—an ardent Catholic and future papal chamberlain—a written, public declaration denying such rumors and once again affirming the Church's readiness to work with the government provided the latter, in turn, "in its administration abstain from anything which might disquiet Catholics and dispose them unfavorably toward the government." [25] Once again, as in its earlier greeting to the President, the Church was making it clear that its proffered support of the government, while sincere and categorical, would be unsentimental and require reciprocity.

The government understood and responded. On November 25, 1926, Prime Minister and War Minister Piłsudski issued an ordinance regulating and facilitating the activities of the military chaplaincy. On December 9, Education Minister and Vice-Premier Bartel followed with an ordinance supplementing in a manner favorable to the Church the provisions of the constitution and of the concordat for compulsory religious education in all elementary and secondary state schools—the state appointing only those teachers who had received ecclesiastical authorization (*missio canonica*).[26] In later years (1930–36), after Bartel's retirement, a Roman Catholic priest—Father Bronisław Żongołłowicz—was to be undersecretary of state in the Ministry of Education. Meanwhile, on February 23, 1927, Justice Minister Meysztowicz prescribed a privileged status for arrested or convicted clergymen.[27] At the turn of the year 1931–32, the government heeded Church protests that a projected matrimonial law, proposed by the Legal Codification Commission, which would have authorized divorce under certain limited conditions, was a "bolshevizing" measure contrary to divine law. The government disclaimed responsibility for the commission's draft law and quietly buried it.

In the sphere of public symbolism, the mutual institutional support of Church and state was advertised. A Catholic religious service was

[25] Quoted *ibid.*

[26] *Dziennik Ustaw Rzeczypospolitej Polskiej,* 1926, No. 124, Item 714, and 1927, No. 1, Item 9.

[27] *Dziennik Urząd Min. Sprawiedliwości,* 1927, No. 5, cited in Jurkiewicz, *Watykan a Polska,* p. 47.

the well-nigh invariable accompaniment of state and military ceremonial occasions. The national holiday of May 3 was also celebrated
as a Church festival, while, in conformity with historic tradition, the
Virgin Mary was acknowledged as "Queen of Poland." Accordingly,
President Mościcki and Prime Minister Piłsudski, respectively, represented the Polish state and the government at the ceremonial corona-
tion of the image of the Virgin in the Ostra Brama shrine in Wilno on
July 2, 1927, at which occasion Piłsudski spoke warmly of Pope Pius
XI and his erstwhile nunciature in Poland.[28] Another significant development testifying to the mutual support of Church and state was
the papal revival—for the modern president—of the historic privilege
of Polish kings to confer the scarlet biretta on those Polish churchmen
or foreign churchmen serving in Poland whom the Pope had elevated
to the cardinalate—a privilege which Mościcki was to exercise three
times.[29]

And yet, for much—probably most—of the Polish clergy this association with the state as embodied in the Piłsudski regime was at best
one of accommodation and convenience, not of enthusiasm and love.
It was a postulate of reason, not a sentiment of the heart. The pull of
National Democratic ideology remained strong, and for many churchmen the Camp of Great Poland would have been the preferred partner. Whereas Primate Hlond represented Vatican rationality in his
good relations with the government, Archbishops Sapieha and Teodorowicz personified the more native, critically disposed, political
sentiment of Polish Catholics.[30] This duality of political inclinations
within the bosom of the Church is illustrated by the fact that a
bishops' pastoral letter of December 5, 1927, issued after the dissolution of the parliament and in anticipation of the new elections, was
worded in a manner which allowed it to be interpreted in two contra-

[28] See his remarks in Piłsudski, *PZ,* IX, 76–77.
[29] In the elevations of Nuncios Lorenzo Lauri and Francesco Marmaggi and
Primate August Hlond.
[30] Sapieha initiated a prolonged quarrel, the so-called Wawel conflict, with
the government when, after Piłsudski's death in 1935, he sought to utilize his
authority as archbishop (since 1925) of Kraków to prevent the burial of the
Marshal in his cathedral's royal crypt. Teodorowicz's hostility to the Piłsudski
regime is vividly demonstrated in Dąbrowski, "Zamach majowy i kryzys
państwa," pp. 2–3.

dictory senses: as an implied recommendation to vote for the Piłsudskist bloc or for its Rightist foes.[31] The letter urged all Catholics to vote, not scattering their ballots but casting them for the political forces solicitous of Catholicism. This advice was ambiguous. The recommendation not to scatter the vote could perhaps be taken as being friendly to Piłsudski, since all the opposing parties, even the demonstratively Catholic ones, were split among many electoral lists. On the other hand, the variegated, catchall Piłsudskist camp was hardly an obvious repository of Catholic ideological expectations. Since the Rightist rumor mills again claimed that in fact the consensus of the Polish Church hierarchy was against the Piłsudskist camp—which was plausible—Pope Pius XI once more stepped into the picture. Piłsudski's celebrated conservative-aristocratic ally, Prince Janusz Radziwiłł, was permitted publicly to announce that his active participation in the Piłsudskist camp enjoyed the clear encouragement of the Supreme Pontiff, who, furthermore, categorically condemned the efforts of certain circles to split its Catholic supporters away from the progovernment electoral bloc through allegedly deliberate misuse of the Polish bishops' pastoral letter.[32] Almost simultaneously, Primate Cardinal Hlond, upon returning to Poland from a conference with the Pope in January, 1928, gave indirect but categorical support to the Piłsudskist camp by prohibiting the clergy of his own overwhelmingly Rightist archdiocese of Gniezno-Poznań from allowing itself to be nominated for office in the forthcoming parliamentary elections.

Though the Nieśwież policy may have been intended primarily to fracture and disorient the Right, it also had the predictable effect of further disappointing and alarming the Left. Piłsudski's apologists professed to be mystified by the Left's negative response to his rapprochement with the conservatives and by its failure to appreciate that this strategy was directed at the common National Democratic enemy.[33] The Left, however, found it difficult to accept Nieśwież

[31] Compare W. J. Rose, *The Rise of Polish Democracy*, p. 175, who accepts the first, pro-Piłsudski interpretation, with Czubiński, *Centrolew*, p. 69, who supports the opposite view.

[32] *Gazeta Warszawska*, February 10, 1928, reprinted in Czubiński, *Centrolew*, p. 71. The Pope had also sent Piłsudski a private message in a similar vein in January. See Léontin, "Deux ans de gouvernement de Pilsudski," p. 256.

[33] Pobóg-Malinowski, *Najnowsza historia*, II, 497–98.

simply as a healthy broadening of the regime's base through the mobilization of supposedly constructive, state-supportive, political forces. Rather, the Left tended to see Nieśwież not only as another repudiation of itself but also as evidence of a dangerous loss of socio-political perspective on Piłsudski's part, as indicating a drift into an intoxicating but illusory atmosphere of historicist romanticism. The Left insisted that it detected here, incipiently, that posture of exaggerated deference toward the wishes of the aristocracy and aloof indifference to the needs of the masses which had once been the fatal flaw of the prepartition Commonwealth. It warned that Poland could not survive between Germany and Russia if her government persisted in repudiating the expectations of the masses. The personality of Piłsudski alone could not forever hold together a regime which increasingly alienated—and itself became alien to—the masses. Indeed, the very dependence of the government on Piłsudski's personal political appeal was already an unhealthy symptom.[34]

Specifically, the Left objected to both the conservative and the authoritarian tendencies which were manifesting themselves in Piłsudski's government. These were matters of substance and of symbol. As offensive to the Left as the inclusion of Meysztowicz and Niezabytowski in the cabinet or the appointments of Wierzbicki and Stecki to head the advisory committees on business and agriculture was the very gesture of Nieśwież, as well as such ceremonial innovations as the regime's demand that the legislators stand during the reading by their respective marshals of the presidential message reconvening the prorogued Sejm and Senate on November 13, 1926. This issue led to a sharp row which was only resolved when Mościcki agreed personally to read his decree—but at his own Royal Castle residence instead of at the Sejm building. The NPR joined the PPS, the Communists, and the Jewish and Slavic minorities in boycotting the ceremony, while Wyzwolenie and Stronnictwo Chłopskie left attendance an optional matter for their members. All in all, only one third of the statutory number of legislators (142 deputies and 42 senators) came to this ten-minute opening ceremony in the Royal Castle—where they were conducted to a chamber from which the chairs had been re-

[34] Porczak, *Rewolucja majowa,* pp. 71–79.

moved, thus guaranteeing the fulfillment of Piłsudski's demand that they stand in deference to the President, who also stood.[35]

A more serious provocation to liberal and Leftist sensitivities was the presidential press decree of November 4, 1926, which authorized fines of 100 to 10,000 złoty and prison sentences of ten days to three months for publishing calumnies of public officials, gossip, false alarms, or anything injurous to the public interest. Application of the decree was to rest in the first instance with the *wojewodas* as agents of the Ministry of the Interior, not with the courts. On December 10 the Sejm voted unanimously to annul this decree and was sustained in its objections by the Senate. The two chambers, in other words, passed a statute of repeal. The government thereupon withdrew the decree but replaced it on May 10, 1927, with a similar if somewhat less drastic one. Again the Sejm overwhelmingly resolved to void it (September 19), with PPS spokesman Herman Lieberman once more leading the fight and with Bartel's own former party, the Klub Praca, abstaining as a quiet manifestation of disapproval toward the government's position. The next day a presidential decree prorogued the legislature before the Senate could confirm the Sejm's vote (and before certain National Democratic censure motions could be considered). Piłsudski, as premier, thereupon stated that the press decree remained in effect since a mere Sejm resolution to the contrary was simply *interna collegii* and had no legal force.[36] Whatever may have been the legal merits of the government's argument, its conduct in this affair was becoming recognizable as its characteristic style of juridical-political casuistry, of manipulating the letter of the law to rationalize political purposes alien to the spirit of the law. An eventual ruling by the Supreme Court against the government's claim of continuing validity for its press decree was mainly of moral significance, for by the time the regime heeded it and accepted the Sejm's repeal resolution as legally definitive early in 1930 (during the final stint as premier by

[35] Details may be found in the Polish and foreign press of October-November, 1926; in Rataj, pp. 422–42; and—in the context of a defense of the government's position—in Malicki, pp. 325–30.

[36] Piłsudski's two letters of September 23 and October 8, 1927, to Sejm Marshal Rataj, in which he presents this legal argument, are omitted from his collected works (*Pisma zbiorowe*) because they were strictly official and were drafted in the Ministry of Justice. However, they are reprinted in Piłsudski, *Przemówienia, wywiady, artykuły, 1926–1929*, pp. 129–35.

the more conciliatory Bartel) fines and confiscations had extensively harassed the opposition press. Between May, 1927, and March, 1930, for example, the Silesian *Polonia* (Korfanty's organ) lost 40,000 złoty as the result of 111 separate confiscations. Hand in hand with such explicit proceedings against this and other papers, there developed a general "understanding" that it was inadvisable for army officers and public officials who valued their careers to become known as readers of certain oppositional publications.[37]

Though the brunt of the application of the press decrees was borne by the Rightist and Right-Centrist papers, and though much of this press was indeed malicious and often slanderous and merited scant sympathy, it was nevertheless the Left, specifically the PPS, which as a matter of civil libertarian principle threw itself into the forefront of the fight against the decrees. The first press decree of November 4, 1926, indeed, became the occasion though not the exclusive cause of the "official" passage of the PPS into formal opposition to the government. The resolution to this effect, adopted on November 10, 1926, by the Party's Central Executive Committee and endorsed the next day by its parliamentary club and its affiliated trade unions, cited as reasons the regime's alleged sellout to big business, latifundist agriculture, and finance capitalism; its contemptuous attitude toward the spirit of parliamentary democracy; and its cavalier disregard for fundamental civil and political liberties.

Yet the passage of the PPS and other Left parties to opposition was to prove even more difficult and far more tortured than the shifting of the conservatives and part of the Church hierarchy into cooperation with Piłsudski. For one thing, his enormous general prestige threatened to make partisan opposition to him a posture of dubious reward. More particularly, however, a deep reservoir of nostalgic sentiment for the former comrade still survived within the PPS. Not only did his general reputation as a "man of the Left" refuse to die, but within each of the parliamentary Left parties his fervent partisans and devoted agents remained active, dedicated, and still strong enough

---

[37] Kopański, p. 151. An extensive discussion of press freedom and its limitations in interwar Poland is contained in the monograph of Pietrzak, *Reglamentacja wolności prasy w Polsce (1918–1939)*. The period 1926–30 is described there on pp. 315–28. For other details, see Czubiński, *Centrolew,* p. 58, and *The Times* (London), November 8, 1926.

to exercise a veto power on party policy through the threat of schism. As a result of all these factors, the shift to opposition was initially apologetic and cautious and the attitude of the PPS toward Piłsudski personally remained for long one of deference and indulgence, as if it could scarcely bring itself to accept his responsibility for the governmental policies which it found so disillusioning and disappointing. After the Meysztowicz and Niezabytowski cabinet appointments, the Supreme Council of the PPS had apologized for a caricature published in its central organ *Robotnik* on October 17, 1926, showing Piłsudski dressed first as a Socialist in cloth cap and worn trousers and then as a traditionally costumed magnate in the company of the two conservative cabinet members. The Supreme Council deemed this illustration, purporting to expose and ridicule Piłsudski's presumed conversion from socialism to reaction (ironically, he had founded the *Robotnik* in 1894), to be inappropriate and unjust.[38] Now, a month later, the PPS had hardly resolved to adopt an attitude of official opposition than it began to explain, to prevaricate, to hesitate, and to regret. On November 11 *Robotnik* gave assurances that the previous day's decision was to be understood as a protest against the composition and policies of the cabinet, not against the person of Piłsudski. In the Sejm on November 16, PPS parliamentary leader Zygmunt Marek took pains to explain that the government would find his party's opposition posture to be a reasonable, realistic, responsible one. As if to illustrate this assurance, the PPS thereupon abstained on the vote over the government's budget estimates for the first quarter of 1927. On December 20, 1926, the Supreme Council of the Party adopted an explanatory resolution stressing that by its parliamentary opposition the Party hoped to force the reconstruction, not the overthrow, of the cabinet and the liberalization of its political and economic policies so as to render them more democratic, more attuned to the needs of the working masses, and more receptive to the aspirations of the ethnic minorities. Emphasizing that it regarded Dmowski's recently organized Camp of Great Poland as the main danger to Polish democracy, the Socialist leadership assured Piłsudski that it was ready and eager to acknowledge and respond to any

[38] Czubiński, "Przewrót majowy," p. 145.

moves by him in the indicated direction.[39] When Piłsudski nevertheless ignored this olive branch, which had been proffered after a sharp
two-day, three-way fight within the Supreme Council among those
who wished to abandon, to sharpen, or to leave unchanged the hitherto formal policy of opposition, the PPS finally steeled itself to oppose
the government's annual budget for the fiscal year April 1, 1927–
March 31, 1928. But even this was still an ambiguous gesture, for the
Socialists knew that the government had at its disposal a sufficient
number of other votes to pass its budget.

From the late spring of 1927 onward the PPS policy toward Piłsudski steadily hardened toward more stable and consistent public opposition, though the persistent rear-guard counterattacks of the Party's
internal Piłsudskists and the desire to avoid an open split with them
and a final rupture with him resulted in occasional halts and retreats.
In May, 1927, for the first time the PPS Supreme Council attacked
the entire government and its policies, making no exception or reser-
vation for Piłsudski personally. In July, the Central Executive Committee criticized him as giving no clear programmatic lead, as letting
himself be swamped by big capitalistic and large agrarian interests, as
permitting others to steer his regime into semifascist directions, as
blurring the decision-making process within his government so
murkily that the nation could not affix responsibility.[40] Even here,
however, the door was still being held open for an eventual reconciliation, for though the tone was indignant, the rhetoric still suggested a
plea for repentance addressed to an errant sinner who had fallen in
with bad company. Ironically, the PPS was shamed into more resolute
and less regretful opposition by the railroad workers, who had been so
instrumental in securing Piłsudski's victory in the May coup but who
in September, 1927, adopted a sharply critical position toward him.[41]
In that same month, on September 24, the PPS leadership finally
steeled itself into expelling Jędrzej Moraczewski, who had refused to

[39] The resolution of December 20 is reprinted from the *Robotnik* of December 21, 1926, in Janowska, ed., p. 21, and in Stęborowski, pp. 62, 68. For the
earlier decision of November 10 and 11 concerning opposition, see Stęborowski, Appendix No. 1, pp. 411–15.
[40] The texts of the PPS statements of May and July, 1927, are reprinted in
Czubiński, *Centrolew*, p. 44.
[41] Roth, p. 22.

accede to Party demands that he resign from Piłsudski's cabinet, in which he was serving as minister of public works. Nevertheless, at the Supreme Council's subsequent plenary session of December 6–7, 1927, a substantial minority of this body (which consisted of forty-four elected members plus the editors of the Party's newspapers and periodicals) denounced the expulsion of Moraczewski. Zygmunt Marek, the chairman of the Party tribunal which had initiated it, thereupon retreated and gave assurances that the expulsion was merely formal. On the insistence of Rajmund Jaworowski, the powerful pro-Piłsudski "boss" of the Warsaw PPS organization, Moraczewski's place on the Party's fifteen-member Central Executive Committee was taken by another Piłsudskist so that the parity of its internal forces could be maintained.[42]

Also in its direct relations with Piłsudski and his government, the PPS was careful not to burn all its bridges behind it even while passing on to more vocal and sustained opposition. Apart from the Piłsudskists *tout court*, a number of the Party's other leaders continued to maintain confidential contacts: Ignacy Daszyński with Piłsudski directly; Mieczysław Niedziałkowski with Bartel.[43] Not until after Daszyński's defeat of Piłsudski's candidate Bartel in the election of March 27, 1928, for the office of marshal of the Sejm were these contacts between the first two principals broken off—on Piłsudski's initiative and with regret and initial disbelief on the part of Daszyński. Not until the "Czechowicz affair" of the spring of 1929, when the PPS, in the person of Herman Lieberman, took the lead in the Sejm's attack on Piłsudski's Finance Minister for his illegal spending of state revenue for Piłsudskist electoral propaganda in 1928, were all substantive political ties between the Socialists and Piłsudski finally ruptured. Indeed, it was in the course of this controversy that the PPS leaders for the first time acknowledged that Piłsudski's May coup had been staged against a lawful government.[44]

The crystallization of the two Left peasant parties' policies toward

42 Czubiński, *Centrolew,* pp. 45–46.
43 Roos, *Geschichte der polnischen Nation,* p. 118; Singer, pp. 48–52.
44 On this "Czechowicz affair," see below, pp. 333–39. The PPS was to revert for the last time to a relatively conciliatory stance during Bartel's final premiership between December 29, 1929, and March 17, 1930. After this, the *sanacja's* authoritarian phase began in earnest and the opposition of the Socialists became irrevocable.

the Piłsudski regime proceeded in a manner analogous to that of the Socialists, though initially with a certain time lag. In contrast to the PPS, these parties still supported the government in the vote over its budget for 1927–28. Wyzwolenie wriggled on the horns of the dilemma of the "good" Piłsudski versus his "bad" entourage (that is, his Nieśwież allies) until June, 1927, when its party congress instructed the parliamentary delegation to adopt a more sharply critical posture toward the government in retaliation for the latter's "deception" of the expectations which the peasantry had earlier reposed in it.[45] The parallel with PPS developments, however, was maintained when Minister of Postal and Telegraphic Services Miedziński—like Moraczewski—chose Piłsudski over his party, resigning from it in December, 1927, and when the Wyzwolenie leaders maintained covert contacts with Piłsudski even after the Party had passed into formal opposition to his regime.

The Stronnictwo Chłopskie, which tended to regard itself more as a class organization of the peasantry than as an ordinary political party and hence was rather zealous to protect its immunity from all urban influences—including those emanating from the PPS—initially dallied behind the latter party and behind Wyzwolenie in adopting an attitude of formal opposition. On June 5, 1927, it organized a peasant congress in Warsaw, attended by 2,000 delegates, at which Piłsudski, Mościcki, and even Sławoj-Składkowski (the minister of the interior) were honored while Meysztowicz, Niezabytowski, and Staniewicz— the ministers, respectively, of justice, agriculture, and land reform— were sharply criticized. Republicanism was hailed, not for any abstract qualities, but as that political structure presumed to be most conducive to the exercise of peasant influence on the government. Conversely, monarchism, fascism, conservative dictatorship, and cliquism were denounced as throttling such influence and restricting the freedom of the toilers, and therefore as politically dangerous. In view of the fact that Nieśwież had provoked rather extravagant rumors that solutions such as those denounced were about to be introduced, and since at least the first two of the three criticized ministers were popularly presumed to favor them, this manifesto of the Stronnictwo Chłopskie peasant congress was an implied warning and plea to

[45] Próchnik, *Pierwsze piętnastolecie*, p. 260; Rek, "Jeszcze o sprawie brzeskiej," p. 8.

Piłsudski not to indulge in any such experiments. For the time being, however, the Party was not prepared to go further than this. Its leaders saw neither logic nor integrity in the PPS and Wyzwolenie stance of official opposition modified by clandestine contacts with Piłsudski. They insisted that the stance of opposition necessarily implied a readiness to work for the ouster of the government and conceded that they were not ready to face or to present this challenge. Piłsudski, they reasoned, would most probably not permit his government to be ousted by legal parliamentary means, and hence any serious effort to bring it down would either elicit a humiliating defeat for the initiators or provoke a renewed bout of civil war. Even in the highly unlikely eventuality of Piłsudski's accepting a political defeat, the beneficiaries of his downfall would almost certainly be not the Left but the old Right-Center coalition, which the poorer peasantry was bound to regard as the least acceptable of all political alternatives. It would therefore be irresponsible to proclaim a pretended opposition to a regime whose ouster one was not prepared to contemplate.[46] While this argument was both more consistent and more candid than the Socialist and Wyzwolenie endeavors to have their cake and to eat it too, the political conclusion to which it led—of supporting Piłsudski simply for fear of worse—eventually proved too frustrating for the inner resiliency of the Stronnictwo Chłopskie. In December, 1927, it finally split. The larger wing, at last driven into opposition by repeated disappointments at the hands of the regime, retained the original party name while the minority which remained accessible to Piłsudski's influence now organized itself as the Związek Chłopski (Peasant Association).

Finally, the small but strategic Klub Praca remained—as was to be expected—that member of the now defunct Left bloc which continued in closest association with the regime. Though it would occasionally abstain during certain parliamentary votes—as, for example, the one on the press decrees of 1927—to show its hesitation over certain governmental initiatives, the Klub Praca substantially remained behind the government until the turn toward tougher and harsher methods of rule at the end of the decade, when the *bartlowanie* gave way to the "colonels." Nevertheless, it did lose three of

[46] *Gazeta Chłopska,* September 25, 1927, quoted in Czubiński, *Centrolew,* pp. 42–43; Mackiewicz, pp. 185–88.

its ten legislators to the opposition ranks. Former Vice-Premier (under Grabski) Stanisław Thugutt quietly withdrew in the autumn of 1926 and two years later rejoined Wyzwolenie.[47] Deputies Ludwik Chomiński and Eugeniusz Śmiarowski, in turn, left in protest against the Klub Praca's readiness to endorse a governmental demand that the parliamentary immunity of four Sejm deputies of the White Russian "peasant-worker party" Hramada (Throng) be canceled preparatory to their trial in the spring of 1928 on the apparently valid charge of secessionist conspiracy and subversive collaboration with the Communist International. The White Russian Hramada, which had been founded on June 24, 1925, and had soon claimed over 100,000—mainly peasant—members, had been effectively broken by sweeping arrests of its leaders and functionaries in January, 1927, but Sejm assent was legally necessary before those who were also deputies could be committed to trial. The PPS and Wyzwolenie, in contrast to the Klub Praca, joined the National Minorities and the Communists in opposing the government's request for this assent, while the Stronnictwo Chłopskie officially abstained on the final vote (February 4, 1927).[48]

Piłsudski, for his part, could view with some contentment the various developments of 1926 and 1927 within the three Polish political orientations. Piast, the most crucial of the Center parties, had been pragmatically docile ever since the close of the coup. As regards the Right, Piłsudski had maneuvered most conservatives into a readiness to exchange their former association with the National Democrats for affiliation with himself. The potential hostility of the Roman Catholic Church had been largely neutralized. Accordingly, the Na-

[47] Thugutt, p. 127, and Singer, p. 73.

[48] There were, however, many unofficial abstentions and the final vote was light, the parliamentary immunities being lifted by votes of 160-odd to 80-odd. On the Hramada, see Jackson, pp. 191–92, 202–8; N. Vakar, *Belorussia* (Cambridge, Mass., 1956), pp. 125–26, 252; Bergman, pp. 73–99; Hass, "Białoruska Włościańsko-Robotnicza Hromada," p. 19; and Oertzen, *Das Ist Polen,* pp. 143–48. The Independent Peasant Party, also closely identified with the Communists, was destroyed simultaneously with the Hramada. See Jarecka, *Niezależna Partia Chłopska,* pp. 94–107. One of the Party's Sejm deputies, Feliks Hołowacz, also ethnically of White Russian origin, had been arrested at the same time as the Hramada roundup, and his parliamentary immunity was lifted together with that of the four Hramada deputies.

tional Democratic movement was isolated for the time being, though it remained both powerful and unreconciled. Indeed, in Dmowski's Camp of Great Poland it had taken on a virulent new expression, which eventually was to exert a moral and intellectual impact on Polish youth far more powerful than Piłsudski initially suspected. For the moment, however, he had successfully deprived the National Democrats of some impressive allies who had formerly lent them both social prestige and financial support. Nevertheless, despite this development and despite the relatively cautious socioeconomic course on which he was embarked—both symbolized by the Nieśwież episode—Piłsudski had neither the interest nor the desire to put all his political eggs into one conservative basket. He was therefore quite content both to keep up his end of the secret contacts with the various Left parties, at least until after election of a successor Sejm to the current one, and to welcome into his fold the various Piłsudskist splinter groups from these parties. Indeed, his major preparatory endeavor for the election of the next legislature was to construct an ark large enough to contain this variegated political menagerie.

CHAPTER XIV

THE NONPARTISAN BLOC FOR COOPERATION WITH THE GOVERNMENT

Piłsudski did not ride to triumph in May, 1926, on the strength of his own organized mass political party. When political power had to be mobilized on his behalf, it came from the parties of the Left bloc and the labor and radical peasant movements which they represented. This was, however, a dual phenomenon. The Left parties supported Piłsudski for general ideological and political reasons, but within each of them, acting as "ginger groups," were lodged nests of Piłsudskists— usually veterans of the First Legion Brigade and the POW—who were more particularly and fervently devoted to the person of the Marshal. This does not mean that these individuals had no political and ideological commitments at all or had been treacherously insinuated into their parties merely to function as Piłsudskist fifth columns. Originally, when joining or rejoining their respective parties in newly independent Poland, they probably never anticipated being obliged to choose between these parties and Piłsudski. Since he enjoyed a generally "Leftist" reputation and the Rightist camp was the common foe, such an assumption was then not unreasonable.[1] With Piłsudski's post-coup refusal to indulge the policy expectations of the Left and his success in winning the endorsement of a large part of the conservative establishment, the position of these veteran Piłsudskists within the Left parties became problematical and in many

[1] Miedziński, for example, had joined Piast before the 1922 elections, at a time when the Party still enjoyed a moderate Left-Centrist reputation as well as Piłsudski's confidence. When Miedziński later left Piast for Wyzwolenie in protest against Witos' turn to collaboration with the National Democrats, he was expressing his own general political reaction as well as the reflex of a loyal Piłsudskist. In other words, Piast had ceased to be congenial to him on both these grounds and his action was more than mere blind obedience to a behest of the Marshal.

cases, as has been shown, was to prove ultimately untenable. By the same token, the Piłsudskist agglomeration was itself becoming more multifaceted. There were now magnate Piłsudskists, peasant Piłsudskists, Socialist Piłsudskists, industrialist Piłsudskists, Catholic Piłsudskists, technocratic Piłsudskists, and praetorian Piłsudskists (the "colonels" proper).

Having committed himself after the coup to a major effort at exercising his power through legal, constitutional channels, Piłsudski had thereby accepted an obligation to put that power to an electoral test sometime after the expiration of the current legislature's mandate in November, 1927. This challenge, in turn, made it necessary to weld his diversified following into a cohesive and disciplined camp in preparation for these elections. Thus it was that he came to build his own party after, rather than preparatory to, his seizure of power. This party, however, could not be a political party like others. For one thing, no serious social and ideological agreement was possible among the great variety of political origins and views represented by all the many types of Piłsudskists. Hence, vague programmatic generality was essential for the new organization. However, this could be wielded dialectically. On the one hand, it was a condition imposed by the diversity of Piłsudskists. On the other, it could be turned into a lure to induce still further defections from the traditional parties. Yet another factor rendering a typical political party unfeasible was the fact that Piłsudski's own political views—seconded and lent some theoretical refinement by Bartel's concept of proper governmental administration—were by now passionately antipartisan and statist. He believed his mission to be the rescue and cleansing of the Polish state from the morass of party life, party strife, party confusion, and party corruption in which it had become mired during the years preceding his coup. His own political machine must therefore be a kind of state-party, capable both of expressing his *sanacja* notions and of subsuming within itself the widest possible spectrum of old and new, genuine and self-styled Piłsudskists. It was given the awkward but candid name of the Nonpartisan Bloc for Cooperation with the Government, generally referred to by its Polish initials as the BBWR (Bezpartyjny Blok Współpracy z Rządem).

While Piłsudski's various utterances before the presidential elections of May 31 and June 1, 1926, had already signaled his general intention to wield power in a demonstratively antipartisan, supposedly "nonpolitical," although still constitutional manner, no organizational impetus was given until January, 1927, when Piłsudski instructed one of his closest political confidants, Walery Sławek—who had earlier participated in the military-conspiratorial preparations for the coup—to proceed to organize what eventually was to be the BBWR. Even then, no real sense of urgency was evident until the late summer, when the expiration of the current legislature and the consequent need to prepare for elections impended.

The core of the BBWR consisted of Piłsudski's ex-Legionary paladins intellectually reinforced and "modernized" by the sponsors and practitioners of the new cult of technocracy—Bartel's parliamentary Klub Praca and the so-called Naprawa (Reform) group organized shortly after the coup among the younger pro-Piłsudskist intelligentsia.[2] To this inner core were assimilated converts from all the earlier political orientations in Poland—conservative, Socialist, peasantist, Centrist, Catholic, even from the ethnic minorities—regardless of whether they came out of conviction, prudence, opportunism, anxiety, or resignation. (The newest converts, who had never before belonged to the Piłsudskist camp and were now generally suspected of joining it to hop on a presumably winning bandwagon, were derisively referred to as the "Fourth Brigade." There had been only three Legion brigades in the war.)

On September 15, 1927, Sławek addressed a confidential conference of conservative aristocrats and intellectuals to explain Piłsud-

[2] The full name was Związek Naprawy Rzeczypospolitej (Association for the Reform of the Republic). Its weekly journal was *Przełom* (Turning Point). Together with the Klub Praca, it formed the Zjednoczenie Pracy Miast i Wsi (Union of Labor in Town and Village) within the BBWR. This provided the technocratic counterweight to the conservative recruits into the Piłsudskist camp and supplied the regime with its official "ideology." The Naprawa generally sought to act as a radicalizing ginger group within the *sanacja,* urging it toward a type of dynamic enlightened despotism in which an untrammeled executive would sponsor economic modernization through rational administration, thereby supposedly serving the interests of all the genuinely productive classes of the society as well as simultaneously strengthening the state. (Naprawa and Klub Praca separated organizationally in January, 1930.) For recollections of the Naprawa, see the memoirs of one of its leaders and the first editor of *Przełom,* Tadeusz Katelbach, *Spowiedź pokolenia,* pp. 138 ff.

ski's and his own general evaluation of Poland's domestic political scene and to solicit their cooperation as representatives of a supposedly "moderate and state-oriented point of view." The occasion was a three-day meeting (September 14–16) on the estate of Count Zdzisław Tarnowski at Dzików (near Tarnów in southern Poland) which attempted to weld various conservative parties and groups into a cohesive phalanx with a common political policy. Two overlapping goals were pursued at Dzików: conservative unity and conservative-Piłsudskist cooperation.[3] It was a politically more articulate gathering than at Nieśwież the year before, with conservative industrial and particularly intellectual leaders more in evidence, though still outnumbered by the agrarian interest. The results generally confirmed the trend which had emerged at Nieśwież. Most of those present agreed with their host, Count Zdzisław Tarnowski, that, despite a certain lack of clarity in particular policies, the present regime was

[3] The following account of the Dzików conference, details of which were long kept secret, draws on the conference minutes in Kersten, ed., pp. 199–215. Part of Count Zdzisław Tarnowski's opening speech is reprinted in Janowska, ed., pp. 25–26.

Apart from Sławek and Piłsudski's adjutant, Major Count Remigiusz Grocholski, and in addition to the host, Count Zdzisław Tarnowski, there were thirty-three other participants in the conference. Among the more active or significant ones were Prince Janusz Radziwiłł, Prince Eustachy Sapieha, Prince Zdzisław Lubomirski, Antoni Baupré (editor of the influential *Czas* [Time]), Count Stanisław Badeni (founder of the *Przegląd Współczesny* [Contemporary Review]), Jan Bobrzyński (editor of the conservative monthly *Nasza Przyszłość* [Our Future]). The industrial element was represented—in addition to Prince Radziwiłł—by Robert Gayer (president of the Łódź Chamber of Industry and Commerce) and Baron Jan Goetz-Okocimski. The academic intelligentsia attending consisted of Professors Stanisław Estreicher (Kraków), Konstanty Grzybowski (later Kraków), Alfred Ohanowicz (Poznań), and Count Adam Żółtowski (Poznań). State functionaries attending privately were Piotr Dunin-Borkowski (then *wojewoda* of Lwów, later of Poznania), Aleksander Morawski (vice-*wojewoda* of Kraków), Count Roger Raczyński (formerly of the diplomatic service, soon to become *wojewoda* of Poznania, vice-minister of agriculture and land reform in 1934–36, and ambassador to Rumania in 1938–39), Józef Wielowieyski (in World War I, secretary of Dmowski's Polish National Committee; envoy to Rumania, 1923–26), and Count Wojciech Gołuchowski (soon to become *wojewoda* of Lwów). The rest were mainly landlords and lawyers, though some of them were eventually to be assigned high state offices by the regime or to be elected to parliamentary mandates under its aegis: Karol Bołoz-Antoniewicz, Seweryn Dolański, Count Wojciech Rostworowski, Józef Targowski, Count Artur Potocki, Count Juliusz Tarnowski, Aleksander Dworski, Count Stanisław Komorowski, Zygmunt Leszczyński, Adam Piasecki, Tadeusz Szułdrzyński, Count Zygmunt Czarnecki, Jan Lipski, Count Stanisław Czacki, Józef Kaden, and Marian Rudziński.

showing greater understanding than any of its predecessors for the problems, needs, and aspirations of the conservatives. Most of them likewise concurred in the judgment of one of their leading intellectual figures, Professor Stanisław Estreicher, formerly rector of the Jagiellonian University in Kraków, that the National Democrats, being a vulgar demagogic rather than a truly moderate party, were not suitable allies for the conservatives. Yet some of them, most articulately represented at Dzików by Professor Count Adam Żółtowski of Poznań University, remained suspicious of Piłsudski and hoped that the conservatives would not irrevocably slam the door on the National Democrats. Thus, of the various conservative-aristocratic clubs represented at Dzików, the Party of National Right (Kraków, Łódź, Lwów, Warsaw), the Association of Conservative State Work (Warsaw), and the Conservative Association (Wilno and the northeastern *kresy*) by and large indicated their readiness to collaborate with Piłsudski, while the lure of the National Democratic alliance remained enticing for many western Christian Nationalists. The East Galician Christian Nationalists of Stroński and Dubanowicz had not even been invited, for they were too closely, and seemingly irrevocably, allied with the National Democrats.

Though Sławek was manifestly eager to elicit conservative endorsement of and support for the Piłsudskist organization in the forthcoming parliamentary elections, he was also acutely conscious of Piłsudski's intention and need to remain master of all the disparate elements in his camp and to avoid antagonizing some by making excessive concessions to others. Thus, despite conservative importunings and complaints, Sławek refused to hold out any hope of scuttling the democratic suffrage—universal, secret, direct, equal, and proportional—which had been bestowed on Poland by the Moraczewski cabinet in November, 1918, and to which the masses in general and the Left in particular were deeply committed. Nor would he even deign to consider the desperate plea of Żółtowski for a wide Piłsudskist–conservative–National Democratic front against the "revolutionary danger." The Piłsudskists' strategy was intended, after all, to cripple the *endecja* by splitting the conservatives away from it—not to become themselves a captive partner of a wide Rightist-conservative coalition and thereby forfeit their capacity to harness elements from all other political positions to the Marshal's chariot. Sławek therefore couched his intervention at Dzików in the form of an appeal for a "state-supportive" and "society-educating" alliance of Piłsudski, the conservatives, and (more tentatively) the Church. Nor would he disavow Leftist support. Rather he professed the hope that a substantial part of the Left, being traditionally also positively disposed toward the state and subscribing to high ideals of public conduct, need not be repelled by such a combination and could, indeed, be associated with it. In conclusion, Sławek pleaded with the conservatives—in their own interest as well as Poland's, for they would otherwise court certain defeat—not to approach the forthcoming elections under their own party banner. Let them instead enter the wide and welcoming Piłsudskist camp and thereby help the Marshal to polarize the contest into one between the new, suprapartisan *sanacja* approach to the problems of Poland and the discredited pre-coup system of multiparty anarchy.

Though no formal alliance emerged at Dzików, the conservatives decided to maintain and develop their contacts with Piłsudski and Sławek. More conclusively, they put a seal on their post-Nieśwież response by resolving to exclude the possibility of a general alliance with the National Democrats in the impending elections. Characteristically, however, the Poznanian Żółtowski reserved the right to interpret this decision as not excluding "local compromises" with the National Democrats where circumstances might so dictate.[4] Sławek, convinced that the conservatives' craving for political influence and economic security must eventually propel them to where effective governmental power was focused, that is, to Piłsudski, confidently sustained his activities among them, even though the aroused and suspicious radical peasant press simultaneously warned that the Polish peasantry would not understand this sort of necrophilic coquetry by the regime with the allegedly defunct landed aristocracy.[5] On October 27 Sławek again represented Piłsudski at a meeting, similar to, though less significant than, the Dzików one, of southeastern gentry (that is, from the Ukrainian-populated area) held on

[4] Kersten, ed., p. 212. Żółtowski, indeed, was to be elected to the Sejm on the National Democratic label in March, 1928.

[5] *Gazeta Chłopska*, September 25, 1927, quoted in Czubiński, *Centrolew*, p. 35.

the Jabłonów property of Count Konstanty Dzieduszycki near Tarno-pol. On December 25 Sławek and General Rydz-Śmigły made a special effort to reconcile the refractory Poznanian and Pomeranian landed proprietors to the Piłsudskist camp at yet another gathering on the estate of Count Taczanowski near Inowrocław in Poznania.[6] On January 16, 1928, finally, Piłsudski personally conferred with Prince Janusz Radziwiłł. The result of all this domestic diplomacy was gratifying to Piłsudski and Sławek in general political terms. The greater part of the conservative agrarian and industrial interests de-cided that they had no realistic option but to endorse, enter, and sup-port the BBWR despite their nervousness about the power and ideol-ogy of its "left Piłsudskist" elements. Despite some "local exceptions" —particularly in western Poland—the National Democrats were for the time being politically and financially abandoned. It was to take several years for the Piłsudskists to learn that this victory was Pyrrhic and illusory.

While his new conservative supporters were fretful over Pił-sudski's failure to repudiate the Leftist elements in his camp,[7] the Left parties as such were painfully and hesitantly adopting a course of opposition because of his refusal to base his power on them or to implement their policy expectations. There were, of course, variations in the type and manner of response of the Left parties. While the Socialists took greater offense at the regime's highhanded politico-administrative style, the Stronnictwo Chłopskie peasant organization appeared more disturbed by Piłsudski's presumed "sellout" to the con-servatives in the socioeconomic realm. Thus, whereas the former party was initially precipitated into formal opposition by the con-troversy over the press decrees—with its civil libertarian and parlia-mentary ramifications—the majority of the latter did not follow until after the Dzików conference and the concessions which they suspected

[6] Czubiński, *Centrolew*, p. 36. For Rydz-Śmigły's later career, see the Bio-graphical Register.
[7] See, for example, the confidential memoir by M. Sobolewski to Prince Janusz Radziwiłł, cited in Czubiński, *Centrolew*, p. 37, and the regretful com-plaints on this score voiced at the Dzików conference.
Radziwiłł (1880–1945), currently a political leader of the conservatives' Party of National Right as well as a vice-chairman of the economically potent Lewiatan, was manifestly coming to be viewed by both sides as the pivotal figure in the Piłsudskist-conservative rapprochement. Further information on him will be found in the Biographical Register.

were there made to the estate proprietors on the issue of land reform.

From the point of view of Piłsudski, Bartel, and Sławek, the regime was neither "betraying" the Left nor—*pace* some of the nervous conservatives—"screening" it. They genuinely saw in the BBWR not an ideologically oriented coalition but—as its title described it—a suprapartisan, or rather nonpartisan, bloc committed to the support of the government. The tasks and policies of this government, in turn, they regarded not as political in the conventional sense—a sense permitting "meaningless" allegations of conservative or radical leanings— but as technocratic-managerial in a new, neutral manner, transcending the old political-ideological definitions.[8] Given these premises, it was quite logical for the BBWR to open its doors wide to anyone, regardless of previous political orientation, prepared to accept this definition of its and the government's functions.

From the PPS, the BBWR drew the committed, veteran Piłsudskists —first Moraczewski and Hołówko, later Jaworowski, Malinowski, and others. Eventually, on October 17, 1928—several months after the parliamentary elections—ten out of the then sixty-three PPS Sejm deputies split away from the parent Party to found a rival group for which they revived the evocative name of Piłsudski's prewar wing of the Party—PPS–Revolutionary Fraction—and with which they affiliated themselves to the BBWR.[9] Jaworowski's Warsaw city Socialist machine and some of the Party organizations in Upper Silesia, together with splinters from those of Kraków, Łódź, and Lublin, initially gave this group a certain amount of rank-and-file support, though most of the membership remained with the parent Party. The earlier defectors from the PPS who had joined the BBWR directly (Moraczewski *et al.*) now aided and patronized this Trojan horse of the PPS–Revolutionary Fraction. The Party loyalists referred to the apostates contemptuously as the "BBS"—a play on PPS and BBWR— or as the *fraki*—implying that they had been motivated to form their so-called revolutionary fraction (*frakcja*) by an opportunistic craving to wear the dress coat (*frak*) of a minister or senior functionary or habitué of the salons of the aristocracy. This imputation was over-

---

[8] See J. Jędrzejewicz, "Myśl państwowa piłsudczyków w okresie 1918–1935."
[9] Their journal was *Przedświt* (Dawn). For additional details of this split within the PPS, see Stęborowski, pp. 148–53, and Tymieniecka, "Rozłam w PPS w 1928 roku," pp. 811–36.

simplified and unjust in so far as it was applied to Moraczewski and Hołówko, both of whom were personally and politically committed to Piłsudski and his policy in a convinced and selfless manner. Moraczewski was genuinely persuaded that the working class stood to gain more from Piłsudski's "suprapartisan" experiment than from a return to the chaotic Sejm system, while Hołówko, whose political passion was the reconciliation of the eastern minorities to the Polish state, was equally certain that they, too, would get a fairer deal from Piłsudski's *sanacja* than from any foreseeable parliamentary coalition.[10] Neither man regarded himself as having retreated from or betrayed his Socialist convictions by opting for Piłsudski over the Party, and both were subsequently alienated and offended by the regime's stooping to limited but definite political terror tactics in the 1930s.[11] Even Jaworowski, a less fastidious and more calloused type, was not so much a "rightist" opportunist as—like his Warsaw following—a Piłsudskist-style nationalist.[12]

The BBWR elicited similar secessions from the two peasant parties of the 1926 Left bloc. From Wyzwolenie came not only the "inner core" Piłsudskist and current Minister of Posts Bogusław Miedziński, but also the agricultural specialist Juliusz Poniatowski and the veteran insurrectionist Antoni Anusz.[13] The defectors from the Stronnictwo Chłopskie were deputies Marian Cieplak, Karol Polakiewicz, Józef Sanojca, Hipolit Śliwiński, and Jan Stapiński (a deputy in 1919–22

[10] See Moraczewski's open letter of November 3, 1927, to the Supreme Council of the PPS, replying to his expulsion, reprinted in Czubiński, *Centrolew,* pp. 45–46; for Hołówko's rationale, see Rzymowski, pp. 322–32. On Hołówko, consult the Biographical Register.

[11] Moraczewski subsequently broke with Jaworowski precisely because he regarded the latter as politically conscienceless. By training and early profession a railroad engineer, Moraczewski had been a deputy to the Vienna Reichsrat for the Galician PPS in 1907–18, a Legionnaire and POW leader in World War I, and minister of communications in the short-lived radical Lublin provisional government of November, 1918, before launching his postwar political career as independent Poland's first prime minister. Further information on him will be found in the Biographical Register.

[12] See Hoffman, pp. 52–54, and Alter, p. 5. An impassioned attack on Jaworowski's Warsaw party machine for alleged hooliganism, terrorism, and corruption—victimizing "honest" workers and Socialists—is the pamphlet by Minkiewicz, *Klika warszawska OKR PPS.* For the Jaworowski issue at the next PPS congress, held at Sosnowiec in November, 1928, see Tymieniecka, ed., "XXI Kongres PPS (1–4. XI. 1928)," pp. 292–96. On Jaworowski, consult the Biographical Register.

[13] For Miedziński, see above, p. 74, n. 33, and p. 232, n. 32. On Poniatowski and Anusz consult the Biographical Register.

and again after 1928). Some of these entered the BBWR directly, others supported it via the satellite Peasant Association (Związek Chłopski).[14]

Even after these losses of the Piłsudskist militants, the Left parties still contained some leaders and members whose general political disposition was to support the Marshal.

Also from the Center parties which had been on the other side of the barricades during the May coup did Piłsudski's BBWR attract some recruits. The "left" National Laborite faction of Ciszak and Waszkiewicz (NPR-Lewica) [15] now became a political adjunct of the BBWR and contributed most of whatever strength Piłsudski commanded in western Poland. The Christian Democratic defection to the BBWR, in turn, was led by Transportation Minister Paweł Romocki. Even from Witos' own Piast Peasant Party there came in October, 1927, a numerically small but prestigious group led by the Party's venerable honorary president, senator Jakub Bojko—a self-educated rustic, a former village teacher, the reputed conscience of the peasant movement—who issued a withering "Manifesto to the Village People" denouncing Witos as having betrayed their interests.[16] Particularly salutary for Piłsudski was the fact that one of the three Piast deputies who endorsed and followed Bojko's step was Marian Dąbrowski, founder, owner, and editor in chief of Poland's biggest and most influential newspaper, the *Ilustrowany Kurjer Codzienny*. Its editorial policy, accordingly, was for the next few years to be

---

[14] Of these five men, Stapiński had the oldest political career, having been an early leader of the Galician peasant movement before the turn of the century. After 1908 he accepted secret financial support from conservative sources which, when exposed, provoked his enforced secession from the main prewar peasant party in 1913. Hipolit Śliwiński was an architect and politician from Lwów who, as a member of the prewar Austrian parliament, had supported Piłsudski's paramilitary preparations for achieving eventual Polish independence. Polakiewicz was a Legion and POW veteran who had worked with Miedziński in organizing the political department of the War Ministry from 1918 to 1921. He had then left to study at Oxford but returned to be elected to the Sejm as a candidate of Piast in November, 1922. He had subsequently joined in the secession from Piast provoked by Witos' Lanckorona Pact with the Right of May, 1923.

[15] See above, pp. 177–78.

[16] Reprinted in Witos, *Moje wspomnienia*, III, 154–55. For a brief biographical sketch of Bojko consult the Biographical Register and see Dunin-Wąsowicz, pp. 33–34. The same author has edited a volume of Bojko's memoirs under the title *Jakub Bojko: Ze Wspomnień* (Warsaw, 1959).

"independently progovernmental." Final confirmation of the BBWR's political magnetism and ideological absorbency was the appearance on its roster of a handful of Roman Catholic priests and clerically inclined laymen, as well as of moderate spokesmen for the ethnic minorities—except the Germans. Thus, as the quinquennial tenure of the current Sejm approached its end in the autumn of 1927 and arrangements were being made for elections in the spring of 1928, the National Democrats stood as the only organized political force in Poland—apart from the semilegal Communist movement and its various "fronts"—from which the BBWR had drawn no significant recruits.

The great and contradictory variety of the BBWR's membership could be accommodated on only one common political denominator— the appeal of strong executive government after a decade of confused parliamentary instability. Sławek might desperately attempt to surround this perfectly obvious and quite respectable, if somewhat prosaic, fact with an aura of ideological profundity and historical necessity by claiming—in the fashion of the day—that the BBWR represented the positive answer of national solidarity to the Marxist challenge of class conflict, that it signified the healthy rejection by resurrected Poland of the fatal prepartition tradition which had elevated opposition per se into a virtue, and that it symbolized the victory of responsibility over demagoguery, of service to the state over the spirit of party.[17] The fact was that in political practice the mission of the BBWR was simply to support Piłsudski. Precisely because this was its only intended function, because its ideological poverty was otherwise so drastic and its ability to express social claims so deficient, the BBWR was able to split but not to replace the political parties, to win the adherence of office seekers but not to attract the youth, to funnel policy problems into the inner councils of the regime but not to articulate, refine, or adjudicate them in the course of its inevitably hollow and formal internal discussions.

At the apex of the regime, whither these problems were directed for solution, a statist-managerial theory of government held sway. Both the technocratically inclined supporters of Bartel and the inner core

[17] Sławek, quoted in Marchand, pp. 14–15. On Sławek, consult the Biographical Register.

of Piłsudskist colonel-praetorians were convinced that Poland's problems were not solvable by ordering the interests and claims of the
various sectors of her civil society through political parties competing in the public and parliamentary arenas. In their view, the im-
maturity of Polish society for such a performance had been too
glaringly exposed during the first few years of her recovered independence. No, Poland's primary need was to emancipate the state
from, and to elevate it above, civil society and to grant the state
apparatus, rather than any part of the society, priority of claim and
jurisdiction. Poland was to be purged, cleansed, and modernized
through state direction, not political competition. She was to be ad-
ministered rather than governed. Interest of state, not of class or
party, would alone be brought to bear in the determination of the
government's political, social, and economic policies.[18]

Alas, this cult of the state was both intellectually and politically
dubious. Operationally, it was useless because unprogrammatic and
undirective. The concept of "interest of state" might under certain
circumstances be adequate as a guide to foreign policy but was not
sufficiently refined to be serviceable for the resolution of serious
domestic socioeconomic policy problems. It might spotlight obvious
national goals—such as industrialization—but could not indicate unproblematical paths to their realization. Therefore it could not relieve
the necessity of making hard political choices. The arena of decision
was simply transferred from the coalition-plastering Sejm to the inner
councils of the regime. While one might acknowledge that the men
ultimately making the regime's policy decisions in these inner councils
believed themselves to be ideologically neutral, while one would credit
them with being motivated by a high sense of public service and duty
to the state, while one would concede that the BBWR as an organization was probably too docile to impinge significantly on their
evaluation of policy imperatives, it is futile to pretend that they were
not making political choices among political options, that they were
simply applying a manifest "interest of state."

On its own terms, furthermore, the regime's exploitation of its

[18] A rationale of these views is presented in the unpublished manuscript by
J. Jędrzejewicz, "Myśl państwowa piłsudczyków w okresie 1918–1935." For a
critique, see Hertz, "The Social Background of the Pre-War Polish Political
Structure."

technocratic theory, of its cult of the state, was in practice halfhearted. A logical corollary to its denial of the validity of parliamentary politics would have been the abrogation of the Sejm. Instead, Piłsudski sought to capture the Sejm through the instrumentality of the BBWR and/or to hamstring it with repeated presidential prorogations. Both of these approaches, however, represented concessions—the latter made with bad grace—to the political-parliamentary rules of the game. The regime's operational—as contrasted to its rhetorical— governmental style was thus a peculiar lockstep of manipulating, undermining, flattering, cajoling, accepting—but not really smashing—the parliamentary and political pattern which it had inherited and which it habitually blamed for the nation's ills. This reflex of restraint expressed Piłsudski's political pragmatism and political conscience. He was aware that after more than a century of foreign subjugation the Polish nation assigned a high prestige to democratic parliamentary institutions despite the unedifying and indeed appalling performance of the party system in restored Poland. The notion of a nonparty parliamentary bloc was thus nicely designed to capitalize on this dual temper of revulsion against the parties combined with commitment to parliamentary institutions. Piłsudski also realized that the nation was eager to demonstrate that it merited independence by emulating the most esteemed of the Great Powers, which in the late 1920s were still the Western democratic states. Finally, he not only shared this national wish to demonstrate Poland's political respectability in Western eyes but was restrained from smashing the constitutional-parliamentary order by his own legal and historical scruples. Several times during these years he appeared to be on the verge of a second coup, this time against the constitutional system itself, only to draw back at the brink. Not until the 1930s was violent repression more or less systematically applied against the enemies of the regime, and not until shortly before Piłsudski's death was a new, authoritarian constitution finally forced upon the country. Piłsudski's craving for power but eagerness to have it by free consent had already been demonstrated in his initial despondency when his intended "armed demonstration" met with armed resistance and again when he declined to accept a politically divisive though arithmetically categorical election to the presidency. So now, too, he could not steel himself to implement his regime's articulated "Platonic" statist-technocratic political theory by tearing up the constitution and liquidating the parties. He was reluctant to personalize his regime officially lest he thereby set a devastating example to any future adventurer and deprive the nation of the necessary institutional framework for its political maturation. Fond though Piłsudski was of quoting Goethe's dictum that a true master reveals himself in his capacity for self-restraint, his major political flaw was his inability to appreciate that his regime's manner of toying with the Sejm and the politicians, of alternating legality with casuistry, flattery with brutality, and wheedling with chicanery, eventually demoralized the public's political ethos at least as much as an explicit dictatorship and direct dismissal of the constitution would have done. While Piłsudski was eager to be the teacher of the nation, his treatment of parliament and the parties was deplorable pedagogically. It could only induce cynicism, provoke rage, or invite opportunism. In short, it perverted the political reflexes of regime, opposition, and public alike.

Piłsudski's insistence that Bartel reappoint two explicitly censured ministers to his cabinet in September, 1926, and his refusal on technical grounds to acknowledge as binding the Sejm vote of a year later to abrogate his regime's press decree proved to be characteristic of the cat-and-mouse game which became his habitual style of dealing with the legislature. At the beginning of his premiership, when he still appeared hopeful that his well-wishers within the Left parties would be strong enough to hold these groups to his support despite Nieś-wież and all the other humiliations and provocations to which he was subjecting the Left, Piłsudski had occasionally been cooperative, charming, and even flattering and ingratiating in his appearances before the Sejm and its commissions.[19] As the Left gradually gravitated—albeit reluctantly—into opposition and the Sejm majority—a "negative" majority because it was internally too incompatible to form an alternative government—became more obstreperous, Piłsudski's attitude became increasingly irascible. Unwilling to dissolve the legislature and unable to work with it, he caused Mościcki repeatedly to prorogue it either to avoid embarrassing interpellations, or to prevent

---

[19] See, for example, his dazzling performance before the Sejm budget committee on December 15, 1926, in Piłsudski, *PZ,* IX, 53–63.

the abrogation of decrees, or to cut off hostile debate. Throughout 1927 the Sejm was prevented from doing further useful work once it had passed the budget. Its exasperated legislators voted on June 20, 1927, to restore to the Sejm its original power of self-dissolution, which had lapsed with the constitutional amendments of August 2, 1926. Yet another prorogation intervened to prevent final action on the matter.[20] Though the Sejm was no longer docile, and therefore this reason among those which had originally motivated Piłsudski's rejection of the Left's importunate demands for a dissolution in the summer of 1926 had lapsed, nevertheless Piłsudski did not now want to risk new elections before the BBWR had been organized and solidified.

Another aspect of Piłsudski's political style, and one closely connected with the building and strengthening of the BBWR, was a quiet purge of the civil service—not the ideologically oriented purge of "reactionaries" which the Left had expected after the coup but an administrative purge to synchronize the bureaucracy with the regime. Once again this campaign was ambiguously extralegal rather than blatantly illegal. A number of provincial governors and county prefects were retired or transferred. In the central administration, the "feudal patrimonies" which the respective governing political parties had crassly carved out for themselves in the various departments before May, 1926, were liquidated and replaced by the regime's own satrapies. Officials were expected to join and to support the BBWR. Particularly energetic in conducting this transformation of the bureaucracy into a reliable bastion for the Piłsudski regime was its long-time minister of the interior, General Sławoj-Składkowski, a pedestrian but tireless administrator for whom Piłsudski's interests were the highest imperatives.[21]

[20] Bernus, "Le Conflict entre le Maréchal Pilsudski et le parlement polonais," p. 546. On July 14, 1927, the formally independent but moderately pro-National Democratic *Kurjer Warszawski* summed up the situation as one in which "the government refuses to dissolve parliament, it does not allow parliament to dissolve itself by its own resolution, and it prevents parliament from effectively performing its legislative work." The motion to restore the right of self-dissolution had been introduced by the PPS and was adopted by a vote of 189 to 10. It appears, therefore, that the National Democrats and the Center abstained, not because they approved of the government's policy and its treatment of the Sejm, but because they were reluctant to face early elections.

[21] See Sławoj-Składkowski's own writings, such as *Kwiatuszki administracyjne, Nie ostatnie słowo oskarżonego,* and *Strzępy meldunków,* as well as Falkenthal, p. 67, and Ahlers, pp. 116, 122. Also consult the Biographical Register.

By the turn of the year 1927–28, Piłsudski at last felt sufficiently confident of his new political machine to hazard elections. He and his BBWR had managed to isolate, neutralize, or split—at least organizationally—the other political camps and institutions. He had behind him the bulk of the society's financial interests. The government's administrative power stood at his disposal. Reinforcing these political cards was the fact that the economic and diplomatic fortunes of Poland appeared to be improving and consolidating. Substantial gains had been recorded over the spring of 1926, gains for which Piłsudski was understandably disposed to reap the credit.

PART FOUR

SOME FUNCTIONAL PROBLEMS

CHAPTER XV
THE COUP AND THE ECONOMY

The first few years of the Piłsudski regime coincided with a palpable and promising improvement of Poland's economic conditions and performance. It was, of course, natural for Piłsudski and his BBWR to capitalize on this phenomenon politically as new parliamentary elections approached early in 1928. It was also understandable that his supporters among the intelligentsia should seek to demonstrate that specifically the May coup had been an economic as well as a political turning point in Poland's history, a turning point from chaos and panic to order and progress.[1] The interplay of political and economic factors is, however, a subtle and complicated problem, one not readily amenable to simple cause-and-effect analysis. It appears correct to state that the impression of stability which was projected by Piłsudski's effective position at the nation's political helm soon produced an economically significant increment of domestic, and especially of international, confidence in Poland. It is also true that the new regime's technocratic-managerial enthusiasts rapidly accelerated or initiated the development of certain crucial state-capitalistic enterprises, such as the port of Gdynia and the Silesia-Dąbrowa-Gdynia railroad line, which had hitherto either languished or been merely under discussion. On the other hand, closer examination of the evidence indicates that the Piłsudski regime was the beneficiary of an economic revival to which its own contribution was relatively modest, which in certain important dimensions had already begun shortly

[1] See the charts and graphs in Bartel, *Wykresy charakteryzujące rozwój życia gospodarczego Polski w latach 1924–1927 włącznie*. Also Krzyżanowski, p. 104; Starzyński, *Rok 1926 w życiu gospodarczym Polski,* p. 113; Pobóg-Malinowski, *Najnowsza historia,* II, 465–72, 502–4.

before its coming to power, and which in others was brought on by the fortuitous fact that the British coal-miners' strike of May-December, 1926, gave a massive stimulus to the Polish coal industry, the benefits of which proliferated throughout the industrial economy.

That the basis for the recovery was laid before the coup—and was probably a delayed local manifestation of the general European economic improvement of the mid-1920s—is suggested by a number of statistical indicators. Foreign trade had begun to revive in the early spring of 1926, with imports spurting sharply in March and exports following from April onward. Domestic industrial production, particularly of textiles and metallurgical products, also began concurrently to recover. Accompanying these phenomena was a rise in industrial employment which, owing to rationalization, was proportionately less than the advance in production. Though budget deficits persisted, their monthly size had been diminishing since the beginning of the year under the conservative, retrenchment-oriented management of Finance Minister Jerzy Zdziechowski. While of dubious value in Keynesian terms, this was regarded as a courageous achievement by contemporaries concerned with the factor of domestic and foreign economic confidence in Poland.[2]

Politically and psychologically, however, this easement of the economic crisis before Piłsudski's coup had not been sufficiently clear or extensive to attenuate the exasperated sense of deterioration which persisted up to and gave momentum to his bid for power. Ominous was the fact that the international exchange value of the złoty continued to plummet at a progressive rate right up to the coup. Polish stock quotations also declined. Business confidence, in other words, was not being stimulated despite the exertions of Zdziechowski. As for the working class, its rise in employment was not only proportionately less than that of production but was countervailed by an overall decline in real wages. Though the number of registered unemployed had begun to fall somewhat in March, the total number of unemployed—including those who were ineligible or had become too

2 For extensive statistics on these items, see Z. Landau, "Wpływ zamachu majowego na gospodarkę polską," pp. 502–18. In a slightly revised and extended form, this article appears as the opening chapter of the same author's *Plan Stabilizacyjny, 1927–1930.*

apathetic to register—remained dangerously high by any politically sophisticated standard.[3]

Piłsudski thus benefited from and then inherited an atmosphere of economic crisis. Interestingly enough, the fact that his own economic views had never been explicitly or publicly stated before the coup was of some advantage to him during its course. In both the conservative and the Leftist camps, powerful interests believed themselves to have good reason to assume that Piłsudski's economic preferences broadly coincided with their own. After the coup, his sphinxlike public silence on economic issues, the composition and tenor of the initial governments which he authorized Bartel to form, and his peculiar combination of cautious consolidation with disquieting allusions to "the street" and "the whip" were further designed to paralyze the various economic and social interests into acquiescence. Eventually they were compelled to realize that Piłsudski had few consistent economic views per se and would habitually subordinate economic problems to the primacy of politics. In this sense, Piłsudski had been honest in insisting before the May, 1926, presidential election that he regarded such labels as "Left" and "Right" as irrelevant.[4]

The applied economic policy of the regime—whether under the premiership of Bartel or Piłsudski—soon emerged as one attempting

[3] Z. Landau and J. Tomaszewski, *Zarys historii gospodarczej Polski, 1918–1939*, p. 106; Ajnenkiel, *Od "rządów ludowych" do przewrotu majowego*, p. 288.

The Piłsudskist historian Pobóg-Malinowski, *Najnowsza historia*, II, 465–72, insists that total unemployment continued to swell right up to the moment of Piłsudski's coup. Without explicitly explaining his calculations, he evidently regarded the dip in *registered* unemployment which was recorded from March onward by the State Labor Exchange (Państwowy Urząd Pośrednictwa Pracy) as illusory of the over-all employment situation. On the other hand, even those historians who do regard the oscillations in the monthly registration statistics as reflecting proportionate changes in the size of the total unemployment pool concede that the latter, despite the dip, remained calamitously large. See Próchnik, *Pierwsze piętnastolecie*, pp. 216–17, and Z. Landau, "Wpływ zamachu majowego na gospodarkę polską," pp. 515–16.

[4] For the conservative pre-coup expectations, see Glinka, "W rocznicę przewrotu majowego." The Leftist hopes are revealed most sharply in the subsequent post-coup charges of betrayal leveled at Piłsudski. See, for example, Daszyński, *W pierwszą rocznicę;* Porczak, *Rewolucja majowa;* Porczak, *Dyktator Józef Piłsudski i "piłsudczycy."* (Porczak was a pseudonym used by Daszyński.) See also p. 241, n. 14, for Starzyński's pre-coup effort to present Piłsudski as an economic "Leftist."

to combine conservative monetary and fiscal policies with state-capitalistic investments in certain social overhead and primary industrial sectors of the economy (for example, transportation and armaments, chemicals and metallurgy). On the one hand, the dogmas of the balanced budget and sound currency were enshrined, both because they were part of the conventional economic wisdom of the day and because they were regarded as crucial in eliciting the confidence of finance capitalism in Poland. They became the only economic myths which Piłsudski simply and dutifully accepted. On the other hand, the technocrats and the "Left" Piłsudskists in the regime were permitted—initially in only a limited number of projects—to proceed with etatist and "mixed" state-private programs of investment and modernization.

In terms of rhetoric and propaganda, the first, orthodox economic posture initially received the greater stress because of the necessity of reassuring both domestic and foreign capital that Poland was a safe country for investment and a deserving candidate for loans. Czechowicz soon calmed the disquiet which his appointment as finance minister had originally elicited in business circles by continuing, on the whole, the ultraconservative fiscal and tax policies of Zdziechowski. Bartel gave assurances that no "doctrinaire" economic or social "experiments" would be attempted.[5] Even Kwiatkowski, who was in fact a master technocrat and the primary mover behind the now spectacularly accelerating construction of the Baltic port of Gdynia and its railroad connections to the Silesian industrial basin (as well as of equally—if not more—ambitious industrial projects in the 1930s), for the time being made pietistic policy speeches, filled with reassuring economic orthodoxies and deprecation of "exorbitant" etatism.[6] When the tenth anniversary of Poland's recovered independence was celebrated in 1928 with the publication of an encyclopedic volume reviewing the decade's achievements and indicating future expectations, its verbal stress was strongly deprecatory of etatism and emphasized instead the virtues of a "sound" economy,

[5] Z. Landau, *Plan Stabilizacyjny, 1927–1930,* pp. 23–28. Simultaneously he promised that the government would not countenance an assault on the legitimate rights of labor.

[6] *Ibid.,* p. 27.

run according to proper commercial principles and free from excessive governmental interference.[7]

This campaign of economic reassurance, powerfully reinforced by the image of political stability which Piłsudski projected and by the Polish coal industry's impressive response to the British coal strike of 1926, successfully restored confidence in Poland. The złoty quickly recovered from its downward plunge and after some readjustments was finally stabilized in October, 1927, as a gold currency worth 8.91 to the U.S. dollar. Its relationship to gold thereafter remained constant until the outbreak of war in September, 1939, and it was readjusted in relation to Western currencies in the 1930s only because these, rather than it, weakened during the Great Depression. By that time, of course, a stiff price was being paid in terms of production stagnation and unemployment for the excessively orthodox and deflationary monetary policy of maintaining at all costs the high exchange-value of the złoty while other countries were devaluating currencies and/or imposing restrictions on their free convertibility. The Polish regime apparently feared that the experience of the hyperinflation of 1923 and the second inflation of 1925 had been so searing and traumatic that even the slightest weakening of the currency or the merest hint of devaluation would panic a brittlely nervous public. Not until 1936 did it introduce some restrictions on currency exchanges and transfers.

In the immediate post-coup years, however, these problems were still in the future and the economic skies were clearing. Foreign capital, particularly American and British, soon demonstrated its satisfaction with the Piłsudski regime through new loans and investments. It is possible that, in addition to suggesting confidence in the stability of the new Polish government and the soundness of its economic policies, this prompt interest on the part of Anglo-American investors and bankers may have had political overtones in

---

[7] *Dziesięciolecie Polski odrodzonej, 1918–1928*, pp. 219, 930. In rebuttal, the technocratic-etatist-Left Piłsudskist "ginger group" that was gathered around the monthly *Droga* (The Way) retorted with a volume of essays emphasizing the positive role of state investment and state control in as relatively backward an economy as Poland's. See Starzyński *et al.*, *Na froncie gospodarczym*. A popularized version of their argument was presented by the Piłsudskist journalist Wojciech Stpiczyński in his volume *Polska, która idzie*, chapter IX.

the sense of reflecting a widely held—and exaggerated—expectation that, in terms of over-all foreign policy, Piłsudski was ready to initiate a Polish-German rapprochement, thereby supporting the current British political endeavors (economically endorsed by American investment policy) of reintegrating Germany into the European concert as a balance to the presumed preponderance of France. By the same token, the French response to Piłsudski's regime was one of suspicion and anxiety.[8]

Though but a pittance in comparison to what was poured into Germany herself during the second half of the 1920s, the credits and loans granted to Poland and the investments made there under American and British capital leadership were a significant contribution to her economic revival.[9] The first break came within less than two weeks of the coup when a substantial British credit was made available to the Łódź textile industry. On June 7, 1926, the London *Financial Times* expressed the optimism which "the City" felt in regard to the new Polish government. Negotiations which had been initiated the preceding November for a major investment in the Silesian zinc industry by the American Harriman interests were speeded up immediately after the coup and were successfully completed on June 26, 1926. At about the same time (July 2, 1926), a new agreement was concluded under which the already existing Franco-Polish consortium to develop Gdynia harbor would draw on

[8] The expectation of a supposed readiness on Piłsudski's part to make concessions to Germany proved false. Nor did the initial British approval of his coup lead to significantly closer British-Polish diplomatic cordiality until the late 1930s. It is true, however, that Franco-Polish relations deteriorated when Piłsudski became dubious of France's reliability as an ally in the event of a future German-Polish crisis. See Korbel, pp. 242 ff., and Komarnicki, pp. 74–75.

[9] Total French private capital investment in Poland remained larger than British and American, but most of this had been invested before World War I in what were then the western areas of the tsarist Russian empire. (The only important capital saved from the massive prewar French investment in tsarist Russia was this Polish fraction.) While the French were willing after 1926 to extend the large enterprises already owned by them since prewar years (mines and foundries, petroleum, textile, and electrical industries), they were generally reluctant to engage in new undertakings—except for the Silesia-Baltic railroad with its politico-economic anti-German implications. Also in the sphere of direct credits and loans to the Polish state, the French henceforth played a secondary role to American and British banking circles—again except for such clearly defense-oriented measures as an armament-and-militarization loan in 1936. See Wellisz, pp. 110, 151–52; Roos, *Polen und Europa,* pp. 239–46.

Belgian and Danish construction-engineering firms to accelerate this work. In mid-October, a large timber-exploitation concession originally granted to a British group in 1924 was extended and renegotiated to provide for the employment of more Polish staff and labor. Suddenly Poland was visited by scores of Western bankers and businessmen—among them the deputy director of the Federation of British Industries—eager to exploit her investment potential.[10]

The most conspicuous expression of foreign confidence in Piłsudski's Poland was the so-called Stabilization Loan of October, 1927. To its prehistory belong two investigatory trips to Poland in 1926—a fruitless one before, and a more promising, comprehensive one shortly after, the coup—by the American financial and budgetary expert Professor William E. Kemmerer, of Princeton University.[11] Upon the submission of the Kemmerer recommendations to both the Polish government and American investment-banking circles, Piłsudski dispatched the vice-president of the Bank Polski, Dr. Feliks Młynarski,[12] and the academic-economist Professor Adam Krzyżanowski, of Kraków University, to New York to initiate serious negotiations for an American or American-led international loan to Poland. The New York talks, which lasted from January to March, 1927, were resumed in Paris in April and successfully concluded in Warsaw during two more rounds of negotiations in June and September-October. Toward the close of the negotiations, Piłsudski and Bartel exercised increasingly attentive political supervision over the technical experts involved in the talks.

As signed in Warsaw on October 13 and 15, 1927, the terms provided for the floating by a group of American and European bankers of a Stabilization Loan for Poland totaling 62 million U.S. dollars and 2 million pounds sterling, of which the sterling was raised in London.

---

[10] For details, see *Frankfurter Zeitung*, May 27, 1926; *The Times* (London), October 19, 1926; Z. Landau, *Plan Stabilizacyjny, 1927–1930*, pp. 45–59, 118–19, 239. In the Polish Stalinist era of the late 1940s and early 1950s, these developments used to be "analyzed" as a sinister plot to betray and enslave Poland to imperialist exploiters. For characteristic examples of the quality of argumentation of those years, see K. Jankowski (K. Lapter), "Droga zdrady narodowej," *Nowe Drogi*, V, No. 2 (March–April, 1951), 69–88, and J. Sołtys, "Kolonia w sercu Europy," *Żołnierz Polski*, No. 4 (January 15–31, 1952), 11.

[11] Z. Landau, "Misja Kemmerera."

[12] See above, p. 17, for Młynarski's vain earlier effort to raise an American loan in the critical summer of 1925.

The dollars were raised as follows: $47 million in the United States, $6 million in Switzerland, $4 million in the Netherlands, $2 million in Sweden, $2 million in France, and $1 million in Poland. The terms were relatively severe, the price of issue being 92 and the rate of interest 7 percent. Redemption was provided by drawing at 103 or open-market purchases and repayment was to be concluded within twenty years. The Poles accepted in the hope that their successful utilization of the loan would maximize international confidence in their country and elicit a flood of investment capital. Simultaneously and closely connected with the loan came a decision by fourteen leading Western central banks to grant Poland a reserve stabilization credit of $20 million. This was mainly a psychological boon and expired in 1929 without ever having been used.

As its name suggests, the Stabilization Loan was utilized in large part (three fourths) to protect and strengthen the currency. The capital of the Bank Polski was increased by 50 percent. Half the fractional treasury notes were withdrawn and the rest were converted into silver coin. A treasury floating reserve fund was created and the floating short-term treasury debt was amortized. The Bank Polski's minimum legal reserve for the złoty was raised from 30 percent to 40 percent (on notes in circulation as well as demand deposits), of which it was henceforth required to hold at least three fourths in gold coin or bullion, the remainder being permitted in holdings in gold-standard countries. Two thirds of the gold cover had to be retained within the Bank Polski's own vaults; the rest might be carried under earmark abroad. With the conclusion of these allocations, only one fourth of the aptly named Stabilization Loan remained available for investment in state-owned enterprises and for agricultural credit.[13]

Although it has been argued persuasively that in the conditions of the mid-1920s an investment credit would have proved more beneficial than the Stabilization Loan,[14] there is no doubt that from the strictly fiscal and monetary points of view the stabilization program underwritten by it proved eminently successful. The currency was solidified, the government's budgets were balanced, the Bank Polski's

---

[13] For details, see Smith, pp. 158–60; Z. Landau, *Plan Stabilizacyjny, 1927–1930,* chapter VIII; Wellisz, pp. 67–69; Zweig, pp. 48–53; Taylor, p. 41.

[14] Z. Landau, *Plan Stabilizacyjny, 1927–1930,* pp. 276–79, where other, earlier protagonists of this position are also cited.

reserves were enlarged, and interest rates were lowered. From the international political point of view, moreover, the loan was a significant demonstration of Poland's capacity to outflank assiduous German efforts to destroy her through a combination of tariff war and credit boycott. As such, it was a categorical success for the Piłsudski regime.

Polish hopes that a truly massive flow of foreign capital (such as was simultaneously being poured into Germany) would follow in the wake of stabilization were to prove only partly justified. Other capital transactions did indeed follow as various Polish municipalities and the province of Silesia, as well as the Polish state railroad system, successfully contracted for extensive foreign loans. Large foreign credits were also granted directly to private Polish industry and banks.[15] But these credits were mainly short-term and were drastically curtailed—indeed, in net terms were reversed into a flight of capital—with the onset of the Great Depression at the end of the decade. In spite of the soundness of her currency, Poland's international political position between Germany and the Soviet Union seemed too precarious to assuage the nervousness of foreign investors at a time of rising international tension and deepening economic crisis. As a primarily agricultural country, moreover, Poland was caught by the Depression in a disastrous price scissors. It was in response to the new problems and challenges presented by the Great Depression that the technocrats within the Polish government succeeded, in the mid-1930s, in imposing on their economically more liberal (or conservative) colleagues a massive extension of etatism as the operative and acknowledged economic ideology of the regime. By the eve of World War II, in consequence, state capitalism was more extensively developed in Poland than in any other European country except the Soviet Union (and possibly Sweden).[16]

In the first post-coup Piłsudskist years, however, these vicissitudes were yet remote. The successful stabilization plan was reinforced and confirmed by Poland's capacity to take advantage of the British coal

[15] For details, see Wellisz, chapter II, and A. Korboński, chapter II.

[16] A factual discussion and sober evaluation of Polish etatism is contained in the unpublished master's thesis submitted at Kent State University in 1952 by Karcz, *Some Aspects of Statism and Planning in Poland, 1921–1939*. See especially chapters VII and VIII for the intensification of the 1930s. On the question of whether or not Poland had more state capitalism than Sweden at the close of this period, compare Taylor, p. 91, and Buell, p. 155.

strike to seize and thereafter to hold new export markets for her coal in the Scandinavian and Baltic countries, as well as in France, Italy, and elsewhere. Though the opportunity to capture these new markets was presented fortuitously, Poland's success in subsequently retaining a substantial share of them in the face of revived British and German competition was an outstanding achievement, earned by the high quality, accurate grading, and prompt delivery of the Polish coal.[17] Not only was this an economic and administrative triumph, but it was also of crucial political significance. With it, Poland slashed through the German effort to strangle her with the noose of the tariff war and, by exporting the bulk of the coal to the new markets by sea through Gdynia, she gave added plausibility and rationality to her claims of requiring and meriting this outlet on the Baltic Sea.[18] Ironically, a number of the Piłsudski regime's spokesmen and apologists, somewhat embarrassed lest the credit for the post-coup economic recovery be ascribed by their opponents and the public to a lucky windfall rather than to the government's own policies and the Marshal's capacity to elicit confidence, tended to minimize the coal-export triumph as a causal factor in Poland's new prosperity.[19]

In one sense, indeed, the coal-export situation was not an unalloyed plus in the economic equation, for with the end of the British miners' strike in December, 1926, and the return of Britain to international coal-export competition in 1927, Poland was able to retain her new northern foreign markets only by selling there below production costs. This was feasible because the effectively cartelized Polish coal industry was able to compensate itself with high domestic prices and to obtain artificially low railroad freight rates on the Silesia-Dąbrowa-Gdynia runs.[20] A considerable burden, however, was

17 For statistics on the Polish share of total coal imports by the north European countries over the next few years, see both Michowicz, p. 239, and Seraphim, p. 86. While not identical, the two sets of figures do closely approximate each other.

18 This was conceded in Seraphim, pp. 80–81, 83. In domestic political terms, the government also hoped with the development of Gdynia to assuage the hitherto militant hostility of the Pomeranian Poles toward Piłsudski.

19 For citations of such Piłsudskist arguments by two authors who reject them, see Michowicz, pp. 211–12, and Z. Landau, *Plan Stabilizacyjny, 1927–1930*, p. 78.

20 For statistical details, see Seraphim, pp. 87–88. While the calculations presented there appear to be accurate and are internally consistent, it should

thereby imposed on the Polish economy. Eventually, after Britain in effect devalued the pound by abandoning the gold standard on September 21, 1931, the competitive price pressure on Poland's coal exports became excessive and was finally alleviated by an agreement of January 1, 1935, between the two national groups of colliery owners to share a specified group of export markets. Under its terms Poland accepted a minority allocation in return for relief from the relentless pressure to depress her export prices ever downward.[21] Similarly, the development of Gdynia, though a proud and impressive achievement, was economically somewhat marred by a lopsided export-import imbalance in the port's total business, as a result of which harbor facilities, as well as arriving railroad stock and shipping tonnage, were not symmetrically, and therefore not fully, exploited.[22]

These were, however, economic flaws which were more than compensated for by the economic and political advantages accruing to Poland as a result of the massive increase of her coal exports and its ancillary benefits. She demonstrated impressive mechanical and organizational efficiency in the mining, transportation, and delivery of the coal, thereby giving the lie to the contemptuous German phrase of "polnische Wirtschaft" as synonymous with chaos and muddle. She diversified her customers. In 1924, for example, 98 percent of Poland's coal exports had gone to the limited, traditional circle of Germany, Austria, Czechoslovakia, and Hungary. This rendered her vulnerable to German economic warfare. By 1931–32, only 20 percent was going to these countries and 80 percent to the newly developed Scandinavian, Baltic, French, Italian, and other markets. Total coal exports rose from 8.1 million tons in 1925 to 14.3 million in 1926 and oscillated between 11 and 15 million for the five years thereafter. Valuable foreign exchange was thereby earned and unemployment was sharply reduced. The local demand for many other industrial products—both producers' and consumers'—was stimulated, and domestic production of these rose proportionately. Railroad

---

be pointed out that the thrust of the article's political argument is to the effect that Poland's coal-export performance was an economic fraud owing to these dumping-like price techniques. Published in the country of the supercartel and in the era of Dr. Hjalmar Schacht, this pretense of indignant contempt for Poland's foreign trade strategy strikes one ironically.

[21] Buell, pp. 178–79.
[22] For statistics, see Douglass, pp. 105–6, and Markert, ed., p. 102.

equipment, for example—including locomotives, tenders, and wagons—ceased to be imported after 1928 as new domestic engineering works filled the demand. The chemical industry, with its sub-branch of artificial fertilizers, likewise expanded to make the country self-sufficient in some categories and to produce for export in others.[23] If Poland's industrial production in 1925 be assigned an index of 100, then for the next three years it rose, respectively, to levels of 112, 130, and 147.[24] Deposits in both state and private banks accumulated rapidly. Significantly, though unemployment fell, wages did not initially rise concomitant with business earnings, thereby also increasing industry's liquid capital.[25]

In the agricultural sector, production and price parity relative to industrial commodities both rose after the disappointing harvest of 1926. So did exports in certain selected cereals (barley, rye), animals (pigs, geese), animal products (butter, eggs), legumes (peas, beans), and fodder.[26] With the onset of the world agricultural crisis in 1929, however, the price scissors opened up so devastatingly against agricultural commodities that the increases in production and exports were thereafter utterly swallowed by the fall in the value of agricultural products.[27] Nevertheless, when Piłsudski's first post-coup elections were held in March, 1928, even agricultural prospects appeared positive.

It is essential to bear in mind that the notion of Poland's economic recovery and progress during the initial post-coup years of the Piłsudski era is relative to her plight during the first half of the decade of the 1920s. In comparison to Western Europe—not to mention North America—Poland remained a poor country of low productivity, overpopulation, underemployment, and underconsumption. The currency was stable—but mass purchasing power remained deficient. The budget was balanced—but at too low a level. Moreover, even in terms

[23] Wirschubski, pp. 702–3. For some statistics illustrating Polish industrial growth in this post-coup period of expansion, see Kwiatkowski, p. 200, and X.X.X., p. 18. On the basis of internal evidence, it appears that the anonymous author of this last article was that Professor Adam Krzyżanowski who had helped to negotiate the Stablization Loan of 1927.

[24] Czesław Klarner, *Przemysł i handel w pierwszym dziesięcioleciu niepodległej Polski* (Warsaw, 1929), p. 34, cited in Drozdowski, p. 119.

[25] Zaremba, p. 102.

[26] For statistics, see Steinert, pp. 612–29.

[27] See Conrad, pp. 421, 432.

of her own economic history, the consequences of the enormous destruction and looting inflicted on her territories between 1914 and 1920, as well as of the dislocations resulting from the redrawing of international frontiers during 1919–21 (virtual loss of the Russian market, partial loss of the German one), were so devastating that even by 1929, on the eve of the Great Depression, many branches of Poland's economy were still short of their prewar levels, though approaching them more closely every year.[28] When viewed against its background problems—uneven development under the partitions, catastrophic biological and material losses during and immediately after World War I, the burdens of confronting postwar German and Soviet hostility—the performance of the Polish economy merits acknowledgment. But it remained a precarious and ponderous economy. The recovery which was initially discernible under Piłsudski proceeded hand in hand with continued vulnerability.

[28] See Frankel, pp. 124–25.

CHAPTER XVI

THE COUP AND FOREIGN POLICY

Palpable improvement combined with persisting hazards—a characterization which has just been applied to Poland's economic situation during Piłsudski's first post-coup years—can be extended as well to her position in the European diplomatic arena.

Poland's resurrection as an independent state after World War I was rendered possible—as Piłsudski had prophetically conjectured on the eve of that conflict [1]—by the triple defeat of all three of her partitioning powers in the course of the war. Recovery by either Germany or Russia (Austria-Hungary having disintegrated beyond repair) and especially an accommodation between them would inevitably be dangerous to Poland and raise again the specter of her partition. Yet Poland by herself was incapable of preventing either the restoration of Germany's and Russia's power or the resumption of their traditional policy of mutual collaboration at Poland's expense—and this is precisely what proceeded to occur. Despite post-1918 differences in public ideologies and political structures, a rapidly reviving Germany and a more slowly resuscitating Russia cooperated with each other and against Poland throughout most of the 1920s. The fact that they were militarily still too weak to truncate or partition her at that time was of scant comfort to Poland, which could hardly fail to be aware of her neighbors' determination to change this military aspect of the power equation in due course. [2]

[1] See the recollection by the Russian Social Revolutionary leader Victor Chernov of a lecture given by Piłsudski in Paris shortly before the war. Chernov, p. 150.

[2] It is true that many Poles had an exaggerated impression of the extent to which Russia had been weakened by World War I, the Revolution, the Civil

Confronted by the dual enmity of her big neighbors, Poland was obviously interested in ensuring that any conflict between herself and either or both of them should not remain localized but should bring powerful friends—equally unwilling to tolerate German and/or Russian hegemony over East Central Europe—to her own support. It was for this purpose that Poland concluded an alliance with France on February 19, 1921 (followed by a secret military convention two days later), and desperately—and for long vainly—strove to interest Britain in her behalf as a factor of stability in an area which in the long run would be regarded as vital also to British interests.[3] Here, however, the Poles constantly came up against a frustration which never ceased to exasperate them, namely, that they could exercise no leverage on the Western powers to oblige them either to honor an obligation or to acknowledge a commitment to Poland. French and British policy toward Poland was to prove simply a function of their policy toward Germany or Russia.[4] Thus, when France decided in the mid-1920s to attempt a rapprochement with Germany, there was nothing that Poland could do to avert this implicit but definite desertion by her Western ally. Two decades later, her government-in-exile was once again powerless to prevent a wartime decision by Britain and the United States that their alliance with the Soviet Union had priority over their commitments to the Polish government and its eastern frontier claims. Meanwhile, in the mid-1920s, Britain viewed the European scene primarily in terms of her desire to revive Germany and to reintegrate her into both the European state system and the pattern of world trade. Britain believed herself to have few or no vital interests in East Central Europe and refused to guarantee the area's post-Versailles frontiers against German revisionist pressure.[5] To

War, and the Communist experiment in government. But though they underestimated her capacity for revival under the Bolsheviks, they did not cease to regard her as a potential threat at some more or less distant point in the future.

[3] For the text of the Franco-Polish political alliance, see Wandycz, p. 393. The same author reconstructs the probable text of the secret military convention on pp. 394–95.

[4] See Kulski, p. 667, and A. C. Rosé, pp. 63–69.

[5] This British attitude was pithily summarized in 1925 by Sir Austen Chamberlain, foreign secretary during the period 1924–29: "For the Polish Corridor, no British government ever will or ever can risk the bones of a British grenadier." Quoted in Henry L. Roberts, "International Relations Between the Wars," in C. E. Black, ed., *Challenge in Eastern Europe* (New Brunswick, 1954), p. 183.

the extent that Britain showed any positive interest in Poland during the 1920s, it was largely as a possible foil against Soviet Russia, and the occasions when she manifested such an interest generally coincided with intermittent periods of British-Soviet tension. France's Polish policy during the interwar period, while more tortured than Britain's, was also ultimately unsatisfactory from Poland's point of view, for reasons to be analyzed presently.

Within limits, Poland could seek to extricate herself from this vise of hostile neighbors and unreliable friends by so developing her own strength as to render the risks of an attack upon her prohibitive to the potential aggressor(s). Simultaneously, she could attempt to organize alliances and coalitions with and among other medium and small powers also threatened by Germany or Russia. The first of these two strategies explains the unremitting Polish efforts to develop the country's economic, demographic, and military potential. It also explains the popularity of the army and the readiness to make sacrifices for its support among all sectors of Polish society. The second strategy was diplomatically ambitious but brought only meager results. Hopes of developing a Polish-Baltic-Scandinavian or Polish-Baltic combination were rendered abortive by Scandinavian and Finnish preference for neutrality and noninvolvement as well as by Lithuania's refusal—encouraged by Germany and particularly by Russia—to reconcile herself to Poland's forcible seizure in 1920 of Wilno (Vilnius, Vilna), a city which Lithuania regarded as her historic capital though her current ethnic–demographic claims to it were weak.[6] Toward the south, Polish-Czechoslovak relations never developed any real warmth or mutual confidence owing to the two countries' quarrel over the economically valuable city and district of Teschen (Cieszyn, Těšín), their contrasting perceptions of Russia's and Hungary's proper roles in Europe (each regarding the other's bête noire with some benevolence), and their contrasting social structures and reciprocally irritating national psychologies.[7] Only with Rumania did Poland conclude a political alliance, signed on March 3, 1921, and renewed

[6] The literature on this complicated Wilno question is vast. See, for example, the debate between the Polish and Lithuanian diplomats Sokal, "Der polnisch-litauische Konflikt," and Sidzikauskas, "Der litauisch-polnische Konflikt."

[7] See Wandycz, *passim,* but especially the concluding chapter entitled "Appraisal—a Pattern of Relations."

periodically, but this, on balance, proved to be more advantageous to the Rumanian than the Polish partner. It pertained exclusively to mutual support along their eastern frontiers, that is, it was directed only at Russia, with which Rumania's relations were even worse than Poland's, and provided no direct support to Poland in relation to Germany.[8] It was, in short, unimpressive. On the whole, therefore, the efforts to create a collective East Central European phalanx of security against Germany and Russia proved disappointing.

European diplomatic developments in the months preceding Piłsudski's coup had starkly emphasized Poland's vulnerabilities in the sphere of foreign affairs. The multilateral Locarno Treaties of October 16, 1925, which partially legitimated, as it were, Germany's anti-Polish revisionism by accepting her legal-political distinction between the validity of her western and her eastern frontiers, had brought to the fore France's unreliability as Poland's ally and Britain's indifference to Poland's security interests in relation to Germany.[9] Half a year later, Germany and Russia reaffirmed their "Rapallo policy" of close cooperation—implicitly but categorically at Poland's expense—with their Berlin Treaty of Neutrality and Nonaggression of April 24, 1926.[10] Simultaneously, Germany was engaged in a major effort to destroy Poland economically through the tariff war and through successful intrigues to prevent American and British financial aid to her.

It is not surprising that this deterioration in Poland's international situation between the spring of 1925 and that of 1926 should occasionally be cited as one of the precipitating causes behind Piłsudski's

[8] The public text of the Polish-Rumanian Convention of March 3, 1921, is in *Survey of International Affairs, 1920–1923* (London, 1925), pp. 504–5. Upon its renewal and transformation into a Treaty of Guarantee on March 26, 1926, and again on January 15, 1931 (text in *Survey of International Affairs, 1926* [London, 1928], pp. 483–85), the wording was revised to render it ostensibly applicable against all aggression, regardless of source. However, the supplementary military convention of 1921, which had envisaged only the hypothesis of a Soviet Russian attack, was never modified, and on the eve of World War II both governments repeatedly indicated that their alliance was not operative against Germany. See *Survey of International Affairs, 1939–1946: The Eve of the War, 1939* (London, 1958), pp. 101, 107, 115, 182–84, 419.

[9] The texts of the Locarno Treaties are in Wandycz, pp. 399–402.

[10] The text of the Berlin Treaty is in Leonard Shapiro, ed., *Soviet Treaty Series,* I (Washington, D.C., 1950), 317–18.

decision to resume power and stage his "armed demonstration" in May, 1926.[11] Though there is no doubt of Piłsudski's disappointment and anger over Locarno and though the general sense of international isolation and danger helped to facilitate his victory, it appears on balance that the foreign situation was but a marginal factor behind Piłsudski's coup, the main causes of which were the internal political and army-command crises. Indeed, on the morrow of his seizure of power, Piłsudski indicated to his personal *homme de confiance* in matters of foreign policy that he did not regard the international situation as carrying any immediate threat to Poland and that he counted on her being able to enjoy and utilize at least five years of peace.[12]

Just as international issues do not appear to have been the principal cause of the coup, so too were its consequences for Polish foreign policy initially less radical than had been widely expected. Piłsudski's National Democratic foes had found it expedient to inflame and capitalize on such drastic expectations of revolutionary change in Poland's diplomatic stance and activity. Their analysis, which was revived in some post-World War II Communist historiography,[13] represented the coup as a British machination designed to achieve the following multiple and interrelated purposes: (*a*) to weaken France in Europe by bringing to power in allied Poland a leader skeptically disposed toward her, (*b*) to assuage and if possible to liquidate German-Polish enmity by bringing to power Poland's leading Germanophile, (*c*) to reorient the primary thrust of Polish policy from defense against Germany to eventual aggression against Russia (with which Britain's relations were chronically poor during most of the 1920s) by bringing to power Poland's most notorious Russophobe. There was, of course, an element of plausibility in the premises on which each of these interpretations rested, but the analysis *in toto* was exaggerated and hence distortive.

British foreign policy in the post-Versailles period was indeed sus-

[11] See, for example, Łukasiewicz, p. 13, and Lipiński, *Wielki Marszałek,* pp. 193–94.

[12] Beck, p. 3. Piłsudski was also relatively optimistic in his remarks of December 15, 1926, to the Sejm's budget committee, as recorded in his *PZ,* IX, 57. For his outrage over Locarno, see *PZ,* VIII, 293, and Beck, p. 268.

[13] See Lapter, "Międzynarodowe tło przewrotu majowego"; Nowiński, p. 5; Arski, pp. 435–43.

picious of and dubious toward France's efforts to protect her security interests through alliances with the "new" states of East Central Europe. To avert French hegemony over the Continent, British governments encouraged the revival of Germany and sought to facilitate her reintegration into the European state system. But British policy was not as systematically anti-French as the above diagnosis suggests nor did it *au fond* prefer Germany to France.[14] London, it is true, quickly welcomed Piłsudski's coup because it hoped that he would prove receptive to a German-Polish *détente* and would strengthen Poland's army and stabilize her government so as to render her more effective against Russia.[15] But this was quite different from the alleged British intention to instigate an armed Polish attack upon the Soviet Union in order to destroy that country's political system and conquer her western territories—supposedly in compensation for the coming surrender by Poland to Germany of her formerly Prussian western areas. Though there was considerable Soviet anxiety on this point, the British government, as of the spring of 1926, was deprecating rather than encouraging the prospect of armed Polish hostilities against Russia.[16] Nor, despite the established fact that the British ambassador to Poland and his military attaché occasionally visited Piłsudski in his Sulejówek "retirement" before the coup, has any convincing proof come to light of actual British complicity in planning or financing the coup.[17] In addition, the assumption

[14] This problem is analyzed in two studies: W. A. Jordan, *Great Britain, France, and the German Problem, 1918–1939* (London, 1943), and A. Wolfers, *Britain and France Between Two Wars* (New York, 1940).

[15] See the report of May 20, 1926, from Konstanty Skirmunt, the Polish envoy in London, published in Z. Landau, ed., "Przewrót majowy w raportach poselstwa RP w Londynie," p. 156. The British also hoped that Piłsudski would prove strong enough to concede what previous Polish cabinets had been unwilling or unable to agree to—that Polish finances be placed under League of Nations (in effect, under British) supervision. See also Morawski, *Tamten brzeg*, p. 165.

[16] For the Soviet anxieties, see the recollections of a Polish diplomat then stationed in Moscow: Poznański, p. 3. For the actual British position, see the obviously inspired editorial in *The Times* (London), May 28, 1926.

[17] Much is made of these pre-coup British visits by the suspicious Frenchman Picardin, p. 358, and by the Communist Wierzbiński, *Warszawa nie odpowiada*, pp. 53–54. Similarly, the prewar Polish diplomat Morawski claims to recall from memory—thirty years after the event—reading a dispatch to the effect that a British envoy in a Near Eastern country had been heard to predict just before the coup that the Witos cabinet would be forcibly overthrown—

of preliminary British connivance in Piłsudski's forcible return to power is rendered improbable by his own attitude toward Britain. Though desirous—like other Polish political figures—of good relations with her, Piłsudski was not particularly pro-British. He never forgot that at Versailles in 1919, during the Polish-Soviet crisis of 1920, and again at Locarno in 1925, Britain had consistently worked against Polish interests.[18] Furthermore, though British economic and financial involvement in Poland quickened after the coup, no substantial increase in political cordiality was discernible until many years later.

The initial French response to Piłsudski's coup was one of dismay and suspicion—partly out of fear lest it tear Poland asunder through civil war, partly because in Paris, too, it was suspected as an attempted Anglo-German seduction of a French ally.[19] Yet the prognoses of a radical change for the worse in Franco-Polish relations again proved exaggerated. It is true that France had reason to regard the political forces composing Witos' deposed Right-Center cabinet—especially its National Democratic contingent—as her own warmest Polish partisans precisely because they viewed Germany as presenting the major threat to Polish survival, whereas Piłsudski, in contrast, was known to regard Russia as enemy number one and to entertain a certain degree of admiration for Germany, or rather for German styles of organization, method, and discipline, which he had come to know well during the wartime association of his Legions with the German army. Piłsudski was also known to resent a certain patronizing air in France's attitude toward Poland and to suspect her ultimate reliability as an ally—particularly after Locarno, when France appeared to have concluded a rapprochement of her own with Germany.

---

to Britain's satisfaction. (Morawski, *Tamten brzeg*, pp. 164–65.) Considering that the Witos cabinet was only two days old when the coup erupted, that British diplomats on Near Eastern assignments would be unlikely to have precise advance information about such a clandestine activity in Poland on such short notice if there were British involvement, and, alternatively, that a British diplomat who babbled about it as this one is alleged to have done would be suspect prima facie as a source of hard information, Morawski's account is too indirect and weak as supposed evidence of British complicity in Piłsudski's coup.

[18] Komarnicki, pp. 74–75.

[19] *Le Temps*, May 14, 1926; Gauvain, "La Crise polonaise," pp. 812–13; Dumont-Wilden, pp. 379–80.

Piłsudski was not, however, alone in his skepticism about France. Indeed, general Polish confidence in the big Western ally had been perceptibly on the wane ever since the electoral victory of the Cartel des Gauches in France in 1924, which had inaugurated the policy of Franco-German reconciliation, one corollary of which was a series of persistent French efforts to narrow the scope and the automaticity of the Franco-Polish alliance.[20] In both its antecedents and its consequences, Piłsudski's coup was thus more a point on a continuum than a pivotal event in Poland's relations with France. On the one hand, the deterioration had set in earlier. On the other, the coup did not lead to an ultimate rupture of the alliance, for neither partner could afford to stand alone against Germany.

Piłsudski, indeed, harbored no a priori objections to the alliance with France. It was he, after all, who had originally concluded it on Poland's behalf in 1921. Had the French treated the alliance as a truly mutual and absolutely firm obligation, Piłsudski would not have been disposed to discount it. He would indeed have been prepared to strengthen and apply it. But this was asking too much of France. First bled white by the war, then abandoned by the United States, persistently restrained by Britain, she lacked the power and, from the mid-1920s onward, the will to sustain the postwar settlement in East Central Europe. Thus a disequilibrium set in between France's far-reaching alliance commitments to Poland and her defensive politico-military posture in relation to Germany. It proved impossible to close this gap either by explicitly abandoning the foreign obligations or by providing herself with an offensive politico-military strategy suitable to honoring them. The gap was blatantly perceptible to all but the most starry-eyed of Francophile Poles. Piłsudski was emphatically aware of it. As a result, the Franco-Polish alliance continued to limp along in an atmosphere of mutual suspicion periodically interspersed with efforts to repair it.

Germany and her revisionist aspirations were, of course, the catalyst of the Franco-Polish irritations. The initial response of German public opinion to Piłsudski's return to power was one of professed optimism that Polish-German differences would now be approached in a more flexible manner by Piłsudski than by the previous Polish

[20] Dębicki, pp. 58–59.

regimes.[21] Rumors erupted to the effect that Piłsudski would return the so-called Polish Corridor and Danzig (Gdańsk) to Germany in return for a free hand to annex Lithuania, with its Baltic port city of Memel (Klajpeda), to Poland. German newspapers which had hitherto been friendly to Lithuania became frigid, the London *Times* hinted in favor of this exchange, and that indefatigable "Pan-European" enthusiast, Count Richard Coudenhove-Kalergi, began to propagate it actively. Interestingly enough, an unofficial but politically well-connected French group was also exploring the same idea.[22]

The scheme was preposterous, as the Wilhelmstrasse must have been aware even if German public opinion was not. Any attempt to realize it would have provoked not only a Polish-Lithuanian clash but also, in all likelihood, another Polish-Soviet war. For this reason alone, no responsible German government could have backed it without being prepared to abandon the Rapallo policy and rupture the association with Russia—a step which awaited the limitless and irrational geopolitical ambition of a Hitler. It would also have implied the renunciation of German claims to Upper Silesia and Memel and to much of Poznania and was therefore again unacceptable to the government of the Weimar Republic. Finally, for Poland, too, it would have been the height of irrationality to initiate such a redrawing of her own frontiers, the only consequence of which would have been to render her a German satellite while embroiling her in a major confrontation with Russia. Foreign Minister Zaleski, therefore, put a stop to this canard and insisted on the inviolability of the Versailles frontier arrangements in their entirety in a major speech delivered on January 9, 1927, at the inauguration of the Polish Society for the Study of International Affairs.[23]

At a more modest and pragmatic level, however, Piłsudski was prepared to seek an easing of German-Polish tensions. In the summer of

---

[21] *Berliner Tageblatt,* May 31, 1926. Other German expressions to this effect are cited in *Kurjer Warszawski,* May 22, 1926.

[22] *The Times* (London), October 7, 1926; Bernus, "La Politique extérieure de la Pologne," p. 100; Korbel, pp. 213–14. One of the members of this French group was the journalist Jules Sauerwein, to whom Piłsudski had granted his first post-coup interviews, published in *Le Matin,* May 24 and 26, 1926, and summarized above, chapter XI. Sauerwein was occasionally used as an unofficial French spokesman by the Quai d'Orsay.

[23] Cieślak, II, 5. See also Chrzanowski, pp. 8–12.

1926 he twice utilized the PPS financial expert Herman Diamand as an unofficial emissary to sound out German Foreign Minister Gustav Stresemann. Diamand, who had been used in a similar capacity by Skrzyński in December, 1925, emphasized Piłsudski's desire for an accommodation with Germany and may have hinted at undefined Polish concessions in return for German support to help Poland win a renewable seat on the Council of the League of Nations.[24] Such semiprivate diplomacy is rarely fruitful in dealing with problems as complex as German-Polish differences, and Diamand's effort proved no exception. Indeed, it may have given the Germans an exaggerated impression of Polish compliancy, for it was followed in the second half of 1926 and the spring of 1927 by a sharp upsurge in German revisionist propaganda against Poland. This was of such intensity that no Polish regime, not even Piłsudski's, could for the time being pursue the feelers for a *détente* lest it appear to be retreating under pressure. Indeed, on at least two occasions, Poland was moved to protest against German Reichstag debates as improper interference in her internal affairs.[25]

The awkward timing of the Germans' propaganda offensive was a characteristic instance of their general tendency to overreach themselves in their contest with Poland—a tendency which had also manifested itself in 1925 with the launching of the tariff war. It was partly an expression of German national arrogance in relation to the Poles and their allegedly contemptible *Saisonstaat,* but, more particularly, it also reflected confidence that Britain would oblige Poland to yield to the German frontier claims. Such German expectations, though understandable, were erroneous. It is true that Britain had from the beginning been critical of the Versailles territorial settlement in East

[24] An attempt to reconstruct the substance of Diamand's remarks from the elusive references to them which appear in the Stresemann *Nachlass* papers has been undertaken in Gąsiorowski, pp. 300–301.

[25] *Ibid.,* p. 306, and Cieślak, II, 12. Piłsudski and Stresemann had a secret but inconclusive discussion in Geneva on December 9, 1927. According to Stresemann's notes of the conversation, Piłsudski desired a settlement of politico-economic issues, such as the disposition of industrial properties in Silesia. Far from indicating any readiness to make Polish concessions to German frontier claims, however, Piłsudski reversed the tables by assuring Stresemann that Poland had no ambitions upon East Prussia. For further details of this meeting, see Jurkiewicz, ed., "Tajne posiedzenie Rady Ligi Narodów w grudniu 1927 r. i spotkanie Piłsudskiego ze Stresemannem," pp. 88–96.

Central Europe and sympathetic toward German protests against it. It is also true that Britain had all along been particularly skeptical about most of Poland's acquisitions of prewar German areas. But this did not mean a readiness actually to sponsor revision unless the revisionist power was able and willing to threaten force—which a still disarmed Germany could not yet do against Poland. What the excessively optimistic German leaders of the Weimar period had to learn was the fact that, when put to a critical test, British policy during the interwar period would back the stronger party. In the 1920s this was the Versailles constellation of France, Poland, and the Little Entente. When the balance shifted to a rearmed and bellicose Nazi Germany during the next decade, Britain was to remain true to form and sponsor Europe's capitulation to Hitler at Munich. Not until the eve of World War II was she to awaken to the dangers of this policy, which, ironically, was the very reverse of her vaunted, historic balance-of-power strategy. In the meantime, another, more specific reason why Britain did not actively promote Germany's frontier claims on Poland was a desire not to weaken Poland in relation to Russia. All in all, Poland's relations with Germany, like those with Britain and France, were thus less affected by Piłsudski's coup than had originally been anticipated. It did not even precipitate a settlement of the tariff war.

The same generalization can be applied to Polish-Russian relations. The initial Soviet response to Piłsudski's coup was one of anxiety lest it signal the start of a British-supported campaign of aggression.[26] The Soviet press agency Tass denied and denounced as provocative Polish reports that the Red Army was massing along Poland's frontier. Soviet nervousness was such that Generals Tukhachevsky and Yegorov left Moscow for Minsk and Kharkov, respectively, to be on hand at operational headquarters in the event of hostilities.[27] But the acute phase of the war scare soon abated as Piłsudski, Zaleski, and

[26] Poznański, p. 3.
[27] *Ilustrowany Kurjer Codzienny*, May 27, 1926. The Tass denial of massive Soviet troop movements is in *Pravda,* May 16. Soviet Commissar for Foreign Affairs Chicherin likewise denied the reports of troop concentrations to German ambassador Brockdorff-Rantzau when they conferred in Moscow on May 16. (Korbel, p. 205.) It will be recalled that Sikorski had utilized such reports as one of the justifications for his refusal to render aid to the Belwederians during the coup.

Bartel all gave earnest assurances that the new government was committed to a policy of peace and harbored no desires for any territorial changes. The Foreign Minister also promised that Poland would never join a bloc directed against the Soviet Union.[28] In December the Piłsudski regime followed up these pacific declarations with the tactful gesture of appointing the ex-lawyer Stanisław Patek, who had made a strong prewar reputation as defense attorney for revolutionaries in the tsarist courts, as its new envoy to the Soviet Union. Some of Patek's onetime "clients" were now members of the Soviet government, and his designation was well received. The Soviet leaders' original fear that Piłsudski's Poland would be but a spearhead for British-inspired aggression against the USSR abated somewhat. Indeed, as British-Soviet relations deteriorated sharply from mid-1926 onward and the Soviets became concerned lest Germany desert them, they were moved to extend tentative feelers toward Warsaw for a rapprochement.

This incipient easing of Polish-Soviet relations was interrupted by another period of tension in 1927. The precipitating cause of the second crisis was the assassination of the Soviet envoy to Poland, Piotr L. Voikov, by an anti-Bolshevik Russian émigré on June 7, 1927, shortly after Great Britain had severed diplomatic relations with the USSR (May 26) and two months after the Soviet embassy in Peking had been raided and its consulate in Shanghai attacked (April 6). Once again, Moscow appeared to suspect that all these incidents formed parts of a concerted British-inspired aggressive provocation. Stalin even compared the assassination of Voikov with that of Archduke Franz Ferdinand at Sarajevo in 1914.[29] Yet this crisis, too, was alleviated and tensions were sufficiently eased over the next year to enable Poland and the Soviet Union to negotiate a series of specific functional agreements, including the exchange of political prisoners, the restoration of Polish cultural objects looted during the eighteenth-century partitions, and a railroad convention. On Soviet initiative the two countries also sponsored the so-called Litvinov Pro-

[28] These various pacific pronouncements are recorded in Piłsudski, *PZ*, IX, 21, and in the European daily press on June 23, July 22, August 1, 1926.

[29] I. V. Stalin, *Sochineniia*, IX (Moscow, 1948), 326. In September, 1927, and May, 1928, there were nonfatal attacks on the Soviet chargé d'affaires and trade mission chiefs, respectively, in Warsaw.

tocol for putting into effect in eastern Europe the Kellogg-Briand Pact even before it became universally "valid." Finally signed on February 9, 1929, by the Soviet Union, Rumania, Latvia, Estonia, and Poland (and adhered to by Lithuania on April 1), the Litvinov Protocol amounted to a nonaggression treaty between the USSR and her neighbors. For the Soviet Union, its significance rested in the relative guarantee against invasion which it gave her, since she was about to turn her attention and energies inward with the first of her monumental five-year plans. Polish satisfaction was prompted by the Litvinov Protocol's regional character: Poland had, in effect, stood as patron and spokesman for the three other original non-Soviet signatories.[30] Though there were still to be occasional troughs in Polish-Soviet relations—often provoked by Polish resentment over Comintern activities, for which the Soviet government blandly disclaimed responsibility, and by Soviet anger over the toleration shown by the Polish government toward anti-Bolshevik émigré groups from the Soviet Union operating in Poland—the fact is that, contrary to all predictions, these relations were on the whole no worse under Piłsudski than they had been before his return to power.

In view of the fact that the coup's impact on Poland's relations with the European Great Powers was thus rather minimal—neither as negative on relations with France and Soviet Russia nor as positive on those with Britain and Germany as had been anticipated—how is the generalization with which this chapter opened—"palpable improvement combined with persisting hazards"—to be justified? The latter half of this statement is virtually self-evident, for the German and Russian threats were ultimately permanent. During the 1920s, Poland's salvation rested in the relative postwar weakness of her two dangerous neighbors. Then, in the 1930s, when they became stronger under Hitler and Stalin, Poland was again reprieved by their mutual enmity until their fateful reconciliation at her expense in August, 1939. As for the palpable improvement in Poland's international status in the first years after the coup, the mere existence of the new Piłsudski regime buttressed the country's international reputation by

[30] H. Laeuen, *Polnisches Zwischenspiel: Eine Episode der Ostpolitik* (Berlin, 1940), pp. 96–97, and Scelle, pp. 19–32. Eventually, Danzig, Persia, and Turkey also signed the Litvinov Protocol, the text of which is in Horak, ed., pp. 158–60.

projecting abroad an image of greater stability and strength than had prevailed under the preceding parliamentary chaos. The Stabilization Loan of October, 1927, was but one illustration of this heightened international confidence in Poland. Then, too, a relative diplomatic victory had been Poland's success in winning election to a renewable, semipermanent, three-year seat on the Council of the League of Nations to "balance" the permanent seat which Germany acquired as a result of joining the League in the aftermath of Locarno. Though some of the groundwork for Poland's election to her seat had been prepared by Skrzyński before the coup, the final effort was Zaleski's, and the success with which it was crowned on September 8, 1926, redounded to the *sanacja* regime's prestige in public opinion. (Ironically, Piłsudski, who was skeptical, even hostile, toward the League of Nations and aware that in this case Poland had gained less than Germany, did not share in the general enthusiasm over this development and on a later occasion was even to express doubt about the wisdom of Poland's utilizing her eligibility for reelection.)[31] Polish public opinion also took considerable pride and satisfaction in the impression—encouraged by the regime—that a proposal submitted by the Polish delegation to the League of Nations in September, 1927, had become the forerunner and basis of the Kellogg-Briand Pact for the outlawry of war.[32]

The most spectacular, if least substantial, of Poland's foreign policy successes in the first years of the *sanacja* era was Piłsudski's personal intervention in ending a Polish-Lithuanian war scare in 1927. Lithuania, it will be recalled, had never reconciled herself to the loss of Wilno to Poland in 1920. She refused to establish diplomatic relations, closed the frontier, and insisted on regarding herself in a formal state of war with Poland. There were, however, no open hostilities, and the issue was simmering rather than seething in the mid-1920s. Shortly after Piłsudski's coup, a number of developments threatened to reopen the quarrel and bring it to a boil. On September 28, 1926, a nonaggression treaty was signed by Lithuania and the Soviet Union. In an accompanying note, the latter power, still nervous about Piłsudski's foreign policy intentions, renewed its long-standing

31 Beck, p. 19.
32 Scelle, p. 26, and Dębicki, p. 61.

acknowledgment of Lithuanian claims to Wilno. In response to a Polish protest of October 13, Soviet Commissar for Foreign Affairs Chicherin on December 6 accused Poland of wishing to establish an anti-Soviet protectorate over the Baltic states and insisted, per contra, on the Soviet Union's own peaceable intentions toward Poland.[33] Then, in the night of December 16, 1926, a military coup d'état in Lithuania replaced a moderate Leftist government with a semi-authoritarian nationalistic one. As the new regime was based on only a minority of the legislature and had scarcely any claims to legitimacy, it was almost bound to try to maximize its popularity by exploiting the national resentment of Poland and sharpening Lithuania's feud with her.

Piłsudski's initial reaction to the Lithuanian coup was one of watchful attentiveness. Indeed, he appears to have hoped that the new authoritarian regime would after all prove strong enough to risk a *détente* with Poland and is reported to have extended secret feelers to it.[34] Nevertheless, the well-nigh inevitable exacerbation in relations was not long in coming. Early in October, 1927, the Lithuanian authorities disaccredited several teachers and closed a number of schools catering to the Polish minority in Lithuania. Seemingly in reprisal though with somewhat suspicious alacrity, the Poles responded in kind, smashing the Lithuanian minority's school system in the Wilno region.[35] Each side arrested alleged subversives of the other's nationality, tempers were mutually inflamed, and early in October Piłsudski rather ostentatiously came to Wilno to participate in the celebrations scheduled for the seventh anniversary of General Żeligowski's seizure of the city for Poland in 1920. On October 15, 1927, Lithuania took her case to the League of Nations, alleging not

---

[33] Cieślak, II, 16, and J. Degras, ed., *Soviet Documents on Foreign Policy,* Vol. II: *1925–1932* (London, 1952), p. 145.

[34] See his press interview of December 24, 1926, reprinted in Piłsudski, *PZ, IX,* 63–65. For a report that in January, 1927, Piłsudski, using a Ukrainian intermediary acceptable to both sides, had vainly offered the new Lithuanian premier a condominium over Wilno in return for the establishment of normal, friendly relations, see [Smal'-Stots'kyi], "Nieznana inicjatywa Piłsudskiego."

[35] For the cross-charges, see Sokal, p. 867, and Sidzikauskas, p. 1068. For a suggestion that the Lithuanians, though the apparent initiators of the crisis, had in fact fallen into a Polish trap of provocation, see Senn, p. 274.

only Polish violation of the Versailles Minorities Treaty of June 28, 1919, but even the existence of a Polish plot against Lithuania's very existence. The matter was placed on the agenda for the December session of the League Council.

German and Soviet support for Lithuania gave the affair an international significance far beyond the local issue at stake. The resulting sense of major crisis was further exacerbated by a press interview of Piłsudski's on November 30, 1927, in which he stated that he had considered mobilizing the Polish army against Lithuania, thus drawing the logical consequence from the latter's insistence that a state of war pertained between the two countries.[36] To emphasize the importance which he attached to the problem, Piłsudski himself came to Geneva on December 9 for the next day's crucial session of the League Council. At that meeting he suddenly turned to the Lithuanian premier, Augustinas Voldemaras, and asked bluntly whether war or peace prevailed between their countries. The stunned and perhaps frightened Voldemaras hastily conceded that it was peace.[37] Though no real improvement in Polish-Lithuanian affairs followed, though the border remained closed, and though diplomatic relations continued to be nonexistent, the settlement of this particular crisis was something of a Polish success and a personal tour de force for Piłsudski. While extensive maneuvering and persuasion by the diplomats of the European powers had helped prepare the way for Voldemaras' retreat, Piłsudski's spectacular ultimatum earned him the sole credit with Polish public opinion. In its combination of theatricality of gesture with insubstantiality in results, Piłsudski's intervention was characteristic of, and in turn appealed to, the more dubious side of Polish romanticism. Neither he nor the nation appreciated the price Poland was paying in terms of her general international reputation by resorting to this brusque manner of dealing with a little neighbor on an issue where Poland's hands were scarcely clean in the first place. Nor were the larger risks of permanently alienating this neighbor in the context of Poland's own vulnerabilities in relation to two hostile Great Powers fully fathomed. Instead, the Poles were bedazzled by

[36] Piłsudski, *PZ*, IX, 97–101.
[37] For firsthand—but varying—descriptions of this episode, see Piłsudski, *PZ*, IX, 101–2, and the items cited in Senn, p. 282, n. 73.

the superficially therapeutic effects of a policy of "power" and "decisiveness." Thus, as Poland's first post-coup parliamentary elections approached in March, 1928, Piłsudski and his BBWR were the beneficiaries of a public sense of gratification over Poland's improved international status as well as her ameliorated economic condition under his stewardship—a sense which in some ways exaggerated the realities.

PART FIVE

CRISIS AGAIN

CHAPTER XVII
THE ELECTIONS OF 1928

The politico-historical function of the Polish parliamentary elections of March, 1928, was to proclaim the nation's judgment on Piłsudski's seizure and subsequent utilization of power as well as on the period of Sejm-party preponderance which had preceded and partly elicited his coup d'état. In preparation for these elections, Piłsudski had, for the first time in independent Poland, formed and identified himself with a particular political organization, the BBWR, instead of permitting his partisans to operate through several, at times mutually oppositional, parties, as had been the case in the first decade of the restored Polish state. Nevertheless, in the public's eye, Piłsudski's earlier, traditional reputation as a man of the political Left still survived to a considerable extent, and the parties of the erstwhile Left bloc sought—partly as a stratagem and partly in reflection of their own persisting illusions—to take advantage of this public impression by utilizing Piłsudski's name and coattails for their own electoral propaganda—to his and his entourage's considerable annoyance.[1] Indeed, the leaders of the Stronnictwo Chłopskie and the Left-NPR had even taken soundings on the possibility of a Piłsudskist–Left bloc electoral coalition. This, however, came to naught; the PPS rejected the notion of a single, combined electoral list, while the *sanacja* camp advanced the unacceptable condition of also including Piłsudski's new conservative supporters.[2]

[1] See Sławoj-Składkowski, *Strzępy meldunków*, p. 75, and Czubiński, *Centrolew*, pp. 77–78.

[2] Próchnik, *Pierwsze piętnastolecie*, p. 271, and Stęborowski, p. 76. The proposed coalition was to consist of the PPS, Wyzwolenie, Stronnictwo Chłopskie, Klub Praca, Naprawa, Left-NPR, and Bojko's defection from Piast. The abortive negotiations for its formation were conducted on the Piłsudskist side by the future prime minister (1929), Kazimierz Świtalski. It appears plausible that the Stronnictwo Chłopskie may have sponsored the coalition idea in order to avert or heal its own schism of December, 1927, over the "Piłsudski question." Once its notion of a "grand" coalition had come to naught, the Party, which had been founded only since the last parliamentary elections of 1922, preferred to stand independently rather than enter a "small" coalition with Wyzwolenie and PPS. Świtalski also maneuvered to prevent this latter possibility by threatening Wyzwolenie with further subversion and defections.

Although the voters were presented with as many as thirty-four "state" lists for the balloting (there had been twenty in November, 1922), their basic choice was among six competing political tendencies: (1) the Piłsudskist camp as represented by the BBWR and some smaller allied groups; (2) the parliamentary Left, slowly and reluctantly moving into opposition but still not averse to capitalizing on Piłsudski's former association with it and its own reciprocal support of his coup; (3) the several Center and (4) Right parties which together had constituted the prevailing parliamentary majority of the pre-coup period; (5) the National Minorities. Also available, though of marginal electoral strength and of minor parliamentary significance, were (6) the parties of the so-called revolutionary Left, including the Communists, their "fronts," and their allies, but also some independently radical groups. To the disappointment of many of Piłsudski's new conservative allies, the democratic "Moraczewski" electoral law of November 28, 1918, providing for universal, secret, direct, equal, and proportional suffrage, was retained in force, as Sławek had indicated it would be at the Dzików conference in September, 1927.

The Piłsudskist camp and its allies participated in the campaign through four different electoral lists. There was, first of all, the main contingent, the BBWR itself, prominently displaying in the persons of its candidates its heterogeneous social and political origins: conservative magnates and self-taught peasants, captains of industry and prewar Socialist underground activists, technocratic intelligentsia and devoted Catholics—even token representatives from the ethnic minorities—all held together by the essential core of Piłsudskist "colonels," of Legion and POW militants. In Poznania and Pomerania, the Piłsudskists also appeared under the label Catholic Union of the Western Areas (Katolicka Unja Ziem Zachodnich), whose list was endorsed for this election by the Polish Catholic-Populist Party (Polskie Stronnictwo Katolicko-Ludowe), a minor group localized in Western Galicia.[3] The Left-NPR now ran in the formerly Prussian areas of western Poland (where their main strength lay) as the National-State Bloc of Labor (Narodowo-Państwowy Blok Pracy),[4] while in the formerly Russian Congress Kingdom territory it entered

[3] The Catholic Union of the Western Areas and the Polish Catholic-Populist Party were led, respectively, by the ex-Christian Democrat and current minister of communications, Paweł Romocki, and by the priest Father Jan Czuj.

[4] Here the Naprawa group (see above, p. 263, n. 2) supported them. For the origins of the NPR split, see above, pp. 177–78.

the BBWR directly. Finally, the pro-Piłsudskist defectors from the Stronnictwo Chłopskie advanced their own list of parliamentary candidates under the Peasant Association label.

With Bartel's Klub Praca subsumed within the BBWR, the parliamentary Left consisted of the PPS, Wyzwolenie, and Stronnictwo Chłopskie minus their defectors. Despite their established record of mutual cooperation, these three parties presented no formal electoral coalition or cartel. Between this "parliamentary" Left and the semilegal "revolutionary" Left led by the Communists, there hovered a number of political groups attempting or claiming to maintain a position more radical than the former but independent of the latter. Such were, for example, the Independent Socialist Labor Party (Niezależna Socjalistyczna Partia Pracy)[5] and the Jewish Labor Association "Bund." The Communists themselves ran officially under the label Worker-Peasant Unity (Jedność Robotniczo-Chłopska), and among their several allies and "fronts" were such groups as the Polish Peasant Self-Help Party (Samopomoc)—the heir of the smashed Independent Peasant Party[6]—and the "Left" wing of the divided Ukrainian Socialist Peasant-Worker Union (Selrob-Lewica).

The Christian Democrats, having gauged the prevailing political wind, declined this time to be identified with their erstwhile partners of the Right (except in Warsaw city) and instead joined with Witos' Piast Peasant Party, equally eager to dissociate itself from the *endecja,* in a Polish Catholic bloc. Only in the province of Silesia did the Christian Democrats stand independently. Abandoned by its former allies as well as by the many conservatives who had opted for the BBWR, National Democracy for the time being found itself in relative political isolation, for which the new militancy of the Camp

[5] In the early 1920s the Independent Socialist Labor Party had belonged to the defunct "2½" International. In April, 1928, shortly after the current elections, it resolved to initiate negotiations for a merger with the PPS over the vehement objections of the leaders of its autonomous Jewish section. The latter feared the loss of their special status in an enlarged and united socialist party, as well as resultant defections of their rank and file to the Bund or the Labor Zionists. They also insisted that many Jewish workers considered the PPS to be anti-Semitic. Except for a miniature rump of the Independents, the merger was concluded despite these objections and despite the fact that in May, 1926, the PPS had alluded to the Independent Socialist Labor Party as a Communist "front." See above, p. 167, n. 26, and the references there cited, as well as Tymieniecka, ed., "XXI Kongres PPS (1–4. XI. 1928)," p. 291.

[6] The Peasant Self-Help "state" list was invalidated by the Supreme Electoral Commission on January 31, 1928.

of Great Poland provided moral-psychological but not numerical-electoral compensation. The National Democrats, too, sought to capitalize on the public's religious sentiments and to make an ideological point by choosing the appellation Catholic-Nationalist for their list. Finally, the National Minorities presented a fractured appearance, on the one hand putting forward a collective bloc list, on the other supplementing and weakening it with a dozen additional particular lists, mainly Jewish and Ukrainian.

The electoral strategy and propaganda of the governmental coalition was set by Piłsudski's intimates Walery Sławek and Kazimierz Świtalski—both members of the "colonels' group," the former being chairman of the BBWR, while the latter currently occupied the less prominent but nevertheless powerful position of chief of the Political Department at the Interior Ministry. The campaign rhetoric of the Piłsudskist camp, as was to be expected, stressed the theme of "saving the state" from the political parties by concentrating on "constructive" technical, economic, and social development rather than on "sterile" party politics, further strengthening the constitutional powers of the president and the executive departments in relation to the legislature, and soliciting universal confidence in Piłsudski's political genius. Despite their annoyance with Leftist efforts to exploit Piłsudski's popularity and reputation, Sławek and Świtalski nevertheless directed the main thrust of their electoral effort in 1928 against the Right.

National Democratic propaganda, in its turn, retorted with demands that Poland's allegedly endangered national and Roman Catholic character be safeguarded and that the authority of government be strengthened without recourse to "personalism." The Piast–Christian Democratic line called for a republican, democratic, representative regime, buttressed by a constitutionally strengthened Senate and stabilized by a revision of the electoral laws such as to strengthen the Polish and weaken the National Minority elements in the parliament, committing itself on the one hand to implementing the land reform law of 1925 and on the other to a program of investments in public works.[7]

The parliamentary Left, oscillating between electoral hope and political apprehension—the former emotion stimulated by a leftward

[7] These points are reminiscent of those made in Witos' brochure of two years earlier, *Czasy i ludzie*. See above, p. 53.

trend in municipal elections throughout 1927, the latter by increasing concern about the regime's ultimate intentions [8]—projected a program composed of predictably extensive economic and social recommendations combined with defensive and disparate constitutional and political warnings. Thus, whereas the three parties of the parliamentary Left could agree in calling for a worker-peasant government, more radical land reform, universal secular education, equality for the ethnic minorities, and abolition of the Senate, they differed on such sensitive issues as those of federalistic autonomy for the ethnic minorities (favored by PPS and Wyzwolenie, not by the Stronnictwo Chłopskie) and the popular election of the president (recommended as suitably democratic by the two peasant parties, opposed by the more Jacobin, Caesarophobic PPS). They also sought to shame the traditional "Left Piłsudskists"—the civilian veterans of the Legions and the POW and the old Socialists—into revulsion against the BBWR by pointing to its internal political contradictions, its hospitality to the very elements that had once sneered at the Legionary movement, and its ostentatious welcome to some of the most regressively conservative strata of Polish society. Simultaneously, the three Left parties presented themselves as valid alternatives to the BBWR for genuine Piłsudskists.[9] The Communists and their affiliates—some of whose lists were invalidated on the eve of the election—issued their predictable calls for the overthrow of the bourgeois state and its analogous class dictatorship. The fragmented National Minorities, despite widespread skepticism toward Piłsudski within the ranks of their Slavic (Ukrainian and White Russian) contingents, nevertheless remained more fearful of, and opposed to, the Rightist *endecja* than the Piłsudskist *sanacja*.

Among the innovations which were introduced in the 1928 campaign as compared to those of 1919 and 1922 was the active, rather than the neutral, engagement of the government. The Piłsudskist organizer, legal expert, and vice-minister of justice, Stanisław Car, was appointed election commissioner-general even though he had not been one of the three nonpartisan judges designated to President

[8] See Ajnenkiel, "Materiały do dziejów politycznych Polski w latach 1924–1927," pp. 432–47.

[9] For examples, see *Robotnik Polski* (Detroit), January–February, 1928; Stęborowski, pp. 82–87; Czubiński, *Centrolew,* pp. 82–88.

Mościcki by the Supreme Court.[10] Then, too, Interior Minister Sławoj-Składkowski made it clear to provincial governors and county prefects that he expected them to utilize their social prestige and administrative authority on behalf of the BBWR in such ways as gracing its rallies, packing local election boards with its partisans, and "getting out" its vote. Indeed, some subsequent bureaucratic promotions were traceable to such successful intervention on behalf of the Piłsudskist lists. Furthermore, on Piłsudski's orders, eight million złoty of state revenue were illegally transferred by Finance Minister Czechowicz to Sławoj-Składkowski to subsidize BBWR electioneering expenditures, quite apart from the enormous financial resources which were being made available by magnates and industrialists and which permitted the veritable flooding of the country with Piłsudskist propaganda. Finally, though it would be erroneous and misleading to assert that the election of 1928 was characterized by overt terror, it is no exaggeration to acknowledge that especially in the *kresy,* the eastern borderlands inhabited by the Slavic minorities, the voting was accompanied by a certain degree of pressure and some chicanery, which supplemented the political effects of such previous steps as the outlawry of the White Russian Hramada a year earlier.[11]

Eager to convey an image of principled solidarity and disciplined effectiveness—perhaps partly in order to countervail the impression of ideological poverty and political incongruity—the BBWR leadership obliged each of its candidates to sign a pledge (1) to support the authority of the president and to work toward the strengthening of executive powers through further appropriate constitutional amendments, (2) to seek no personal, partisan, or class advantages from matters of state (an implied slap at other, allegedly corruptly para-

[10] Stanisław Car (1882–1938) was the *sanacja's* legal expert, notorious for interpretations which bent, without formally violating, the constitution. He had been head of the Chancellery of the Chief of State during Piłsudski's incumbency from 1918 to 1922, was subsequently editor of the legal journal *Palestra* (Bar) and procurator to the Supreme Court, and again chief of the Presidential Civilian Chancellery in 1926, under Mościcki. From December 22, 1928, until December 7, 1929, and again between March 29 and August 23, 1930, Car was minister of justice. Further information on him will be found in the Biographical Register.

[11] In the capital, the Right-leaning daily *Gazeta Warszawska* (Warsaw Gazette) was confiscated on three different occasions during the electoral campaign and toward its close published an issue consisting entirely of cooking recipes.

sitical, parties), (3) to treat BBWR colleagues with the respect proper among those who shared a common concern for the state, (4) to be guided by the advice of Piłsudski in the matter of organizing and joining parliamentary clubs. This last point is somewhat puzzling, since it implies the possibility that Piłsudski might choose to partition his bloc and instruct his supporters to enter various parliamentary groupings, presumably to capture and control them from within—a reversion to an earlier state of affairs.

Participation in the elections was considerably higher in 1928 than in 1922, thanks in part to a decision by the Ukrainians of Eastern Galicia not to repeat their former boycott. Of the eligible Sejm electorate, 78.3 percent cast ballots in 1928 compared to 67.9 percent in 1922, while in the senatorial case the equivalent proportions were 63.9 percent (1928) and 61.5 percent (1922). The prevailing conditions of relative economic prosperity, governmental stability, and international prestige for Poland reinforced the attractiveness of those lists most closely identified with Piłsudski—the BBWR and its allies. Out of a total number of 11,408,218 valid ballots cast in the Sejm elections of March 4, and of 6,390,531 in the senatorial voting a week later, the four pro-*sanacja* lists collectively polled 25.2 percent and 31.7 percent, respectively, the BBWR alone receiving 21 percent and 28.8 percent.

The parliamentary Left, however, also did well, owing partly to a lingering though rapidly obsolescing tendency of the electorate to identify it with Piłsudski and partly to a popular urge to repudiate the Right and Center politicians who had dominated the pre-coup governments. The three parliamentary Left parties, accordingly, drew 25.7 percent of valid Sejm and 21.6 percent of senatorial ballots.[12] (In 1922, when the Stronnictwo Chłopskie did not yet exist, PPS and Wyzwolenie had together polled 21.2 percent [10.8 percent plus 10.4 percent] and 16.8 percent [8.3 percent plus 8.5 percent] of the votes cast for Sejm and Senate.) Center and Right, on the other hand, were severely punished. The joint Piast Peasant–Christian Democratic list drew only 6.7 percent of both Sejm and senatorial ballots,

---

[12] The strengths of the PPS, Wyzwolenie, and Stronnictwo Chłopskie contingents were, respectively, 13 percent, 7.3 percent, 5.4 percent (Sejm) and 11.2 percent, 6.1 percent, 4.3 percent (Senate).

whereas in 1922 Piast alone had drawn 13.2 percent and 12.2 percent of Sejm and Senate votes. In that earlier year the Christian Democrats had run within the general Right bloc, which had then been supported by 28.9 percent of the Sejm and 39.1 percent of the senatorial votes. Now, in 1928, the Right shared Piast's defeat, its portion of votes for the Sejm declining to 8.6 percent (8.1 percent for the Catholic Nationalists and 0.5 percent for the Monarchists) and for the Senate to 9.3 percent (9.2 percent plus 0.1 percent).

The public's urge to punish the preponderant pre-coup constellation and to repudiate Piłsudski's explicit enemies extended also to the unreconciled National Laborite rump, which now polled only 2 percent and 2.2 percent of Sejm and Senate votes, in contrast to the 5.3 percent and 5.2 percent drawn by the full party in 1922. The National Minority lists collectively received 22.2 percent of Sejm and 24.2 percent of Senate votes, which does not include certain minor parties, such as the Jewish Bund (0.7 percent of Sejm votes) or the Ukrainian Left-Selrob (1.2 percent), whose support came from the minorities but who are more properly identified by politico-ideological than by ethnic criteria. Many Jews, incidentally, voted for the BBWR rather than for their "own" parties in this election. In 1922, when the Ukrainians of Eastern Galicia had boycotted the election, the National Minority lists (again excluding the distinctive Bund and pro-Communist groups) had drawn 18.6 percent of Sejm and 19 percent of Senate votes.

The calculation of the pro-Communist vote in 1928 depends on what proportion of the invalidated ballots (320,142 and 116,931) is estimated as intended for Communist and "front" lists and on whether the unhyphenated Selrob (1.6 percent and 1.3 percent), then succumbing to the Shumskyite Ukrainian nationalist deviation, is numbered with the Communist "fronts" or with the several National Minority groups. In the latter case, 3.7 percent of the valid Sejm and 0.8 percent of the valid Senate votes remain as the clearly identifiable pro-Communist proportion, though the supporters of other small parties, particularly among the ethnic minorities (for example, a White Russian group named Zmahanne [Struggle]) were also sympathetically inclined toward the Soviet Union as the presumed champion of their grievances and hopes. Moreover, judging on the basis of the official criteria for invalidation of lists and votes and of the location of most such invalidations, it appears probable that the bulk of the invalid ballots had been intended for Communist and "front" lists in the eastern constituencies. In effect, therefore, it is conceivable that as much as 6–7 percent of the total (valid and invalid) Sejm vote and 2–3 percent of the total Senate vote was pro-Communist in 1928. (In 1922 the explicitly Communist proportion of the vote had been 1.4 percent and 0.9 percent for Sejm and Senate respectively.) Finally, a number of minor and local groups accounted for the remaining 5.2 percent of valid Sejm and 3.5 percent of valid Senate ballots in 1928 which are not tabulated with the six basic political groupings.[13]

[13] Among them were the Polish Radical Party, the Independent Socialist Labor Party, and several local or provincial splinters not affiliated to "state" lists. The data and percentages given above are taken or extrapolated from Groth, tables 13, 17, 32, and 33, and p. 242. In conrast to Groth, however, the above calculations incorporate the Sejm vote for local Communist "fronts" in Łódź and Lublin (0.6 percent) into the pro-Communist rather than the miscellaneous column. The raw results in 1928 were as follows:

	Sejm	Senate
Total ballots	11,728,360	6,507,462
Valid ballots	11,408,218	6,390,531
Void ballots	320,142	116,931
I. BBWR	2,399,032	1,842,537
Catholic Union of the Western Areas	193,323	12,749
National-State Bloc of Labor	146,946	132,039
Peasant Association	135,276	36,118
II. PPS	1,481,279	714,956
Wyzwolenie	834,448	391,979
Stronnictwo Chłopskie	618,503	274,097
III. Piast and Christian Democrats	770,891	426,179
National Labor Party (NPR)	228,088	143,806
IV. Catholic–National List (Endecja)	925,744	589,905
Monarchists	53,623	4,661
V. National Minority Bloc	1,438,725	1,063,888
Labor Zionists	30,945	
Jewish National Union of Galicia	240,780	123,090
All-Jewish National Bloc	174,978	94,609
Russian List	133,196	38,065
Ukrainian National Alliance	8,887	231
Ukrainian Socialist and Peasant Bloc	268,677	148,431
Ukrainian Labor Party	44,919	
Shumskyite Ukrainian Selrob	179,536	80,502
VI. Communists	217,298	48,346
List No. 37 in Łódź and Lublin (approximate)	67,000	
Left-Selrob	143,475	
VII. Miscellaneous or unaffiliated		
Independent Socialist Labor Party	21,929	
Polish Radical Party	44,560	6,423
Jewish Bund	80,219	
Other	525,941	217,920

The election thus amounted to a repudiation of the pre-coup Right-Center hegemony and an endorsement of both Piłsudski and the parliamentary Left. The camp specifically associated with the Marshal emerged as the nation's largest—though not as its majoritarian—political constellation. In the western, central, and southern areas of the country, the Piłsudskist and Leftist lists drew votes away from the Right and Center parties, while toward the east there was a variation on this theme. Here the BBWR triumphed at the expense of *all* other lists—Right, Center, Left, and even, relative to their much increased participation, National Minorities.[14] Significantly, this was the region where governmental intervention and administrative irregularities had been most frequent. It is also of some interest to note that for the first time the PPS managed to elect its deputies in the western provinces of Poznania (two) and Pomerania (one), a result which was undoubtedly facilitated by the regime's having broken the pre-coup Rightist stranglehold on the local administrations.

The composition of the new legislature was as follows:[15]

	Sejm	Senate
I. BBWR	122	46
Left National Laborites	5	
Peasant Association	3	
PPS–Revolutionary Fraction (after October, 1928)	10	
Piłsudski camp total	140	46
II. PPS (63, less 10 after October, 1928)	53	10
Wyzwolenie	40	7
Stronnictwo Chłopskie	26	3
Parliamentary Left total	119	20

[14] *Ibid.*, pp. 224–28.

[15] *Ibid.*, tables 34 and 35, and T. and K. Rzepecki (Rzepeccy), pp. 217–25, 231. In addition to the secession of the Revolutionary Fraction from the PPS and its accession to the Piłsudskist camp in October, 1928, and the division, in the next month, of what had originally been a joint Ukrainian–White Russian nationalist club into its constituent components (developments which are already recorded in the accompanying list), the other significant shifts of partisan affiliation which were to occur during the life of this parliament were the defection of three BBWR deputies to the Stronnictwo Chłopskie in July, 1930 (which may have been a faked, Trojan horse defection), and of one Ukrainian Socialist, the lone deputy of the Ukrainian Labor Party, to the Left-Selrob Communist "front" in 1928.

To compare the political composition of this legislature with that of its predecessor, consult above, p. 6, n. 3.

	Sejm	Senate
III. Christian Democrats	15	6
Silesian Christian Democrats	3	
Piast	21	3
National Laborites	14	3
Center total	53	12
IV. National Democrats	34	9
Christian Nationalists	3	
Right total	37	9
V. German Nationalists	19	5
German Socialists	2	
Jewish Club	13	6
Russian Club	1	
Ukrainian Nationalists	29	9
Ukrainian Socialists and Radicals	8	1
Shumskyite Ukrainian Selrob	4	1
White Russian Nationalists	4	2
National Minority (non-Communist) total	80	24
VI. Communists (5, plus 2 on List No. 37 in Łódź)	7	
List No. 37 in Lublin	1	
Left Ukrainian Selrob	2	
White Russian Worker-Peasant Club (heir to Hramada)	5	
Communist and "front" total	15	0
Grand Total	444	111

From the Piłsudskist point of view, the electoral outcome was a mixed blessing and an inconclusive victory. The BBWR and its satellites had indeed emerged as the largest constellation but had failed to achieve a majority or even to reach the goal of 160 Sejm seats which Sławek had indicated in his confidential remarks to the Dzików conference the previous September.[16] To the extent that there was a triumph, it was reaped by all the groups which had backed the May coup and thus had to be shared by the explicitly Piłsudskist camp with the parliamentary Left—both Socialist and radical peasantist. By the same token, nemesis struck specifically the Right and Center members of the pre-coup "Lanckorona coalition," not—as the Piłsudskists had hoped—all the "old" parties across the entire pre-BBWR

---

[16] Kersten, ed., p. 211.

political spectrum.[17] The results thus indicated considerably stronger approval of the coup than of Piłsudski's subsequent efforts to restructure the pattern and style of Polish political life to his own characteristic mold. Furthermore, in the context of the incipient mutual alienation of the Piłsudski camp and the parliamentary Left from each other, the failure of either to win a clear and unequivocal majority was ominous, despite their parallel successes relative to the Right and the Center. The capacity of the Polish political system either to accommodate itself or to offer effective resistance to the Piłsudski experiment was thrown into doubt. Heightening this uncertainty were the polymorphous nature and the disparate constituency of the Piłsudski camp. It indeed enjoyed some support in almost every sector of the society, but most workers, most peasants, most of the petite bourgeoisie, most of the Roman Catholic clergy, and most of the ethnic minorities had remained outside and even alien to it. Would the backing of the conservative stratum on the one hand and of the technical intelligentsia on the other (assuming, for the moment, their reliability) prove sufficient to compensate for the softness and spottiness of intermediate, class-related, social support in a country finding itself in the socioeconomic transitional stage that characterized interwar Poland? In the context of Piłsudski's reluctance to institute an explicit dictatorship as the capstone to his coup and his entourage's technocratic-managerial outlook, and given his decision, instead, to try to rule through and within the established constitutional-parliamentary machinery, the prospects for an affirmative answer to this question were rendered doubtful by the inconclusive outcome of the 1928 elections.

[17] Piast, of course, had already been punished for its alliances with the Right and its foot-dragging on land reform by the secessions of Dąbski's and Bryl's groups in 1923 and that of Bojko in 1927.

Within the National Minority sector of the political spectrum, the Ukrainians doubled their Sejm representation—thanks to greater participation than in 1922—and the Germans also increased theirs slightly. The Jewish Club, on the other hand, lost heavily—partly as a result of the entrance of the Ukrainians into the lists in greater numbers, partly because many Orthodox Jews voted for the BBWR. Nevertheless, some Jewish observers hailed the election results even though their own Sejm delegation declined from 34 to 13, because at least the hated and feared National Democrats had been trounced. See, for example, two articles by a certain W. S. entitled "Wybory uczą" and "13 = 34" in the Polish-language Jewish weekly *Dzwon,* I, No. 1 (March 15, 1928), 5–6, and No. 2 (March 25, 1928), 1–2.

These ambiguities and problems were thrown into relief by aspects of the organizational business attendant upon the opening of the new legislature. On March 13, 1928, Piłsudski addressed a caucus of some of the recently elected BBWR deputies and senators in Sławek's Warsaw residence. Priding himself, on the one hand, on his self-restraint at not having proclaimed by fiat a new constitution on the morrow of the May crisis, and insisting that he was not in principle or in general a partisan of rule by decree, Piłsudski on the other hand made it clear that he expected a sharp reversal in the traditional relationship between the legislative and executive branches of Poland's government. The hitherto dominant and arrogant Sejm must become moderate and deferential toward the president and the cabinet. In particular, the constitutional authority of the president must be expanded yet again, while the cabinet must have discretionary authority in the areas of foreign policy, legal codification, and administrative rationalization.[18]

To achieve even this relatively modest grant of decree powers in specifically defined areas, not to mention his more sweeping constitutional and political ambitions, Piłsudski and the BBWR would require allies in one or more of the other major Sejm groupings if the path of constitutional legality were not to be abandoned. Within the parliamentary Left, there was still considerable sentiment for finding some sort of *modus vivendi* with Piłsudski, its former comrade and cowinner in the recent elections, and thereby restoring the victorious coalition of May, 1926.[19] Piłsudski, however, declined to make any overtures with a view to negotiating a compromise program and instead expected the Left, and perhaps a large majority of the new parliament in general, to render unrewarded support to him and his so-called nonpartisan camp. Not only did Piłsudski choose to ignore the fact that the parliamentary Left had also emerged as a victor from the elections, but he apparently discounted, or was oblivious toward, the consideration that the new Sejm could regard itself as validly representative of the nation's political mood and hence would

[18] Piłsudski, *PZ,* IX, 104–7. A prefatory note concedes that this is a drastically truncated version of Piłsudski's remarks on this occasion. For a summary admittedly based on hearsay but giving a much tougher impression, see the memoirs of the occasionally overly imaginative French ambassador to Warsaw at this time, Laroche, p. 52.

[19] This was conceded even by the staunchly anti-Piłsudskist Herman Lieberman at the Twenty-first PPS Congress in November, 1928. Alter, p. 5.

prove less docile and more self-confident than its chastened post-coup "lame-duck" predecessor. The first test was to come over the election of the marshal of the Sejm.

Piłsudski approached this issue with the understandable but unwarranted assumption that the largest Sejm delegation, in this case his own BBWR, had a moral right to designate the chamber's presiding officer. His initial preference for the post was Bogusław Miedziński, who, however, demurred on the grounds that he lacked the stature and the authority to be acceptable to the Sejm. Piłsudski thereupon decided upon Kazimierz Bartel, apparently expecting that the nomination of this relatively prestigious and conciliatory figure would be acknowledged by the Sejm in general and by the parliamentary Left in particular as a gesture of moderation. He did not, however, consult the other Sejm groupings before making or publicly announcing this selection. They, in turn, declined to endorse it and instead advanced competing nominations of their own.[20] Whatever he may have expected from the Rightist, National Minority, and Communist camps, there is no doubt that Piłsudski was stunned and enraged when the parliamentary Left also advanced its own candidate in the person of the senior PPS leader Ignacy Daszyński. BBWR leaders Bartel, Miedziński, and Sławek all warned Daszyński that, if he persisted in his candidacy, he risked provoking Piłsudski into repudiating the policy of ruling within the constitutional framework. At a stormy session of the PPS parliamentary club, the Daszyński candidacy was nevertheless sustained as a necessary gesture of independence for the Party and the Sejm in the face of Piłsudski's proprietary attitude toward both.[21]

[20] Pobóg-Malinowski, *Najnowsza historia,* II, 516. The nomination of Bartel was announced two weeks before the scheduled opening of the new legislature. Piłsudski's decision reportedly offended Rataj, the marshal of the previous Sejm, who was eager to succeed himself and expected as much in reward for the critical, if "disinterested," assistance he had given Piłsudski in facilitating the transfer of power at the close of the May coup. Malicki, p. 346.

[21] Próchnik, *Ignacy Daszyński,* p. 79, and Pobóg-Malinowski, *Najnowsza historia,* II, 516. It appears that Lieberman was instrumental in stiffening Daszyński and the majority on this issue. Piłsudski vented his anger in several ways, at least one of them petty. On March 27, 1928, while opening the session of the new Senate in his capacity as prime minister, Piłsudski violated the established custom of inviting the oldest senator to preside over the first, organizational session of the chamber pending its election of a marshal. The oldest senator was the Socialist Nestor, Bolesław Limanowski, who had prepared for

With Bartel and Daszyński obviously the leading contestants, the other candidates for the Sejm marshalcy were the National Democrat Aleksander Zwierzyński, the Ukrainian nationalist Ivan Lyshchynskyi, and, rather oddly, two Communists, Konstanty Sypuła and Adolf Warski-Warszawski. Two ballotings were necessary on March 27 before a majority of valid votes was achieved. The results were as follows:

	First Ballot	Second Ballot
Bartel	136	141
Daszyński	167	206 (elected)
Zwierzyński	37	37
Lyshchynskyi	28	
Sypuła	13	13
Warski-Warszawski	4	
Valid ballots	385	397
Invalid ballots	49	36
Absent ballots	10	11
	444	444

Far from automatically eliciting general, unsolicited assent, the candidacy of Piłsudski's nominee had proved embarrassingly weak. Indeed, since the occasion was still several months before the open defection of the PPS–Revolutionary Fraction to the Piłsudski camp, loser Bartel had in fact drawn only a handful of votes in addition to those of the *sanacja* contingent *stricto sensu* as of March, 1928. This small increment (first six, then eleven) may well have consisted of some of these soon-to-be seceders from the PPS and almost certainly of a few Christian Democratic and some Piast deputies. The Piast leaders were indeed once again repeating their stance of the presidential elections of 1926, that is, endorsing Piłsudski's preference. Nevertheless, Daszyński, in winning, appears to have added the support of a large part of the Center and the National Minorities to his own parliamentary Left base, although most of the blank ballots were manifestly cast by Center and/or National Minority deputies. It is note-

this ceremonial occasion a speech emphasizing the need to adhere to democratic principles despite all temptations to abandon them. Piłsudski passed him over and instead invited Maksymilian Thullie—like Bartel and Mościcki a professor at the Lwów Polytechnic, a former Christian Democrat now elected on the BBWR list—to preside over the session. In the Sejm, such a stratagem of pique was averted by the fact that the oldest deputy was the ex-Piast defector to the BBWR, Jakub Bojko.

worthy that neither of the principal protagonists struck a bargain with the National Democratic Right.

In the simultaneously held elections for the rather less significant office of marshal of the Senate, the results were different. Here a proportionately stronger BBWR contingent was helped by a handful of Christian Democratic and Jewish senators to elect its candidate, Dr. Julian Szymański (a professor of ophthalmology at the Stefan Batory University in Wilno), by 54 votes against 25 for the Socialist Stanisław Posner, 8 for the National Democrat Stanisław Głąbiński, and 5 for the Piast Peasant Andrzej Średniawski, with 7 ballots invalid and 12 absentees.

Most of the Piłsudskist camp reacted with extremely bad grace to the rebuff inflicted on it by the Sejm. When Daszyński's election as marshal was officially announced, the cabinet ministers and the BBWR deputies ostentatiously marched out of the chamber. The Piłsudskist press organ *Głos Prawdy* accused the Sejm in general and the Left in particular of having repudiated the idea of governmental-legislative cooperation.[22] Only the Naprawa group of younger, technocratically oriented radicals, aware that the realization of their modernization plans for Poland and the maintenance of their own position within the Piłsudskist camp required "an opening" to the Left, initially put a good face on Daszyński's election, denying that it was tantamount to a repudiation of Piłsudski and insisting that the possibility of eventual cooperation between the government and its current parliamentary opposition remained open.[23]

As an interpretation of the intention of the Left and part of the Center, this judgment was essentially correct. The candidature of Daszyński had been advanced as a gesture of independence, not of defiance,[24] and in the subsequent months the Left shunned further

[22] See the citations from its editorials in Stęborowski, pp. 103, 108–9. *Głos Prawdy* had been expanded from a weekly to a daily after the coup.

[23] *Przełom,* April 1, 1928, cited in Stęborowski, p. 109.

[24] Próchnik, *Ignacy Daszyński,* p. 80. Daszyński, indeed, was leader of that wing of the PPS which was most reluctant to oppose Piłsudski and most eager for a reconciliation with him. The two men had originally met within the PPS in 1896, the year before Daszyński was first elected to the Vienna parliament from Galicia. Further information on Daszyński will be found in the Biographical Register.

provocation of Piłsudski and strenuously avoided a possible but assuredly explosive arrayal of the several opposition groups into an operational "negative majority." In his speech accepting the election, Daszyński had not only promised to conduct the office in a nonpartisan manner but had also urged loyal and harmonious cooperation between the Sejm and the government. Simultaneously, his and his party's response to the temporary but forcible and illegal eviction by the police of some obstreperous Communist deputies from the Sejm chamber at the time of Piłsudski's formal opening remarks was, after some reflection, mild and inconsequential.[25] During the next few weeks, the Left first joined part of the Center and the National Minorities in forcing the government to retreat on a proposed tax reform involving three new levies, but then avoided a showdown by permitting final passage of the provisional budget for 1928–29. Toward the turn of the year, PPS, Wyzwolenie, and Piast once again maintained this cautious stance by withholding their support from two Rightist motions of censure against (*a*) Finance Minister Gabriel Czechowicz for his earlier illegal expenditure of public funds to subsidize the BBWR electoral expenses and (*b*) the partisan election commissioner-general during that campaign, Stanisław Car, who had become minister of justice on December 22, 1928. The respective spokesmen of these parties, in explaining their stands, emphasized, that, while they, too, condemned the actions for which the censure motions were being introduced, they were not willing to serve as the tool or the auxiliary army of the Right or to permit it to dictate the

[25] The Communists had greeted Piłsudski with shouts demanding the release of political prisoners and the abolition of the "fascist regime." Piłsudski, after three warnings, had them ejected by the police under the direct command of Interior Minister General Sławoj-Składkowski—a clear violation of the privileges and immunities of the Sejm. Amidst the ensuing confusion, a Ukrainian Socialist Radical and a Wyzwolenie deputy were also ejected by the police— the latter perhaps in error. For descriptions of the incident, see Sławoj-Składkowski, *Strzępy meldunków,* pp. 75–82, and Malicki, pp. 342–43. In view of the fact that several days before the convening of the Sejm Piłsudski had instructed Sławoj-Składkowski to prepare a police unit for some such eventuality, it is possible that he anticipated the Communist initiative and planned to utilize it in a manner which might impress the Sejm and intimidate it into electing Bartel as its marshal. Witos, however, believed that Piłsudski was genuinely surprised and unnerved by the incident. See Witos, *Moje wspomnienia,* III, 173–74.

timing and the issue of a serious struggle between the parliament and the regime.[26] The censure motions failed.

By this time, however, that is, by the turn of the year 1928–29, the Left-Center effort at "judicious" and "responsible" opposition, while holding open the option of mutual toleration, indeed of possible cooperation, with the government, was rapidly becoming untenable. Not only did it impose heavy internal tensions upon the parties involved, but it was increasingly mocked by the growing ascendancy within the Piłsudskist camp of elements itching for a showdown with the parliament and the parties per se and scornful of any *modus vivendi* short of the latter's utter surrender. Piłsudski, characteristically, hesitated at length between this tough policy, recommended by his "colonels," and the more moderate, constitutional one represented within his *sanacja* by the Bartel-led intelligentsia contingent and by some of the "old-fashioned," legality-oriented conservative aristocrats. Piłsudski's own legal-historical scruples over the form and sources of law, if not about its substance and spirit, for long inhibited him from an outright, naked assault on a political-constitutional system which he preferred instead to overawe, to undermine, and to intimidate.

[26] See the citations from the speeches of M. Niedziałkowski (PPS), M. Róg (Wyzwolenie), and J. Dębski (Piast) in Pobóg-Malinowski, *Najnowsza historia,* II, 518, and Stęborowski, pp. 175–76. The Stronnictwo Chłopskie, as usual more direct and less artful than its Left partners, supported the Right's censure motion against Car, as did the Christian Democrats, the National Laborites, the Ukrainians, the German Socialists, and the Communists. In their abstention on this vote, PPS, Wyzwolenie, and Piast were joined by the Jews and the German Nationalists, while the BBWR and the PPS–Revolutionary Fraction opposed the motion. There were many absentees.

The immediate provocation of the censure motion against Car, to whom the opposition was already predisposed to be hostile since the elections, was a dispute reminiscent of the one over the validity of the presidential press decree of May 10, 1927. On February 6, 1928, Mościcki had issued a decree pertaining to the structure of the court system. It was to go into effect on January 1, 1929. A majority of the Sejm, concerned over its possibly negative impact on the independence of the judiciary, resolved on December 18, 1928, to suspend the decree. Four days later, Car became minister of justice. The Senate failed to act on the Sejm resolution until mid-January, 1929, at which time Car announced that the proper deadline for action had passed and that the presidential decree had gone into effect on January 1, since the Sejm resolution to the contrary had been unsupported by the Senate and was therefore without legal validity. Promptly on January 18, Mościcki retired the president of the Supreme Court, Władysław Seyda (known to be a National Democrat), and replaced him with Leon Supiński, hitherto president of the Court of Appeals in Warsaw. There then followed the abortive censure motion against Car.

CHAPTER XVIII

TOWARD BRZEŚĆ

Piłsudski's personal reaction to Daszyński's election as marshal of the Sejm had been frigid. Though as prime minister he consented to an exchange of formal visits with the new head of the legislature (April 4, 1928), he soon ended the secret political contacts which he had until then maintained with Daszyński as a senior PPS leader. Toward the end of May, his political lieutenants were appealing to "sensible" pro-Piłsudskist elements latent within the opposition parties (they appear to have had the parliamentary Left most particularly in mind) to break with the "anachronistic" stance of sterile opposition and instead to rally to the regime "in the interests of the state." [1] By October this campaign had culminated in the defection of the PPS–Revolutionary Fraction to the *sanacja*. Meanwhile, on June 27, 1928, five days after the close of the Sejm's budget session, Piłsudski had transferred the premiership to Bartel, but had accompanied this gesture with an angry press interview.[2] In strong and crude language he vitriolically denounced the Sejm, its deputies, and the prevailing constitutional distribution of power between government and legislature,

[1] Stęborowski, pp. 115–16, citing Sławek (leader of the BBWR) and Stpiczyński (editor of *Głos Prawdy*).

[2] Reprinted in Piłsudski, *PZ*, IX, 109–19, from *Głos Prawdy*, July 1, 1928.

Two new faces now appeared in Bartel's cabinet. Kazimierz Świtalski and Alfons Kühn replaced Dobrucki and Romocki as the ministers, respectively, of education and communications. Half a year later, on December 22, Stanisław Car took over the justice portfolio from Meysztowicz. Kühn, unlike these other two, did not emerge from Piłsudski's praetorian-"colonels" entourage. Rather, he was a typical Bartel recruit—a technical expert in electrification, having been director of the Warsaw tramway system since 1918, with moderate Leftist political leanings, having belonged to the PPS in his youth. He was to serve as minister of communications from June 27, 1928, to September 5, 1932, and as acting minister of public works from March 20 to July 1, 1932. He died in Warsaw on January 27, 1944.

and openly speculated that Poland would have been spared much misery, including the May coup, if he had established a purifying dictatorship at the conclusion of the Polish-Soviet campaign of 1920 instead of returning the country to the clutches of her allegedly corrupt politicians and their prostituted Sejm. Piłsudski closed the interview with a warning that this time his resignation of the premiership must not be misunderstood, even though once again he was refraining from resort to force: he stood at the president's disposition in case of need (a statement which provoked rumors of another coup), and he would in any event continue his *de facto* control of Poland's foreign policy.

The Left opposition, on the one hand wishing to draw hope from the return of the supposedly more sympathetic Bartel to the premiership, on the other hand disturbed by the simultaneous elevation to the cabinet of a leading representative of the hard "colonels" group (Świtalski), responded to Piłsudski's abusive and menacing attack with characteristic ambivalence. Daszyński replied that, if Piłsudski was truly as frustrated by the Sejm as he claimed to be, then three courses were open to him: new elections, yet another coup, or, preferably, the cooperation of his camp with the parliamentary Left so as to achieve a stable and positive legislative majority. A day after its articulation, this overture-qua-challenge of Daszyński's was promptly sharpened to the point of negation by the PPS theoretician and publicist Niedziałkowski, who insisted as a preliminary condition that Piłsudski's current style of political manipulation and domination be liquidated in favor of democracy. Whatever Bartel's preferences might have been, it appears unlikely that the "colonels" would have been prepared to work with the Left at this juncture even without Niedziałkowski's correction of Daszyński's invitation. In any event, immediately after this exchange, Sławek declared to the BBWR parliamentary club that cooperation with the Left was impossible.[3]

The discrepancy between the attitudes of the two Socialist leaders reflected not only different interpretations of the preceding personnel changes in the government but varying assessments of the general polit-

[3] Daszyński's and Niedziałkowski's articles in *Robotnik,* July 4 and 5, 1928, and Sławek's speech of July 6 are quoted and summarized in Stęborowski, pp. 134–36. Subsequent exchanges between Niedziałkowski and Sławek became so sharp that on November 13, 1928, the BBWR leader sent the PPS leader a challenge to a duel—which was declined as contrary to Socialist ethics.

ical situation and its drift. One wing of the PPS still continued to believe in Piłsudski's essential "leftness" and to prefer an alliance with
the asserted left wing of the BBWR over one with the Centrist or
right-of-center parties such as Piast, the National Laborites, perhaps
even the Christian Democrats. These parties, in turn, had for the two
preceding years been perceptibly drawing away from the categorical
Right but were simultaneously being so alienated by the manifestly
antiparliamentary tendencies of Piłsudski's regime, with which they
initially had sought a rapprochement, as to become potential recruits
for a Center-Left alliance against it and in defense of the constitutional order. The other PPS phalanx (to which, ironically, Niedziałkowski was rather a latecomer) was disillusioned with Piłsudski
and had concluded that the "colonels" were in any event setting the
pace for his policy and driving it inexorably toward dictatorship,
against which trend the Left must organize the combined resistance
or all the old parties with a principled commitment to democratic
politics, including even such otherwise unlikely and ideologically distasteful partners as the above-named Centrist and right-of-center
parties. One may note a parallelism between the expectations of the
first PPS group, continuing to hope for a rapprochement with a
supposedly still Leftist Piłsudski, and the opposite but symmetrical
assumption of some of the conservatives at the Dzików conference
the previous year, contemplating an alliance with him on an essentially
conservative basis. Complementing and reinforcing this wishful view
of Piłsudski and of the BBWR core as fundamentally "Leftist" was
a fear among those PPS leaders who subscribed to it that Piłsudski's
attractiveness to their members was still so massive as to enable him
to disintegrate the Party should it become excessively aggressive toward him. Not until after the defection of the PPS–Revolutionary
Fraction in October, 1928, when the Piłsudskists had, as it were, done
their worst but the Party had nevertheless survived substantially intact, did this anxiety abate and the paralysis within the PPS unfreeze.
Henceforth, under the prodding of the oppositionally inclined wing,
the Party and its allies moved—albeit not without occasional regretful
backward glances—toward a policy of systematic and sustained opposition, a trend which was both propelled by and in turn provoked
the simultaneous emergence of the "tough" school within the Piłsud-

skist camp. The trend also dovetailed with the apparent estrangement of the Centrist parties from the National Democratic-led Right
and the dissolution of some initial Centrist hopes (parallel to those
on the Left and among the conservatives) for a special partnership
with the Piłsudskist camp.

An initial step was the formal reconstitution on November 14,
1928, of the original parliamentary Left bloc of 1926, this time without Bartel's Klub Praca and under the new name Coordinating Commission for the Defense of the Republic and Democracy (Komisja
Porozumiewawcza dla Obrony Republiki i Demokracji), composed of
the PPS, Wyzwolenie, and Stronnictwo Chłopskie. The name and the
date suggest that the formation of this coalition may have been precipitated by an ominous demand of October 31 by BBWR leader
Sławek for substantial constitutional revisions. The Coordinating
Commission, while scrupulously avoiding contacts with the Communists and their "fronts," did confer with Leftist groups among the
ethnic minorities. Despite its publicized "defensive" intentions, its formation took the Piłsudskists aback. Early in February, 1929, the
Left followed up this challenge by initiating the reduction in the Sejm
of the discretionary fund allocated for the fiscal year 1929-30 to the
War Minister (Piłsudski) and the outright elimination of the one for
the Interior Minister (Sławoj-Składkowski).[4] No formal censure
motions were pressed, and the ministers, in turn, did not make their
original budgetary request an issue of confidence, choosing, instead,
to absorb the financial slashes without resigning. Both the opposition
and the government, in other words, were hesitant to come to grips
with each other and were groping their way into a constitutional
twilight zone. Then, on March 20, 1929, the Left led the Sejm in

---

[4] Both Piłsudski and Sławoj-Składkowski responded that those who had voted
these curtailments of their funds apparently wished to facilitate foreign espionage in and against Poland by depriving them of the means to counter it.
Sławoj-Składkowski further challenged the opposition to show the courage of
its grievances by censuring him directly. A senatorial effort to restore his (but
not Piłsudski's) fund was rejected by the Sejm in its final budgetary vote of
March 25, 1929. Piłsudski then sought to capitalize on Polish patriotism and
turn the affair into a propaganda weapon against his political foes. A general
public appeal for funds to protect the nation against hostile espionage was
launched and raised a million złoty. The amount by which Piłsudski's own
fund had been reduced was just under two million. For details see Piłsudski's
remarks to the Senate budget committee on February 28, 1929, reprinted in his
PZ, IX, 132–43, and Malicki, pp. 361–69.

probing somewhat more purposively for the limits of the regime's self-confidence by resurrecting and this time successfully pressing the suggestion, earlier sponsored in vain by the Right, that Finance Minister Czechowicz be punished for his illegal budgetary excesses and transfers during the 1928 election campaign. However, instead of politically censuring the entire cabinet, and specifically Piłsudski, whose orders Czechowicz had rather unwillingly obeyed, the Sejm was still too cautious (or cowardly) to do more than impeach the latter on technical charges before a quasi-judicial Tribunal of State—a unique case in the interwar history of Poland.

This "Czechowicz affair" was exceedingly intricate, and only a bare outline need here be given to clarify the political issues at stake beneath its veneer of judicial inquest.[5] Gabriel Czechowicz, it will be recalled, had been the *sanacja's* finance minister from the formation of Bartel's initial post-coup government until after the presidential election of Mościcki and then once again, after a four-month interval, since the formation of Piłsudski's first cabinet on October 2, 1926. Coming into office with a somewhat "Leftist" reputation as being oriented more toward economic expansion than financial caution, he soon established himself as an economist of considerable technical ability and shared in the general credit claimed by, and given to, the regime for Poland's relative economic successes since mid-1926. During the fiscal year April 1, 1927–March 31, 1928, Czechowicz had permitted various governmental (executive) bodies to spend 563 million złoty in excess of the legislatively authorized budget. The money came from the revenue surplus of the currently good economic year. While this was a noticeably large sum, amounting to over 28 percent of the legal budget of almost 1,975,000,000 złoty, the fact of excessive expenditures was not unusual per se, and the conventional manner of correcting such situations was a retroactive legalization by the Sejm through the appropriation of supplementary funds upon the finance minister's presentation of his accounts. This, however, Piłsudski forbade Czechowicz to do on the rationale that the improved health of the Polish economy was the exclusive achievement of his regime, which was therefore morally entitled to dispose of the resultant budg-

[5] A recent compilation of only the most crucial documents runs to over three hundred closely printed pages. It is Z. Landau and B. Skrzeszewska, eds., *Sprawa Gabriela Czechowicza przed Trybunałem Stanu.*

etary surpluses at its own discretion since no new tax burden would fall upon the citizen as a result of nonappropriated expenditures made from nonanticipated revenue surpluses.[6] (The Piłsudskist propaganda organs insisted that the bulk of the 563 million excess złoty spent with Czechowicz's permission had been productively invested in the development of the port of Gdynia and comparable projects.) [7] This bizarre and somewhat medieval argument (the king was "living off his own"), constitutionally monstrous though it might be to the Sejm deputies and modern lawyers, did not appear to be particularly disturbing to the general public. After all, under the partitions Poles had become accustomed to not being given an accounting of how governments spent revenues, and Piłsudski's proprietary attitude toward their own state was reminiscent of a still older Polish szlachta tradition. Piłsudski did not even find it necessary to explain or correct or apologize for the most serious transgression of all in this affair—the fact that, at his own express instructions, eight million złoty had been diverted by Czechowicz to defray BBWR electioneering expenses during the period December, 1927–February, 1928.

Aware that the issue was one to which the nation would be aroused only with difficulty, and politically still hesitant to burn their bridges to the regime, the Left and Center parties had rejected and postponed several Rightist demands for a showdown with the regime throughout 1928. Their resolve to maintain this stance of discretion was buttressed by indications that both Czechowicz and Bartel, apparently embarrassed by the position in which Piłsudski was placing them, wished him to relent and permit them to obtain retroactive absolution from the Sejm for the excessive expenditures. As late as November 28, 1928, Bartel had promised to present the necessary accounts, and the Sejm on December 5 had accepted his declaration without setting an official time limit for its implementation (such as the Right had wanted to insert), though the Left parties indicated in the accompanying debate that their patience would be strained if the government delayed its accounting beyond the second reading of the coming

[6] See Piłsudski's affidavit of June 1, 1929, to the Investigating Judge for the Tribunal of State, reprinted in his *PZ,* IX, 157–62, and Z. Landau and B. Skrzeszewska, eds., *Sprawa Gabriela Czechowicza,* pp. 73–76.

[7] Pomarański, *Józef Piłsudski* (13th ed.), p. 52, and *Głos Prawdy,* February 26, 1929.

1929–30 budget—a warning which was, of course, without binding legal effect.

When the final reading of the 1929–30 budget came and went on February 11, 1929, without the hoped-for governmental petition for supplementary appropriations to cover the 1927–28 excesses and with no accounting of the same, the worm suddenly turned. As indicated earlier, the parliamentary Left was now ready to probe the limits of possible opposition more determinedly. Yet, still fearful of the possible consequences of a direct political attack on Piłsudski, it opted instead for the flanking tactic of impeaching the technically guilty but politically secondary Czechowicz. Its motion to this effect was presented to the Sejm by the three Left parties composing the Coordinating Commission for the Defense of the Republic and Democracy on February 12 and forwarded for action by a vote of 220 to 132 to the Sejm budget committee on February 26, despite the exasperated protests of Bartel that this sudden vindictiveness against Czechowicz, coming so shortly after these same parties had quite deliberately persuaded the Sejm not to confront the government with a definite deadline for regulating the affair, was in bad faith, hypocritical, and craven.[8] Pertinent though this reply may have been as a comment on the moral and political attitude of the opposition, it failed to account for the facts that a whole year had elapsed since the illegal expenditures were incurred and that Piłsudski appeared to have no intention of permitting an accounting to the Sejm at any forseeable time. In other words, he was manifestly not interested in providing the Sejm with an avenue for honorable retreat.

On March 14, 1929, the Sejm budget committee, by a vote of 18 to 9, recommended favorable action on the Left's impeachment motion and simultaneously nominated three lawyer-deputies to serve as prosecutors.[9] On March 20, a few days before recessing until the end of October, the Sejm took the final necessary legal step to institute the impeachment proceedings by endorsing these recommendations by a

---

[8] K. Bartel, *Kilka uwag o praktyce parlamentarnej w Polsce,* p. 6, and Z. Landau and B. Skrzeszewska, eds., *Sprawa Gabriela Czechowicza,* pp. 8–9.

[9] They were Herman Lieberman (PPS), Jan Pieracki (National Democrat), and Henryk Wyrzykowski (Wyzwolenie). The commission's report is published in Z. Landau and B. Skrzeszewska, eds., *Sprawa Gabriela Czechowicza,* pp. 305–10. Czechowicz's defense attorney was Franciszek Paschalski, who had served in the same capacity for the Piłsudskist Lieutenant Błoński in 1924.

vote of 239 to 126, the majority stretching from Right through Center to parliamentary Left, on to the Communists, and including as well the Ukrainians and the White Russians. As in the Sejm marshal election of March, 1928, Lieberman of the PPS once again took the lead in organizing the victorious anti-Piłsudski coalition. Czechowicz, in apparent anticipation of the outcome, had already resigned his portfolio on March 8, simultaneously submitting a memorandum to the Sejm budget committee in which he made—somewhat more diplomatically—the same points as had Bartel a few days earlier, acknowledged that formally and technically he had violated the laws, but insisted that this was rendered necessary by the prevailing politico-administrative climate and had, in any event, been permitted his predecessors. He concluded with the ironic reflection that the first and only finance minister in restored Poland against whom impeachment proceedings had been launched was also the first one under whom the budget had been consistently balanced and the currency reliably stabilized.[10]

The case was now transferred to the Tribunal of State, consisting of the president of the Supreme Court, eight persons selected by the Sejm, and four by the Senate. (At least half of the selected members were statutorily required to hold university degrees in law.) It convened on April 5, 1929, spent two months (until June 5) collecting written evidence and affidavits, then held public hearings of an array of witnesses—including Piłsudski, Daszyński, Sławoj-Składkowski, Kwiatkowski, the accused, and others—from June 26 to 29. On June 29 it handed down an ambiguous and inconclusive ruling, affirming that the government was indeed bound by and to the budget as voted by the legislature and was accountable to the Sejm for all expenditures but that the Sejm must itself first made an evaluation of the merits of Czechowicz's expenditures, that is, must determine whether

---

[10] The Czechowicz memorandum is published *ibid.,* pp. 303–5. The concluding point was driven further and more polemically by Adam Krzyżanowski, the professorial economist, BBWR deputy, and member of the Sejm budget committee, who contrasted the present punishment of the successful Czechowicz with the conferral in 1925 of the Order of the White Eagle on W. Grabski, under whom (as Krzyżanowski put it) Poland had gone bankrupt. Upon resigning the Finance Ministry, Czechowicz became director of the Land Bank in Warsaw. In May, 1930, Czechowicz broke with the Piłsudskist camp, charging the current ministers with economic incompetence and political myopia in face of the Depression. Further information on him will be found in the Biographical Register.

they had been politically, administratively, or financially necessary by
virtue of *raison d'état,* before the Tribunal could judge him.[11] From
this anticlimax the affair never recovered. The currently recessed Sejm
was due to reconvene on October 31, but when that day arrived,
Daszyński refused to open it on the grounds that Piłsudski was seeking to intimidate it with armed force. When it eventually convened on
November 5, Mościcki promptly suspended it for a month. December
5 brought with it a cabinet crisis, followed by a decision to postpone
the Czechowicz problem until the 1930–31 budget had been proc-
essed. Then came a spring and summer of great political tension
characterized by repeated presidential prorogations and culminating,
after the presidential dissolution of the legislature on August 30,
1930, in a period of governmental terror against the opposition (the
Brześć crisis). The subsequent elections of November 16 and 23,
1930, were characterized by sufficient intimidation to give the BBWR
at last absolute parliamentary majorities of 247 out of 444 deputies
and 76 out of 111 senators, who on January 26 and 27, 1931, retroactively appropriated the necessary funds to clear the accounts of the
budget year 1927–28 and thereby dispose of the Czechowicz affair.

However, Piłsudski had not waited for this denouement or even for
the Tribunal's ruling on June 29, 1929—which, under the circumstances, was a favorable one for his regime—before responding to
what he professed to regard as the impermissible provocation on the
Sejm's part in performing "ritual murder" on his finance minister. In
response to the Sejm vote of February 26, 1929, forwarding the Left's
impeachment motion to its budget committee for processing, as well
as in response to the Sejm's prior curtailment of the discretionary
funds of the ministers of war and the interior, Piłsudski had appeared
on February 28 before the Senate budget committee to unburden
himself of insults and warnings directed at the Sejm deputies and,
incidentally, of complaints about his allegedly ignorant and corrupt
predecessors as war minister.[12] To the Sejm decision of March 20 to
proceed with the impeachment trial, Piłsudski had responded with a
press interview of incredible abusiveness and cloacal vulgarity on

[11] *Ibid.,* pp. 289–91.
[12] See note 4 above.

April 5 [13] and, more seriously, with the reconstruction and "hardening" of the government on April 14. Świtalski [14] now replaced Bartel
as premier and three new "colonels" were brought into the cabinet,
thus definitely tipping the *sanacja's* scales toward this group and provoking rumors of a second Piłsudskist coup to liquidate the Sejm
altogether.[15] Piłsudski now also sundered the last of his remaining
concealed contacts with the PPS and rebuffed Daszyński when the
latter, still reluctant to accept the rift as final, came secretly to the
Belweder on June 24 to urge on Piłsudski a BBWR-PPS-Wyzwolenie
reconciliation in the face of the worsening economic situation (the
Great Depression was setting in).[16] Determined to undermine and

[13] This notorious "bottom of the eye" interview is reprinted in Piłsudski,
PZ, IX, 143–54. In response to it, Daszyński wrote an open letter to the outgoing Premier Bartel, asking if it conformed to Bartel's notion of the sound
political and moral reeducation of the public that had become one of the
much-touted slogans of the *sanacja.* Daszyński also argued that the Czechowicz
affair would never have arisen if the government had presented its accounts
and requested post-factum cover for the excess expenditures. Próchnik, *Ignacy
Daszyński,* p. 82.

[14] Świtalski was a Legion veteran and a member of Piłsudski's inner entourage of "colonels," having served as his political aide in the office of the Chief
of State after 1918. A major in the reserves before the 1926 coup, he briefly
headed Mościcki's Civilian Chancellery after it, until his translation to the
directorship of the Political Department of the Interior Ministry. Świtalski held
the latter position until his "elevation" to the cabinet as minister of education
on June 27, 1928. He served as prime minister from April 14 to December 7,
1929. Further information on him will be found in the Biographical Register.

[15] Mackiewicz, p. 196. The new "colonel"-ministers were: Ignacy Matuszewski—Acting Finance (in place of Czechowicz); Aleksander Prystor—Labor
(in place of Jurkiewicz); Ignacy Boerner—Posts (in place of Miedziński, who
became editor of the semiofficial *Gazeta Polska*). Świtalski's previous portfolio
of Education went to Sławomir Czerwiński. Information on all these men will
be found in the Biographical Register. The rest of the cabinet remained
unchanged: Piłsudski (War), Sławoj-Składkowski (Interior), Car (Justice),
Zaleski (Foreign Affairs), Niezabytowski (Agriculture), Staniewicz (Land
Reform), Kwiatkowski (Industry and Commerce), Moraczewski (Public
Works), Kühn (Communications).

[16] When this overture—which in effect betrayed the newly agreed-upon
stance of the parliamentary Left—was made public by Piłsudski in September,
the embarrassed Daszyński insisted that he had made it in a nonpartisan capacity, from strictly patriotic motives, as Sejm marshal and at the urging of
his brother-marshal of the Senate, Szymański, because no one else dared tell
Piłsudski the harsh truth about the economic situation. However, Daszyński
had never ceased to hope for PPS-Piłsudskist reconciliation, and his offer of
PPS and Wyzwolenie support (incidentally, without the prior assent of either
party) was hardly disinterestedly nonpartisan. As recently as November 10,
1928, and February 9, 1929—the decennial anniversaries of Piłsudski's return

compromise the impeachment trial, Piłsudski forbade those of his cabinet colleagues who had been summoned as witnesses to give any substantive testimony and then, in his own written affidavit and oral declaration to the Tribunal, insisted that he alone bore responsibility for the excess expenditures and challenged the Sejm and the Tribunal to punish him instead of the scapegoat Czechowicz.[17] In the face of the multiple and persuasive political and polemical Piłsudskist counterattack, the Tribunal reported out its evasive verdict on June 29, 1929.

Though this round had, in effect, been won by Piłsudski and though it had strengthened the protagonists of a tougher course within his camp, it had not by itself resolved the major substantive political dilemmas with which he had for quite some time been reluctant to come to grips—dilemmas on which were now about to be superimposed the Depression-provoked economic difficulties of which Daszyński had sought to warn Piłsudski on June 24, 1929. The Sejm being in recess from the end of March until the end of October, 1929, the new "colonel"-dominated Świtalski cabinet had no early opportunity for an immediate overt test of strength with the legislature. It was confronted, however, with increasingly ominous economic clouds which provided a pretext for smashing, by administrative action, the traditional PPS control over the hitherto autonomous workers' sickness-compensation fund banks. By displacing the elected governing bodies of these fund banks with appointed commissars (often from the PPS–Revolutionary Fraction), Labor Minister Prystor, a "colo-

---

to Poland from German imprisonment and of his convening the Constituent Sejm—Daszyński had praised him warmly in commemorative speeches, and as late as August 15, 1930—on the eve of the Brześć crisis—Daszyński yet again spoke in a conciliatory tone about Piłsudski. The latter did not reciprocate these benevolent sentiments. In later years he attacked Daszyński passionately with word and pen and even caused his passport for foreign travel to be withheld in the 1930s. See Piłsudski, *PZ*, IX, 193–94, 225–30, 271–315, and Chernov, p. 146.

[17] Sławoj-Składkowski, *Strzępy meldunków*, p. 141. Piłsudski's affidavit of June 1 and his oral testimony of June 26 are reprinted in his *PZ*, IX, 157–62 and 176–83, as well as in Z. Landau and B. Skrzeszewska, eds., *Sprawa Gabriela Czechowicza*, pp. 73–76 and 116–22. It was in the second of these interventions that he referred to the impeachment as a "ritual murder." Here he also denounced the constitution and the statutes from which the Sejm and the Tribunal derived their authority.

nel," not only attacked the key opposition party at a vulnerable point and reinforced the regime's own labor cohort but also achieved control over substantial financial resources—estimates vary from one-fourth to one-half billion złoty.[18] Simultaneously, BBWR leader Sławek was seeking to sustain the psychological pressure in this skirmish-type warfare by threatening to "break bones" unless the legislators would in the future prove more accommodating to the government's demands, particularly its increasingly emphatic insistence on constitutional changes—to which Piłsudski had most recently alluded in his oral declaration to the Czechowicz Tribunal.[19]

Against this background of maneuvers and threats but also of continuing hesitations, it was hardly surprising that the opposition should decline two invitations extended by the regime in September, 1929, to confer with it on the economic situation and on constitutional revisions. The first, issued by Świtalski on September 4, was declined by the Right on September 11 and collectively—this was significant— by the six Polish parties of the Center and Left (Christian Democratic, Piast, National Laborite, PPS, Wyzwolenie, and Stronnictwo Chłopskie) on September 14. Suspecting bad faith, they replied that the proper forum for such a discussion on economic problems was not an *ad hoc* all-party conference but rather the Sejm itself, to which, moreover, the government should present its own draft budget. As this rejection, however, had been preceded by considerable discussion among the parties of this emerging Center-Left (Centrolew) coalition, Piłsudski sought to ventilate their disagreements and torpedo the alliance by revealing Daszyński's confidential proposal to him of June 24 of BBWR-PPS-Wyzwolenie collaboration to confront the nation's economic problems. Adopting a tone of cosmic sadness, Piłsudski remonstrated that he was baffled by the rejection of Świtalski's proposal, which was, after all, but a follow-up on and an extension of Daszyński's original overture.[20] The effect of this intervention was, as in-

[18] For details, see X.Y.Z., "Chronique polonaise," VII, No. 4, 105–6; Malicki, p. 464; Czubiński, *Centrolew,* p. 139; Stęborowski, pp. 254–55, 314.
[19] Sławek in July, 1929, quoted from *Głos Prawdy,* No. 169, in Porczak, *Dyktator Józef Piłsudski i "piłsudczycy,"* as serialized in *Robotnik Polski* (Detroit), December 7, 1930.
[20] Piłsudski's "to a dying world" interview, reprinted from *Głos Prawdy,* September 22, 1929, in his *PZ,* IX, 185–92.

tended, to sow discord among the opposition. Within his own party, Daszyński's action proved divisive and he was forced to a rather lame explanation. Wyzwolenie announced that he had had no right to speak for it. The National Democrats and the Christian Democrats crowed over this latest evidence of continued clandestine collusion among the "May companions," and Witos reminded his Piast Party that the PPS, by virtue of its participation in the forcible overthrow of his own government in 1926, shared responsibility for the current situation.[21] Significantly, when the second of the regime's two invitations to all-party conferences was extended, this time by Sławek on September 20 to discuss constitutional revisions, the opposition parties again declined—but separately (except for Piast and the Christian Democrats). The fragile foundations of the nascent six-party Center-Left coalition had been exposed.

Now, however, it was the Piłsudskists' turn to overplay their hand. After more than seven months of recess, during which much combustible political tinder had piled up, the Sejm was due to reconvene for its regular budget session on October 31, 1929. In an effort to overawe the Sejm and thereby smother in advance a predictable assault on the government, it was decided that Świtalski would be diplomatically ill on that day and that Piłsudski would substitute for the Premier in reading the presidential decree convening the Sejm. As the appointed day dawned, Warsaw was electric with tension, its garrison had been placed in a state of alert, and the galleries of the Sejm chamber were crowded to capacity.

Preparatory to Piłsudski's arrival, a substantial number of army officers—eyewitness estimates vary from eighty to one hundred and twenty—assembled in the vestibule to the Sejm building, allegedly to honor their Inspector General and War Minister, the First Marshal of Poland. Other groups of officers were gathered in even larger numbers at nearby points—the Ujazdowski Hospital, the Frascati Park, the Square of the Three Crosses, the end of Wiejska street.[22] Piłsudski

[21] See note 16 above; Stęborowski, pp. 340–42; and Czubiński, *Centrolew,* p. 145.

[22] Czubiński, *Centrolew,* p. 148. Piłsudski, in his subsequent report of November 7 on this incident, claimed that not quite eighty officers were involved. Daszyński complained on October 31 to the President of more than ninety and later to the Sejm itself of over one hundred officers. The chief of the Sejm

entered the Sejm building through the cordon of saluting officers and made his way to the cabinet's anteroom to await the designated time of opening the session. Sejm Marshal Daszyński, his attention drawn to the military demonstration, sent one of his functionaries into the vestibule to order the officers to leave and then summoned the interior minister, General Sławoj-Składkowski, to repeat this demand. Finally, after an acrimonious confrontation with Piłsudski himself, Daszyński refused to permit the Sejm to be opened under the attempted intimidation, as he expressed it, "of bayonets, carbines, revolvers, and swords." In his subsequent report to the Sejm, Daszyński widened this charge of armed intimidation to allege that the officers had forcibly entered the building, overpowered the Sejm Marshal's Guard, and excluded other persons having legitimate access.[23] This was in fact untrue, and even his original enumeration of the officers' weapons was an arrant exaggeration—some of them wore ceremonial side arms as part of the regulation uniform. Indeed, certain circumstances suggest that the officers were already leaving the building before the Daszyński-Piłsudski showdown when they were provoked into remaining by a second, brusque demand by Daszyński's functionary to depart forthwith. Furthermore, army officers in even greater numbers had been permitted to congregate in the Sejm vestibule on previous occasions to render homage to Piłsudski.[24]

However, Daszyński had reason to inflate and exploit the current incident. In personal political terms, a firm, even truculent, stance would go far toward restoring his reputation after the recent painful fiasco of the revelation of his June 24 overture to Piłsudski. In more general political terms, an attempted military intimidation of parliament, however obliquely mounted, was (in contrast to budgetary

---

Marshal's Guard reported the high estimate of one hundred and twenty. (Piłsudski, *PZ*, IX, 196–99, and Malicki, pp. 405–8.) The Warsaw garrison commander at this time was Colonel Bolesław Wieniawa-Długoszowski.

[23] Piłsudski, *PZ*, IX, 192–99, and Sławoj-Składkowski, *Strzępy meldunków*, pp. 151–57.

[24] For example, when he was sworn in as war minister on May 16, 1926; when he was nominated prime minister on October 1, 1926; when he appeared before the Senate budget committee on February 28, 1929. Of course, these earlier occasions were not as manifestly intimidating in purpose as the current one.

manipulations) a matter to which the Polish nation was historically conditioned to be quite sensitive. And, indeed, public opinion proved firmly hostile to the officers. There were protest demonstrations in Warsaw and other cities, even the BBWR was somewhat disoriented, and the official governmental communiqué rather weakly called for a clarification of Daszyński's and Piłsudski's contradictory versions of the episode.[25] Piłsudski had blundered and was immediately penalized. The opening of the Sejm was first postponed to November 5, then, over opposition protests, was again suspended by Mościcki for another month. When the Sejm was eventually convened, the chamber promptly overthrew the Świtalski cabinet on December 6 by a vote of 243 to 119 on a motion introduced by the six parties of the now reunited Center-Left constellation—the first occasion since Piłsudski's coup d'état that a cabinet had been ousted by the Sejm. Piłsudski, seeing the handwriting on the wall, had attempted to conduct an orderly retreat and mitigate the blow. On November 7, he had issued an order to the army declaring the incident closed without injury to the honor of the officers involved, and on November 9 he published a long and warm reminiscence recalling his revolutionary comradeship with the PPS against tsarist Russia during the Russo-Japanese War a quarter of a century earlier.[26]

In initiating what he presumably had intended as a minor show of force to save the Świtalski cabinet—and the gathering of troops at other points in the vicinity of the Sejm building confirms that intimidation was indeed intended—Piłsudski had manifestly not thought through the possible consequences of his maneuver. He had misjudged Daszyński as on May 12, 1926, he had misjudged Wojciechowski. Underestimating the pride and integrity of these former comrades from the prewar underground independence movement, he overrated his own presumed continuing power and influence over them. Still

[25] Malicki, pp. 409, 429–30.

[26] Piłsudski, *PZ*, IX, 199–206. The specific occasion which he invoked was a revolutionary demonstration of November 13, 1904, in Warsaw, organized by himself and other PPS leaders against the tsarist mobilization of Poles for the war in the Far East. This was the first armed violence of the Russian Revolution of 1905. Significantly, Piłsudski concluded his reminiscence with the observation that "in history, a witty pleasantry (*dowcip*) sometimes goes further than force."

seared from the fratricidal strife of 1926, with less at stake this time, and—as always—reluctant to appear to be violating the fundamental sources of the law, Piłsudski retreated. In sum, he paid an excessive political price for the superfluous demonstration of what was well known—that the army supported him. Not only did this officers-in-the-Sejm episode lead directly to a reconsolidation of the struggling young Center-Left alliance, which had been almost dispersed a few weeks earlier, but it also stimulated a serious drive to unify the political peasant movement of the three peasant parties within the larger coalition. This latter development, rendered possible by the earlier detachment of Piast from the Right, and secondarily encouraged by the deceptive example of the apparent political triumph of Iuliu Maniu's National Peasant Party in Rumania in November, 1928, was eventually to lead to the amalgamation of Piast, Wyzwolenie, and Stronnictwo Chłopskie into a united Peasant Party (Stronnictwo Ludowe) on March 15, 1931.

Meanwhile, Piłsudski drew a logical inference from his misfired 18 Brumaire and the attendant defeat of Świtalski by recalling to the premiership the more conciliatory Bartel, who dropped from the cabinet all but one of the ministers most objectionable to the parliamentary opposition—Sławoj-Składkowski, Car, Moraczewski, and Niezabytowski (but not the bête noire of the PPS, Prystor, who remained at Piłsudski's express wish). Their replacements were in every case more acceptable: Henryk Józewski (Interior) had earned a liberal reputation by virtue of his relatively enlightened policy toward the local Ukrainians while *wojewoda* of Volhynia; Feliks Dutkiewicz (Justice), previously president of the Appeals Court, was reputed really to care about justice and lawfulness; Maksymilian Matakiewicz (Public Works) was one of Bartel's favored technocratic types, the professor of hydro-engineering at the Lwów Polytechnic; Leon Połczyński (Agriculture) was a former Christian Democratic senator.[27] Significantly, the formation of this cabinet had been preceded for the first time since May, 1926, by presidential consultations with the opposition parties. In his inaugural speech on January 10, 1930, Bartel

[27] Sketches of all these men will be found in the Biographical Register.

assured the Sejm of his "goodwill" and clearly differentiated his political theory from that of the "colonels" by emphasizing that the state bureaucracy and administrative machinery must be politically neutral and not be used as the arm of any party—not even the government party. His interior minister (Józewski) endorsed this position and his finance minister (Matuszewski) was conciliatory to the point of praising some of his pre-coup predecessors.[28] As a palpable demonstration of his wish to govern in a constitutional manner, Bartel now withdrew the controversial presidential press decree of May, 1927.[29]

The Center-Left opposition parties were in a dilemma as to how to respond. Desirous, on the one hand, to strengthen Bartel's hand against the "colonels" and to influence Piłsudski in the same direction, their rational course appeared to be one of moderate, nonprovocative accommodation to the new cabinet as proof that the Sejm was capable of constructive work. On the other hand, they were strongly tempted to interpret the recent developments as indicative of the rout of the regime and hence to try to push their advantage to the point of forcing a change in the governmental system per se, in other words, to overplay their hand as Piłsudski had overplayed his in October with the officers-in-the-Sejm episode.

Initially, the more tolerant, cooperative approach prevailed. The Czechowicz affair, having been referred back to the Sejm by its Tribunal for a determination of the possible necessity for the former Finance Minister's technical illegalities, was allowed to remain dormant, and instead the Sejm applied itself to processing the 1930–31 budget with exemplary dispatch, thereby spiting the "colonels," who were unreconciled to Bartel and who egged on the BBWR to snipe at him. Piłsudski, meanwhile, held his peace, allowed his conciliatory recollection of working with the PPS for Polish independence in 1904 to stand as his last public statement for several weeks, and—in sharp contrast to his sabotaging "colonels"—remained cordial toward Bartel. Whether he was simply biding his time till the budget was passed or whether he was genuinely tolerant of the revived *bartlowanie* style is

[28] Próchnik, *Pierwsze piętnastolecie*, pp. 341–42; Singer, p. 101.
[29] Other conciliatory gestures by Bartel at this time are alluded to in Ajnenkiel, "Z dziejów kartki wyborczej," p. 20.

an open question. Certainly both the Center-Left parliamentary opposition and Piłsudski himself had for long been hesitant to square off
for an ultimate showdown and test of strength. Suddenly in March,
however—perhaps as the inadvertent result of a miscalculation in the
mutual testing and probing over political and constitutional readjust-
ment by the two sides, perhaps as the consequence of a deliberate
challenge by one or the other—the relations between government and
parliament precipitously worsened. On March 12, 1930, Premier
Bartel, seriously ill of kidney disease, presumably offended by the
"colonels'" intrigues against him via the BBWR and irritated by the
continued Center-Left rhetoric demanding a broadening of his recent
concessions into a fundamental change of the system, delivered himself of an exasperated retort. He accused the deputies of being an
"abomination," utterly incapable of rising to the demands of the hour
and the needs of the state. The final straw had been the announcement that the PPS would sponsor a censure motion against Prystor
(Labor) and the Christian Democrats and National Democrats one
against Czerwiński (Education). Two days later Bartel warned that
the life of his entire cabinet and, by implication, the survival of his
final experiment in nondictatorial government were at stake in the
impending votes—to no avail. The opposition, now apparently convinced that the tide had turned in its favor with Piłsudski's retreat the
previous autumn, took up Bartel's warning as a challenge. The Right
joined the Center and Left parties (the Stronnictwo Chłopskie alone
abstaining) to vote the censure of Prystor by 192 to 120 on March 14.
Bartel immediately resigned, rendering the motion against Czerwiński
redundant. There followed two weeks of stalling and diversions as
Piłsudski permitted Senate Marshal Szymański and his own younger
brother Jan to go through the motions of seeking a resolution to the
crisis—but in fact obstructing their efforts, which in any event were
hardly promising in view of the opposition's expectations.[30] Piłsudski
was but awaiting the end of the parliamentary session. Promptly with
its close, he sponsored the formation of a new "hard" cabinet under
the premiership of BBWR leader Sławek. The censured Prystor and

[30] For Piłsudski's rather transparent sabotage of Szymański's attempted
mediation by imposing extravagant conditions, see his *PZ,* IX, 214–15. The
more diplomatic but quite firm statement of position by the Center-Left parties
is reprinted as Appendix No. 2 to Czubiński, *Centrolew,* pp. 301–3.

the about-to-be censured Czerwiński remained at their posts, Car reverted immediately to the head of the Justice Ministry, and, on June 3, Sławoj-Składkowski returned to the Ministry of the Interior.[31] Bartel's last cabinet had proved but an interruption, not a reversal, in the drift of power toward the "colonels." The end of the *bartlowanie*, of semiparliamentary government, and of cat-and-mouse games between the government and its opposition also coincided with the end of the relative economic prosperity of the initial post-coup years. The resultant hardship and discontent provided social support for the opposition, with which the government was about to collide violently.[32]

The opposition of the National Democratic-led Right to the Piłsudski regime, if not necessarily to all of its policies, was a given constant, subject to little if any modification or adjustment. With the departure of its onetime conservative allies in the aftermath of the coup and its electoral setback in March, 1928, the Right had lost the central role in the struggle between government and Sejm for the time being. It was to reemerge in the 1930s as the Piłsudski camp's primary ideological adversary in the contest for the allegiance and control of Polish society—a contest, as it were, in which the one antagonist "owned" the state apparatus and the other commanded the loyalty of the nationalistic younger generation. In the meantime, however, in the conflict of the turn of the decade to determine the locus of sovereignty within (and the nature of) the Polish political system, the role of the Piłsudski government's pivotal opponent was to be taken over by the developing Center-Left parliamentary coalition.

A preliminary turning point in the formation of this constellation

[31] The return of Sławoj-Składkowski to the Interior Ministry indicated that Piłsudski expected to schedule early elections and desired a tough minister to "make" a BBWR victory of them. Another change was the demotion of the technocrat Kwiatkowski—Mościcki's and Bartel's protégé but never liked by Piłsudski—from minister to acting minister of industry and commerce. At the next cabinet reshuffle in August he was dropped altogether, not to reemerge until after Piłsudski's death.

[32] Labor Minister Prystor acknowledged that as of the end of March, 1930, officially registered unemployment stood at 297,440, which was 119,000 more than in March, 1929, while the reserves of the unemployment compensation fund stood significantly lower than the previous year. Industrial production was to be 18 percent lower in 1930 than in 1928 and 31 percent lower the next year. Rural pauperization would overwhelm the countryside on a catastrophic scale in the 1930s.

had been the 21st Congress of the PPS held at Sosnowiec on November 1–4, 1928, shortly after the defection of the PPS–Revolutionary Fraction to the Piłsudski camp. Here it was concluded that, as the Party was relentlessly being obliged to move into ever firmer opposition to the regime, the time had come to seek allies and that the preferred allies should be the Wyzwolenie and Stronnictwo Chłopskie peasant parties rather than the Bund and the Communists or—and this was more controversial—the left wing of the BBWR. Thus the stage was set for the formation in the middle of the month of the above-mentioned Coordinating Commission for the Defense of the Republic and Democracy.[33] In the course of the next year's various episodes of friction and tension between the government and the opposition, this new bloc was expanded into the originally fragile but eventually viable (though never absolutely firm) Center-Left alliance by adding the National Laborite, Piast, and Christian Democratic parties to the three original Left members.[34]

Controlling nearly two fifths of the Sejm in a situation where the government's relations with the Right and the Communists were chronically hostile and those with the Slavic minorities steadily worsening, the Center-Left alliance now became the pivotal parliamentary force of opposition to the Piłsudski camp's drift toward greater political and constitutional authoritarianism. After playing the central role in the overthrow of the Świtalski and Bartel cabinets, the Center-Left constellation had then firmly if unprovocatively affirmed its demands for a fundamental change in the governmental style and system when Szymański consulted it in the course of his abortive attempt at mediation. This was followed by a Center-Left demand of May 9, 1930, endorsed by 149 deputies—one more than the constitutionally necessary minimum (Article 25)—that Mościcki reconvene the Sejm in extraordinary session to take up the nation's political and economic problems. Mościcki was legally obliged to comply *pro forma,* but immediately upon opening the session on May 23 he prorogued it for

[33] The crucial PPS discussion is in Tymieniecka, ed., "XXI Kongres PPS (1–4. XI. 1928)," pp. 289–96.

[34] Once he had been persuaded of the need for open and sustained opposition to the regime, PPS leader Niedziałkowski became the key organizer of this Center-Left coalition. From the peasant movement, former Sejm Marshal Rataj emerged as a strong supporter. See Ciołkosz, p. 34, and Modelski, p. 2.

a month and then on June 20 closed it altogether, thus effectively preventing its functioning. The Center-Left parties responded to the first prorogation of May 23 with a sharp attack on Mościcki for thus violating the apolitical requirements of his presidential office.[35] More fatefully, they decided that strictly parliamentary opposition was insufficiently effectual in view of the provocative aggressiveness of the "colonels" and the manifest partisanship of the President, and hence resolved to summon the masses into action in a series of huge protest rallies, the first of which was scheduled for June 29 in the form of a Congress for the Defense of Law and the Freedom of the People to be held in Kraków, a city with a proletariat loyal to the PPS and a village hinterland supporting Piast. On June 20, immediately upon Mościcki's ultimate closing of the Sejm session, the Center-Left deputies and senators met in preliminary session in Warsaw to discuss strategy for the Kraków congress. They decided to link their own political grievances to the economic tribulations of the masses by attributing the latter to the regime's stubbornly dictatorial and confidence-eroding style of rule.[36]

Though the government sought to sabotage the Kraków congress by various deceptions, such as sending forged telegrams over the signatures of Piast and PPS leaders to local party organizations ostensibly announcing the respective party's withdrawal from sponsorship of the congress owing to the alleged betrayal of the other party, and though the simultaneous summoning by Cardinal Kakowski of the First Polish Eucharistic Congress to Poznań introduced a diversion for the religious members of the Center parties, particularly the Christian Democrats, nevertheless the Kraków congress attracted an attendance of many thousands of the city's citizens and pilgrims from the

[35] For the text, see Appendix No. 4 to Czubiński, *Centrolew*, pp. 305–6. The letter of the 149 Center-Left deputies to Mościcki demanding a special Sejm session is reprinted in Malicki, pp. 472–73. The Right had declined to endorse it as too moderate and the National Minorities remained neutral—an understandable tactic in view of the fact that the Center-Left coalition had as yet demonstrated little strength and the consideration that its Center members were not known for friendliness to ethnic minority aspirations.

[36] The Center-Left statement of June 20 is reprinted as Appendix No. 7 to Czubiński, *Centrolew*, pp. 311–14, and the earlier summons to the Kraków congress as Appendix No. 5, pp. 306–8. An abbreviated English text of the latter is available in Sokalski, *The Cracow Congress and the Brest-Litovsk Trial*, p. 3.

rest of the country, as well as extensive international interest, embarrassing to the regime. It began with a small indoor meeting in the Old Theater, addressed by a wide spectrum of political leaders, at which an antiregime manifesto was adopted, and concluded with a huge rally of acclamation in the Plac Kleparski, a central city square, that culminated in mass processions to the Mickiewicz monument and the Wawel castle.[37] The manifesto proclaimed a united and relentless struggle against what it termed the *de facto* dictatorship of Piłsudski, warned that another attempted coup on his part would be resisted by force and that no external obligations incurred by such a putschist regime would be honored, and demanded the ouster of the allegedly perjured and biased Mościcki. It insisted that the end of the dictatorship and the resumption of genuinely parliamentary government were necessary conditions for the solution of Poland's economic problems and the maintenance of her international independence. In conclusion, however, lest some of these demands elicit charges of national disloyalty, it cautioned that any external attempt to take advantage of Poland's domestic difficulties by seeking to impose negative frontier revisions on her would be firmly resisted.[38]

Exhilarated by this apparent moral and propagandistic triumph, the Center-Left leaders decided on August 21 to follow up and expand

[37] The most effective speeches were made by the rival peasantist leaders, Thugutt and Witos. Daszyński did not attend but sent a message of solidarity, styling himself "Marshal of a Sejm condemned to enforced inactivity." The Kraków congress had originally been suggested by Piast but the PPS quickly became its main organizer. The ex-Legion Chaplain Panaś who had reacted so passionately to the 1926 coup also addressed the outdoor rally.

Some leading French political figures, as well as thirty-eight British Labour MPs, sent greetings. There are various estimates of attendance. The generally reliable anonymous X.Y.Z., "Chronique polonaise," VII, No. 8, 269, claims 20,000 Cracovians were joined by 30,000 from elsewhere. The Piłsudskist Malicki, pp. 473–74, counters with a total of 5,900—which seems spurious because of its suspicious precision. Witos, *Moje wspomnienia,* III, 183, estimates 25,000 and concedes that this is lower than other participants were claiming. Subsequent Polish historians, e.g., Tomicki, p. 23, generally agree on an estimate in the vicinity of 30,000. Attendance at mass rallies is, of course, notoriously difficult to establish with any precision.

[38] The manifesto of the Kraków congress is reprinted as Appendix No. 8 to Czubiński, *Centrolew,* pp. 314–15, and is available in English translation in M. Kridl *et al.,* eds., *For Your Freedom and Ours* (New York, 1943), pp. 247–48.

the congress by scheduling more than a score such mass protest meetings in various towns and cities for September 14. Piłsudski, however, had had enough. On August 11 he had ordered Interior Minister Sławoj-Składkowski to investigate the Center-Left deputies and prepare dossiers with a view to their possible arrest and imprisonment.[39] The Kraków congress' threatened repudiation of future foreign commitments incurred by an "illegal" government and its explicit attack on Mościcki had provided the regime with an opportunity to accuse the congress organizers of sedition and subversion.[40] Nor was Piłsudski in a mood to be deterred by the Sejm's refusal of a governmental demand that the parliamentary immunity of eighteen of its Center-Left leaders be lifted so that they could be tried together with fifteen other organizers of the congress.[41] By August 22 Sławoj-Składkowski had prepared the requested dossiers, a day later the Sławek cabinet resigned, and on August 25 Piłsudski himself took on the premiership with a cabinet of the same hard hue. He was now formally and publicly at the helm in the showdown on which he was determined.[42] For all his many ambivalences and occasional miscalculations, it could not be said of Piłsudski that he shirked responsibility for his own decisions in a crisis. On August 26 he gave the first of a series of nine ferocious interviews designed to persuade the public of the utter depravity of the parliamentary opposition and virtually in-

[39] Sławoj-Składkowski, *Strzępy meldunków,* p. 205.

[40] In 1928 the Rumanian National Peasant Party, then in opposition, had successfully resorted to the stratagem of warning would-be foreign creditors that any loans extended to the incumbent Liberal Party government would not be honored by a future National Peasant one. In November the Liberals fell, in large part as a result of their failure to secure foreign credits. The Center-Left threat of 1930 in Poland was more conditional, referring as it did to foreign obligations incurred by the Piłsudski regime should it stage yet another putsch against the constitutional order.

[41] X.Y.Z., "Daszyński ou Piłsudski?" p. 425.

[42] New ministers were: Czesław Michałowski (Justice), whose appointment was rendered necessary by Car's last-minute loss of nerve and his refusal to sign arrest warrants for the Center-Left leaders; Leon Kozłowski (Land Reform), in place of Staniewicz, who was uncomfortable with the government's toughening policy; Stefan Hubicki (Labor), replacing Prystor, who, in turn, moved over to Industry and Commerce in place of Kwiatkowski, who was now definitely dropped from the cabinet; Mieczysław Norwid-Neugebauer (Public Works); Józef Beck (deputy premier without portfolio). Sketches of all but Michałowski will be found in the Biographical Register.

citing to violence against it,[43] and on August 30 Sejm and Senate were dissolved and new elections scheduled for November. On September 1 Piłsudski personally made the final selection of the opposition leaders to be arrested before these elections.[44]

Though this last preparatory action was kept secret, the Christian Democrats—the most clericalist party of the Center-Left opposition and its rightist anchor—who had all along been lukewarm, wavering, and divided in their commitment to the Socialist-led coalition, now correctly gauged the many other straws in the wind and quit the coalition on September 8. The reason given officially was the failure of their partners to guarantee the Polish-papal concordat of 1925 in the Center-Left electoral platform currently being drafted. Behind this undoubtedly true disagreement, and symbolized by it, there lurked a more general sense of ideological incompatibility, ecclesiastical influence, and, finally, the intimidation of Christian Democratic leaders by the drift of political events.[45] Though there were other tremors of vacillation within the coalition, notably on the part of some Piast leaders still hankering for the older Center-Right phalanx, some Stronnictwo Chłopskie ideologues uncomfortable at the immersion of their peasant "class movement" in such a basically "political" opposition led by the suspect party of the urban proletariat, and some PPS militants preferring the Communists as allies, nevertheless the five Center-Left parties remaining after the Christian Democratic defection cohered sufficiently to present a joint electoral manifesto to the nation on September 10, focusing their denunciations on both the assertedly reactionary and the lawlessly dictatorial tendencies of the regime, its socioeconomic and politico-administrative policies.[46]

---

[43] The interviews were published in *Gazeta Polska* between August 27 and December 14, 1930, and are reprinted in Piłsudski, *PZ,* IX, 217–70. The most explicit instigation to violence was in the first interview (pp. 221–22) and was almost immediately followed by the brutal beating up of Stronnictwo Chłopskie leader Jan Dąbski by "unknown" culprits in officers' uniforms. Dąbski, a vice-marshal of the outgoing Sejm, never fully recovered, and died of these wounds on June 5, 1931. Further information on him will be found in the Biographical Register.

[44] Sławoj-Składkowski, *Strzępy meldunków,* p. 223.

[45] See Stęborowski, p. 408, n. 19.

[46] The text is reprinted as Appendix No. 9 to Czubiński, *Centrolew,* pp. 315–18.

As for the shufflings within the coalition, there was indeed to be another

The manifesto had been agreed to barely in time. During the night of September 9 came the first arrests, initially of nineteen opposition deputies and senators, followed within the next few days by over sixty more.[47] Those arrested were apprehended in secrecy, without proper warrants, on specious charges of common and political crimes, under the transparent excuse that their parliamentary immunity had lapsed with the recent dissolution of the legislature. The most prominent ones were detained illegally and incommunicado in the fortress-prison at Brześć (Brest-Litovsk) under deliberately brutal and degrading conditions. Several thousand lesser activists of the opposition were also arrested in the course of the ensuing electoral campaign; the Center-Left rallies scheduled in over a score of towns for September 14 were bloodily repressed; the member parties' offices were ransacked and their publications confiscated; and approximately a million of their supporters were disfranchised through the arbitrary invalidation of Center-Left electoral lists in several districts, costing the coalition perhaps as many as fifty Sejm seats. Though one grand councilor of Dmowski's Camp of Great Poland was among the Brześć prisoners (the pre-coup National Democratic *wojewoda* of Volhynia, Aleksander Dębski), the brunt of the repression was borne by the Center-Left and the Slavic National Minorities. Piłsudski's erstwhile allies of 1926 had become his particular bêtes noires.

Piłsudskist diversion within the Stronnictwo Chłopskie (in addition to the split of December, 1927) in October, 1930, led by two of the three deputies who had apparently defected from the BBWR to the Stronnictwo Chłopskie in July. (See above, p. 320, n. 15.)

The recommendation of the PPS radicals for an alliance with the Communists was rejected by the Socialist leadership and was unacceptable to the Communists, then in the throes of their "social fascist" phobia.

In contrast to these Center-Left inconstancies stood the unity and stridency of the *endecja* Camp of Great Poland, now even more radically Rightist than in 1928 while simultaneously playing on the Centrist nostalgia for the old alliance of 1923–28.

[47] The most important of these prisoners were: (*a*) the six PPS leaders, N. Barlicki, A. Ciołkosz, S. Dubois, H. Lieberman, M. Mastek, and A. Pragier (M. Niedziałkowski was beaten up but not arrested); (*b*) the two Wyzwolenie leaders, K. Bagiński and J. Putek; (*c*) the Stronnictwo Chłopskie leader, A. Sawicki (J. Dąbski having earlier been severely beaten); (*d*) the National Laborite K. Popiel; (*e*) the two Piast leaders, W. Witos and W. Kiernik; (*f*) the Christian Democrat W. Korfanty; (*g*) the National Democrats A. Dębski and J. Kwiatkowski; (*h*) the Ukrainians V. Tselevich, D. Paliev, O. Kohut, I. Lyshchynskyi, and A. Vyslots'kyi; (*i*) the BBWR deputy J. Baćmaga, who was charged with embezzlement. All had in one way or another aroused Piłsudski's personal ire.

Superficially, the tactic of intimidation proved successful. The BBWR won absolute majorities of 247 (out of 444) and 76 (out of 111) seats in the Sejm and Senate elections of November 16 and 23. Though the Right partly recovered from 1928, the National Minorities and especially the parties of the Center-Left coalition lost severely.[48] More significantly, the coalition's bluff had been called, for the masses failed to rise to the defense of the imprisoned and tortured leaders in Brześć. The Center-Left attacks on Piłsudski's regime had been sufficiently sharp and damaging to provoke it to revenge and to give it the pretext for charging subversion, but they had been unaccompanied by serious preparations to resist by force its violent response, symbolized in the expression "Brześć." "Brześć" signaled the end of Piłsudski's uneasy four-year lockstep with constitutional parliamentarism. The

[48] In the 1930 elections, 74.8 percent of eligible Sejm electors and 63.4 percent of senatorial ones cast valid ballots. The following results are drawn from Groth, tables 40, 41, 46, and 47, and from Próchnik, *Pierwsze piętnastolecie,* pp. 392–96.

	SEJM (NOVEMBER 16)			SENATE (NOVEMBER 23)		
	Votes	Per-cent	*Seats*	*Votes*	Per-cent	*Seats*
Total	11,816,413					
Valid	11,333,795	100.0	444	6,797,188	100.0	111
I. BBWR	5,292,725	46.7	247	3,715,273	54.6	76
PPS–Revolutionary Fraction	74,096	0.7		10,510	0.2	
II. Center-Left	1,965,864	17.3	82	882,636	13.0	14
(PPS)			(24)			(5)
(Wyzwolenie) united into			(15)			(4)
(Stronnictwo one party						
Chłopskie) March 15,			(18)			
(Piast) 1931			(15)			(2)
(NPR)			(10)			(3)
III. Christian Democrats	430,074	3.8	14	160,444	2.4	2
IV. Nationalists (Endecja)	1,443,165	12.7	63	882,215	13.0	12
Monarchists	1,816					
V. German Bloc	309,713	2.7	5	236,471	3.4	3
Jewish Economic Bloc	150,146	1.3	1	148,522	2.2	
Jewish National Bloc	184,968	1.6	4	79,358	1.2	
Jewish Rights Bloc	246,840	2.2	2	146,726	2.2	
Jewish Socialist Bloc	71,123	0.6				
Jewish Labor Zionists	19,206	0.2				
Ukrainian–White Russian Bloc	725,984	6.4	21	434,042	6.4	4
Ukrainian Peasants	11,465	0.1				
VI. Communists	232,000	2.1	4			
Self-Help ("front")	23,000	0.2	1			
Miscellaneous	151,610	1.4		100,991	1.4	

authoritarian era now began in earnest. "Brześć" thus became a turning point in interwar Polish political history as significant, in its way, as had been "the May events" of 1926.

In the long run, however, Piłsudski paid a heavy moral price for the immediate political victory ensured him by "Brześć." Though the masses did not rise in protest, nevertheless the specific manner of his taking sole and autocratic possession of the state apparatus cost Piłsudski dearly within civil society. Poles had been historically conditioned to acute sensitivity in the face of such savageries as the repeated clubbing into unconsciousness of the sixty-year-old Lieberman for his prosecution of "the Marshal's minister" (Czechowicz), the forcing of ex-ministers Witos, Kiernik, and others to clean out latrines with their bare hands until they fainted, the refusal to permit the PPS youth leader Stanisław Dubois to attend the burial of the premature baby which his wife had miscarried under the shock of his unexplained nocturnal arrest, the merciless beating of Wyzwolenie deputy Kazimierz Bagiński for "betraying the Marshal" (he was a Legion and POW veteran of World War I and a pioneer hero of the Polish air force in 1920), the infliction on a terrified Lieberman and Popiel of a mock execution, and so on. These and other atrocities committed in the Brześć fortress-prison severed a moral tie between Piłsudski and his nation which the 1926 coup, per contra, had not done.[49] Furthermore, Brześć, unlike that earlier recourse to force, did not stimulate expectations of drastic yet necessary improvements in the body politic. It was felt to be a gratuitous abuse of power, not a purgative seizure of it. Already rapidly losing the nationalistic youth to Dmowski's Right-radical nostrums, Piłsudski had now repelled the influential intelligentsia of virtually all political hues, sacrificed the support of many of his prestigious conservative allies, driven an ultimate chasm between himself and his earlier Socialist and Left peas-

---

[49] The atrocities were in part exposed in the Polish press and, where it was censored, in the *Robotnik Polski* (Detroit) and the anonymous "Chronique polonaise" column of *Le Monde Slave* (Paris) during the autumn and winter of 1930–31. One of the first systematic exposures in English appeared in 1931 in H. H. Tiltman, *The Terror in Europe* (New York, 1931), pp. 350–54. The Brześć trial itself also yielded many devastating revelations when it was eventually held. Two stenographic records of the trial proceedings—neither apparently complete—have been published: *Sprawa brzeska* and *Proces brzeski*. The prisoners Pragier and Witos have also published their recollections of the affair.

antist partners, and even shaken the confidence of some of his immediate coworkers. Moreover, simultaneously with Brześć, he was destroying whatever credit he may still have possessed (thanks to his onetime sponsorship of federalism) with the Slavic minorities by seeking to break the Ukrainian nationalist movement through a series of brutal dragonnadelike military "pacifications" of the disaffected eastern districts between mid-September and the end of November, 1930.[50]

Indeed, the Piłsudskists now attempted to utilize the leverage of Polish nationalism against the Center-Left opposition by seeking to identify the latter in the public's mind with the ethnic minorities. Thus, five Ukrainian nationalist leaders had been among the political prisoners rounded up for detention at Brześć during the night of September 9, 1930; a *sanacja*-sponsored electoral *feuilleton* simultaneously referred to the Center-Left bloc as a "sackful of Judases"; and when eleven of the Brześć prisoners were eventually put on trial in October, 1931, the proceedings were officially designated as "the case of Hersch Lieberman *et al.*—again an anti-Semitic allusion.[51] The Polish Center-Left strategists had indeed been so loath to be identified with the non-Polish minorities in the public mind that they had refrained from any references to this problem in their joint elec-

[50] The literature—mainly polemical—on the cycle of Ukrainian sedition and Polish repression in 1930 is voluminous. See, for example, Feliński, pp. 158–73; Santoro, *passim;* Tarnopolsky, chapters III–V; Un Polonais, pp. 364–383; X.Y.Z., "Chronique polonaise," VII, No. 10, 98–138; Prudhommeaux, pp. 36–38; Pobóg-Malinowski, *Najnowsza historia,* II, 533–41.

[51] "Haniebny dokument," pp. 21–22.
Similarly designed to destroy the public standing of the Brześć political prisoners was their incarceration jointly with the erstwhile BBWR deputy Józef Baćmaga, accused of embezzlement. For an argument that even he may have been the victim of a provocation, see Czubiński, *Centrolew,* p. 214.
The trial of eleven Brześć prisoners took place in Warsaw from October 26, 1931, to January 13, 1932. The defendants had been free on bail since December, 1930. They were charged with preparing a coup d'état; no common crimes were alleged in the eventual indictment. Ten were found guilty in a judgment which somewhat damaged the Polish judiciary's reputation for fearlessness and impartiality. Ciołkosz, Dubois, Mastek, Pragier, and Putek were sentenced to three years' imprisonment, Barlicki, Kiernik, and Lieberman to two and a half years, Bagiński to two years, and Witos to one and a half. Sawicki was acquitted. Rather than serve any part of their sentences, Bagiński, Kiernik, Lieberman, Pragier, and Witos fled to Czechoslovakia. Thenceforth their popularity, especially that of Witos, rose to near-legendary (and quite exaggerated) proportions. The embarrassed government eventually pardoned them as a gesture of national reconciliation on the eve of World War II.

tion manifesto of September 10, 1930—most probably on the insistence of the Center phalanx, to which the Left then acquiesced. All this rather chillingly suggests the extent to which Dmowski's Right-radical xenophobia was beginning to course through the bloodstream of the entire Polish body politic, ideologically embarrassing even some of its staunchest foes.

Nevertheless, this depressed state of Polish–ethnic minority relations failed to serve Piłsudski as a lever with which to stave off the consequences of the Brześć outrages. The conscience of the nation had been violated. Led, appropriately enough, by the faculty of the ancient Jagiellonian University at Kraków, the academic intelligentsia of the several institutions of higher education protested passionately and movingly against the Brześć atrocities, and they were joined therein by the leading members of the nation's literary intelligentsia.[52] The Warsaw Lawyers' Guild and the Union of Polish Jurists protested and were dissolved. Among the professors-in-government who had originally given the regime its aura of suprapolitical expertise and nonpartisan dedication, many defected. Piłsudski's first and perennial post-coup premier, Kazimierz Bartel (Lwów Polytechnic), testified for the defense at the Brześć trial. His durable minister of land reform, Witold Staniewicz (Wilno University), resigned from the BBWR, as did the economist and conegotiator of the 1927 Stabilization Loan, Senator Adam Krzyżanowski (Kraków University), and two less prominent intelligentsia-deputies of the Naprawa ginger group. Even President Mościcki, with whom Bartel and his other former colleagues at the Lwów Polytechnic forcefully intervened, was sorely troubled. Matching the prestige of the intelligentsia in interwar Poland was the station of the historic magnate families, and among them, too, Piłsudski suffered damaging withdrawals. Prince Zdzisław Lubomirski, his original preference for the presidency in 1926, berated Piłsudski

[52] The protest of the Kraków professors, on which were modeled those of other universities, is appended to *Proces brzeski,* pp. 805–7, and translated in Sokalski, *The Cracow Congress and the Brest-Litovsk Trial,* pp. 7–9. For a reminiscence about its drafting by one of its sponsors, see Lednicki, "Z dziejów pewnego protestu." The most eloquent protests by the nonacademic intelligentsia were those of the writers Antoni Słonimski, Andrzej Strug, and Julian Tuwim. The most significant exceptions to this near-unanimous condemnation of Brześć by the intelligentsia were the novelist Juliusz Kaden-Bandrowski, the ethnographer-romancer Wacław Sieroszewski, and the poetess Kazimiera Iłłakowiczówna.

over Brześć. Prince Janusz Radziwiłł, the virtual godfather of the Nieśwież coalition, was appalled, as were many of the legality-oriented, "old-fashioned" conservatives. Even among Piłsudski's own entourage, where public defections were avoided, there were those who wavered, among them his ex-Socialist expert on eastern minority affairs, Tadeusz Hołówko.[53]

Indeed, Piłsudski himself appears to have been ashamed of Brześć. After the devastating facts of the prisoners' treatment came to light, he never again delivered himself of one of those virulent public attacks on the Sejm and the political parties which he had made so notorious in the preceding years. Already on September 29, 1930, he was ruminating to his cabinet whether a more ameliorative course was not, perhaps, preferable,[54] and he did, after all, permit the (albeit defective) elections of a new parliament to be held. Four years earlier, on the morrow of his coup d'état, Piłsudski had said he wanted to test whether Poland could, despite everything, be ruled without recourse to the whip. Now Brześć had finally come as his negative answer to the question, but it had failed to provide a solution to Poland's fundamental politico-historic problems or even to serve as a resolution of his own doubts and ambivalences about power, force, and law. Intellectually more sophisticated and morally more sensitive than the uninhibitedly totalitarian Hitler and Stalin, Piłsudski was in due time to make an acknowledgment pertaining to Brześć of which they would have been incapable. "Poles," he avowed in an autobiographical conversation with Artur Śliwiński, whom he had also considered as a potential president in 1926, "have an instinct for freedom. One cannot rule Poland by terror." [55] His *sanacja* may have lacked the social dynamism of neighboring Nazism and Bolshevism, but Piłsudski was also free of their totalitarian ferocity.

---

[53] These examples of the repercussions to Brześć are culled from *Proces brzeski* and *Robotnik Polski* (Detroit), *passim;* Morawski, *Tamten brzeg,* p. 159; Zbyszewski, "Nieznane 'testimonium' o Piłsudskim," p. 47; Léontin, "Le Gouvernement de Piłsudski au pouvoir," p. 25; X.Y.Z., "Daszyński ou Piłsudski?" p. 426; Pobóg-Malinowski, *Najnowsza historia,* II, 532; Juryś, p. 4; Roos, *Geschichte der polnischen Nation,* p. 123.

[54] Sławoj-Składkowski, *Strzępy meldunków,* p. 241.

[55] For the full account of this conversation, which took place in November, 1931, see Śliwiński, pp. 367–73.

CONCLUSION

By 1926 resurrected Poland was ripe for dictatorship. The political system was in chaos, the economy in disarray, public morale in despair. As a result of the partisan bitterness accompanying and shaping its drafting, the constitution of 1921, despite such virtues as its political republicanism, legal egalitarianism, and civil libertarianism, as well as its contribution to the drawing together of the long-separated Polish parts of three empires, had fatally maldistributed institutional power in the state and had subsequently failed to elicit that general public acceptance and veneration which is an essential element of national unity in successful democracies. The all-too-numerous political parties were behaving with an irresponsibility reminiscent of the szlachta confederations of the prepartition Commonwealth. The antigovernmental reflexes which had been further indulged under the partitioning powers now expressed themselves in the form of intrigues, conspiracies, and poor citizenship on the part of both the public and the politicians—most prominently and devastatingly the latter. The chronic cabinet instability and the resultant paralysis of governmental power had produced a condition suggestive of Rousseau's description of an earlier Poland:

L'affaiblissement de la législation s'est fait en Pologne d'une manière bien particulière et peut-être unique. C'est qu'elle a perdu sa force sans avoir été subjugée par la puisance exécutive. En ce moment encore la puissance législative conserve tout son autorité; elle est dans l'inaction, mais sans rien voir au-dessus d'elle. La Diète est aussi souveraine qu'elle l'était lors de son établissement. Cependant, elle est sans force; rien ne la domine; mais rien ne lui obéit.[1]

Though the Witos cabinet formed on May 10, 1926, was un-

[1] Jean-Jacques Rousseau, *Considérations sur le Gouvernement de Pologne* (London, 1782), pp. 49–50.

deniably legal, and though its prime minister, at any rate, probably intended to demand extensive constitutional corrections, the personnel of this cabinet and the Right-Center party coalition which composed it were too discredited by that time to elicit the necessary general recognition of its validity and legitimacy. Nor was any other parliamentary coalition by then feasible or capable of winning national confidence. Poland was indeed ready for dictatorship. Who would supply the dictator?

As a result of his dramatic prewar and wartime leadership of the struggle for Poland's resurrection as an independent state, Józef Piłsudski was without comparable challengers as candidate for this role. In particular, since his earliest activities on behalf of Polish independence had been conducted through the instrumentality of the always patriotic and nationalistic PPS, he could count on a reservoir of sympathy within the ranks of the Polish Left for his intervention in politics. His enemies and the Left's enemies largely, albeit not entirely, overlapped—though not for identical reasons. Yet he enjoyed a national prestige and moral authority extending far beyond the Left and quite unmatched by any of the would-be strong-man candidates favored by Right or Center. In addition, his long years of commanding the prewar Riflemen and wartime Legions and POW had provided Piłsudski with a core of praetorians whose primary political affiliation was to his person.

Yet Piłsudski long hesitated to stage a coup d'état against the crumbling parliamentary political system. His frequently brutal utterances and occasionally barbarous political actions during his last decade should not obscure the recognition that he was not a mere tinhorn strong man and coarse *Realpolitiker* in the cheap conventional sense. Not unlike Bismarck, who also preferred to screen an acute sensibility with the pretended bluntness of a gruff *Junker,* Piłsudski adopted an abrupt, gnarled, and seemingly thickheaded szlachta manner that veiled a fine sense for the imponderables of history. Twice before 1926 he had toyed with the idea of making a coup against the Sejm and had refrained, explaining:

I won't do it because I can't be certain that my life will be long enough to permit the ordering of the state's affairs. If I were to break the law, I would be opening the door to all sorts of adventurers to make coups and putsches. It is my pride, my moral crest, that I established law in Poland or (at least) that I created the necessary conditions for the nation freely to develop its legislative productivity, but I have never violated legality.[2]

Similarly, it will be recalled, he had initially forbidden his followers to organize a conspiratorial Piłsudskist network within the army.[3] Piłsudski was thus eminently aware of the possible demoralizing and pattern-setting consequences of an illegal recourse to force for the solution of domestic political crises, an awareness which in large part explains his depression and disorientation when the intended show of force, or "armed demonstration" of May 12, 1926, degenerated into civil strife, leaving him open to the accusation of having resurrected one of Poland's more disastrous prepartition traditions, that of the *rokosz*, or armed rebellion by a gentry faction against the government.[4] Piłsudski's eagerness retroactively to "legalize" the coup by interpreting his election to the presidency as its legitimation and his reluctance to exploit his triumph in a revolutionary manner are also partly ascribable to this concern not to inaugurate a chain reaction of lawlessness and insurrection. The incumbent Sejm and Senate were to be given one more, ostensibly free, opportunity to demonstrate that Poland could be governed in a responsible and parliamentary manner. Once before, in 1922, Piłsudski had retired from public political office (and in 1923 from military office) in part because he wished the nation to learn to organize itself without him. But for the confluence of the politico-economic and the crucial army

[2] Remarks made in 1922 to the journalist-politician Antoni Anusz, published by him in the *Kurjer Poranny*, May 27, 1926, and quoted in Woyszwiłło (pseudonym of Pobóg-Malinowski), *Józef Piłsudski*, pp. 172–73. The two earlier occasions when Piłsudski had considered a coup were in 1920 over the Wilno issue and in 1922 at the time of a serious constitutional crisis.

[3] See above, p. 75, n. 35.

[4] The fact of the coup was immensely embarrassing to Piłsudski and the Piłsudskists. Among the rationalizations which the latter have advanced for it—apart from the credible argument that he had hoped an "armed demonstration" would suffice—are: that Piłsudski came from his country home to Warsaw on May 12, 1926, to place himself under President Wojciechowski's protection; that he came merely to describe the alleged night attack on his house; that his was a preventive coup to forestall a civil clash even more severe than the events in Kraków of November, 1923, a clash that would inevitably have been provoked by Witos' Right-Center government. This third argument is objectively plausible though it is probably not a valid description of Piłsudski's subjective motives.

command crises in the next years, he might not have reemerged to seize power in 1926.

As it was, this seizure of power, this return as potential dictator, was unaccompanied by any political goals and social purposes apart from *sanacja*. What was *sanacja*? Formally, it implied (1) the alleged immunization of the army from political influences—which meant in practice the transformation of the army into Piłsudski's own instrument and a reflection of himself; (2) the healthy cleansing and administrative professionalization of the state apparatus—which came to mean its infusion with a technocratic-managerial (and again anti-political) stance; and (3) the laudable but vague admonition, expressed by Piłsudski himself during the first night of the coup, that "there must not be too much injustice in the state toward those who labor for others, there must not be too much wickedness, lest the state perish" [5]—which eventually came to mean the Nieśwież-BBWR strategy of seeking to form an allegedly nonpolitical phalanx of all classes and parties supposedly prepared to elevate general state interests above particular partisan and social ones. (Piłsudski's traditional National Democratic enemies were a priori presumed to be unequal to this test.) Piłsudski's resumption of power thus took the form of an uneasy yoking of excessively specific to exceedingly general purposes: on the one hand, purging the army and polity of particular undesired personnel; on the other hand, regenerating moral excellence in the service of the state. Though he would attempt to make a virtue of his and the new regime's freedom from ideological preconceptions [6]—to the distress of his recent supporters on the Left—Piłsudski and Poland were to pay a heavy price for this absence of a clear, long-run, middle-range political program in the *sanacja*.

Piłsudski was sufficiently sophisticated and serious to be aware of this gap, to perceive the contradiction between his goals for Poland, which were ultimately those of a free, law-abiding, and pluralistic democracy structured with a public-spirited traditional "establishment," [7] and the commandeering, forceful, even violent methods

---

[5] Piłsudski, *PZ*, IX, 9.
[6] *Ibid.*, pp. 11–33.
[7] *Ibid.*, pp. 21–22, 47–48.

which he felt himself drawn to utilize. Though anxious to assert the prerogative of state institutions above, and their immunity from, partisan politics, he had caused a part of the army to indulge in mutiny against the constitutional authorities. Though eager to establish the primacy of the president in the political system, by his coup Piłsudski had ousted one incumbent and had then denigrated the office by contemptuously declining to fill it upon being elected to it. Though wishing to raise the dignity, respect, and morale of all public functionaries, he berated the Sejm legislators in incredibly abusive terms and eventually treated them in scandalously brutal fashion. Though sedulous to inculcate on the nation a sense of legal norms, he bent, manipulated, and violated the law in the pursuit of his immediate political aims. Piłsudski liked to see himself primarily as the teacher of the Polish people, educating them to civic virtue,[8] but the example which he set tended to subvert the maturing of true citizenship. In a sense, his regime proved to be one long, extended coup d'état against the constitutional and parliamentary principles of a democracy. Piłsudski's awareness of these contradictions accounts heavily for the irascibility and moodiness of his later years. Yet the fault did not lie exclusively or even primarily in his personality but "in his stars." Historical, political, social, economic, and international circumstances all conspired to lengthen the odds against a happy resolution of Poland's interwar problems.

The seeds of both the personal and the general tragedy of Piłsudski's *sanacja* were already germinating at the time of the May coup. It was Piłsudski's and Poland's misfortune that the Marshal's best years were then already behind him. The protean underground freedom fighter, the versatile rebel, the energetic wartime Legion commander, the wide-visioned Chief of State, was now, despite his immense prestige and his large horizons, prematurely cantankerous, embittered, and rigid. Having had no clear advance idea of how far his "armed demonstration" would carry him, Piłsudski was somehow lacking in dignity in his successive responses to the eruption of fratricidal fighting—the initial despair, then the frantic casting about for mediators, finally the shrill attempts to throw all responsibility on his opponents. Afterward he failed to give a strong lead. On the

[8] W. Baranowski, "Rozmowy z Piłsudskim," *Wiadomości Literackie,* XV, No. 767 (July 3, 1938), 1.

morrow of the fighting, he could have exploited the collective national catharsis to rally the Polish people around himself, activate them politically, elicit rededication, demand sacrifices, and accomplish much.[9] But, distrusting the spontaneity of the masses, he chose to do the opposite, to impose political passivity on the nation, reserving the responsibility of governing to himself, to the technocratic elite recruited by Bartel, and to his own immediate coterie of "colonels." The function of the BBWR was to neutralize the established political parties and to insulate the regime from antagonistic social and ideological pulls and pressures—not to draw the nation into participant political activism. Though a number of "new" recruits (often careerists of the so-called Fourth Brigade) were accepted and were promoted quite high up in the *sanacja* pyramid, the regime managed in a deeper sense tragically to isolate itself. Piłsudski and his entourage succeeded in asserting their monopoly ownership of the state apparatus and its power structure, but they lost control and leadership over Polish society to the allegedly corrosive political parties. The achievements of his regime—undeniable despite their immolation in the 1939 catastrophe—were a series of structural and diplomatic reclamations achieved within and by the state apparatus, for example, the constitutional amendments of August, 1926, the resuscitation of military morale, the professionalization of the civil bureaucracy, the reintegration of all preponderantly Polish-populated areas—including the western regions—into one political system, the balancing of budgets, the raising of Poland's international prestige and self-confidence. But no fundamental social problem was solved or even seriously tackled in Piłsudski's lifetime.

Given his reluctance to take the nation into genuine confidence and political partnership, Piłsudski might have done better to establish an explicit dictatorship on the morrow of the coup rather than lead the country through the demoralizing and unedifying pseudo-parliamentary charade which eventually culminated in the Brześć outrage. This dictatorship need not have been "Leftist" to achieve some positive "revolutionary" corrections. However, such a solution was inhibited both by Piłsudski's own scruples, fears, and hopes and by a general national craving to demonstrate that the reborn Poland was, despite

[9] See Micewski, p. 156, and J. Romer, p. 326.

the coup, sufficiently mature to emulate successfully the Western tradition of constitutional parliamentarism. Hence, the coup fell between two stools. It was a potentially revolutionary action whose revolutionary potential was immediately denied and repressed by its author, abetted by the "responsible" Polish political community.

What did Piłsudski believe himself to be expressing and accomplishing by his *sanacja?* His political theory (never systematically articulated) presumed, in a classic but obsolete tradition, the conceptual and even the organizational separability of the state and civil society. His own interests were concentrated exclusively on the former, a concentration certainly maximized by his conviction that the neglect of her *state* institutions had been responsible for the death of the old Polish-Lithuanian Commonwealth.[10] Concern with the state meant, for Piłsudski personally, concern with three issues: military affairs, foreign affairs, and executive administration. He regarded a properly organized political system as one in which these issues are independent of and above social forces and economic classes. Toward the latter he believed himself to be genuinely neutral and disinterested, a result of being, indeed, uninterested. Hence he could recruit into his cohort persons of moderate, radical, and conservative social and economic views. Beyond its unanimity on the basic question of "strong" and "immune" state institutions, the Piłsudski camp agreed to disagree on other issues.[11] This was one of the reasons why it did not regard itself as a political party but rather formed around itself the Nonpartisan Bloc for Cooperation with the Government.

This concentration on "state" issues proved to be ambivalent. It enabled Piłsudski and his entourage to take, to hold, and to maximize their political power, but it blunted their sense of knowing what to do with it. With no cohesive social ideology, they lacked a sense of historical direction. Their response to the Great Depression, for example, was one of stunned and prolonged rigidity at the level of socioeconomic policy. Their reaction to the resultant political ferment provoked by the Depression, by their inability to cope with it,

[10] Piłsudski, *PZ,* VIII, 266–69.
[11] See J. Jędrzejewicz, "Myśl państwowa piłsudczyków w okresie 1918–1935," for a defense of this perspective, and Górski, "Legenda Józefa Piłsudskiego," for an attack on it.

and by their continued refusal to relinquish or even to share power was the sterile one of Brześć and then of the Bereza Kartuska concentration camp.

Yet the fixation by Piłsudski and the Piłsudskists on "state" as contrasted to "social" issues had not originated simply as an abstract or immature or merely subjective political preference. It was induced in the pre-1914 years when the Piłsudskists were a relatively isolated band of rebels while the bulk of the Polish nation remained immersed in that "positivist" concentration on "organic" social work into which it had recoiled in reaction to the defeat of the "statist-romanticist" insurrection of 1863 against tsarist Russia. The fixation was then confirmed during the first years of World War I when the Legionnaires were shocked to find that their struggle and their sacrifices for the resurrection of an independent Polish state were still not understood or shared by the majority of their countrymen—at least not until the later, to them the morally anticlimactic, phases of the war.[12] Hence Piłsudski and the Piłsudskists emerged from the war into independent Poland with a profound elitist self-awareness, a conviction that they alone had fathered and mothered the reborn state and that only they bore ultimate responsibility for nurturing it to maturity. The obverse of this aloof sense of mission for the safety of the state was a somewhat distant, patronizing attitude toward the other classes and strata that had continued to wallow in their social interests and had proved incapable of rising to the vision and challenge of independent statehood. Hence they could not really be entrusted with its protection now.

On this issue of their role in, and their responsibility for, the state, there is a great psychological and a significant sociological continuity between the modern Piłsudskist-Legionnaires and the prepartition szlachta. They both came to believe in and to act on the principle "Polska—to my" (We are Poland), admittedly not without a certain justification. It is also no accident that the inner core of Piłsudski's entourage, like the Marshal himself, originated from the szlachta-

---

[12] When the Legions entered Warsaw in 1915 after participating in the successful offensive of the Central Powers to expel the Russian armies from central Poland, Colonel Sławek had to endure overhearing a Polish mother pointing him out to her little girl, not as a patriotic hero, but as "one of those men who wants to kill your daddy." Quoted in Roos, *Geschichte der polnischen Nation,* p. 25.

become-intelligentsia families of the *kresy,* where the memories of the old Commonwealth and its traditions of aristocratic stewardship of power over "immature" social and ethnic elements had remained particularly vivid, albeit romanticized. The classic szlachta contempt for business, trading, and bourgeois values which they also imbibed from these origins confirmed their more immediately political reasons for ignoring "social" in favor of "state" concerns. At the same time, their heritage and training did not dispose them to, or equip them for, the give-and-take of parliamentary politics.

It is thus clear that the rift in the interwar Polish body politic which was exposed by Piłsudski's coup and which hardened in subsequent years was not one between the army and the civilians but rather one between the Piłsudskist "state-bearing" elite and the rest of society.[13] The Piłsudskists—even the "colonels" and, in a sense, the Marshal himself—were not a professional military caste but rather a political intelligentsia which had retooled for military action before and during World War I in order to create the Polish state. Relations between those of them who stayed in the postwar army and those who transferred their activities to the civilian branches of the state apparatus remained comradely. Within the resurrected state they were enabled to play a power role quite disproportionate to their relatively small numbers thanks to their cohesion, their self-confidence, and their sense of righteousness based on genuine sacrifices for the cause of independent Polish statehood, as well as to the feebleness, brittleness, and disorganization of the political parties, the political institutions, and the parliamenary political structure. Their utter dedication to the charismatic Piłsudski gave focus, élan, and authority to their political actions. After his death in 1935, their ideological poverty and lack of social anchorage, which his immense prestige had till then veiled, were exposed. The now overly bureaucratized and somewhat ossified, though still remarkably Spartan, *sanacja* regime learned to its alarm that in its monopolistic concentration on *state* power it had lost control over, direction of, and influence upon the nation's *social* classes and forces to the despised "mere" politicians—National Democratic and quasi-fascist, peasantist and Socialist. The desperate efforts of

[13] For an extended discussion of the problem treated in this paragraph, see the two articles by Hertz, "The Social Background of the Pre-War Polish Political Structure," and "The Case of an East European Intelligentsia."

Piłsudski's epigoni to stem and reverse this marooning ebb of social support and public confidence by such stratagems as the organization of the Camp of National Unity (Obóz Zjednoczenia Narodowego) in 1936–37 proved sterile, since the nation would not be fooled by such blatant attempts to combine advanced demagoguery with continued proprietary exclusivism of political power. (It must also be conceded that among the older Piłsudskist generation there was some reluctance to indulge in this scandalous aping of the totalitarian devices of the country's neighbors.) Only the increasingly ominous international situation, which gave the regime a respite by allowing it to capitalize on the patriotic impulses of the otherwise politically divided nation, averted the serious domestic upheavals toward which Poland was demonstrably heading in the late 1930s as the bourgeois youth became increasingly Rightist-radical, the peasantry and proletariat mutinous, the intelligentsia and aristocracy disillusioned, and the minorities seditious.

It thus appears that the person of Piłsudski was crucial for the viability of the *sanacja* system, though not necessarily—at least not after its first decade of independence—for the survival of the Polish state. Though his own direct supervisory control was focused only on military and foreign affairs and occasionally on "issues of principle" in executive-legislative relations, Piłsudski was altogether basic to the *sanacja* system in both its *bartlowanie* and its "colonel" manifestations. The fourteen cabinets of the nine years between his coup and his death were rotated at his command, and the function of the ministers was not to make general policy but to implement his ideas and to supply the technical expertise which he lacked. Always formidable and often perspicacious, Piłsudski possessed a rare ability to elicit the ardent loyalty and the passionate belief in his genius of otherwise sober and critical persons—even though he treated them curtly and witheringly, indeed savagely, in his later years. These dedicated men of his inner entourage were by no means born flunkeys. Most of them were intelligent, discerning, and self-confident. Piłsudski's hold on their devotion is evidence of an extraordinarily imposing personality. Among the wider public, his prestige was also immense. Without recourse to ranting demagoguery or a contrived "cult of the individual" or, in turn, to chauvinistic flattery of the Polish nation, Piłsudski was nevertheless acknowledged by it as the state's founder and its guardian. Even when disillusionment with the policies, or rather the lack of adequate policies, of his government overtook the masses, they continued to repose vast confidence in the person of the increasingly testy but ultimately selfless, benevolent, and protective *dziadek* (grandfather).

Piłsudski's origins in the Polish-Lithuanian szlachta of the eastern marches undoubtedly contributed much to shaping his impressive personality. Not only his vast Jagiellonian political vision and his deliberate identification with the anti-Muscovite insurrectionary tradition of 1794, 1830, and 1863, but also his psychological readiness to sacrifice much for a great and romantic idea, his contempt for "trading" in business or politics, and his confident habit of command and expectation of being obeyed are all traceable to his consciousness of this genealogical heritage.[14] The subsequent years of organizing the PPS underground revolutionary movement against tsarist Russia instilled the conspiratorial habits of secretiveness and suspiciousness which thereafter remained characteristic of Piłsudski. The military fighting and political maneuvering of the war years 1914–20 left him with a penchant for sudden, seemingly incalculable actions, for the *coup de main,* the preemptive stroke, taken on the basis of a principle, an idea, an attitude, for the achievement of a specific long-range or short-range goal, but never planned or explained in terms of a general program. Then, in the wake of these years of intense strain to impose his will and his dream on a recalcitrant and resisting world, Piłsudski developed a curious interest in spiritualism. He engaged in occult psychic experiments and believed himself to be endowed with intermittent powers of clairvoyance and thought transference.[15] Politically,

[14] Some interwar German commentators subscribing to the "national character" school of interpretation have ascribed to the "Lithuanian strain" in Piłsudski such supposedly un-Polish traits as his circumspection, stubbornness, tenacity, and Spartan asceticism. While this seems forced, it must be acknowledged that he felt most at home with other "easterners" and did not fully understand the ways of the Galicians, Silesians, Poznanians, and Pomeranians (nor they his). See Forst de Battaglia, "Pilsudski," and Henrici, "Der Werdegang des Marschall Pilsudski."

[15] A. Piłsudska, *Wspomnienia,* pp. 278–79, and W. Grzybowski, "Spotkania i rozmowy z Józefem Piłsudskim," p. 99. In 1927 Piłsudski professed to Grzybowski that during the Polish-Soviet campaign of 1920 a disembodied

this expressed itself in—or rather it confirmed—his conviction that he bore a special destiny of responsibility for Poland. It does not, however, appear to have seduced him into basing particular political decisions on any presumed mystical intuition.

Despite these traits of highhandedness, of tortuousness, of abruptness, of messianism, there was a deep vein of humanity in Piłsudski's nature. Behind his contempt for the Polish politicians of his own time, there pulsed a vibrant hope in the next Polish generation. Unlike the neighboring dictators, he was capable of rising above power and politics, of love for his family, of regard for cultural and intellectual achievement. In his first radio broadcast, on the eighth anniversary of independence (November 11, 1926), he gave his listeners not the expected martial exhortation but an impromptu fairy tale for the listening children about his mare Kasztanka (Little Chestnut) amidst the Legionnaires.[16] When the bones of the great romantic poet Słowacki were returned to his homeland from Parisian exile and reinterred in the royal crypt of Kraków's Wawel castle on June 28, 1927, Piłsudski rose to the occasion with a profoundly moving oration—lyrical, dignified, thoughtful, lettered, and utterly apolitical.[17]

Yet it is in political terms that Piłsudski must ultimately be judged. It appears, at first glance, plausible to evaluate him within a comparative framework, to juxtapose him to the leaders of the newly emergent countries of post–World War II vintage on other continents and to match his *sanacja* to their several experiments at "guided democracy." A note of caution is, however, in order. While European statesmen did indeed view Poland after World War I as a country very much "on trial," one that somehow had to justify its existence in a way even beyond what was expected of the other so-called successor states, she was, in fact, and felt herself to be, not a new but a restored state, profoundly conscious of her past political sovereignty and her traditional participation in the culture of Europe. And it is here that Piłsudski's achievement lies. By virtue of his activities before and during World War I, he had been instrumental in the re-creation of this state. Regardless of whether or not his coup was the only

voice had announced to him the death at that very moment but far away of his former adjutant, Major Stanisław Radziwiłł.

[16] Piłsudski, *PZ*, IX, 48–52.

[17] *Ibid.*, pp. 72–76.

possible and feasible resolution to the then darkly disintegrative condition of that state's body politic, it is a fact that the coup's success and its consequences allayed definitively the danger that Poland would indeed prove but an ephemeral *Saisonstaat*. Despite all the socioeconomic failures of the *sanacja* regime, despite its semidictatorial (but not totalitarian) [18] political tendencies, despite Piłsudski's own tortured ambivalences in matters of legality, power, and liberty, and despite his ultimate, and ironic, defeat at the hands of Dmowski, Witos, and Daszyński in the struggle for the minds of the younger interwar generation, Piłsudski must in justice be acknowledged as meriting primary credit for the fact that today the notion of a Europe without a Polish state is no longer conceivable.

---

[18] This is an important distinction. Though circumscribed and badgered, free political parties and trade unions, an independent press, an autonomous judiciary, and parliamentary usages and elections all survived despite such ominous countertrends as Brześć, Bereza Kartuska, the "pacification" of the Ukraine, and official concessions to popular anti-Semitism. While the pre-coup Polish system may have been little better than a semidemocracy, the post-coup government was no worse than a semidictatorship.

APPENDIX

THE COMMUNIST PARTY OF POLAND AND PIŁSUDSKI'S COUP

Whereas the influence of the Communist Party upon Polish political developments in the 1920s was meager, the impact of Piłsudski's coup upon the internal history of the Party was immense. It therefore appears appropriate to append to the main analysis of Piłsudski's coup and its consequences the following discussion of the interrelationship between the Communist Party and the coup.

The Communist Party of Poland (Komunistyczna Partia Polski—KPP) labored under a triple handicap of apparent antipatriotism in the early years of national independence. It was the heir of the Luxemburgist Socialist tradition of rejecting the resurrection of an independent Polish state as allegedly unviable and undesirable. It was identified in popular eyes with the historic national foe, Russia, which as recently as 1920 had once again—this time in Bolshevik rather than tsarist guise—appeared to be determined to crush the newly restored Poland. Finally, it was committed by the international Communist line to advocating the cession of Poland's eastern *kresy*—largely populated, it is true, by non-Poles—to the Soviet Union.[1] This triple burden of seeming sedition proved to be a heavy mortgage upon the Party.[2]

Formed in December, 1918, by the fusion of Rosa Luxemburg's old Social Democracy of the Kingdom of Poland and Lithuania with a part of the so-called Left wing of the then PPS, the KPP, by May, 1926, had

[1] In 1923, indeed, the KPP—presumably under pressure from Moscow—made two serious organizational concessions to this line by authorizing the formation of autonomous Communist subparties for the Western Ukraine and Western White Russia (KPZU and KPZB) in the *kresy*. In the second half of the decade there was to come a period when—at least in terms of membership figures—these two tails threatened to wag the dog by outnumbering the Polish core of the parent KPP. This was at a time when the party line on separatism for the *kresy* had already compromised communism with Polish nationalists but before the initially quite strong Ukrainian and White Russian confidence in the Soviet Union's nationality and peasant policies had been eroded by the Stalinism of the 1930s.

[2] See J. K. Kwiatkowski ("Ren"), *Komuniści w Polsce: Rodowód-taktyka-ludzie* (Brussels, 1946), *passim*.

undergone a series of fluctuations in its line toward various issues and of upheavals in its leadership ranks, which were tortured and bitter even by the prevailing international Communist standards of the day.[3] An exacerbating contribution to these internal rifts was the fact that after February, 1919, the Party was technically illegal and existed in semiunderground conditions of persecution, although it could and did participate in the electoral, parliamentary, and trade union systems through the subterfuge of "front" organizations and labels. By the eve of Piłsudski's coup there were, indeed, six "regular" Communists and at least a dozen identifiable "frontists" or "fellow-travelers" of the Party in the Polish Sejm. Another factor which tended to complicate and sharpen the internal vicissitudes of the KPP was the chronic penchant of its leaders for intervening gratuitously (from Moscow's perspective) in the domestic developments of other Communist parties—for example, defending the opposition leaders Trotsky and Brandler in the Russian and German parties, respectively— thereby eliciting, in turn, Comintern, that is, Russian, purges of the KPP leadership.[4]

In its attitude toward Piłsudski and the Polish parliamentary Left during the years prior to the coup, the KPP oscillated between cautious invitations for joint collaboration against the Right and vituperous denigration of its potential associates. Such fluctuations in the KPP's posture were a function of three factors: (*a*) the convulsions within its own leadership ranks, with the "rightist" majority being readier for collaboration with Piłsudski and the parliamentary Left than the "leftist" minority; (*b*) the presumed waxing and waning of an ostensibly revolutionary situation in Poland; and (*c*) genuine confusion over how to evaluate Piłsudski politically. Was he a "fascist militarist" or the (possibly unwitting) "leader of the democratic petite bourgeoisie"? Was he the Kornilov or the Kerensky of Poland?

In August, 1923, at a time of deepening economic crisis and mounting

[3] For details, see Reguła, chapters II–IV; Carr, Vol. III, Part I, pp. 183–202 and 380–95; and Dziewanowski, *The Communist Party of Poland,* chapters IV–VI.

Until its Third Congress in March, 1925, the Party's official name was Communist Workers' Party of Poland (KPRP)—the reference to workers reflecting the classic Luxemburgist emphasis on the urban proletariat as the essential and necessary bearer of revolution. In this appendix, however, the abbreviation KPP will be used for the sake of convenience to refer to the Party throughout the interwar period.

[4] The Fifth Comintern Congress of June–July, 1924, appointed a special Polish Commission to hold an inquest on the KPP. It was chaired by Stalin, whose report of July 3, 1924, is in his *Sochineniia,* VI (Moscow, 1947), 264– 72. A year later, however, in June, 1925, the KPP leaders were again taking it upon themselves to issue critical pronouncements—which contradicted the current Comintern line—on internal developments in the Bulgarian, French, and German Communist parties. See Reguła, pp. 101–13, 148–49.

political unrest that was shortly to culminate in the insurrectionary events of early November in Kraków and other Polish cities, the Second Congress of the KPP, meeting for safety's sake in Soviet Russia, issued to the PPS and to the Wyzwolenie Peasant Party a restrained invitation for collaboration against Witos' unedifying and ill-omened Right-Center cabinet.[5] At about the same time, the secretary of the Party's Central Committee, a member of the KPP's "rightist" majority, left-handedly but apocalyptically appealed to the PPS and the Piłsudskists to join with the Communists in a united struggle

against the government of the bourgeoisie and the rich peasants. . . . To the Piłsudski parties (in whose readiness to fight we have little belief but in whom wide masses still repose their faith) we offer the united struggle—not for the sake of Piłsudski but of this clear-cut class program. We need not fear that, in the event of victory in our common struggle, we would thereby have merely worked for Piłsudski. A second Moraczewski government, coming to power as a result of a real struggle by the worker and peasant masses against the bourgeoisie, would not be a repetition of the first [of November 18, 1918–January 16, 1919], but would be bound to become a step toward the dictatorship of the proletariat.[6]

From mid-1924 until the second half of 1925, however—an interval during which the "leftist" faction had, with Comintern support, temporarily achieved ascendancy in the Party leadership—such Communist appeals to Piłsudski and the parliamentary Left were to be replaced by undifferentiating execration of all non-Communist political camps.[7] Yet this was not to be the end of such oscillations, for the wheel turned once more before Piłsudski's coup when Moscow reinstalled the Party's "rightists," who alone had some credit with and influence upon the wider masses, to the leadership toward the end of 1925.

During the first half of 1926, as the Skrzyński government, after a hopeful launching, was manifestly foundering, and as Poland, in consequence, was obviously drifting toward a severe political crisis, the freshly reinstated "rightist" leaders of the KPP adopted a stance of militant hostility against the bourgeois-peasant Right-Center coalition. This attitude was combined with a complicated endeavor to "expose" the parliamentary Left as lacking any serious social program while simultaneously "drawing . . . the more radical and sincerely idealistic Piłsudskist elements over . . . to

[5] *KPP: Uchwały i rezolucje,* I, 211–24, 243–51.

[6] E. Brand (pseudonym of Henryk Lauer), "Pilsudskis Glück und Ende," *Kommunistische Internationale,* IV, No. 28–30 (1923), 47–48.

[7] See, for example, G. G. L., "Die KP Polens nach dem fünften Kongress der Komintern," *Kommunistische Internationale,* VI, No. 1 (January, 1925), 105–8; A. Maletzky, "Der weisse Terror in Polen," *ibid.,* No. 1 (January, 1925), 121–25; L. Domski (pseudonym of Henryk Stein), "Die Lage in der KP Polens und die Aufgaben der Partei," *ibid.,* No. 3 (March, 1925), 368–72; L. Domski, "Stabilisierung oder Revolution?" *ibid.,* No. 8 (August, 1925), 897–905.

the revolutionary side" (that is, toward KPP influence).[8] The Communists' last theoretical prognosis on the developing situation was an authoratative statement in the April, 1926, issue of the official Comintern journal by Julian Leński-Leszczyński, a veteran "leftist" who was currently also transforming himself into Stalin's particular Polish mouthpiece. The substance of his statement was that, whereas Piłsudski's social base in Poland was less resilient than that of the National Democrats, it was broader and included the large and radical, albeit confused, petite bourgeoisie, which oscillated between socialism and Bonapartism, between Bolshevism (*sic*) and chauvinism. The Piłsudskist camp, Leński concluded, could indeed be described as a kind of Polish National Bolshevism which the KPP should win over to the side of the proletarian revolution while simultaneously "exposing" its cult-leader, Piłsudski.[9]

In that same month of April, 1926, the Political Bureau of the KPP Central Committee resolved that "we support the struggle of all democratic elements—not excluding the Piłsudskists—to the extent that they combat fascism in the defense of republican-democratic institutions and of worker-peasant demands." [10] Some middle-echelon Party functionaries even went so far as to advance the slogan "a worker-peasant government headed by Piłsudski." Whether they were indeed carried away by genuine euphoria and enthusiasm or whether their motivation—as had been the case with the overtures to Piłsudski of 1923—was less faith in Piłsudski as a genuine revolutionary than the conviction that the KPP must harness the presumed dynamic potential of the current situation by capitalizing on the masses' misplaced but definite faith in their hero Piłsudski is a question to which contradictory answers have been advanced.[11] In any event, it is apparent from Leński's analysis that, on the eve of the May coup, the KPP leaders regarded the Piłsudski camp not only as a lesser evil than its enemies (which was rational) but also as a potential object of Communist manipulation (which was illusory). Piłsudskist agents, in turn, were doing their best to confirm Communist (as well as Socialist and Left peasantist) hopes of benefiting from a victory of the Marshal over his Right-Center enemies in the impending showdown. The leading Piłsudskist "reassurers" in this campaign were Floyar-Rajchman, Sławek, Stamirowski, Stpiczyń-

---

[8] *KPP: Uchwały i rezolucje,* II, 354–58. Carr, Vol. III, Part I, p. 392, notes that this strategy "carried some disconcerting echoes of the 'Schlageter line' of 1923 in Germany."

[9] J. Leschtschinski (Leński-Leszczyński), "Die nächsten Aufgaben der KPP," *Kommunistische Internationale,* VII, No. 4 (April, 1926), 375–78.

[10] Quoted in Reguła, p. 167, who says that the resolution was drafted by the "rightist" leader Adolf Warski-Warszawski.

[11] Cf. *ibid.,* p. 166, with the recollective contribution of Tadeusz Daniszewski to the discussion in Kowalski, "Rozwój sytuacji wewnętrznej w KPP po przewrocie majowym 1926 r.," p. 160.

ski, and Wieniawa-Długoszowski. They spoke of nationalizing industry, purging corrupt elements from the state apparatus, and legalizing the KPP, among other steps. Communist leaders either permitted themselves to be persuaded by these suggestions or developed the equally convenient and comforting theory that Piłsudski was really interested only in army matters and hence again relatively "safe" to support.[12] Indeed, some Polish Communist leaders became concerned lest Piłsudski prove to be politically too aloof and fail to resist in time a coup d'état which they expected to come from the National Democratic–Christian Democratic direction.[13]

Thus when Piłsudski's "armed demonstration" was launched on May 12, 1926, the KPP, despite its self-consciously crisis-oriented sensitivities and rhetoric, was no less taken by surprise than were the other Polish political groups. Yet it reacted with great alacrity. Convinced that neutrality or passivity would not only be "objectively" fatal but would also bring down upon the Party the wrath of the Comintern's Moscow headquarters (as had been the case with the Bulgarian Communist Party in an analogous predicament three years earlier),[14] the KPP leaders immediately summoned the proletariat to render armed support to Piłsudski's "revolutionary armies," called upon all parties of the Left—Polish and ethnic minority, worker and peasant—as "respected comrades and citizens" to form a united front led by a joint worker-peasant committee which should prosecute the civil war against the Right-Center government, and speedily endorsed—indeed, anticipated—the railroad and general strikes.[15] A mass

[12] A. Warski-Warszawski in *Trybuna,* May 8, 1926, cited in Świerzewski, p. 6; also Kowalski, "Rozwój sytuacji wewnętrznej w KPP po przewrocie majowym 1926 r.," pp. 128, 132–33.

[13] See, for example, two pseudonymous reports, carrying Warsaw datelines, in the Comintern's *Internationale Presse-Korrespondenz:* "Faschistische Vorbereitungen in Polen" and "Die Regierungskrise in Polen," in *Inprekorr,* VI, No. 39 (March 9, 1926), 532–33, and No. 66 (April 30, 1926), 996–97, respectively.

[14] In June, 1923, the Bulgarian Communist leadership had been excoriated by Moscow for deciding that an armed clash between the "petit bourgeois" Peasant Union of Alexander Stamboliski and a "military–fascist–big bourgeois" coalition led by Alexander Tsankov was merely an internal struggle within the bourgeoisie, in the outcome of which the proletariat had no stake and the Communist Party no interest. With the Communists standing by as passive observers, the Tsankov group won. Four months later it smashed a belated insurrection which Moscow had forced the Bulgarian Communist Party to launch against it. See J. Rothschild, *The Communist Party of Bulgaria* (New York, 1959), chapters VI–VII. In the Polish case, the Comintern's Polish Commission subsequently agreed that a repetition of the "Bulgarian error" of neutrality would have been disastrous. See "Der Faschistische Umsturz in Polen und die KP Polens," *Kommunistische Internationale,* VII, No. 8 (August-September, 1926), 706.

[15] *Czerwony Sztandar,* May 13, 1926, cited in *Dokumenty chwili,* II, 9, and in Kowalski, "Rozwój sytuacji wewnętrznej w KKP po przewrocie majowym 1926 r.," p. 135. The PPS, incidentally, immediately rejected the KPP appeal

meeting, convened by the Communists in Warsaw's Plac Bankowy (Bank Square) on May 14, expressed "fraternal greetings and assurances of solidarity" to Piłsudski's troops but was nevertheless dispersed by Sławoj-Składkowski's police, as were other Communist attempts to organize the masses or to intervene in the fighting.[16] Even more spectacular was a personal visit by Communist leader and Sejm deputy Jerzy Czeszejko-Sochacki at Piłsudski's headquarters to offer his and the Party's services in the fighting.[17] This overture, too, was rebuffed, and Communist attempts to participate in or to exacerbate the military developments of the coup in the Warsaw, Lublin, and Volhynian areas were suppressed by Piłsudski and the army commanders associated with him.[18] Indeed, not only was Piłsudski able easily to dispose of such Communist efforts at intervention, but he was able to capitalize on them by presenting himself a few days later to the hitherto dubious and skeptical French government as Poland's reliable bulwark against the menace of a Bolshevik take-over.[19]

While the KPP leaders' view of Piłsudski as the "lesser evil" when compared to the Right-Center coalition was valid and their apprehension that aloofness from or hostility toward his "armed demonstration" would alienate the masses was plausible, such outright and unconditional support as they offered him went considerably beyond their own dignity or interest and verged on mere "'tail-endism." They were caught up in a fatally euphoric mood, however, superciliously regarding Piłsudski as the programless and unwitting catalyst of "the revolutionary battle of the masses against the latifundists and the capitalists"—a battle which would soon evolve beyond his intentions and out of his control. "Objectively," therefore, Piłsudski—described as the focus of the aspirations of Poland's petite bourgeoisie (including part of the peasantry and numbers of workers) and as the leader of her democratic intelligentsia—was serving the Communists' purposes.[20] (The reverse, of course, happened in fact to be the case.)

---

for joint action. That the Communists went to Piłsudski's support even before the Socialists is boasted in a report datelined Warsaw, May 17, by Axel (a pseudonym), "Die Maikämpfe in Polen," *Inprekorr,* VI, No. 76 (May 21, 1926), 1209–10.

[16] Ortel, p. 114, and Sławoj-Składkowski, "Wspomnienia z okresu majowego," p. 152. Also *Kurjer Warszawski,* May 15, 1926, and *Dokumenty chwili,* I, 13. There was a report in the *Ilustrowany Kurjer Codzienny,* May 18, 1926, that the PPS had helped the police to break up the Communist demonstrations.

[17] "Jak się zachowali komuniści w dniach majowych?" *Robotnik Polski* (Detroit), January 22, 1928, p. 2; Daszyński, *W pierwszą rocznicę,* p. 31; Fiderkiewicz, *Dobre czasy,* p. 309. Czeszejko-Sochacki was severely reprimanded for this overture by Moscow and eventually, in the 1930s, was liquidated in the Soviet Union, together with the other Polish Communist leaders.

[18] AKL, 2/1; *Ilustrowany Kurjer Codzienny,* May 17, 1926.

[19] Laroche, p. 41.

[20] Axel, "Die Maikämpfe in Polen," *Inprekorr,* VI, No. 76 (May 21, 1926), 1209 (dateline: Warsaw, May 17).

Given this delusive prognosis of the situation, the sudden end of the fighting on May 15 and Piłsudski's rapid and skillful measures (accepted by his Right-Center enemies) to close the coup before it could lead to genuinely revolutionary consequences were bound to hit the KPP leadership like an unpleasantly sobering and disillusioning cold shower—as was keenly reflected in the pages of the Party's daily *Czerwony Sztandar* (Red Standard) from May 16 onward.[21] In Moscow, meanwhile, the prevailing attitude toward Piłsudski, as manifested in both the news reports and the interpretive articles in *Pravda,* had from the beginning of his coup been far more cautious—perhaps because the Bolshevik leaders of the Comintern and the Soviet government were naturally inclined to be particularly concerned over the foreign-policy implications of a bid for power by this notorious Polish Russophobe. While the fighting was still in progress, Karl Radek began a series of sober—and largely accurate—analytical background articles on the divisions in Poland's army and society, concluding a few days later with some wishful but hardly triumphant and barely hopeful reflections to the effect that history might nevertheless have some damaging surprises in store for the seemingly victorious Piłsudski, "the last Mohican of Polish romanticism." [22] Such sour-grapes witticisms notwithstanding, there is no doubt of Radek's awareness that Piłsudski had, for the moment at least, outflanked and exposed the Polish Communists. On May 15 the Comintern's Polish Commission, while agreeing with the decision of the KPP "rightist" leaders that passive neutrality in relation to the coup would have been disastrous, insisted that unconditional support for Piłsudski was also impermissible and that the KPP should dominate the entire situation by taking the lead in the fight against the Witos regime and in the organization of a bloc of all Leftist and democratic forces, thereby forcing Piłsudski toward dependence on this Communist-led phalanx and simultaneously "deepening" the conflict toward a real, social revolutionary, civil war. This was, of course, a utopian counsel of revolutionary perfection, far beyond the capacity or the opportunity of the KPP to implement, and it was likely extended more as a gesture of ideological piety and as an alibi for the Comintern than as a serious contribution to political strategy. A day later, with the fighting in Warsaw concluded and the Piłsudski-Bartel government installed, the Comintern's Polish Commission decided with some alacrity that KPP support for the coup had been an unmitigated blunder.[23] The Soviet Commissariat of Foreign Affairs was simultaneously manifesting considerable anxiety about the possible implications and consequences for Soviet security of Piłsud-

21 *Czerwony Sztandar,* cited in Ortel, p. 114.
22 Radek in *Pravda* (Moscow), May 15, 18, 28, and June 2, 1926 (all front-page articles). See also Radek and Stefanovich, *passim.*
23 Unpublished archival documents cited in Kowalski, "Rozwój sytuacji wewnętrznej w KPP po przewrocie majowym 1926 r.," p. 135.

ski's return to power in Poland.[24] Three weeks later, on June 8, Stalin—who appears to have been held responsible for the Polish debacle by the recently united opposition coalition of Trotsky, Zinoviev, and Kamenev within the Soviet leadership—utilized the occasion of a speech to railroad workers in Tiflis, Soviet Georgia, to criticize the KPP for having supported Piłsudski and to place the entire responsibility for this alleged error on the Polish leadership. Interestingly enough, in this speech—in which, incidentally, he gave an incisive and largely correct, if brief, analysis of the social and political antagonisms between the Piłsudskists and their *endecja* enemies and predicted that, though the former had proved stronger militarily, the latter would eventually trump them ideologically—Stalin still referred to Piłsudski and his camp as petit bourgeois rather than (as subsequently became compulsory in Communist rhetoric) as fascistic.[25] Later in June the Comintern's Polish Commission analyzed the KPP's "opportunist errors" of May at great length, and in July the Executive Committee of the Communist International (ECCI) formally criticized and condemned them.[26]

Despite this virtually unanimous condemnation by leading Soviet personalities and Comintern bodies, the "rightist" majority of the KPP Central Committee initially insisted that its "line" toward Piłsudski's coup had been, "by and large," correct. Indeed, at the first post-coup Central Committee meeting, held in Danzig on May 23–26, 1926, the leadership not only reaffirmed its commitment to its recent actions but instructed the six-member Communist Sejm delegation to vote for Piłsudski in the impending presidential election, despite Communist disappointment with his moderation, lest the KPP incur the wrath of the masses by failing to support their hero.[27] Though this decision was overruled by the Comintern's Polish Commission and the six Communist deputies instead cast their presidential votes on May 31 and June 1 for their own imprisoned comrade Stanisław Łańcucki and then for the fellow-traveling Independent Peasant Party deputy Alfred Fiderkiewicz, the KPP nevertheless considered it politic and necessary to issue a rather embarrassed public

[24] See above, p. 302.

[25] I. V. Stalin, *Sochineniia*, VIII (Moscow, 1948), 168–72. Even before Stalin personally took to the lists in this controversy, one of his current shield-bearers in the Comintern, the German Communist Ernst Thälmann, had published an angry and rather ineptly argued attack, "On the Tactics of the KPP," in *Pravda* (Moscow), May 30, 1926, p. 1.

[26] The analysis by the Comintern's Polish Commission of June, 1926—an interesting and quite impressive document—was published as "Der Faschistische Umsturz in Polen und die KP Polens," *Kommunistische Internationale*, VII, No. 8 (August–September, 1926), 701–13. See also the resolution of the Polish Commission of January 21, 1927, reprinted in *KPP: Uchwały i rezolucje*, II, 377–78.

[27] Reguła, pp. 172–73, and Kowalski, "Rozwój sytuacji wewnętrznej w KPP po przewrocie majowym 1926 r.," pp. 136–37.

declaration "to the workers and peasants" virtually apologizing for not supporting Piłsudski's candidacy.[28] The Warsaw organization of the KPP even participated—though without Central Committee authorization—in a parade honoring Piłsudski which the PPS had organized in the brief interval on May 31 between Piłsudski's election to, and declination of, the presidency. At a Central Committee session of June 10–12, the "rightist" majority—albeit now on the defensive—again insisted that, as Piłsudski had acted as leader of the radicalized petite bourgeoisie in May, the KPP policy of supporting him had been, "in general," correct.[29]

During subsequent months, however, under the compound impact of disillusionment with Piłsudski and admonitions from Moscow, the KPP reversed its evaluation of the May coup and its own stance at the time. By the end of June, the Communist and "frontist" deputies in the Sejm were using its pulpits as a forum from which to denounce the Piłsudski-Bartel regime as having betrayed the expectations of the masses who had put it in power. During July they attacked the government's proposed constitutional amendments. By August and September the "rightist" Central Committee leaders were in retreat and were prepared to concede that in May they had overlooked the international situation and hence the dangerous implications for the Soviet Union of Piłsudski's British-endorsed victory, and to admit that they had erroneously exaggerated the strength and function of the petite bourgeoisie in a revolutionary situation. By now, however, their "leftist" rivals, with the bit in their teeth and confident of Comintern, that is, Soviet, support, refused to accept such a *mea culpa* as adequate and in October demanded a thorough overhaul of the leadership. Interestingly enough, however, though the Soviet rulers of the Comintern were also condemning the May *policy* of the Polish "rightists," they initially refrained from imposing a purge of the *persons* who had conducted it—perhaps because the leader of these "rightists," Adolf Warski-Warszawski, took upon himself the responsibility for the May fiasco and made no attempt to trace it back to Moscow.[30]

Thanks to this initial Muscovite abstention from administrative intervention in the KPP's internal rift, the "rightist" numerical majority on the Central Committee felt able to fight back and to charge that the "leftist" demand for a leadership purge could only provoke chaos and fractional

[28] "Erklärung der kommunistischen Abgeordneten zu den Staatspräsidentenwahlen in Polen," *Inprekorr,* VI, No. 82 (June 8, 1926), 1307.

[29] Kowalski, "Rozwój sytuacji wewnętrznej w KPP po przewrocie majowym 1926 r.," pp. 137–38.

[30] Dziewanowski, *The Communist Party of Poland,* p. 330, n. 5, cites material in the Trotsky Archives at Harvard University in support of this suggestion. There is a brief hint to the same effect in L. Trotsky, *Moya Zhizn,* II (Berlin, 1930), 273–74. On the other hand, Reguła, p. 179, says that Moscow, having already inflicted several leadership upheavals on the KPP in previous years, feared that yet one more might so demoralize the Party—coming on the heels of the May debacle—as possibly to prove fatal.

strife. In the absence of direct Comintern intervention, the quarrel dragged on at least until the Sixth KPP Central Committee Plenum of June, 1929 (and by another reckoning until the Fifth KPP Congress of August-September, 1930), when the "leftists," benefiting from and capitalizing on the general Comintern swing toward the ultra-leftist line of "social fascism," of disdaining all non-Communist forces of the democratic Left as more dangerous even than the overt Right and fascist camps, at last captured control of the KPP and ousted their rivals from all leading positions. The struggle had been characterized by extreme personal bitterness and ideological hairsplitting—probably an ironic consequence of the fact that the points ostensibly at issue, that is, the responsibility for the "May error" and the proper definition of the Piłsudski camp as "fascist" or "petit bourgeois verging toward fascism," were rather synthetic. The strain of the quarrel upon the Party may be gauged from Bukharin's admission at the Sixth Comintern Congress in the summer of 1928 that, but for pressure from the Moscow international headquarters, the KPP would have formally split in two. As it was, the two sides conducted a virtual guerrilla war against each other's cells and committees.[31] The denouement of the struggle was destined to be grotesquely calamitous. In the mid-1930s, during the Great Purge, the surviving leaders of both KPP factions were indiscriminately liquidated by Stalin. No other Communist party was as heavily decimated in this bloodbath as the Polish one.

In addition to the stark tragedy of its eventual extirpation at Stalin's hands, yet another historic irony was in store for the KPP. With the onset of the Great Depression, the Party and its "fronts" came for the first time to enjoy some substantial appeal to, and influence upon, the masses of indigent Polish peasants and unemployed workers, as well as the younger intelligentsia.[32] But just at this very moment, when a united front with

[31] The polemical literature spewed forth from this rift is vast and repetitive. Some items were cited in footnote 7, above. Others are: A. Warski, "Die Vierte Konferenz der KPP," *Kommunistische Internationale,* VII, No. 2 (February, 1926), 132–38; "Erklärung abgegeben von der Minderheit des ZK der KPP," and "Erklärung der Delegation der KPP an das Präsidium der Siebten Erweiterten Exekutive der KI," *Inprekorr,* VI, No. 155 (December 21, 1926), 2782–83; speeches by various KPP delegates to the Seventh Enlarged ECCI Plenum, November–December, 1926, in *Inprekorr,* VI, No. 152 (December 14, 1926), 2731; No. 160 (December 30, 1926), 2922–23; VII, No. 4 (January 11, 1927), 92; "Das Ergebnis der Parteidiskussion der KPP," *Kommunistische Internationale,* VIII, No. 40 (October 5, 1927), 1933–43; EKKI (ECCI), "Offener Brief an die Mitglieder der KPP," *ibid.,* IX, No. 42 (October 17, 1928), 2584–95. Many hitherto unpublished aspects of the rift were exposed in the recent symposium led by Kowalski, "Rozwój sytuacji wewnętrznej w KPP po przewrocie majowym 1926 r.," especially pp. 138–52.

[32] Strobel, pp. 70–85. Even the Piłsudskist historian Pobóg-Malinowski, *Najnowsza historia,* II, 562–65, 638–41, concedes an increase in Communist mass support at this time. The elections of 1930 were unfree, and hence their official statistics fail to reflect this accretion of Communist influence.

radical peasantist and Socialist parties might have brought with it an effective accretion of the KPP's power, the twin victories of the "leftist" faction organizationally and of the "social fascist" line ideologically propelled the Party into a sectarian line of self-isolation. The main enemy was now declared to be not the increasingly rabid *endecja,* not even Piłsudski's hardening *sanacja,* but rather the democratic Center-Left coalition, which was denigrated by the Communists with limitless vilification and sneering contempt even at the very moment its leaders were being tortured and humiliated in the cells of the Brześć prison-fortress.[33] The wheel had thus turned full circle. When the KPP had attempted to associate itself with the Piłsudskist and parliamentary Left coalition intermittently between 1923 and 1926, it was still too weak and disreputable among the Polish population to exercise effective leverage. By the time it came to enjoy a modest degree of general influence during the Depression years, it refused to exploit its opportunities rationally and instead deliberately cut itself off from its potential allies. By the time this policy was reversed, the Party stood on the eve of its assassination at Stalin's hands. In sum, thanks to its own errors and the liabilities flowing from its dependence on Moscow, the KPP consistently stood at variance with the demands of the "objective situation" during the interwar decades.

[33] *KPP: Uchwały i rezolucje,* Vol. II, chapter V, *passim; Inprekorr* and *Kommunistische Internationale,* 1928–34, *passim;* Reguła, chapter VI, especially pp. 243–44.

BIOGRAPHICAL REGISTER

ANDERS, Władysław (1892–   ), in World War II, was commander of the Polish army recruited on Soviet soil in 1941 and evacuated the next year to the Near East and thence to North Africa. In 1944 he commanded the Polish Second Corps at the battle of Monte Cassino in Italy and in 1945 was commander in chief of all Polish armed forces owing allegiance to the government-in-exile in London. At the end of the war Anders declined repatriation to Communist Poland and chose exile in Great Britain.

ANUSZ, Antoni (1884–1935), had belonged to the Piłsudskist fraction of the prewar PPS as a young man and had been exiled to Siberia by the tsarist authorities for his participation in the revolutionary events of 1905–7. Returning to Poland in 1918, he became a high official in the Ministry of Industry and Commerce, joined the Wyzwolenie Peasant Party (before the war he had been a Socialist), and was elected on its label to the Sejms of 1919–22 and 1922–27. During the Polish-Soviet campaign of 1920 he was a member of the Council for the Defense of the State. In 1928 Anusz was elected to the Sejm on the BBWR label.

BARTEL, Kazimierz (1882–1941). During the 1930s, as Piłsudski's system became increasingly semidictatorial and culminated in the authoritarian "colonels' regime" of the last half of the decade, Bartel, having been prime minister of five cabinets, withdrew to his professorship, from which he criticized the disturbing fascistic and anti-Semitic trends then gaining ground in Polish society. Embittered, he declined a portfolio offered him after Piłsudski's death by Poland's last civilian prewar premier, Marian Zyndram-Kościałkowski, in the spring of 1936. The Germans murdered Bartel together with his professorial colleagues in Lwów on July 3, 1941.

BECK, Józef (1894–1944), a Legionnaire and POW veteran, had been Polish military attaché in Paris and Brussels (1922–23) but was withdrawn on French insistence under obscure circumstances. Active in Piłsudski's 1926 coup, he had then served as chief of the Marshal's personal staff in the War Ministry. As deputy premier after August, 1930, Beck coordinated cabinet work for Piłsudski. In December, 1930, he became vice-minister of foreign affairs and full minister of that portfolio from November 2, 1932, until the Polish catastrophe of September, 1939— a period during which he conducted a highly controversial foreign policy. He was also a senator after 1935. Having retreated into Rumania with Mościcki, Rydz-Śmigły (*q.v.*), *et al.* in September, 1939, Beck died there of tuberculosis on June 5, 1944.

BNIŃSKI, Adolf (1884–1942), after his defeat as the Right's candidate for president in 1926, remained *wojewoda* of Poznania until 1928. He subsequently was a senator from 1935 to 1938, president of Poland's Catholic Action, chairman of the landowners' association, and, from 1937 to 1939, leader of the Conservative Union. The delegate of Sikorski's (*q.v.*) government-in-exile to the Polish underground, Bniński was executed by the Germans on July 7, 1942.

BOERNER, Ignacy (1875–1933), son of a Lutheran pastor and an engineer by training, was an early member of the Piłsudskist wing of the prewar PPS. Very active in Russian Poland in the revolutionary year 1905 (he had headed a so-called insurgent republic in the Sandomierz-Opatów area), Boerner had served in the Legions during World War I and at its conclusion negotiated, on Piłsudski's behalf, the peaceful withdrawal of the German army from Congress, that is, ex-Russian, Poland. In 1919 he conducted Piłsudski's secret negotiations with the Bolsheviks at the height of the Denikin threat to both sides. Polish military attaché in Moscow (1923–24), military liaison officer to the Ministry of Industry and Commerce (1925–29), an acknowledged expert on war industry, he served as minister of posts from April, 1929, until his death.

BOJKO, Jakub (1857–1943), unlike many other politicians of the peasant movement, never cut his village roots or became too sophisticated for them. Though personally religious, he attacked the clergy for siding politically with the landlords. With Stapiński and Bolesław Wysłouch (by 1925–27 a senator belonging to Bartel's Klub Praca), Bojko had been one of the original leaders of the Galician peasant movement in the last quarter of the nineteenth century. He had served in the Galician Diet and the Austrian Reichsrat before World War I. As a member of Piast, he was vice-marshal of the Polish Constituent Sejm (1919–22) and vice-marshal of the Senate (1922–27). In 1928 he was elected to the Sejm on the BBWR label. Retiring from politics in 1935, he died in his native village in his eighty-sixth year.

BORTNOWSKI, Władysław (1891–   ), as a senior general, was in command of those Polish forces which occupied Czechoslovakia's part of the Cieszyn area of Silesia at the time of the Munich crisis in October, 1938.

In September, 1939, at the beginning of World War II, he led the Pomeranian army group which, together with Kutrzeba's Poznanian army group, flung itself in a violent counterattack against the Germans during the second week of the campaign, delaying and temporarily threatening their advance on Warsaw. Bortnowski was wounded and captured. After the war he took up residence in the United States.

BORUTA-SPIECHOWICZ, Mieczysław (1894–   ), as a general in World War II, was first active in an underground organization in the Soviet-occupied part of Poland immediately after the September, 1939, catastrophe. Then he commanded a division in Anders' army. After its transfer in 1942 from the Soviet Union to the Near East, Boruta-Spiechowicz was detached to take over the command of another Polish corps then being organized in Scotland. His relations with Anders appear to have been somewhat frictional.

CAR, Stanisław (1882–1938), minister of justice in 1928–29 and 1930, was elected to the Sejm in 1930 on the BBWR label and became the chamber's vice-marshal and chief *rapporteur* of its Constitutional Commission. In this latter capacity Car emerged as the primary legal architect of the Polish constitution of April 23, 1935. He was marshal of the Sejm during the last three years of his life, 1935–38.

CZECHOWICZ, Gabriel (1876–1938), after his break with the Piłsudskist camp in 1930, founded a short-lived Polish Radical Party. His last political affiliation was with the oppositionist Stronnictwo Pracy (Party of Labor—not to be confused with Bartel's earlier Klub Praca), an amalgam of former Christian Democrats, National Laborites, and "Hallerites." Czechowicz joined it in 1937 but died in January, 1938. Some of his earlier—and fairly radical—critiques of Polish economic policy had been published under the pseudonym "G. Leliwa." He had been a high officer in the Finance Ministry since 1919. As director of its Tax Department in 1925, he had organized the national administration of taxation and was undersecretary at the time of his first nomination as finance minister by Bartel on May 15, 1926.

CZERWIŃSKI, Sławomir (1885–1931), a Protestant, a member of Piłsudski's prewar Rifleman organization, had been a director of Polish gymnasiums in Piotrków and Ostrowiec during World War I. In independent Poland he had remained in the field of education, first as a functionary in the Ministry (1919–23), then as "visitor," that is, inspector, of teacher-training seminaries (1923–28), then as vice-minister of education (1928–29), before becoming minister from April, 1929, until his death on August

4, 1931. In his capacity as minister, Czerwiński sought to instill into the educational curriculum a Polish Great Power cult, as well as the near-deification of Piłsudski.

DĄB-BIERNACKI, Stefan (1890–   ), an army inspector after 1930, commanded an army corps in the September, 1939, campaign but was alleged by his nominal subordinate Anders (*q.v.*) to have psychologically collapsed under the pressure of events (Anders, pp. 14–16). Upon making his way to France (via Hungary) after the surrender of his corps, he was arrested by Sikorski (*q.v.*) and held for a time in prison.

DĄBSKI, Jan (1880–1931). A cofounder and, until his break with Witos in 1923, a leader of the Piast Peasant Party, Dąbski formed the Stronnictwo Chłopskie in 1926 and led it until his death following a beating by *sanacja* toughs. In 1920–21 he had been vice-minister of foreign affairs, in which capacity he had led the Polish delegation at the Riga peace negotiations with the Soviets. He was vice-marshal of the Sejm in 1928–30.

DASZYŃSKI, Ignacy (1866–1936), had become a Socialist in the 1880s, prior to his university studies at Kraków and Zurich. Editor since 1894 of the Galician Socialist journal *Naprzód* (Forward), he soon earned a reputation as the "tribune" of Polish socialism owing to his journalistic and especially his oratorical skills. A member of Piłsudski's independence-oriented wing of the PPS after the 1906 split, a patron of Piłsudski's Rifleman organization before World War I (thanks to his influence as deputy to the Vienna Reichsrat since 1897 and Kraków municipal councilor since 1902), at the close of the war Daszyński headed the abortive Lublin provisional government of Socialists and radical peasantists founded on November 7, 1918. A week later he was asked by Piłsudski to be Poland's first prime minister. The vigorous opposition of the Right, however, forced Daszyński's withdrawal in favor of his less controversial PPS colleague Moraczewski (*q.v.*), who formed what is conventionally regarded as the first official Polish cabinet on November 18, 1918. In subsequent months, Daszyński supported the Piłsudskist position in constitutional and foreign political issues, that is, he argued for a strong executive and an expansionist, federalistic, policy toward the east. A Sejm deputy since 1919, he was vice-premier during the crisis of the Polish-Soviet campaign of 1920, vice-marshal of the Sejm (1922–28), marshal of that chamber (1928–30), and throughout a leading figure in the PPS—in which capacity he had actively supported Piłsudski's May, 1926, coup. A brilliant orator but an unoriginal thinker, Daszyński probably made his most significant contribution to modern Polish history through his founding in December, 1922 (in response to the murder of Narutowicz), of a Polish Workers' University (TUR) to raise the cultural and intellectual level of the proletariat. Poor health forced Daszyński's withdrawal from active politics in 1931, and he died on October 31, 1936.

DĘBSKI, Jan (1889–), was chairman of the Piast parliamentary delegation for 1928–30 and after 1932 was active in the Polish Naval and Colonial League (headed by General Orlicz-Dreszer, *q.v.*).

DUTKIEWICZ, Feliks (1872–1932), had been exiled to Siberia by the tsarist regime for political subversion before World War I but had nevertheless been permitted to function as a judge in Irkutsk and Krasnoyarsk. By 1917–18 he was in Bessarabia, where he commanded the militia in Kishinev (Chişinău). Representing the local Poles in the Bessarabian Diet, he was the only minority deputy to support the affiliation of the province to Rumania. In independent Poland he was a judge or functionary in the Justice Ministry until his death on May 25, 1932. As acting minister (1929–30), he insisted on the independence of courts and procurators from government and politics.

FABRYCY, Kazimierz (1888–1958), was second (1926–31) and first (1931–34) vice-minister of war, and then became an army inspector. He commanded the Carpathian army group in the September, 1939, campaign and later served with the Polish forces in the Near East. He died in London.

GALICA, Andrzej (1873–1945), served as a Piłsudskist Sejm deputy and senator throughout the 1930s. Toward the close of the interwar period, he belonged to the extreme wing of the Camp of National Unity (see the entry for S. Skwarczyński). Galica had retired from the army in 1931 and died in Poland at war's end without having held a command either in the September, 1939, campaign or subsequently with the underground Home Army (Armia Krajowa).

GĄSIOROWSKI, Janusz (1889–1946), served as chief of the General Staff from December, 1931, until January, 1936, and commanded a division in the September, 1939, campaign.

GLIWIC, Hipolit (1878–1943), ceased to be a cabinet minister within a few weeks of the 1926 coup but remained politically influential thanks to his industrial-entrepreneurial connections. He was vice-marshal of the Senate and chairman of its budget committee on behalf of the Piłsudskist camp in 1928–30, but during the late 1930s he was affiliated with the oppositionist Stronnictwo Pracy (Party of Labor). Active in the civilian activities of the underground during World War II, he was arrested by the Germans on April 9, 1943, took poison, and died the next day.

GRABSKI, Stanisław (1871–1949), and Władysław (1874–1938). During World War II, as chairman of the Polish exile parliament in London from 1942 to 1945, Stanisław Grabski became a leading protagonist for Polish-Soviet collaboration as essential to Poland's continued existence. He returned to Poland at war's end and became vice-chairman of the Communist-sponsored Krajowa Rada Narodowa (National Council of the Homeland) in 1945–46, the relatively free years before the full totalitarian, Stalinist crackdown. He died in Warsaw in May, 1949. His brother Władysław, the former premier, had died there in March, 1938.

GRAŻYŃSKI, Michał (1890–1966), was associated with the Naprawa (Reform) group within the Piłsudskist camp. In the late 1930s he urged more dynamism and political liberalism upon the increasingly rigid and authoritarian "colonels' regime." He became minister of propaganda (a portfolio innovated at the outbreak of the war) on September 3, 1939, and after the Polish collapse made his way to France.

GRZĘDZIŃSKI, January (1892–   ), formerly Piłsudski's adjutant, broke with the "colonels' regime" after the Marshal's death, founding (1936) and editing the oppositional weekly journal *Czarno na Białym* (Black on White). In 1965 he republished his reminiscences of the May, 1926, coup and was in political and legal difficulties with the Polish government.

HALLER, Józef (1873–1960), after his retirement from the army in 1926, was active in political opposition to Piłsudski and served as minister of education in Sikorski's London government-in-exile from 1939 to 1943. He died in London.

HOŁÓWKO, Tadeusz (1889–1931), was born in Semipalatinsk, Central Asia, where his father had been exiled by the tsarist Russian authorities for participating in the Polish insurrection of 1863. He had been recruited into Piłsudski's PPS–Revolutionary Fraction while a student in St. Petersburg and Kraków before World War I. During the war he had served in Piłsudski's underground POW and had also retained and deepened his Socialist affiliations. In November, 1918, he had been vice-minister of propaganda in the Left-wing provisional government which Daszyński (*q.v.*) briefly organized in Lublin before Piłsudski's return to Warsaw from German internment. Hołówko had also helped edit the radical manifesto issued by that abortive government. Subsequently devoting himself to the ethnic minorities problem and to developing a federalistic solution to Poland's relations with the Lithuanians, Ukrainians, and White Russians, he was twice nominated by the PPS for Sejm elections (1919, 1922) and was soon elected to the Party's Supreme Council and Central Executive Committee (1924). Early in 1925 he went to Paris for a year of study but returned toward the end of the year and participated in the 1926 coup. From 1927 to 1930 Hołówko was head of the Eastern Department of the Ministry of Foreign Affairs, in which capacity he worked strenuously for Polish-Ukrainian reconciliation. Elected to the Sejm in 1930 on the BBWR ticket, he became vice-president of the bloc under Sławek. Yet Hołówko was deeply disturbed and almost provoked to break with the government by its mistreatment of Left and Center opposition leaders illegally imprisoned in September, 1930, in the fortress-jail at Brześć. Less than a year later, on August 29, 1931, he was assassinated—ironically, by Ukrainian nationalists determined on unconditional independence for their nation rather than for a federal relationship with Poland.

HUBICKI, Stefan (1877–1955), a medical doctor by training, had been active in the Polish independence movement before World War I and been repeatedly arrested by the tsarist authorities. Drafted in 1917 into the First Polish Corps in the Russian army, he had utilized this opportunity for organizational work on behalf of Piłsudski's underground POW. In May, 1918, he was involved in an abortive plot to arrest the corps commander, General Dowbór-Muśnicki, to prevent his capitulation to the Germans. Hubicki then served the Piłsudskist cause in Moscow and Paris during 1918 and 1919 and was a senior medical officer in the Polish army (1919–28), vice-minister of labor (1929), and minister of labor and social welfare (1930–34). Under the dual pressure of the Depression and the government's deflationary response to it, his ministry proved unable effectively to alleviate the social and economic misery of its proletarian "constituency." In Hungary during World War II, Hubicki helped Polish refugees and facilitated Marshal Rydz-Śmigły's (*q.v.*) clandestine return to Poland from Rumania in the summer of 1941. Fleeing before the Germans into Slovakia in 1944, Hubicki returned to Poland at the end of the war to function for another decade as a provincial doctor.

JAWOROWSKI, Rajmund (1885–1941), had been a militant in Piłsudski's prewar Revolutionary Fraction of the PPS, in which capacity the tsarist police had exiled him to Siberia in 1906–9. A Rifleman, then a Legionnaire and POW activist during World War I, he had again served at the front in the Polish-Soviet campaign of 1920 and been a member of the Polish delegation to the subsequent Riga peace conference in 1921. A Sejm deputy (1922–30), vice-president (1919–26) and president

(1927–31) of the Warsaw Municipal Council, chairman of the PPS Warsaw District Committee and member of the Party's Central Executive Committee from 1919 until the schism of 1928, Jaworowski was to reunite his Revolutionary Fraction with the parent PPS in the underground resistance movement against the Germans after September, 1939.

JÓZEWSKI, Henryk (1892–   ), born in Kiev, knew and understood Ukrainians and their aspirations. A POW veteran, he was Piłsudski's personal choice as *wojewoda* of Volhynia both before and after his stint (December, 1929–June, 1930) as interior minister. Having turned the province into a relative showpiece of Polish-Ukrainian amity, he was dismissed as a result of Rightist and military pressure in June, 1938.

KLEEBERG, Franciszek (1888–1943), in 1939 commanded the last operational Polish field forces to remain in combat on Polish soil. After battles with both Soviet and German armies, he finally surrendered to the latter on October 5, when his ammunition was exhausted. He was killed by the Germans for conducting conspiratorial activities while a prisoner of war.

KOZŁOWSKI, Leon (1892–1944), a professional archaeologist and untalented politician, had served in the Legions and the POW during World War I, after which he became professor of prehistory at the Jan Kazimierz University in Lwów. A BBWR Sejm deputy after 1928, he served as minister of land reform (1930–32), as vice-minister (undersecretary of state) of finance (1932–34), briefly as interior minister in June, 1934, and as prime minister from May 15, 1934, until March 28, 1935. Thereafter he became a senator and a partisan of Sławek's (*q.v.*) intraregime opposition to the government after Piłsudski's death. It was during Kozłowski's premiership that the notorious Polish concentration camp at Bereza Kartuska was organized. His role during World War II was to be enigmatic and controversial. Captured by the Soviets at Lwów in September, 1939, he was held prisoner there and in Moscow until released in August, 1941, to join the Anders (*q.v.*) army then being organized on Soviet soil. Kozłowski made no secret of his bitter feelings against the Soviets, in whose prisons he had lost an eye and several teeth, and in November, 1941, he crossed over to the German lines, for which a Polish court-martial condemned him to death *in absentia*. On January 11, 1942, he gave a press conference in Berlin, arranged by the German Ministry of Foreign Affairs, at which he vigorously attacked the Soviet regime without, however, endorsing the Nazi one. He died in Berlin under somewhat obscure circumstances, allegedly of wounds suffered during an Allied air raid.

KUKIEL, Marian (1885–   ), in World War II, succeeded Sikorski (*q.v.*) as defense minister of the Polish government-in-exile (London) after the latter's death in an airplane crash on July 4, 1943. At the end of the war Kukiel remained in England, becoming director of the General Sikorski Historical Institute and president of the Polish Historical Society.

KURCYUSZ, Tadeusz (1881–1943), in World War II, controlled for a time the Narodowe Siły Zbrojne (National Armed Forces), a fascistic underground band which concentrated on killing Communists and Jews rather than fighting Germans. He died in Warsaw.

KURYŁOWICZ, Adam (1890–   ), a member of the PPS since 1909, of its Supreme Council from 1921 to 1939, and of its Central Executive Committee from 1928 to 1939, was to head his Socialist railroad workers' union until 1937. A Sejm deputy (1922–30, 1934–35), he was active during World War II in the Polish resistance against the Germans, who imprisoned him. At the end of the war Kuryłowicz rejoined the PPS Supreme Council and Central Executive Committee, resumed his leadership of the railroad workers' union, and was vice-chairman (1945–46) and secretary-general (1947–48) of the central Polish trade union organization. A member of the National Council of the Homeland (1945–47), a Sejm deputy (1947–50), minister of labor and social welfare (1946–47), Kuryłowicz was a member of the Central Committee of the new Polish United Workers' Party (Communists and Socialists) from 1948 to 1954.

KWIATKOWSKI, Eugeniusz (1888–   ), reemerged after Piłsudski's death as finance minister and vice-premier in charge of all economic matters. In the last prewar years, 1935–39, Kwiatkowski devoted himself to the rapid state-capitalistic industrialization of Poland. He spent the war years in Rumanian internment but returned to Poland in 1945 to serve for two years as director of a governmental commission on coast and harbor problems.

MAKOWSKI, Wacław (1880–1942), was elected Sejm marshal after the last prewar Polish elections in November, 1938. He fled to Rumania in September, 1939, and died in Bucharest in December, 1942.

MATAKIEWICZ, Maksymilian (1875–1940), a colleague of Bartel and Mościcki at the Lwów Polytechnic, had been a professor there since 1908 and subsequently also dean and rector. He served in the Austrian army in World War I and in 1918–19 participated in the Polish defense of Lwów against the Ukrainians. He died there on February 3, 1940.

MATUSZEWSKI, Ignacy (1891–1946), a veteran of both the tsarist army and Piłsudski's POW—he had been twice wounded during World War I and had helped organize the Polish military units in Russia after her 1917 revolution—had then served in independent Poland as military expert on the Polish delegation to the Riga peace conference with the Soviets in 1921 and as military attaché in Rome in 1924. Leaving active military service, he had been a director of a department in the Foreign Ministry (1926–28) and envoy to Hungary (1928–29) before taking over the Finance Ministry (April, 1929–May, 1931). A contributing editor to the *Gazeta Polska* in the 1930s, Matuszewski helped bring the Polish gold reserves to safety in the West after the September, 1939, catastrophe. Settling in the United States during World War II, he was a tireless Cassandra, warning against the Sikorski government's policy of attempted rapprochement with the Soviet Union. He died in New York City.

MODELSKI, Izydor (1888–1962), upon his enforced retirement from the army in 1927, was active in the Sikorski-Haller opposition to the Piłsudski regime. During World War II he became vice-minister of war under Sikorski (*q.v.*) in the Polish government-in-exile in London. In July, 1945, he returned to Poland to take up service under the other, Soviet-sponsored Polish government (which Great Britain and the United States recognized on July 5). In October, 1945, Modelski was sent by that government to Great Britain to head the military mission for the repatriation of Polish troops in the West. In May, 1946, he came to the United States as Poland's military and air attaché. He resigned from these functions on August 15, 1948, simultaneously requesting political asylum in the United States. See U.S. Congress, House Committee on Un-American Activities, 81st Congress, 1st Session, Hearings of March 31 and April 1, 1949.

MORACZEWSKI, Jędrzej (1870–1944), by profession a railroad engineer, was a PPS deputy to the Vienna Reichsrat (1907–18) and a Legionnaire and POW activist in World War I. Minister of communications in Daszyński's (*q.v.*) radical Lublin provisional government in November, 1918, he had then been appointed independent Poland's first prime minister by Piłsudski. After his expulsion from the PPS in 1927, Moraczewski founded—with government backing—a new trade union organization in 1931 to compete with the one standing under the aegis of the PPS. Known as the Association of Professional Associations (Związek Związków Zawodowych), it enjoyed some support among teachers and white-collar workers. In 1936, after Piłsudski's death, it broke with the regime, which it accused of antilabor bias and thuggery. The government, in turn, persecuted the organization and frequently confiscated its paper, *Front Robot-*

niczy (Labor Front). See Moraczewski, "Nieznany list." Moraczewski was killed on August 8, 1944, aged seventy-four, in the course of the German-Soviet fighting around Sulejówek, where he had long lived as Piłsudski's neighbor.

MORAWSKI, Witold (1896–1944), a colonel, was fated to be executed by the Germans in the Mauthausen concentration camp for having organized escapes and resistance by Polish prisoners of war as well as for involvement in the plot of July 20, 1944, to assassinate Hitler. He had been Polish military attaché in Berlin and Bucharest in the interwar period.

NIEDZIAŁKOWSKI, Mieczysław (1893–1940), one of the leading theoreticians and politicians of the Polish Socialist movement, succeeded Perl as editor of *Robotnik* in 1927. He organized workers' battalions in the defense of Warsaw during the September, 1939, campaign and was subsequently a leading activist in the underground resistance movement. The Germans executed him on June 21, 1940, simultaneously with Rataj (*q.v.*).

NORWID-NEUGEBAUER, Mieczysław (1884–1952), promoted to army inspector after the 1926 coup, later served as minister of public works between 1930 and 1933. In 1941, in London, Norwid-Neugebauer published a pioneer study of the September, 1939, campaign in Poland, in which he had been unable to participate owing to an assignment at the time as chief of the Polish military mission to Britain.

ORLICZ-DRESZER, Gustaw (1889–1936), active in the Polish independence movement since 1906, had deserted from the tsarist Russian army in August, 1914, to join Piłsudski's Legions. Having shown daring and initiative in World War I, in the Polish-Soviet campaign of 1920, and in the coup of May, 1926, he was rapidly promoted by Piłsudski. An army inspector (1930–35), he was also active in propagating Polish overseas interests and would-be colonial ambitions. Yet his political reputation was that of a Leftist and a democrat. Named inspector of air forces in 1936, he died in this capacity in a plane crash on the Baltic coast.

PASZKIEWICZ, Gustaw (1892–   ), in the late 1930s, as a general, commanded a division active in the often brutal "pacification" of the Ukrainian-populated areas of southeastern Poland. In September, 1939, he escaped to Rumania and subsequently commanded a tank brigade in North Africa under Anders (*q.v.*), who loathed him but was unable to achieve his removal until after the death in 1943 of Paszkiewicz's protector, Prime Minister General Sikorski. (See Anders, pp. 179,

193, 200.) Paszkiewicz returned to Poland after the war and became notorious for his ferocity in the suppression of anti-Communist guerrilla bands. (See S. Korboński, *W Imieniu Kremla* [Paris, 1956], pp. 306–8.)

POŁCZYŃSKI, Leon (1867–   ), had made his first political mark as a publisher of Polish journals in prewar Prussian Pomerania. After independence he had served as vice-minister for the former Prussian areas before his election to the Senate in 1922. He was minister of agriculture in 1930–32.

PONIATOWSKI, Juliusz (1886–   ), a Legion and POW veteran, had been minister of agriculture in the radical Lublin provisional government in November, 1918, and once again for the period July, 1920–February, 1921, in the official Polish government. He was destined to resume this portfolio for the years 1934–39. In the emigration after the September, 1939, defeat, Poniatowski went to the United States, from which he returned to Poland in 1957.

PRYSTOR, Aleksander (1874–1941), like Piłsudski, had studied medicine at Russian universities in his youth and had early joined the PPS to fight for Polish independence. Active in the Warsaw branch of the terroristic-paramilitary section of the PPS during and after the 1905 revolution, he was held under Russian arrest from 1912 to 1917. In independent Poland he was vice-minister of labor (1918–19) and was then active in the Polish seizure and administration of Wilno, his native district, during 1919–20. Subsequently attached for a time to Piłsudski's Inner War Council, he was again assigned to central staff work after the 1926 coup, first in the office of the inspector general, then at the War Ministry—each time within Piłsudski's closest circle. Labor minister (1929–30), minister of industry and commerce (1930–31), Prystor was prime minister from May, 1931, to May, 1933. During all these years in the cabinet he fiercely fought his erstwhile party, the PPS. A Sejm deputy (1930–35), a senator (1935–39), Prystor was marshal of the Senate (1935–38). He died of dysentery in Soviet imprisonment in October, 1941.

RADZIWIŁŁ, Janusz (1880–1945). Born in Berlin, active in the German-sponsored Polish Regency in 1918, a political leader of the conservatives' Party of National Right as well as a vice-chairman of the economically potent Lewiatan, in interwar Poland he was a BBWR Sejm deputy and chairman of the Sejm foreign affairs committee (1928–35), and a senator (1935–39). A partisan of German-Polish reconciliation during these years, he rejected German feelers to become a Polish quisling after September, 1939, and died in Poland in January, 1945.

RATAJ, Maciej (1884–1940), ceased to be Sejm marshal in 1928. In World War II he was active in the underground resistance movement and represented the Peasant Party in its political directorate until his execution by the Germans on June 21, 1940, together with Niedziałkowski (*q.v.*).

RYDZ-ŚMIGŁY, Edward (1886–1941), succeeded Piłsudski as inspector general of the armed forces upon the latter's death on May 12, 1935, and as marshal of Poland on November 10, 1936. He was the leading political personality of the Polish state from Piłsudski's death until the lost campaign of September, 1939, in which he was commander in chief of the Polish forces. Upon his defeat, he fled to Rumania (September 17–18), apparently hoping to be permitted to proceed to France. Instead, he was interned. Rydz-Śmigły escaped to Hungary on December 15, 1940, and from there secretly made his way back to Poland sometime during the period August–October, 1941. The commander of the underground Home Army (Armia Krajowa) declined, however, to acknowledge or to meet him. Rydz-Śmigły died in Warsaw on December 12, 1941, and was buried there three days later under a false name ("Adam Zawisza").

SIKORSKI, Władysław (1881–1943). At the outbreak of war in 1939, Sikorski, who had been in opposition to the *sanacja,* offered his services to Rydz-Śmigły (*q.v.*) but was declined. He thereupon left for France (via Rumania) where, after the German-Soviet occupation of Poland, he formed on September 30 a government-in-exile in which he was defense minister and commander in chief as well as prime minister. Upon the fall of France he transferred this government to London. On July 4, 1943, Sikorski was killed in an airplane crash at Gibraltar while returning to England from an inspection tour of General Anders' (*q.v.*) corps in the Near East.

SKWARCZYŃSKI, Stanisław (1888–), in the last years before World War II, was a political figure of some importance, succeeding Colonel Adam Koc as head of the government-sponsored Camp of National Unity at the turn of the year 1937–38. In that capacity, however, General Skwarczyński presided over the depoliticization of this hitherto semi-totalitarian movement (founded on March 1, 1937) and its transformation into a mere propaganda auxiliary to the army.

SŁAWEK, Walery (1879–1939), born in the Ukraine, had been active in the terrorist-paramilitary organization of the PPS during the years of insurrectionary ferment under tsarist rule from 1905 to 1908. During this period he had been severely wounded when a bomb which he was assembling exploded in his face (June 9, 1906). He was then active in the Galician PPS from 1908 until the outbreak of World War I, when he joined the First Legion Brigade. In 1915 he transferred his activities to the underground POW until his arrest by the Germans in July, 1917. After the restoration of Polish independence, he took the staff officers' course at the Superior War Academy and was assigned to the personal staff of Chief of State Piłsudski, whose closest political friend he had meanwhile become. (They had first met at a PPS congress in Wilno in 1902.) Upon Piłsudski's ostensible retirement to Sulejówek in May, 1923, Sławek went on the military reserve list. After the May, 1926, coup, he briefly returned to active military service but retired from the army in 1927 to organize the BBWR for Piłsudski. Elected to the Sejm in 1928, he thrice served as premier: March 29–August 23, 1930; December 4, 1930–May 26, 1931; March 28–October 12, 1935. He was also designated by Piłsudski as Poland's next president. After Piłsudski's death (May 12, 1935), however, Mościcki refused to vacate the presidency, thus thwarting Sławek's expectation of inheriting Piłsudski's mantle, and Sławek came to lead the internal opposition within the Piłsudskist camp to the dominant duumvirate of President Mościcki and Marshal Rydz-Śmigły (*q.v.*). He made the fatal political error of dissolving his own instrument, the BBWR, on the rather naïve ground that the new constitution which had come into effect on April 23, 1935, had rendered the BBWR obsolete by subsuming and formalizing its previous political function of protecting the government from the Sejm. In effect, this amounted to Sławek's political suicide. Though elected marshal of the Sejm on June 22, 1938, in which capacity he represented not only the internal opposition within the Piłsudskist camp to the ruling faction but also the extra-parliamentary Left opposition to the regime of Piłsudski's epigoni, Sławek became despondent over political developments since Piłsudski's death and committed suicide on April 2, 1939. His wish to found a new organization to bridge the gap of estrangement between the regime and the nation had been prohibited by the government, which had furthermore arranged his defeat in the Sejm elections of November 6, 1938. In the last hours of his life Sławek had even vainly sought readmission into the PPS. But the Brześć brutalities of 1930 lay between him and the PPS as an unbridgeable chasm. Sławek was personally incorruptible and politically somewhat artless. The lodestar of his life was a childlike devotion to Piłsudski. Without him, Sławek had no bearings. For a brief biographical sketch, see Schaetzel, *Pułkownik Walery Sławek.* My sources for his last desperate approach to the PPS are an interview with the late Dr. Otton Pehr of that party (July 16, 1963), and Jędrzejewiczowa, p .7.

SŁAWOJ-SKŁADKOWSKI, Felicjan (1885–1962), was interwar Poland's last prime minister and again interior minister, holding these portfolios from May 15, 1936, to September 30, 1939. A physician by training, he had belonged to Piłsudski's prewar PPS–Revolutionary Fraction and had served as a medical officer with the wartime Legions. Chief of the Army Medical Corps (1924–26), Piłsudski's commissar for Warsaw in the 1926 coup, Sławoj-Składkowski was second vice-minister of war and chief of Army Administration during the interval between his incumbencies as a cabinet minister (1931–36). Interned in Rumania in September, 1939, he escaped to the Near East and in 1947 came to Great Britain, where he died on August 31, 1962.

SOSNKOWSKI, Kazimierz (1885–   ), in September, 1939, commanded in the Lwów-Przemyśl area in the south. After the Polish catastrophe he made his way via Hungary to the West, where he was in charge of liaison between Sikorski's exile government and the underground resistance in Poland until August 18, 1941. He succeeded Sikorski (*q.v.*) as commander in chief of the armed forces after the latter's death in July, 1943, but was dropped from this post on September 30, 1944, as an abortive gesture toward reconciliation between the "London Poles" and the Soviet government, of which he was a vehement foe. After the war Sosnkowski settled in Canada.

ŚWITALSKI, Kazimierz (1886–1962), after his stint as prime minister in 1929, served as marshal of the Sejm (1930–35), senator by presidential nomination, and vice-marshal of the Senate under the new constitution of April 23, 1935. He was also *wojewoda* of Kraków province in 1936. A military prisoner in Germany during World War II, he returned to Poland at the end of the war, was arrested in 1948, and died in Warsaw on December 28, 1962, of wounds suffered in an auto accident.

WACHOWIAK, Stanisław (1890–   ), during World War II, was a Polish Red Cross official who, on behalf of the Home Army command, negotiated an agreement with the Germans in September, 1944, to evacuate noncombatant civilians from insurrectionary Warsaw. Few Varsovians availed themselves of this opportunity to leave their city.

WIENIAWA-DŁUGOSZOWSKI, Bolesław (1881–1942), educated at the universities of Lwów, Berlin, and Paris, a physician and an artist by training, a poet by inclination, the Polish translator of Baudelaire, had embarked on his military-political career through service with the Piłsudskist Riflemen, Legions, and POW before and during World War I. During and after the war he was Piłsudski's adjutant and always remained one of his special favorites. In addition to his cavalry command, he served as military attaché in Bucharest and on the staff of the inspector general during the interwar period. Polish ambassador to Italy (1938–40), Wieniawa-

Długoszowski was under consideration as a possible president-in-exile after the September, 1939, catastrophe but was passed over. Named envoy to Cuba by the Sikorski government, he committed suicide *en route,* in New York City, on July 2, 1942.

WITOS, Wincenty (1874–1945), though in exile in Czechoslovakia from the end of the Brześć trial until 1939, remained the undisputed political leader of the then organizationally unified Polish peasant movement—a recognition which he had achieved through decades of representing peasant interests and the peasant image in the Galician Diet (1908–14), the Vienna Reichsrat (1911–18), and the Polish Sejm (1919–30). Thrice prime minister of Poland (1920–21, 1923, 1926), Witos was at the time of his death a figurehead vice-chairman of the Communist-sponsored National Council of the Homeland—in which organization his National Democratic cabinet colleague of May, 1926, Stanisław Grabski (*q.v.*), served the same function.

ZALESKI, August (1883–   ), was foreign minister in 1926–32 (he was replaced by Beck, *q.v.*) and again in Sikorski's (*q.v.*) government-in-exile in 1939–41. He resigned in protest against Sikorski's failure to elicit from Stalin an explicit recognition of the pre-1939 Polish-Soviet frontier. In 1947 Zaleski became president of the Polish government-in-exile, which continued to maintain itself in London, though recognized by only a handful of small states. Internal quarrels within the emigration weakened his authority after 1954.

ŻELIGOWSKI, Lucjan (1865–1947), was a Piłsudskist Sejm deputy in 1935–39 and a member of the exile Polish National Council in London during World War II. In the course of the war, however, he became a convert to the ideas of Polish-Soviet and Pan-Slavic fraternity. Together with General Gustaw Paszkiewicz (*q.v.*), Żeligowski shortly after the end of the war issued a public appeal to Polish soldiers in the West to return home.

ŻYMIERSKI, Michał (1890–   ), upon being released from the five-year prison term for embezzlement to which a Piłsudskist court-martial had sentenced him in 1927, went to France for a few years, where he engaged in smuggling arms to the Loyalist side during the Spanish Civil War. Having returned to Poland in 1939, he repeatedly offered his services to the London-affiliated underground Home Army (Armia Krajowa) in 1941 and 1942 but was rebuffed. He then threw in his lot with the Communist underground and in 1943 became commander of its People's Guard (Gwardia Ludowa), in which he took the alias "Rola." His fortunes followed those of the Polish Communist movement as he rose to become commander in chief of the Polish army (July 21, 1944), defense minister (January 1, 1945), and marshal of Poland (May 3, 1945). On November 9, 1949, he was suddenly replaced as commander in chief and defense minister by Soviet Marshal Konstantin Rokossovsky. In 1953 Rola-Żymierski was arrested for alleged contacts with American intelligence services but was not, apparently, ever placed on trial. Rehabilitated in 1956, he was named vice-president of the Polish National Bank.

BIBLIOGRAPHY

Though substantial, this bibliography is a selected rather than a complete one. Instead of listing all items consulted in the course of research, or even all items cited in footnotes, I have chosen, on the one hand, the most substantial and serious scholarly studies which any student of the domestic political history of interwar Poland would wish to consult, and, on the other hand, the most controversial and/or polemical arguments which have emerged from and are pertinent to the ongoing debate in Poland and within the Polish political emigration abroad about the proper evaluation of Piłsudski's coup d'état and the subsequent regime inaugurated by it.

UNPUBLISHED MATERIALS

"Akta Komisji Likwidacyjnej" [Documents of the Commission to Investigate the Military Events of the Coup]. 25 folios in the archives of the Józef Piłsudski Institute of America, New York.

Cieślak, T. "Historia polskiej diplomacji w latach 1926–1939, cz. II [History of Polish Diplomacy during 1926–1939, Part II]. Mimeographed. Warsaw, 1960.

Gitman, J. "The Jews and Jewish Problems in the Polish Parliament, 1919–1939." Doctoral dissertation, Faculty of the Graduate School, Yale University, 1962.

Groth, A. J. "Parliament and the Electoral System in Poland, 1918–1935." Doctoral dissertation, Faculty of Political Science, Columbia University, 1960.

Jędrzejewicz, J. "Myśl państwowa piłsudczyków w okresie 1918–1935" [The Statist Thinking of the Piłsudskists in the Period 1918–1935]. Typescript in the archives of the Józef Piłsudski Institute of America, New York. Dated 1935.

Jellenta, S. O. "Relacja z udziału w przewrocie majowym 1926 r." [Report of My Participation in the May, 1926, Coup]. Typescript in the archives of the Józef Piłsudski Institute of America, New York. Dated December 28, 1936.

Karcz, J. F. "Some Aspects of Statism and Planning in Poland, 1921–1939." Master's thesis, Kent State University, 1952.

Kmicic-Skrzyński, L. "Przewrót majowy 1926 roku" [The May Coup of 1926]. Typescript in the archives of the Piłsudski Historical Institute, London. Dated July 9, 1961.

Korboński, A. "Foreign Capital in Polish Industry, 1918–1939." Master's thesis, Faculty of Political Science, Columbia University, 1954.

Krok-Paszkowski, H. "Relacja" [A Report]. Typescript in the archives of the Piłsudski Historical Institute, London.

Modelski, I. "Maciej Rataj." Typescript in the possession of K. Bagiński. Dated June, 1956.

Mościcki, I. "Wspomnienia" [Memoirs]. Typescript in the archives of the Piłsudski Historical Institute, London. Written in Switzerland after December, 1939. (Another part published, *q.v.*).

Piłsudski, J. "Wypowiedzi Marszałka Józefa Piłsudskiego w sprawach organizacji naczelnych władz wojskowych oraz relacja pani marszałkowej Aleksandry Piłsudskiej" [Pronouncements of Marshal Joseph Piłsudski Pertaining to the Organization of the Military Supreme Command as Well as a Report by Mme Aleksandra Piłsudska]. Typescript in the archives of the Piłsudski Historical Institute, London. Dated 1952.

Skwarczyński, S. "Relacja" [A Report]. Typescript in the archives of the Piłsudski Historical Institute, London.

Sokalski, W. "The Polish Peasant Party, 1926–1931." Master's thesis, Faculty of Political Science, Columbia University, 1948.

Tarnopolsky, W. "The Polish-Ukrainian Conflict in Eastern Galicia in 1930 and Its Repercussions in the League of Nations." Master's thesis, Faculty of Political Science, Columbia University, 1955.

Walkowicz, L. T. "Przewrót majowy, początkiem walki przeciw demokracji w Polsce" [The May Coup as the Beginning of the Struggle Against Democracy in Poland]. Typescript in the archives of the Józef Piłsudski Institute of America, New York. Dated May 12, 1951.

Żeligowski, L. "Akta" [Papers]. Folios in the Archiwum Akt Nowych, Warsaw.

PUBLISHED MATERIALS

A. L. "Socjalizm polski na drodze ku konsolidacji" [Polish Socialism on the Way Toward Consolidation], *Dzwon* [Bell], I, No. 10 (June 30, 1928), 2–3.

Ahlers, J. *Polen: Volk, Staat, Kultur, Politik, Wirtschaft.* Berlin, 1935.

Ajnenkiel, A. "Materiały do dziejów politycznych Polski w latach 1924–1927" [Materials for a Political History of Poland in the Years 1924–1927], *Historia i nauka o konstytucji* [History and Knowledge of the Constitution], V, No. 6 (1957), 432–47.

—— *Od "rządów ludowych" do przewrotu majowego: Zarys dziejów politycznych Polski, 1918–1926* [From the "People's Government" to the May Coup d'Etat: An Outline of the Political History of Poland, 1918–1926]. Warsaw, 1964.

—— "Z dziejów kartki wyborczej" [From the History of an Election Note], *Mówią Wieki* [The Centuries Speak], IX, No. 1 (January, 1966), 17–21.

—— "Z dziejów reformy rolnej w Polsce, 1918–1939" [From the History of Land Reform in Poland, 1918–1939], *Mówią Wieki* [The Centuries Speak], VI, No. 5 (May, 1963), 6–8.

Alter, W. "XXI Kongres PPS" [The 21st PPS Congress], *Nasza Walka* [Our Struggle], II, No. 1 (January, 1929), 3–6.

Anders, W. *Bez ostatniego rozdziału* [Without a Final Chapter]. Newtown, Wales, 1949.

Anusz, A. *Rola Józefa Piłsudskiego w życiu narodu i państwa* [The Role of Joseph Piłsudski in the Life of the Nation and of the State]. Warsaw, 1927.

Arski, S. *My pierwsza brygada* [We Are the First Brigade]. Warsaw, 1962.

Badeni, S. "O Generale Rozwadowskim" [About General Rozwadowski], *Wiadomości* [Information], XVI, No. 789 (May 14, 1961), 1.

Bąkowski, K. "Zapiski krakowskiego adwokata" [Notes of a Cracovian Lawyer], *Mówią Wieki* [The Centuries Speak], V, No. 6–7 (June–July, 1962), 17–19.

Balcerak, W. "Polska polityka zagraniczna wobec układów lokarneńskich" [Polish Foreign Policy Toward the Locarno Treaties], *Przegląd Zachodni* [Western Review], XV, No. 6 (November–December, 1959), 259–97.

Baranowski, W. *Rozmowy z Piłsudskim, 1916 r.–1931 r.* [Conversations with Piłsudski, 1916–1931]. Warsaw, 1938.

Barbier, J.-B. *Un Frac de Nessus.* Rome, 1951.

Bartel, K. *Kilka uwag o praktyce parlamentarnej w Polsce* [Some Remarks on Parliamentary Practice in Poland]. Warsaw, 1929.

—— *Niedomagania parlamentaryzmu* [The Deficiencies of Parliamentarism]. Warsaw, 1929.

—— *Wykresy charakteryzujące rozwój życia gospodarczego Polski w latach 1924–1927 włącznie* [Charts Characterizing the Development of Polish Economic Life in the Years 1924 Through 1927]. Warsaw, 1928.

Bartel, P. *Le Maréchal Pilsudski.* Paris, 1935.

—— "Josef Pilsudski," *Les Oeuvres Libres,* No. 146 (August, 1933), pp. 235–308.

Beck, J. *Dernier rapport: Politique polonaise, 1926–1939.* Neuchâtel, 1951.

Bednarczyk, T. "Generał Sikorski a K.B." [General Sikorski and the Security Corps], *Po Prostu* [Stated Simply], No. 426 (March 17, 1957), p. 7.

Bełcikowska, A. *Stronnictwa i związki polityczne w Polsce* [Political Parties and Associations in Poland]. Warsaw, 1925.

—— *Walki majowe w Warszawie 11 maj–16 maj 1926* [The May Fighting in Warsaw, May 11–16, 1926]. Warsaw, 1926.

Benedykt, S. "O przełomie majowym" [On the May Coup], *Wiadomości* [Information], XIV, No. 667 (January 11, 1959), 1.

Berbecki, L. *Pamiętniki* [Memoirs]. Katowice, 1959.

Bergman, A. "Białoruska Włościańsko-Robotnicza Hromada (1925–1927)" [The White Russian Peasant-Worker Hramada, 1925–1927], *Z Pola Walki* [From the Field of Struggle], V, No. 3 (1962), 73–99.

Bernus, P. "Le Conflict entre le Maréchal Pilsudski et le parlement polonais," *Journal des Débats Politiques et Littéraires*, XXXIV, No. 1753 (September 30, 1927), 546.

—— "Pilsudski et la politique polonaise," *Revue de Paris*, XXXVI, No. 12 (June 15, 1929), 779–95.

—— "La Politique extérieure de la Pologne," *Journal des Débats Politiques et Littéraires*, XXXIV, No. 1717 (January 21, 1927), 99–100.

Bojan-Błażewicz, W. *Przewrót majowy w Polsce: Na podstawie dokumentów urzędowych* [The May Coup in Poland: Based on Official Documents]. New York, 1926.

Bojko, J. *Ze wspomnień* [From the Memoirs]. Edited by K. Dunin-Wąsowicz. Warsaw, 1959.

Brudkowski, J. *Stanisław Wojciechowski*. Warsaw, 1926.

Brus, W. *Polska, 1918–1926* [Poland, 1918–1926]. Paris, 1946.

Buell, R. L. *Poland: Key to Europe*. New York, 1939.

"Bystander." "Pilsudski and Poland," *The Contemporary Review*, CXXX (July, 1926), 22–30.

Carency, J. de. Pseudonym of K. Smogorzewski, *q.v.*

Carr, E. H. *Socialism in One Country, 1924–1926*. Vol. III, Part I. London, 1964.

Cepnik, H. *Józef Piłsudski, twórca niepodległego państwa polskiego* [Joseph Piłsudski, the Creator of the Independent Polish State]. Warsaw, 1935.

Chernov, V. "Joseph Pilsudski," *Foreign Affairs*, XIV, No. 1 (October, 1935), 146–55.

Chrzanowski, L. *Les Evénements de Pologne et le Maréchal Pilsudski*. Geneva, 1926.

Chrząszczewski, A. *Od sejmowładztwa do dyktatury* [From Sejm Preponderance to Dictatorship]. Warsaw, 1930.

—— "Kartki z mego pamiętnika" [Notes from My Diary], *Tygodnik Zachodni* [Western Weekly], II, No. 19 (1957), 1–2; No. 20 (1957), 1–2; No. 21 (1957), 2, 7; No. 22 (1957), 2; No. 23 (1957), 2.

—— "Uwagi w sprawie 'Granatów nad Belwederem'" [Observations to the Question of "Shells on the Belweder"], *Za i Przeciw* [For and Against], IV, No. 30 (July 24, 1960), 14. (The polemic of the deputy chief of Wojciechowski's Civilian Chancellery against his military adjutant, H. Comte, *q.v.*)

Ciołkosz, A. *Trzy Wspomnienia* [Three Reminiscences]. London, 1945.

Comte, H. "Belweder—Maj 1926" [Belweder—May, 1926], *Stolica* [Capital City], XVII, No. 19 (May 13, 1962), 14–15; No. 20 (May 20, 1962), 19.

—— "Granaty nad Belwederem" [Shells on the Belweder], *Za i Przeciw* [For and Against], IV, No. 22 (May 29, 1960), 11; No. 23 (June 5, 1960), 11; No. 24 (June 12, 1960), 11.

Conrad, H. "Farm Aid in Poland," *Foreign Agriculture,* II, No. 9 (September, 1938), 409–32.

"Coup d'état de Varsovie, Le," *Le Monde Slave* (N.S.), III, No. 7 (July, 1926), 1–32.

Czarkowski-Golejewski, K. "Walki majowe i audiencja w Belwederze" [The May Fighting and an Audience in the Belweder], *Wiadomości* [Information], XVI, No. 789 (May 14, 1961), 1.

Czubiński, A. *Centrolew* [Center-Left]. Poznań, 1963.

—— "Przewrót majowy 1926 roku" [The May Coup of 1926], *Zeszyty Naukowe Uniwersytetu im. Adama Mickiewicza* [Scholarly Pamphlets of the Adam Mickiewicz University], No. 13 (1958), pp. 77–151.

—— "Wielkopolska i Pomorze wobec zamachu stanu w maju 1926 r." [Poznania and Pomerania in Relation to the Coup d'Etat in May, 1926], *Studia i materiały do dziejów Wielkopolski i Pomorza* [Studies and Materials for the History of Poznania and Pomerania], VI, No. 1 (1960), 153–207.

Czy Wiesz Kto to Jest? [Who's Who in Poland?] Warsaw, 1938.

Dąbrowski, S. *Zagadnienie obrony narodowej w wojnie nowoczesnej: Organizacja rządu i naczelnego dowództwa* [The Problem of National Defense in Modern War: The Organization of the Government and the Supreme Command]. Poznań, 1925.

—— "Zamach majowy i kryzys państwa" [The May Coup and the Crisis of the State], *Tygodnik Warszawski* [Warsaw Weekly], II, No. 23 (June 9, 1946), 2–3.

Daszyński, I. (under the pseudonym M. Porczak). *Dyktator Józef Piłsudski i "piłsudczycy"* [Dictator Joseph Piłsudski and the Piłsudskists]. Kraków, 1930.

—— (under the pseudonym M. Porczak). *Rewolucja majowa i jej skutki* [The May Revolution and Its Consequences]. Kraków, 1927.

—— *Sejm, rząd, król, dyktator* [Sejm, Government, King, Dictator]. Warsaw, 1926.

—— *W pierwszą rocznicę przewrotu majowego* [On the First Anniversary of the May Coup]. Warsaw, 1927.

—— *Wielki człowiek w Polsce: Szkic psychologiczno-polityczny* [A Great Man in Poland: A Psychological-Political Sketch]. Warsaw, 1925.

Dawson, C. "Pilsudski's Seizure of Power in Poland," *Current History,* XXIV, No. 4 (July, 1926), 586–91.

Dębicki, R. *The Foreign Policy of Poland, 1919–1939.* New York, 1962.

Delmas, Y. *L'Evolution constitutionelle de la Pologne depuis 1919.* Paris, 1936.

Deutscher, I. *The Tragedy of Polish Communism Between the Wars.* London, n.d. [1958?]

Diamand, H. "O aktualnej sytuacji politycznej" [On the Current Political Situation], *Dzwon* [Bell], I, No. 4 (April 5, 1928), 1–4.

Dmowski, R. *Przewrót* [Overthrow]. Warsaw, 1934.

Dokumenty chwili. Vol. I: *12 do 16 maja 1926 r. w Warszawie* [Documents of the Times. Vol. I: May 12–16, 1926, in Warsaw]. Warsaw, 1926.

Dokumenty chwili. Vol. II: *Od Belwederu do Zamku* [Documents of the Times. Vol. II: From the Belweder to the Castle]. Warsaw, 1926.

Dołęga-Modrzewski, S. Pseudonym of S. Kauzik, *q.v.*

Douglass, P. *The Economic Independence of Poland.* Cincinnati, 1934.

Dreszer, Z. "Czy zamach majowy był dziełem tajnej organizacji?" [Was the May Coup the Work of a Secret Organization?], *Polityka* [Politics], IX, No. 23 (September 25, 1938), 4–5.

Drobner, B. *Moje cztery procesy* [My Three Lawsuits]. Warsaw, 1962.

Drozdowski, M. "W sprawie badań nad gospodarką Polski przedwrześniowej" [On the Question of Research on the Economy of Pre-September Poland], *Przegląd Historyczny* [Historical Review], XLVIII, No. 1 (1957), 117–25.

Dubanowicz, E. *Rewizja konstytucji* [Revision of the Constitution]. Poznań, 1926.

Dumont-Wilden, L. "La Crise polonaise," *Revue Politique et Littéraire (Revue Bleue),* LXIV, No. 12 (June 19, 1926), 377–80.

Dunin-Wąsowicz, K. "Jakub Bojko i jego wspomnienia" [Jacob Bojko and His Memoirs], *Mówią Wieki* [The Centuries Speak], II, No. 10 (October, 1959), 33–34.

Dymek, B. "Z polityki polskiego Stronnictwa Ludowego 'Piast'—Pakt Lanckoroński 17. V. 1923" [From the Politics of the Polish People's Party Piast—the Lanckorona Pact of May 17, 1923], *Zeszyty Historyczne: Uniwersytet Warszawski* [Historical Pamphlets: Warsaw University], II, (1961), 143–60.

Dzendzel, H. "W dniach zamachu majowego" [In the Days of the May Coup], *Tygodnik Demokratyczny* [Democratic Weekly], No. 415 (1961), p. 5; No. 416 (1961), p. 6.

Dziennik Ustaw Rzeczypospolitej Polskiej [Official Gazette of the Polish Republic]. Warsaw, 1918– .

Dziesięciolecie Polski odrodzonej, 1918–1928 [A Decade of Restored Poland, 1918–1928]. Kraków-Warsaw, 1928.

Dziewanowski, M. K. *The Communist Party of Poland*. Cambridge, Mass., 1959.

—— "Piłsudski's Federal Policy, 1919–1921," *Journal of Central European Affairs*, X, No. 2 (July, 1950), 113–28; No. 3 (October, 1950), 271–87.

Eichler, A. *Polen, ein Volk in Waffen*. Berlin, 1929.

Falkenthal, H. *Das Parlament der polnischen Republik von 1919–1930*. Bydgoszcz, 1932.

Feliński, M. *The Ukrainians in Poland*. London, 1931.

Fiderkiewicz, A. *Burzliwe lata* [Stormy Years]. Warsaw, 1963.

—— *Dobre czasy* [Good Times]. Warsaw, 1958.

—— "Wyprawa posłów polskich" [An Expedition by Polish Deputies], *Polityka* [Politics], II, No. 40 (October 4, 1958), 4.

Folkerts, W. *Die staatsrechtliche und politische Stellung des Präsidenten der polnischen Republik*. Jena, 1929.

Forst de Battaglia, O. "Pilsudski," *Nord und Süd*, LII, No. 2 (February, 1929), 126–40.

Frankel, H. *Poland: The Struggle for Power, 1772–1939*. London, 1946.

Garlicki, A. "N.P.Ch." [The Independent Peasant Party], *Mówią Wieki* [The Centuries Speak], I, No. 11 (November, 1958), 38.

—— "Obóz Wielkiej Polski" [The Camp of Great Poland], *Mówią Wieki* [The Centuries Speak], II, No. 6 (June, 1959), 32.

Gąsiorowski, Z. "Stresemann and Poland before Locarno" and "Stresemann and Poland after Locarno," *Journal of Central European Affairs*, XVIII, No. 1 (April, 1958), 25–47; No. 3 (October, 1958), 292–317.

Gauvain, A. "La Crise polonaise," *Journal des Débats Politiques et Littéraires*, XXXIII, No. 1682 (May 21, 1926), 812–14; No. 1684 (June 4, 1926), 895–96.

—— "Le Prétendu mouvement monarchiste en Pologne," *Journal des Débats Politiques et Littéraires*, XXXIII, No. 1706 (November 5, 1926), 748–49.

Głąbiński, S. *Wspomnienia polityczne* [Political Memoirs]. Pelplin, 1939.

Glinka, W. "W rocznicę przewrotu majowego" [On the Anniversary of the May Coup], *Polityka* [Politics], I, No. 11 (May 8–14, 1957), 6–7.

Górnicki, W. (under the pseudonym F. Wierzbiński). *Warszawa nie odpowiada* [Warsaw Does Not Answer]. Warsaw, 1960.

—— "Ostatni rokosz w Warszawie" [The Last Rebellion in Warsaw], *Świat* [World], VI, No. 20 (May 13, 1956), 8–9; No. 21 (May 20, 1956), 8–9; No. 22 (May 27, 1956), 20–21.

Górski, J. "Legenda Józefa Piłsudskiego" [The Legend of Joseph Piłsudski], *Nowa Kultura* [New Culture], XI, No. 40 (October 2, 1960), 5; No. 41 (October 9, 1960), 9, 11; No. 42 (October 16, 1960), 4.

Goryński, M. "Joseph Pilsudski: The Coup d'Etat of an Idealist," *The Review of Reviews*, LXXIII, No. 437 (June–July, 1926), 528–32.

Grabski, W. *Dwa lata pracy u podstaw państwowości naszej (1924–1925)* [Two Years of Work at the Foundation of Our Statehood, 1924–1925]. Warsaw, 1927.

Grabski, W. J. "Ostatnie rozmowy Piłsudskiego z Wojciechowskim" [The Last Conversations of Piłsudski with Wojciechowski], *Kierunki* [Directions], V, No. 19 (May 15, 1960), 3, 11.

Grobicki, J. "Dwa niedoszłe zamachy" [Two Abortive Assassination Attempts], *Zeszyty Historyczne* [Historical Pamphlets], III (1963), 93–102.

Grudziński, A. "Cyfry mówią" [Numbers Speak], *Wiadomości* [Information], XIV, No. 675 (March 8, 1959), 6.

Grzędziński, J. *Maj 1926*. Paris, 1965. (Volume XIV in the series *Dokumenty*, published by the Institut Littéraire.)

―― "Fragmenty pamiętnika" [Fragments of a Memoir], *Tygodnik Illustrowany* [Illustrated Weekly], LXXII, No. 20 (May 17, 1936), 388–90; No. 21 (May 24, 1936), 405–6; No. 22 (May 31, 1936), 415–16; No. 23 (June 7, 1936), 443–44; No. 24 (June 14, 1936), 461–62; No. 25 (June 21, 1936), 485–86; No. 26 (June 28, 1936), 495–97.

Grzybowski, K. "Parlamentaryzm polski w dwudziestoleciu (1918–1939)" [Polish Parliamentarism in the Two Decades 1918–1939], in *VIII Powszechny Zjazd Historyków Polskich: Historia Najnowsza Polski* [Eighth General Congress of Polish Historians: Contemporary History of Poland], pp. 229–64.

Grzybowski, W. "Premier Kazimierz Bartel" [Prime Minister Kazimierz Bartel], *Kultura* [Culture], No. 13 (1948), pp. 99–114.

―― "Spotkania i rozmowy z Józefem Piłsudskim" [Encounters and Conversations with Joseph Piłsudski], *Niepodległość* [Independence] (N.S.), I, (1948), 89–100.

Haller, J. *Pamiętniki* [Memoirs]. London, 1964.

Haller, S. *Wypadki warszawskie od 12 do 15 maja 1926 r.* [The Warsaw Events of May 12 to 15, 1926]. Kraków, 1926.

Halpern, L. *Polityka żydowska w Sejmie i Senacie Rzeczypospolitej Polskiej, 1919–1933* [The Jewish Policy in the Sejm and Senate of the Polish Republic, 1919–1933]. Warsaw, 1933.

"Haniebny dokument" [A Shameful Document], *Nasza Walka* [Our Struggle], VII, No. 6–7 (December, 1930), 21–22.

Hass, L. "Białoruska Włościańsko-Robotnicza Hromada" [The White Russian Peasant-Worker Hramada], *Mówią Wieki* [The Centuries Speak], II, No. 8 (August, 1959), 19.

―― "Generał Władysław Sikorski wobec zamachu majowego" [General Władysław Sikorski in Relation to the May Coup], *Mówią Wieki* [The Centuries Speak], V, No. 3 (March, 1962), 23.

—— "Kształtowanie się lewicowego nurtu w Polskiej Partii Socjalistycznej na tle sytuacji wewnątrzpartyjnej (listopad 1923–maj 1926)" [The Formation of a Leftist Current in the PPS Against the Background of the Internal Party Situation, November, 1923–May, 1926], *Kwartalnik Historyczny* [Historical Quarterly], LXVIII, No. 1 (1961), 69–102.

—— "PPS Lewica, 1926–1931" [The Left PPS, 1926–1931], *Mówią Wieki* [The Centuries Speak], II, No. 3 (March, 1959), 1–7.

—— "PPS Lewica, 1926–1931" [The Left PPS, 1926–1931], *Najnowsze Dzieje Polski: Materiały i Studia z okresu 1914–1939* [Contemporary History of Poland: Materials and Studies of the Period 1914–1939], IV (1961), 59–99.

—— "Zamach majowy 1926 r." [The May Coup of 1926], *Mówią Wieki* [The Centuries Speak], IV, No. 10 (October, 1961), 1–5; No. 11 (November, 1961), 14–18.

Hauke-Nowak, A. "Nieznany raport o telefonach, telegrafie i radiu w czasie przewrotu majowego 1926 roku w Warszawie" [An Unknown Report about the Telephones, Telegraph, and Radio at the Time of the May Coup of 1926 in Warsaw], *Mówią Wieki* [The Centuries Speak], VI, No. 2 (February, 1963), 12–15.

Hełczyński, B. "Prezydent Ignacy Mościcki widziany oczami szefa jego kancelarii cywilnej" [President Ignacy Mościcki as Seen Through the Eyes of the Chief of His Civilian Chancellery], *Niepodległość* [Independence] (N.S.), VI (1958), 228–33.

Henrici, W. "Der Werdegang des Marschall Pilsudski," *Osteuropa*, VI (1930–31), 463–68.

Hertz, A. "The Case of an East European Intelligentsia," *Journal of Central European Affairs*, XI, No. 1 (January–April, 1951), 10–26.

—— "The Social Background of the Pre-War Polish Political Structure," *Journal of Central European Affairs*, II, No. 2 (July, 1942), 145–61.

Hincza, S. Pseudonym of L. Stolarzewicz, *q.v.*

Hoffman, E. Pseudonym of E. Szerer, *q.v.*

Hołówko, T. *Ostatni rok* [The Past Year]. Warsaw, 1932.

Horak, S., ed. *Poland's International Affairs, 1919–1960: A Calendar of Treaties, Agreements, Conventions, and Other International Acts, with Annotations, References, and Selections from Documents and Texts of Treaties.* Bloomington, 1964.

Hurwicz, E. "Joseph Pilsudski," *Neue Rundschau*, XXXXI, No. 7 (July, 1930), 1–14.

Huyn, H. *Tragedy of Errors.* London, 1939.

Iłłakowiczówna, K. *Ścieżka obok drogi* [The Path Alongside the Road]. Warsaw, 1939.

Jabłoński, H. "Z tajnej dyplomacji Władysława Grabskiego w r. 1924" [From the Secret Diplomacy of Władysław Grabski in 1924], *Kwartalnik Historyczny* [Historical Quarterly], LXIII, No. 4–5 (1956), 440–55.

Jabłoński, T. *Zarys Historii PPS* [An Outline of the History of the PPS]. Warsaw, 1946.

Jachieć, F. "10 pułk piechoty w wypadkach majowych 1926 r." [The Tenth Infantry Regiment in the May Events of 1926], *Wojskowy Przegląd Historyczny* [Military Historical Review], V, No. 2 (1960), 337–45.

Jackson, G. D., Jr. *Comintern and Peasant in East Europe, 1919–1930*. New York, 1966.

Janowska, H., ed. *Przewrót majowy: Pierwsze lata rządów sanacji (1926–1928)* [The May Coup: The First Years of the Sanacja Regime, 1926–1928]. Warsaw, 1960.

Jarecka, S. *Niezależna Partia Chłopska (1924–1927)* [The Independent Peasant Party, 1924–1927]. Warsaw, 1961.

—— "Stosunek Niezależnej Partii Chłopskiej do przewrotu majowego i Piłsudskiego w świetle materiałów policyjnych" [The Relation of the Independent Peasant Party to the May Coup and Piłsudski in the Light of Police Documents], *Wieś Współczesna* [Contemporary Village], I, No. 2–3 (April–May, 1957), 151–57.

Jędrzejewiczowa, C. B. de C. "Tomasz Arciszewski," *Robotnik Polski* [Polish Worker], LXVI, No. 6 (June, 1962), 3, 6–7.

Jordan-Rozwadowski, A. *Generał Rozwadowski*. Kraków, 1929.

Józef Piłsudski, 1867–1935. Kraków, 1935.

Jurkiewicz, J. *Watykan a Polska w okresie międzywojennym, 1918–1939* [The Vatican and Poland in the Interwar Period, 1918–1939]. Warsaw, 1958.

Jurkiewicz, J., ed. "Tajne posiedzenie Rady Ligi Narodów w grudniu 1927 r. i spotkanie Piłsudskiego z Stresemannem" [A Secret Session of the Council of the League of Nations in December, 1927, and a Meeting of Piłsudski with Stresemann], *Sprawy Międzynarodowe* [International Affairs], XIII, No. 2 (February, 1960), 88–96.

Juryś, R. "Proces brzeski" [The Brześć Trial], *Prawo i Życie* [Law and Life], No. 22 (1957), pp. 4–5.

Kagan, G. "Agrarian Regime of Pre-War Poland," *Journal of Central European Affairs*, III, No. 3 (October, 1943), 241–69.

Karbowski, W. "Wypadki majowe w 1926 r." [The May Events in 1926], *Wojskowy Przegląd Historyczny* [Military Historical Review], IV, No. 2 (1959), 328–78.

Karpatowicz, L. "18 Brumaire'a Józefa Piłsudskiego?" [The Eighteenth Brumaire of Joseph Piłsudski?], *Więź* [Link], IV, No. 5 (May, 1961), 84–112.

Katelbach, T. *Spowiedź pokolenia* [Confession of a Generation]. Lippstadt, 1948.

—— "Loże" [Masonic Lodges], *Zeszyty Historyczne* [Historical Pamphlets], III (1963), 199–208.

Kauzik, S. (under the pseudonym S. Dołęga-Modrzewski). "Ś.p. Stanisław Wojciechowski" [The Late Stanisław Wojciechowski], *Orzeł Biały* [White Eagle], May 23, 1953, p. 3.

Kersten, K., ed. "Protokół konferencji grup konserwatywnych z udziałem przedstawicieli marszałka Piłsudskiego w Dzikowie w dniach 14–16 września 1927 r." [Minutes of a Conference of a Group of Conservatives with the Participation of Representatives of Marshal Piłsudski in Dzików, September 14–16, 1927], *Najnowsze Dzieje Polski: Materiały i Studia z okresu 1914–1939* [Contemporary History of Poland: Materials and Studies of the Period 1914–1939], II (1959), 199–215.

Kirchmayer, J. *Kampania wrześniowa* [The September Campaign]. Warsaw, 1946.

Kisch, E. E. "Warszawa w dzień po przewrocie" [Warsaw on the Day after the Coup], *Świat* [World], V, No. 20 (May 22, 1955), 6–7.

Koitz, H. *Männer um Pilsudski*. Breslau, 1934.

Komarnicki, T. "Piłsudski a polityka wielkich mocarstw zachodnich" [Piłsudski and the Policy of the Western Great Powers], *Niepodległość* [Independence] (N.S.), IV (1952), 17–92.

Kopański, S. *Moja służba w wojsku polskim, 1917–1939* [My Service in the Polish Army, 1917–1939]. London, 1965.

Korbel, J. *Poland Between East and West: Soviet and German Diplomacy Toward Poland, 1919–1933*. Princeton, 1963.

Kościałkowski, S. "Marian Zdziechowski," *Kultura* [Culture], No. 195–196 (January–February, 1964), 166–84.

Kowalski, J. *Zarys historii polskiego ruchu robotniczego w latach 1918–1939. Część I, lata 1918–1928* [An Outline of the History of the Polish Labor Movement in the Years 1918–1939. Part I, 1918–1928]. Warsaw, 1959.

—— "Rozwój sytuacji wewnętrznej w KPP po przewrocie majowym 1926 r." [The Development of the Internal Situation in the Polish Communist Party after the May Coup of 1926], *Z Pola Walki* [From the Field of Struggle], VI, No. 4 (1963), 123–79.

Kownacki, P. *Gdyby dziadek żył* [If Grandfather (Piłsudski) Were Alive]. Wilno, 1940.

Kozłowski, E. *Wojsko polskie, 1936–1939: Próby modernizacji i rozbudowy* [The Polish Army, 1936–1939: Efforts at Modernization and Development]. Warsaw, 1964.

KPP: Uchwały i rezolucje [The Communist Party of Poland: Decisions and Resolutions]. Vol. I (1918–23). Warsaw, 1953. Vol. II (1924–29). Warsaw, 1955.

Krasuski, J. *Stosunki Polsko-Niemieckie, 1926–1932* [Polish-German Relations, 1926–1932]. Poznań, 1964.

Kruszewski, C. "The German-Polish Tariff War (1925–1934) and Its Aftermath," *Journal of Central European Affairs,* III, No. 3 (October, 1943), 294–315.

Krzyżanowski, A. *Rządy marszałka Piłsudskiego* [Marshal Piłsudski's Government]. 2d ed. Kraków, 1928.

Kukiel, M. "Jeszcze o majowej wojnie domowej i generale Zagórskim" [Once Again about the May Civil War and General Zagórski], *Wiadomości* [Information], XIV, No. 693 (July 12, 1959), 6.

―― "Jeszcze o przełomie majowym [Once Again about the May Coup], *Wiadomości* [Information], XIII, No. 678–79 (March 29–April 5, 1959), 16.

Kulski, W. W. "The Lost Opportunity for Russian-Polish Friendship," *Foreign Affairs,* XXV, No. 4 (July, 1947), 667–84.

Kumaniecki, K. *Odbudowa państwowości polskiej: Najważniejsze dokumenty, 1912–styczeń 1924* [The Restoration of Polish Statehood: The Most Important Documents, 1912–January, 1924]. Warsaw-Kraków, 1924.

Kutrzeba, S. *Polska odrodzona, 1914–1928* [Revived Poland, 1914–1928]. 4th ed. Warsaw, 1935.

Kwiatkowski, E. "Der wirtschaftliche Fortschritt Polens," *Nord und Süd,* LI, No. 3 (March, 1928), 191–207.

Łańcucki, S. *Moje wspomnienia* [My Memoirs]. Vol. I. Moscow, 1931.

Landau, R. *Pilsudski, Hero of Poland.* London, 1930.

Landau, Z. *Plan Stabilizacyjny, 1927–1930* [The Stabilization Plan, 1927–1930]. Warsaw, 1963.

―― "Misja Kemmerera" [Kemmerer's Mission], *Przegląd Historyczny* [Historical Review], XLVIII, No. 2 (1957), 270–84.

―― "Pożyczka dillonowska" [The Dillon Loan], *Kwartalnik Historyczny* [Historical Quarterly], LXIV, No. 3 (1957), 79–85.

―― "Władysław Grabski a pożyczki zagraniczne" [Władysław Grabski and Foreign Loans], *Kwartalnik Historyczny* [Historical Quarterly], LXVI, No. 4 (1959), 1185–1205.

―― "Wpływ zamachu majowego na gospodarkę polską" [The Influence of the May Coup on the Polish Economy], *Przegląd Historyczny* [Historical Review], LIII, No. 3 (1962), 502–18.

Landau, Z., ed. "Przewrót majowy w raportach poselstwa RP w Londynie" [The May Coup in the Reports of the Legation of the Polish Republic in London], *Kwartalnik Historyczny* [Historical Quarterly], LXVI, No. 1 (1959), 154–58.

Landau, Z., and B. Skrzeszewska, eds. *Sprawa Gabriela Czechowicza przed Trybunałem Stanu* [The Gabriel Czechowicz Affair before the Tribunal of State]. Warsaw, 1961.

Landau, Z., and J. Tomaszewski. *Zarys historii gospodarczej Polski, 1918–1939* [An Outline of the Economic History of Poland, 1918–1939]. 2d ed. Warsaw, 1962.

—— "O polityce zagranicznej Polski w latach 1924–1925" [On the Foreign Policy of Poland in the Years 1924–1925], *Kwartalnik Historyczny* [Historical Quarterly], LXVIII, No. 3 (1961), 725–38.

Lapter, K. "Międzynarodowe tło przewrotu majowego" [The International Background of the May Coup], *Sprawy Międzynarodowe* [International Affairs], IX, No. 5 (May, 1956), 43–60; No. 6 (June, 1956), 54–71.

Laroche, J. *La Pologne de Pilsudski: Souvenirs d'une Ambassade, 1926–1935.* Paris, 1953.

Lednicki, W. "Z dziejów pewnego protestu" [From the History of a Certain Protest], *Wiadomości* [Information], X, No. 507–8 (December 25, 1955), 10.

Léontin, L. (Argoutine). "Deux ans de gouvernement de Pilsudski," *La Paix par le Droit,* XXXVIII, No. 6 (June, 1928), 245–58.

—— "Les Evénements de Pologne," *La Paix par le Droit,* XXXVI, No. 7–8 (July–August, 1926), 293–99.

—— "Le Gouvernement de Pilsudski au pouvoir," *La Paix par le Droit,* XLII, No. 1 (January, 1932), 23–29.

Lewandowski, J. *Federalizm: Litwa i Białoruś w polityce obozu belwederskiego (XI, 1918–IV, 1920)* [Federalism: Lithuania and White Russia in the Policy of the Belwederian (Piłsudskist) Camp, November, 1918–April, 1920]. Warsaw, 1962.

Ligocki, E. "Ze wspomnień o Władysławie Sikorskim" [From (My) Recollections about Władysław Sikorski], *Świat* [World], XIII, No. 4 (January 27, 1963), 14–15; No. 5 (February 3, 1963), 8–9.

Lipiński, W. *Wielki Marszałek* [The Great Marshal]. Warsaw, 1936.

—— "Wywiad u marszałka Piłsudskiego w Sulejówku z dn. 10. II. 1924 r." [An Interview with Marshal Piłsudski in Sulejówek on February 10, 1924], *Niepodległość* [Independence] (O.S.), VII, No. 15 (1933), 63–80.

Lisiewicz, M. "Związek wojskowy 'Honor i Ojczyzna'" [The Military Association "Honor and Native Country"], *Bellona,* XXXVI, No. 3 (July–September, 1954), 47–53.

Loessner, A. *Josef Piłsudski.* Leipzig, 1935.

Lubodziecki, S. "Sprawa Michała Żymierskiego" [The Michał Żymierski Affair], *Kultura* [Culture], No. 39 (January, 1951), 112–19.

Łukasiewicz, J. *Polska w Europie w polityce Józefa Piłsudskiego* [Poland in Europe in the Policy of Joseph Piłsudski]. London, 1944.

Machray, R., *Poland, 1914–1931.* London, 1932.

—— "Poland and Pilsudski," *Fortnightly Review,* DCCXVI (N.S.) (August 2, 1926), 166–76.

Maciejowski, J. *Dlaczego Marszałek Piłsudski nie chciał być Prezydentem Rzplitej Polskiej* [Why Marshal Piłsudski Did Not Want to Be President of the Polish Republic]. Warsaw, 1926.

Mackiewicz, S. *Historja Polski od 11 listopada 1918 r. do 17 września 1939 r.* [History of Poland from November 11, 1918, to September 17, 1939]. London, 1941.

Malaparte, C. *Coup d'Etat.* New York, 1932.

Malicki, J. *Marszałek Piłsudski a Sejm* [Marshal Piłsudski and the Sejm]. Warsaw, 1936.

Marchand, R. *Le Maréchal Pilsudski et la Pologne actuelle.* Paris, n.d.

Markert, W., ed. *Polen: Osteuropa-Handbuch.* Cologne, 1959.

Matuszewski, I. *Wybór pism* [Selected Writings]. London–New York, 1952.

Mercik, W. "Wspomnienie z wypadków majowych" [A Reminiscence from the May Events], *Zeszyty Historyczne* [Historical Pamphlets], III (1963), 103–11.

Mettler, C. *Józef Piłsudski.* Fribourg, 1938.

Micewski, A. "Sanacja-Endecja," *Więź* [Link], III, No. 11–12 (November–December, 1960), 141–61.

Michowicz, W. "Wpływ strajku górników angielskich z 1926 r. na przemysł węglowy w Polsce" [The Influence of the English Coal Miners' Strike of 1926 on the Coal Industry in Poland], *Zeszyty Naukowe Uniwersytetu Łódzkiego* [Scholarly Pamphlets of Łódź University], Series I, Pamphlet 7 (1957), pp. 209–46.

Mieszkowski, J. "Zamach majowy 'Towarzysza Ziuka' " [The May Coup of "Comrade Joe"], *Prawo i Życie* [Law and Life], No. 2 (1958), pp. 4–5.

Minkiewicz, R. Pseudonym of K. Romin, *q.v.*

Moraczewski, J. "Nieznany list" [An Unknown Letter], *Mówią Wieki* [The Centuries Speak], I, No. 8 (August, 1958), 29–34.

Morawski, K. *Tamten brzeg* [The Other Shore]. Paris, 1962.

—— *Wspólna droga* [Common Road]. Paris, 1962.

—— "Przewrót majowy" [The May Coup], *Wiadomości* [Information], XII, No. 566 (February 3, 1957), 1–2.

Mościcki, H., *et al.*, eds. *Dziesięciolecie odrodzenia Polskiej Siły Zbrojnej, 1918–1928* [A Decade of Restoration of the Polish Armed Forces, 1918–1928]. Warsaw, 1928.

Mościcki, I. "Wspomnienia" [Memoirs], *Niepodległość* [Independence] (N.S.), VI (1958), 188–204. (Another part unpublished, *q.v.*)

Nagel, F. *Mai 1926.* Warsaw, 1935.

Nagórski, Z., Sr. *Ludzie mego czasu* [People of My Time]. Paris, 1964.

Niemczyk, B. *Rachunek sumienia* [Examination of Conscience]. 1st ed., Wilno, 1940; 2d ed., New York, 1941.

Niewiadomski, E. *Kartki z więzienia* [Notes from Prison]. Poznań, 1923.

Nowiński, T. "Zagraniczne sprężyny" [Foreign Contrivers], *Prawo i Życie* [Law and Life], No. 8 (1958), p. 5.

Oertzen, F. W. von. *Das Ist Polen*. Munich, 1932.

—— *Marshall Pilsudski*. Berlin, 1934.

Okulicz, K. "Eustachy Sapieha," *Tydzień Polski* [Polish Week], March 30, 1963, p. 3.

Ortel, Z. "Kluby sejmowe wobec przewrotu majowego 1926 r." [The Sejm Clubs in Relation to the May Coup], *Wojskowa Akademia Polityczna im. F. Dzierżyńskiego: Zeszyty Naukowe: Seria Historyczna* [Scholarly Pamphlets of the Felix Dzerzhinsky Military-Political Academy: Historical Series], No. 7 (1962), pp. 112–27.

"Ostatnie dni Rydza-Śmigłego" [The Last Days of Rydz-Śmigły], *Polityka* [Politics], III, No. 16 (April 18, 1959), 10.

Ostrowski, K. "Paradoksy Romana Knolla" [The Paradoxes of Roman Knoll], *Wiadomości* [Information], XII, No. 571 (March 10, 1957), 6.

Piątkowski, H. *Wspomnienia z 'wypadków majowych' 1926 roku* [Reminiscences from the "May Events" of 1926]. London, 1962.

Picardin, J. "Le Coup d'état polonais," *Revue Hebdomadaire*, XXXV, No. 6 (June, 1926), 345–59.

Picheta, H. "Przełom majowy" [The May Coup], *Tydzień Polski* [Polish Week], May 9, 1959, p. 3.

Pietrzak, M. *Reglamentacja wolności prasy w Polsce (1918–1939)* [Regulation of Press Freedom in Poland, 1918–1939]. Warsaw, 1963.

Pietrzak, M., ed. "Jak doszło do wojny domowej" i "Przewrót majowy" [How It Came to Civil War *and* The May Coup], *Kwartalnik Historyczny* [Historical Quarterly], LXVI, No. 1 (1959), 127–54.

Piłsudska, A. *Memoirs*. London, 1940.

—— *Wspomnienia* [Memoirs]. London, 1960.

Piłsudski, J. *Pisma zbiorowe* [Collected Writings]. 10 vols. Warsaw, 1937–38.

—— *Przemówienia, wywiady, artykuły, 1926–1929* [Speeches, Interviews, Articles, 1926–1929]. Warsaw, 1930.

Pobóg-Malinowski, W. (under the pseudonym J. Woyszwiłło). *Józef Piłsudski*. Warsaw, 1937.

—— *Najnowsza historia polityczna Polski, 1864–1945* [Contemporary Political History of Poland, 1864–1945]. 1st ed., Vol. I, Paris, 1953; Vol. II, London, 1956; Vol. III, London, 1960; 2d enlarged ed., Vol. I, London, 1963.

Podoski, B. "Organizacja naczelnych władz obrony państwa: Szkic historyczny" [The Organization of the Supreme Authority of Defense of the State: Historical Sketch], *Niepodległość* [Independence] (N.S.), VII (1962), 181–99.

Polonais, Un. "En Galicie orientale," *Le Monde Slave* (N.S.), VII, No. 9 (September, 1930), 364–83.

Polski Słownik Biograficzny [Polish Biographical Dictionary], Vols. 1–10 (A-Jun). Warsaw, 1935–65.

Pomarański, S. *Józef Piłsudski.* 7th ed., Warsaw, 1931; 13th enlarged ed., Warsaw, 1936.

Popiel, K. "Wybór Prezydenta I. Mościckiego" [The Election of President I. Mościcki], *Zeszyty Historyczne* [Historical Pamphlets], IX (1966), 46–51.

Popławski, W. "Maj 1926—chodzę po ulicach Warszawy" [May, 1926—I Walk Through the Streets of Warsaw], *Tydzień Polski* [Polish Week], May 9, 1959, p. 3.

Poralla, C. "Marshall Pilsudski," *Zeitschrift für Politik,* XXIV, No. 2–3 (February–March, 1934), 81–99.

Porczak, M. Pseudonym of I. Daszyński, *q.v.*

Poznański, K. "Wypadki majowe widziane od strony Moskwy" [The May Events as Seen from the Perspective of Moscow], *Wiadomości* [Information], XII, No. 586 (June 23, 1957), 3.

Pragier, A. "H_2O i bomba Trojanowskiego" [H_2O (Honor and Native Country) and Trojanowski's Bomb], *Wiadomości* [Information], X, No. 481 (June 19, 1955), 2.

—— "Ostatni rząd przedmajowy" [The Last Pre-May Government], *Wiadomości* [Information], XX, No. 1004 (June 27, 1965), 2.

—— "Sąd nad Korfantym" [Judgment on Korfanty], *Wiadomości* [Information], XVII, No. 835 (April 1, 1962), 3.

—— "Spisek" [Plot], *Wiadomości* [Information], X, No. 478 (May 29, 1955), 2.

—— "Wierzyć" [To Believe], *Wiadomości* [Information], X, No. 479 (June 5, 1955), 3.

Proces brzeski [The Brześć Trial]. Toledo, Ohio, n.d. (With an Appendix of Sejm Interpellations, pp. 797–805, the Protest of the Professors of the Jagiellonian University, pp. 805–7, and a Protest Letter by A. Świętochowski, pp. 807–16.)

Proces Eligjusza Niewiadomskiego [The Trial of Eligiusz Niewiadomski]. Warsaw, 1923.

Próchnik, A. *Ignacy Daszyński.* Warsaw, 1946.

—— *Pierwsze piętnastolecie Polski niepodległej* [The First Fifteen Years of Independent Poland]. Warsaw, 1957.

Pronin, D. I. "Land Reform in Poland 1920–1945," *Land Economics,* XXV, No. 2 (May, 1949), 133–45.

Prudhommeaux, J. "Les Hontes du régime Pilsudski," *La Paix par le Droit,* XLI, No. 1 (January, 1931), 36–38.

Radek, K., and R. Stefanovich, *Perevorot v Pol'she i Pilsudski* [The Coup in Poland and Piłsudski]. Moscow-Leningrad, 1926.

Rataj, M. *Pamiętniki* [Memoirs]. Warsaw, 1965.

Ratyńska, B. "Geneza wojny celnej polsko-niemieckiej" [The Genesis of the Polish-German Tariff War], *Najnowsze Dzieje Polski: Materiały i Studia z okresu 1914–1939* [Contemporary History of Poland: Materials and Studies of the Period 1914–1939], VI (1963), 77–103.

Recouly, R. *La Pologne de Pilsudski.* Paris, 1935.

Reddaway, W. F. *Marshal Pilsudski.* London, 1939.

Reguła, J. A. *Historia Komunistycznej Partji Polski w świetle faktów i dokumentów* [History of the KPP in the Light of Facts and Documents]. 2d enlarged ed. Warsaw, 1934.

Rek, T. "Jeszcze o sprawie brzeskiej" [Once Again about the Brześć Affair], *Prawo i Życie* [Law and Life], No. 26–27 (1957), p. 8.

—— "Sprawa Bagińskiego i Wieczorkiewicza" [The Affair of Bagiński and Wieczorkiewicz], *Prawo i Życie* [Law and Life], No. 17 (1958), pp. 4–5.

Retinger, J. H. *All about Poland: Facts, Figures, Documents.* London, 1941.

Romer, E. *Rady i przestrogi, 1918–1938* [Advice and Admonitions, 1918–1938]. Lwów, 1938.

Romer, J. *Pamiętniki* [Memoirs]. Lwów, 1938.

Romeyko, M. "Maj 1926: Zwierzenia Generała Kutrzeby" [May, 1926: The Confidences of General Kutrzeba], *Świat* [World], IX, No. 19 (May 10, 1959), 6–7.

—— "Pierwsze dni niepodległości i zamach stanu" [The First Days of Independence and a Coup d'Etat], *Kultura* [Culture], No. 158 (December, 1960), pp. 81–100.

—— "Przed i po maju 1926 r. Ze wspomnień oficera sztabu generalnego" [Before and after May, 1926: From the Reminiscences of an Officer of the General Staff], *Wojskowy Przegląd Historyczny* [Military Historical Review], VII, No. 1 (1962), 274–316; No. 2 (1962), 203–38; No. 3 (1962), 262–301; No. 4 (1962), 259–94; VIII, No. 1 (1963), 251–83; No. 2 (1963), 194–223; IX, No. 1 (1964), 227–54; No. 2 (1964), 300–42; No. 3 (1964), 193–224; No. 4 (1964), 126–55; X, No. 4 (1965), 211–53; XI, No. 1 (1966), 241–77.

—— "Ze wspomnień attaché wojskiego" [From the Reminiscences of a Military Attaché], *Wojskowy Przegląd Historyczny* [Military Historical Review], IV, No. 3 (1959), 208–28; No. 4 (1959), 279–300; V, No. 1 (1960), 261–82; No. 2 (1960), 264–89; No. 3 (1960), 225–74.

Romin, K. (under the pseudonym R. Minkiewicz). *Klika warszawska OKR PPS* [The Clique of the Warsaw District Committee of the PPS]. Warsaw, 1928.

Romin, S. *Józef Piłsudski.* Paris, 1926.

Roos, H. *Geschichte der polnischen Nation, 1916–1960.* Stuttgart, 1961.

—— *Polen und Europa.* Tübingen, 1957.

—— "Józef Piłsudski i Charles de Gaulle," *Kultura* [Culture], No. 151 (May, 1960), pp. 11–20.

Rosé, A. C. *La Politique polonaise entre les deux guerres.* Neuchâtel, 1945.

Rose, W. J. *Poland's Political Parties, 1919–1939.* Surbiton, 1947.

—— *The Rise of Polish Democracy.* London, 1944.

Rosenberg, K. (under the pseudonym K. Wrzos). *Piłsudski i piłsudczycy* [Piłsudski and the Piłsudskists]. Warsaw, 1936.

Roth, P. "Die innerpolitische Entwicklung in Polen seit dem Staatsstreich Pilsudskis," *Osteuropa,* III, No. 1 (1927–28), 16–26.

Rudomimo, G. *See* Vonsovski, B., and G. Rudomimo.

Rzepecki, J. *Wspomnienia i przyczynki historyczne* [Reminiscences and Historical Contributions]. Warsaw, 1956.

—— "Jeszcze o maju 1926" [Once Again about May, 1926], *Wojskowy Przegląd Historyczny* [Military Historical Review], V, No. 2 (1960), 346–49.

—— "Rozejście się Sikorskiego z Piłsudskim w świetle korespondencji Izy Moszczeńskiej z sierpnia 1915 r." [The Parting of Sikorski from Piłsudski in the Light of the Correspondence of Iza Moszczeńska of August, 1915], *Kwartalnik Historyczny* [Historical Quarterly], LXVII, No. 3 (1960), 728–39.

Rzepecki (Rzepeccy), T., and K. Rzepecki. *Sejm i Senat, 1928–1933.* Poznań, 1928.

Rzepecki (Rzepeccy), T., and W. Rzepecki. *Sejm i Senat, 1922–1927.* Poznań, 1923.

Rzymowski, W. *W walce i burzy: Tadeusz Hołówko na tle epoki* [In Struggle and Storm: Tadeusz Hołówko Against the Background of the Epoch]. Warsaw, 1933.

Santoro, C. *Through Poland During the Elections of 1930.* Geneva, 1931.

Scelle, G. "Pacte Kellogg et protocole Litvinov," *Le Monde Slave* (N.S.), VI, No. 4 (April, 1929), 1–32.

Schaetzel, T. *Pułkownik Walery Sławek* [Colonel Walery Sławek]. Jerusalem, 1947.

—— "Przełom majowy" [The May Coup], *Wiadomości* [Information], XVI, No. 684 (May 10, 1959), 6.

—— "Ustalenie faktów" [Establishing the Facts], *Wiadomości* [Information], XIV, No. 698 (August 16, 1959), 6.

Senn, A. E. "The Polish-Lithuanian War Scare, 1927," *Journal of Central European Affairs,* XXI, No. 3 (October, 1961), 267–84.

Seraphim, P. H. "Der polnisch-englische Kohlenkampf in Nordeuropa und seine wirtschaftliche und politische Bedeutung," *Osteuropa,* X, No. 2 (November, 1934), 80–91.

Sidzikauskas, V. "Der litauisch-polnische Konflikt," *Nord und Süd,* LI, No. 12 (December, 1928), 1061–72.

Sieroszewski, W., *et al.,* eds. *Idea i czyn Józefa Piłsudskiego* [Idea and Deed of Joseph Piłsudski]. Warsaw, 1934.

Sikorski, W. "Kartki z dziennika" [Notes from a Diary], *Żołnierz Polski* [Polish Soldier], No. 13 (July, 1957), pp. 4–6; No. 14 (July, 1957), pp. 14–15.

"Sim." "W obliczu wyborów" [In the Face of the Elections], *Walka* [Struggle], V, No. 1–2 (January–February, 1928), 1–3.

Singer, B. *Od Witosa do Sławka* [From Witos to Sławek]. Paris, 1962.

Skotnicki, J. *Przy sztalugach i przy biurku* [At Easel and Desk]. Warsaw, 1957.

Skrzeszewska, B. *See* Landau, Z., and B. Skrzeszewska.

Skwarczyński, T. "Generał Sikorski podczas przewrotu majowego" [General Sikorski During the May Coup], *Polityka* [Politics], III, No. 31 (August 1, 1959), 1.

Sławoj-Składkowski, F. *Kwiatuszki administracyjne i inne* [Administrative and Other Small Flowers]. London, 1959.

—— *Nie ostatnie słowo oskarżonego* [Not the Last Word of the Accused]. London, 1964.

—— *Strzępy meldunków* [Scraps of Reports]. Warsaw, 1938.

—— "Wspomnienia z okresu majowego" [Reminiscences from the May Period], *Kultura* [Culture], No. 116 (June, 1957), pp. 95–116; No. 117–18 (July–August, 1957), pp. 143–73.

Śliwiński, A. "Marszałek Piłsudski o sobie" [Marshal Piłsudski about Himself], *Niepodległość* [Independence] (O.S.), XVI, No. 43 (September–October, 1937), 367–73.

[Smal'-Stots'kyi, R.] "Nieznana inicjatywa Piłsudskiego" [An Unknown Initiative by Piłsudski], *Kultura* [Culture], No. 103 (May, 1956), pp. 124–27.

Smith, L. "The Zloty, 1924–1935," *Journal of Political Economy,* XLIV, No. 2 (April, 1936), 145–83.

Smogorzewski, K. *Le Jeu complexe des partis en Pologne.* Paris, 1928.

—— (under the pseudonym J. de Carency). *Joseph Pilsudski: Soldat de la Pologne restaurée.* Paris, 1929.

—— *La Pologne restaurée.* Paris, 1927.

Sokal, F. "Der polnisch-litauische Konflikt," *Nord und Süd,* LI, No. 10 (October, 1928), 861–72.

Sokalski, W. *The Cracow Congress and the Brest-Litovsk Trial.* Washington, D.C., 1955.

Sokulski, H. "Wojna celna Rzeszy przeciw Polsce w latach 1925–1934" [The Reich's Tariff War Against Poland in the Years 1925–1934], *Sprawy Międzynarodowe* [International Affairs], VIII, No. 9 (September, 1955), 54–65.

Sołtys, J. "Za kulisami przewrotu Piłsudskiego" [Behind the Scenes of Piłsudski's Coup], *Żołnierz Polski* [Polish Soldier], No. 3 (January 18–24, 1952), p. 12.

Sopicki, S. *Sprawa żydowska w Polsce ze stanowiska polskiego stronnictwa Chrześcijańskiej Demokracji* [The Jewish Question in Poland from the Viewpoint of the Polish Christian Democratic Party]. Kraków, 1926.

Sprawa brzeska, 1930–1932 [The Brześć Affair, 1930–1932]. Katowice, 1932.

Sprawa Józefa Muraszki: Zabójstwo Bagińskiego i Wieczorkiewicza [The Joseph Muraszko Affair: The Murder of Bagiński and Wieczorkiewicz]. Warsaw, 1926.

Srokowski, W. "Obrona Belwederu" [The Defense of the Belweder], *Kultura* [Culture], No. 115 (May, 1957), pp. 87–104.

Starzewski, J. *Józef Piłsudski: Zarys psychologiczny* [Joseph Piłsudski: A Psychological Profile]. Warsaw, 1930.

Starzyński, S. *Rok 1926 w życiu gospodarczym Polski* [The Year 1926 in the Economic Life of Poland]. Warsaw, 1927.

Starzyński, S., *et al. Na froncie gospodarczym* [On the Economic Front]. Warsaw, n. d. [1928?]

Stawecki, P. "O dominacji wojskowych w państwowym aparacie cywilnym w Polsce w latach 1926–1939" [On the Dominance of Military Personnel in the Civilian State Apparatus in Poland in the Years 1926–1939], *Wojskowy Przegląd Historyczny* [Military Historical Review], X, No. 3 (1965), 328–46.

Stęborowski, S. P. *Geneza Centrolewu* [The Genesis of the Center-Left]. Warsaw, 1963.

Stefanovich, R. *See* Radek, K., and R. Stefanovich.

Stein, W. "Bitte rechts herum, vorne ist Revolution: Im warschauer Strassenkampf," *Vossische Zeitung,* May 20, 1926.

Steinert, H. "Polens Ausfuhr von landwirtschaftlichen Erzeugnissen," *Osteuropa,* V, No. 9 (June, 1930), 612–29.

Stolarzewicz, L. (under the pseudonym S. Hincza). *Pierwszy żołnierz Polski odrodzonej* [The First Soldier of Revived Poland]. Warsaw, 1935.

Stpiczyński, W. *Polska, która idzie* [Poland as She Goes]. Warsaw, 1929.

Strobel, G. W. "Arbeiterschaft und Linksparteien in Polen 1928–1938," *Jahrbücher für Geschichte Osteuropas,* X, No. 1 (April, 1962), 67–102.

Stroński, S. *Pierwsze lat dziesięć* [The First Ten Years]. Lwów-Warsaw, 1928.

Strumph-Wojtkiewicz, S., *et al. Warszawa w ogniu* [Warsaw Aflame]. Warsaw, 1926.

Stünzner, O. "Polens Heer," *Osteuropa,* X, No. 11–12 (August–September, 1935), 675–87.

Świerzewski, S. "Oczami świadka 'operacji wojskowej' Piłsudskiego" [Piłsudski's "Military Operation" Through the Eyes of a Witness], *Prawo i Życie* [Law and Life], No. 5 (1958), p. 6.

Szerer, E. (under the pseudonym E. Hoffman). "Rozłam w PPS" [Breach in the PPS], *Nasza Walka* [Our Struggle], I, No. 2–3 (September–October, 1928), 52–54.

Taylor, J. *The Economic Development of Poland, 1919–1950*. Ithaca, 1952.

Thugutt, S. *Wybór pism i autobiografia* [Selected Writings and Autobiography]. Glasgow, 1943.

Tomaszewski, J. "Polityka stabilizacyjna Władysława Grabskiego, 1923–1925" [The Stabilization Policy of Władysław Grabski, 1923–1925], *Najnowsze Dzieje Polski: Materiały i Studia z okresu 1914–1939* [Contemporary History of Poland: Materials and Studies of the Period 1914–1939], I (1958), 77–102.

——— *See also* Landau, Z., and J. Tomaszewski.

Tomicki, J. "Centrolew" [Center-Left], *Mówią Wieki* [The Centuries Speak], III, No. 11 (November, 1960), 21–24.

Tommasini, F. *Marsz na Warszawę* [The March on Warsaw]. Warsaw, 1929.

Tymieniecka, A. "Rozłam w PPS w 1928 roku" [The Breach in the PPS in 1928], *Kwartalnik Historyczny* [Historical Quarterly], LXXII, No. 4 (1965), 811–36.

Tymieniecka, A., ed. "XXI Kongres PPS (1–4. XI. 1928)" [The Twenty-first PPS Congress, November 1–4, 1928], *Najnowsze Dzieje Polski: Materiały i Studia z okresu 1914–1939* [Contemporary History of Poland: Materials and Studies of the Period 1914–1939], VI (1963), 289–96.

Verax. "Le Maréchal Pilsudski," *Revue des Deux Mondes,* XCVIII (August 1, 1928), 503–22.

Vonsovski, B., and G. Rudomimo. *Kuda Pilsudski vedet Pol'shu?* [Whither Is Piłsudski Leading Poland?] Minsk, 1927.

W. S. "13 = 34," *Dzwon* [Bell], I, No. 2 (March 25, 1928), 1–2.

——— "Wybory uczą" [Elections Teach], *Dzwon* [Bell], I, No. 1 (March 15, 1928), 5–6.

Walewski, J. "Omyłka Wincentego Witosa [Wincenty Witos' Error], *Kultura* [Culture], No. 197 (March, 1964), pp. 115–20.

Wandycz, P. S. *France and Her Eastern Allies, 1919–1925*. Minneapolis, 1962.

Wapiński, R. "Działalność Narodowej Demokracji na Pomorzu Gdańskim w latach 1920–1926" [The Activities of National Democracy in Danzig Pomerania in the Years 1920–1926], *Zapiski Historyczne* [Historical Notes], XXIX, No. 1 (1964), 7–37.

Wellisz, L. *Foreign Capital in Poland*. London, 1938.

Werder, A. "Ostatnie wypadki w Polsce" [The Latest Events in Poland], *Walka* [Struggle], III, No. 5–6 (May–June, 1926), 105–8.

Wierzbicki, A. "Uwagi o przewrocie majowym" [Remarks on the May Coup], *Najnowsze Dzieje Polski: Materiały i Studia z okresu 1914–*

1939 [Contemporary History of Poland: Materials and Studies of the Period 1914–1939], IX (1965), 205–25.

Wierzbiński, F. Pseudonym of W. Górnicki, *q.v.*

Więzikowa, A. "Powstanie i geneza Stronnictwa Chłopskiego, 1923–1926" [Eruption and Genesis of the Peasant Party, 1923–1926], *Zeszyty Historyczne: Uniwersytet Warszawski* [Historical Pamphlets: Warsaw University], II (1961), 280–310.

Wirschubski, G. "Die Entwicklung der polnischem Industrie," *Osteuropa,* V, No. 10 (July, 1930), 693–706.

Witos, W. *Czasy i ludzie* [Times and People]. Tarnów, 1926.

—— *Moje wspomnienia* [My Memoirs]. 3 vols. Paris, 1964–65.

Woyszwiłło, J. Pseudonym of W. Pobóg-Malinowski, *q.v.*

Wrzos, K. Pseudonym of K. Rosenberg, *q.v.*

Współpraca rządu z sferami gospodarczemi państwa [Collaboration of the Government with the State's Economic Spheres]. Warsaw, 1927.

X.X.X. "Joseph Pilsudski," *Le Monde Slave* (N.S.), VI, No. 7 (July, 1929), 3–33. (Probable author was A. Krzyżanowski.)

X.Y.Z. "Chronique polonaise," *Le Monde Slave* (N.S.), VII, No. 4 (April, 1930), 104–28; No. 8 (August, 1930), 258–90; No. 10 (October, 1930), 98–138; VIII, No. 3 (March, 1931), 422–58.

—— "Daszyński ou Piłsudski?" *Le Monde Slave* (N.S.), VII, No. 9 (September, 1930), 409–37.

Zakrzewska, B. "Za kulisami przewrotu majowego" [Behind the Scenes of the May Coup], *Mówią Wieki* [The Centuries Speak], VII, No. 2 (February, 1964), 34–36.

Zaremba, Z. *PPS w Polsce niepodległej* [The PPS in Independent Poland]. Warsaw, 1934.

Zbyszewski, W. "Generał Haller," *Kultura* [Culture], No. 156 (October, 1960), pp. 106–11.

—— "Nieznane 'testimonium' o Piłsudskim" [An Unknown "Testimonium" about Piłsudski], *Zeszyty Historyczne* [Historical Pamphlets], IV (1963), 45–51.

Zdziechowski, J. "Wspomnienia o Stanisławie Wojciechowskim" [Reminiscences about Stanisław Wojciechowski], *Dziennik Polski* [Polish Daily], April 23, 1953, p. 2.

Zdziechowski, M. "Ze wspomnień o Józefie Piłsudskim" [From (My) Reminiscences about Joseph Piłsudski], *Myśl Polska* [Polish Thought], III, No. 1 (January 1–15, 1938), 2–3.

Zweig, F. *Poland Between Two Wars*. London, 1944.

Zyndram-Kościałkowski, W. "Moje wspomnienia o Kazimierzu Bartlu [My Reminiscences about Kazimierz Bartel], *Wiadomości* [Information], XIV, No. 684 (May 10, 1959), 2.

INDEX